KAMA MUTA

This book describes a ubiquitous and potent emotion that has only rarely and recently been studied in any systematic manner. The words that come closest to denoting it in English are *being moved* or *touched*, *having a heart-warming feeling*, *feeling nostalgic*, *feeling patriotic*, or *pride in family or team*. In religious contexts when the emotion is intense, it may be labeled *ecstasy*, *mystical rapture*, *burning in the bosom*, or *being touched by the Spirit*. All of these are instances of what scientists now call 'kama muta' (Sanskrit, 'moved by love'). Alan Page Fiske shows that what evokes this emotion is the sudden creation, intensification, renewal, repair, or recall of a communal sharing relationship – when love ignites, or people feel newly connected. He explains the social, psychological, cultural, and likely evolutionary processes involved – and how they interlock.

Kama muta is described as it manifests in diverse settings at many points in history across scores of cultures, in everyday experiences as well as the peak moments of life. The chapters illuminate the occurrence of kama muta in a range of contexts, including religion, oratory, literature, sport, social media, and nature. The book will be of interest to students and scholars from a number of disciplines who are interested in emotion or social relationships.

Supplementary notes can be found online at: www.routledge.com/ 9780367220945

Alan Page Fiske is Distinguished Professor in the Department of Anthropology at the University of California, Los Angeles, CA, USA.

KAMA MUTA

Discovering the Connecting Emotion

Alan Page Fiske

Routledge
Taylor & Francis Group

LONDON AND NEW YORK

First published 2020
by Routledge
2 Park Square, Milton Park, Abingdon, Oxon OX14 4RN

and by Routledge
52 Vanderbilt Avenue, New York, NY 10017

Routledge is an imprint of the Taylor & Francis Group, an informa business

British Library Cataloguing-in-Publication Data
A catalogue record for this book is available from the British Library

Library of Congress Cataloging-in-Publication Data
A catalog record has been requested for this book

ISBN: 978-0-367-22093-8 (hbk)
ISBN: 978-0-367-22094-5 (pbk)
ISBN: 978-0-367-22095-2 (ebk)

Typeset in Bembo
by Deanta Global Publishing Services, Chennai, India

Visit the eResources: www.routledge.com/9780367220945

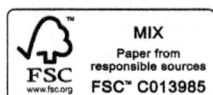

MIX
Paper from
responsible sources
FSC
www.fsc.org   FSC™ C013985

Printed in the United Kingdom
by Henry Ling Limited

CONTENTS

THE EMOTION

You give birth to your baby and you hold her; she looks at you, cuddled against your chest, secure and calm.

You're at a poetry lounge where the poet on the stage differs from you in gender, age, ethnicity, and dress. He's reading a poem he wrote about being avoided and excluded by people who reject him simply because of his appearance, and the hardships he faced when his parents were killed in an auto accident. You know just what he experienced, since you were an outsider because of a prominent facial scar, and your mother died, leaving you in a foster home; you suddenly identify with him intensely.

You are driving through a small town and you see a sign boosting the high school basketball team. With a pang of deep nostalgia you wistfully remember the sense of connection you experienced on your high school team: the one-for-all and all-for-one spirit, the devotion of the fans, and your girlfriend rushing out to hug and kiss you at the end of every game.

You are gathered with others from your community at the annual commemoration of the martyred heroes who bravely faced certain death, sacrificing themselves to protect you all. With heartfelt patriotism, you join in singing the national anthem.

You are hiking on a trail when you hear someone crying, and you come upon a five-year-old girl with a broken arm and bruises on her face and neck. You ask her what happened and, sobbing, she tells you her father beat her up because she stopped hiking to look at a butterfly. Your heart goes out to her; you just want to comfort and care for her.

In worship, you suddenly feel a rapturous union with God; you and He are one.

In the quiet forest, you listen to the wind and you feel yourself merge with nature.

*

Your true love proposes marriage.

Suddenly you see a litter of four wonderfully cute and playful puppies; you sit down and one by one they come up and climb into your lap. As you stroke their soft fur they lick you, curl up, and fall asleep in your lap on top of each other.

You've got a bad flu, and you've barely been able to get out of bed. After three days you drag yourself outside to take in your mail. Three hours later an elderly neighbor – whom you only know from greetings exchanged on the sidewalk – knocks on the door. You get up and open the door; she's brought you homemade soup, fresh-baked bread, and a vase of flowers from her garden. She says, "Excuse me, but I saw you were ill. This is the 'love soup' my mother always made for us when we were sick, and I always made for my children and grandchildren when they weren't feeling well. It will make you well."

You've just had a huge, drawn-out fight with your boyfriend and you're wondering whether he's going to end the relationship and move out, which would devastate you. As you're walking alone in the dark he texts you that he's sorry, you're perfect, and he wants to be with you forever.

A tornado destroys your neighborhood and you can't find your sister – she was in her room, which was crushed flat by a giant tree. Then you hear her calling your name, you turn, you see her running toward you, and she jumps into your arms, crying with joy.

You go to an Alcoholics Anonymous meeting where, for the first time, you tell your story. It's difficult to stand up and tell about what you have done to yourself and your family, but you manage to get through it. By the end, you see tears on the faces of some of the listeners, and several come up, give you big hugs, express their affection and support, and tell you how much they appreciate your sharing.

Your unit is pinned down by a machine gun and nearly out of ammunition; the enemy are about to overrun your position. One soldier grabs a bunch of grenades, says, "I'm not going to let you all die here," and runs toward the machine gun, tossing grenades to blow it up as he's riddled with bullets.

*

You see a video of a dog who faithfully comes and waits at a train station every evening for ten years for his dead owner to come home.

After a very long flight, you're sitting in the baggage claim, next to a tired soldier in camouflage with a bandaged head. A four-year-old girl comes running across the room, cries, "Daddy!!," and jumps into his arms. His wife joins them, kisses him fervently, and the three of them start singing a silly song as they dance together.

It's your daughter's wedding. You remember vividly when at six she had leukemia; she was so sick and you were sure she'd die – you never thought you'd see her fully recover as she did. The groom is a terrific guy, and they love each other deeply. They can't stop smiling joyfully at each other as they say their vows.

*

In the midst of the protest marchers you feel one with the cause – moved by the movement. The social movement transcends the individuals in it; your identities merge so that you feel an intense sense of belonging.

At a rave, high on Ecstasy, dancing with everyone else to the beat of the electronic dance music, you love everyone around you. You hug strangers, strangers give you back rubs, and everyone shares their drinks.

You're listening to an extraordinary performance of Chopin's *Nocturne*. The musicians are inspired, the rapt audience is entirely absorbed; you feel rapturously enveloped, transported, and transformed into oneness — experiencing a fusion of yourself, the music, Chopin, the conductor, the performers, and the whole audience.

You're at your mother's funeral, desolate with grief, but now fondly remembering the songs she sang you as she brushed your hair. When her best friend stands up to speak of her memories of your mother, you realize how much she loved her, too. And looking around, you appreciate how in life and now in death, your mother always brought everyone together – she was the link that connected everyone, and still is. You are consoled by the thought of her in heaven with Jesus, while you look forward to joyously joining her in heaven when you die.

This book is about the emotion you may experience in such events. It's an emotion that people all over the world frequently feel, but that doesn't have a consistent name and isn't mentioned in textbooks or handbooks of emotion. People feel this emotion when they suddenly *connect,* and it motivates long-term connections among the people feeling it. This previously unrecognized emotion connects everyday social relations, peak moments in the life-cycle, literature, fine arts, social media, marketing, politics, and religion. As a characteristic human emotion we all share, it connects all humanity

For a few videos, photos, and an audio recording that often evoke this emotion, see the links from Online Note 0.1.

TYPOGRAPHIC NOTE

The typography should be self-evident, but to forestall any ambiguity, here are the conventions of this book:

Italics designates words in English and in other languages when I am drawing attention to the semantics of natural language. That is, italics indicate vernacular lexemes whose ordinary usage is in some way problematic or whose meanings I wish to reflect on.

<u>Underlining</u> is for emphasis (since I use italics to designate vernacular lexemes).

'Single quotes' generally designate names for the constructs of other researchers and theorists; that is, words and phrases used in a technical scientific sense but not part of the theory proposed in this book. Single quotes are used only the first time a technical term is introduced in a chapter.

> Boxed paragraphs are informants' first-person accounts written for this book. They are not field notes, but texts in the informants' own words. (Some were minimally copyedited and then cleared with the informant.)

Tinted boxes mark major conceptual points.

Endnotes within the book are indicated with superscript numbers in the usual manner. They are located at the end of each chapter.

Online supplementary materials are available at www.routledge.com/9780367220945. They are structured as extended endnotes and indicated as Online notes.

PREFACE

Ways to read this book:
My aims and your uses for it

I hope that reading this book will be as joyful as it was to write it. At the same time, it should be intellectually intriguing. It will be satisfying and provoke your curiosity. It should open your eyes so you see your life and the world more clearly, and ask new questions about it. It will help you understand a wonderful emotion that you have often felt and often observed, yet rarely thought about. (There isn't even a definite emoji for it!) At the same time, this book offers a great many opportunities to *feel* this wonderful emotion as you read about others' experiences of it and recall your own experiences. You may find that you'll read passages out loud to share them with family and friends. And beyond that, this book can help you become a connoisseur of this emotion. Before we began our research we hardly noticed this emotion. As my colleagues in the Kama Muta Lab and I have studied and talked to people about it, we have found ourselves becoming more sensitive to it – we have become more aware of feeling it, we feel it more deeply and with more refined nuance, we have more joy in it, we remember our experiences of it more fully. I hope this will also happen to you, the reader. Most of the peak experiences of life are moments when people feel this emotion, so reading this book will illuminate the moments that make life most meaningful. It may even facilitate your having these profound experiences.

This book encompasses a great range of phenomena because it aims to illuminate their common core, together with how they contrast with each other and what is distinctive about each. Because of the breadth of the phenomena encompassed, I cannot go deeply into any of them. However, for the reader intrigued by a phenomenon, and for the specialist, I provide extensive supplementary material online. To grasp the theory and recognize the scope of the emotion, there is no need to read any of the online material, but it provides more depth. I have formatted this material online so as to make it quickly and intuitively accessible, and to facilitate browser bookmarking, all online supplementary material is available at www.routledge.com/9780367220945. References to the online materials are indicated as such.

The deepest insight will result from reading the whole book, because all of the phenomena interlock to form a cohesive whole. And I hope that every chapter is engaging. But I imagine that many readers will initially be attracted to the book for what it says about a particular phenomenon, such as cuteness, sentimentality in literature, political oratory, Sufism, or peak experiences, for example. Those readers with a very specific focus will find that it is not necessary to read the whole book beginning to end in order to get the key idea. One can jump straight into a topical chapter, then move on to peruse another topic, or dig into the theory. Step by step over the course of the book, I build up an integrated theory of the psychological, cultural, and evolutionary aspects of this emotion. The theory connects the many manifestations of this emotion that I consider, shedding light on each by showing how they comprise parts of a greater whole. But even without mastering the details of the theory or discovering all of the homologies and interconnections, readers interested in particular phenomena are likely to find each chapter illuminating in its own right. For readers who do not read the book from beginning to end, or who forget concepts introduced in previous chapters, a glossary at the end defines the key theoretical terms.

I hope that everyone will enjoy this book, and that it will especially interest cultural, social, psychological, and evolutionary anthropologists; cultural, social, cognitive, clinical, and evolutionary psychologists and emotion researchers; social historians; sociologists of culture and cohesion; scholars in religious studies; political scientists; media and marketing researchers; and just about everyone in the humanities, whether their focus is art, literature, poetry, classics, theater, cinema, dance, phenomenology, or the philosophy of mind. This book offers insights into all of these realms, and more.

This book has eleven complementary aims:

I aim to present a general theory of social emotions, a theory that integrates psychology, social relations, culture, evolution, and development.

I plan to show that a social emotion cannot properly be described – let alone explained – without reference to the full range of its cultural implementations.

I aim to show that vernacular words make poor scientific constructs, and specifically, that English emotion terms do not precisely correspond to natural kinds of emotions.

I offer a psychocultural theory of how ritual and related cultural processes create social solidarity at the level of dyads, families, communities, and nations.

I illuminate the emotional bases for many religious practices and civic memorials.

I explain important facets of social movements, support groups, and sports.

I shed light on a key emotional foundation of literature, oratory, marketing, and other arts and media.

I intend this book to exemplify the merit of an approach to psychology that begins with observation, description, and comparison of naturally occurring behavior across disparate contexts, truly diverse cultures, and long spans of history. From this inductive foundation, I illustrate how researchers can fruitfully orient focused ethnographies, interviews, surveys, and controlled laboratory experiments to validate, correct, or refute the inductively constructed theories.

Through the example of one emotion and the cultural forms the at resonate with it, I aim to show that many cultural institutions, practices, roles, narratives, and artifacts are cultural adaptations to evolved psychological dispositions. In particular, an emotion can be the substrate out of which grow these cultural systems – the emotion is a crucial aspect of the niche to which they are culturally adapted.

Conversely, through our analysis of one emotion, I aim to illustrate how psychosocial dispositions are naturally selected adaptations to culturally transmitted systems that are cultural adaptations to the evolved psychological dispositions. Each is adapted to the other, with cultural systems constituting the environment to which social psychological mechanisms adapt biologically, while innate social psychological dispositions constitute the environment to which cultural systems adapt though cultural evolution.

I have structured the book so that descriptions of the phenomena are interspersed with theory. Thus I build with bricks, then mortar, another course of bricks, and so on. The phenomena provide the inductive basis for the theory, the theory illuminates the phenomena, which in turn enrich the theory, revealing new patterns in the phenomena. In other words, our approach is inductively nomothetic. I propose some theoretical principles – dynamic 'mechanisms' – with two complementary facets: in one respect, the principles are parsimonious, elegantly concise, and precise <u>descriptions</u> of similarities among a wide range of phenomena that were previously not recognized as related. Thus, in a limited and tentative way, our description aims to do for some psychological, social, and cultural phenomena what Newton's principle of gravity did for physical dynamics when he showed that a simple formula describes ballistic trajectories, acceleration of falling objects, planetary and lunar orbits, the oscillation of pendulums, flotation, and the downward flow of liquids. Gravitation can be construed as a remarkably comprehensive yet parsimonious description, or it can be construed as an <u>explanation</u> of the phenomenon it encompasses – an explanation by elegantly parsimonious formal general description. Likewise, in a second respect, our kama muta theory can be construed as an explanation of some of the causal dynamics of love, solidarity, devotion, and compassion. (Of course, I'm far from reaching Newton's level of precision!)

This means that our goal is <u>not</u> to fully describe, much less understand, all of the aspects or all of the interacting determinants of any <u>particular</u> event, activity, or experience. I do not believe that our kama muta theory, or any one theory, could alone explain why a particular event occurs, let alone <u>all</u> of what occurs in any particular instance. There are always many factors impinging and interacting to shape events, activities, and experiences; explaining these particularities is the task of idiographic accounts. An idiographic account is necessarily a representation of the confluence of nomothetic principles as they jointly shape events. No one principle alone determines what happens on any one occasion. Gravity is a universal principle, but objects do not always accelerate toward nearby masses; to explain the trajectory of any particular object, one often needs to take into account friction, wind currents, solar pressure, thrust (operating according to Newton's second and third laws), fluid lift, or the intentions of the bird. Likewise, I simply posit that kama muta is <u>one</u> of the factors influencing any particular instance of human sociality.

Thus the thesis of the book is that each of the many kinds of events and practices that this book comprehends is significantly shaped by the kama muta mechanism. This has an intriguing converse corollary: that the kama muta mechanism is a mechanism that by its nature operates in all of these phenomena. Four analogies: we would not know what oxygen is if we only recognized it as the agent of oxidation in rust, without identifying its role in combustion, photosynthesis, respiration, and so forth. We would not know what Varicella zoster virus is without recognizing that it is the virus that causes chickenpox <u>and</u> causes shingles. We would not understand what oxytocin is if we only knew its function in causing contractions in labor, without knowing its function in maternal and pair bonding. We would misunderstand marriage if we saw only its function in regulating sex, without being aware of how it organizes property, production, and consumption, how it often functions in determining the kin group to which children belong, and how it frequently works as a mechanism of alliance between groups.

Recognizing the operation of the kama muta mechanism is essential to understanding any of the phenomena encompassed by this book. But conversely <u>we cannot understand what the kama muta mechanism is without appreciating that it operates in all of these phenomena</u>. That is, the kama muta mechanism is something that has the potential to shape each and all of these phenomena. So, for example, if we only recognized the kama muta mechanism's operation in shaping responses to art (e.g., Konečni 2005, 2011; Levinson 2006; Nusbaum et al. 2014), we would not properly understand what the kama muta mechanism is. If we only recognized the kama muta mechanism's operation in response to the perception of morally beautiful events (Haidt 2000, 2003a; Haidt & Keltner 2004; Pohling & Diessner 2016; Thomson & Siegel 2016), we would not correctly understand what the kama muta mechanism is. If we only appreciated the kama muta mechanism's operation when core values are challenged but realized (Cova & Deonna 2014; Strick & Van Soolingen 2017; Cova, Deonna, & Sander 2017), or when overcoming adverse circumstances (Tokaji 2003), we would not correctly understand what the kama muta mechanism is. Because the kama muta mechanism is the mechanism that, by its nature, responds to <u>all</u> of these – but <u>only</u> when love suddenly ignites. If we think of the kama muta mechanism as a function in the mathematical sense, it is essential to its definition that it is a function that takes as its domain all of the phenomena that this book encompasses (see Chapter 10).

Some readers may open this book because of their interest or expertise in a particular phenomenon that I discuss. I hope they will find that what I write about it resonates with their deeper knowledge of the phenomena, while shedding new light on it. Once they have the book open, I hope they will discover unexpected congruence between their phenomena and the others I discuss. Looking just beneath the surface, we see that all the trees are connected through their roots, a forest comprising a single organism.

We have found that our conceptualization of kama muta resonates with our experience of it. But our conceptualization is discrepant with some strong intuitions; our theory contradicts a lot of implicit folk–psychology, especially superficial categories based on the vernacular lexicon. This is just how science works – by transcending naïve commonsense understandings, replacing them with more rigorous, consistent, and valid constructs. So this book will mesh with your experience, yet replace your intuitions with deeper and often surprising insights that enable you to more truly understand yourself, your relationships, and society.

Many languages have at least one word or phrase that refers to an emotion that people experience in many of these social situations. In English we can say that a person is *moved*, *touched*, *stirred*, *heart-warmed*, experiences *rapture*, gets *the feels*, or has *tender* feelings. Of course, these words have somewhat different meanings, and people use each of them somewhat imprecisely and inconsistently. People may use any one of these words to refer to different emotions on different occasions – they do not invariably refer to kama muta. Furthermore, these words don't have exact translations in other languages, and sometimes can't really be translated at all. Vernacular emotion words in different language differ in their prototypes and the scope of their referents. In any case, no vernacular language has a single word or phrase that encompasses all of these experiences and excludes all other emotions, or that corresponds precisely to the emotion construct as we theorize it. Hence we draw on a dead language and denote it *kama muta*, which is Sanskrit for 'moved by love.'[1] We have adopted *kama muta* as a scientific term whose meaning we can fix precisely and use consistently, much as scientists often borrow Latin or Greek terms. In Chapter 4, I define the kama muta construct.

The universality of the core experience of kama muta is a central point of this book, while at the same time we explore the great cultural variety of subjective interpretations, performances, and meanings of the kama muta experience. In this book my goal is to carve nature at the joints, identifying an emotion that is a natural kind, yet a natural kind that is culturally informed and personally experienced in each instance. I posit that humans have an innate psychological disposition to experience kama muta. The evidence I present here suggests that this evolved psychology is adapted to function according to cultural precedents, prototypes, and precepts that specify when and with whom people feel kama muta, and what it means when they do. Conversely, throughout the book I show that there are myriad institutions, practices, roles, narratives, arts, and artifacts that have culturally evolved to evoke kama muta, to orient it, to shape it, and to give it meaning. These cultural systems are culturally adapted to the evolved psychology of kama muta, which in turn is biologically adapted to them by natural selection. They have co-evolved and are mutually dependent. I begin to analyze these co-evolutionary processes in Chapter 10, and then in depth in Chapter 17 and Online Note 17.1. I will show that to understand kama muta – or any other social emotion – we must understand the total domain of culturally-informed, culturally-promising social relationships in which it arises, together with the manner in which it maps these social opportunities onto the culturally congruent range of motives. For the present, it is enough to keep in mind the concept that we cannot understand kama muta until we recognize how it functions (is adaptively integral) in many kinds of social relationships in many disparate cultures and historical epochs. The reason is that the kama muta disposition is a function (in the mathematical sense) whose input consists of sudden intensifications of culturally informed social relationships, and whose output consists of culturally fruitful motives.

In later chapters, I will also address how kama muta experiences function at the societal level. Humans are extraordinarily cooperative in a huge variety of culturally particular ways – more than any other animal. How is this possible? The heart of the matter is that people have strong feelings of identity, belonging, trust, devotion, and compassion with some other persons and groups. What is the source of this solidarity – this love? Remarkably often, it arises in kama muta.

I will explore how kama muta supports and gives form to family, friendship, cuteness and caring responses to baby humans and other animals, religious devotion, support groups, social movements, patriotism, and loyalty to comrades in combat. I will show that kama muta is vital to literature, art, cinema, video, marketing, and sports. And I will explain how kama muta does this. Neither popular culture nor science have recognized that kama muta is a fundamental force in social life, but that's what it is – an emotion fundamental to human social life.

A young actress from Kansas, asked to think about *moving* or *touching* experiences, came back after a few minutes with this list, which neatly summarizes many of the events that evoke kama muta in everyday American life:

Family.

Physical touch.

When the [6-year-old] girl I nanny for gets so excited to see me. Makes me feel like I really influence her life.

Volunteering, especially animal shelters.

Performing and seeing the smiles on people's faces.

Hearing the words 'I love you' from people close to me.

Online notes

1 Links to kama muta-evoking media

Notes

1 Sanskrit agglutinates the two words, so कามमूत could be transliterated as *kamamūta* or *kāmamūta*; but for our technical term, we separate the two words, following English orthography. In the Romanized orthography of Sanskrit, *mūta* indicates the long *u*, pronounced like the vowel in 'mew.' By using *kama muta* as our scientific name for the emotion, we do <u>not</u> mean to imply that Sanskrit speakers themselves used काममूत just as we conceptualize here, or that they used it any more precisely or consistently than any other vernacular term in any language. We could just as well name this emotion K, or anything else. We just need a fresh, unique name for the concept that we can define purely with respect to our theory and our methods for identifying it, without being encumbered by the vague and shifting penumbra of any language's emotion lexemes – which we discuss in Chapter 7.

ACKNOWLEDGMENTS

This book is the fruit of the collaborative research of the Kama Muta Lab (kamamutalab.org), directed by Beate Seibt and Thomas Schubert at the University of Oslo, in collaboration with me and with the participation of a wonderful set of students there and at UCLA. The ideas and studies of this group have enabled whatever understanding of kama muta we currently have, and made this book possible. It's a continuing joy to study kama muta with Thomas and Beate.

More particularly, the people who have contributed to this book include Mersalla Akbari, Zoya Owais Andrabi, Mariam Bakheet, Andrew Beatty, Annette Bening, Johanna Katarina Blomster, Robert E. Buswell Jr, Ethan Cristensen, Ilker Dalgar, Ipek Demirdag, Julien Deonna, Alessandro Duranti, Brittany Florkiewicz, Michael Frishkopf, Mark Gallagher, Rowan Hong, Katherine Kinzler, Matthew M. Gervais, Brian Gould, Asmir Gračanin, Jon Haidt, Nicholas Haslam, Camilla Helen Heiervang, Camille Hendricks, Taylor Henry, Hilda Hoem, Bonnyjean Hoffert, Morris Hoffman, Deborah Kapchan, Luiza Kinzerska-Martinez, Katherine Kinzler, Stephanie Jamison, Jerrold Levinson, Tanya Luhrmann, Catherine Lutz, Autumn McGrath, Lisa Mendelman, Rita Miguel, Ryan Morris, Selene Nafisi, Alex Purves, Pat Reilly, Michele Piazza, Jennifer Pierre, Rachel Rabin, Joseph Reiff, Gabriel Rossman, Ali Navid Said, Victoria Schönefeld, James Schultz, Kamilla Knutsen Steinnes, Madelijn A. Strick, Diane Sunar, Håkon Tandberg, Gregory Verini, Ad Vingerhoets, Benedicte Walle, Lei Zhu (朱磊), and Janis Zickfeld. Miranda Gilmore, Rowan Hong, and Michelle Piazza kindly read the final draft; they caught errors and made helpful comments that I tried to respond to. I appreciate the University of California, Los Angeles, for generously supporting my sabbatical year and, every year, my time for research. I am grateful to the University of Oslo and the psychology faculty, in particular, for kindly hosting me for my sabbatical year and my other fruitful and pleasant visits. Coffee Tomo, Blue Bottle

Coffee on Abbot Kinney, Caffé Luxxe on Montana, and Tim Wendelboe's Café provided perfect cappuccinos, thoughtful and hospitable baristas, and conducive milieux for writing. Students in classes, seminars, and independent study projects at the University of California, Los Angeles, and at the University of Oslo contributed innumerable insights and accounts of their kama muta experiences, while perceptively probing the theory. Thank you, all!

PART I
The feeling

1

CUTENESS AND COSMOS

Contemplant un jour un beau bébé de deux ans, frais et rose, aux cheveux bouclés, qui dormait paisiblement en plein air, caressé par le soleil d'une douce matinée en printemps, j'ai été 'ému.'

[Observing one day a beautiful two-year-old baby, fresh and pink, with curly hair, sleeping peacefully outside, caressed by the sunshine of a mild spring morning, I was 'moved.']

(Claparède 1930:335)

If kama muta has a prototype, it is the experience of hearing, seeing, and/or holding an infant. Indeed, 'imprinting' or 'attachment' to one's infant is presumably the primordial evolutionary function of kama muta. Responses to blog queries such as "how does it feel to hold your newborn baby for the first time" on sites such Yahoo! Answers indicate that many English–speaking mothers and fathers weep when they first see and hold their newborns. On another website a woman writes of her childbirth:

As the labor progressed, three things helped me more than anything else: Alex fed me ice chips, which were hugely refreshing. He put cold damp paper towels on my forehead and wiped my face during each contraction, which felt wonderful and helped distract me from the intense pressure. Most of all, I responded enormously to his positive encouragement. He'd say things like, 'You're doing a great job; you're so amazing; I'm so proud of you; our sweet baby boy is coming into the world because of you.' (Those words still make me tear up!) Every time he'd say something buoying, I'd feel a huge new wave of energy. I was amazed at how well positive encouragement helped, and I was so grateful to him.

So it was at 12:40pm that the doctor placed teeny Toby into my arms. He was purplish-red and wet and crying, and my heart felt like it was going to burst. He felt soft and smooth, and I was weeping and laughing. It was so magical to be cuddling our sweet sweet baby in my arms after nine months. I would have a million babies just for that moment.

Remembering that day still makes me weepy.[1]

But the cuteness of any child, animal, cartoon character, doll, or stuffed animal can evoke kama muta. People are often instantly attracted to others' infants and toddlers, as well as kittens, puppies, and other baby animals that match the neotenous *Kindchenschema* (Lorenz 1943, 1988:164–165). Lorenz described the *Kindchenschema* as a gestalt comprising relatively large head compared to body size, a high and protruding forehead, large eyes, chubby cheeks, a small nose and mouth, short and thick extremities, and a plump body shape. Sounds and smells are probably also important (Kringelbach et al. 2016), as is a certain configuration of clumsy awkwardness in locomotion. Many breeds of dogs are tailored expressly to the *Kindchenschema* template – buyers prefer cute dogs and breeders select for this schema.[2]

The cuter the image of an infant or child, the more participants rate themselves as motivated to take care of the infants depicted (Glocker et al. 2009; Nittono et al. 2012; Sherman et al.; Coan 2012). Similarly, Volk and Quinsey (2002) found that the younger the age of the face depicted in a photograph (aged six months to six years), the more viewers expressed hypothetical willingness to care for and to adopt the depicted child. The immediate motivations evoked by seeing cute babies are to feed them, touch and hold them, and keep them warm, which are exactly what a newborn needs. Bodily contact between parent and child is the primary medium for this permanent attachment or bonding, and it is our impression that these moments of cuddling the baby are frequently the events in which parents and other family members report kama muta.

People tend to perceive cute beings as helpless, physically weak (Lorenz 1943), naïve, warm, and kind (Berry & McArthur 1985), and hence vulnerable and needing care. Susan T. Fiske and colleagues' extensively and cross-culturally supported Stereotype Content Model posits that the perception of a person or category of person's warmth and low competence evokes the perceiver's pity and sympathy toward the person(s), in turn eliciting helping and protective behavior (Cuddy, Fiske, & Glick 2007; S. Fiske 2010; S. Fiske 2012). And there is direct evidence that facial cuteness does evoke help-related behavior, such as returning lost resumes (Keating et al. 2003). Dijker (2014) theorizes that there is an adaptive psychological disposition to feel "sympathy" when a person perceives that another person is cute and vulnerable. Dijker posits that this disposition has evolved because it prevents harm to kin. Dijker suggests that the emotion of being moved is closely related to the tender feelings prompted by cute targets. Indeed, one intriguing American study found that the more "attractive" (cute?) an infant, the more affectionate and attentive the mother was, measured by her objective actions (Langlois et al. 1995).

The International Affective Picture System consists of 606 photographs intended to evoke the full range of human emotions (Bradley & Lang 2007). A large sample of American participants rated each of the photos on what the authors call "valance" by selecting a schematized "manikin" from an array that varied in facial expression and body position. Of all 606 photos, the seven photos rated most positive were photos of, respectively: puppies, bunnies, a kitten, a human baby, a seal, a human baby, and another human baby. This suggests that the cuteness kama muta response to images is very strong indeed.

Kamilla Knutsen Steinnes (2017) interviewed (in Norwegian) seven women who were at an animal shelter near Oslo and were interacting with cute animals at the time she interviewed them. In response to questions about their feelings at the moment, four spontaneously labeled their emotion *rørt*, the nearest term to the English *moved*, which is the word that Norwegians typically use to name kama muta experiences. Most of the sensations that are characteristic of kama muta (see Chapter 2) were reported by most of the seven women (Steinnes 2017:13). Table 1.1 summarizes the sensations they reported.

One 56-year-old respondent said that "Whenever I get that feeling after spending time with her [informant's cat], I just want to do kind things for others.

TABLE 1.1 Sensations of women interacting with animals at an Oslo animal shelter

Sensation	Total	Number of women (N = 7)		
		Volunteered information	*Reported when specifically asked*	*Observed*
A floating, buoyant feeling	7	5	2	0
Moist eyes, teary-eyed	6	2	3	1
A warm feeling	6	5	1	0
Tears, crying	5	1	2	2
A feeling in the chest	5	3	2	0
Goosebumps, chills	4	1	3	0
Hand on chest (observed)	4	0	0	4
Choked up	3	0	2	1
Difficulty speaking	3	2	0	1

Source: Steinnes 2017.

I get really friendly" (2017:12; all quotations translated by Steinnes). She also said,

> I have certainly felt it [the feeling] before. [Interviewer: When?] After the birth of my first and second child. … Other times that I've felt this same emotion is when I was in love. I just feel happy. It's pure bliss, this feel-good experience. I feel like I'm helping the animal and I receive plenty in return. She [informant's cat] appreciates my affection and care, you know. She talks to me, purrs, and I can just tell how much she is enjoying herself. It's really rewarding.
>
> *(Steinnes 2017:13)*

Another, age 26, said,

> I would compare it with my boyfriend. You know, the feeling I have here right now [at the animal shelter surrounded by seven kittens] is the same as what I usually feel around him. I feel safe and completed. It is reassuring somehow. It might not be the exact same because these are two completely different situations. But I do think the feeling is the same in both. For me anyway.
>
> *(2017:13)*

A 16-year-old informant "compared the feeling to the same one she experienced when she celebrated Christmas Eve with her family. She highlighted unity, love and happiness to describe the feeling she felt in both contexts." (2017:13) And she described the pleasant sensation of warmth from inside. Narratives relating to caretaking and parental protection surfaced in five out of the seven interviews. One woman told how she and her dog have a child-parent relationship: "He is like a small child. I feel this maternal instinct coming to life in me, I want to protect him, to take care of him." (Informant F, age 24) Another woman described the mutual caretaking bond she had formed with her cat: "She can always tell when I need her. She comes over and takes care of me, just like I take care of her. She puts her paws around my neck, almost like she is giving me a hug" (Informant G, age 23).

Steinnes (2017) also ran a study using data kindly provided by Ad Vingerhoets and Tim Wildschut, combined with new data she collected. Participants rated seven photos of young animals and seven of adult animals. Dutch participants were asked how much the image evoked felt physical sensations or made them feel moved (*Wekt dit plaatje lichamelijke beroering op?*) and how much it touched them (*Raakt dit plaatje u?*). Norwegian participants were asked (in English) to rate how cute each image was. Across the 14 images, cuteness ratings were correlated with how moving it was ($r = .73$, $p = .003$) and how touching it was ($r = .82$, $p < .001$). In another study she pretested videos of animals to select four especially cute videos and four not particularly cute ones. Then she showed the videos to a Norwegian sample and a US American sample. As predicted, the cute videos evoked significantly more intense sensations typical of kama muta (see Chapter 2); higher ratings of being *moved, touched,* and *heart-warmed*; more positive ratings of the valence of the participant's feelings; and stronger motivation to form or strengthen close relationships (all $p < .001$). There were no significant differences between the results from the samples of Norwegians and US Americans.

When preparing this study, we noted that most of the videos on the Internet that social media users found especially cute depicted affectionate interaction between an animal or human baby and another animal or person. We wanted to test whether affectionate interaction indeed makes videos both cuter and evokes stronger kama muta responses. So, for another study, Steinnes (2017, Steinnes et al. 2019) made pairs of comparable videos; one of each pair showed affectionately touching or licking between two cute puppies, cute kittens, or one cute animal and a human hand. The other video in each pair showed the exact same two animals or animal and a hand moving, but not touching or otherwise interacting. As predicted, the Norwegian participants rated the videos depicting affectionate interactions as cuter, and as evoking more intense sensations typical of kama muta; and responded with higher ratings of being *moved, touched,* and *heart-warmed* ($p = .004$ and $p < .001$, respectively). Moreover, ratings of the sensations partially mediated the effect of video type on cuteness ratings, and ratings of *being moved, touched,* or *heart-warmed* also partially mediated the effect of type of video on cuteness ratings. That is, as predicted, two components of the kama muta response to the videos substantially affected how cute the videos seemed to participants.

What Steinnes' research shows is that the emotional responses that people have to kittens, puppies, bunnies, baby hedgehogs, and the like consists of at least four of the components of kama muta: a distinctive set of physical sensations, especially a warm feeling in the chest, moist eyes or tears, and goosebumps; a definitely positive feeling; labels such as *moving, touching,* and *heart-warming*; and motivation to strengthen close relationships or form new ones. I'll have a lot more to say in this book about the kind of relationship that for the moment I am just calling "close"; our conceptualization of the nature and dynamics of that relationship were the foundations for Steinnes' research. I think that the joy of kama muta in response to images and videos of cute animals and human babies, as well as in response to social events, is a major motivation for posting, sharing, and liking social media content (for a similar idea about *being moved* by social media, see Dale et al. 2017). We will look into that a bit more in Chapter 8.

It is intriguing that there is no definite standard English, Norwegian, or German lexeme for the emotional response to cuteness (though the Uralic languages – Hungarian, Finnish, and Estonian – do have lexemes for precisely this). However, there is an English slang word, *squee,* that comes pretty close. The leading results of a Google search for *squee* are images and compilations of images of truly cute kittens, dogs, and cats cuddling with dogs. *Squee* is also used to denote the screams of *fangirls* and *fanboys* when they see and hear singers and bands they love. On the Internet, some young speakers of English use the phatic *squee* for the response to cuteness, indexically naming the emotion onomatopoetically by the *squeeee!* sound that some girls and young women may utter when they see a cute animal or event. *Squee* also denotes the utterance and emotion of *fangirls* (and sometimes *fanboys*) make or feel when they see or hear their idol.[3] It is notable that the same lexeme is used for both the emotional response to cuteness seen on the Internet and the emotional response of fans seeing their celebrity idol – and that both uses are onomatopoeia for the sound of the exclamation, suggesting that people in these two situations utter the same sound and feel the same emotion. This is not conclusive evidence that the predominant or ideal emotion is the same in the two contexts – many words are polysemic – but it's a strong hint that the emotions are the same or apperceived as very similar. Note further that *squee!* is a phatic – a speech act (performative utterance) that, as the Wikipedia article on phatic expression elegantly puts it, "performs the important function of establishing, maintaining, and managing bonds of sociality between participants."[4] To vocalize the exclamation *Awww!*, or type *squee!* on social media, is not just to communicate information, but to <u>declare that one feels an emotion, and hence that one is the kind of person who feels this emotion about this social relational event</u>. Furthermore, these vocal or typed phatics <u>invite</u> the listener or viewer to join in the emotion, and, perhaps, to intensify the listener or viewer's *close* relationship with the kitten or idol, <u>and with the speaker</u>. This illocutionary effect makes them what Rett (2018) calls "emotive markers."

It is not obvious how one might account for the absence of any accessible, prevalent oral lexeme for kama muta that occurs in this particular domain, cuteness. But it is notable that even without a universal accessible term for the emotion, BuzzFeed employs several Beastmasters who pick out the cutest videos and photos to display prominently on its web site (Baron 2014).

I hadn't seen my 20-month-old grandson for 4 months, and didn't really expect him to remember me. But when I arrived he immediately agreed to letting me take him from my daughter's arms, and put his head down against my neck and snuggled. Later when my daughter and he were going out, he came and took my hand to bring me along.

He loves chocolate, but the next day, when my daughter gave him a tiny chocolate treat after changing his diaper, rather than eating it, he kept it in his little hand and, when he got down, brought it out and fed it to me.

(A. P. Fiske)

Kama muta is evoked by cute features, but probably it is strengthened by the perception that the infant or child needs to be cared for, fed, or held. People may feel a kama muta 'tenderness' when they see or hear about a person who is helpless, injured, lost, fleeing, frightened, hungry, or otherwise vulnerable – especially a cute child or animal that is in jeopardy. That is, vulnerability seems to amplify the response to cute physical features of the target. This emotional experience is probably an important motive to rescue, donate to, or adopt humans and animals – or simply be attentive and kind.

Reading this passage, a UCLA undergraduate made the following connection:

> Maybe this explains why fangirls tend to latch on to male characters with angsty backstories or that they see as being in distress. You see it in fanfiction all the time—male characters like the Winter Soldier/Bucky Barnes from the Marvel Cinematic Universe are portrayed as being even more distressed in fanfics than they are in the source material and (usually) this angst is followed by "fluff" or the "hurt" is followed by "comfort". The fact that the Winter Soldier has killed hundreds of people is ignored because he has been through so much emotional and physical trauma. It is as though the perceived emotional vulnerability of these characters enhances fangirls' sense of connection and attraction to them. Back when I was a frequent user of the teen-girl dominated social media platform Tumblr, fans of the Winter Soldier, the 10th or 11th Doctor from the long-running BBC sci-fi classic *Dr. Who,* and other popular films and television shows would frequently post "gif sets" of their favorite male characters in distress and would affectionately refer to these 30 to 50-year-old men as "my sweet baby angel," "my son," or "my child" in the captions or tags. I no longer speak the lingo, but when you type "my son" into Tumblr these posts are now also accompanied by "so soft," "sad puppy," and "my precious little angel muffin." The Tumblr bloggers also still appear to be putting flower crowns on characters they love.
>
> (Rowan Hong)

People often feel kama muta in response to cute faces and clumsy infantile movement, especially when the cute babies (human or other animals) play, or snuggle. A baby's kiss or offer to share his food, or a kitten's lick, can also evoke a kama muta experience. Even an idea can be cute enough to evoke a little kama muta. Lewis Carroll's *Through the Looking Glass* opens with Alice talking to her kittens as if they were children and then as if they were friends, pretending they are responding, as one of them plays with a ball of yarn that Alice constantly has to roll up again. She scolds and kisses the kitten she is holding. Then Alice says to the kitten,

> Do you hear the snow against the window-panes, Kitty? How nice and soft it sounds! Just as if someone was kissing the window all over outside. I wonder if the snow LOVES the trees and fields, that it kisses them so gently? And then it covers them up snug, you know, with a white quilt; and perhaps it says, 'Go to sleep, darlings, till the summer comes again.' And when they wake up in the summer, Kitty, they dress themselves all in green, and dance about – whenever the wind blows – oh, that's very pretty!'
>
> *(Carroll 1897:18)*

I was going to Central Station one evening, and I took the tram. There was a drug addict, carrying a lot of plastic bags. After a couple of stops a drunk man came on the tram; he began speaking very rudely to the addict, insulting him loudly, telling him to get off the tram. He kept saying nasty things to him. I wanted to tell the drunk to stop but I didn't know what to do. I was angry but embarrassed. Then, while the tram was going, an old lady about 80 got up and walked up to the drunk man, pointed her walking stick at him. She told him to "stop talking like that, you can't say those things, behave like a human being." She told him to go away, and he got off at the next stop. Then the other passengers started saying to the addict, "Sorry that you experienced that. You shouldn't be treated like that." Several of them, maybe ten, went up and shook his hand, and several hugged him; people said good bye to him as they got off. I was very moved by that. Also a bit sad that the addict has to experience that. When I get moved I feel as if I'm about to cry, though I don't. When you get moved you feel that your heart is warm [gestures repeatedly toward her heart].

(Ina Emily Swann Rønneberg, dictated to ApF)

Need can be visible or audible. Calls and crying, especially in a child-like voice, evoke kama muta.

William McDougall (1919, 1923) argued that there are seven primary emotions, one of which is "the tender emotion," a concept very similar to our construct of kama muta. He construed it to be the expression of the maternal instinct common to birds and mammals that a human prototypically feels "when he hastens to comfort a little child sobbing in distress"(1923:328), or more broadly, when a person perceives something delicate or helpless that evokes a protective response (1923:335; see also 424). He posited that tenderness is evoked by the expression of need:

> it is important to note that the object which is the primary provocative of tender emotion is not the child itself, but the child's expression of pain, fear, or distress of any kind, especially the child's cry of distress; further, that this instinctive response is provoked by the cry, not only of one's own offspring, but of any child. Tender emotion and the protective impulse are, no doubt, evoked more readily and intensely by one's own offspring, because about them a strongly organized and complex sentiment grows up. But the distress of any child will evoke this response in a very intense degree in those in whom the instinct is strong. ...
>
> In the human being, just as is the case in some degree with all the instinctive responses, and as we noticed especially in the case of disgust, there takes place a vast extension of the field of application of the maternal instinct. The similarity of various objects to the primary or natively given

object, similarities which in many cases can only be operative for a highly developed mind, enables them to evoke tender emotion and its protective impulse directly—*i.e.*, not merely by way of associative reproduction of the natively given object. In this way the emotion is liable to be evoked, not only by the distress of a child, but by the mere sight or thought of a perfectly happy child; for its feebleness, its delicacy, its obvious incapacity to supply its own needs, its liability to a thousand different ills, suggest to the mind its need of protection. By a further extension of the same kind the emotion may be evoked by the sight of any very young animal, especially if in distress ... [this] instinct ... is the source of the only entirely admirable, satisfying, and perfect human relationship, as well as of every kind of purely disinterested conduct.

In a similar direct fashion the distress of any adult (towards whom we harbour no hostile sentiment) evokes the emotion; but in this case it is more apt to be complicated by sympathetic pain, when it becomes the painful, tender emotion we call pity; whereas the child, or any other helpless and delicate thing, may call it out in the pure form without alloy of sympathetic pain. It is amusing to observe how, in those women in whom the instinct is strong, it is apt to be excited, owing to the subtle working of similarity, by any and every object that is small and delicate of its kind—a very small cup, or chair, or book, or what not.

(McDougall 1919:58–59)

McDougall's "tender emotion" is precisely kama muta when it is evoked by cuteness and vulnerability; he does not realize that innumerable other things can evoke kama muta. Without citing McDougall, Batson and colleagues (Batson, Fultz, & Schoenrade 1987; Batson et al. 2007; Batson 2010) likewise connected being moved with sympathy, compassion, tenderness, warmth, and soft-heartedness. They define and measure the personality trait of 'empathic concern' as emotional responsiveness to encountering vulnerable or needy persons. And in our research, this self-reported personality trait is consistently correlated around $r = .32–.35$ with participants' ratings of how *moved* or *touched* they feel when viewing kama muta-evoking video clips or remembering moments in their lives when they shed tears because of a positive experience. The self-reported trait of empathic concern is also correlated with participants' reports of warmth in the chest, with tears, and with goosebumps or chills when watching kama muta videos or remembering personal episodes of positive tears (Zickfeld et al. 2017; Zickfeld et al. 2019).

Moving experiences with adult animals

People may have kama muta experiences with characters they read or hear about, or with real or imagined ones they perceive in movies, television, or videos – actors, or animated or cartoon characters. They may also feel kama muta in encounters with animals. I often sit outside at a café in Los Angeles with my two exceptionally appealing retriever-Chow mix dogs. From time to time a passerby will look at them, stop, and say something like "Awww! How cute! May I pet them?" Typically one or both of the dogs comes over to the speaker, leans against her, then lies down, and soon rolls over on his back for a tummy-rub. If the petter stops or moves to leave, the dog gently reaches out with his paw to touch her, appealing for her to keep petting. With her voice, her body language, and her contented smiles, the petter shows that she is enthralled, calls her friends to join her, and often speaks of missing her dog back home, or the desire to get a dog herself. She may ask if I come here often and say that she wants to see the dogs again. I previously had two Newfoundland dogs in succession; they are huge, long-furred dogs with giant heads and soulful eyes. 'Newfies' love children and instinctively lie down when approached by a toddler. These dogs, too, often elicited this *awww* response. I think that this is a mild kama muta experience evoked by suddenly falling in love with the animal. It's quite similar to the response that many people have upon seeing a cute human infant or toddler. It doesn't ordinarily reach the intensity that provokes tears, goosebumps, or other overt physiological sensations, but the feeling is qualitatively the same as more intense kama muta experiences. And the motivational effects are the same, only milder.

An Australian surfer (putting both hands to her chest) described this mix of kama muta and '*awe*' when she's in the ocean, a "very profound experience that I have with the ocean and I think a lot of surfers feel the same way"; she feels "part of nature and the world and connected."

The other day, like dolphins came and swum right up right up to the surf board and we were like super close to them and you could see them just playing and having a good time and they were just like jumping and some of them were floating and it was that pure joy that we feel when we're surfing, the dolphins were experiencing the <u>same</u> thing right next to us, and moments like that are definitely very heart-warming.

(Hannah Wang, transcribed from an audio recording)

Exceptional kama muta encounters with animals can be profound. As a woman stood looking through the underwater glass wall of an aquarium, a Beluga whale came right up to her, face-to-face, making eye contact with her; she described her experiences with phrases such as "connection, communication, permanent change in perception of love, extremely powerful" (DeMares 2000:91). DeMares (2000:95) interviewed informants who had had profound, life-changing "peak experiences" with cetaceans. All five informants reported "an enduring sense of connectedness with the animal or animals which is generalized to all others of the species." A woman who does dolphin-assisted therapy reported a personal experience with a wild dolphin:

> when the dolphin is side to side with you and looks you in the eye, and you just have the opportunity to be with the dolphin in a very special way. After that experience, when I see pictures of dolphins, or I see videos of dolphins, my heart has the same feeling as when I was in the water.
>
> *(DeMares 2000:95)*

Observing orcas in the wild, a man reported:

> We really saw that close harmony that existed within the pod. Frequently … there wouldn't be just one or two coming together, there might be three, four, or five. All moving in unison just right in front of us. Literally cresting, breathing at the same time, and then going down under. In very close proximity, so you'd see quite a few orca fins all at once as they moved en masse under the water again.
>
> *(DeMares 2000:95; ellipses by DeMares)*

Informants reported what DeMares characterizes as "non-duality/wholeness" and "unconditional love." Another woman made contact with a dolphin who took care to swim along at her slow pace as she walked on the beach:

> And it didn't take but a couple of seconds before I started to have a feeling that I've never had before at this level. It was love, exponentially enhanced to a point that I can't describe … I just stood there and realized that tears were falling off my chin. The feelings were so powerful and so filling.
>
> *(DeMares 2000:96–97)*

Another woman spoke of her feeling of affinity, a bond between herself and the orcas, a sense of harmony among the orcas and between the orcas and their environment – a circle of harmony that she felt included herself (DeMares 2000:97). Another woman went orca-watching with her son, who had come to town to confront her about their conflicted relationship. As soon as the boat went out, they encountered

> a mother and an adolescent son named Slick and Mike [who began] breaching in tandem off the bow of the boat. … And [my son] and I were both in tears, and we felt very much that these whales were responding to our process.
>
> *(DeMares 2000:98; brackets and ellipses by DeMares)*

Although DeMares did not investigate physical sensations, he mentions other informants who shed tears as well.

One of the dolphin viewer mentions that after having a special feeling alongside a dolphin, she has the same feeling in her heart when she sees photos or videos of dolphins. Many viewers sometimes seem to feel kama muta from photos or videos of animals even when they've never encountered the species up close, or at all. Depictions in art may have similar effects on occasion.

Humans sometimes form strongly affectionate relationships with animals – they love their pets and may become deeply attached to wild animals. When a person 'falls in love' 'head over heels' with an animal, suddenly feeling an exceptional bond, the person feels kama muta. In an online study where participants watched short video clips, a video of a reunification between two men and a lion was one of the most *moving* for people from Portugal, China, and Israel. Likewise, videos of people saving a baby elephant and the baby then reuniting with its mother, as well as of an elephant herd giving a last goodbye to a dead baby elephant, both *moved* audiences in Norway and the US (Seibt et al. 2017).

Do highly social animals have this feeling, too – toward their offspring, mates, or their human? Few, if any, non-human animals are definitely known to shed tears, and it's not obvious how a researcher would determine whether they have warm feelings in the center of the chest, are choked up, or feel buoyant afterwards. However, three primatologists have independently told us of an intriguing phenomenon they have repeatedly observed. Chimpanzees forage in shifting subgroups that separate and rejoin after several hours or a few days. When chimpanzees who are 'friends' meet up again after a separation, their hair stands up. Then they may hug or groom each other. The only written source I have been able to find is Frans de Waal, describing "reunion euphoria." First he quotes Cynthia Moss on joyous elephant reunions after separation, then he continues: "The greeting ceremonies of chimpanzees, both in the wild and in captivity, are well known: they involve charging about with erect hair, loud hooting, kissing, and embracing" (de Wall 1996:174). Perhaps chimpanzee reunion piloerection is homologous the human reunion goosebumps.

Humankind, nature, and the cosmos: Feeling one with the wild

Cute and vulnerable infants, children, animals, adults, and even small things evoke a sense of wanting to take care of them. It is our own concern and care for the needy creature that *moves* us. What happens, then, when, from a new perspective, something that appeared big and strong suddenly appears small and vulnerable? This is exactly the experience that many astronauts describe looking down on the earth. One writer who interviewed astronauts paraphrased their emotional experience when looking out at earth as a feeling of "unity with nature, transcendence, and universal brotherhood" (Hunt 2015:73; quoted in Yaden et al. 2016:3). Yaden et al. (2016) quote astronauts' descriptions of their extraordinarily intense emotions seeing the earth from space:

an overwhelming sense of oneness and connectedness.

(Edgar Mitchell, 2016:2)

abiding concern and passion for the well-being of Earth.

(Edgar Mitchell, 2016:5)

in outer space, you develop an instant global consciousness, a people orientation, an intense dissatisfaction with the state of the world, and a compulsion to do something about it.

(Edgar Mitchell, 2016:5)

I had another feeling, that the earth is like a vibrant living thing. The vessels we've clearly seen on it looked like the blood and veins of human beings. I said to myself: this is the place we live, it's really magical.

(Yang Liu, 2016:3)

yet when I first looked back at the earth, standing on the moon, I cried.

(Alan Shepard, 2016:3)

You ... say to yourself, 'That's humanity, love, feeling, and thought.' You don't see the barriers of color and religion and politics that divide this world.

(Gene Cernan, 2016:3)

You identify with Houston and then you identify with Los Angeles and Phoenix and New Orleans ... and that whole process of what it is you identify with begins to shift when you go around the Earth ... you look down and see the surface of that globe you've lived on all this time, and you know all those people down there and they are like you, they are you—and somehow you represent them. You are up there as the sensing element, that point out on the end ... you recognize that you're a piece of this total life.

(Rusty Schweikart, 2016:3)

When you go around the Earth in an hour and a half, you begin to recognize that your identity is with that whole thing.

(Rusty Schweikart, 2016:5)

Before I flew I was already aware how small and vulnerable our planet is; but only when I saw it from space, in all its ineffable beauty and fragility, did I realize that humankind's most urgent task is to cherish and preserve it for future generations.

(Sigmund Jahn, 2016:3)

The feeling of unity is not simply an observation. With it comes a strong sense of compassion and concern for the state of our planet and the effect humans are having on it. It isn't important in which sea or lake you observe a slick of pollution or in the forests of which country a fire breaks out, or on which continent a hurricane arises. You are standing guard over the whole of our Earth.

(Yuri Artyushkin, 2016:3)

From space I saw Earth—indescribably beautiful with the scars of national boundaries gone.

(Muhammad Ahmad Faris, 2016:3)

The Earth is dramatically beautiful when you see it from orbit, more beautiful than any picture you've ever seen. It's an emotional experience because you're removed from the Earth but at the same time you feel this incredible connection to the Earth like nothing I'd ever felt before.

(Sam Durrance, 2016:3)

During a space flight, the psyche of each astronaut is re-shaped; having seen the sun, the stars and our planet, you become more full of life, softer. You begin to look at all living things with greater trepidation and you begin to be more kind and patient with the people around you.

(Boris Volynov, 2016:6)

Note that in addition to a wonderful sense of oneness with the whole earth, five astronauts report feeling that the earth is vulnerable, so it needs their protection and care. They remember perceiving the earth as "small and vulnerable" and realizing the "fragility" of the earth made it clear that "humankind's most urgent task is to cherish and preserve it for future generations"; feeling "abiding concern and passion for the well-being of Earth"; "an intense dissatisfaction with the state of the world, and a compulsion to do something about it." They could almost have been describing their feelings about seeing kittens or holding their newborn infant – their affective devotion and moral commitment to caring has about the same tenor. For more details on astronauts' kama muta moments, see Online Note 1.1.

Some of the most profound experiences of kama muta are generated by the sudden intensification of a relationship of unity in which a person feels one with all humans, with 'nature,' the earth, or the whole cosmos (Marshall 2005). Encountering wild animals, looking out over a beautiful 'natural' landscape, walking in the woods, sitting by a pond or a river, or staring up at the myriad stars on a clear night in the mountains, one may lose the sense of being a separate individual – evoking kama muta (see Laski 1961:187–190, 1980). One may feel that one belongs to a vast timeless universe in which the self is merely a transient illusion. Ultimately, one is not separate: all is one. Marshall's review of "mystical" experiences with nature reported in English-language sources summarizes 17 often-reported features, including 7 shown in Table 1.2.

In his textual expansion of the table of 17 features, Marshall makes it clear that the characteristic feelings are "positive" and "affirmative," "dominated by bliss,

TABLE 1.2 Seven of the seventeen features Marshall identified in "mystical" experiences with nature

Unity	Feeling part of the whole; the whole contained within; everything intimately connected; community
Self	Relaxation of individual identity; identification with persons, animals, plants, objects, even the entire cosmos; discovery of deeper self
Knowledge	Intuitive, all-encompassing knowledge ('knew everything'); insights into order, harmony, and perfection of the world; ... feeling that one has 'come home'
Love	All-embracing love; sense of being deeply loved
Beauty	Extraordinary beauty; everything equally beautiful
Body	Sensations through the body or at places along the spine
Miscellaneous feelings	Bliss, joy, elation, uplift, peace, relief, gratitude, wonder, power, fearlessness, humor, surprise, insignificance, humility, unworthiness, awe, terror, discomfort with sheer intensity

Source: Marshall 2005:27; see also 48–81.

joy, reassuring insights, balancing perspectives, love" (2005:80). One of the other features Marshall lists is an altered sense of time, or timelessness. He states that mystical experiences of nature are "usually fairly brief, lasting from moments to hours, although traces may last for days, weeks, or longer. ... Experiences often start abruptly, but gradual shifts are also described" (Marshall 2005:72). The other nine of Marshall's 17 features don't seem to be essentially related to these, and don't closely correspond with other researchers' characterizations of mystical experiences. Of course, there is a dialectical relation between the features used to define the category and those that are observed to occur in instances of it. All students of mysticism agree that the sense of union is either the defining feature or one of the essential defining features. In Chapters 11 and 13 we will see that mystical experiences in the world's religions often evoke kama muta.

Hudson (1918: 209–235) describes the emergence of his consciousness of this feeling beginning at age eight; growing up on the Argentine pampas, he first felt it, apparently, in regard to a particular large black snake, and then more definitely in devotion to a particular species of rare, but not exceptionally beautiful, wild-flower. By age nine, Hudson reports that he developed a very strong mystical feeling for trees, particularly locust trees in the moonlight.

Based on his journals of his first experiences in the Sierra Nevada mountains in the Yosemite region in 1869, every page of John Muir's (2004) account is filled with his joyous sense of oneness with the place. He constantly refers to the animals as "people" and to the ineffable but total connection he feels with the mountains, lakes, rivers, trees, and meadows. Muir does not describe his own physical sensations, but his exultation and devotion are transparent and explicit.

He repeatedly expresses his wish to stay forever, to experience more, to return to explore further, and his deep sense of belonging. There are indications of 'awe' at the massive Yosemite peaks, 4,000-foot cliffs, and giant trees, but the predominant theme is union with nature, experienced over and over every day. He delights in the visits of every personified insect and identifies with every flower. In one passage, looking at the red clouds around Mt Dana, Mt Gibbs, and Mammoth Mountain, he rejoices at the "infinite lavishness and fertility of Nature."

> I watched the growth of these red-lands of the sky as eagerly as if new mountain ranges were being built. Soon the group of snowy peaks in whose recesses lie the highest fountains of the Tuolumne, Merced, and North Fork of the San Joaquin were decorated with majestic colored clouds like those already described, but more complicated, to correspond with the grand fountainheads of the rivers they overshadowed. The Sierra Cathedral [Cathedral Peak], to the south of camp, was overshadowed like Sinai. Never before noticed so fine a union of rock and cloud in form and color and substance, drawing earth and sky together as one; and so human it is, every feature and tint of color goes to one's heart, and we shout, exulting in wild enthusiasm as if all the divine show were our own. More and more, in a place like this, we feel ourselves part of wild Nature, kin to everything.
>
> *(Muir 2004:134)*

The infinitude of stars in the night sky clearly seen far from any light, at high altitude on a clear night, may evoke this sort of feeling in some, as may a spectacular sunset. Experiencing a total eclipse of the sun, people may "feel a sense of immense connection with the Universe" (Russo 2012:56) that in some cases involves goosebumps or tears. Informants seeing a total eclipse say things such as:

> The emotional rush is literally out of this world.
> Love for all. …
> I feel as if I could/should run up the shadow to the Sun—as if that is where I belong; where I came from
> I feel I am at one with the cosmos.

Experiences of nature vary, and often involve a mix of emotions, such as kama muta combined with an awed feeling of being tiny, trivial, and impermanent in an immense cosmos – the experience of a sudden intensification of an authority ranking relationship with the universe. That is, just like the sudden intensification of connection that is felt as kama muta, something approximately named by the English vernacular *awe* occurs when people suddenly feel deference and respect before a tremendous eminence that is vastly superior to them. (On *awe*, see Chapter 19).

The person encountering and feeling one with some greater trans-human whole apperceives this whole as something profoundly <u>there</u>, given, ineluctable, perhaps unknowable or eternal. That is what evokes kama muta. But every such experience is afforded or impeded, shaped, and interpreted through the person's cultural framework. While the human disposition to feel kama muta is an evolved adaptation universal to the species, culture informs the specific features of the relationships that underlie it, the beings or entities who relate in those relationships, the opportunities for intensification of the relationships, the significance of the intensification, and the manner of performing it. (I address these cultural aspects in Chapters 4, 10, and 17). 'Nature,' 'planet earth,' 'the universe,' and such are not simply immanent entities; they are the cultural constructions of particular historical processes, political forces, and economic configurations. So, likewise, is the separation from 'nature' that contemporary Westerners of some social classes often feel – a separation that affords sudden 'reconnection' in kama muta. In contemporary environmentalism, 'earth' is now our common heritage to sustain, but less than a century ago for many in the West, it was something savage that civilized, scientific people were responsible for conquering, controlling, and taming. Technologically sophisticated nineteenth century Western men felt certain they were destined to exploit the earth's resources. In the Christian tradition before that, everything existed to serve man. Yet the experience of late nineteenth century transcendentalists and contemporary environmentalists like ourselves is that we humans are members of an interdependent community – and in moments of our lives when we 'realize' this, we may feel kama muta.

Intriguingly, kama muta can also occur when abstract, even mathematical thinking evokes a sense of the wholeness of everything. For Arthur Koestler's sensitive report of this, see Online Note 1.2.

Peak experiences

Most Americans from time to time have 'peak experiences' in which the self merges with nature or the cosmos (Maslow 1962, 1970; Davis 1998). "It is quite characteristic in peak experiences that the whole universe is perceived as an integrated and unified whole" (Maslow 1970:59). Furthermore, "the peak-experiencer becomes more loving and more accepting" (1970:67) and people who are religious feel "gratitude or an all-embracing love for everybody and everything, leading to an impulse to do something good for the world, an eagerness to repay, even a sense of obligation and dedication" (1970:68).

In a 1970 representative sample of 1,000 residents of the San Francisco-Oakland area, respondents were asked whether or not they had "ever had the feeling that you were in close contact with something holy or sacred"; 76% said they had. When asked they had ever "experienced the beauty of nature in a deeply moving way," 82% said they had. And 38% responded affirmatively to the question asking whether they had ever had the "feeling that you were in harmony with the universe" (Wuthnow 1978:61). Eighty-eight percent reported that they had had at least one of these experiences. Many respondents had had such experiences in the past year (47%, 70%, and 76%, respectively), suggesting that they are not rare in most lives. In each case, somewhat less than half of these experiences had had a "lasting influence on my life." Apparently, these experiences have motivational effects, evoking loving-kindness: the deeper and more lasting the effect of the experience on a respondent's life, the more likely they were to report working for social change, helping to solve social problems, or helping people in need. These results may well include social desirability and demand effects, but they are consistent with other surveys (Panzarella 1980; see Chapter 11 and Online Note 1.3).

There's no way to know what proportion of these peak experiences involved kama muta, but it seems likely that a great many did, and other studies of peak experiences offer many glimpses of kama muta. Studying peak experiences, Ho et al. (2013) asked Portuguese and Chinese adults to "Think of the most wonderful or joyful experience of your life up through the age of 14." In each culture, more than half of these experiences were experiences of "interpersonal joy" consisting of "family togetherness, friendship, birth of a sibling, having a mentor, being a mentor, recovery of family member from illness, peer camaraderie." Norwegians most frequently report the peak experiences of their lives to be "family togetherness, the birth of a baby sibling or cousin, and romantic bliss," report Hoffman, Iversen, & Ortiz 2010). People often shed "tears of joy" on such occasions. Hoffman, Garg, and González-Mujica (2013) asked a sample of 131 mostly urban and educated Indian informants to report an occasion when they had felt "tears of joy." Among the reports, 20% were occasions of non-romantic affection, 12% the birth of a child, 12% a reunion (typically with kin at a holiday or celebration), 8% romantic affection, and 8% identification with a movie or other media narrative. In addition, 16% reported a moment of personal achievement, often in the company of good friends or family (see Chapter 5 for a discussion of the solidarity that achievements often generate). A mostly Australian nationality sample of 298 responded to the question, "Have you ever had a peak experience in a love relationship, for example: an experience of profound oneness, incredibly intense joy during sexual contact or arising from loving your partner?" (Woodward, Findlay, & Moore 2009:436). Two-thirds of respondents reported "peak experiences … which involved mystical sexual or loving experiences, feelings of sexual 'oneness' with a partner, intense passion or intense feelings of closeness and belonging, and out of the ordinary positive feelings such as overwhelming joy or happiness" (2009:436). Some of these involved tears of joy, and many may have been kama muta. For example, one informant reported,

> Several times since October last year our love-making has moved me to tears of great happiness. The experience is overwhelming. I am totally focused on my husband and there is a sense of 'time has stopped.' There is a blending of the physical, mental and spiritual in a very special way. I feel as I move 'out there' that there is someone or something very beautiful 'out

there.' Afterwards I feel very loving and close to my husband and part of something very special in the universe.

(Woodward, Findlay, & Moore 2009:437)

When kama muta is strong, it is memorable. When kama muta is extremely strong, it may be a highpoint of human life, making life both joyful and richly meaningful; for Marghanita Laski's accounts of what she calls "transcendental ecstasy," see Online Note 1.3. In Chapter 9, I describe the peak experiences of communal sharing that unexpectedly arise in disaster.

One aspect of mystical union with nature that I have to leave for future research is the role of art in <u>preparing</u> people to feel this, and in evoking it directly. Many landscape and nature paintings have the potential to evoke kama muta in sensitive viewers open to feeling it, especially classical Japanese painting and woodcuts. Some cultural traditions cultivate and value a kama muta sensibility. Portrayals of domestic and pastoral scenes may also evoke kama muta. How often do kama muta experiences motivate artists to paint, make woodcuts or lithographs, or sculpt? How many artists are motivated to create art in order to share their kama muta experiences with viewers, intending to give viewers the same joyous feeling of connection with nature that they have felt? In Chapter 8, I will return to art; we will see that even non-representational art can evoke strong kama muta in some viewers. In Chapter 11, we will explore *transcendent mystical* experiences of *ecstasy*, which correspond in most respects to peak experiences, except that the experiencer understands them as 'religious' and often as feelings of union with divinity. But there are no essential differences in the emotion itself.

Many people – adults as well as children – have a teddy bear or doll they snuggle up to at night. When she heard about the concept of kama muta, one colleague told us about cuddling with hers:

Whether I have experienced *kama muta* before? I believe I experience it every single night when I go to bed and find my *Wuschel* waiting there for me. Yes, even as an adult, I derive a deep sense of pleasure when I touch this very special cuddly toy that takes me back into my childhood. There is nothing quite like putting it on my neck and having its cold surface (due to its lacking fur) touch my skin. It has a soothing influence and can even give me goosebumps or cause me to chuckle for luck.

(A professor)

Every experience is culturally situated and culturally informed. Birth is culturally organized. Even random encounters with cute animals occur because humans domesticated, bred, and keep animals <u>for</u> their cuteness. Likewise, the identification with animals in *nature* is fostered by cultural representations and sensibilities about certain *wild* animals. The feeling of *belonging* and being part of *nature* or *the earth* or *the cosmos* is fostered by cultural models of those entities. However, the sorts of kama muta experiences presented in this chapter mostly are evoked by encounters in situations that were not primarily 'designed' or 'tailored' to evoke kama muta, and that people may not engage in with the principal intent to feel kama muta. Ordinarily one does not get pregnant and deliver a baby or become an astronaut chiefly in order to feel kama muta. And, of course, the primary function of space programs is not to give astronauts kama muta experiences. Conversely, at least until recently, 'modern' delivery practices and maternity ward architecture were not primarily designed to afford kama muta. Nurses briefly showed the newborn to the mother, then took it away to be weighed and measured, and brought it to a nursery, where the father could view it through a window, and from which the infant was intermittently brought to the mother to nurse. In contrast, the rest of this book describes practices, institutions, roles, arts, and artifacts whose primary function is precisely to evoke and orient kama muta. We shall see that cultures have evolved many systems to evoke kama muta, and much of the kama muta people experience is due to engagement in these practices that are culturally reproduced precisely because they reliably and strongly evoke kama muta. Moreover, we shall see that the devotion and commitment generated by kama muta is a principal source of social solidarity – it is an essential glue that bonds human dyads and groups.

Although this emotion is not widely recognized or distinguished by contemporary emotion theorists, there are some prescient early accounts. The Scottish philosopher–psychologist Alexander Bain's (1859) detailed characterization of "the tender emotions" corresponds rather well with kama muta (see Online Note 1.4). Later, without giving it a name, William James (1902) characterized a kama muta-like emotion that occurs in the core experience of religion when a person is in union or communion with a deity or some more encompassing wholeness (see Chapters 2 and 11). As I noted above, William McDougall (1919) again identified "the tender emotion" as one of the seven primary emotions; everything he wrote about the tender emotion corresponds to kama muta.

Among early accounts, the depiction of the emotion by the Swiss psychologist Édouard Claparède (1930) stands out for its sensitivity. While fully appreciating that there is no one-to-one correspondence between lexemes and emotions, Claparède indicated that the emotion he aimed to describe is the one most commonly denoted by the French *être ému, être remué*, and German *berührt sein* (whose literal physical meanings are, respectively, 'be moved, be stirred,' and 'be touched'). However, he immediately notes that the expression *être ému* is also used for social fear, as when one is about to speak in public or knocks on the door of a hierarchical superior, and for the sadness one feels when paying a condolence visit or reading about the death of a worker who supported many children. He observes that these meanings of the lexeme are entirely distinct from the emotion he is concerned with.

As a prototypical example of the emotion, he gives the audience response to a solemn patriotic ceremony when the flag is displayed, or the feeling of people in the crowd listening to the traditional reading of the names of the heroes who died for their country. Claparède observes that he has felt this emotion attending a similar ceremony abroad, though he felt no true patriotic sentiment. He mentions the impact of a preacher on his listeners. In the theater, one often feels this emotion at a reconciliation scene, when, for example, a wife finds and takes back the husband who left her, or in a scene where two friends, after a murderous quarrel, make up, one extending his hand to the other and asking for forgiveness. Claparède cites a scene in a play when a son tells his father that, when he was about to commit suicide, hearing his father's voice stopped him. And one feels this when reading newspaper accounts of human brotherhood or generosity which touch (*touchent*) us, such as during the World War when a Catholic chaplain risks his life to save a Protestant chaplain, or vice versa. Claparède felt this emotion lightly but distinctly when he read that a woman in a nearby village was celebrating her hundredth birthday, surrounded by her children and grandchildren. He also felt it one sweet spring morning upon seeing a beautiful two-year-old sleeping in the open air, caressed by the wind. The emotion can accompany action, as when one extends one's hand to a person one has injured, and might have hugged him, if custom allowed. Children don't feel this emotion, perhaps because they lack a special social sensibility. When he was about ten, Claparède reports, he was astonished to see his father crying at a patriotic ceremony.

The sensations of this emotion, Claparède notes, are sudden tears, a slight trembling of the lips, a softening or relaxation of the body, "with a light constriction of the thorax, as if one were holding back a sob" (1930:334; my translation); this half-sob interferes with speech (1930:338). Feeling this emotion, one is happy. In a subsequent footnote to his discussion of the James-Lange theory of emotion (1930:343), Claparède raises the question of whether shivers on one's back listening to moments of beautiful poetry, music, or oratory should count as instances of the emotion of beauty or solemnity, or mere bodily sensation. But he does not appear to regard this *frisson* as a sensation of the "pure emotion" that is his specific focus.

The emotion can be as brief as one or two seconds, typically four or five seconds, but, Claparède supposes, never more than 15 or 20 seconds. Nevertheless, it can recur several times in succession.

He notes that there is often surprise or relief in the situations that evoke the pure emotion he's describing, but neither is essential to the emotion. Claparède (1930) posits that the emotion in question is "pure," without any of the qualities of fear, anger, astonishment, anxiety, shame, pity, compassion, or even joy. It has sensations that overlap with sadness and grief (1930:344), but its intimate significance makes it distinct. What makes it distinct from all other emotions and affective states is that it is neutral, without any direction or biological function. It is the emotion of the pure shock, simple disorder, disruption, turmoil, confusion (*trouble*) that characterizes all emotion, but unlike all other emotions, without any value or meaning for the person. Claparède asserts that this emotion has no adaptive function in adjusting the actions of the person to the circumstances that evoke it.

Though he describes a fairly wide range of elicitors, Claparède's account ignores all religious experiences and is limited to the manifestations of the emotion in the culture of upper-middle-class men in Switzerland and Germany of his day. From my perspective, I judge that he was mistaken to claim that the emotion does not have any intrinsic meaning, that it is not adaptive, and does not even motivate any behavioral response. Yet he presciently recognized what causes this emotion, precisely specifying that it is evoked by scenes that highlight "human solidarity, a communion of souls, a generous action, or people becoming closer (*rapprochement*)" (1930:336). Young children probably do feel it, though we do not yet have good evidence about this.

* * * * *

Participants feel this emotion at weddings in many cultures, and so do those who later see photos or videos of the wedding. Memories of transitions and other special moments of family life often evoke nostalgic feelings of this kind, and there appear to be similar emotional moments of imagining the future bliss of marriage and parenthood. In many respects, weddings and other lifecycle rites of passage feel 'designed' to evoke this particular emotion. Furthermore, there is a definite sense that key participants, especially women, *should* feel this emotion, and that the wedding is better, more successful, the more they do. This is clear from personal experience, journalists' reports, and popular blogs at sites such as "Pass the Tissues": Brides on What Made Them Cry at Their Weddings; Will You Cry at Your Wedding? (Did You?); Surprising Moments That Make One Cry on Their Wedding Day; Nostalgic Moments That Make a Bride Cry on the Happiest Day of Her Life.

People often feel this emotion when seeing the first ultrasound images of their baby, giving birth, others' infants, kittens, encounters with wild animals, mountain landscapes, celestial events and night skies, the view of the earth from space, cuddling with their teddy bear – people can suddenly connect to all of them, feeling care, compassion, closeness, and connection. This evokes a distinct emotion. What are the sensations of this emotion? What are the signs of kama muta – what does it look and <u>feel</u> like?

Let's see – and feel.

Online notes

1.1 Kama muta evoked by connecting to humanity.
1.2 Koestler's kama muta upon reconstructing Euclid's proof.
1.3 Laski's description of moments of "transcendental ecstasy."
1.4 Bain's 1859 description of "the tender emotion."

Notes

1 http://cupofjo.com/2010/09/our-birth-story/
2 This paragraph and the following ones rely directly on Steinnes (2017), whose MA research we supervised. See also Steinnes et al. 2019.
3 http://tvtropes.org/pmwiki/pmwiki.php/Main/Squee
4 https://en.wikipedia.org/wiki/Phatic_expression

2

THE SIGNS AND SENSATIONS

In listening to poetry, drama, or heroic narrative we are often surprised at the cutaneous shiver which like a sudden wave flows over us, and at the heart-swelling and the lachrymal effusion that unexpectedly catch us at intervals. In listening to music the same is even more strikingly true.

(James 1890:457)

James (1890:470) then writes of

the diffusive wave of reflex effects which the beautiful object sets up. A glow, a pang in the breast, a shudder, a fulness of the breathing, a flutter of the heart, a shiver down the back, a moistening of the eyes, a stirring in the hypogastrium [lower abdomen], and a thousand unnamable symptoms besides, may be felt the moment the beauty *excites* us. And these symptoms also result when we are excited by moral perceptions, as of pathos, magnanimity, or courage. The voice breaks and the sob rises in the struggling chest, or the nostril dilates and the fingers tighten, whilst the heart beats, etc., etc.

These are almost exactly the sensations and signs of kama muta, when it is at least moderately intense. Yet people may have little or no bodily reaction to the most common mild experiences of kama muta. But when kama muta is intense, people typically have some of the following sensations and signs:

- A warm or other feeling in the center of the chest;
- Moist eyes, tears, or weeping;

- A 'choked-up' feeling of a constricted throat or 'lump in the throat,' difficulty speaking, or speaking in a creaky voice;
- Chills, thrills, or goosebumps (also called chicken skin, horripilation, piloerection);
- A deep breath or pause in breathing;
- A phatic exclamation – an emotive marker – such as *awww*;
- Moving one or both hands over the center of the chest;
- Especially strong experiences may be followed by a feeling of lightness, buoyancy, or exhilaration.

In scores of experimental studies, with several thousand participants, we consistently find this integrated set of sensations (see especially Zickfeld et al. 2019). As I presented in the previous chapter, Norwegian and American participants report these sensations when viewing videos of cute kittens and puppies (Steinnes et al. 2019). Participants from 19 countries, responding in 15 languages, watching any one of a variety of kama muta-evoking videos, or recalling an episode when they shed tears because of something positive, commonly report warmth in the chest, moist eyes or tears, and goosebumps or chills when they say a video or episode made them feel *moved* or *touched* (or translations of these terms in the participants' languages; Seibt et al. 2017; Zickfeld et al. 2019). We have not yet collected quantitative data from unschooled or non–'modern' populations.

When watching any of several kama muta-evoking videos, in time series analyses of data from 909 participants, there are high moment-to-moment correlations between the points in time (3–second intervals) when different groups feel, respectively, warmth in the chest, moist eyes or tears, and goosebumps or chills (Schubert et al. 2016). That is, for example, the higher the mean level of one set of participants' reports of feeling warmth at a given 3-second moment, the higher the mean level of a different set of participants' reports of tears and goosebumps at that particular moment. (Each participant rated only one thing.) In further time series analyses, the moment-to-moment means of a separate set of participants' ratings of *being moved or touched* correlate with the reports by the other groups of, respectively, warmth, tears, and goosebumps at each moment. These experimental results from large samples of American participants support the supposition that, separately and together, this set of key sensations indeed index kama muta. We shall see many ethnographic, historical, and textual examples of this set of sensations throughout this book.

William Braud (2001:101) describes the sensations:

I am witnessing a scene or occurrence that calls forth tears of wonder-joy. It is a scene or activity that moves me deeply. Tears quickly fill my eyes. My skin erupts in gooseflesh, hairs standing on end. Something literally takes my breath away; I gasp, involuntarily. Chills run up and down my spine. I feel a tingling around my eyes, my head, and the back of my neck. The tone of the experience is positive. Toward the end of the experience, or afterwards, there may be some sadness. In the midst of the experience I feel love and compassion. My heart goes out to what I am witnessing. I feel gratitude. I feel a yearning, a poignancy, an intensity. Around me, and between me and the provoking event, there is what I can only describe as a thickness, as though the surrounding air somehow has a greater density. The experience comes upon me—unexpected, spontaneous. My attention is focused strongly upon what I am witnessing, what is provoking these feelings. I am strongly aware of the feelings themselves and the sensations that are being provoked. Other things fade from my attention. The rest of me pauses, shuts down temporarily. If I try, later, to describe the event that initially brought forth the wonder-joy tears, the tears may occur even more strongly than they did initially, and I weep. Sometimes, I am unable to relate the incident that originally provoked the tears—the feelings and the weeping are too intense. I must cease, and allow the feelings to subside before I am able to continue.

Exhilaration is also characteristic. For example, reporting past experiences, people say that after watching cat videos, they feel more *energetic* (Myrick 2015). In an experimental design, Janicke, Rieger, and Connor (2018) found that participants who watched an 'elevating' video reported more 'vitality' afterwards, compared to a control of nature images. They measured elevation with ratings on *touched, moved, emotional, meaningful, compassion, inspired,* and *tender.* They measured vitality with ratings on *sleepy, tired, drowsy, wide-awake,* and *wakeful* (reverse coding the first three).

Of course, a person may feel one of these individual sensations in conjunction with emotions other than kama muta. Tears may occur from fear, pain, rejection. Goosebumps or chills may occur from *awe,* perception of something uncanny, dust in eyes, or simply being exposed to chilly air or water (see, for example, Cairns 2013 on Greek awe-full shudders.) It is the *combination* of these sensations and signs that indexes kama muta. The bodily experience of any particular kama muta experience usually involves some subset of these sensations. I imagine that people tend to feel, exhibit, acknowledge, and remember more of these sensations and signs the greater the significance of the relationship, the more it intensifies, and the more rapidly it does so. They may also experience more of them the more temperamentally prone the person is to kama muta, and the more willing they are to experience, acknowledge, and communicate or share kama muta. Many people do not have any of these bodily responses in very mild kama muta experiences, and some people seem to have few or none of these sensations, even when they have strong experiences of kama muta. So far as we are aware, and so far as Darwin observed about 'tenderness,' there is no specific facial expression distinctive to kama muta.

Love, tender feelings, etc.—Although the emotion of love, for instance that of a mother for her infant, is one of the strongest of which the mind is capable, it can hardly be said to have any proper or peculiar means of expression; and this is intelligible, as it has not habitually led to any special line of action. No doubt, as affection is a pleasurable sensation, it generally causes a gentle smile and some brightening of the eyes. A strong desire to touch the beloved person is commonly felt; and love is expressed by this means more plainly than by any other. Hence we long to clasp in our arms those whom we tenderly love. We probably owe this desire to inherited habit, in association with the nursing and tending of our children, and with the mutual caresses of lovers.

(Darwin 1872:215)

It seems to us that the movement of the palm(s) to the chest that often occurs in kama muta is the "inherited habit" of the fact that "we long to clasp in our arms those whom we tenderly love."

Many people describe the feeling in the center of the chest (in the area of the sternum) as 'warm,' but others describe feelings of swelling or movement there, and others simply can't describe what they are feeling there. We don't yet know what the source of that sensation is, or how it is sensed. Also, we don't yet know whether chills/thrills are just another label people use for goosebumps, or whether one can have one without the other (we're collecting data on that). Likewise, we don't yet know whether in this emotional context being choked up, having a lump in the throat, difficulty speaking, and speaking in a creaky voice[1] are distinct phenomena that can each occur in this emotion without the others, or are just labels for the same phenomenon; and we don't know whether or not these throat and speaking sensations are consistent part of a package that includes shedding tears, or can occur separately. (That, too, we're studying.)

The vocable *aww!* (phonologically /ɔː/, /ɑː/) can be drawn out for emphasis. It is an emotive marker (Rett 2018) used by speakers of English (Buckley 2016), German, Swedish, Norwegian, and other languages.[2] However, I expect that the phonology of this vocable may differ across languages. For example, informants tell us the vowel is more open in Hungarian. In the contemporary US, girls and young women are more likely to utter this interjection than males or older women. When they feel ecstatic kama muta, audiences engaged with Arab *ṭarab* music – and even a famous *ṭarab* singer when she is moved by her own singing – often utter an exclamation transcribed as *Āh! Āh* (Racy 2003:128). Goddard (2014:61) observes that "many Australian Aboriginal languages have high–frequency interjections connected with compassion and 'fellow feeling', like Yankunytjatjara *Ngaltutjara!* or Warlpiri *Wiyarrpa!* (roughly) 'poor thing!'" All over Africa and the Middle East, women ululate together at kama muta-evoking events such as a birth, wedding, or reunion, or accomplishment, and in some cultures at certain religious events. Ululation is a high-pitched warbling sound in which the tongue moves rapidly side to side. A woman almost never ululates alone; when one woman starts ululating, even before they know what the ululation is about other women join in the ululation as they come gather where they heard the ululation start. Ethnological exploration of the situations in which women ululate strongly suggests that the emotion they are performing is kama muta. For a survey of the contexts and cultures where ululation occurs, see Online Notes 2.1 and 2.2. One imagines that, in addition to attracting women to share the first ululators' kama muta, the experience of ululating together amplifies the kama muta that each participant feels. But there has yet been very little research on ululation and its emotional functions.

Autumn McGrath interviewed a young Spanish and English bilingual woman after showing her a video of a cute tiny kitten trying to walk.

'I did feel like [touching heart] I wanted to say "ayyy" when I was watching the kitten video. I don't remember if I did or not. ...

Hmm ... I might say "ayy" if I saw a dog. I do that with dogs a lot. Or small fluffy animals. Small children that are dressed really cute or something cute. A cute video I've seen of either one of those things. [voice raises] Usually I think it has a lot to do with babies or something and little animals. Or if I saw a guy do something cute for a girl. Yeah, it's usually that. Or romance stuff.'

Autumn: What do you mean by romance stuff?

'Like chivalry? If I see a guy go out of his way to do something really sweet for a girl. I can't really ... I guess I'm biased that way because I don't usually feel like that if a girl did something like that for a guy. Or maybe if a child did something cute for a parent. Acts of affection like that.'

Right after she said this a man pulling a Radio Flyer wagon with two pugs sitting inside of it rolled by where we were sitting outside of LuValle and I pointed it out. She said 'ayy!' and we both laughed.

'So I say "ayy" when there are cute things like those dogs [laughs]. See, look at my dog. He's sooo cute' [shows me her phone's photo background].

Another young woman, a Spanish and English bilingual linguistic anthropology major, said she and others speaking Spanish respond to cuteness with *ayeeeee*. (This phatic can be written similarly to a shorter and perhaps lower-pitched interjection of disapproval: *ay*.) A Korean and English bilingual male reported that the corresponding interjection Korean females utter in response to cuteness would be *oeuhhh* or *uhh*, (어우), while a Korean and English bilingual female transcribed the sound that Korean females would make in response to cuteness as *ohuhh*, which Autumn indicated "sounds like *owuhhh* with a softer, rounder 'o'." It would be intriguing to do further research among monolinguals in more languages, audio-recorded so as to produce proper phonetic transcriptions.

Such phatic interjections, and to some degree the tears and hands over the heart, are declarations of the speaker's claim to be experiencing kama muta, and at the same time invitations to listeners to feel kama muta. *Aww!* and its equivalents in other languages are performative utterances whose illocutionary force is to claim to experience kama muta: the speaker declaims, 'I suddenly feel an intensification of communal sharing!' (On illocutionary aspects of utterances, see Austin 1975. On interjections as illocutionary acts, see Wilkins 1992.) By implication, the speaker is portraying herself as a loving, affectionate person, motivated to care for the current target and by implication other targets like it, such as kittens, infants, the romantic partner who brings flowers, fictional characters who generously sacrifice for each other, loved ones who re-unite. Moreover, like other interjections, *aww!* purports to be an automatic, sincere, and direct reflection of a genuine emotion. It is ideally supposed to be heartfelt, not merely a tactical performance – a 'spontaneous' and therefore 'genuine' 'expression' of an 'internal' feeling. That nominal immediacy and spontaneity is precisely what gives *aww* its illocutionary force as a declaration: 'I'm truly kama muta.' Nonetheless, once it becomes a speech habit associated with the kama muta experience, a person may sometimes say it even when alone.

Many emojis function similarly as illocutions or emotive markers (Rett 2018) declaring the 'spontaneous' emotional responses of the author. Some emojis seem to declare, 'see, I feel kama muta!' (♥, 😎, and 😺). Such emojis invite the recipients to experience kama muta with the sender, while asserting, 'I'm a tender-hearted person.'

Kama muta tears and the hand-over-heart gesture have the same illocutionary force; because they are perceived to be 'spontaneous,' 'genuine,' and hence unpremeditated – and may be experienced that way – these signs function as performative indices of compassion and affection. They declare 'I care.' In a sense, the kama muta *awww*, tears, and hand-over-heart are vows of love. At least a little bit of love, for now.

Let us return to Braud's beautiful description of the feeling. Based on his own experience and reports of twelve others, Braud (2001:101–102) identifies "tears of wonder-joy" as "indications and expressions of love" (2001:103).

> always, there are the tears. Often, there is gooseflesh. Sometimes, there are the chills and thrills—electrical or tingling feelings in the spine, arms, shoulders, neck, and back. (The French have a special term for this—*frisson*: shiver, shudder, quiver, thrill.) More rarely, there is an involuntary gasp, an irregularity in breathing, or a vocalization ("oh!" or "ah!" or "uh!"). Some report a feeling of warmth throughout the body. Others report warm, soft colors. Still others report a pulsing, expanding, aliveness in the chest area that may extend for three to four feet. Sometimes there is a quiet, gentle sobbing.
>
> In connection with this experience, all report positive affect. There are feelings of joy, peace, and awe; feelings of love, compassion, empathy, and

acceptance; feelings of unity, union, oneness, closeness, connection, and immersion. Some report a congruence of themselves and all life. There are feelings of gratitude, blessedness, intensity, yearning, poignancy. Some report feeling cleansed, renewed, a beginning. For some there is a feeling of being at home, of recognition, of safety. Others experience a lightness, a spaciousness, an expansion, a feeling of being uplifted, soaring. Some feel a release, freedom. There may be feelings of deep satisfaction; of being accompanied and not alone; of being fulfilled, loved, fully seen, known, held, released from the need to be fully responsible for one's own way or in charge; of daring to be vulnerable. More rarely, there is an experience of the facade cracking, of the surreal, of timelessness. There may be a paradoxical appreciation, a holding of opposites: joy/sadness, bitter/sweet, tragic/beautiful, confused/clear, amazed/normal. Some report sadness near the end of the experience.

In terms of attention, there is a 'stopping' at various levels. Attention is very focused, one-pointed—focused on the precipitating event and on the experience itself. Awareness of all else fades. Yet, there is awareness of a fuller spectrum of existence.[3]

Kama muta experiences have a rapid onset and short duration; the subjective feel and the sensations often reach full intensity with a few seconds after onset and typically begin to decline within less than a minute, or at most a very few minutes.[4] However, it can be re-evoked by repeating the original event, remembering or re-imagining it, or encountering another one. Watching a Pixar movie or participating in a wedding, one may feel kama muta over and over again, but not continuously. Some consummatory sensations such as orgasm are followed by a refractory period during which the person is not susceptible to re-experiencing the sensation. We have not observed this in kama muta; rather, each experience of kama muta seems to potentiate subsequent experience of it. The opening scene in the movie *Up* sets up the viewer to feel kama muta again and again.

Kama muta is sweet – positive and meaningful. When a song evokes it, people want to listen again. When a ritual evokes it, people come back to participate again. People also like to share the experience with people they care about. Seeing a kama muta video online, people call others over to see it with them or post it to their Facebook page. Hearing about a kama muta movie or opera, people invite close friends to come see it with them – to have a good cry together as they watch. The girl who sees cute puppies and exclaims "Aww. How adorable! They're so cute! May I pet them?" is likely then to call her friends over to join in her experience of kama muta, wanting them to love and pet the puppies, too. When people experience the kama muta of loving union with their divinity, they want to bring others to have the experience too.

With a few exceptions, Western folk psychology, social science, and humanities have understood crying (including tears, sobbing, and weeping) as 'expressions' of 'sadness' or 'distress' and, concomitantly, as a 'negative' experience (see, for example, the research reviewed in Vingerhoets and Bylsma 2015). This understanding of crying may make it seem out of place in an emotion experienced overall as 'positive' – an emotion that people often seek to experience, pass on to their friends, and actively share with those they love. The apparently problematic appearance of weeping in kama muta is intelligible if we recognize that the core implicit social relational function of weeping is pleading for love: weeping is a request for support, empathy, connection, caring, and compassion (Kottler 1996; Hendriks et al. 2008). Essentially, weeping says, 'I need you, take care of me, comfort me' (what is called the "signal value of crying faces"; see, e.g., Hendriks, Croon, & Vingerhoets 2003; Zickfeld & Schubert 2018).

People shed tears when they are terrified, in physical pain, isolated, in social distress, grieving a separation or the break-up of a relationship, or mourning death. Newborn children typically cry as soon as they take their first breath. Some infants cry frequently, but children cry less as they grow older, and apparently women cry more than men – across the vast majority of cultures. What do these conditions have in common? The answer is clear when we consider the prototype, the helpless crying infant. Tears are a plea for love – for compassion and caretaking. Crying is not simply a surface 'expression' of an internal state, much less an hydraulic 'release' of a 'pent-up' emotion: it is a relational act. "Human beings need behaviors that move us toward each other and keep us there. Crying is one of the most powerful and essential of those behaviors" (Nelson 2005:26). Crying says 'come hold me and care for me, comfort, cuddle, caress, rock, feed me, or relieve my pain' (see Hendriks, Croon, & Vingerhoets 2008; Balsters et al. 2012). In other words, crying is an attempt to evoke kama muta in receptive perceivers. This seems to be the evolutionary function of tears, but tears are nonetheless culturally informed, with meanings in friendship, art, politics, and religion that I extensively explore (see especially Online Note 2.7 and Chapters 5, 8, and 15).

But what about the tears of grief and loss? We usually don't have strong emotions about water, but if you're in the desert and discover that all the water has leaked out of your canteen, thoughts of cold drinks become very salient and attractive. If your home is destroyed by a tornado, from time to time you may dream of how wonderful it was; the image and feeling of the cozy hearth may spring to mind – although you took it pretty much for granted until then. Across a wide range of basic needs, deprivation increases desire. When what we lack is suddenly made salient by a reminder, or just abruptly recalled, our desire suddenly intensifies – sometimes overwhelmingly. Parched, if we see an oasis mirage, we vividly imagine cool water in our throat – and the more thirsty we are, the more watery mirages we see. Thinking of her infant, a mother's milk lets down and leaks from her nipples. Imagining her lover in her arms, a woman becomes sexually aroused. When we imagine or hope for a delicious meal, we salivate. Like other appetites, social relational desires generate sensations that reproduce the sensations of their fulfillment. Indeed, since social relationships consist of mental models – perceptions, interpretations, motives, emotions, evaluations – in an essential psychological sense, relationships exist whenever and to the extent that people represent them. Hence we can relate to a person on a cellphone – even after she goes out of range. When we send an e-mail or leave a message for someone, we are relating to him – though later we might discover he has closed his account, or had died before we sent our message. Many of people's most intensely felt relationships are with deities, spirits, ancestors, as well as absent or deceased family members and friends. When these loving union relationships suddenly intensify, we feel kama muta.

Thus intensification of imagined love may be major aspects of 'longing,' 'missing' someone, being 'homesick,' 'mourning,' 'grieving,' and 'sorrow.' When a person's longing, missing, homesickness, mourning, grief, or sorrow begin suddenly or rapidly increase in intensity, the person is likely to feel kama muta. To feel separation or loss, we must vividly imagine what we are missing. Grief can only be generated by representing what we lack, and the deepest grief is that generated by a wonderfully real sense of what we wish we had, and perhaps used to have. To put this in perspective, compare it with the converse. Consider the kama muta experience of reunion with a soldier or a lost child – the kama muta is especially heartfelt because we feel joy and relief along with and in contrast to the horror of imagining that the loved one might not have returned. Kama muta results from the sudden restoration of the loving relationship against the prior fear and still-felt ground of the possibility that the person returned to us might not have come back safe and sound. Kama muta results from sudden temporal intensification of love though some sort of affectionate interaction, but also from a sudden dramatic contrast between what is and imagining what might have been. Likewise, we may feel kama muta when we face the imminent prospect or fact of a serious separation from the one(s) we love, grave danger to them, or their death. I can formalize this by positing that kama muta results from a sudden increase in the difference between the currently experienced love and sense of the previously weaker relationship, the threatened loss of the partner or harm to them, or the actual loss of the person. We feel kama muta when we sense how contingent the loving relationship is – we feel deeply connected right now, but once were not, or know that it might not have been, and soon or someday will no longer be.

In short, separation, longing, loss, grief, and mourning occur only when people vividly feel what they lack and desire; when the missing relationship is affectionate, and the feeling comes on suddenly, people experience kama muta. In contrast, a person may focus purely on her pain, suffering, bleak future, desolation, and despair; this purely negative representation does not generate kama muta. When authority-ranking, equality-matching, or market-pricing relationships are jeopardized, suspended, attenuated, or lost, or newly created, renewed, restored, or intensified, people may have strong emotions, but these emotions are distinct from kama muta (see Chapter 19).

From this it follows that tears and crying in distress may be pleas for loving-kindness that a person needs and hopes for, and whose possibility the distressed person hence represents. At the same time tears and crying of separation or loss involve not simply grief, but, against the background of grief, the vividly evocative memory of the wonderful loving care that the tearful person once had, or hopes to have again.

Of course, there are multiple levels of intention in tears, as in every social act. The tearful person may simply cry without consciously intending to evoke loving-kindness, or a person may be reflective about their need for loving-kindness and indeed use tears tactically to get sympathy or help. In some cultures crying at marvelously moving performances in turn becomes a sign of the observer's sophisticated artistic sensibility or her admirably compassionate moral sentiments.

In some cultures in Brazil, New Zealand, the Andaman Islands, and elsewhere, women (and in some cultures men, too) weep when a traveler arrives from an arduous journey, at reunions, at reconciliations, and at peace-making rituals (Frazer 1918: Vol 2, 86; Radcliffe-Brown 1922; Metraux 1947; Urban 1988). In Le Mans in 1793 when the opposing Girondins and Montagnards ceased fighting, to make peace they met in the town square, embraced, and wept, while the watching crowd wept with them (Vincent-Buffault 1986:87; for more on tears of friendship and patriotism in revolutionary France, see Online Note 2.7). These formal, ritualized weeping practices apparently build on more spontaneous, less culturally shaped manifestations of kama muta-evoking crying. Likewise, in quite a number of cultures around the globe, women, especially, have perfected weeping into an esthetically appreciated art form (e.g., Salmond 1974; Tiwary 1978; Abu-Lughod 1986; Urban 1988; Tolbert 1990; Desjarlais 1991; Grima 1992; Briggs 1993; Clark-Decès 2005). These forms of weeping lament seem to be culturally perfected to optimally evoke kama muta, and indeed women often perform laments on occasions when CS intensification is called for. Along with kama muta, lamenting also typically performs and evokes the sadness of loss.

Love is a warm feeling in the heart

I had received a text from my friend Darcy a few weeks ago asking for my current address, and stating that she would be sending me something in the mail and that I should keep an eye out for it. I knew she was in the midst of wedding planning – we had talked extensively about it months prior – so I assumed what she was sending was a save the date. We have been friends since high school, and we are still close but don't talk as regularly as we would like, especially since I moved to California. ... I kept checking the mail each day after receiving that text, until one afternoon about a week later when I saw a package had arrived in front of my door. My heart immediately started pounding and jumped to my throat and I thought, 'Maybe she is inviting me to be a part of her bridal party!!' I rushed to open it up, and inside was a link to an adorable bridal party invitation video that her and her fiancé made, a card detailing the responsibilities, and a beautiful decorated glass to commemorate the occasion. I got goose bumps as I took each item out, and tears sprung to my eyes. I also felt very warm and had a huge smile on my face. My chest felt tight but my body also felt very light and floaty. I was very stressed that week preparing for my dissertation proposal defense (which was the next morning), so I do wonder if that affected how moved I was at that moment. I felt so grateful for our friendship, and very nostalgic too at the beauty of how long we have been friends and how wonderful a gift it was that I am going to be able to share this special day with her after talking about it idealistically so many years earlier. After about 5 minutes, I decided to call her on the phone and though she only had a few moments, we gushed about how excited we were and my heart seemed to feel even tighter but also warmer and lighter. After hanging up (it was probably a 5 or 6 minute conversation) I still felt light and warm and smiley for up to 20 minutes after, even though the goose bumps and tears had faded since the end of the phone call and the heart tightness started to fade soon after.

(Jennifer Pierre)

In English, people often speak of kama muta as *heartwarming*, or as having something *tug at your heart strings*; similarly, compassion can be expressed as *My heart goes out to you*. To indicate sincerity of gratitude or sympathy, English speakers declare *heartfelt thanks*, or a person may express the motivational sincerity of various affiliative sentiments by indicating that they are *from the bottom of my heart*. German, French, Spanish, and Italian have similar heart sincerity metaphors (Pérez 2008). Something that arouses intense compassionate kama muta is *heart-rending*. Japanese speakers my emphatically indicate kama muta by saying *kokoro o ugokasareru*, 'something moved my heart.' (For a lot more exploration of the metaphors for kama muta, see Chapter 7.)

Beyond words, there are gestures, images, and other signs for kama muta that focus on the center of the chest. A popular Western motif in art and greeting cards depicts Cupid shooting an arrow into the heart of a person, who thus instantaneously falls passionately in love (Conti 2006). This is a visual image of narratives from Greek and Roman mythology. Despite Cupid's use of a weapon, the motif is not intended to represent aggression or injury; quite the contrary. The vision of Cupid as a cute baby may evoke a bit of kama muta in the viewer, representing the kama muta of the suddenly infatuated lover(s). But why use a god (visible to the listener to the narrative or the viewer of the art but generally imagined to be invisible to the characters depicted) shooting an arrow into the heart as a motif for suddenly falling in love? Perhaps because people abruptly falling in love have a sudden, mysterious sensation in the heart.

Like the other primary emotions, the tender emotion cannot be described; a person who had not experienced it could no more be made to understand its quality than a totally colour-blind person can be made to understand the experience of colour-sensation. Its impulse is primarily to afford physical protection to the child, especially by throwing the arms about it; and that fundamental impulse persists in spite of the immense extension of the range of application of the impulse and its incorporation in many ideal sentiments.

(McDougall 1919:57–58)

Contemporary people experiencing strong kama muta often place one or both hands over the center of the chest for a moment or two, usually with the hand flat. This gesture may derive from the kama muta sensation in the chest. But it seems more likely to be a hold-the-baby-to-the-chest reflex derived from maternal primate infant-carrying, which would be consistent if the phylogeny of kama muta is that it originated as maternal care motivation, then evolved into paternal and then sibling care motivation, and then became flexibly extended as a mechanism for bonding beyond kin. In many species of primates, though not all, mothers hold their young infants against their chest, especially when locomoting; older infants often ride on the back. A number of species of primates, including bonobos and chimpanzees, also 'hug' their 'friends' at times.

In many cultures of North and Northwest Africa, Anatolia, and across the Middle East at least as far as Afghanistan, this gesture has culturally evolved into a performative act of affection and commitment. Men and women place their right hand over the center or left-center of their chest to indicate friendship, esteem, sincerity, appreciation, thanks. People in this region commonly use the hand over heart gesture in greeting or leave-taking. Qureshi (1995:121) describes contemporary Pakistanis and Indians listening to *qawwal* who, from his description, apparently experience kama muta; in the early phase of the emergence of the emotion, they typically place a hand on the chest to indicate the image of the spiritual guide (*sheikh*) in the heart (see Chapter 13). Conservative Muslims – who do not shake hands with the opposite gender – use the hand-to-heart gesture as a sociable greeting to persons of the opposite gender. A 2004 *Los Angeles Times* article dated March 27 reports that

It won't take long for friends and families of returning U.S. troops to notice how Iraq has changed the soldiers just as the soldiers have changed Iraq. One change will be evident the minute Lt. Col. Michael T. Mahoney of Lompoc, Calif., and other GIs greet people in their hometowns. After shaking hands, it's a good bet that they will press their right hands solemnly over their hearts. They're not having chest pains or overcome with emotion. Instead, the soldiers have adopted a vital ritual of everyday life in Iraq: Arabs place their hand on their heart after a handshake to convey sincerity and respect, to show that the greeting comes from the heart.

The hand-on-the-heart gesture has become second nature to many U.S. troops in Iraq.[5]

Contemporary Turks use the hand to heart gesture to indicate 'You are one of us, I thank you, I will never forget, solidarity'; 'compassion'; I mean this 'from my heart'; 'gratitude.' Traditional Turkish men, especially, use the gesture in indicating 'I must depart, but leave with you in my heart,' or in appreciation for an offer that one declines, where it indicates: 'I appreciate your kind offer or invitation, and I do not wish to separate myself from you by refusing it.' Women, especially, place their hand over their heart to indicate 'I'm touched.' Young Turks use the gesture to say 'I'll take care of it, depend on me, you can count on me,' for example, when assuring a friend 'I'll pay for our dinner,' or when committing to help someone. When asked about the gesture, one Turkish graduate student who studies relational models theory exclaimed, "It's definitely communal sharing!" (Oral personal communication.) I might add that the gesture is <u>a promise</u> of communal sharing (on communal sharing, see Chapter 4).

A similar gesture indicated romantic attraction in twentieth century Puerto Rico. A 1931 listing of "Hispanic" gestures includes this one:

> *Infatuation*—A second mannerism of the Porto Ricans, especially the women, is the gesture accompanying the remark '*Es un tipo*,' referring to a handsome or charming person of the male sex. It consists mainly in the placement of the right hand on the heart, and a simultaneous vertical extension of the left forearm to the chin level, with the palm open and facing forward, and fingers relaxed. As the words are spoken the head is thrust somewhat to the left and backward, simultaneously with a light upward shrug of the shoulders, and an entranced heavenward gaze of the eyes.
>
> *(Kaulfers 1931:256)*

Parzuchowski et al. (2014:238) write, "In Poland ... not only is 'with hand over heart' (*z ręką na sercu*) an idiomatic expression of honesty used at the end of any dubious statement, but the 'hand-over-heart' gesture is also a common emphasis of sincere intentions." This gesture has an impact on those who perform it and on those who observe it: Polish participants using this gesture were more honest in their assessments of others' attractiveness and more willing to admit their lack of knowledge, while being perceived as more honest and trustworthy (Parzuchowski et al. 2014; Parzuchowski & Wojciszke 2014). Thus, in all of these cultures the hand-over-heart gesture is a performative declaration, 'I feel kama muta about you and commit myself to the bond between us.' Similarly, in all kinds of settings, people now use the heart sign made with the thumbs and forefingers of the two hands to sign, 'I love you' to a lover, family members, or friends.

In another cultural conventionalization of the spontaneous hand-to-heart gesture in many Western cultures, people place the right hand over their heart during the national anthem. Americans also do so when saying the pledge of allegiance to the flag and the nation, which starts the day in most American schools. Politicians communicate affectionate solidarity with people in a crowd by placing a closed hand over the heart, often followed by pointing to the person addressed. Bill Clinton did this as he walked to the podium to speak at the 2016 Democratic National Convention.

At the 2016 Democratic National Convention, Khizr Khan gave a short speech. From the United Arab Emirates, Kahn is the father of Captain Humayun Khan, who died in Iraq in 2004 protecting his unit from a car-bomber. In greeting the audience and in expressing his appreciation for the audience's support, Khizr Kahn used this gesture repeatedly.[6] Video shows delegates in the audience moved to tears as they listen to him. In the 2016 presidential campaign, Hilary Clinton adopted the gesture, right hand to the heart.

> It's a gesture unfamiliar from her past campaigns, but it's a favorite this time around. In Columbus, Ohio, and Omaha, Mrs. Clinton spoke of her late father, and up went her hand, placed over her heart.
>
> At the Democratic National Convention, when she took the stage to wild applause, she cued the audience on how grateful, moved and humbled she felt by putting her hand to her heart, once, twice, then a third and fourth time.
>
> *(Stanley 2016)*

It might appear that this movement of the palms to the center of the chest may be related to the more general experimental phenomenon that 'positive' stimuli increase 'approach' motivation. People seem to mentally represent *liking* as *closer*, and hence as congruent with 'bringing closer to one's torso.' That is, approach motivation results in a reduction in response latency for acts that decrease the distance between oneself and the positive stimulus, compared to acts that increase the distance from the positive stimulus (Seibt et al. 2008). As an instance of this approach motivation making people want to get physically closer to a positive stimulus, the kama muta hand-to-heart gesture may represent bringing an appealing object – an infant, child, family member, or friend – to one's chest. However, in a meta-analysis of 29 studies, Phaf et al. (2014:13) found only a small effect size, and concluded that "there seems to be little evidence for a direct or automatic link between affective information processing and arm flexion and extension." "The results of the meta-analysis argue against an immediate, unintentional, implicit, stimulus-based, and evolutionary based or automatized, link between affect and approach and avoidance, and against a direct link with arm flexion and extension, respectively" (2014:14). They conclude that the small effects of affect on approach or avoidance depend on instructions to consciously appraise the valence of the target. In a qualitative review of the literature, Krieglmeyer, De Houwer, and Deutsch (2013), also found a very small effect size. They also conclude that latency of arm flexion versus extension as such does not respond automatically to the valance of the target, but – consistent with Seibt et al. (2008) – that there is an "automatic pathway from evaluation to distance-change behavior" (2008:280). That is, "evaluations automatically trigger responses that cause a compatible distance change, regardless of the specific muscles involved (i.e., arm flexion or extensions)" (2008:283). In a meta-analysis of 58 studies, Laham, Kashima, Dix, and Wheeler (2015:1085) likewise concluded that "the link between affective stimuli and muscle movements is not direct or 'hard-wired', but rather indirect and malleable as a function of contextualising information" such as motivational framing and response label. In particular, the latency of hand-toward-body responses to positive stimuli is only reduced when participants are told to evaluate stimulus positivity and shown that moving the hand toward the body indicates *liking* or *positivity*.

What does this imply? Quite apart from the cultures and contexts discussed earlier in which the hand-to-heart gesture is conventionalized to mean affiliation or loyalty, the kama muta hand-to-heart motion occurs spontaneously without any overt framing of the motion as indicating *liking* or *positivity*. And the gesture does not actually displace the evoking stimulus. So it probably does <u>not</u> result from a very general mechanism of compatibility of a flexion and inward rotation of the shoulder response with implicit or explicit emotive evaluation. Rather, it seems most likely to be a distinct and specific <u>cuddle-the-infant and hug-the-loved-one reflex</u>. The gesture could also be learned by observation, imitation, and playacting.

The HAND-OVER-THE-HEART MEANS LOVE trope is prominent in Western art. Gombrich (1966:394–395) reproduces a 1924 Käthe Kollwitz anti-war poster in which the figure makes this gesture with the left hand, while the raised arm calls for action. Kendon (2004:47) reproduces an engraving from de Jorio's 1832 book on Neapolitan gesture, based on a painting that de Jorio commissioned. It shows a young woman holding her right hand over her left upper chest, telling a professional letter writer what to write to her husband; de Jorio says that her gesture indicates her love. Indeed, this gesture of loving commitment has long been a visible trope in Western religious art (Gombrich 1966:394–395). Depictions of the infinitely loving Jesus and of the Virgin Mary prominently display their stylized hearts. Also, paintings and sculptures of Mary when she is not holding Jesus often depict her holding her hands crossed over her upper chest. This is particularly prevalent from the early 1400s until the late 1600s in paintings of the angel Gabriel announcing to Mary that she will bear the child of God. Mary Magdalene is also often shown making this same gesture. In Lorenzo di Credi's *The Annunciation* c.1480–1485, it is Gabriel who holds his hands across his upper chest. In David Gerard's *The Nativity with Donors and Saints Jerome and Leonard*, ca. 1510–1515, Joseph's hands are crossed in front of his chest as he looks at the infant Jesus. Paintings of the last supper of Jesus and his disciples may show them with their hands over their hearts. There are many other distinguished European paintings that depict this gesture; see Online Note 2.3.

Folk art today continues to include images of the Virgin Mary making this gesture. The gesture with this meaning is not universal, but it is widespread. See Online Note 2.4 for an exploration of the cultural distribution of the hand-over-heart gesture.

It seems that this is also likely to be the semiotic source of the meaning of ♥, 'love,' on Valentine's cards and decorations, in contemporary texting, and on T-shirts. In all these ways, the fact that people all have similar kama muta sensations affords a medium for communicating the emotional state, for the illocutionary declamation of the caring motivation that accompanies kama muta and the commitment to the relationship that ensues. The kama muta feeling in the center of the chest is evidently the source of the representation of love as being 'in' or coming 'from' the *heart*. Feeling a sensation in the middle of the chest while knowing that their heart is located there affords the sense that the feeling of love, commitment, and sincerity is a state of the heart.

In a number of languages, one may speak of a person who is loved as 'my heart': "*¡Corazón mío!*" in Spanish; "*mein Herz*" in German; "*mon (petit) coeur*" in French; "*cuore mio*" in Italian; and "sweetheart" in English" (Pérez 2008:47). Similarly, to act so as to make someone love the speaker is "Eng. To win somebody's heart; Sp. Robarle el corazón a alguien; It. Conquistare il cuore di qualcuno; Fr. Gagner le coeur de quelqu'un; Ger. Jemandes Herz gewinnen" (Pérez 2008:47).

Moreover, love is specifically <u>warmth</u> in the heart. In English, one speaks of *heart-warming* experiences, and a *warm-hearted person*. Similarly, German has *warmherzig sein*. As we shall see in Chapters 13–15, Methodists, Mormons, and Sufis understand a warm feeling in the heart as <u>the</u> definitive evidence of God's love. When we evoke kama muta in our lab with videos, or ask participants about their everyday experiences, the most commonly reported sensation is "warmth in the center of the chest." In a combined sample, n = 4115, of mostly US and Norwegian participants (with some Israeli, Portuguese, and Chinese participants), 51% reported some sort of warm feeling, and 24% reported strong warmth (4 or 5 on a scale of 1–5; the proportions are similar when we simply ask about bodily warmth, without specifying location). In a separate set of data from 3543 participants, we found that in all 19 nations, in all 15 languages in the study, ratings of warmth in the chest are highly correlated with the other bodily sensations of kama muta (two of the 76 predicted correlations were marginal), correlated with the labels for it in every language and nation, invariably correlated with positivity of the experience, invariably correlated with the appraisal that a CS relationship has suddenly intensified, and invariably correlated with CS motivations (Zickfeld et al. 2019). In other words, people in 19 nations speaking 15 languages (from six language families) tend to report warm feelings in the chest when they feel kama muta, whether the kama muta is evoked by watching one of our video stimuli, (in 12 countries) or from recalling personal experiences in their own lives (in 7 countries). Overall, women reported a bit more warmth in the chest than men, though not in every country. In all 12 countries where participants watched videos they reported more warm feelings in the chest when watching the kama muta videos than when watching watch awe-inspiring, amusing, or sad videos. (The sole exception among these 36 predicted contrasts occurred in Japan, where there was no significant difference between chest warmth in kama muta and sad videos). In all seven countries where we elicited memories, participants reported more warmth in the chest when remembering an event in which they shed tears because of something positive than when they shed tears because of something negative.[7]

This warm sensation affords the metaphor KINDNESS AND COMPASSION ARE WARMTH. IJzerman and Semin (2009) propose that this metaphor may also be afforded by the experience of being held during infancy and cuddling throughout life, although those experiences would seem to better afford a coziness metaphor that, in fact, is not prevalent. The experience of being held does not explain why people feel KINDNESS AND COMPASSION ARE WARMTH IN THE CENTER OF THE CHEST – which is what people report: The adjective 'warm' is synonymous with 'warm-hearted,' which the held-and-snuggled hypothesis does not easily explain. In 1952, Solomon Asch conducted a series of experiments to show that the trait words 'warm' and 'cold' are the most central trait descriptors in impressions of people. S. T. Fiske (2010, 2012) explained that we perceive people and groups as *warm* when they are allies and collaborators whose goals and interests are aligned with ours. We perceive people and groups as *cold* when they are antagonists in completion with us.

In addition to the English characterization of experiences of kama muta as *heart-warming* or giving one *a warm glow*, the converse is also true: love, friendship, loyalty, patriotism, and other close bonds are metaphorically *warm feelings*. This sensation is probably the source of locutions and folk concepts such as *heart-throb*, *heart-felt* sentiments, *my heart goes out to someone, speaking from the heart, heart-to-heart talk, big hearted, warm-hearted, heavy heart, cold-hearted, heartless, holding* or *keeping someone in one's heart, hearty welcome*. Likewise, *bleeding heart* is a derogatory epithet indicating that a person is excessively and inappropriately compassionate. Similarly, in German a person feeling kama muta may describe the situation as *herzergreifend* ('heart gripping') and *herzerweichend* ('heartrending'). You could also say that an action *kommt von Herzen* ('comes from the heart') for a gesture or something that moves you. To 'heart' someone is *herzen* and a person that one is in love with is *Herzilein*. Just as in English one says that a kind, honest, and caring person has his 'heart in the right place,' in German one says that someone has *das Herz am rechten Fleck*.[8] Likewise, in Ancient Greece, the emotion that people felt when reunited with loved ones, or when nostalgically reviving the solidarity of warrior fellowship, was represented as occurring in the *phrén*, 'upper chest'. (We'll explore these Greek accounts in the next chapter.)

In English, we say, for example, 'my grandfather was a warm man,' meaning that he was kind, compassionate, and loving. When a person is said to greet another 'warmly,' this means that the person displays genuine gladness to see the other, as they would if they felt kama muta. Mandarin has many more 'warmth' metaphors that make fine distinctions about the nature and performance of devotion and commitment. Lucy Zhao describes these:

> In Chinese, the phrase that roughly translates *warm-hearted* is *rè qín* 'warm family member = warm-hearted', or *rè qín sī huǒ* 'warm family member like fire = very warm-hearted' if describing someone who is *very* warm-hearted – *sī huǒ* means 'like fire'. ...

> In Chinese, the expression *rè chéng* 'warm honest' essentially carries the same meaning as *rè qín*, but also connotes honesty and possessing a genuinely good-hearted nature, indicating that the person being described is genuine in his or her warm disposition. By contrast, *rè qín* merely refers to *acting* warmly, regardless of whether this attitude is true to one's individual nature. The phrase *rè qié* 'warm keen' carries the same meaning of *warm-hearted* that *rè qín* expresses, but it also connotes being eager to help, meaning that one who is *rè qié* is so kind and caring that they are keen to help out anyone in need. Going one degree further than *rè qié* is to describe one as *rè xīn cháng* 'warm heart (and) intestines', which literally means that one's heart is so full of warmth that its heat warms the intestines beneath it. *Rè xīn cháng* refers to one who is so warm-hearted and eager to help that they in fact *do* help, implying that one is an accomplished philanthropist versus one who merely has the *intent* to help.
>
> (Zhao 2012:5–6)

In addition, Mandarin has a term, *wēn*, 'lukewarm,' that indicates a temperature that is warm, but less warm than *rè*.

> The Chinese phrase *wēn hé* refers to a personality that is warm, but also has aspects of humbleness and leniency, indicating that this person is well composed, their warmness coming from their calm and understanding disposition. *Wēn shùn* 'lukewarm passive' is very similar in meaning to *wēn hé*, differing in that *wēn shùn* emphasizes that one is devoid of all stubbornness, this lenient passivity making them easy to get along with. *Wēn róu* 'lukewarm soft' is essentially identical in meaning to *wēn hé*, but with one exception: *wēn róu* may only refer to the softness of women (you would get laughed at if you used it to describe a male!), whereas *wēn hé* is a neutral term that may refer to anyone. *Wēn hòu* 'lukewarm sincere' is very similar to *wēn hé* as well as to *wēn shùn*, except that it carries aspects of a forgiving personality, indicating that this person is so humble and not wanting to offend that he or she does not even hold grudges. *Sòng wēn nuǎn* 'to give lukewarmth = to uplift someone's mood' carries strong connotations of being warm-hearted, but also nudges toward the direction of lending a helping hand. It means that an individual is so selfless and caring that they will sacrifice their own happiness to make someone else feel better; their

modesty allows them to view other people's happiness as more important than their own, and thus they make this sacrifice without self-regard or hesitation.

(Zhou 2012:9).

Mandarin and Cantonese also have the lexeme 溫情, *wēnqíng*, 'tender loving care, kindness, affection', where 溫, *wēn*, means 'warm,' as a temperature term, and 情, *qíng*, is 'emotion, sentiment'.[9] One Shanghainese informant, seeing the Thai Medicine video, reported his sensation as 心老暖的, *xīnlǎonuǎndè*, 'feeling warm in the heart.'[10] Another informant said that this could also be translated 'You make my heart warm,' and that it would be a very affectionate emotional statement that one would make to a loved one.

Mandarin and English both have 'cold' (*lěng*) metaphor antonyms to 'warm' (*rè*); they are used to characterize lack of compassion and lack of caring. It is also notable that "*xīn liáng* 'cool heart' refers to one who is experiencing such great disappointment that they give up all hope" (Zhou 2012:17).

Our hypothesis that English 'warm' and Mandarin *rè* metaphors arise in the kama muta feeling of warmth in the center of the chest is supported by the Mandarin metaphors that Zhou (2012) mentions which locate the warmth in the *xīn*, 'heart'. This hypothesis predicts that similar 'warmth' and 'heart' metaphors, separate and combined, should be widespread across language families, including ones that are unrelated to English and Mandarin and unlikely to have borrowed the metaphors from or lent them to either language. Consider also Latin:

> When orientated towards the meaning 'warm-er', the state verb *tĕp-ē-re* 'be lukewarm' means 'start feeling the warmth of love'. But when oriented in the opposite direction, the same state verb means 'be less warm than before, start losing warmth in love, have a moderate degree of love' (Ov. Rem. Am. 629 and Met. 11,225.)
>
> *(Fruyt 2013:28).*

Speakers of Gĩkũyũ, a Central Bantu language in the Niger–Congo family, use the metaphors *wendo nĩ ngoro*, 'love is heart,' and *wendo nĩ ũrugarĩ*, 'love is warm' (Gathigia 2010; Gathigia does not indicate whether Gĩkũyũ speakers speak of 'warm hearts').

Using a small but unspecified number of respondents' answers to a questionnaire, Vejdemo and Vandewinkel (2016) systematically investigated figurative extensions of temperature terms in English, Ibibio (Benue-Congo family), Kannada (Dravidian), Japanese, Mandarin Chinese, Eastern Ojibwe (Algonquin), and (based on Vandewinkel's introspection as a native speaker) Swedish. They found that English, Swedish (*varmt hjarta*), Japanese, and Ibibio (*mmeme esit*, though *esit* has a broader meaning than 'heart') use 'warm' lexemes to describe the 'heart' of caring or kind persons. Mandarin refers to a generous person as having a 'hot heart.' Kannada does not figuratively extend its warm term to hearts. Nor does Ojibwe, in which figurative language is said to be rare, but Ojibwe say that a person with a kind regard for someone looks on that person with very warm eyes (*á-kámá ánjên mmèmè mmèmè*), and a gentle, peaceable, mediating voice is 'warm.' Like the English, Swedish, and Japanese, Ojibwe (*daki-de'è*) say that an <u>un</u>caring person has a 'cold' heart.

Intrigued by these instances, we informally tested our hypothesis using a large edited book on temperature representations in diverse languages (Koptjevskaja-Tamm 2015a). We asked the question, "Where there is at least one term for 'warm,' how frequently, and in what languages and language families, is the 'warm' term used to attribute 'love, affection, cordiality, compassion, kindness, sincere desire for connection,' or other CS sentiments?" From Koptjevskaja-Tamm (2015a) and a few statements we incidentally collected from informants when exploring kama muta, I constructed a table of languages that definitely do and ones that apparently do not use 'warm' terms to denote kind persons, actions, and attitudes (see Online Notes 2.5 and 2.6).

There are 31 languages in the Koptjevskaja-Tamm (2015a) book whose temperature language (though not always temperature metaphors) is well-described, and we have added 9 more to the table). Of these 40 languages, in 32 there is at least one attested term that denotes 'warm', as distinct from 'hot', 'neutral,' and 'cold.' Among these 32 languages, one source does not discuss metaphors at all, and 6 indicate either that the 'warm' terms are not used metaphorically or that they are not used for humans, actions, or speech. Of the 25 remaining languages, 22 use one or more physical 'warmth' terms metaphorically to characterize actions, speech, or persons. <u>In 21 of the 22, the 'warm' term metaphorically means something like 'kind, compassionate, affectionate, or cordial'.</u> (In the GurenƐ language of northern Ghana, *wam* (borrowed from English?) means 'active, cautions, respectful, responsible.') <u>In 14 of these 21 languages, the 'warm' lexeme can readily be used to characterize a person's 'heart' or chest, in particular.</u> (In the other seven languages we do not have evidence that the term cannot be used for the heart; the sources do not say one way or the other.)

In general, these can be treated as minimum proportions in this sample for WARMTH = AFFECTION, KINDNESS, or CORDIALITY, since only a few of the chapters draw on a large corpus of speech or writing to comprehensively consider the temperature metaphors used in the languages analyzed: quite possibly some other such metaphors exist but were not mentioned in the chapters that do not systematically, much less exhaustively, analyze the full usage range of 'warm' metaphors.

While the 40 languages considered here are not a random sample of the world's languages, they come from ecologically, technically, and socially diverse cultures widely dispersed across the world, from 5 subfamilies of Indo-European, 2 subfamilies of Uralic, and 6 other language families. With the exception of possible Nganasan *hekǝ*, which might be a translation of a Russian metaphor, there is nothing to indicate that any of these metaphors have been borrowed from other languages.

Reading the sources reveals a converse pattern. Contrasting with 'warm' in many languages, 'cool' lexemes may metaphorically indicate 'not affectionate, not cordial.' In some languages, 'cool' may metaphorically indicate 'calm, reasonable,' or have other meanings. But we have found no language in which 'cold' or 'cool' metaphorically means 'affectionate, cordial, kind, loving, generous.' So far as we have seen, if a language uses any temperature lexeme metaphorically to describe a person's affectionateness, cordiality, kindness, or compassion – in general, or with specific reference to the heart – it is always a lexeme whose literal basic meaning is 'warm.'

Altogether, there are about 7100 living languages in about 152 families (Simons & Fennig 2017). Thousands more languages must have died out without ever leaving written traces. If our sample of 40 languages is to any remote degree representative, this suggests that the metaphor AFFECTION, KINDNESS, AND COMPASSION ARE WARMTH may have been independently invented, adopted, and diffused across language communities hundreds and likely even thousands of times in human history. More particularly, we can extrapolate to infer that AFFECTION, KINDNESS, AND COMPASSION ARE WARMTH IN THE HEART was invented, adopted, and diffused in hundreds and probably thousands of language communities. So we can infer that warmth in the chest has been a kama muta sensation around the world for millennia – a sensation so salient and consistent that people have very often used the sensation to name the motives and social–relational attitudes that emerge from kama muta.

One might ask whether and why the other sensations of kama muta do not give rise to any common metaphors for compassion, kindness, and related 'loving' devotion motives or moral commitments. Why does one not ordinarily characterize a caring person metaphorically as *TEARFUL, *MOIST EYED, *SHIVERY, or *GOOSEBUMPY, for example? These sensations are common in kama muta – only slightly less common than warmth in the center of the chest. However, so far as we know, warmth in the center of the chest occurs only in kama muta, while moist eyes and tears can occur in sadness, fear, and pain; goosebumps and shivers can occur in fear, and in spooky experiences of the uncanny. Though not everyone experiences heartwarming in kama muta, and few experience it every time they feel kama muta, evidently its distinctiveness and frequency are sufficient to afford the metaphor AFFECTION, KINDNESS, AND COMPASSION ARE WARMTH, especially WARMTH IN THE HEART. However, note that this metaphor and others like it seem not to be intuitive to American children under about age 8–9, who may actually deny that *warmth* and other physical terms could be used metaphorically to characterize non-physical qualities of persons (Asch & Nerlove 1960). If this is so, then the metaphor must be sustained by its intuitive resonance among older speakers.

What we do not know, however, is the physiology, neurobiology, or neurochemistry of the sensation of HEART WARMTH. What occurs in the chest? What could be warming up? How do we sense it? Subjective reports of this sensation seem to place it inside the chest, not on the skin, but to check I did some pilot research on chest skin temperature with several participants. I showed them videos that generally evoke kama muta and asked them to report when they had warm feelings in the chest. I used a sensitive thermal video camera that recorded skin temperatures at a resolution of approximately 0.1°C, and then I meticulously and repeatedly eye-balled the videos. There was no detectable change in skin temperature anywhere on the chest of any participant at the moments when they reported warmth in the chest, nor at any small temporal offset.

Sensory nerves tuned to warmth are limited to the skin and esophagus; there are no known warmth-sensing nerves in the heart or anywhere else in the chest. No one reports kama muta warmth that they attribute to the esophagus – kama muta doesn't evoke the sensation of swallowing a warm drink. So where is this *warmth*? And if something truly is warming up in the chest, how would we sense it? If some level(s) of the sensory system are spoofing warmth in the chest, what are the neural systems doing this, how are they doing it – and why are they creating this illusion? It's a mystery. If researchers can solve this mystery, perhaps we could devise sensors that would detect this sensation and provide a biomarker of the kama muta emotion. If this becomes possible, and if this biomarker occurs only in kama muta, it would be the first physiological signature ever discovered for any emotion.

Any of the sensations or signs of kama muta can be endowed with various cultural meanings. Because they are salient to observers as well as the person experiencing kama muta, tears are especially prone to be given cultural significance. In eighteenth and nineteenth century Europe, for example, tears were socially salient signs of cultural sophistication, love, friendship, political allegiance, and patriotism; see the detailed account in Online Note 2.7. In Chapter 15 we will see that early and Medieval Christians perceived tears as gifts from God and signs of devotion to him. But at other times, male tears, especially, have been derided as signs of weakness.

Online notes

2.1 Ululation: The sound of women's kama muta in Africa and the Levant.
2.2 Occasions for Ululating.
2.3 European paintings depicting the hand over the heart.
2.4 The cultural distribution of the hand-over-heart gesture.
2.5 Metaphors in many languages of kind people as 'warm' or 'warm hearted.'
2.6 'Warm' metaphors for persons, actions – and hearts.
2.7 Tears mediating European art, friendship, love, and politics.

Notes

1 For an explanation of the phonology of creaky voice, along with descriptions and theories of speakers' uses of creaky voice in various languages, see Mendoza-Denton 2011.
2 This phatic kama muta *aww* must be distinguished from the intensifier *aww*, as in *Aww, heck!* or *Aww! Please!* or *Aww! That sucks!*, which is uttered with a lower and flatter pitch contour.

3 Although his phenomenology is superb, Braud's <u>conceptualization</u> differs from ours. He posits (2001:106) that, "Tears of wonder-joy are somatic concomitants of my profound gratitude for encountering clear, pure, unambiguous instances or manifestations of the innocent, unspoiled, uncomplicated, and artless. Such tears are an appreciation of what could be or should be but has been missed, or from which we have gone astray—of what is less common than it could be." Poetically, he suggests that "wonder-joy tears may be signals or signs of an encounter with the numinous—an unplanned, unavoidable encounter with the Real."

4 We do not rule out the possibility that there are cultural practices, structured experiences, personal histories, or personality traits that enable kama muta experiences to last longer than a few minutes. But we haven't yet found any definite instances of continuous, sustained kama muta experiences.

5 Rotella, Sebastian 2004. Taking Iraqi Customs to Heart." *Los Angeles Times* 27 March. https://www.latimes.com/archives/la-xpm-2004-mar-27-fg-heart27-story. html.

6 https://www.youtube.com/watch?v=9ws7Vujn0p8.

7 This warmth-in-the-chest result is from an analysis conducted for this book; it is not reported in Zickfeld et al. 2019.

8 Our thanks to Janis Zickfeld for bringing to our attention these German and Polish locutions.

9 Source: en.wiktionary.org.

10 The video shows a man and his daughter helping a boy who has just stolen medicine for this mother, and later the boy, who has grown up to be a doctor, helping the man and his daughter. It is a Thai commercial for life insurance.

3

UNIVERSAL NARRATIVE PROTOTYPES OF REUNION, CULTURALLY ADAPTED TO EVOKE KAMA MUTA

Western wind, when wilt thou blow
That the small rain down can rain?
Christ, that my love were in my arms
And I in my bed again.

(Anonymous, 16th century)

Joyful weeping at reunions is depicted on several occasions in the Old Testament, though the details are opaque (Frazer 1918:Vol. 2, 82–84; Bosworth 2015). In assessing the sanity of King George III of England in 1788, it was considered an indication of the good prospects for his recovery that he wept when he was allowed to see his daughters (Dixon 2015:128). The parliamentary select committee observed that the emotions he displayed were those "which might naturally take place at the sight of relations or friends" (Dixon 2105:128, quoting from *The Times*, 16 January 1789). Twelve years later James Hadfield, an intermittently insane retired army officer, attempted to assassinate the King. To argue that he was currently sane, his barrister claimed that if Hadfield's 18-month old son were brought into the courtroom, Hadfield would "instantly burst into tears and shew every symptom of parental affection" (Dixon 2015:129, quoting from the London paper *The Morning Chronicle* of 27 June 1800). For king or assassin, crying when reunited with one's children meant sane normality.

Discussing "love and tender feelings, &c." Darwin (1872:216) noted that tears are evoked by sympathy for the imagined distress of a heroine, as well as "sympathy with the happiness of others, as with that of a lover, at last successful after many hard trials in a well-told tale." Drawing primarily on canonical literature in the major written literary traditions of the world, Hogan (2003) posits that this "romantic tragi-comedy narrative prototype" is the most salient and prevalent of four universal narrative prototypes.[1] Hogan loosely adopts the cognitive science concept of 'prototype,' defining literary prototypes as ones that "share all our standard criteria for verbal art. They share all the properties we consider 'normal' for literature" (Hogan 2003:6). Although the "we" here is Hogan's reference group of literature scholars and critics, he makes a deeper claim that the four narrative plots are universal prototypes in the sense that they have sustained the interest of their audiences as paradigms: they are widely shared, highly esteemed, and "establish evaluative standards and structural principles" in their literary traditions. Furthermore, they have endured for many centuries.

Hogan argues that the universality of the romantic union tragi-comedy narrative prototype results from the fact that reunion of separated lovers is a prototype of "personal" "happiness." Another type of happiness is "social," which generates a second universal narrative prototype of the rightful ruler who is finally restored to his (or her) place in "heroic" narratives. Heroic narratives commonly pair this with the restoration of the community's domination over other communities. Two other prototypical narratives grow out of the happiness prototype of sufficient food, and the happiness of discovering the moral problem underlying collective suffering. Hogan (2003:100) finds that "heroic and romantic tragi-comedy are the prominent forms of canonical and popular narrative in all traditions"; of these two, romantic tragi-comedy is the more prototypical and prevalent. It is the barriers to reunion that make these two narrative prototypes engaging, so that the ultimate reuniting of the protagonists evokes strong kama muta in them and in the audience.

In short, the most universal literary form consists of

> two lovers who cannot be united due to some conflict between their love and social structure, typically represented by parental disapproval. This conflict often involves a rival, as well, a suitor preferred by the interfering parents. The lovers are separated, frequently through exile and imprisonment. This separation often involves death or imagery of death. In the end, they are reunited, sometimes following a direct conflict with and defeat of the rival. It may happen that the reunion of the lovers takes place in the afterlife.
>
> *(Hogan 2003:101)*

This meshes with Frijda's (1988:88) proposition that *being moved* occurs when "Latent attachment concerns are awakened; expectations regarding their non-fulfillment are carefully evoked but held in abeyance; and then one is brusquely confronted with their fulfillment." The other three narrative prototypes are often combined with the romantic, so that their respective tensions and fulfillments amplify each other. For example, the reunion at the end that reunites the lovers often reconciles the lovers with their parents, and reintegrates the hero into his community (Hogan 2003:235).

Hogan extends his theory to argue that lyric poetry treats junctural moments in implied narratives, particularly romantic and heroic narratives. Lyric poetry reflects the critical assessment of an agent's position in such a narrative at a crucial juncture. This occurs not only in secular poetry, but also in devotional lyrics with a narrative of separation, longing, and mystical union with a god – notably in Hindu *bhakti* poems and Sufi *ghazals* (Hogan 2003:169–170; we explore these further in Chapters 12 and 13). He illustrates the poetic distillation of the romantic tragi-comedy with this *bhakti* poem:

> When he comes back
> to my arms
> I'll make him feel what nobody ever felt
> everywhere
> me
> vanishing into him
> like water
> into the clay of a new jar
>
> *(Hemacandra n.d. – classical Sanskrit)*

Independently of Hogan, Booker (2004) induced a taxonomy of seven plots in Western literature, popular books, and movies. Does the appeal of some of these plots derive from their evocation of kama muta experiences?

> Of course the supreme symbol of completion in story telling is the union of two people, hero and heroine, masculine and feminine, to make a whole: because they are seen as complementary in a more fundamental way than anything we know. Only when this has been achieved can hero and heroine together succeed to the kingdom: because the two have finally become one.
>
> *(Booker 2004:235)*

Neale (1986) makes a similar point about melodrama. A close look at both Hogan and Booker's basic plots shows that all consist of tales of challenges that render CS problematic, concluding in the sudden restoration of the CS bonds (see Online Note 3.1).

It is not only 'folk' and 'literary' narratives that rely on making the audience hope a couple will be able to be together in blissful love. Contemporary Western culture is highly focused on the vicissitudes of romantic love. Falling in love, unreciprocated love, threats to love, jealousy, betrayal, and problems in love, loss of love, and nostalgia for former lovers are the predominant themes of popular culture. These kama muta-evoking themes are the appeal of what critics call 'sentimental' literature, which I discuss in Chapter 8. The vicissitudes of love are the themes of a great many popular songs and prominent in poetry, short stories, novels, movies, television serials and 'reality' shows, news features, magazine stories and columns, articles, blogs, YouTube and BuzzFeed videos, and stand-up comedy, as well as ballet, opera, and theater. Many depict misery and suffering: problematic love, challenges to love, disappointments, and mourning for lost love. This may evoke compassionate kama muta, when the reader or viewer's *heart goes out* to the vulnerable, needy protagonist, or the kama muta of identification when the viewer recognizes her own experience in the suffering of the protagonist.

Appreciation of kama muta was the core of late eighteenth century and early nineteenth century literature, including the German *Sturm und Drang* movement and other Romantic movements, and kama muta performances were essential to friendship and politics; for details, see Chapter 10.

Reunions that evoke kama muta occur in everyday life, too:

> My one-year-old nephew ran up to me as soon as I got back home, with an ecstatic smile on his face … I found it amazing how he seems to remember who I am, and to see how much he's grown in such a short time. It was one of those great 'awwwwwww moments.'
>
> (UCLA freshman)

These themes are prevalent in narrative arts precisely because they evoke kama muta. That is, the more effectively a story evokes kama muta, the more people attend to it, remember it, tell others about it, seek to re-experience the story, and bring others to hear or see it with them. Creators of the most kama muta-evoking stories gain prestige, fame, and wealth; this motivates people to create stories that best evoke kama muta. Thus the kama muta emotion is a niche to which innumerable cultural constructions constantly adapt: the more a cultural construction evokes kama muta, the more people reproduce that construction. Chapters 10 and 17 explicate this cultural evolutionary process.

In our own experiments, we have shown participants a Google commercial of Pakistani and Indian friends, separated for over 60 years, reunited. And we have shown a YouTube video of a baby elephant rescued from a hole, running to rejoin its mother (Seibt et al. 2016; Seibt et al. 2018). Both evoke kama muta. Norwegians call this *gjensynsglede*, 'joy of seeing again' – to see the sentiment, just Google *gjensynsglede* images; it's also a Twitter hashtag.

> [Viewers] do not and did not cry about [the dog] Lassie (Knight, 1938) being hopelessly lost (although that is sad and causes tension). They cry when it is clear that Lassie will successfully make her way home. By the same token, they do not cry during *The King and I* (Rodgers & Hammerstein, 1961) when they learn that the king is dying (although that fact is saddening), but they do tend to cry when he and Anna reconcile their differences before his death.
>
> *(Efran & Spangler 1979:66)*

But beyond the emotional response evoked in the audience, there's a question about the prototype narratives such as the romantic tragi-comedy and basic plots such as comedy: what emotions are <u>the characters themselves</u> represented as experiencing? In contemporary Western cultures, we know that long-separated lovers' often experience strong kama muta when at last they are safely back together, and fiction represents them feeling this emotion when they reunite. Is this unique to the modern world? Let's look at classical Greek narratives to see whether friends, lovers, and families are depicted as experiencing kama muta when they reunite after a long and stressful separation.

Recognizing Odysseus

When we first started to explore kama muta, we didn't know whether it was an emotion people experienced beyond or before contemporary Western culture. We also weren't sure whether we could identify kama muta in other cultures or historical eras – when communal sharing relationships suddenly intensify, do non-modern or non-Western people cry, have warm feelings in the upper chest, get goosebumps or chills, or feel their hair stand up? Is kama muta everywhere an extremely positive experience that people actively seek to experience, especially together? Were audiences elsewhere and at other times in history as attracted to depictions of kama muta as contemporary Western audiences are? One of the first places we looked was in Homer and classical Greek theater.

Scenes of recognition ($\alpha\nu\alpha\gamma\nu\dot{\omega}\rho\iota\sigma\eta$, *anagnōrisis* – roughly, 'ceasing not to know') were pivotal turning points in the *Odyssey*, in the Greek drama discussed by Aristotle in his *Poetics*, and in Greek and related novels of the first four centuries of the current era (Perrin 1909; Gainsford 2003; Konstan 2009:320–321; Montiglio 2013).[2] In these recognition scenes the central characters have been separated for many years and one or both are believed or feared to have died. They have typically suffered great hardships over long journeys, and sometimes are currently in mortal danger. Then when they are finally together again, often at least one of the characters doesn't recognize the other and is about to kill him or her. When one of the characters already knows or discovers who the other character is, he typically tests the other's loyalty to make certain that the unknowing one's love remains steadfast – which it is, despite every inducement to forsake the relationship. When they recognize each other they scream with elation, hug and hold each other, weep with joy, and often kiss. Those who are reunited may be siblings, parent and child, lovers or spouses; sometimes they are master and faithful household servants or retainers. When they are spouses or lovers, embraces are sometimes followed by making love. Clearly recognition reunions belong to Hogan's (2003) tragi-comedy narrative prototype and Booker's (2004) comedy plot type.[3]

There are many indications that the reunited characters are represented as experiencing kama muta. The ancient Greeks wept in extended laments at joyful events, especially when reunited after a long separation from people they loved (Föllinger 2009:28). "The joy about a homecoming or an unexpected return" (2009:28) are the most common occasions for weeping, for example, as Odysseus's shipmates do when he unexpectedly returns safely (Homer 2018:Book 10, 408–418). Likewise, when at last Agamemnon comes home from Troy, "Then joyfully he stepped foot in his country, and touched and kissed the earth of his dear home, He wept hot floods of tears, from happiness" (Homer 2018:Book 4,520–522, Wilson translation.) Let's explore signs of kama muta in the characters re-uniting when Odysseus comes home, and consider how the text is crafted to evoke kama muta in the listener or reader.

After almost 20 years of fighting in Troy and overcoming innumerable obstacles on his way home, eventually Odysseus reaches his island, Ithaca. As Book

16 begins, Odysseus, disguised as a beggar, is sitting with his old swineherd, Eumaios, who has not recognized him. Odysseus's son Telemachos has long been away searching for Odysseus; no one in Ithaca knows whether either Odysseus or Telemachos are alive.

> These two in the shelter, Odysseus and the noble
> swineherd, stirred the fire at dawn, and arranged their breakfast,
> and sent the herdsmen out with the pasturing pigs. At this time
> the clamorous dogs came fawning around Telemachos, nor did
> they bark at him as he came, and great Odysseus noticed
> that the dogs were fawning; above them he heard the loud noise of footsteps.
>
> Immediately he spoke in winged words to Eumaios:
> 'Eumaios, someone is on his way here who is truly
> one of yours, or else well known, since the dogs are not barking
> but fawning about him, and I can hear the thud of his foot- steps.'
> His whole word had not been spoken when his beloved
> son stood in the forecourt. Amazed, the swineherd started
> up, and the vessels, where he had been busily mixing
> the bright wine, fell from his hand. He came up to meet his master,
> and kissed his head, and kissed too his beautiful shining
> eyes, and both his hands, and the swelling tear fell from him.
> And as a father, with heart full of love, welcomes his only
> and grown son, for whose sake he has undergone many hardships
> when he comes back in the tenth year from a distant country,
> so now the noble swineherd, clinging fast to godlike
> Telemachos, kissed him even as if he had escaped dying,
> and in a burst of weeping he spoke to him in winged words:
> 'You have come, Telemachos, sweet light; I thought I would never
> see you again, when you had gone in the ship to Pylos.
> But come now into the house, dear child, so that I can pleasure my
> heart with looking at you again when you are inside;
> for you do not come very often to the estate and the herdsmen,
> but you stay in town, since now it seems you are even minded
> to face the deadly company of the lordly suitors.'
>
> *(2018:Book 16, 1–29)*

Telemachos does not recognize his father Odysseus. Eumaios sacrifices a pig and serves it to Telemachos, Odysseus, and Eumaios's men. Then Telemachos sends Eumaios to secretly tell his mother, Penelope, that he has returned safely. After Eumaios departs, Athena appears to Odysseus and transforms his appearance, making him younger, tall, strong, and well-dressed. Telemachos is awed. Then Odysseus reveals his identity, telling Telemachos that he is Telemachos's father; Odysseus kisses his son and his tears splash on the ground (2018:Book 16:178–224). It takes a moment, but when Telemachos realizes that this is truly his father, he hugs him, sheds tears, and the two of them utter a pulsating cry.

One after another, Odysseus's herdsmen, his dog, and his servants recognize him, and finally his wife Penelope accepts that it is truly he; they each clearly display kama muta. When his long-neglected dog Argos, once a great hunter but now abandoned on a dung heap, sees Odysseus, Argos raises his head and ears, wags his tail in recognition, and dies. We don't know if we can characterize the dog's emotion as kama muta, but we feel kama muta when we read this. Kama muta moments ensue one after another as successive member of Odysseus's household recognize him. Online Note 3.2 provides all the moving details of Homer's account.

Homer's Odysseus is not the only classical Greek work to depict the kama muta experiences of recognition reunions. Joyfully reunited characters in the plays of Aeschylus, Sophocles, and Euripides often embrace each other and often weep (Shisler 1942:287–288, 291; Wright 2005). "Euripides even uses the suggestion of hair rising on the head to help show Helen's joy at meeting Menelaus (Helen 632–633)" (Shisler 1942:288). Hair rising would not likely be under an actor's control, nor visible to an audience, even if the actor's hair was uncovered, so evidently Euripides' stage directions meant to indicate the emotional state of the character. Likewise, it is particularly interesting that all three playwrights specify weeping in a number of reunion scenes. Actors wore masks in Greek drama, so weeping on stage could only be conveyed by the dialog, or the actor's gesture or posture (Montiglio 2013:230) – unless perhaps it was conveyed by a creaky voice. Thus in providing the stage direction that the actor weeps, or her hair stands up, Aeschylus, Sophocles, and Euripides can only have intended to characterize by its physical signs the kama muta emotion the actor should convey to the audience. Indeed, without specifying joyful tears, hugs, kisses, or hair standing up with joy, Homer had no way to describe the emotions of his characters and the playwrights had no way to tell the actors the emotion to be performed: there was no word or phrase for kama muta in ancient or classical Greek. Though their climactic scenes depicted and evoked kama muta, the emotion had no name.

In sum, Greek recognition scenes suddenly, joyfully – and with great relief to participants and their audience or readers – restore, reinstate, and rekindle intense loving relationships (Montiglio 2013:225). These recognition scenes evoke tears in the reunited, who shed 'sweet' tears, as spouses 'weep with love' on their wedding night (Konstan 2009). In some cases the tragic chorus or watching crowd weep or joyfully celebrate along with the central characters (Montiglio 2013:153–154). When they recognize each other, the reunited characters sometimes experience something intense in the *phrén*, the upper chest. Sometimes they have trouble speaking at first. Surely they felt kama muta, although they had no name for the emotion itself. Apart from Euripides' instruction that Helen's hair rise in joy at being reunited with Menelaus, apparently there is no mention of goosebumps or chills in these scenes. Perhaps in actual reunions, or listening to and watching these fictional scenes, ancient and classical Greeks had goosebumps or chills, but they didn't regard those sensations as significant. Perhaps for some reason they did not have kama muta goosebumps or chills. Or perhaps they *are* mentioned in some texts; classical scholars may find them once they look, along with representations of the other sensations of kama muta.

Early modern Western fiction extensively developed the recognition scene, often involving separated lovers who recognized each other after overcoming a succession of tribulations. Early modern novels also elaborated a theme from these first novels: "blood's call" (Montiglio 2013:126–130, 234–238). The idea was that close 'blood' kin, who naturally love each other, would 'naturally' recognize each other in some intuitive way. This representation of love as a shared essential substance is another manifestation of consubstantial assimilation, a concept I discuss in the next chapter.

Although the ancient Greeks had no name for the kama muta experience as a psychological state, they depicted it often and appreciated its impact on protagonists and audiences. And they definitely had an appetite for it: it was an emotional experience they explicitly hungered for, intentionally and explicitly engaged in, and sated themselves with. That is, it was a positive emotion that they sought to experience together. When Telemachos recognized Odysseus they "had a desire for mourning" (2018:Book 16, 215), and when Penelope heard the disguised Odysseus tell of meeting Odysseus, Penelope took "pleasure of tearful lamentation" (2018:Book 19, 251), and when she finally recognized him, it "still more roused in him the passion for weeping" (2018:Book 23, 231). When the palace serving women recognized Odysseus and warmly held and kissed him, "sweet longing for lamentation and tears took hold of him" (2018:Book 22, 500–501). Similarly, when Menelaus speaks of mourning for his men who died in the Trojan War, he says that at times his *phrén* 'satisfies/ delights/gladdens/cheers/has full enjoyment of weeping/wailing,' (*góos phrén terpomai*, γόῳ φρένα τέρπομαι), and he 'quickly takes his fill of icy lamentation' (*aiyhrós kóros kruerós góos*, αἰψηρὸς δὲ κόρος κρυεροῖο γόοιο; Homer 2018:Book 4,102–103). Menelaus's declaration arouses in Telemachos the 'desire/passion/ longing/yearning to weep' for his father (*imeros ornumi góos*, ἵμερον ὦρσε γόοιο; 2018:Book 4, 113). These phrases are used to describe the states of mind (or rather, state of *phrén*) of heroes at many other points in the Homeric epics (for example, 2018:Book 4:194, Book 15, 398–401; *Iliad*: Book 4, 102, Book 24, 507–514). In particular, the characters actively sought to mnemonically re-experience the comradely solidarity of soldiers in battle. Heroes also shed tears of yearning when they think about a spouse or family member they love from whom they are separated (Föllinger 2009:28–29).

Death is the final voyage, but people experience vivid reunions with the dead. In Chapter 9 I explore how memorial sites, monuments, and mementos bridge the gap between the living and the dead, often reuniting them affectively. Beyond these material means, in a great many cultures, conversation with the deceased is a common and normative practice. Clients visit mediums who go into trance and then adopt the personas of the client's deceased family members, or the persona of spirits or deities (Bourgignon 2008; Lewis 2003). The client typically experiences this as a vividly direct conversation with, say, his mother or son. At least one ethnographic film shows clients weeping during and after such conversations; perhaps they feel purely sad, but it appears that speaking with their loved ones is evoking kama muta (Connor, Asch, & Asch 1986). It is plausible to imagine that one of the things that sustains the role of spirit medium is clients' attraction to the possibility of kama muta experiences when, through the medium, they reunite with deceased loved ones. Kama muta through spirit mediumship certainly occurs, as one informant recounts in Online Note 3.3. I will briefly return to it in Chapter 16.

* * * * * *

Listeners, readers, and audiences are more attentive to some narratives than others; people remember and retell some narratives more than others. And story-tellers who tell especially appealing stories attract big audiences. The more a story evokes kama muta, the more it spreads and the longer it endures. In Dan Sperber's conceptual framework, a story or other cultural practice or artifact that evokes kama muta would be termed a "contagious" "attractor" (Sperber 1996; Claidière & Sperber 2007). Furthermore, story-tellers with intuitive or articulate sensibilities about what makes a narrative appealing will improve stories they hear, transforming the narrative to make it evoke kama muta more frequently and more strongly. One aspect of this is that, like everyone else, story-tellers and those who quote them enjoy giving kama muta to their audiences; 'sharing' kama muta is intrinsically joyous. In complement to this, audiences and critics may evaluate narratives according to how well they evoke kama muta, demanding ever more powerful stories. This active (conscious or unreflective) tailoring of narratives to better evoke kama muta, along with selective attention, memory, and demand – thereby increasing the prevalence of such stories – is an example of what Claidière and Sperber (2007) call a "cultural attractor." In any case, it seems clear that the human disposition to kama muta is an essential component of the substrate that a great many narratives grow out of – without this emotional disposition, people probably would not want to tell and would not listen to many of the most popular stories. Perhaps, without kama muta, there would be a lot less story-telling.

In Chapter 8 I will return to literature and other arts of kama muta. But at this point let us step back and conceptualize what it is that evokes kama muta and what kama muta motivates. How does the evolved psychological propensity for kama muta become realized in socially transmitted cultural forms? And precisely what is kama muta?

Online Notes

3.1 Hogan and Booker's identification of the plot that universally evokes kama muta.

3.2 Kama muta moments when Odysseus's family and servants recognize him.

3.3 Kama muta evoked by reconnecting with a deceased great-grandmother.

Notes

1 In Hogan's use of the terminology of literary analysis, a narrative is a *tragedy* if the prototypical narrative is truncated before the couple can be reunited, or before the hero defeats the usurper and returns in triumph. The full, completed narrative that culminates in re-uniting the lovers is a tragi-comedy.
2 Alex Purves kindly and astutely guided us to this phenomenon and explained its cultural context.
3 This is the clear literary prototype of *anagnōrisis* (recognition). However, Aristotle and others sometimes also use the term *anagnōrisis* in a much broader sense when they discuss scenes in which the characters recognize important facts, or recognize something horrible (as in *Oedipus Rex*).

PART II

The basic theory and everyday experiences

4

HOMO MOVENS: WHAT EVOKES KAMA MUTA EXPERIENCES, AND WHAT MOTIVES EMERGE?

The merit of benevolence, arising from its utility, and its tendency to promote the good of mankind, has been already explained, and is, no doubt, the source of a *considerable* part of that esteem, which is so universally paid to it. But it will also be allowed, that the very softness and tenderness of the sentiment, its engaging endearments, its fond expressions, its delicate attentions, and all that flow of mutual confidence and regard, which enters into a warm attachment of love and friendship: It will be allowed, I say, that these feelings, being delightful in themselves, are necessarily communicated to the spectators, and melt them into the same fondness and delicacy. The tear naturally starts in our eye on the apprehension of a warm sentiment of this nature: Our breast heaves, our heart is agitated, and every humane tender principle of our frame is set in motion, and gives us the purest and most satisfactory enjoyment.

(Hume 1777:M 7.19, SBN 257)

The kama muta response to one's own infant, to cuteness, and to reunion with a loved one result from a dynamic transition in social relationships in which people suddenly become 'closer.' More precisely, **kama muta occurs when there is a rapid emergence, renewal, restoration, or intensification of a communal sharing relationship** (hereafter "CS intensification"). A communal sharing relationship is one in which two or more persons interact with reference to something they have in common that makes them socially equivalent (Fiske 1991, 1992, 2004a). In strong CS relationships, people feel they have some essential substance in common that makes them the same. CS is a feeling of love, solidarity, and identity in which people are kind to those of their kind. Depending on how people culturally implement CS, they may share resources (what's mine is yours – it's all ours), share work (let's all pitch in, everyone doing whatever they can), responsibilities (we are jointly account-able), share goals and outcomes (we're in this together, win or lose), or share mutual care and compassion (your happiness is my happiness, your suffering is my suffering). Participants in a CS relationship may take collective moral responsibility for each other's actions, as well as for avenging any insult or harm done to any of them. CS is often multi-faceted, including all or many of these aspects, but in some cases people implement CS to coordinate just one aspect of one domain. For example, we may share the use of a park without coordinating anything else in a CS manner.

Intense CS includes parental love, deep romantic love, and the devotion and loyalty that may bind soldiers in a small unit in wartime. Other examples of CS include membership in an athletic team; the sense of solidarity with a school or a community; and racial, ethnic, or national identity. The kindness of a stran-gers may create a momentary CS that affords kama muta. Institutionalized CS relationships include the *compadrazgo* of godparent with the godchild's parent, blood brotherhood, and membership in age sets of the sort that were common among East African pastoralists. We may speak loosely of a 'CS relationship,' but we do not mean 'relationship' in the colloquial sense. We also may speak loosely of persons being 'in' a CS relationship, but CS is not a container. Any aspect of any social interaction may be organized with reference to something socially significant that the participants have in common. We may have a joint responsi-bility for a task without sharing our beds with each other. We may seek to make a decision by consensus without eating commensally. Or we may share a joint without pitching in to pay for it. The CS coordination and sentiments may be momentary or life-long. Relating in a CS manner with respect to some aspect of an interaction does not imply anything about other aspects of the interaction, which may be organized according to any of the other three relational models.

Affectively, CS consists of sentiments of compassion and caring. CS is affec-tionate. The suffering of one is the suffering of all of us, while each one's joy is the joy of all. Morally, the sentiment is 'one for all and all for one.' The welfare of the dyad or group comes before the welfare of individual participants. This is why the self-reported trait of empathic concern for the needy consistently correlates with ratings of *being moved* or *touched* and the three core sensations of kama muta that occur with the sudden intensification of CS (Zickfeld et al. 2017; Zickfeld et al. 2019).

The validity of the CS construct, along with the other three relational mod-els, has been supported by hundreds of studies by hundreds of researchers using diverse methods, and the construct has been persuasively applied to illuminate a great many social phenomena.[1] But it is only recently that we have come to recognize what happens when CS suddenly intensifies.

Erik Ridderström is a barista in an Oslo café that serves what may be the best coffee in the world. He has worked in retail service since he was 14, beginning part time in a cheese shop. Whenever a customer is especially thoughtful or appreciative, he gets goosebumps on his forearms. He reacts this way, for example, when someone brings back their empty cups, because he feels a sense of 'togetherness' – which he hopes is mutual. From his first days in the cheese shop, he remembers this goosebumps feeling whenever he had the sense that, although only 14, older customers treated him with 'respect' as a person. This feeling is what makes him always want to work out-front in customer service. In the café he may have the feeling perhaps every other day. It is the same sensation he feels when his girlfriend returns after an absence. He frequently had the same feeling when he was in China for a year at age 18, whenever a shopkeeper, despite the hectic pace of business, took the time to connect across languages and cultures.[2]

The intensification can be initiated by the person herself, by someone else doing something that makes her feel closer, or by observing someone else doing something that makes that person feel closer to another person. So in *first-person kama muta*, a person experiences kama muta when she suddenly feels new or renewed CS with someone. In *second-person kama muta*, a person experiences kama muta because she perceives that someone feels new or renewed CS with her. In *third-person kama muta*, a person feels kama muta when she observes others feeling new or renewed CS for each other – and she identifies with the people she observes. (That identification itself is a form of CS, but the identification may be stable.) In third-person kama muta, the CS relationship between the observed others may in fact be new or renewed, and that is often the case, but it could simply be new to the observer, or their CS newly catches her attention. *First-person plural kama muta* occurs when doing, being, or creating something together makes them feel one. It is only the triggers that differ among first-, second-, third-person, and first-person plural kama muta; the kama muta emotion itself is the same. Examples of first-person kama muta are a person encountering a beautiful sleeping infant or seeing a cute kitten playing with a feather. Examples of second person kama muta are receiving a marriage proposal or a huge and unexpected kindness. Third-person kama muta occurs when a person reads a story, watches a movie, or sees a soldier return from combat to be reunited with his family. The *we* of first-person plural kama muta occurs among eight oarsmen and a coxswain, players in a jazz band, protesters marching in a demonstration, or soldiers drilling in synchrony.

Often two or more of these types occur together. For example when lovers both make a huge effort to be reunited, they each feel both first- and second-person kama muta; if there is an audience, the audience feels third-person kama muta. If Jane has a new lover Tom, and because Tom loves Jane, he makes a specially sweet effort to get close to Jane's young son, all three of them may feel kama muta. And Jane in particular may feel first-person kama muta watching how cute her son is when he responds to Tom, second-person kama muta because she recognizes that Tom's attention to her son shows how much Tom loves her, and third-person kama muta because she sees that her son and Tom are suddenly closer. In these examples there are three different social-relational cognitive processes operating, so it is useful to distinguish among them by keeping in mind who has initiated the intensification of what CS relationship(s) with whom. Then we can proceed to analyze how they affect each other. This is helpful especially in the many instances of recursive or meta kama muta.

There are also reflexive instances of kama muta, such as may occur in mindful self-compassion when a self-critical, self-derogating person suddenly feels compassionate love for herself. Other interesting reflexive instances apparently include those in Pepys' (2003) seventeenth-century *Diary* when Pepys seems to be recording events in his life framed so as to evoke kama muta in his future self. Online Note 4.1 provides the intriguing details.

If you review the examples with which I began the book, you will see that they are divided into first, second, and third person, and first person plural (*we*) instances, concluding with an instance that consists of all four. Holding one's baby for the first time, nostalgic experiences, union with divinity, or having cute puppies curl up in your lap are first person experiences: one's own feelings of communal connection with someone (or some animal, spirit, or deity) suddenly intensify. The 'warm glow' that some donors report feeling from such compassionate acts as donating blood (Ferguson 2015) or organs may be the experience of first-person kama muta, named for the sensation it evokes in the center of the chest. When someone unexpectedly brings you "love soup" or sacrifices his life to save you, the emotion is evoked by the second person's surprising intensified CS expression or action toward you. Observing the soldier's reunion with his family, or your daughter marrying the love of her life, are third party experiences: you are watching others suddenly intensify their CS relationship. If you are responding to the puppies' attraction to you, we could classify the experience as second person kama muta, while if you come across sleeping puppies and are instantly attracted to them, it would be first person kama muta. Of course, you and the puppies could be simultaneously attracted to each other. Steinnes (2017, Steinnes et al 2019) showed that first person and third person kama muta combine; people feel kama muta when they see cute puppies or kittens, and their kama muta responses are even stronger when they observe CS (stroking or licking or cuddling) between the animals, or between a person and the animals.

In third-person kama muta, the observer may have a CS relationship with a real person, or a pet. Or the CS relationship between observer and target may consist of identification with a celebrity, a fictional character, or a deity represented in a narrative or image. Whatever the nature of the being that the observer identifies with, the sudden intensification of that being's CS relationship with another being tends to evoke a wonderful feeling of kama muta in the observer.

People often feel kama muta without being in face-to-face interaction with a living person. For example, people may feel first- or second-person kama muta when their own CS relationship intensifies with a singer or actor who is not actually aware of the person. Likewise, people may feel first- or second-person kama muta when their own CS relationship intensifies with a collectivity or imagined community such as a town, nation, club, university, or military service (see Anderson 2006). And people may have very strong kama muta when they feel united with a deity.

Typically the intensification of CS is socially valued; the greater the compassion, kindness, generosity, and self-sacrifice, the more moral approbation it receives. For this reason, it seems, some scholars have posited that 'elevation' occurs <u>only</u> when a person <u>perceives</u> an act of "moral beauty" (Haidt originally posited that it was evoked by "spiritual purity"; Haidt 2000, 2003a, 2003b; Haidt & Keltner 2004). Similarly, Cova and Deonna (2014; Cova, Deonna, & Sanders 2017) posit that 'being moved' is evoked by the "realization of core values," especially when their realization appeared to be problematic. That is, the Haidt and Cova and Deonna constructs define emotions that result from <u>observation</u> of others' exceptional moral acts. Such conceptualizations exclude innumerable instances of kama muta when the CS intensification is not morally extraordinary, along with all the instances when the exemplary CS actions are directed to or initiated by the person feeling kama muta. Both theories also imply that elevation or being moved would occur when a person observes a supererogatory act that does not consist of <u>CS</u> intensification. So their theories posit that elevation or being moved would occur when a person observes exemplary obedience or leadership that intensify an authority ranking relationship; morally beautiful turn-taking or repayment of an obligation that intensify an equality matching relationship; or validation of the moral value of proportionality in market pricing, such as praiseworthy repayment of a mortgage or a perfectly calculated prison sentence. These acts might evoke emotions, but not kama muta.

Haidt and colleagues (Haidt 2003a, 2003b; Algoe & Haidt 2009) include "touched" and "moved" among the descriptors of "elevation," which is the sentiment at the pinnacle of the purity dimension of morality. Haidt's construct of "elevation" has been measured with scales including items asking about being "moved" and "touched" (Haidt 2000, 2003a, 2003b; Algoe & Haidt 2009; Pohling & Diessner 2016; Thomson & Siegel 2016). However, our interviews and participant observation show that kama muta is evoked by kittens, by viewing the first ultrasound of one's baby, participating in Sufi worship, listening to poems that tell of suffering that the listener identifies with, sharing intimate secrets about fears and traumas, gathering for holiday meals, or seeing commercials that evoke nostalgic memories (Fiske, Schubert, & Seibt et al. 2017a, 2017b).

These are not instances of observation, nor are the acts "morally beautiful." People also feel kama muta when they observe cruelty or hear a person recounting cruelty they have suffered – and the observer, having shared that experience of cruelty, deeply identifies with the sufferer. Also, acts that are morally virtuous in the framework of Authority Ranking, Equality Matching, or Market Pricing seem not to evoke kama muta. For example, a soldier obeying an order to expose himself to certainly fatal enemy fire evokes *awe*, but not kama muta – unless the observer perceives the soldier's ultimate motive to be CS devotion to saving his comrades.

The concept of elevation is defined as a state that results from observing others' actions, as entirely a third-party emotion. In contrast, people frequently feel kama muta in the first- and second-person and in the first-person plural 'we', as a result of interactions in which they are deeply engaged as participants. We found that in 132 Americans' reports of a recent experience of "positive tears," we found that they rated the events they witnessed (or read or saw on screen) as no more *moving* and *touching* than events in which they personal participated (Seibt et al. 2017). For example, they reported *being moved* when going trick-or-treating with a child, at graduation, when receiving a happy birthday phone call from an ex-husband, and when remembering working closely with friends to lose weight for a wedding. I recently felt kama muta when I returned home after two months abroad and the baristas in one of my favorite American cafés shouted out, "Oh, look who's here! It's Alan!"

Moreover, large samples of American participants reported feeling *moved* or *touched*, as well as having warm or other feelings in the chest, tears, and goosebumps, when they watched videos in which the characters suddenly become closer, but don't do anything morally remarkable (Schubert et al. 2016). For example, many participants felt strong kama muta when watching a video of people who had raised a lion cub in London, then released it into the wild, and then, going to look for it after a long gap, having an affectionate reunion with the lion; a video of performance art in which Marina Abramović, sitting silently looking at whoever sits opposite her, when her former lover sits down, after a pause, reaching out to hold his hand; and one in which, after people help a baby elephant get out of a water hole, it runs to its mother. Kama muta experienced when people watch such morally ordinary events, or hold a kitten, graduate from college, or take their children trick-or-treating, are not instances of "elevation" as Haidt and colleagues have defined it. But our experiments show that they definitely evoke kama muta. There is certainly a moral facet of kama muta, but it is limited to the morality of CS: the goodness of loving-kindness. (On CS morality versus the moralities of the other three fundamental relational models, see Rai & Fiske 2011).

However, consistent with our theory of kama muta, note that Janicke and Oliver (2017) have recently shown that beyond perception of moral beauty, 'elevation' is also evoked by portrayals of connectedness, love, and kindness. Janicke and Oliver measured elevation with seven self-report items labelling the participants' emotion: "touched, moved, emotional, meaningful, compassion, inspired, and tender." These are all labels that an English speaker would be likely to use for kama muta.[3]

It appears that occasionally people experience kama muta responses to something they were not paying any conscious attention to. A Norwegian informant told us about an event in which she noticed she was shedding tears while writing with headphones on, and only then played back the song to see what had evoked her kama muta (see her account in Online Note 4.2). Another time she was singing and found herself choked up and tearing, which led her to stop and attend to the lyrics that she had been singing without attending to. Four other informants (one Norwegian, one Finno-Norwegian, two Americans) have told us that they also have experienced kama muta without initially being aware of what evoked it. That is, they noticed themselves crying, and/or getting goosebumps, felt 'moved' or 'rørt,' and searched for what was evoking it. The first two informants reported that while studying and listening to music they have found themselves crying and/or getting goosebumps, felt rørt, but didn't know what they'd heard that made them feel that way because they had not been consciously attending to the music. Then they played back the song and discovered what made them kama muta. In another case, a UCLA undergraduate woman reported this:

> I was visiting Seattle for the first time and was looking around the city. There was a restaurant by the Public Market that overlooked the ocean and I felt so at peace while I was outside there and walking around. I realized that I had goosebumps ... like chills, and I was just having a moment. But then I got teary-eyed and I didn't know why. I wasn't sad but I was just, [pauses] you know, having a moment [laughs, looking up]. Um, and I realize now that it's because I was just so excited and I felt like I was at home there in that place. I've always wanted to live in Seattle so I was excited for that trip but I feel like talking about it now I might have been feeling just at home. I could see myself there. I've never really felt that way before but maybe when I first visited UCLA and just knew this was the school for me. But yeah I could just imagine and picture myself picking up my produce at that market and going home and having a dog and all of those wonderful things! ... Just a life by myself. I really want a pug though! A cute little black pug and a little apartment. I have no idea what kind of job I'll have but I just really feel like I belong there.

Two other Norwegian accounts report experiences in which they evidently experienced kama muta while their reflective mind assessed the situation as embarrassing – in fact, as a vicariously mortifying failure to evoke kama muta. Consciously, they felt embarrassed, and not rørt or moved. The stories were from a couple, who heard each other's accounts, so they're not entirely independent, but we discussed them in detail so the descriptions feel reliable. Both began their stories by saying that they had experienced goosebumps of embarrassment. The guy is in a band and he was listening to a recording of another band that he's friends with and that has released songs on the same album as his own band. His friends' band was playing a love song badly, pronouncing the French badly too, and he felt embarrassed for them. At the same time he felt goosebumps on his arms and a feeling in the chest similar or identical to what he feels when "moved" (he was discussing this in English). The woman told about watching a popular Norwegian talk show in which the guest was telling what he clearly intended to be a moving sob story, while she felt embarrassed by how trite it was and how flat the story felt [here she mimed her reaction at the time, lowering her head and hiding her face in her hands in vicarious shame]. Yet at the same time she felt goosebumps and the "moved feeling" in her chest.

Similarly, in a Culture Gabfest (2016) podcast on Slate Plus,[4] Dana Stevens reported "crying at something embarrassing yesterday and was hiding the fact from my daughter, I can't remember now what it was, but was some, you know, some YouTube video or something." Julia Turner spoke about crying not only at great art, but at "manipulative narratives" in commercials and television shows that feel like "a debased entertainment that I can't feel good about crying at ... I'm not proud about those tears."

These events suggest that the processes that evoke kama muta can occur outside of and independent of conscious awareness, and may be inconsistent with the person's conscious judgments. Many psychological processes are inaccessible to any direct reflective conscious awareness (Carruthers 2011). But these events raise some important issues about the nature of kama muta, and by extension, other emotions. In each of these cases, the person unconsciously 'felt' an emotion first, and only then noticed the sensations, which led them to reflectively interpret the experience as an emotion. Similarly, there are many reports of people not feeling pain despite severe injury, or not feeling fear despite great danger, until after a crisis. Are there instances of kama muta when the sensations are too mild, or the person is too preoccupied by something else (an emotion, or a problem that fully loads their cognitive processes), or too intently in flow, to notice the sensations at all, so that they never become reflectively aware of being emotional? That is, could a person be too distracted to <u>ever</u> become conscious of a kama muta episode? If so, would the unconscious kama muta generate the same sentiments of devotion and moral commitment that emerge from conscious experiences – and would these <u>motives</u> be conscious? Are the people who rarely have any physical sensations of kama muta especially prone to unconscious experiences of it?

When I say that the intensification of CS that evokes kama muta is "sudden," I mean a transformation or realization of the CS that becomes apparent in a few seconds, or at most a minute or two. The intensification may be sudden because it is unexpected, and unexpectedness affords kama muta. But the intensification may also be fully anticipated – as, for example, in the third-person kama muta that occurs when viewing the same video for the thirtieth time. The concluding kama muta-evoking scene of a video, TV episode, or movie that one has watched many times is readily retrieved from episodic memory and often quite vivid when imagined, so it presents no new information to the viewer. Everyone involved in a wedding knows what will happen, yet may still feel very strong kama muta at key moments. This raises the intriguing question about just what it is that is "sudden" in these familiar moments of "sudden intensification of CS" that evokes kama muta. Evidently the apperception of sudden intensification is based on cognitive processes that are not limited to declarative-explicit knowledge: the mechanism that evokes kama muta responds to aspects of a situation which are not wholly represented in either episodic-narrative memory or semantic-conceptual memory.

CS intensification varies in magnitude (the difference between the initial and the final intensity of the CS) and in the rapidity of change (the rate of change, i.e., acceleration). Starting points also vary: the intensification can be from zero (no initial CS) to some positive level, or can begin at some higher prior level. I don't know what effects these variables have on kama muta.

The "intensification" of a CS relationship that evokes kama muta experiences may consist of the emergence of a purely mental representation of CS when a person is feeling the loneliness of separation or loss. In this case, intensification is the figure–ground contrast between a suddenly remembered, anticipated, or imagined feeling of CS coming to mind in the midst of a state of sorrow or hunger for connection. Although perhaps nothing has changed in the world, when a person feels the lack of CS, the sudden appearance of a memory of CS is often sufficient to evoke kama muta. Hence, as mentioned earlier, kama muta often occurs at funerals and memorial services when desolate grief abruptly shifts to the re-experience of love for the lost one. And it occurs when one is separated (in time and space, or otherwise) from a loved one – and suddenly feels love for them. Often conjoined with this first-person kama muta in memorial services is the mourner's second-person experience of others' caring support for her, along with her third-person discovery of others' love for the deceased, and the observation of the sudden emergence of unexpectedly warm CS bonds among the mourners. Events that English-speakers call *nostalgia* are often kama muta evoked by the sudden emergence of the mnemonic feeling of CS with some person or group, typically accompanied by episodic memories of the CS relationship.

My students recently told me about that the sudden cognitive representation of CS evokes kama muta when fans *ship* fictional characters. *Shipping* is imagining and communicating (verbally or in posts online) that two characters have a close CS relationship, although that relationship is not portrayed in the original TV series, movies, books, or comics. The imputed relationship is often the fictional characters' *OTP: one true pairing*; the characters are inherently destined to be together in this perfect pair. The relationship that the fans construct for the pair is generally romantic, typically erotic, and often homoerotic. It is common for female fans to imagine and promote the idea that two male characters have a homosexual relationship. When fans represent a ship or OTP, they typically represent a stable, indefinitely enduring relationship – the fans don't generally focus on the moment that the characters form, intensify, or recognize their CS relationship. But the <u>cognitively abrupt</u> enthusiastic representation of the ship or OTP often evokes kama muta that is apparent in the *fangirling* of the shippers: the fans wave their hands back and forth while squealing *awww!* This shared fan-girling may in turn suddenly intensify the CS among the communicating fans, evoking further kama muta.

I was walking home from the grocery store the other night and I heard this baby crying. All of a sudden I had this very overwhelming feeling, a mixture of extreme happiness and sadness, which I found rather strange. The baby's crying sounded like my little sister Maddi when she was a baby. What's strange is that Maddi is actually turning 21 at the end of the month, so I've heard a lot of different babies crying over the past 21 years, none of which evoked this kind of feeling. It brought me to tears. Happy and sad tears. It made me happy cause I hadn't thought about her at that age in such a long time, and man was she a cute little baby. It made me sad for the exact same reason.

(Hana Lash)

In short, the sudden intensification that evokes kama muta may consist of:

The creation of a new CS relationship, for example, when parents see the first ultrasound of their infant, or when the infant is born, or when people respond to a terrorist attack by opening their doors and harbor anyone who can't get home. Other examples are induction into an identity-defining group, acceptance into a support or recovery group, and, I believe, the generous hospitality (*xenia*) that classical Greeks and Arabs for thousands of years have ideally extended to even the most bedraggled strangers.

Extraordinary, supererogatory, or unexpected acts of CS devotion, generosity, kindness, compassion, or courage, for example, when a person drops everything to help a friend in a crisis, or when a soldier sacrifices himself to save his comrades.

The profound deepening of devotion to an existing CS relationship or display of commitment to it, for example, when a loving couple's relationship is deepened by a marriage proposal and acceptance, or raising a child together. This also occurs for example, when an athlete's victory makes him feel deep gratitude toward his supporters and for the adoration of his fans.

The renewal of a CS relationship after a long or traumatic separation, especially if the survival of one or both parties was uncertain, there was uncertainty about whether they would meet again, doubt about whether the relationship could be renewed, or when one or more participants steadfastly or bravely overcame challenging obstacles that stood in the way – ideally represented in the romantic tragi-comedy narrative prototype and the comedy plot – as in Odysseus's return to Penelope, Telemachos, and his loyal retainers; when a soldier returns from combat to her family; or a pilgrim, after enduring hardships, reaches Mecca.[5]

The restoration, rectification, or revival of a problematic CS relationship that was stressed, breached, or had apparently ended, for example, when a couple who broke up get back together again, or a sinner feels forgiven and regains God's love.

The vivid, deeply felt recollection or imagination of a CS relationship, for example, when a person remembers his relationship with the beloved whose loss he is mourning, when a woman remembers her first love (or her first dog), or she imagines living 'happily ever after' with the perfect partner, in the perfect family. This also occurs when a ritual or anthem strengthens patriotism or solidarity with an identity group.

When people suddenly intensify their CS relationship in any of these ways, they are likely to experience kama muta. And as I noted, hearing about, reading about, or seeing any of these first- and second-person events also tends to evoke third-person kama muta in the observer. Arthur Koestler (1964) generated a similar list of occasions that embody "the logic of the moist eye," neatly presenting the occasions in mid-twentieth-century Western Europe when communal sharing relationships suddenly intensify, and noting the characteristic signs of kama muta:

A. *Raptness.* Listening to the organ in a cathedral, looking at a majestic landscape from the top of a mountain, observing an infant hesitantly returning a smile, being in love—any of these experiences may cause a welling-up of emotions, a moistening or overflowing of the eyes, while the body is becalmed and drained of its tensions. A few steps higher on the intensity-scale, and the 'I' seems no longer to exist, to dissolve in the experience like a grain of salt in water; awareness becomes de-personalized and expands into 'the oceanic feeling of limitless extension and oneness with the universe' [quoting from an unspecified Roman Rolland letter to Freud]. ...

To be 'overwhelmed' by love, wonder, or devotion, 'enraptured' by a smile, 'entranced' by beauty—each verb expresses a passive state, a surrender. ...

B. *Mourning.* A woman is notified of the sudden death of her husband. She is stunned, unable to believe the news. Then she finds some relief in tears. ...

And again, the emotion originates in the experience of 'belonging to,' 'being together,' of a communion which transcends the boundaries of the self. Resentment, guilt, unconscious gratification, may, of course, enter into the widow's mixed feelings, but we are concerned at the moment only with her experience of identification and belonging. That experience, and the emotions generate by it, have not come to an end with the husband's death;

on the contrary, they have at the same time become more intense and frustrated. ...

The urge to transcend the self's boundaries, to break out of its insulation always carries a certain amount of frustration. ... [T]here are cases of mourning where the worship of the dead partner, with or without hope of reunion in the after-life, creates a more harmonious, if imaginary, communion that the actual partnership ever did. ...

C. *Relief.* A woman whose son has been reported by the War Office as missing suddenly sees him walking into her room, safe and sound. ...

Obviously there are two processes involved here. The first is the sudden, dramatic relief from anxiety; the other an overwhelming joy, love, tenderness. Some writers on the subject are apt to confuse these two reactions—to regard *all* joyous emotion as due to relief from anxious tension. But clearly a tender reaction would be expected in any case form the mother on her son's return—even if he were merely returning from a day at school, and there had been no previous anxiety. Vice versa, relief from anxiety in itself, though always pleasant, does not create tender feelings overflowing in tears. What happened in the present case is that the agony the woman endured had increased the intensity of her yearning and love; and that relief from anxiety had increased all out of proportion the gratification she would have felt on his return after an absence under normal circumstances.

D. When a woman weeps *in sympathy* with another person's sorrow (or joy), she partially identifies herself with that person by an act of projection, introjection or identification—whatever you like to call it. The same is true whether the 'other person' is a heroine on the screen or in the pages of a novel.

(*Koestler 1964: 273–278; italics in original*)

Experiencing or perceiving the actual or potential intensification of a CS relationship typically evokes kama muta – but not invariably. When someone does something unexpectedly or extraordinarily kind for a person, the person usually intensifies her CS relationship with the donor. But the kindness is not likely to evoke kama muta if the recipient infers that the benefactor has ulterior motives: if, for example, she perceives that the benefactor is engaged in a con or is attempting to entrap her into sexual slavery. In such cases, the recipient does not perceive the other's nominal CS intensification to be 'genuine.' Or she may perceive the other's initiative to be genuine, but she does not want or feel any CS intensification, for example, if she abhors or feels contemptuous of him. Despite receiving a genuine benefaction, she may not feel kama muta if she regards any CS relationship between them to be a serious transgression, for example, an invitation to have an affair with her brother-in-law. Observing third parties' sudden intensification of CS, the observer is not likely to feel kama muta if she despises them, for example, if they are Nazi torturers. Or she may feel jealous: a woman does not feel kama muta if she sees another woman kissing her boyfriend. There any many such moderators of kama muta, and we do not know exactly how to conceptualize them beyond positing that ordinarily a person does not feel kama muta unless they are open to (want, accept, morally approve) the potential CS intensification. But the process is probably more subtle; a person might feel kama muta even while judging that the CS intensification is inappropriate. People have multiple evaluative frameworks, conflicting desires, and competing motives at the same time.

Throughout the book we will explore many intriguing cultural and historical practices that have arisen around the world to create kama muta–inducing experiences. These practices orient the kama muta so as to foster socially important bonds, give the kama muta meaning, and resonate with sophisticated esthetic and moral frameworks. In one sense, the bulk of this book is an exploration of the vast range of CS relationships that suddenly intensify, and the great variety of circumstances in which they suddenly intensify. To know what kama muta is, we have to grasp the whole domain of circumstances in which it can arise. If we know of it only in one sphere (say, worship, or when reading narratives in an experimental lab), we simply don't know what kama muta is. That's because to characterize the psychological, social, cultural, and biological aspects of kama muta, we need to understand what can cause it, what consequences it can have, and what meanings people can give it. Remember the tale of the blind men trying the describe an elephant, each touching only one part of it. If we are only aware of the kama muta that occurs, say, when people see others' extraordinarily virtuous CS actions, or only when people see core CS values realized under adverse circumstances, we have only touched the tail of the proverbial elephant, so we'll think that kama muta is a rope. It's not a rope; it's a whole elephant whose parts function together to constitute a living organism. And these highly moral elicitors of kama muta are just the tail end of the giant creature: most of kama muta isn't in the tail.

Equivalence among bodies makes persons socially equivalent: Consubstantial assimilation

Along with these actions and thoughts, there are innumerable things people can say and gestures they can perform that afford at least a little intensification of CS: prayers, blessings, vows, putting hand over heart, and the like. But more powerful than words or other actions, there is a singular performative *medium* of creating, renewing, and sustaining CS. The most powerful and pervasive mode of intensifying CS is to give people the feeling that their bodies are one (Fiske 2004b; Fiske & Schubert 2012). The sense that one's body is equivalent to the bodies of others makes one feel socially equivalent. This sense of equivalence occurs when people feel the sameness of their essential substances, body motions, or surfaces. A mother often feels this at the birth of her child, when the infant emerges from her body, and when she holds and suckles her infant with the milk of her body – and presumably the infant feels something like this when nursing in his mother's arms. Parent and child feel this when cuddling, waking up together, when the parent washes and grooms the child. Infant and caretaker feel this when the caretaker rocks the child and when the child is snuggled against them, moving rhythmically together as the caretaker walks, digs, hoes, grinds, pounds, draws water from a well, or dances. Adults feel their bodies are one when they dance, move in ritual synchrony, or do military drill together. Infant and caretaker feel a oneness of substance when they feed each other, as do adults when they drink and eat commensally, or share tobacco and other drugs, especially when the substances they ingest are ritually marked, like the smoke from a peace pipe. Worshippers may feel this when they share sacrificial offerings with their ancestors or gods, or consume what they construe to be the god's body and blood. Blood brothers feel this when they mix their blood and ingest it. Initiates bond when they shed blood together and when their genitals are modified in the same manner. Caressing, kissing, hugging, even shaking hands does this a bit. Equivalent scars, tattoos, and removal or modification of teeth have the same effect. To a lesser extent, there are similar effects of having the same coiffure, body paint, uniform, or clothing. People bond when they perceive themselves to share the same 'blood' or 'genes', father's 'bones' or mother's milk, skin color or hair type, physiognomy, disease, disability, or addiction. Moreover, the most intimate, affectionate sex is a merging of bodies and sharing of substance – which brings us back full circle to the beginning of life.

> In short, one body = one social self, and one social self = one body. People connect to each other by assimilating their bodies to each other, making themselves one substance together. Hence, the technical term for this mode of forming, mentally representing, and communicating communal sharing relationships is *consubstantial assimilation* (Fiske 2004b; Fiske & Schubert 2012). Consubstantial assimilation is an indexical constitutive sign. That is, a person's body signifies the social person, so that making bodies equivalent makes the social persons equivalent. For example, two traditional Africans who cut themselves, mix their blood into beer, and consume it in a blood-bonding ritual become one social person: they become devoted and committed to sharing their resources, sharing sexual access to their wives, hosting, feeding, protecting and defending each other. Parents who create a child with the substance of their bodies typically become devoted and committed to the child. When the baby is born, suddenly commencing and realizing the new CS relationship, they may feel the strongest kama muta they have ever experienced. We will encounter a great many culturally elaborated rituals of consubstantial assimilation throughout the book, each of which is constituted so as to strongly and reliably evoke kama muta that supports locally important CS bonds.

For contemporary Westerners and many others, genes have become the most essential essence defining one's CS relational identity. Commercial genetic tests are now available that offer to reveal your ethno-geographic and national ancestry. A promotion video produced by the travel site Momondo, using DNA testing by Ancestry.com, shows people talking about their identities, providing spit samples for genetic testing, and two weeks later seeing their results (Momondo 2016). As they look at the graphs and maps showing who they are, genetically – what nations they 'come from' – the participants tear-up joyfully, apparently feeling kama muta from the sudden CS connection with their ancestors and ethno-geographic kinship groups. When the hosts tell two of the participants that they are genetic "cousins," the woman and the man both evidently feel strong kama muta, and she, who identifies as a Kurd, ululates – a sound that women make in this part of the world when they feel kama muta (see Chapter 2 and Online Note 2.1).

In short, CS relationships are naturally, primarily, universally, and most evocatively cognized, communicated, constituted, and conducted through consubstantial assimilation. Consubstantial assimilation motivates CS especially powerfully. When an act of consubstantial assimilation suddenly intensifies CS, the participants (and observers who identify with them) experience kama muta. However, humans are symbolic animals, and abstract, arbitrary symbols, especially language, can also foster CS: all it takes is your child saying, 'I love you, dad.' Martin Luther King Jr's "I Have a Dream" oration, raising a national flag, and many anthems and songs evoke kama muta.

We should keep in mind the fact that communal sharing relationships may be very close without therefore evoking kama muta: it is the sudden intensification of CS that evokes kama muta. The steady, taken for granted sense of being one body, one being, does not activate it – the steep increase does. The derivative (slope) of the intensity of CS is the trigger. Acts of consubstantial assimilation probably often cause this steep increase in CS feeling, evoking kama muta more powerfully, more consistently, and more universally than any other kind of symbolic action. But it's also important to recognize that consubstantial assimilation does not always generate kama muta experiences. Feeling a person's mouth on your lips can evoke kama muta – or be totally disgusting (Fiske & Schubert 2012). All kinds of factors may distance people from the consubstantial assimilation experience, block its effects, or completely reverse them. To feel kama muta, people have to be prepared for and disposed to relating communally. Sex can make people feel totally one, but physically similar actions occur in rape. And people can have sex with indifference, feeling neither intimacy nor horror. Eventually we should go back one more step in the causal chain to discover what disposes people to be open to the potential for consubstantial assimilation. Voluntary choice is one factor, but not the only one. And there is no reason to stop at investigating the disposing factors; we should then proceed to ask, in turn, what produces those disposing factors, and so on, causes behind causes. But in this book we will have to be satisfied with a causal sequence that begins with consubstantial assimilation, newly creating a CS relationship or suddenly increasing the intensity of existing CS. That's as much as I can manage in one book.

Kama muta's psychosocial and adaptive functions

Out of kama muta come devotion and commitment to the communal sharing relationship that has suddenly intensified. When a person experiences kama muta they are motivated to enhance, revive, or redress the CS relationship that intensified, or create a new CS relationship. Kama muta makes a person implicitly or explicitly more greatly value the CS relationship that they feel is intensifying in first or second person instances. In third person instances, people are inclined to more greatly value CS relationships with the persons they observe intensifying their relationships and more greatly value relationships that resemble the one they observe intensifying. If we can paraphrase the kama muta feeling as "Wow! This CS is wonderful," we can paraphrase the resultant CS motivation as "I really want to take care of this person (these people) and do everything to deepen and preserve my relationship with them." Of course, typically these sentiments are not declaratively articulated, but that's how they would be translated into semantic declamations. Narrowly defined, kama muta consists of feeling CS intensify, producing the affective intention to dedicate oneself to that relationship. But the experience and the motivation are all of a piece; they are analytically distinct, but subjectively integral, aspects of one emotion.

Compare kama muta to non-social-relational affects. When you're hot and thirsty, you experience a certain sensation when you swallow a cold drink. When you're famished and you start to eat a delicious meal, you have a somewhat similar sensation. When you're exhausted and you lie down to rest on a soft bed where you can sleep, you have another feeling something like those. And there's a related feeling when you make it home safely after a trying or dangerous journey. Adopting Lorenz's (1988) terminology, these are *consummatory emotions*: they are cues that the organism has just experienced something adaptively beneficial: a striking change for the better. When this happens it is important to remember how it happened and what circumstances afforded the opportunity for it, and it is adaptively necessary to establish the motivation to seek or create similar experiences. Orgasm is the conceptual prototype of the consummatory experience, and it may not be going too far to say that orgasm is to sexual relations as kama muta is to communal sharing relations.

Emotions are experiences of adaptive motives. Social relationships require frequent tactical shifts to make the most of opportunities and challenges; the relational motives of social emotions motivate tactical action to function effectively in partnerships, groups, and networks. More than for almost any other vertebrate, human fitness depends on cooperatively coordinated social relationships. So human psychology has evolved to make the creation, restoration, improvement, or loss of crucial social relationships exceptionally emotional so as to motivate people to adopt adaptive relational tactics (Keltner & Haidt 1999; Fiske 2002, 2010; Stellar et al. 2017). Appetitive emotions reflect relationships that people need, while satiation moods reflect the stabile satisfactory state of important relationships. Anxious or depressive social moods reflect relationships in jeopardy, or the needs that follow loss. Anger reflects other's transgressions, and self-punitive emotions reflect one's own actual or prospective transgressions. In short, social relational emotions direct people to act tactically to make their relationships adaptively beneficial (see Chapter 19).

Because intense CS relationships are, and long have been, extraordinarily important for human survival and reproduction, it is easy to see how natural selection generated a rewarding feedback emotion that motivates people to devote and commit to the sudden intensification of CS relationships. Consider the adaptive necessity of the mother's bonding to her newborn infant. The embarrassment, vulnerability, fear, pain, and exhaustion of childbirth are not conducive to warm appreciative devotion to the newborn whose birth caused the distress. But mammalian fitness depends on immediate committed devotion to the infant. Something has to motivate that, immediately creating a strong, reliably enduring bond to the infant. Maternal bonding motives must do that, and in pair-bonding mammals, paternal bonding must be strong and immediate as well. In the few mammals that form affectionate pair bonds, both partners must overcome the fear and aversion that they have toward conspecifics, transforming this into devotion. While other mammals copulate and separate, mammals with this psychological adaptation copulate, bond, and jointly care for offspring. In a few mammals, the mechanism of maternal bonding and pair bonding evidently evolved to create bonds among sibling 'helpers' who care for the next set of their parents' offspring, as in several canids; these packs actively share food, bringing prey back to the den or regurgitating for the pups and their 'baby-sitter'. In many primates, as well as elephants and other genera, enduring bonds between mothers and daughters result in troops of matrilineally related kin that stay together and defend each other against predators and against other troops of conspecifics. Chimpanzee troops are composed around a core of male kin. Toothed whales also form kin-based pods that protect each other and some, such as the orcas that prey on marine mammals, actively share food. Occurring among several diverse phyla, this convergent evolution of enduring bonds that generate cooperative groups indicates that maternal-bonding mechanisms can readily be selected to function in this way. Humans have evolved this beyond kin-based bonding into human kama muta, enabling humans to create the other CS relationships they need among non-kin. What is unique about the human kama muta adaptation is its flexibility and generativity: humans form innumerable CS bonds with mates, offspring, kin, and innumerable other partners and groups, depending on culture and life experience.

Evolutionary psychologists generally assume that adaptive cognitive-motivational 'modules' are very narrow, such that each one addresses a very specific evolutionary 'problem.' There is rarely, if ever, any principled grounds or analytic demonstration to support such assumptions about how narrow the scope (domain or input) must be for an adaptive module to functional adaptively. Nor is there much consideration of the merits of considering adaptive <u>opportunities</u> rather than environmentally and phenotypically defined 'problems.' Our theory posits that the flexibility and generativity of the psychosocial mechanism of kama muta are just what makes it so adaptively – and socially – beneficial: it can create innumerable CS dyads and groups to enable myriad ways to live in every ecosystem, and to create whole new modes of subsistence by transforming existing ecosystems (see Chapters 10 and 17). No rigid modules of fixed and limited scope can do this (Fiske 2000).

More generally, emotions are motivational signals about important issues deserving our attention, action, or re-calibration (Frijda 1988, 2006). They can signal opportunities or threats, so they can be positive or negative. Positive social-relational emotions indicate social relational opportunities (Fiske 2002, 2010; Keltner & Haidt 1999). That is, sociomoral emotions evoke action to create, sustain, transform, redress, sanction, or terminate relationships in an adaptive manner. When we look at Frederickson's (2013) list of positive emotions, she identifies amusement, love, and gratitude as indicating opportunities for social bonds. From a relational models theory perspective (Fiske 1991, 1992), amusement is not specific to any model. It can improve all symmetrical relations, CS, EM, and MP, because it helps to find common ground. The other two are more specific to CS. Love is described by Frederickson as being characterized by shared positivity, mutual care, and biobehavioral synchrony. Thus, love indicates a working, shared CS relationship – although the concept "love" probably conflates the kama muta emotion and affection, which is more like a mood. Gratitude, according to Frederickson, emerges when another person is recognized as the source of one's good fortune. Simão and Seibt (2014) show that gratitude is an emotion of CS relationships. Thus, gratitude indicates being cared for by a CS partner. I suggest that there is a third positive emotion related to CS, namely, kama muta. Kama muta indicates that another person cares for oneself, or that one should care for someone, so (to use the terminology that evolutionary psychology borrowed from economics) one should 'invest' in the relationship.

The person whose loyalty and devotion to a person or group motivates them to be hospitable, kind, and generous, or who will stand by you, defend you, and avenge those who harm you – that person is an invaluable ally who merits your loyal devotion. The strategic assessment of the relational appeal of an heroic or assiduous person may be fully conscious, but probably it is usually computed without much conscious reflection. The culturally informed adaptive significance of the CS relationship with the target is not so much thought as felt. Like other social and moral emotions (Fiske 2002, 2010), kama muta is an immediate motivational proxy for the long-term adaptive significance of a social relational tactic – devoting and committing to CS – in a given sociocultural situation. In this case, what is adaptive is to form or enhance a CS relationship with the target, and commit to that relationship. The desirability of that adaptive tactic is experienced as kama muta.

In sum, the function and effect of first- and second-person kama muta, I posit, are to motivate current and long-term effort to devote and commit to the CS relationship whose sudden intensification evoked it. Presumably derivative and later evolved, third-person kama muta functions to motivate potential CS relationships with the persons observed, persons resembling them, and persons with whom they have CS relationships. The logic is that if the observed persons' relationship is so wonderful, they are good prospects as partners for one's own CS relationships – and CS relationships with people like them might be worth cultivating, too. As one participant who watched a set of our video stimuli commented at the end, "can't wait to hug and say I love you to all my loved ones; thank you guys for enlightening me, seeing this video material; things don't matter love is all that matters."

The disposition to experience kama muta is adaptive only when it responds appropriately to the cultural signs of intensification of the specific CS relationships that have specific promise in locally particular contexts of each person's particular culture. That is, kama muta is biologically selected to resonate with culture-specific, community-specific signals. It is this sensitivity to the CS relationships that matter in each particular culture, community, and context that makes the kama muta disposition biologically adaptive. Moreover, the kama muta disposition enhances a person's fitness only to the extent that that the devotion and commitment it evokes are tailored in a culturally congruent manner. Should a person experiencing kama muta acknowledge paternity, take up arms and fight alongside the person, become an evangelist, marry the person, or what? Kama muta doesn't work adaptively unless it motivates culturally and situationally appropriate action. In Chapters 10 and 17 I'll analyze this in greater depth. For now, the essential idea is that the social psychological adaptation maps culturally propitious opportunities onto culturally fruitful motives.[6]

The cultural constitution of an evolved psychological adaptation

In our species, which might well be called *Homo movens*, evolved psychological adaptations are only adaptive if they are tuned to the cultural context in which they function. For example, the human capacity for language enables people to learn and use a particular culturally transmitted language; to use this capacity people must learn not only the phonology, lexicon, and semantics, but how language is used: when to say what to whom. No-one speaks universal grammar, which is, in fact, unspeakable because it is indefinite. Likewise, no one feels universal kama muta. Every experience of kama muta is informed by the culture and oriented by the specific cultural context. To extend the analogy, the innate capacity for language makes infants and children sensitive to the <u>specific</u> phonology, lexicon, semantics, illocutionary practices, and sociolinguistics of one (or more) <u>particular</u> language(s) – but still unable to communicate in all other languages. Similarly, the innate capacity to feel kama muta makes *Homo movens* sensitive to the specific precedents, prototypes, paradigms, and precepts for the sudden intensification of communal sharing that occur in their particular social system. My culture enables me, personally, to feel kama muta when I visit the Vietnam Veterans Memorial, but unable to feel kama muta evoked by being in love with Krishna, participating in the *hajj*, performing a blood-brotherhood ritual, getting a gang tattoo, or listening to Kaluli *gisaro* songs. By the same token, my culture makes my kama muta experience at the Vietnam Veterans Memorial distinct from my kama muta experience cuddling kittens and my kama muta experience of Christmas morning with my family.

It appears to us felicitous to use the construct "kama muta" to encompass all of the experiences that share most of the following features: they result from sudden intensification of CS, are positive, people want to share them, they generate CS devotion and commitment, they generally evoke some of the characteristic sensations and signs, and people tend to label them with the relevant lexemes. In the terminology I use here, all such experiences are one "emotion," kama muta. But it would not matter conceptually if one adopted a more cultural-social constructivist terminology and called the (typical?) Kaluli experience listening to *gisaro* songs one culture-specific, context-particular 'emotion,' while labelling (typical?) American Vietnam Veterans Memorial experiences another, distinct 'emotion.' And one could make much finer distinctions among different emotional experiences, of course – every experience has some unique aspects. Scientific terminology is arbitrary; it just has to be precise, clear, and consistent. Which means we cannot rely on vernacular lexemes such as the natural language terms *moved*, *touched*, or, for that matter, *emotion*. What matters most is that we make clear what we want "kama muta" to mean, and what we mean when we define it as "one emotion" (see Fiske 2019).

To posit that kama muta is one, distinct emotion, does not in any way imply that it exists in isolation, experienced without any other affect. People may experience multiple emotions at the same time, and different combinations may have distinct emergent, synergistic properties beyond the sum of the properties of the constituent emotions. Furthermore, emotions occur in sequences – often culturally paradigmatic sequences. I have noted many contexts in which grief, despair, or fear precede, and indeed greatly afford, kama muta, for example, in reunions. Depending on the culture, context, and metarelational models that are operating, experiencing kama muta may lead to embarrassment or shame if the person feels that they should not be experiencing kama muta, or should hide it. In contrast, experiencing and displaying kama muta may indicate that the person is sophisticated and sensitive, so that he feels pride. Likewise, a person who performs kama muta with great virtuosity, such as in an opera or movie, may feel pride, while a poor performance may lead to shame.

A worshipper who experiences the kama muta of a loving divinity generally will feel a sense of security and often relief, her anxiety washed away. Kama muta at a grave, memorial site, or ceremony may lead to sorrow for those who sacrificed themselves or otherwise perished. If a person at the grave, memorial site, or ceremony judges that he should not have survived while others perished, or wishes he could change places with them, he may feel guilt. Among the Kaluli, a person who experiences kama muta may become enraged at the person who evoked it – or, in other circumstances such as psychotherapy or support groups, a person who experiences kama muta may be grateful to the one who evoked it. In oratory, at a dance performance, or visiting a memorial site, people who experience kama muta may then be *awed* by those who powerfully evoked it.

I have emphasized that the kama muta of one person or group often evokes others' kama muta. But it may also evoke different emotions in others. Co-religionists who could not make a pilgrimage may be envious of those who do, and then tell of their kama muta. Fellow worshippers who do not feel a divinity's love may be envious of those who do, or may even feel humiliated that they themselves do not. And a person who observes another's kama muta without feeling any may feel separated from or inferior to those who do. Or they may feel smugly, pridefully superior to those who 'break down' and display their 'weakness' by 'losing control.' On the other hand, a person may take pride in the kama muta of a family member or friend who feels touched by divinity, or ashamed of – or angry at – a family member or friend who 'can't keep it together' and 'falls apart' when they are not supposed to. Just as a person in the audience may be *awed* by an orator or performer who evokes her kama muta, she may be *awed* by (or envious of) the orator or performer's evocation of kama muta in others, whether she herself feels kama muta or not.

Kama muta may be the offspring of other emotions. Pride, humiliation, envy, or avarice may motivate someone to prepare a great speech, sermon, or song, or to create a terrific movie, in order to evoke the audience's kama muta, and then take advantage of the audience's emotion. Envy of others who have felt the love of divinity, or fear of going to hell, may dispose people to seek situations such as revivals or confession that afford kama muta. An alcoholic or addict may attend a recovery group because he is frightened by his future, feels guilt about what he is doing to his family, is ashamed of his addiction or is *awed* by an authority who orders attendance. Motivated by any of these or other emotions, his participation in such a group affords kama muta. Similarly, he may be driven to attend by the anger, shame, or fears of his family. In the narratives discussed in the previous chapter, the listener or reader's anxiety, frustration, or sadness about the protagonists' separation potentiate the listener or reader's kama muta when the protagonists are reunited (see Fiske, Schubert, & Seibt 2017a). Similarly, one's distress when separated from a loved one affords the kama muta one feels when reunited – or when one simply remembers how much one loves the one who is away. ('Remember' is an inadequate word, because the rekindling of the feeling of love is not a dispassionate cognitive reconstruction of mere knowledge.) Likewise, at a memorial service or funeral, the sadness that pervades the event is the dark ground against which the contrasting figure of kama muta moments brilliantly flashes: it is precisely this contrast that evokes kama muta. In short, kama muta is distinct from other emotions, but other emotions can be precursors or contexts that afford it, or consequences of it.

These and other sequential intrapersonal and metarelational processes are important aspects of emotions which we should explore. However, these sequences have major methodological implications. If not well-timed, self-reports, memories, observations, and physiological measurements of kama muta could easily be distorted by these sequential processes if researchers mistakenly tap an emotion that precedes or follows kama muta. Short- or long-term memories of kama muta could be overridden or concealed behind memories of later emotions. If feeling kama muta evokes pride, participants may over-report what they felt. And if kama muta leads to shame, informants may well conceal or under-report their kama muta. Moreover, if asked to report how they felt in an episode that involved a number of emotions in sequences, people may report that the <u>episode</u> (taken as a whole) was sad, distressing, or otherwise *negative*, despite the fact that the specific kama muta moments within it were singularly *positive* in valence.

Positing that "kama muta" is "one emotion" does <u>not</u> mean that all experiences of it are identical in all respects. Indeed, experiences of kama muta are always informed by the culture and context in which they occur, and hence differ accordingly. There are no generic kama muta experiences: every one occurs due to a particular culturally informed intensification of a culturally particular CS relationship. (I, for one, will not have kama muta with a *xenia*, blood brother, *compadre*, age-set mate, handball teammate, or with Krishna, the Buddha, Allah, Jesus, or the Virgin Mary – because I have no such CS relationships.) An intensification of CS is necessarily realized with respect to cultural prototypes, precedents, paradigms, and precedents. Just as there is no generic human language, only particular languages, and as there is no generic utterance, only particular utterances, there is no generic kama muta. Instances of kama muta are particular with regard to nine cultural parameters:

1. The beings or entities with whom the CS forms
People form CS relationships with all sorts of individual persons and animals – present, represented, remembered, or imagined; with groups of co-present people; with "imaginary communities" such as nations, ethnicities, or social movements; with immaterial beings such as deceased relatives, saints, and deities; with fictional characters; with nature, the earth, or the cosmos; and so on. Likewise, people notice CS relationships among such beings and entities. These beings or entities and the CS relationships with them are always informed and sometimes entirely constituted by the person's culture. When the sudden intensification of any of these CS relationships evokes kama muta, the experience of it is always shaped by the cultural nature of the beings or entities and the relationship with them. The CS relationships between the Buddha and his followers represented in the Jataka tales, and the sudden intensification of the CS in particular, are culturally constructed. The modern nation is a culturally constituted entity that is essential to any experience of patriotic kama muta. People who live in a culture without the Chicago Cubs cannot feel the fans' kama muta when 'we' win the World Series for the first time in 108 years.

So one could construct a taxonomy of kama muta experiences according to the beings or entities with whom the CS relationship intensifies: for example, animals versus humans versus divinities versus nature versus the whole of exist-ence. One could reasonably make finer distinctions among the animals, for example, contrasting kama muta evoked by cute *Kindchenschema* infants versus adults, or kittens versus puppies. One could make another taxonomy according to whether the CS relationship that suddenly intensifies is in the past (nostal-gia), present, or imagined in the future. Or again, whether it has a sexual flavor or not. One could also differentiate between dyadic kama muta, kama muta in a group, and kama muta with an indefinitely extended whole. Of course, one could distinguish between a person's kama muta with this individual versus another individual – or on this occasion versus that occasion; they certainly dif-fer subjectively. The distinctions that are fruitful to make depend on the sort of understanding one seeks.

2. The implementation of the CS relationship: What sort of CS is it? What comprises devotion and commitment?

Cultures provide the prototypes, precedents, paradigms, and precepts for how, when, and where to engage in CS with a Sufi saint or a fan group. Moreover, cultures provide the preos that constitute a person, representation, place, or memory as a Sufi saint or a fan group, and particular ones with unique cul-tural and historical attributes. Significantly, cultures present the preos for how, when, and where to enact the devotion and moral commitment that kama muta with a Sufi saint or a fan group generates. Does devotion mean giving certain foods at certain altars on certain occasions, or posting certain sorts of images on Facebook? The CS with one's deity has different qualities and entails different actions from CS with one's newborn infant, where devotion comprises changing her diapers and making sure she's vaccinated. For the Cubs fans, devotion means making sure that the players on the team that won the World Series *never have to buy a beer in this town again*, as the expression goes.

3. The cultural practices, institutions, roles, narratives, artifacts, and art that function to evoke kama muta

Sentimental literature, romantic poetry, war memorials and commemoration rites, Pentecostal worship, weddings, marketing using cute animals and chil-dren, and innumerable other cultural activities are tailored to evoke kama muta. Evoking and orienting kama muta is a major function of these activities. They have culturally evolved along diverse paths into more or less unique forms. Many chapters of this book are devoted to such practices, institutions, roles, narratives, artifacts, and art whose manifest or latent function is evoking kama muta. The bottom line is that the CS relationship and its sudden intensification are psycho-socioculturally constructed. In some cultures, giving a puppy is likely to evoke kama muta oriented to the cuteness of the puppy and the kindness of the donors in giving something so cute. In other cultures the tender puppy may evoke kama muta in the recipient when he and the donor delightedly eat it. In either case, the kama muta is afforded by the prevailing precedents and prototypes for giving puppies.

4. The incidental affordances of kama muta

All sorts of cultural activities provide occasions when people may suddenly intensify CS relationships, although that sudden intensification is only incidental to the purposes or functions of the activities. The military benefits of combat rotation leave afford kama muta when soldiers return to their families. Ultrasound images made to screen for medical issues afford kama muta experiences when the parents see their infant for the first time. The acquisition of a guard- or guide-dog puppy affords kama muta that is incidental to the aims of the purchaser. Driving to a ski slope affords feeling kama muta if one's car skids off the road into a tree, and a passerby takes great risk to rescue the victims. The opportunities vary depending on the culture and context.

5. The constitutive signs that suddenly intensify particular forms of CS

Presenting a bouquet of flowers may intensify a romantic CS relationship – if there are cultural precedents for using flowers to show love. Being circumcised or excised while showing stoic courage may intensify the initiate's CS with co-initiates and kin – if there are cultural paradigms for initiation rites of this sort. The culmination of a pilgrimage may evoke kama muta – if there are cultural prototypes that make the arrival after an arduous journey a sign of devotion to the deity of the place that is culturally constituted as sacred. The exchange of rings and vows evokes kama muta only if there are cultural precepts and precedents that make those acts constitute 'marriage,' and make marriage mean loving CS (rather than, say, pure authority ranking). Then looking at the wedding album or video commemorate the kama muta – if the culture provides photography and these uses of it. A diploma or a class ring may legitimate, remind, inscribe, and proclaim the kama muta of graduation, while a circular scar around the face with a diagonal scar from nose to cheek may legitimate, remind, inscribe, and proclaim the kama muta of becoming an adult Moaaga (Moose person, in Burkina Faso; *Moose* is pronounced **MOH**-say)

6. What sort of person one's CS intensification contributes to making, and other ramifications for the self

An initiation rite makes the initiate an adult member of a particular community or age set, abruptly intensifying that CS relationship. Feeling *touched by the Spirit* makes a person an exemplary Pentecostal, while feeling *burning in the bosom* contributes to making one an exemplary Mormon. Feeling kama muta when listening to the Grateful Dead is an important facet of being a Deadhead. Feeling patriotic and Marine kama muta at a commissioning ceremony gives one a sense of being a Marine, as a core identity. Participating in the chants and eight-clap at a UCLA football game may evoke kama muta that makes a participant feel that she is a *Bruin*. The person may have the experience only once, infrequently, or quite regularly, but however frequent the kama muta is, it often constitutes one as a particular sort of person. One's peak kama muta experiences make up important aspects of who one is: a mother, wife, friend, suffragist, and revolutionary, for example.

7. The ramifications of the CS intensification for other social relationships

People have models of how social relationships should or should not be interconnected; in every culture there is a syntax for combining relationships (Fiske 2010). Among these metarelational models are precepts and prototypes that link CS relationships, and their sudden intensification, to other relationships. A Sufi sheikh or saint's kama muta with Allah attracts many followers who want his guidance to emulate his experience; the sheik's kama muta evokes admiration and awe (see Chapter 13). As a result, the followers bring gifts and support this sheikh, who acquires political stature. White readers of *Uncle Tom's Cabin* felt kama muta at Eva's compassionate kama muta with her household slaves and the slaves' grateful kama muta evoked by Eva's love for them; this motivated readers to feel compassion for slaves and hence engage in the abolitionist movement (see Chapter 8). Presumably the readers' abolitionism was also partially mediated by the shame they felt about slavery. These motives had huge political and economic consequences. The mother of a newborn intensifies her CS with the baby's father, siblings, or grandparents when she observes the kama muta that the baby evokes in them – but only if and when she observes this, depending on how the culture structures childbirth and infant care practices. At the most basic level, there are varied cultural models for who witnesses kama muta displays, and how they should participate or respond. An African or Middle Eastern woman may ululate to share her kama muta with family and neighbors, who are expected to be moved to join her, ululating as they come together. A YouTube viewer may announce her kama muta response to a video or live experience by sharing it on social media; this sharing influences how her friends perceive her, while it informs their relationship with her. Conversely, cultural paradigms of male concealment of kama muta limit its ramifications for other relationships, except when a man is shamed by his display of it.

8. Folk models and significance of the emotion

When a Krishna worshipper gets goosebumps (today, or in classical texts), South Asians interpret this as a sign of the worshipper's love for Krishna and her feeling of Krishna's love for her. This means that she has reached the most desired religious state that is the aspiration of all worshippers. Signing the constitution in 1792 that made France a nation of liberty, equality, and fraternity, the delegates, tears as they kissed the constitution indexed their patriotic devotion and commitment. Around 1770–1840, men's tears in the theater indicated the quality of the play and the sophisticated sensitivity of the weepers. African or Middle Eastern women should and do ululate when an important CS relationship suddenly intensifies; joining in the ululation, family and neighbors reinforce the emotion and perform their solidarity with the core participants. Conversely, when an older Norwegian man or a Bedouin in the Western Desert of Egypt stolidly conceals his kama muta, he is sustaining the imperturbable self-control expected of him. Conversely, an Andaman Islander would be censured for failing to publicly weep while sitting on the lap of a spouse returning from a voyage.

The paradigms, precepts, and paragons of each culture indicate the expected sensations and their implication, while providing parameters for the evaluation of feeling and displaying kama muta, as a function of gender and context. Art, song, dance, theater, rituals, narratives, and other media comprise prototypes and precedents for kama muta. Moreover, the linguistics of kama muta, especially the lexicon, profoundly inform how people understand, remember, and represent kama muta experiences and the disposition to experience it.

9. Its performance

There are many commonalities in what people do when they experience kama muta, but there are also considerable variations and dramatic particulars. In many Methodist revivals, Pentecostal churches, and Sufi worship at some times and places, people enact very strong kama muta by exuberant movement, or loud non-verbal utterance, or running around, often followed by collapse and stupor. When feeling kama muta in certain contexts (but not others) Western women, especially young women, are prone to say *awww*. African and Middle-Eastern women ululate in many kama muta circumstances, while in some cultures, men fire guns into the air. In some cultures and contexts, feeling kama muta leads to hugging or kissing, while in other cultures or contexts, people would not even consider doing so.

Every chapter of this book illustrates several of these nine cultural facets of kama muta.

These facets of kama muta are empirically intertwined, but it is still useful to have an analytic schema such as this as a tool for comparing and contrasting kama muta experiences. To make contrasts, one could distinguish the emotional experiences according to the kinds of CS relationship that intensifies, the kinds of cultural practices that function to afford it and the kinds of situations that incidentally evoke it, the kinds of ramifications of the experience for the self and for other social relations, the kinds of folk models of it, and/or the kinds of performances of it. We could construct innumerable meaningful taxonomies by making broader or more granular distinctions with respect to each of these aspects of kama muta experiences, or any combination of these aspects. For some descriptive and analytic purposes, any or all of these distinctions are important, so one should attend to the differences where they matter. (Indeed, this book is organized into chapters and sections based on such distinctions.) Whole fields of scholarship are focused on subtypes distinguished by differences on one or more of these aspects, and in fact scholars find that for some descriptive and explanatory purposes it is necessary to make very fine distinctions about one or more of these aspects of kama muta. For example, it may be illuminating to discriminate among the kama muta experiences afforded by different kinds of poetry, or the practices of different Sufi saints. Furthermore, no doubt individual life histories, personalities, and circumstances affect kama muta experiences, sometimes profoundly. Psychotherapists, biographers, friends, and family need to be aware of these specifics. My emphasis on the commonalities among all of these experiences across all of these cultural, personal, and circumstantial variations does not mean that I aim to deny or minimize the variations. However, I believe that it is crucial to understand the whole scope of human kama muta experiences, their universal psychosocial mechanisms, and the manner in which they are culturally informed and imbued with meaning. This global understanding provides the crucial framework <u>within which</u>, <u>with reference to which</u>, we can interpret the particular cases. Only if we see the whole scope of kama muta across *Homo movens* can we make sense of what occurs in each unique case; appreciating what that case <u>is</u> means seeing how that case compares and contrasts with other cases of kama muta. For example, comparing and contrasting with respect to the nine cultural facets presented above.

The analogy with sex is illuminating. Sexual desire has an evolved biopsychological foundation, and there are universal aspects of sexual attraction (along with individual differences). But at the same time, in important respects sexual attraction is culturally shaped. Is a man more or less attractive to women after he has tossed the severed head of an innocent stranger (Rosaldo 1980, 1984)? Does it make a woman more or less attractive if she dresses and acts like a helpless little girl (*kawaii*; Nittono, Fukushima, Yano, & Hiroki Moriya 2012; see also Steinnes 2017)? Moreover, the many cultural practices, institutions, roles, arts, and artifacts that function to arouse sexual desire vary greatly across culture and history – as do those that function to evoke kama muta. Kama muta evoked by the sudden intensification of CS with different beings and entities has very different meanings – different implications for the self, different metarelational implications, different valuations. Similarly, for a given person, there are very different meanings of being sexually attracted to an adult man; an adult woman; a spouse versus non-spouse; a person of a given clan, social class, religion, or 'race;' a ten-year-boy; a ten-year-old girl; a spouse's adult child; a husband's brother; a spouse's adult same-sex sibling; a deceased husband's brother; a priest; a student; a superior officer; the wife of a blood brother, age-mate, or *xenios*; a lactating mother; a particular divine being; a sheep; and so on. Beyond being attracted to any of these partners, having sex with them has further significance. And each of the innumerable culturally abetted ways of 'having sex' with them has substantially distinct meanings. These meanings are not given by nature: they are constructed by culture, yet, so-constructed, become objective social facts that a person must deal with. In important biological, psychological, and social respects, 'sexual attraction' is a universal natural kind. In other, equally important respects, 'sexual attraction' is always deeply embedded in social structures, informed by culture, situationally particular, and dyadically distinctive. These natural and cultural aspects of sex are not dissociable: it is in the nature of human sex to be culturally significant in culturally particular ways, while the culture of sex is built on and powered by its psychophysiology. The social implications of sex depend simultaneously on its cultural meanings and its biological nature.

Likewise, kama muta has both universal and specific aspects – aspects that are analytically distinct, but inseparable in actual practice. This book aims to address both. At the same time that I show how kama muta is a universal natural kind, I show how cultural practices function to evoke it, cultural affordances shape the CS relationships that can be intensified, and cultural meanings give distinct significance to kama muta with each sort of being in each context, for each kind of person. The socially constitutive properties of kama muta depend on both nature and culture together.

For want of a more precise scientific construct, in this book and our other work on kama muta, we follow conventional practice in psychology and anthropology by using the vernacular lexeme "*emotion*" when we characterize kama muta as "a distinct and particular emotion." Our characterization of kama muta makes it clear why we posit that kama muta is an <u>emotion,</u> but this characterization only partially addresses the supposition that kama muta is <u>an</u> emotion. In what sense are all of the experiences described in this book <u>one and the same</u> emotion, rather than instances of many different emotions, some of which perhaps extend beyond the boundaries of the kama muta construct that we delineate? Using any of the nine principal cultural facets of kama muta, or other aspects of it, one could reasonably construct a taxonomy that would divide kama muta into any number of entities that one could posit to be distinct "emotions." For example, would it make sense to distinguish among the emotions evoked by sudden intensification of CS with different partners? If so, what distinctions should we make? Is a Swiss patriot's kama muta when feeling suddenly one with Switzerland (see Claparède 1930) distinct from an American patriot's kama muta when feeling suddenly one with the United States of America? Are both types of kama muta distinct from the kama muta of a civil rights participant's kama muta when feeling suddenly one with the cause? Is kama muta evoked by cute kittens different from kama muta evoked by puppies? Cute human babies? Cute interactions between kittens and babies? Kittens dressed as babies or kittens appearing to hide their eyes like a human baby? Why say that kama muta is <u>an</u> emotion, not 2, 20, 200, or an indefinite number of 'different' 'emotions'? Where should we draw the lines that delineate 'an' emotion, distinct from other emotions? More generally, what sort of scientific taxonomy of emotion is most fruitful? It is far from obvious what makes some set of experiences precisely <u>one</u> emotion, rather than a subset of an emotion, or several distinct emotions.

The answer may be that for certain explanatory purposes a broad set of experiences are causally or functionally equivalent, while with respect to other causes and functions, they are distinct. 'Anxiety disorders' share common features, but there are subtypes whose distinctions are crucial with respect to aspects of etiology, suffering, prognosis, and treatment. Similarly, for many scholarly purposes, it is most useful to designate 'chemical elements' such as 'carbon' and 'uranium.' Those elemental constructs are essential for characterizing all chemical processes and biological processes. However, for certain purposes, it is essential to distinguish among the 15 isotopes of carbon, ^8C to ^{22}C, and among the six isotopes of uranium, ^{232}U to ^{238}U (there is no ^{237}U). There are multiple frames of explanation, sometimes requiring different distinctions. So I certainly acknowledge that for some explanatory or interpretive purposes, it may be perfectly sensible, and indeed illuminating, to delineate one or more subtypes of kama muta. A student of religion may be interested in the particularities of kama muta evoked by the love of, and for, Krishna, in contrast to the love of, and for, Jesus or Allah. Or the scholar may want to contrast specific features of kama muta evoked by the love of, and for, Krishna at different points in history, in different Vaishnavist traditions, at different temples, or in different rituals. For such scholarly purposes, it is entirely appropriate to give the subtypes their own names.

Nevertheless, some constructs at some levels of inclusion are more generally informative than others; the criteria are the consistency of their causes and their consequences, or their functions. As a set, a construct is valid and valuable to the extent that all elements of the set have the same causal or functional relations with other valid sets. In this case, if CS is a valid construct, then kama muta is a valid construct to the extent that it is always caused by the sudden intensification of CS relationships. Likewise, kama muta is a valid construct to the extent that all instances of kama muta – across cultures, contexts, and history – are correlated with warm feelings in the chest, tears, goosebumps, et cetera. The kama muta construct is further validated to the extent that all instances of kama muta – evoked by intensification of CS with all sorts of beings and wholes – produce sentiments of devotion and moral commitment to CS relationships. The construct will be validated to the extent that whatever the specific CS relationship that suddenly intensifies to evoke kama muta, people consistently want to give and participate together in the kama muta, such that joint participation further intensifies CS among participants. Further, kama muta is a valid construct to the extent that perceiving kama muta in others tends to evoke kama muta in the perceiver. If we find evidence that all sorts of instances of kama muta consistently (and in contrast to other positive emotions) involve activation of the agranular anterior insula, or specifically involve cascades of μ-opioids in conjunction with dopamine and oxytocin, that will further validate the construct. And so on.

From Michelle Rosaldo (1980) and Catherine Lutz (1988) to Paul Ekman (1992) and Lisa Feldman Barrett (2017), many emotion researchers have used the term *emotion*, along with specific types such as *anger*, *happiness*, *liget*, or *fado*, to denote the experiencers' or perceivers' linguistic usage – their lexical labelling of experiences. Many have also apparently assumed that vernacular terms and the folk concepts that they denote each actually correspond to distinct psychological (or sociocultural psychological) mechanisms. In short, many 'emotion' researchers have used the English vernacular term *emotion* to denote the recognition, categorizing, and naming of sensations. Sometimes they have recognized that the recognition, categorizing, and naming of sensations occurs with reference to social situations. That is, the academic term 'emotion' has been used to denote the vernacular meanings – the everyday usage – of words; in effect, for many researchers, an 'emotion' consists of a dictionary definition framed by speakers' explicit or implicit folk psychology.[7] Researchers have often gone beyond this, assuming that vernacular lexemes and the typically unarticulated folk concepts that they denote delineate real psychological entities or processes.

Our *kama muta* construct is not an 'emotion' in that sense (Fiske 2019). Our research, and this book, is not much concerned with vernacular <u>names</u> for, or processes of naming, one's interoceptive sensations, others' facial expressions, or situations. Except for considering metaphorical consistency across languages, and for methodological purposes, we are <u>not</u> studying the everyday usage of dictionary definitions of lexemes such as *moved, touched, proud, nostalgic, bewegt sein,* בלל עגנ, *olema puudutatud,* 感动, or *terharu.* True, people often use these lexemes to denote kama muta experiences, but in each language they also use other words to denote kama muta, and sometimes use these words to denote emotions that are <u>not</u> kama muta. Indeed, we are interested in a psychosocial cultural entity that people sometimes cannot name, or for which they have many distinct context-specific names. We agree with Barrett, Wierzbicka, and most psychological anthropologists, that vernacular lexemes are socially constructed, and hence are more or less specific to particular languages, cultures, historical periods, and contexts. <u>But in contrast to these researchers, our core aim is **not** to explain how people use vernacular lexemes.</u> Likewise, the social construction of folk concepts and taxonomies is a legitimate and interesting topic of study, but it is not **our** core topic, as such. We are interested in word usage primarily as a methodological tool – as only one among several separately imperfect ways of identifying kama muta events. We have to use vernacular language to listen to and communicate with our informants, respondents, and participants – but we do not assume that they use their lexemes precisely or consistently. So we never rely on verbal labels alone. (For a detailed exposition of these issues, see Fiske 2019.)

Moreover, the encompassing concept, 'emotion,' is itself an English vernacular lexeme; there is no reason to assume a priori that it is a psychologically distinct, scientifically meaningful construct. Psychologists certainly do not agree on what *emotion* means or even what sorts of affects the term encompasses (Scherer 2005; Moors 2010). Online Note 4.3 inspects the fallacy us directly adopting *emotion* as a scientific construct.

So let us now define kama muta.

What kama muta is

1. Kama muta is evoked by the perception of a sudden intensification of communal sharing between the participant and another being (human, animal, deity) or entity (the earth, the cosmos), or by the observation of a sudden intensification of communal sharing between third parties (Schubert et al. 2016; Seibt et al. 2016; Seibt et al. 2017; Steinnes 2017). "Intensification" may consist of a rapid temporal increase in the strength of a CS bond; the creation of a new CS bond; or the figure-ground contrast that occurs when memory, anticipation, or imagining of CS springs forth against a background of separation, longing, or loss.
2. It is a positive emotion in five respects:
    a. People report liking it, rate it as positive, and have no consistent tendency to rate it as negative (Darwin, 1872:216; Batson et al. 1987; Frijda

2001; Haidt 2003a, 2003b; Cova & Deonna 2014; Menninghaus et al. 2015; Schubert et al. 2016; Seibt et al. 2016; Seibt et al. 2017; Fiske, Seibt, & Schubert 2017a, 2017b; Steinnes 2017);

b. People actively seek it out, and seek to re-experience it (e.g., rowers' experience of 'the boat' – Brown 2013; Gabrielsson 2001; Oliver & Raney 2011; Hanich et al. 2014; Menninghaus et al. 2017; Vuoskoski & Eerola 2017);

c. People want to give it to others whom they care about;

d. People want to experience it together with others, which intensifies it (note the Spanish and Portuguese terms *comovido*, 'to be moved together');

e. In many cultures, in appropriate circumstances, the emotion is culturally valued or even prescribed for at least some people, such as *kawaii* for contemporary Japanese women, patriotic sentiment for European men between about 1770 and 1840, the feeling of union with God for worshippers attending Methodist revival meetings in the great awakenings, and the feeling of *ḥāl* for Sufis, or *salṭanah* for Egyptians listening to *ṭarab* music.

3. When it is mild, many people experience few or no sensations and display few if any signs, but when it is strongly felt, most (but not all) people usually have some of the following sensations and/or show some of the following signs:

A pleasantly warm, swelling, heavy, or other feeling in the center of the chest ('heart') (Tan & Frijda 1999; Haidt 2003a, 2003b; Schnall et al. 2010; Cova & Deonna 2014; Zickfeld 2016; Pohling & Diessner 2016; Thomson & Siegel 2016; Schubert et al. 2016; Fiske, Schubert, & Seibt 2017a, 2017b; Zickfeld 2016, Zickfeld et al. 2019).

Moist eyes, tears, or weeping (Schubert et al. 2016; Seibt et al. 2016; Seibt et al. 2017; Zickfeld et al. 2017a; Steinnes 2017; Mori & Iwanaga 2017; Wassiliwizky et al. 2017; Zickfeld et al. 2019).

Goosebumps, body hair standing up, chills, or shivers (Panksepp 1995; Juslin & Laukka 2004; Konečni 2005; Benedek & Kaernbach 2011; Nusbaum et al. 2014; Menninghaus et al., 2015; Laeng et al. 2016; Mori & Iwanaga 2017; Schubert et al. 2016; Seibt et al. 2017; Fiske et al. 2017a, et al. 2017b; Mori & Iwanaga 2017; Benedek & Kaernbach, 2011; Wassiliwizky et al., 2017a; Wassiliwizky et al. 2017b; Zickfeld et al. 2019).

Choked up (lump in throat), with difficulty speaking or a creaky voice (Konečni 2005; Cova & Deonna 2014; Fiske et al. 2017a, 2017b).

Placement of one or both open hands to the chest, palm inwards (Fiske ct al. 2017a, 2017b).

A deep breath and/or a pause in breathing (Fiske et al. 2017a, 2017b).

In some contexts, a phatic utterance such as *awww!* (as I noted in Chapter 2, the sound varies across languages), or ululation (Fiske et al. 2017a, 2017b).

> **Feelings of buoyancy, lightness, floating, rising** (often at the end or afterwards; Fiske et al. 2017a, 2017b; Zickfeld et al. 2019; Fiske 2019).
>
> **Exhilaration, being energized, optimism** (often at the end or afterwards; Fiske et al. 2017a, 2017b; Zickfeld et al. 2019; James 1902; Ingold 2015; Myrick 2015; Janicke, Rieger, & Connor 2018).

Though all of these sensation and signs are common in kama muta, experiences of *all* of these sensations and signs *together* are very rare, if they ever do all occur together.

4. Devotion motivation and a sense of moral commitment emerge: people aim to strengthen, repair, and sustain the focal communal sharing relationship and their other communal sharing relationships, and feel one with others (Batson 1991; Batson et al. 1988; Haidt 2003a, 2003b; Tan 2009; Cox 2010; Schnall et al. 2010; Cova & Deonna 2014; Cova et al. 2016; Menninghaus et al. 2015; Oliver et al. 2015; Janicke & Oliver 2015; Strick et al. 2015; Zickfeld 2016; Pohling & Diessner 2016; Thomson & Siegel, 2013, 2016; Steinnes 2017).

5. In English, depending on the context and depending on with whom the communal sharing relationship suddenly intensifies, people may label the experience as *being moved, touched, having a heart-warming* experience, having a *poignant* experience, feeling *tenderness, nostalgia, ecstasy, rapture, being touched by the Spirit* (Fiske, Schubert, & Seibt 2017a, 2017b). People may speak of team *pride* or *patriotic* sentiments. However, people also use each of these lexemes for other emotions, and do not always give kama muta the same name, so the labels are by no means definitive. Each language has a different set of lexemes that may typically denote kama muta, though languages partition the emotion domain differently, with different degrees of specificity (Zickfeld et al. 2019; Fiske 2019; see Chapter 7).

6. There are more or less distinctive neuroanatomical and neurochemical systems involved, including peripheral physiology, though we do not yet know what they are.

7. There are, or were, adaptive functions that resulted in natural selection for the disposition to experience kama muta, and to experience it generatively, in the intensification of all sorts of communal sharing relationships.

8. There are ontogenetic pathways, interlocking with culture, through which kama muta develops, though we know little about them yet.

The definition of a construct is only useful to the extent that it enables one to delineate a valid entity. The validity of the entity denoted *kama muta* is what our research program, and this book in particular, aims to establish.

Negative affect leading up to, accompanying, or following kama muta

When people report an event in which they experienced kama muta, they sometimes report negative emotions, including sadness, anger, guilt, or embarrassment. Given our theorization that kama muta itself is inherently a purely positive emotion, how can this be?

I mentioned above that kama muta can occur in the course of an episode that included negative emotions before or after the kama muta moment(s). For example, a person might be sad or worried about a loved one who is absent, and then feel kama muta when reunited with them. If we ask the person to remember and report how they felt 'at the reunion,' the person may take 'at the reunion' to include some hours or minutes before the moment of being reunited. If so, in addition to (or instead of) recalling and reporting the positivity of the brief kama muta moment at the end, the person may label the event as a whole negative, because there was, indeed, a long period of worry before the few seconds of wonderfully positive kama muta. As we saw in Chapter 3, a similar process is operating in the audience or reader of the universally popular narrative prototype of a couple separated by social and other obstacles, yet who ultimately reunite in person, or who, dying, reaffirm that their love is paramount over all. If Odysseus had never left, or he had left but his family had been certain of his safe and easy return, and if he had not struggled to overcome so many hardships on his journey home, there would not have been kama muta moments when he returned.

Similarly, the person participating in a funeral or a memorial service or visiting a memorial monument generally feels sad about the loss of the deceased. Likewise, a person who nostalgically misses someone they love, but are separated from, feels sad about being apart. Against this ground of sorrow, however, there may be moments of mnemonic love, moments when the person feels again the love of the person they miss. This figure-ground contrast evokes kama muta. But because the moments of kama muta are brief (though they may occur again and again), if one recalls visiting the memorial, one may report the visit – evaluating it as a whole – as distressing. In short, when kama muta is generated by the sudden re-emergence of CS against a prior state of worry or sadness, memories and reports of the negative emotions may overwhelm memories of the totally positive but brief kama muta moments. Note also that the vivid memories of one's love for the departed that evoke kama muta may then also quickly amplify the sadness that one feels about the separation from them.

As we shall see in Chapters 5, 8, and 11–15, when two or more people suddenly suffer together, or recall and recount suffering that they discover they have in common, this commonality may suddenly intensify the CS relationship among them. The suffering and its remembrance evoke negative affects, but the sudden connection among fellow sufferers generates kama muta that in itself is entirely positive. So here again the negative affect affords a positive kama muta moment.

While we don't yet definitely understand the process, it seems that people may feel kama muta when their *heart goes out* to a needy, vulnerable, frightened, or suffering person or animal (McDougal 1919; Lorenz 1943; Berry & McArthur 1985; Dijker 2014; see Online note 8.2). That is, a person's feeling of empathic concern may evoke sudden CS that motivates compassionate care-taking (on the correlation of <u>trait</u> empathic concern to kama muta, see Zickfeld et al. 2017). In such an event, the vulnerable or suffering person is in a very negative affective state, while their distress evokes empathic distress in the compassionate observer. This compassionate concern is a form of CS; suddenly intensifying, it generates kama muta.

So, for example, when my toddler has fallen and is crying, when I pick him up and comfort him I may feel kama muta, and he may, too. A person lost, fearful, in pain, or otherwise distressed is prone to feel strong kama muta when rescued, cared for, and comforted. But that does not imply that distress is a <u>necessary</u> precursor to kama muta; a person who is safe and happy can nonetheless feel kama muta when someone is especially loving to her.

Finally, perceiving or displaying one's own kama muta can result in shame or embarrassment if one judges that one should not feel kama muta, or should not reveal it. (Or, on the contrary, one may be proud to note or to display the sensitivity evident in one's proclivity to kama muta.)

In sum, as we have seen in previous chapters and will see again and again in subsequent chapters, negative affects are absolutely not <u>necessary</u> precursors or contexts for kama muta. Kama muta often occurs without any prior or concurrent negative affects. I was perfectly content, reading, before the moment when my two-year-old grandson came up and silently took my hand to bring me along with him for a walk. My girlfriend and I were having a wonderful time together on a holiday when, out of the blue, I proposed to her.

Online notes

4.1 Pepys' kama muta when he imagines his future self feeling kama muta reading his diary.
4.2 Kama muta evoked by a song the listener did not consciously hear.
4.3 *Emotion* is a vernacular lexeme that does not correspond to a definite class of mental phenomena.

Notes

1 See www.rmt.ucla.edu.
2 Alan Fiske, fieldnotes.
3 We'll come back to the elevation construct in Chapter 10. For the theory that moral evaluation is evaluation of social relationships, see Rai & Fiske 2011; for consideration of emotions that may occur when relationships other than CS intensify, see Chapter 19. For further elucidation of the contrast between the elevation construct and kama muta, see Janicke-Bowles, Schubert, and Blomster 2020.
4 https://slate.com/author/dana-stevens/16
5 On kama muta in the culmination of pilgrimage, see Chapter 16.
6 That is, in formal mathematical terms, the kama muta disposition is the psychosocial function mapping the set of all culturally signaled sudden intensifications of culturally implemented CS relationships onto the set of culturally congruent devotion and commitment motives (the co-domain, range, or output). The domain (input) is CS intensifications, the co-domain (output, range) is motives to devote and commit to CS. The set of all input-output pairs is technically called the graph of the function. In other words, kama muta transforms CS intensifications into corresponding motives. One cannot understand a function if we only know one or a few input-output pairs. So we cannot understand the psychological mechanism that is the kama

muta disposition if we only know how one or a few kinds of CS intensification map onto one or a few CS motives. In Chapters 10 and 17 we more fully characterize this conceptualization of the kama muta disposition as a function.

7 Lexemes are not used merely to denote pre-existent things; words are often, perhaps typically, not used purely referentially, but uttered to <u>do</u> things – to constitute aspects of social relations (Austin 1975). Emotion lexemes, in particular, are often used as pleas, claims, or judgments of virtue. See Fiske 2019.

5

COMPASSION, HEROISM, AND VICTORY

When a person sees the first ultrasound of her baby, gives birth, or is smitten by an adorable kitten, she suddenly creates a new communal sharing relationship and is likely to feel first–person kama muta. When long-separated partners reunite, they suddenly renew their previously stressed CS relationship and are likely to experience both first- and second-person kama muta, while their audience is likely to feel third-person kama muta. Formulating our theory that kama muta is the product of sudden intensification of CS relationships stimulated us to go out and look at other kinds of intensification, such as the sudden deepening of a relationship, exceptional kindness and compassion, and forgiveness (see Konečni 2005). Do these kinds of rapid CS intensification also evoke the kama muta experience?

Cry dates

> During finals week at UCLA, I came back from a full day of classes and found that my roommate, Madelyn, had stocked our room with chocolate, pretzels, and wine. Earlier in the day I had run into Madelyn in a busy hallway and she looked at me wide-eyed and said 'Can we just cry later?' I laughed and replied 'Oh, definitely.' Upon my return I knew that we were going to have a Cry Date.
>
> We went out for dinner and when we arrived back in our room, we sat down on the floor together with cozy blankets. We started out simply talking about how our days went, the finals we had, and what we had planned for the next day. But things transitioned from a casual conversation when I asked her, 'How are you *really* feeling?' Madelyn began to tell me about being stressed,

but moreover, that she was amazed how we were actually at UCLA and were almost finished with our first quarter. We talked about where we had come from and how much our lives had changed since attending community college. It was deeply nostalgic and I teared up as I told her about my experiences and how I had arrived at this point.

When I began community college, I had just been through a traumatic life event, moved out on my own, and was working full-time. My GPA continued to sink as time went by and it wasn't until two years had passed that I had realized what kind of a life I was leading myself into. I faced a great amount of anxiety, but persevered, maintaining a 4.0 GPA for the following two years. It wasn't until transfer applications were a month from being due that I decided to apply to UCLA. It had never occurred to me that my hard work could possibly be enough to make up for past mistakes. A professor I spoke with was baffled by this and said, 'UCLA is where you belong.'

Sitting on the bedroom floor, I relived all of the tumultuous feelings I had during those four years in community college. I used to be embarrassed by this and felt that I had failed. Yet, I was sitting with my roommate and discussing how far we had made it. We actually did it! We both cried. I was overwhelmed with inspiration and I was moved upon recalling those memories of everything that had played a part in how I had gotten to the place that I was at.

(Autumn McGrath)

Young women in Southern California and probably elsewhere in the US occasionally get together with one or more close friends with the explicit intention of having a *cry date* (McGrath 2015). Not everyone uses this or any other specific phrase to refer to these events, and sometimes the intention to cry together is mutually understood but not made verbally explicit. In these events the women get together, perhaps beginning by just chatting about anything, and then beginning to disclose very personal, private concerns, problems, experiences, or emotions. The trusting intimacy of these disclosures evokes tears that quickly merge into hugs. Often the intensification of the CS relationship is amplified by sharing food, particularly desserts or 'junk food.' Sometimes the experience is afforded by beginning with a 'chick flick – a 'tear-jerking' movie that is romantic and perhaps depicts personal struggle courageously overcome. Young women watch such movies together with the definite hope of being moved to tears together. Sometimes participants prepare for the cry date by bringing tissues or wearing waterproof mascara. Young women may also exchange confidences and cry together spontaneously, without prior planning. In either case, they engage in one or more bouts of crying, often feel choked up, and have a light or warm feeling in the center of the chest. Afterwards the participants typically feel buoyant, light, and exhilarated. It is invariably a positive experience (McGrath 2015).

Cry dates are events where the participants' joint intent is to experience kama muta, and to experience it not just in parallel, but to mutually facilitate each other's kama muta, and furthermore, to enhance their mutual kama muta by sharing the experience so that their emotions resonate. Alongside the consubstantial assimilation of commensal eating and drinking, and of hugging, what typically evokes the participants' kama muta is revealing secrets or disclosing hardships, suffering, and fear. Notably, this is called 'sharing.' Sometimes what the participants reveal are traumatic events that they are ashamed of, or that are in some ways humiliating, such as being cheated on or dumped by a boyfriend, or other betrayals or abuse. Revealing such matters puts the teller at the listener's mercy, making her vulnerable to ridicule or gossip; this manifestation of trust typically moves the listener. Often the participants 'can relate' to each other's experiences, emotions, moods, and attitudes; it is moving to discover that one is not alone. When someone has shared similar distressing experiences that had previously shamed and potentially isolated them, those very events can forge a bond with listeners who reciprocate by telling congruent secrets. Overcoming obstacles is often part of the trope: cry date partners bond through the troubles and fears they have transcended – often worries about being accepted, or fears of being disdained or excluded. The pride of 'I did it! Just like you!' and the joy of 'We did it!' make the victors feel wanted and welcome to CS relationships that otherwise eluded them.

Several UCLA students have reported engaging in more or less structured events like these, more or less explicitly intended to consist of experiencing kama muta together – as the Spanish and Portuguese say, _comovido_. We don't know the geo-cultural extent of this unobtrusive cultural practice within or beyond North America. A Bosnian-born Norwegian young woman reported that she engages in similar practices with Bosnian-Norwegian girlfriends (but not with native Norwegians) in which they pick out tear-jerking movies, bring tissues and ice-cream, tell each other intimate troubles, and cry together. She didn't have a name for this practice. An analogous, apparently independent recent cultural invention is _rui-katsu_, tear-seeking gatherings in Japan, at which people assemble to watch sad and heart-warming videos in order to cry together (Shimbun 2013; St. Michel 2015). Many of these events are organized by therapists or others who charge fees for attending. One service provides a choice of guys – their photos are online – who will come to your workplace, show you and your colleagues tear-jerking videos, and then personally wipe away your tears; the company name, _Ikemeso_, combines _ikemen_, 'hot guy', with _mesomeso_, 'crying' (Wilson 2015).

In some northern European cultures people are reserved in their emotional expression; men, especially, rarely express affection explicitly, except when they're drunk, or at special occasions such as wedding, retirement, or decade-birthday toasts. Then they are allowed, almost expected, to express their affection, evoking kama muta in themselves, the person they express affection for, and everyone listening. Norwegians recount innumerable such kama muta-inducing wedding toasts. Here's another informant's account of something more like a cry date, occurring in the Norwegian prototypical framework of inebriation licensed and expected kama muta.

Norwegians, especially men, present themselves as emotionally tough. And there is a lot of heavy drinking in Norway. In 2010 my classmates and I from Sandnes, all about 18, were on a class trip to Berlin; people had just gotten back to our hotel after a night out and were gathered in the lobby. I was astonished to see five of my male classmates had started to tear up; I had certainly never before witnessed any of the boys in my class crying. Within a couple of minutes almost the whole class was gathered tightly together in a corner, crying loudly. Apparently, it all started with two boys hugging and telling each other how much they appreciated the other's friendship; more boys rapidly did the same, and the girls joined in soon after. At some point one boy suddenly recalled his aunt, who had died a year ago, and started to cry. My classmates told me that then many started crying as they recalled their own departed loved ones, while others cried because they felt bad for everybody else who had lost someone they really loved. This incident seemed to bring the class closer together, at least for a little while.

(Kamilla Knutsen Steinnes)

Norwegians say that they don't often explicitly express strong affection when they are sober, but are quite prone to when drunk; doing so is called *I love you-drita* – '(very) drunken I-love-you.' Informants report that sufficiently intoxicated Norwegians are prone to say I love you to anyone around. When Siri Leknes heard about our kama muta concept, she immediately told us about *I love you-drita*, saying,

> the basic idea is that when in a state of alcohol intoxication you are overwhelmed with a desire to say how much you love and appreciate someone. This would most frequently occur with friends. But it could certainly occur with someone that you have recently bonded with, for instance over a drink at a bar or a party.

Later, once the Norwegian participants are sober, these loving statements are not taken to mean much. To conclusively determine how often *I love you-drita* evokes kama muta, we will have to conduct extensive participant observation.

* * * * *

Many cultures of the insular Pacific grow what in English would be called *compassion*, *empathy*, or *sympathy* beyond the transitory emotional experience into a general cultural ethos of *arofa* that ideally envelopes most everyday social relations, both as a sentiment and a paradigm for social relations (Levy 1973). People should be sensitively caring. Such cultivation fosters a disposition to experience what appears to be the core emotion, kama muta, informs the experience of it, and orients it. But it does more: it colors much of everyday social life, the self, identity, and art.

> I have spoken of affection, sympathy, concern. The Tikopia have one word which covers these concepts and similar ones: *arofa*. Grief, gratitude, moral support, pride in, appreciation of another, all these are also included under this term. In fact, this is the term for social warmth, the social emotion.
>
> *(Lee 1959:45)*

In other Pacific cultures the concept is equally central, but has other names. For example, see Kirkpatrick (1985) about *ka'oha* in Marquesas; Lutz (1995) about *fago* on Ifaluk Island in Melanesia; Young (1999) about *nuakabubu* on Goodenough Island in eastern Papua New Guinea; and Throop (2010) on *runguy* on Yap. We do not know how – or even for sure whether – this cultural emphasis on compassion is constructed through kama muta moments, or how the cultural focus on compassion affords and informs kama muta experiences.

Charity volunteers, caretakers, and therapists

> I was helping out with Meals on Wheels deliveries, doing research on kama muta. At one delivery an old man came out onto the small porch to greet Carol and me, offering his name and hand to me, as we had not yet met. He was quite the talker, although I did not understand the context and history of most of what he was talking about. Then, noticing my polite but nevertheless confused look, he told me that his wife had passed away last week. He then began telling me about her and how they had been together for 67 years and she was such an important part of his life. It then reached a point where he stopped talking, wiping tears from his eyes. I felt a deep urge of closeness and compassion with this man as I tried to fight off shedding tears myself.
>
> (Ryan Morris)

Many people volunteer to help needy people. Why do they do that? Participant observation in a Meals on Wheels program revealed that helping someone needy can make the helper feel kama muta (Morris 2015). Both drivers delivering meals and recipients were eager to see each other and recipients often confided in the drivers, telling of their trials and tribulations. Recipients often shared hearty hugs with drivers. The sentiment that English speakers call *gratitude* generally grows out of, and reinforces, CS relationships (Simão & Seibt 2014, 2015). And indeed the recipients' heartfelt expressions of gratitude and evident feelings of kama muta for what they received often evoked kama muta experiences in the volunteers, interviews and observations showed. And evoked kama muta in the ethnographer himself when he observed the gratitudinous kama muta. Even if the recipients said little, drivers sometimes felt some kama muta just from knowing that the recipients were getting what they needed. As the volunteers said, helping "just feels good." Kama muta heartened volunteers, sustaining them and making it all worthwhile.

Among American participants, the more a person feels empathic concern for people in need or distress, the more the person tends to report *being moved or touched*, having warm feelings in their body or specifically their chest, getting moist eyes or tears, and getting goosebumps or chills when watching kama muta-evoking videos (Zickfeld et al. 2017; Zickfeld et al. 2019). This implies that people who are most likely to volunteer to help the needy are the very people who are most prone to feel kama muta when CS suddenly intensifies in other ways, such as through expressions of gratitude.

Volunteers who care for the dying often have experiences of "grace" that may be kama muta, and that may motivate the volunteers (Gowack & Vale 1998). Moreover, kama muta experiences may be palliative for the dying. We don't yet know, but we imagine that kama muta experiences foster all sorts of charitable volunteerism, providing the key motivation sustaining innumerable civic organizations. Kama muta experiences may attract and sustain helping professionals such as doctors, nurses, home-care aids, emergency medical technicians, rescue teams, Peace Corps and Doctors Without Borders volunteers, psychotherapists, marriage and family counselors, day care workers, drug counselors, social workers, clergy, hot-line volunteers, and in some communities at some points in history, firefighters and police. Frequent or strong kama muta experiences probably reduce 'burnout' and make professional life more meaningful. In psychotherapy, both therapists and patients often have significant experiences of 'tenderness' (in Norwegian, *ømhet*; Jon Monson and Øle Solbakken, personal communication 21 October 2015). Many of these experiences may be kama muta.

Treating a Syrian boy who was suffering from a severe traumatic experience, Lauren Ban had an intense kama muta experience when he eventually trusted her and created a ritual they performed together to address his trauma; see her sensitive report of this in Online Note 5.1. Other therapists whom Lauren has interviewed have recognized and remembered moments when they felt kama muta in therapy. Furthermore, when the patient sees the therapist's kama muta tears, it may greatly strengthen the therapeutic relationship. We are currently studying this.

One Australian therapist, Sarah, responding to a questionnaire about kama muta that Lauren gave her, told of the following case:

> An example of such experience is the following. A client was telling me about her childhood sexual abuses which were truly horrific. When she revealed to me some graphic content which have never been shared with anyone else, I could see that my client was feeling very vulnerable and scared. My response was to validate the client's experience in a person-centred way and with this I was touched and felt a genuine warmth and lump in my throat. My eyes welled with tears (usually this doesn't happen to me but something about this client got to me). I maintained eye-contact and told her that I feel sad for the little girl inside of her who experienced these abuses, whilst also affirming her resilience. I remember feeling like I wanted to hug her, but I didn't.
>
> In response to a question about this, Sarah responds:
>
> Yes, I think it strengthened the bond between us. She could see through my response to her, that I care about her and that I believe her story. I think she has felt safer and more trusting in the therapeutic process. The connection that I felt with this client definitely enhanced rapport, which helped with the therapy more broadly. Even though we have continued processing trauma and I have helped her develop skills to manage everyday stressors etc., the subtle therapy is happening alongside all of this; development of a trusting and open relationship, being believed and seeing that she is of importance.

Given that charity volunteers, caretaking professionals and therapists experience kama muta, sometimes profoundly, we may ask to what extent kama muta motivates these activities. Do people care for others in considerable part because of the kama muta experiences that emerge from doing so? What role does kama muta have in sustaining compassionate roles?

In Chapter 12 we consider possible kama muta experiences in dialectical behavioral therapy and mindful self-compassion training.

Addiction recovery groups and support groups

Let's look at how trusting revelation of shared suffering unites participants in Alcoholics Anonymous. AA meetings are often remarkably warm and welcoming. The entire culture of AA and similar groups is one of inclusion:

I was doing participant observation on kama muta in an Alcoholics Anonymous meeting. I'd had several weeks of ups and downs in my perception of whether or not my research was valid, whether the people I was studying wanted me there, whether I could truly be a participant observer in a setting that seemed so far separated from my own personal experience and feeling. As usual, I arrived, politely greeted the members waiting for the meeting to begin, and took my seat ready to observe from what felt more like an outsiders perspective than a participant of the meeting. The first part of the meeting went as usual. Members told their stories and struggles, and I did my best to understand and relate to what they were saying and how other people might be feeling as they recognized familiar themes in the struggle being shared. The short intermission began where I would normally do my best to join in on conversations and become a real part of the group; a task that was generally proving difficult for me. Then, unexpectedly, I was tapped on the shoulder by an older woman who was usually quiet and who up until this point I had only exchanged a few greetings with. I turned around and looked at her in surprise. She looked up and smiled at me with a genuineness that kept my gaze and thoughts affixed on her when she calmly said, 'You being here comforts me.' I very much wanted to give her a hug in addition to my now uncontrollable smile and shock upon hearing this, however I caught myself and thought it best not to do so. From this point on, I felt like I had a place in the group and I knew that what I was searching for was truly in this group as I truly felt it myself.

(Ryan Morris)

Ryan found that he felt kama muta in the surprisingly warm acceptance and inclusion he encountered – despite having made it clear to everyone that he's not alcoholic, but was simply doing fieldwork I asked him to do. But warm acceptance alone doesn't explain why Alcoholics Anonymous works, at least in the sense that it is a self-reproducing organization that attracts millions of participants, has diffused over the world, and has endured for decades. How does AA work?

In general, when a person's communal sharing relationship with a group suddenly intensifies, a sense of commitment to the group emerges out of the kama muta. That motivates people to adhere to obligations and responsibilities that are inherent in the CS group. Thus kama muta-evoking practices and narratives can be used to get people to adhere to group norms. Furthermore, kama muta experiences are attractive: people seek this experience and they make efforts to experience it with others, drawing in their associates. Thus anything that evokes kama muta experiences can be used to sustain attendance. If transgression of group norms means some degree or feeling of exclusion, then the desire to belong and partake in kama muta-evoking practices generates a major second-order motivation to adhere. In addition, as we shall see with regard to poetry reading in Chapter 8, hearing of others' hardships, suffering, endurance, and overcoming obstacles often evokes kama muta. The participants in cry dates, addiction recovery groups, and probably support groups of all sorts typically arrive feeling alone, isolated by their misfortune, cut off from others who do not understand their suffering, avoiding others who might discover their stigmatized condition (see Ricoeur 1967). When they get together in a welcoming, non-judgmental, accepting atmosphere; when they hear others tell of suffering that they recognize as their own suffering; when they develop the trust to reveal their humiliations, their degrading victimization, or personal failures; when their peers listen compassionately and show that they understand because they have been through the same hard times – then their CS relationship ignites. This experience of love igniting is kama muta. Discovering with surprise that one is not alone – that others have suffered similar traumas, shame, suffering, or loss – transforms such isolating experiences into connecting bonds: what previously made one separate abruptly unites the persons with those who have those experiences in common. Moreover, listeners feel kama muta at the trust demonstrated by the teller's revelation of embarrassing, degrading secrets. Their mutual kama muta experience is enhanced by their overcoming their traumas and suffering *together*, with mutual support.

Participants' desire to recount such stories of struggle and triumph, moving the audience to identify with them, can help participants maintain their efforts in the face of great challenges. And participants do not want to disappoint those who love and identify with them. These features mean that institutions and practices evoking kama muta are likely to endure and diffuse, gain membership, and support self-control by transforming it into loyalty. For these reasons, narratives and practices that evoke kama muta likely to be are vital constituents of addiction recovery and other support groups in contemporary Western society.

Alcoholics Anonymous meetings are characterized by an "ethos of relaxed camaraderie" marked by informal dress and speech (Swora 2004). People say they feel 'at home' and that, in general, participants *speak from the heart*, 'spontaneously.' "AA stories and AA story-tellers create community" (Swora 2004:366). "When one tells one's story to others, one creates a relationship between performer and audience. ... The emergent social structure includes all listeners" (2004:368). That CS relationship, that CS social structure, result from the reiteration of individual stories of alcoholic depravity and degradation, prayer, and providential intervention by another alcoholic, resulting in abstinence maintained by the solidarity of AA gatherings. Often the stories include stumbles and, again, another alcoholic extending a hand to bring the speaker back into the fold. Thus each recovering alcoholic identifies with each story as a version of his or her own, creating re-intensified CS binds.

By hearing these stories over and over, AA participants learn how to tell their story of overcoming obstacles and achieving sobriety by depending on God's love, along with continuing attendance, speaking, and support in AA meetings.

> Healing in AA is marked by new understandings of one's drinking past and their sober present, and this happens as they learn to tell an acceptable AA life story. In this manner, they acquire the identity of 'sober alcoholic' and join a community of others like them.
>
> *(Swora 2004:377)*

> In the process of socialization into AA, the newcomer must learn not only how to tell his or her story, he or she must learn how to listen to the stories of others. In listening to the speaker's story, the listener should look for ways in which the story resonates with his or her own experiences, how this new interpretive scheme makes sense of not only the storyteller's life, but the story-listener's life as well. The listener should 'identify, not compare.' AA members describe the process of identification with the expression 'If you go to enough meetings and warm a chair, you will hear your own story.' By identifying with others, one learns to identify oneself. In recognizing others, one recognizes oneself.
>
> The process of mutual identification is very satisfying for many AA members, and this fact provides a clue as to why many members continue to relish AA stories (and collect AA speaker tapes) even years into their sobriety. AA members find a good AA speaker's performance edifying precisely because they identity with the speaker's account of his or her drinking, crisis, and recovery. That is, they experience the story they hear and the story they have or tell as both evidence for their participation in something larger than themselves.
>
> *(Swora 2004:379)*

> [F]inding meaning and coherence in one's suffering [leads to] finding oneself as a member of a moral community, as part of a larger whole.
>
> *(Swora 2004:380)*

Being an alcoholic is "who we are," and indeed, participants begin each narrative with, "My name is X, I'm an alcoholic." Every time a participant hears a 'new' personal version of their shared story, or receives an unexpected kindness extended by another member, their CS relationship intensifies and they feel kama muta.

Addiction and its attendant afflictions and transgressions are degrading; they isolate the sufferer from the family, community, and other CS groups she would otherwise belong to.

By the time alcoholics come to A.A., they usually have shame, guilt, and many regrets about past transgressions, and feel alienated from those around them. According to an A.A. member with 11 years of sobriety, the telling of the drunk-a-log is an antidote to these feelings:

To me, telling my story gave me an incredible feeling of being accepted by a group. All these awful things I had inside didn't have to be secrets any more. When the group accepted my story, all the shame I had melted away.

(50-year old woman, field conversation, 3/19/92)

The purpose of relating drunk-a-logs to potential A.A. members is to get listeners to see commonalities between their own experience and that of the speaker. This purpose of the stories of A.A. members is explicitly stated in the preface to *The Big Book*:

(Alcoholics Anonymous, 2001)

If you have a drinking problem, we hope that you may pause in reading one of the forty-four personal stories and think: 'Yes, that happened to me'; or more important 'Yes, I've felt like that'; or most important, 'Yes, I believe this program can work for me too.'

(1976:xii)

Thus, *The Big Book* (Alcoholics Anonymous, 1976) shows the reader that his or her individual life story has a place in the A.A. community's narrative on alcoholism.

(Humphrys 2000:500; references in original)

Learning to tell a 'personal' and 'sincere' redemption narrative transforms the teller from an isolated individual to a member of a community of people who have the same bodily experience of suffering. This is crucial not only in addiction-recovery groups, but in mental health support groups (Rappaport 1993). The narrative of a degraded self transformed though participation and commitment provides an essentializing identity shared with everyone else in the support-group community, in contrast with everyone else in the world. When participants telling their story see that others care and identify with their suffering, degradation, and destructive compulsion, and when participants hear the story of another's corresponding suffering, degradation, and destructive compulsion, CS often suddenly intensifies so they feel kama muta.

Participants assimilate with each other through the consubstantial essence of their distinctive and inherent bodily nature: alcoholism, drug addiction, a particular type of cancer, mastectomy, AIDS, or tuberculosis, along with addictions and afflictions that participants understand to be biological: OCD, depression, schizophrenia, bipolar disorder, and all sorts of inherited genetic disorders. A serotonin imbalance, a gene, a virus or bacillus, or a kind of cancer are corporeal substances that make a body equivalent to other bodies with the same corporeal substance. People with a given disease further assimilate to each other by virtue of the medications they ingest or inject; they have equivalent drug substances in themselves. Furthermore, people with such conditions assimilate through the consubstantiality of their distinctive pains, their symptoms, and the physical signs of the disease. All these experiences make their bodies alike. Whenever they suddenly assimilate by attending to these consubstantiations, the resultant intensification of CS tends to evoke kama muta.

A core theme of the 1999 movie *Fight Club* is what we would call the need for CS and the odd forms of consubstantial assimilation that people use to constitute CS relationships. The movie takes the consubstantial assimilation of illness-based support groups to an absurd extreme, showing two of the main characters each attending numerous support groups for different afflictions that they don't have, but pretend to. They both attend the groups because they love the compassion, belonging, hugs, and shared tears – the kama muta. But the main character (who is never given a name) is irritated that Marla is attending, too. He confronts her, telling her that she should stay away because he can't cry when she's there: she's just a tourist who is only pretending to share the defining illnesses of any of the support groups. The irony is that he can feel kama muta with the true sufferers in each group, despite not actually sharing any of their afflictions himself. He, too, has no consubstantial assimilation with the true members, but by pretending, can still enjoy kama muta with them – except when Marla is there. In a further irony reflecting the kama muta foundation of addiction recovery groups, both he and Mara are "addicted" to the recovery groups. The main character suddenly stops going to all the support groups when he discovers the even more powerful CS-creating effects of the consubstantial assimilation of shared bloodshed in the brutal fighting that constitutes the Fight Club. Marla finds CS of a sort in a passionate sexual relationship with the main character's alter ego. (*Fight Club*, directed by David Fincher, is based on the novel with the same name by Chuck Palahniuk.)

It would be interesting to know whether those who design recovery programs or run support programs either reflectively or intuitively construct these practices so as to more consistently and strongly evoke kama muta. Are they designed to evoke kama muta so as to attract participants and motivate them to support each other, and to recover? Would such programs be successful – to the extent that they are – without the human propensity to kama muta? Would they even exist at all?

Forgiveness

Denver District Judge Morris B. Hoffman of the Colorado Court writes about events in sentencing hearings that he believes are kama muta experiences for convicted criminals and others in the courtroom:

> The most moving courtroom experiences I've ever had have come during sentencing hearings in homicide cases, when family members of murder

victims told their loved ones' killers that they forgave them. ... Of the roughly three dozen homicide cases I've presided over, I can remember four where at least one member of the victim's family expressed forgiveness. Nothing victims say at a sentencing hearing has more impact, not just on the audience, the lawyers, and the judges, but especially on the defendants. It can be shocking to watch a murderer sit emotionless as his victim's survivors try to express their profound loss. But on those occasions when a survivor said, 'I forgive you,' in all four cases the murderer broke down and wept.

(Hoffman 2014:188)

When Judge Hoffman recounted this to me, we both felt kama muta.

After trials conclude, Judge Hoffman meets with juries to debrief them. When the jury has convicted a defendant of a serious crime, there are nearly always some jurors who cry during this debriefing. Apparently they feel compassionate kama muta for the suffering that they have had to impose on the defendant by sentencing him to a long prison term. At least, that's Judge Hoffman's interpretation. He e-mailed a listserv of fellow judges in several US and other common law jurisdictions, asking what reactions they had observed. Several other judges reported instances of defendants breaking down in tears when forgiven by their victim's survivors, or when the survivors asked for leniency in sentencing, though not every defendant did so (M. Hoffman, oral communication, 2 April 2015, and personal communications, 6 April 2015 and 5 June 2015). In England from around 1750 to 1850, it was not uncommon for judges to cry in sympathy with a defendant when they condemned him to death (Dixon 2015:174–178). Konečni (2005) posits that forgiveness, selfless sacrifices, and generosity all make people feel *moved*. Certainly experiences of reconciliation are not limited to courtrooms; for an example, see Online Note 5.2 for a true story about an encounter at the Los Angeles Museum of Tolerance.

* * * * *

So far, kama muta experiences appear to be prevalent and deep when seeing the first ultrasound image of one's baby, when the baby is born, when one sees cute infant humans or other animals, in Greek recognition reunions, in cry dates, addiction recovery groups, volunteer services to the needy, and when families forgive the murderers of their loved ones. The plots of the most culturally salient and widespread types of narrative are evidently precisely crafted to evoke kama muta in the characters and the audience. The variety of these events, which have little in common other than the sudden intensification of a communal sharing relationship, supports our contention that it is, indeed, sudden intensification of a CS relationship that evokes kama muta. However, we soon noticed that people are also moved by heroism. And will discuss below that fact that modern Olympic winners, Academy Award winners, and other victors sometimes cry on the podium. Why? If kama muta is generated by sudden intensification of CS, why does heroism evoke kama muta? If weeping at happy events is a sign of kama muta, why are winners weeping – what CS relationship has suddenly intensified? Up to this point, we've been asking whether sudden intensification of CS is sufficient to evoke kama muta; so far, the answer seems to be, 'yes, it is sufficient.' But is sudden CS intensification *necessary* to kama muta? Early in our research on kama muta we wondered whether winners weeping and people being moved by heroism were exceptions (or worse, contradictions) to our theory. If we see kama muta, can we infer that a CS relationship has intensified?

Sports and war

> There is no paucity of religious metaphor invoked to offer commentary on the social context and psychological impact of football. It is also well accepted that football can stimulate a range of emotional reactions from goose bumps to tears or rapture.
>
> *(Smith 2006)*

Many basketball fans were affected and still remember 12 April 2013, when Kobe Bryant tore his Achilles tendon but, despite the excruciating pain, stayed in the game to shoot two free throws, and sink them both. Baseball fans remember when Kurt Gibson, despite injuries to both legs so bad he could hardly hobble to the plate, went to bat in the bottom of the ninth inning in the 1988 World Series – and hit a walk-off home run. In 2004, Curt Schilling pitched and won two post-season games with ankle injuries so bad that his sock was drenched in blood. Ice hockey fans remember center Gregory Campbell in a 2013 playoff game, who slid to block a slap shot with his leg; the shot broke his fibula, but he continued on the ice for 40 seconds, successfully defending against a power play.[1] These are extreme examples at the top levels of professional sports, but in every ice hockey, rugby, and American football game, and often in basketball, baseball, and other sports, many players take excruciating hits for the team. Fans and teammates sometimes seem to feel kama muta when this happens, and when they remember and tell about it later. Indeed, it appears that the kama muta evoked when a player *takes one for the team* is a significant attraction of such sports for fans, and for players themselves. Systematic study of emotions evoked by 'taking one for the team' would be fruitful. What role do such kama muta experiences play in motivating athletes to play team sports, and fans to watch? Does it enhance fans' or players' identification with the team?

Emerging from innumerable hours of grueling practice together, moments of exquisitely perfect team coordination can evoke kama muta.

Sports that require training, some degree of hardship and joint endurance, as well as coordination among team members, seem propitious for a feeling of *kama muta*. For many years during my childhood and adolescence, I played Handball in a team in Germany (I encourage non-European readers to watch some Handball game excerpts online). We would meet at least twice a week for training, and have at least one match against another team on the weekend. The highlights of these matches were – at least for me – the moments when we performed strategic moves that required multiple players to act in unison or fulfill a carefully rehearsed series of consecutive moves, thereby outwitting our adversaries. Even for people sitting on the sidelines or in the audience, seeing such a coordinated enactment succeed would almost inevitably prompt them to break out in cheers and exclaim how "beautiful" this series of moves was.

(Jana Gallus)

Some of the most memorable heroic kama muta-evoking acts are those of men who courageously face great risks together or sacrifice themselves together for their community. In the Battle of Thermopylae, the Greek force under Spartan King Leonidas stayed to fight and delay the enormous Persian invasion force, thereby saving the body of the Greek army and protecting their homeland, despite the certainty they would all die doing so. Even 2500 years later, imagining this may evoke a twinge of kama muta. The most kama muta-evoking fictional case is Shakespeare's *Henry V*: Facing battle against a superior force, King Henry tells his fearful men that they should be proud to fight this battle together, and will be forever united by the experience. Anyone lacking the courage should simply depart now, but "He today that sheds his blood with me shall be my brother" (quoted in full in Online Note 5.3).

In any case, *accounts* of heroic courage tend to evoke kama muta in listeners, renewing listeners' commitment to the group for which the heroes have risked or sacrificed themselves. Heroic acts typically become prototypes for successors of the heroes – prototypes which leaders promote with medals, monuments, and speeches whose purpose is to commemorate the heroism, indefinitely re-evoking kama muta and the patriotism it rekindles (see Claparède 1930). That in turn may unite people behind the leaders who evoke the kama muta experience with the monuments they erect, the memorial rituals they perform, and their speeches (which I discuss in the next chapter).

Presumably heroic acts also evoke a second emotion in many observers: *awe*. Making sacrifices for the common good intensifies communal sharing. When an athlete 'takes one for the team' or plays on despite a painful injury, she invigorates the bond with her teammates and between team and fans. When a warrior 'has the back' of his comrades, taking great risks or willingly dying to protect them, he vitalizes the CS that binds them to each other – and to the corps and nation he fights for. This evokes kama muta. And when people learn of such heroic acts they often feel kama muta, too. Media, leaders, and politicians may mobilize this kama muta to attract an audience; evoke loyalty, nationalism, or patriotic dedication; and enhance their AR prestige. Political or religious leaders also present instances of exemplary self-sacrifice or dedication to evoke kama muta in order to morally educate and motivate their followers.

There is another kind of consubstantial assimilation that sometimes operates among soldiers, sailors, and airmen. Very strong CS relationships can form when people work hard together, but especially when they move in rhythmic synchrony, over and over (Fiske 2004b; Cohen, Mundry, & Kirschner 2013; Brown 2013). Military drill, rowing, synchronized workouts, and dancing can do that. McNeil (1995) describes vivid memories of the sense of oneness he felt sometimes on the drill field when the whole unit moved as one person. McNeil shows that what we recognize as the CS relationship created by synchronous rhythmic movement can transform a set of conscripts who are total strangers into a unified *body* that is a true *unit*. Military drill creates the loyalty to each other that motivates a group of men to 'have each other's back,' no matter what the cost. No doubt there are gradual, cumulative effects of long hours of synchronous movement, and it requires a great many hours of practice together, individual talent, and even a certain collective gift to enable a body of humans to 'sync' so they become one. Even with aid of music, moving in perfect synchrony is a skill that is slowly perfected, and not everyone is capable of. But when a group moves in sync they can experience kama muta.

> Joe Rantz lay dying. ... I knew that he had been one of nine young men from the state of Washington—farm boys, fishermen, and loggers—who shocked both the rowing world and Adolf Hitler by winning the gold medal in eight-oared rowing at the 1936 Olympics. ... His voice was reedy, fragile, and attenuated almost to the breaking point. ...
>
> But it wasn't until he began to talk about his rowing career at the University of Washington that he started, from time to time, to cry. He talked about learning the art of rowing, about shells and oars, about tactics and technique. ... It was when he tried to talk about 'the boat' that his words began to falter and tears welled up in his bright eyes. ...
>
> Finally, watching Joe struggle for composure over and over, I realized that 'the boat' was something more than just the shell or its crew. To Joe, it encompassed but transcended both—it was something mysterious and almost beyond definition. It was a shared experience—a singular thing that had unfolded in a golden sliver of time long gone, when nine goodhearted young men strove together, pulled together as one, gave everything they had for one another, bound together forever by pride and respect and love. Joe was crying, at least in part, for the loss of that vanished moment but much more, I think, for the sheer beauty of it.
>
> *(Brown 2013:13)*

More than 70 years after the rapturous experience of rowing on that crew, Joe Rantz was nostalgically re-experiencing kama muta, the emotion he had felt at the moment when the crew rowed in perfect unison as one man. And what they again felt together when they stood at the podium in 1936 in the Berlin Olympic Stadium, received their gold medals, and listened to the Star-Spangled Banner:

> As Joe watched the flag rise with his hand over his heart, he was surprised to find that tears had crept into the corners of his eyes. On the podium Moch [the coxswain] choked up too. So did Stub McMillin. By the time is was over, they were all fighting back tears.
>
> *(Brown 2013:354–355, based on a contemporary undated clipping of a story by Gail Wood in the* Daily Olympian *[a Washington state newspaper]; see Brown's note on 2013:391)*

Weeping winners and their weeping fans

A UCLA gymnast performed an amazing dismount that no one had ever done before; her teammates mobbed her, hugging and telling her how wonderful she was. They all felt so close and you could see how they totally supported each other. She was moved, her teammates were moved, all the fans were moved.

(UCLA undergraduate)

When athletes, singers, actors, and other media figures win, they often weep – at the moment of their victory or, especially in international games, on the winners' podium while their national anthem plays. Weeping and even being choked up when receiving Oscars, Emmys, and certain other awards is culturally meaningful: it is interpreted as indicating at the same time being *overwhelmed* by the honor, and showing that the person is a *sensitive, feeling, human* person *in touch with their feelings.* The prototype and precedents of winning and weeping incorporate hands to the chest, and hugging teammates, supporters, or family. Apparently weeping winners are experiencing kama muta. But why? Early in our research on kama muta, when we first thought about winner weeping, we were perplexed, and a bit uneasy. Was winner weeping an exception or even disproof of the communal sharing-intensification theory of kama muta, we worried? On the face of it, the winner of a major victory in sports or entertainment should simply be feeling pride at their supremacy. We assumed, that is, that winners might be feeling an emotion of sudden intensification of an authority ranking relationship in which their victory make them superior. (On authority ranking, another of the four fundamental relational models, see Fiske 1991, 1992, 2004a.) That's what we assumed, none of us having won an Olympic event, an Oscar, or anything remotely like it. So we read every interview with a weeping winner we could find, and then went to the World Cup Ski Championships in Oslo to listen to and interview the winners, as well as second- and third-place finishers.

What we found showed us how little we understood the feeling of victory at the top levels of competition! It turns out that some winners, together with their families, supporters, fans and compatriots, feel strongly that they have won 'for' their CS groups, such that the victory abruptly affords intensified identification. The winning individual or team wins on behalf of those who have been devoted to them. Victor and close supporter feel that the victory validates their mutual 'belief in each other' – their steadfast patience and faithful commitment to the sacrifices, dedication, and arduous training required. A team that wins together feels especially bonded, as is often evident in their hugs or piling onto each other. But in a sense any serious athlete is the embodiment of a dedicated team, as any performer is the figurehead of a collective effort. It is typical for victors to say just this in their 'thank you' speeches and interviews. And this may not be just pro forma courtesy. When the winner deeply appreciates that their victory was made possible by their supporters, and when the victory is a victory <u>for</u> their supporters, celebrated <u>with</u> their supporters, they feel kama muta. Many media photographs show winners weeping in kama muta.

Weeping winners consistently refer to the obstacles and hardships they overcame, the doubts, and, above all, the support and faith of their family and supporters. For example, in the 2008 Beijing Olympics, the grandmother of Dominican Republican Felix Sanchez's died the morning of his race. "I ran but I ran badly and I made a promise that day that I would win a medal for her. It took me four years" (Preece 2012). In the London 2012 Olympics he indeed won the 400 meter hurdles and wept on the podium.

> No one thought I had a chance to get on the Podium, let alone win it. ... I was focusing on, almost, redemption, and accomplishing it all for my grandmother. ... [Stepping up to the winner's podium at the awards ceremony] is the toughest moment because this is when it all settles in {tearing up during interview}. ... I was just thinking about grandmother and it was almost like she was, she was happy – and crying tears of joy. It made it tough to hold back my tears.
>
> *(Preece 2012)*

At the same 2012 London Olympics, cyclist Chris Hoy of Great Britain also cried on the winner's podium.

> It's quite overwhelming. We knew it was possible, but it doesn't come out of the blue. It was an immensely proud moment to do it in front of a home crowd. It's a once in a lifetime opportunity. We enjoyed it and we gave it our all. I dug deeper than ever before, I didn't want to let the boys down.
>
> *(Slater 2012)*

In modern sports kama muta is a common response to victory by an individual or a team; see Online Note 5.4.

In an online discussion with some native speakers of Malay about the word *terharu*, which nicely translates kama muta, one informant wrote:

> I think 'terharu' is most commonly used, like Juan said, when someone does something nice to you when you least expected it (e.g. a surprise birthday party). However, I think something like what happened in the Olympics yesterday also made people 'terharu.' Our country has always won a medal in the badminton, but we lost in the London Olympics 4 years ago. Yesterday was Indonesia's Independence Day (Aug 17th); and for Indonesia to have won our first gold medal this year during our Independence Day brought tears and joy to a lot of people back home. As the players themselves have said, that gold was a gift to our country. My family and I (at the least) felt very 'terharu' when we heard their words and I'm sure a lot of people was too. So in some ways, 'terharu' usually arises from any bittersweet moment. It can be (and is often) a private and personal thing, but it can also be a shared experience depending on the context.
>
> *(Gabriella Aliifa Thohir; for more on the Malay lexeme*
> terharu, *see Chapter 7)*

In the Olympics, the first winner weeping seems to have occurred in 1956 and 1964, when swimmers wept; by 1996, Olympic winners on the podium wept in droves (Dixon 2015:305). In Great Britain, land of the stiff upper lip, winning athletes crying apparently began around 1968, when team Captain Bobby Charlton, having scored two goals, led Manchester United to victory in the European Cup, and wept; they were the first British team ever to win (Dixon 2015:265ff.). In 1973, when the underdog rugby team Sunderland AFC won a semi-final match against Arsenal, the winning players wept and hugged each other, as did their fans. Scotsman Andy Murray reached the Wimbledon finals in 2012 – the first British player to do so in 74 years; after he lost the final, while thanking his fans he wept so much that he repeatedly couldn't speak; his fans cheered him and his weeping, while British newspapers declared that his show of feeling had won the nation's heart (Dixon 2015:307.) (That same year, Conservative politician Boris Johnson declared that he cried with patriotism at the opening of the London Olympics (Dixon 2015:306–307); see also Claparède 1930). The first Academy Award winner to cry was none other than John Wayne, in 1970, followed by Gene Hackman in 1971; in 1979, Jon Voight cried when he won (Dixon 2015:268). By the 1990s, weeping was the de rigueur demonstration of humble gratitude for the victory and appreciation for team, supporters, and nation. The prototype of the weeping-winner was firmly established as a precedent for winning comportment.

In sum, it is clear that athletes, actors, and singers feel kama muta when they have the sense that a victory or scoring a goal makes them one with their teammates, coaches, parents, supporters, university, or nation. The winner may feel that she could not have won without the support of these CS groups, so that the victory is not individual, but rather 'our' collective victory. When a <u>team</u> wins, this is literally true, intensifying their feeling of unity. All this ignites kama muta. In many respects, weeping winners in sports and entertainment are playing out Hogan's (2003) *heroic* narrative prototype and Booker's (2004) *overcoming the monster* plot that I discussed in Chapter 3. Indeed, is it going too far to suppose that the institutions of Emmy, Oscar, and Grammy awards, together with sports tournaments and the Olympics, are to some degree more or less intentionally constituted <u>so as to evoke kama muta</u> in winners and audiences? Certainly tearful, choked-up gratitude for supporters and collaborators has become the paradigm performance for award winners. Winners are supposed to show that they *feel the love* of their fans.

In each event, most competitors lose – losing is the ground against which the foregrounded figure of winning stands out. To lose is to fail one's supporters and hence feel unacceptable – the loser wants to avoid his CS partners and group, who for their part feel uncomfortable in his presence. In contrast, the winner is suddenly appreciated, affirmed, acknowledged, approved, recognized, and validated. When he wins, all existing CS relationships are instantly intensified, myriad new CS relationships appear, and potential CS relationships are everywhere. When a victor wins against great odds, overcoming obstacles with determination, defying setbacks, coming from behind, enduring pain and making great sacrifices, everyone identifies with the hero. People applaud him. Everyone wants to affiliate with a winner – he is welcome everywhere. Everyone is eager to be his friend – all doors are open to him. The winner is always included. Furthermore, the winner is not just popular, but attractive and sexually desirable. Everyone recognizes him, wants to shake his hand, hug him, buy him a drink – or sleep with him. Fans and admirers imitate the winner of major competitions, for example by wearing jerseys in his team color, with his number and name. People scramble for everything he has touched, treasuring and collecting his memorabilia. The sudden intensification of CS is a temporal dynamic: the CS relationship rapidly emerges or grows. But the intensification also consists of a <u>contrast</u> effect where the wonderful performance is the figure against a ground of expected, ordinary, commonplace, banal, or flubbed performances. A poor or muffed performance is embarrassing – the performer feels shame, the sense of being unacceptable, unfit to belong. An outstanding performance rises out of this jeopardy. If winning were not difficult, problematic, or uncertain, it would evoke less kama muta.

Short of final victory, other accomplishments may evoke kama muta. When a player scores a goal, hits a home run, makes a tough or crucial basketball shot – or makes a difficult block, save, or defensive play – teammates often slap the player's hand or hug him. Such acts of consubstantial assimilation enact the sudden intensification of CS that results from the outstanding play. At the moment of an important or spectacular team victory, players may join in a collective huddle-hug or pile up on top of each other in a heap. In short, the dynamic social psychology of winner weeping precisely fits our theory. Rather than being an exception, as we first feared, winner weeping provides further support for the theory, showing that kama muta is prominent in yet another context.

Winner weeping also perfectly illustrates our contention that cultures provide institutions and practices to evoke kama muta. Sports and playoffs and championships, film and Oscars, television and Emmys, music and Grammys are all culturally constructed. They were created during a particular era in particular cultures. The victor weeping when he wins for his US college or high school team is feeling the sudden intensification of a CS that doesn't exist in Europe or other regions that don't have university- or school-based teams at all. Many traditional cultures did not have competitive sports, nor entertainment awards. Evoking kama muta is not the predominant function of sports, but it is one of its functions. Evidently, some of the practices and artifacts of award ceremonies in fact historically evolved partly because they evoked kama muta experiences. The national anthems and flags that precipitate Olympic winner weeping were invented in modern European cultures, as were nations themselves.

There are also varying cultural precedents and prototypes for winner weeping in different sports. For example, among team sports, it appears to be much more common in soccer than in basketball, baseball, or American football (though there may be locker room crying in these sports). Norwegians think of themselves as reticent about expressing emotions, but their reserve breaks down when they win gold medals in skiing – especially when they beat Sweden. Winners apparently are more likely to cry in front of home crowds than when they win in other countries.[2] It appears that winners' weeping at the presentation of awards is a relatively recent historical development (Dixon 2015). It would be interesting to study the development of winner weeping as children participate in different sports, in different competitive practices, and in different cultures. How do children observe and imitate cultural precedents and prototypes for winner weeping, and how do their observations shape their subjective experience of winning? In any case, people often perceive tears to be signs of devotion; in Chapter 15 we will consider how early and Medieval Christians perceived tears as gifts from God and signs of genuine loving worship of him. In eighteenth and nineteenth century Europe, secular tears were socially salient signs of cultural sophistication, love, friendship, political allegiance, and patriotism (see again Online Note 2.5).

One might fruitfully explore the extent to which kama muta motivates participation in sports, and sports fandom. In what manner do kama muta experiences attract participants and shape their participation? It seem that players and fans are significantly sustained by the moments of kama muta evoked by the joyful unity of 'we scored!' and 'we won!!'

* * * * *

Here and in all of the situations I discuss in this book, kama muta does not always appear as a pure, unadulterated Platonic type. In any given event people may feel kama muta simultaneously with other emotions, and may experience a series of emotions one after the other. Often, we assume, the winner of a major victory feels the intensification of authority ranking as *pride*, while her audience feels *awe* looking up to her. But often winners and fans also weep with kama muta because the victory makes them suddenly feel the oneness of communal sharing.

The kama muta of achievement is by no means limited to sports and performing arts awards. Observing an icon's accession to the top of the realm caused viewers to weep in 1952 – the 26-year old Queen Elizabeth II's coronation.

> Something extraordinary, which may perhaps even have been unique, happened in England … The people involved themselves. Through their television sets they found means, on that day, to participate in the service, and commonly, very commonly I am told, those who were watching were moved to tears … We were all one.
>
> *(Christopher Salmon 1953. The Trumpets Have Sounded.*
> The Listener *11, quoted in Webster 2005:97)*

Exemplary, extremely difficult or dangerous achievements may also generate kama muta. For example, when someone is the first to climb a mountain or fly across an ocean, or achieves an exceptional theatrical or musical performance, the quickening of attraction and identification among supporters or audience may evoke kama muta in them. The moment when people saw Neil Armstrong walk on the moon, he made American identity exceptionally salient and significant, and made Americans proud to be Americans. The moon landing felt like 'our' unique, historic achievement – and indeed that was the political aim of the program to land men on the moon. Because it was "seen live, unedited, and everywhere, it became a genuine experience of global intimacy" (Rothman 2014) so that the moon landings and safe returns drew humankind together. They were not just American achievements, they were <u>human</u> achievements. Furthermore, through their camera we saw the globe of the earth as the astronauts saw it and we realized that this delicate planet is the home we all share, and must nurture together.

Online notes

5.1   A psychotherapist's kama muta.
5.2   Kama muta at the Los Angeles Museum of Tolerance.
5.3   He today that sheds his blood with me shall be my brother.
5.4   Kama muta in victory.

Notes

1   I owe these insights to Kai W. Fiske.
2   *Wall Street Journal* http://www.wsj.com/articles/SB100008723963904436592045775 75401395853744.

6

STRATEGIC EVOCATION OF KAMA MUTA

In the first five chapters, I've treated kama muta experiences as something that more or less just happens to people. People are particularly likely to experience strong kama muta when they engage in practices that have culturally evolved to evoke kama muta, and indeed people are drawn to participate in such practices because they seek the kama muta experience. (We'll explore these processes in depth in Chapters 10 and 17.) In Chapter 3 we considered the possibility that story-tellers and writers might (reflectively or intuitively) craft their narratives to evoke kama muta, thereby making their stories more appealing. We were thinking about kama muta in this almost esthetic framework that is one of the joys that makes life meaningful. But then I came across elaborate staging and publicity by a Chinese state-owned television station who presents "Moving China" awards for self-sacrificing compassionate action. This program of awards was moral education propaganda. Then I noticed a series of MyCall posters on the Oslo buses and trolleys depicting cute children and grandmothers, asking (in different languages on different posters) "Is there someone you should call?" The posters were ads for mobile phone service. We found the posters *touching*, and in the *warm glow* we felt, one of us bought a MyCall SIM card. Later I listened to Michelle Obama, Bill Clinton, and Barack Obama's speeches at the Democratic National Convention. I felt kama muta, as I was supposed to. I was *moved* (at least for a little while) to get more involved, to work to elect Hillary Clinton. In an experiment just before the 2016 elections, we found that commercials for the candidates evoked kama muta, and the more kama muta viewers felt, the more support they expressed for the candidate (Seibt et al. 2018).

And so we realized that there is another aspect of kama muta. People sometimes have instrumental motives for evoking kama muta experiences in others. Evoking kama muta can be a tool that people more or less self-consciously use for political, commercial, or interpersonal purposes. People may respond as intended.

Or if it is done too obviously or clumsily, the audience may feel manipulated. People who recognize ulterior motives – especially motives they judge to be illegitimate – may resent attempts to make them feel kama muta and resist feeling it. An audience also may resent and resist being manipulated because they just don't like others *playing with their emotions*, or because the audience regards the devices employed – such as the plot line or the dialog – as trite, or regard responding to be beneath their dignity. So there are risks in using kama muta instrumentally. Nevertheless, much oratory, propaganda, and marketing aims to evoke kama muta in order to move the audience to do what the promulgator wishes. And it may work.

Oratory

In 1783, after fighting ceased at the end of the American Revolutionary War, General George Washington and his troops waited in Newburgh, New York, for the peace negotiations in Paris – and waited to be paid. The troops had not been paid for a long time and they expected to be demobilized and sent home without their pay. They deeply mistrusted the Congress's promise of a pension. Indeed, as they knew, the Confederation Congress had hardly any money, and no authority to collect revenue. There was serious prospect of a mutiny, even a march on the Congress in Philadelphia and a coup. An anonymous letter about the army's grievances circulated among the officers, calling for a meeting to decide upon action. When he saw the letter Washington ordered his officers to postpone the meeting for three days, and when they met after this delay, he unexpectedly walked in on them and delivered a short address. He sympathized with their grievances but rejected the proposal for a military solution that the writer of the anonymous letter advocated. Here's what Washington said to his restive officers.

> The way is plain, says the anonymous addresser. 'If war continues, remove into the unsettled country; there establish yourselves and leave an ungrateful country to defend itself.'—But who are they to defend? Our wives, our children, our farms and other property which we leave behind us? or, in this state of hostile separation, are we to take the two first (the latter cannot be removed) to perish in a wilderness with hunger, cold and nakedness? .... by the dignity of your conduct, afford occasion for posterity to say, when speaking of the glorious example you have exhibited to mankind—'had this day been wanting, the world had never seen the last stage of perfection to which human nature is capable of attaining.'
>
> *(Wikisource, Newburgh Address)*[1]

Washington's appeal to the patriotism, honor, and concern for the soldiers' families apparently had his audience wavering, but not definitely persuaded. So he pulled out a letter to read from a congressional representative that explained the Congress's good intentions and the problems it faced in fulfilling their obligations to the army. But Washington had difficulty reading it. He took out his glasses, which few of the officers knew he needed, saying, "Gentlemen, you will permit me to put on my spectacles, for I have not only grown gray but almost blind in the service of my country." This display of vulnerability, with its reminder of the sacrifices he had made alongside his men, evoked kama muta in almost all, and Major Samuel Shaw reported that "There was something so natural, so unaffected, in this appeal, as rendered it superior to the most studied oratory; it forced its way to the heart, and you might see sensibility moisten every eye" (Shaw 1847:104) After reading the letter, Washington left the meeting. The officers decided to wait and trust in Congress. By evoking kama muta in his officers, Washington quelled a mutiny and preserved a fledgling nation.

Leaders often want to mobilize their followers to make great efforts for a cause such as a political campaign, a social movement, or a war – led by the mobilizer himself. Evoking kama muta is an effective way for leaders to do this, motivating potential and current followers to commit or rededicate themselves, while strengthening the perception of the leader as a core member, primus inter pares. Giving a speech that evokes kama muta rallies the listeners, while thereby simultaneously reinforcing the authority relationship between speaker and audience – because loyalty to the speaker feels like a natural expression and display of the loyalty to the group that the kama muta promotes. Memorialization of the sacrifices, suffering, and bravery of those who gave their lives for the motherland is a prototypical oratorical means to do this. Readers are expected to feel kama muta when hearing or reading Alfred Lord Tennyson's famous 1854 "The Charge of the Light Brigade," a stirring, often quoted poem about the dutiful courage of a cavalry brigade that was wiped out in the Battle of Balaclava during the Crimean War.

Abraham Lincoln, Winston Churchill, Franklin Delano Roosevelt, John F. Kennedy, and Martin Luther King Jr.'s speeches drew on the kama muta sentiment evoked by sacrifice for the community, calling forth kama muta in listeners in order to motivate them to rededicate themselves to collective effort, suffering, and potential sacrifice. Adolf Hitler's oratory did this very effectively. Online Note 6.1 analyzes other political oratory evoking kama muta.

When great orators speak, audiences applaud and cheer; these responses sometimes seem to index kama muta; see Online Note 6.2 for a review of research on this. Researchers have identified the rhetorical devices that seem to be especially effective for evoking kama muta; see Online Note 6.3.

On rare occasions, especially in a crisis when people seek unity in a common cause, a great charismatic speaker can evoke significant kama muta with substantial social effect. Jesse Jackson's speech at the 1988 Democratic National Convention had that impact:

> As he has stirred voters all across America this year, the Rev. Jesse Jackson moved friend and former foe alike tonight with his revival-style speech to the Democratic National Convention. ... By the time he was finished there were tears and cheers of passion flowing through the hall of a sort

that Michael S. Dukakis simply does not spark. 'I can hardly speak' … a white delegate from Mississippi said, choking back tears, his face red with emotion. He threw himself into the arms of a black Mississippi delegate.

(New York Times *1988, cited in Shamir, Arthur, &* House *1994:30; ellipses in Shamir et al.)*

The *Boston Globe* for 21 July 1988 also reported that "several of those watching had tears in their eyes," and the Washington Post referred to "reaction shots on all three networks of teary–eyed onlookers" (quoted in Shamir, Arthur, & House 1994:31). How did Jackson evoke such powerful kama muta experiences in his audience? Jackson repeatedly referred to past Democratic presidents who "brought us together" and "unified us," and spoke of "common ground" 14 times (Shamir, Arthur, & House 1994:32–33). In his speech, Jackson uses the word "together" 14 times, "America(n)" 23 times, "common" 30 times, "our" 41 times, "we" 113 times (American Rhetoric 2019).

Perhaps the most kama muta-invoking speech in English is Martin Luther King Jr.'s "I have a dream" address from the steps of the Lincoln Memorial during the 1963 March on Washington. The speech concluded with these famous passages:

I have a dream that one day on the red hills of Georgia, the sons of former slaves and the sons of former slave owners will be able to sit down together at the table of brotherhood. …

With this faith, we will be able to transform the jangling discords of our nation into a beautiful symphony of brotherhood. With this faith, we will be able to work together, to pray together, to struggle together, to go to jail together, to stand up for freedom together, knowing that we will be free one day. …

And when this happens, and when we allow freedom to ring, when we let it ring from every village and every hamlet, from every state and every city, we will be able to speed up that day when *all* of God's children, black men and white men, Jews and Gentiles, Protestants and Catholics, will be able to join hands and sing in the words of the old Negro spiritual:

Free at last! Free at last!

Thank God Almighty, we are free at last![2]

(American Rhetoric.com)

Without Martin Luther King, Jr., and Jesse Jackson's gift for evoking kama muta, would the civil rights workers' dedication been sustained, would the American public been moved to insist on civil rights, and would the movement have transcended the great hurdles it faced? Certainly their oratory, along with the hymns of the movement, persuaded many an American to feel, "Oh, deep in my heart, I do believe, We shall overcome someday."

Pushed by the popular response to King, President Lyndon Johnson's 1965 address to a joint session of Congress on voting rights legislation focused in large part on equality matching, while also invoking the authority of the presidency and the will of God. But these were steps in his argument that the nation must be inclusive, respecting the basic rights of all. With passing allusions to market pricing, Johnson builds from equality matching through authority ranking to communal sharing, evoking kama muta that contributed to the political pressure that enabled the voting rights act to pass. Online Note 6.4 quotes the major kama muta passages from the speech.

I have focused on the verbal aspects of oratory, but that's not all there is to charismatic invocation of kama muta. The impact of a speech depends on much more than rhetoric or semantics. The social emotional effects of a speech depend on the biography, role, personality, age, ethnicity, appearance, postures, and gestures of the speaker; on the qualities of the speaker's voice; on costume, architecture, acoustics, cinematic technique, and technology of communication; and certainly on the cultural situation and historical moment. There is also the stagecraft: audiences may feel a little kama muta when family members demonstrate their affection and dedication by introducing the politician, or by hugging, kissing, or holding hands with them. Cute children help. Similarly, politicians sell themselves by kissing babies, by visiting the ill, the wounded, and victims of disaster, or by attending funerals and memorial events. These heartwarming displays make the politician 'genuine' and loveable. It would be fruitful to investigate the efficacy of such techniques to evoke kama muta, as a function of the culture, audience, situations, and relational history of the participants.

Do politicians and other speakers have the explicit aim of evoking kama muta, and are they reflectively aware of the techniques that they use to do so? To some extent, in certain respects, yes. Hitler (1939:715–716) articulated part of the mechanism, and many politicians, preachers, or other leaders have more or less clearly articulated recipes for stirring rhetoric. In media, speechwriters, journalists, and commentators reflect on what makes a rousing speech. Furthermore, in contemporary Western culture there are professional 'inspirational speakers' whose occupation consists of giving speeches that evoke kama muta. They must have ideas about how they do it, whether those ideas are entirely correct or not. It would be interesting to systematically study the explicit theories of cultural specialists in rhetoric, and compare their theories and evidence with ours. Equally interesting would be to explore the cognitive and social processes through which rhetorical specialists discover, develop, change, and transmit implicit procedural competence in verbally evoking kama muta.

In any case, as we consider these speeches, we see something more than leaders making audiences feel kama muta. Kama muta makes leaders. The orator becomes primus inter pares precisely when and because he evokes deep kama muta among his followers. Furthermore, stirring speeches contribute to the creation of imagined communities such as ethnic groups, races, gender identities, occupation and interest groups, political parties, cities, states, and nations.

Anderson (2006) argued that nations consist of communities that are constituted in the minds of those who identify with them. Modern societies, particularly, are comprised of 'groups' of persons who never materially encounter and are not even personally cognizant of most of the other individuals in them. But all communities are the products of 'imagined' identification, that is, mental representations of CS – and not dispassionate representations, but emotionally felt, morally motivated commitments to them. Anderson poses the question of why people kill and die for their nations, pointing to the importance of printed books and newspapers sold to consumers whose reading gives them a sense of belonging to discrete nations with mapped boundaries and enumerated populations. But this literacy-mediation theory is insufficient and incomplete. It is incomplete because it doesn't tell us why reading creates social bonds. When the readers experience shared kama muta moments, this links them in CS relations – especially when the suddenly intensifying CS consists of patriotic pride and identification. Texts create imagined communities specifically when reading those texts intensifies CS with those communities and hence evokes the devotion and commitment arising in kama muta. But imagined communities are not based on texts alone: they are created, sustained, and enhanced by all sorts of kama muta-inducing speech and ceremonies. Nations and other social groups depend significantly on political oratory that evokes shared mental representations of them, along with narratives of crucial past and necessary future suffering for them. Charismatic oratory elicits emotional *motivation* to loyally support and sacrifice for the nation, for a cause, and certainly for new revolutionary communities. When orators suddenly create, enhance, or restore CS solidarity, they are creating an identity, a belief in an imagined community. Communities exist just to the extent that people imagine them – and devote themselves to the whole that they imagine themselves to belong. To a significant degree, nations, political parties, social movements, races, and revolutions are made of kama muta.

This is visible in the creation of new nations. Kwame Nkrumah led the Gold Coast Colony to independence as the new nation, Ghana, in 1957. At that point, most of the rest of Sub-Saharan Africa still consisted of colonies under European rule. On the eve of Ghana's independence, after a speech by Nkrumah, everyone walked out of the parliament building just before midnight to observe the moment of transition. A month later, back in his Montgomery, Alabama church, Martin Luther King Jr. preached about the obstacles that had faced the Ghanaians in their struggle for independence, and how they had worked together to overcome those obstacles. Then he recalled the moment:

> As we walked out, we noticed all over the polo grounds almost half a million people. They had waited for this hour and this moment for years.
>
> As we walked out of the door and looked at that beautiful building, we looked up to the top of it. And there was the Union Jack flag of the Gold Coast, the British flag, you see. But at twelve o'clock that night we saw a little flag coming down and another flag went up. The old Union Jack flag

came down and the new flag of Ghana went up. This was a new nation now, a new nation being born. And when Prime Minister Nkrumah stood up before his people out in the polo ground and said, 'We are no longer a British colony, we are a free sovereign people,' all over that vast throng of people we could see tears. And I stood there thinking about so many things. Before I knew it, I started weeping. I was crying for joy. And I knew about all of the struggles, and all of the pain, and all of the agony that these people had gone through for this moment.[3]

(King 2007:159–160)

In contemporary political campaigns, television commercials probably are more important than oratory. Political ads often use devices that may evoke kama muta in viewers. In the 1996 and 1999 Israeli elections, the great majority of ads employed intimacy themes: words of intimacy, intimate situations, families of politicians, nonverbal expressions, and children (Marmor-Lavie & Weimann 2008). Religious parties and left-wing parties used these intimacy devices more frequently than other parties. Two studies that we did just before the 2016 presidential election experimentally demonstrate the political impact of kama muta (Seibt, Schubert, Zickfeld, & Fiske 2018). We picked television commercials that news reports and social media comments characterized as *heartwarming* and *inspiring*. Online participants rated the ads as *moving*, *touching*, and *heart-warming*; appraised the ads as increasing the communal sharing among the characters in the commercial; reported sensations of tears, goosebumps, and warmth in the center of the chest; and reported stronger intentions to vote for the candidate. The effect of the ads on intention to vote for the candidate was partially mediated by the labels and sensations. What is perhaps surprising a week before the election is that kama muta evoked by the ads even moved voters in the direction of intending to vote for the candidate that they did not initially indicate supporting.

The Moving China Award

The political uses of kama muta-evoking narratives extend beyond efforts to attract voters or mobilize political movements and nationalism. By presenting exemplary prototypes of dedication or self-sacrifice, leaders and media may evoke kama muta in order to change attitudes, enhance nationalistic pride, or revitalize commitment to a social movement or institution. Representations of martyrs and saints move revolutionaries and worshippers to renew their commitments. This is pervasive in religious education and preaching, as well as propaganda. Furthermore, invoking kama muta-evoking paragons is moral education: the paragon is an inspiring prototype for how the audience should act. The audience's kama muta ideally motivates them to follow the heroic precedent, in part because they may identify with the hero, and in part because the adulation that the hero receives can make people in the audience think, 'If I do that, people will praise and admire me, just like that!' Let's consider a contemporary secular practice. The state-owned Industrial and Commercial Bank of China is the world's largest bank. China Central Television, also state-owned, is the largest broadcaster in China. Since 2002, with the sponsorship of the Industrial and Commercial Bank of China, China Central Television has annually given ten recipients the "Touching China Award" or "Moving China Award" (they use both English translations for *gǎn dòng zhong' guo*, 感动中国.[4] The awards are presented in a grand televised spectacle, with videos posted online for each recipient. They have selected, for example,

A teacher who saved two students from being hit by a bus, but lost both her legs in the effort.
A Uygur street vendor who lives extraordinarily frugally to save money with which he has helped over 160 students continue their studies and establish a scholarship fund.
An adopted girl who, since age eight, has been selflessly taking care of her paralyzed adoptive mother.
The late leader of the Chinese nuclear program, whom Premier Wen Jiabao praised: "You have devoted your whole life to the development of the country and service to the people. Your loyalty and unselfish dedication to the country and people will encourage younger generations and their descendants forever."

For more examples, and responses from the public, see Online Note 6.5.

China is not the only nation whose leadership has aimed to evoke kama muta for political ends. As I noted earlier, innumerable politicians, heads of state, and other leaders and preachers have endeavored to mobilize and direct their audiences by evoking kama muta. Before and during World War II, the military leadership of Japan promulgated the metaphor that dying for the emperor and nation was the fall and scattering of cherry blossoms (Ohnuki-Tierney 2002). Cherry blossoms were (and remain) emblematic of Japan, and at the same time iconic of the delicate ephemerality of life – the fall of their petals is a metaphor for death. Toward the end of the war when defeat was immanent, *tokkōtai* (kamikaze) pilots and torpedo helmsmen were exhorted to sacrifice themselves for their emperor and nation, repel the enemy, and, falling like cherry blossoms, be memorialized in the Yasukuni shrine for eternal worship. Ohnuki-Tierney (2002) does not say whether the promulgation of this ideology incorporated either the term 感動, *kando* ('moved'), or the stronger phrase, *kokoro o ugokasareru* ('something moved my heart'), but the emotion that the military leaders were promoting may have been kama muta.

Most people regularly read or listen to kama muta-evoking moral education narratives and regularly view kama muta-evoking images of moral paragons who suffered or died for their fellow humans or for their god. Where? In every holy text, religious icon, and sermon. China has repressed 'religion' but maintained the practice of motivating morality by exhibiting exemplary acts of CS devotion that operate through the same emotion. When they wage popularly supported wars, other states and media do the same every time they award and publicize a medal to a hero. Social movements that advocate diversity and rights also use commercials to evoke kama muta to motivate people to join and support their campaigns. For example, the 2015 Irish Marriage Equality Campaign produced some ads that were quite evocative; see Online Note 6.6.

* * * * *

Sports fans raptly watch, avidly read and talk about, and long remember the courageous performances of player prototypes who stoically play on through injuries for the sake of the team. Soldiers never forget the sacrifices their buddies make for each other, while their communities and nations honor these paragons with medals and statues. Media, politicians, and leaders evoke these heroic acts of CS, stirring their audiences with paradigmatic narratives of determination and destiny, of courageous struggle against obstacles or enemies. Religious texts and sermons do the same. Egalitarian social movements attract adherents by evoking kama muta – and so do racist, xenophobic, and jihadist movements. Such rhetoric contributes crucially to the formation and invigoration of social and revolutionary movements, political parties, racial and ethnic identities, religions, nations, and sometimes one-world consciousness.

Moving merchandise

Political leaders and preachers are not the only ones who use kama mute to move people to action. The kama muta experience can be used to sell morals and causes, but also to solicit donations and sell commodities. Foundation and university fundraisers present touching images of their work and their needs. Advertisements and commercials often aim to evoke kama muta that will attract the audience to their product. Marketing often further promises that purchasers will have lovely kama muta experiences when they use the product. These appeals are by no means limited to rhetoric or text; in modern and contemporary media there are abundant images and videos intended to move people to buy, contribute, or do something. Kama muta is probably the vital component of the marketing factor "engagement" with television or radio shows, and especially the "emotional bonding" aspect of engagement (for a discussion of engagement and how it's measured, see Napoli 2011:88–108). These measures are used to assess whether shows should be produced and the price at which a station sells commercials in them.

Animal shelters, environmental foundations, and charitable organizations present images of cute animals, or desperate children, appealing for compassionate donations. Commercials for flowers and jewelry often indicate that the product will evoke kama muta in the recipient. In the 1980s the American Bell Telephone Company marketed long-distance phone calling with an extensive campaign to

"Reach out and touch someone." Print ads and television commercials[5] showed grandparents talking to a grandchild, a son at college talking to his mom at home, or excited young girls dressed in halos and white dressed for a performance talking to a teacher nun. Inside the trolleys, the Norwegian office of the International Organization for Migration has posters showing visually non-Norwegian ethnic people joyously reunited with their families in non-Norwegian locales. The text in these posters suggest that if you miss your home and family, IOM will pay for you to return – and, it is implied, not come back to Norway.

In a campaign themed "There are gifts you can't wait to give," Tiffany's has run a commercial showing a handsome, well-dressed young man in a taxi stuck in New York traffic, anxiously looking at his watch and checking the contents of a small Tiffany box.[6] These scenes alternate with ones of a beautiful young woman putting on make-up, donning a gorgeous dress, and checking her watch with an expression of concern. The man leaves the stuck taxi, runs down the sidewalk and reaches the bottom of the steps to a house, just as the woman emerges from it; she smiles in relief and joy, and he draws the box out of his pocket. The commercial ends, but we know he is about to propose to her. The wedding dress maker La Sposa has a series of posters for store windows consisting of untitled photographs of a beautiful bride in a long wedding dress with train, holding a bouquet. Behind her holding her train, or beside her, are two cute young girls in white dresses and fairy wings. All smile joyfully as they look into the camera. It's impossible not to smile back at them, touched by the scene.

In Munich, SOS Children's Villages (*Kinderdorf*) used a moving sidewalk to appeal to people to sponsor their children. On the balustrade beside riders were images of small children of diverse ethnicities reaching up to the handrail. On the handrail moving along with riders are faces of the children looking and reaching up, so that riders resting their hand on the rail are touching the children's hands or faces. On the handrail is written *Nehmen Sie ein kind an die Hand. Werden Sie SOS-pate* ('Take a child by the hand. Become an SOS godfather'). Similarly, Roma beggars in Norway often display images of young children who putatively would be supported by money given to the beggar. In a number of cultures, children themselves do much of the begging, and children with prominent disabilities are often particularly successful, presumably in part because their vulnerability, need, and suffering evoke compassionate kama muta.

Readers will encounter innumerable other instances of media campaigns and smaller scale marketing utilizing kama muta. The product or service itself may be promoted as kama muta: returning to your family in your home country, for example, or adopting a needy deserving child. The product may be the vehicle mediating kama muta, like the mysterious jewelry in the Tiffany box the anxious man is bringing to the eagerly waiting woman. Often marketing promotes a product simply by pairing it with a stimulus that evokes kama muta: selling the wedding dress by displaying it in a scene with the adorable girls attending the bride, or selling baby food by alternating images of the product with scenes of cute infants – or simply placing images of cute infants on baby food, and images of cute puppies on dog food. (See this wonderful commercial for Pampers disposable diapers: A Newborn Journey of Firsts.[7]) For several decades, Eastman Kodak promoted its cameras and films as the way to 'preserve' "Kodak Moments" of kama muta, and this is still one of the uses of contemporary amateur photography and video as well as professional wedding photography and videography.

I can't say whether invoking kama muta actually increases sales, but evidently marketing executives buy campaigns that evoke kama muta. It might pay to study which customers' purchases of what sorts of items and services are influenced by kama muta marketing – if any actually are. And what is the impact of kama muta marketing on corporate image?

* * * * *

Politicians, preachers, motivational speakers, media producers, marketing creatives, and advertising executives are in the business of evoking kama muta. We know something about the rhetorical devices and narrative structures that these professionals use, but there is a lot more to learn about their cultural practices and folk-psychology of kama muta. It would be fruitful for linguistic, cultural, and cognitive anthropologists to explore how these kama muta professionals write, talk, and think about kama muta. (For example, see journalist Zach Baron's [2014] participant observation with the Beastmasters at BuzzFeed who pick out the cutest videos and photos.) How do they declaratively conceptualize and semantically articulate emotion concepts and motives that intersect with kama muta? Or, in designing their campaigns, do they rely purely on intuition, and if so, how do their intuitions emerge and how are they individually and socially structured? Many interesting studies could be done on what these kama muta professionals intend, how they think, how they are socially organized, and how they pursue their objectives. These are anthropological and sociological issues. Doubtless psychologists could learn a lot about emotions from these kama muta professionals, too. Conversely, kama muta professionals will have a lot to learn from emerging psychological research. So will 'consumers' choosing whether to buy political agendas and products marketed with kama muta.

Obviously people do not know the kama muta concept. But people do think and strategize about emotions and motives, and people also have emotion-oriented habits and skills that they do not articulate. So it could be illuminating to explore the ethnopsychology of kama muta, such as, for example, folk theories of what *moves* or *touches* or *stirs* people to action. What sort of kama muta-related skills, habits, narratives, associations, and concepts are prevalent among politicians, religious leaders, artists and writers, architects and designers, marketing creatives, and ordinary people trying to influence others? Are there folk theories or rules of thumb that people use to evoke and utilize kama muta? Conversely, what are the skills, habits, narratives, associations, and concepts relevant to seeking kama muta? Do people know how to find the drivers of kama muta that work for them, and if so, how and when do they seek them? How does all this differ as a function of culture, history, roles, institutions, and social class?

Online notes

6.1 Political oratory evoking kama muta.

6.2 Applause that communicates the audience's kama muta.

6.3 Oratorical charisma.

6.4 Lyndon Johnson's evocation of kama muta to motivate the passage of the Civil Rights Bill.

6.5 The "Moving China" Award.

6.6 The marketing campaign to promote marriage equality in Ireland.

Notes

1 https://en.wikisource.org/wiki/Newburgh_address.

2 From AmericanRhetoric.com.

3 Compare with the moment when the new French Republic was formed after the Revolution and the French delegates wept as they signed the new constitution, and kissed it (see Online Note 2.5).

4 E.g., http://english.cntv.cn/special/movingchina/homepage/index.shtml.

5 E.g., https://www.youtube.com/watch?v=OapWdclVqEY.

6 http://adsoftheworld.com/media/tv/tiffany_co_the_gift.

7 https://youtu.be/lDSJRPDG8C0.

PART III
Getting deeper into it

A PIVOTAL IDEA

Kama muta is a long-run cause of the cultural practices that evoke it

We have observed that people giving speeches, staging the Moving China Award, and formulating marketing campaigns aim to evoke kama muta in order to motivate people to do something. The psychological propensity to kama muta is a necessary condition for this: the emotion is a cause of these activities. Does this give us any hints about the other cultural practices considered in this book? Why do people engage in cry dates, recovery and support groups, social service volunteerism, and vocations, sports, and fandom? Why do people tell and listen to stories in which loving protagonists struggle to be reunited? There can be no one answer – people have multiple, and more or less distinct, motives for doing each of these things, people differ in their motives, and motives change over time. But clearly the opportunity to experience kama muta is a major attraction – sometimes *the* major attraction – that draws people to them. This delightful emotion makes participation worthwhile, sustaining participants through the inevitable intervals that intervene between the peak emotional moments (when supplementary motives may also help sustain participants' engagement). Each instance of the emotion is momentary but evokes more enduring devotion and commitment to the social relationships involved in the activity – and induces people to ardently seek to re-engage in the activity in order to re-experience the emotion. Consequently, this emotion appears to be crucial to the sociocultural reproduction and diffusion of these activities, and hence their prevalence worldwide. The emotion also seems to shape the cultural evolution of these activities, such that variants that most strongly evoke the emotion spread most rapidly, attract the most adherents, and motivate the most avid participation (see Chapter 17). In other words, to a considerable extent, it seems likely that all of these activities have become pervasive practices *because* they evoke the emotion. People do these things partly – sometimes primarily – in order to experience kama muta. People are only partially aware of this motivation, and can't always readily name the emotion, but if you ask they can usually tell you about the wonderful feeling of it.

The kama muta moments vary from barely perceptible to extremely intense and memorable peak experiences that give meaning and purpose to life. These kama muta experiences are 'positive' in every sense: people report that the feeling is good, they remember it fondly, and they want to re-experience it. It is motivating – people make considerable effort to have kama muta experiences. Furthermore, people want to give kama muta to other people they care for, and seek to experience kama muta *together with* others. It seems to be potentially stronger and more rewarding when experienced collectively, perhaps because experiencing kama muta together evokes it recursively – recognizing that one shares a kama muta experience with others tends to intensify the CS relationships among people sharing the kama muta. Moderate to intense kama muta is memorable, and people are eager to tell others about kama muta experiences – which typically evokes kama muta in the listeners or readers. Thus people reproduce their kama muta experiences and recruit others to join and recreate kama muta practices. I theorize that many people do these things in large part for the kama muta experiences these activities afford. Kama muta moments make them rewarding and meaningful.

Kama muta in these activities indirectly makes them very attractive in another manner: beyond the moment, the emotion generates relatively enduring affective devotion and moral commitment to socially significant CS relationships. Kama muta in worship generates cohesive congregations that have all kinds of intrinsic and extrinsic appeal to members. Kama muta from marching in a protest together bonds participants, creating communities that are rewarding in many respects. Family and friends' kama muta cements essential ties that sustain vital kinship and affiliation. Memorial events evoke patriotic kama muta that sustains politically important national bonds, while kama muta from participation in mass gatherings creates cohesion that fosters mutual support and dedication to social movements (see Claparède 1930). Friendships grow out of kama muta moments that result from caring for people or animals – or just sharing images of cute kittens. Teammates and fans who experience kama muta thereby facilitate warm ties among people who would otherwise be strangers. In short, not only is kama muta appealing in itself, but people are attracted to kama muta-evoking practices because the kama muta in these practices enables them to form worthwhile social bonds. Those who feel kama muta together take care of each other.

In short, kama muta is a part of what people are seeking in worship, pilgrimage, and memorial events; celebrating birthdays and anniversaries; going out into 'nature'; marching or rowing in synchrony, and dancing; telling, listening to, and watching stories, and looking at social media; engagement in sports; caring for pets; caring for needy and vulnerable people. These activities have four attractions:

1. The likelihood of joyous <u>kama muta experiences</u>.
2. Mediated by these kama muta experiences, along with other, more gradual bonding processes that may occur once people assemble, the security and support of <u>CS relationships</u>.
3. Through the presence of other participants attracted by the kama muta experiences and the CS relationships that ensue, all of the other appeals and advantages (and disadvantages) of <u>social gatherings</u>.
4. Participants actively <u>recruit converts</u> and <u>welcome new participants</u> in order to feel kama muta more strongly together with others.

The first attraction is direct; the second follows from the first, while the third follows from the first and second. The fourth attraction results primarily from the reinforcement of kama muta that occurs when it is experienced together with others. I hypothesize that in many cases the first attraction is the one that most strongly motivates engagement in impractical events of the types listed. In any case, the others depend on the first, which is our focus in this book. Humans are utterly reliant on the benefits of trusting cooperation, so there are clear adaptive benefits to the disposition to experience kama muta, together with the disposition to recruit others to join in these experiences (see Chapter 17).

The joyous kama muta moments of these activities, albeit frequent at times, are sometimes so small as to be barely noticeable, and hence rather taken for granted after a while. One might say that such events are merely a bit 'sweet' or 'touching.' Some kama muta moments are noticeably 'heartwarming.' Some are quite 'moving,' grabbing the person's full attention. And a few are profound, life-transforming, peak 'mystical' experiences of 'rapture' or 'ecstasy' that people marvel and reflect on for the rest of their lives. But kama muta is an emotion; as such, the apperception and the sensations are brief, typically lasting no more than a matter of seconds or at most a very few minutes. But the CS *motives* that emerge from the emotion endure beyond this moment, often apparently lasting for days, months, or, occasionally, for many years. People may simply feel more affiliative and kind for a little while, or they may feel deeply compassionate for a long time. But in all cases, kama muta is rewarding – people want to experience it again. So when engaging in a cultural activity evokes kama muta, people want to engage in the activity again. The stronger and the more frequent – and the more predictable – the kama muta, the more motivated people are to engage in the activity that produced it. To a considerable extent, these cultural activities exist just because they often evoke kama muta (see Chapters 10 and 17).

But before we can explore this causal effect of the emotion in more of these activities, we have to address a lexical issue: the reification of vernacular words.

7

HOW NOT TO REIFY WORDS

> Some psychologists, indulging our natural tendency to reïfy whatever we name, seem to assume that we have to recognize 'an emotion' of distinctive quality corresponding to every name used in popular and literary description of emotional experience.
>
> *(McDougall 1923:314)*

Are you getting used to thinking about *kama muta*, perhaps even beginning to fondly use the term to understand your own experience – or do you read the words with faint irritation, mentally translate 'being moved,' and wonder whether our use of the term *kama muta* is just scientific pretension? Does the term clarify our concept, or obfuscate it? Before we go on to the following chapters where we explore kama muta experiences in other domains of social life, in this chapter let's go deep into the issues of scientific nomenclature. We really have to do this, but actually it turns out to be a lot of fun to think about how words correspond – or don't correspond – to entities or processes in the real world. Also, thinking about the words we use for the phenomenon helps us to think more clearly about the phenomenon itself. It helps us transcend our messy, inchoate, opaque speech habits, clearing the way for us to articulate exactly what kama muta is, theoretically and empirically. In philosophical terminology, analysis of the lexical practices opens the way for us to get a better grasp on the ontology.[1]

We needed to coin a new term, *kama muta*, to denote our construct for eight reasons:

1. Because everyday speech is imprecise and inconsistent (D. Fiske 1981; S. Fiske 1995):
   - A person uses the same word more or less differently on different occasions,

- Different people use the same word in more or less different ways,
- There are substantial dialectical differences in the use of words,
- There is change over time in the meanings of words, sometimes very rapid change.

2. Because there are many English words whose meanings intersect with the phenomenon, there is no good reason to pick just one, and no way to know which one to pick (see Weidman, Steckler, & Tracy 2017).
3. a. Because none of the English words that come closest to denoting the phenomenon translate one-to-one into other languages.
   b. Because, that is, different languages divide the world of affect into different categories; their taxonomies of affect don't exactly correspond with those of other languages, and sometimes aren't even close (for the evidence that this is true of all affects, see Wierzbicka 1999).
4. Because there is no reason to ethnocentrically assume that English words just happen to pick out natural kinds in the world, while other languages based on different taxonomies are less valid.
5. Because some languages have no specific term that is consistently and distinctively used to refer to the kama muta phenomenon.
6. Because there are contexts in which English speakers feel kama muta, but call it something else and don't realize it is the same emotion as, say, *being moved* (such as *nostalgia*, *rapture*, or, in a collective context, team, community, or patriotic *pride*) – and other languages also have different words for the same emotion in different contexts.
7. Because there are contexts in which people feel kama muta, but don't have any vernacular name at all for the feeling (such as when speakers of English, German, or Norwegian see a cute kitten or infant; or, again, when looking out into the sky and feeling one with the cosmos).
8. Because, across the natural and human sciences, newly recognized constructs have always required the coinage of new scientific terms to precisely, consistently, and clearly denote the new theoretically defined constructs.

Let's consider these issues (see also Fiske, Schubert, & Seibt 2017b and 2017c; Fiske 2019). In English, the principal lexemes that may (but do not always) refer to the experience of kama muta are *being moved*, *being touched*, *stirring*, *heartwarming*, *tug at your heart strings*, one's *heart goes out to* someone or some animal, *tearjerking*, *rapture*, *tenderness*, and *entrance(d)*. Interestingly, people may describe this experience more or less specifically as *being emotional*. A contemporary slang term is *the feels*; in religious contexts, people often call occurrences of kama muta events *mystical* experiences. Kama muta does not correspond to the denotations of any of these individual vernacular terms, their union, nor their intersection. And people may sometimes use each of these terms to designate other emotions, moods, or attitudes that are not kama muta.

In Chapter 1 we observed that when researchers elicit self-reports of 'peak experiences,' most of these consist predominantly of strong kama muta events (Maslow 1962, 1970; Keutzer 1978, Wuthnow 1978; Davis 1998; Woodward, Findlay, & Moore 2009; Hoffman, Iversen, & Ortiz 2010; Hoffman, Garg, & González-Mujica 2011; Ho et al. 2013). In Online Note 1.3 I reviewed indications that when Laski (1961, 1980) asked English respondents about experiences of 'transcendent ecstasy,' many (perhaps most) of the experiences that people recounted were occasions when they evidently felt strong kama muta, as are many of the experiences that researchers have called "mystical." I review other experience labelled *'mystical'* or *rapturous* in Chapter 11. All of these terms often, but not always, denote kama muta experiences, though the people experiencing them, and the scholars who write about such experiences, restrict the terms 'peak experiences,' 'ecstasy,' 'mystical,' and 'rapturous' experiences to emotional moments that are exceptionally intense – yet without exploring whether there is any natural boundary between these and less intense experiences that are otherwise qualitatively congruent with them. Our view is that there kama muta experiences vary greatly in intensity, and there is no discontinuity between the most intense kama muta experiences and less intense ones. So it does not make sense to use a distinct scientific term for intense kama muta.

There are a number of vernacular lexemes for kama muta that are limited to specific contexts. While English speakers often use the terms listed above to refer to kama muta experiences that occur in social relationships with other humans or in response to media and narratives, people may not be able to find <u>any</u> name for kama muta they experience in 'nature,' such as watching a sunset, looking up at the night sky, or standing on a mountain top looking out on a beautiful and immense landscape. Likewise people refer to infants and baby animals that evoke kama muta as *cute* or *adorable*, and say that a baby human or animal, or the creature's friendliness, is *so sweet*. But these are adjectives for the being that evokes the emotional response; English speakers usually don't have any term for the evoked emotional experience as such. (*Tenderness* comes close, but English speakers rarely come up with this term to describe how they feel when they see cute human or animal babies.)

An English-speaking informant asked to list *moving* or *touching* experiences generally will not mention experiences of *patriotic feeling*, *national pride*, *team pride*, or *fan spirit*, for example. It simply doesn't occur to people to think of those experiences as *moving* or *touching*. (Sometimes people whose feelings would be named *patriotism* or *fan spirit* are feeling simultaneous kama muta and *pride* in the other sense of the word – the sudden intensification of a superior position in a legitimate and valued hierarchy, because they've *come up in the world*.) But collective and parental *pride* are forms of kama muta. This is illustrated below by the Toonocracy "Man Tears" Sticker from Facebook; it shows a father sitting with his arm behind his son, smiling and shedding a tear of pride at something his son is reading – perhaps a letter of admissions to a university.

I also suspect that when people feel especially *cozy* they are often feeling mild kama muta, but one wouldn't list *cozy* moments among one's moving or touching experiences, despite the fact that artifacts, places, events, and calendrical occasions such as birthdays, anniversaries, or religious holidays celebrated with family may evoke kama muta. When kama muta is evoked by fond memories of lost loves, childhood best friends, or former family togetherness, English speakers call it *nostalgia*. There are many occasions when one lovingly remembers departed travelers or sailors who may never return, or recalls the sense of belonging one once had in a close community (on memorials and mementos, see Chapter 9). (In Portuguese and Galician, a tragic version of this emotion is *saudade*.) These feelings of *nostalgia*, *wistful reminiscence*, and *longing* often denote the mnemonic re-experience of old CS sentiments. And indeed people rate *being moved* as conceptually similar to *nostalgia* (Menninghaus et al. 2015). "The self almost invariably figures as the protagonist in nostalgic narratives and is almost always surrounded by close others" in relationally important events (Zhou et al. 2008; Wildschut et al. 2010). Also, "nostalgia restores an individual's social connectedness," attachment security, and perception of social support. Nostalgia can trigger the mnemonic feeling of past loves (Wildschut et al. 2006). Wildschut and colleagues found that "communal" themes predominate in the episodes whose recall evokes nostalgia. In several studies, Sedikides and colleagues (2006:4) found that in nostalgia people "feel loved, protected, socially supported, connected to others, and trusting of others," along with feelings of "warmth or comfort."

After sketching his vivid recollections of boyhood butterfly-collecting and his lifelong enchantment with Lepidoptera, Vladimir Nabokov concludes a short memoir:

> I confess I do not believe in time. I like to fold my magic carpet, after use, in such a way as to superimpose one part of the pattern upon another. Let visitors trip. And the highest enjoyment of timelessness—in a landscape selected at random—is when I stand among rare butterflies and their food plants. This is ecstasy, and behind the ecstasy is something else, which I cannot explain. It is like a momentary vacuum into which rushes all that I love, a sense of oneness with sun and stone, a thrill of gratitude to whom it may concern, perhaps to the contrapuntal genius of human fate or to the tender ghosts humoring a lucky mortal.
>
> *(Nabokov 1948)*

I found out tonight (via a text message, she wasn't emotionally ready to talk about it yet) that my best friend since childhood has breast cancer. My initial reaction wasn't to freak out, or cry from the thought of possibly losing her. Instead, I found myself writing her a response text about all the wonderful high points and struggles of our past 25 years of friendship. How much we've changed, learned and grown. How we can sometimes go long periods without seeing one another (she lives hundreds of miles away), yet can always pick up the friendship right where we left off. And that, of course, I was there for her, for whatever, always.

I think that while writing that I felt very kama muta: tears, goosebumps, lump in throat, general feeling of lightness after (rather than despair). And I think it was because, in writing it, I fully realized how dear this relationship is to me, and it made me feel suddenly closer to her than ever before.

(Young woman studying kama muta)

Nostalgia and spirit mediumship (see Online Note 3.3) illustrates the fact that people may feel CS-relationship emotions about people who are no longer living. We saw in Chapter 3 that people very often have similar sentiments about historical, mythical, or fictional characters. I will show in Chapters 11–16 that people experience strong kama muta when they suddenly feel love from or for deceased or immaterial beings such as saints, angels, Jesus, Mary, God/Allah, Hussain ibn Ali, Krishna, the Buddha, or a bodhisattva/bodhisatta. What evokes kama muta is the sudden intensification of a CS relationship, regardless of whether that relationship is with a person who is alive or dead, present or absent, and regardless of whether the being is real or imagined. The sudden emergence of a memory or schema of intense CS is more than sufficient to evoke kama muta.

In short, there are innumerable lexemes that speakers or English or another language may use for kama muta, depending on dialect, historical period, age, gender, context, and the intensity of the experience. But English speakers do not invariably restrict any of these lexemes to kama muta; people also sometimes use each of these terms to denote other emotions, moods, attitudes, and evaluations – and to present themselves as having various desirable mental states and affinities. Even psychologists studying emotions are remarkably inconsistent in the vernacular lexemes that they ask participants to rate when measuring a given emotion – often using the same lexeme in items measuring <u>different</u> emotion constructs (Weidman, Steckler, & Tracy 2017). Limiting ourselves to denotations, it is helpful to present these nomenclature issues visually. Figure 7.1 schematically depicts the intersections of the construct of the experience of kama muta with related affective experiences denoted by vernacular English terms. The figure certainly does not represent all English terms that can be used to denote kama muta. Moreover, a purely schematic two-dimensional representation of a many–dimensional space, the figure is not intended to be precise or to capture all the set intersections (for example, in multidimensional space, *awe* intersects with *stirring* and *rapture*). The sizes of the ellipses are not based on any usage data. Rather, Figure 7.1 indicates how <u>kama muta intersects with but does not correspond one-to-one with any English vernacular term</u>, or with any set of terms. No term denotes all kama muta experiences (represented as the interior of

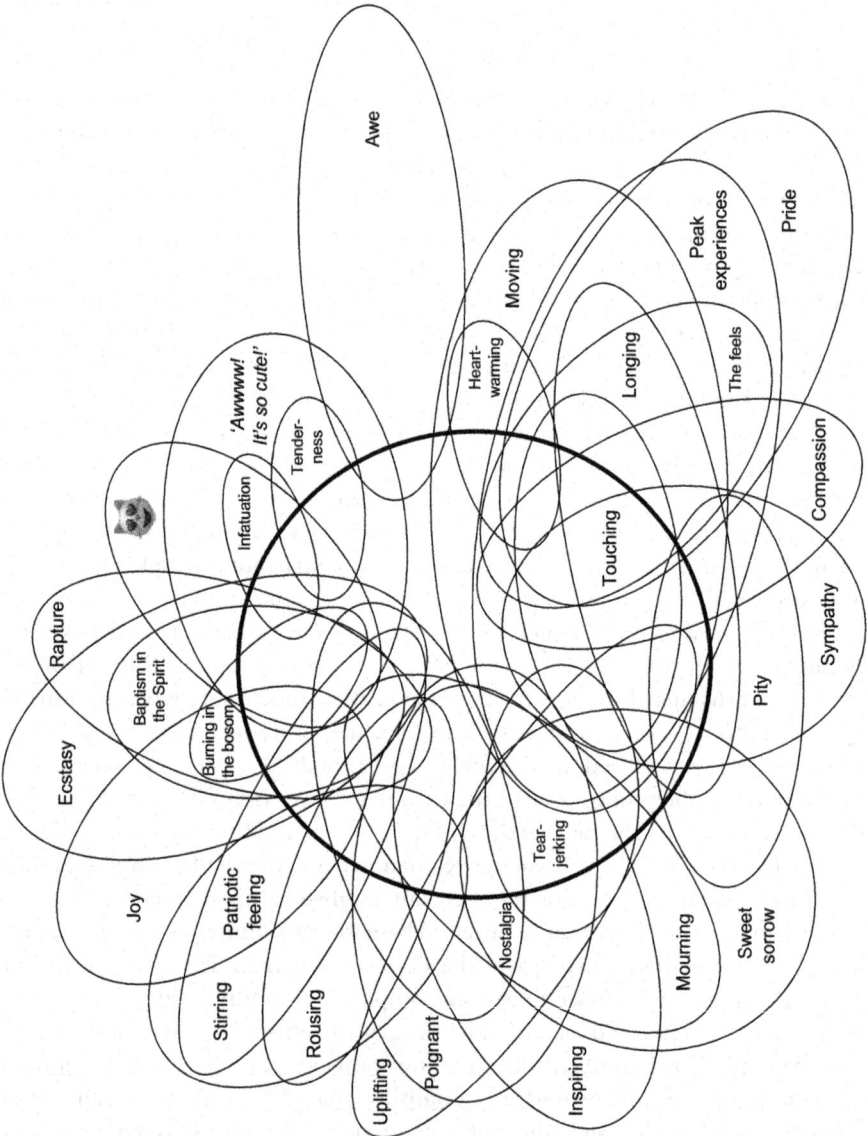

FIGURE 7.1 Schematic of the denotational fields of some of the English vernacular terms related to kama muta. Bold circle indicates kama muta.

the kama muta circle), and every term denotes some experiences of other emotions (represented as outside the circle).

And it is not just in everyday vernacular usage that people differ in how they denote the same emotion; emotion researchers are almost equally inconsistent. Figure 7.1 diagrams just one emotion, kama muta, but the picture gets even messier if we consider vernacular words used for many different emotions: emotion researchers themselves do not agree on what vernacular lexemes refer to what emotions. This is evident in Weidman, Steckler, and Tracy's (2017) Venn diagrams of the different words researches have used to measure the same emotion and the different emotions that have been assessed using the same word. Analyzing a representative sample of 467 articles published in *Emotion* from 2001–2011, Weidman, Steckler, and Tracy (2017) found that in a great many cases different researchers used the same item to measure purportedly distinct emotions – yet many studies measured an emotion with a single item, based on just one emotion term. They found that 51 of the 65 (78%) emotions measured were assessed with at least one word or phrase that was also used to measure an overlapping emotion; these 51 emotions were each measured with a set of words that were used to measure an average of 4.96 distinct emotions, across studies (Median 4, SD 3.55, Range: 2–17) (Weidman, Steckler, & Tracy 2017:282). And this is from articles in just one journal over a span of only ten years!

It is interesting to note that the terms that English speakers sometimes use for kama muta include not just emotional states (e.g., *touched*, *moved*) as such, but also qualities of stimuli and situations (e.g., *cute, adorable, sweet, poignant, heart-warming, tear-jerking, stirring*) that evoke emotional states that may have no name. What do you call the feeling you have when you watch a *tear-jerking* movie, or you react strongly to seeing or holding a cute baby or kitten? Other terms denote not simply an internal state or a quality of a stimulus, but the significance of an event, especially its religious meaning (e.g., *feeling touched by the Spirit, rapture*). Most terms are more or less restricted to certain contexts: *nostalgia* is only used to refer to an emotional state (generally kama muta) evoked by memory; kama muta emotion at a wedding cannot felicitously be called *feeling patriotic*, nor can one say, *Awww! It's so cute!* when listening to the national anthem as one's flag goes up the pole. (Of course, these situations may differ with respect to the emotions that people tend to feel in addition to kama muta.) Note that within the construct represented by the bold kama muta circle there is a region that is not within the scope of any English lexeme. Note also that people use many of these words to denote moods, attitudes, and so forth – not just emotions.

Moreover, researchers generally assume that their participants mean each of these words just the same way as the researchers conceptualize them, so that participants can give valid (and reliable) reports of precisely what emotion they experience – often using just one word. I doubt that informants can give precise, entirely consistent, clearly distinct, reliable, or entirely valid names to their emotions. Figure 7.1 depicts just one language, and only some of the intersecting lexemes in it. I posit that similar figures could be drawn for any language, though languages differ in how dense or sparse the lexemes are in the region of kama muta (and in the broader zone of emotions in general), and in how much of the kama muta construct is covered by common and mentally accessible lexemes. And corresponding figures could be drawn for any other psychological construct (on the ambiguity and unreliability of participants labeling psychological states, see D. W. Fiske 1986; S. T. Fiske 1995).

What the static figure cannot depict, but is essential to keep in mind, is that vernacular terms are dynamically fluid in their denotations: what they mean depends on the historical moment, the dialect, the idiolect of the speaker, the social relational situation and its performative opportunities, in conjunction with the speaker's options and intentions (see point 1 in the list of reasons for coining a technical term). In contrast, as a scientific construct, kama muta should have a stable, consistent denotation — that's the function of scientific nomenclature.

In a similarity map of lexicalized English folk emotion concepts, kama muta is near emotions or attitudes related to needing, seeking, or experiencing CS: *empathy, sympathy, compassion, sadness, longing, infatuation, being smitten*. Because kama muta occurs when CS relationships suddenly intensify, and this suddenness is sometimes unexpected, kama muta is also near *surprise*. People sometimes use the term *moved* or *stirred* for *awe* or *amazement* (though they don't use *touched* in these senses). Kama muta is almost always a pleasant, attractive emotion that people report enjoying, like to repeat experiencing, give to others they like, and want to experience together with others they like. Hence it is related to the vernacular terms *joy, pleasure,* and *happiness*. In contrast to some earlier approaches (Tokaji 2003, Hanich et al. 2014), we believe that kama muta is not necessarily evoked by a simple 'mixture' of sadness and joy, and indeed is not related at all to non-social relational sadness or joy. Rather, as we saw when discussing the universal themes of literature in Chapter 3, people experience kama muta when the sadness *of separation or loss* suddenly transforms into *the joy of CS togetherness*; it is this dynamic process that generates kama muta. Likewise, kama muta can result from the *nostalgic* memory or imagination of wonderful CS relationships when the partner is departing, absent, or dead, or the relationship has broken up. In our experiments, when participants rate their emotions continuously as they watch videos, positivity consistently cross–correlates moment-to-moment with ratings of *being moved or touched*, with *moist eyes or tears*, with *goosebumps or chills*, with feelings of *warmth in the chest*, and with the rated *closeness* of the characters in the video (Schubert et al. 2016). The moment-to-moment correlation of negativity with each of these aspects of kama muta differs greatly from video to video, with the aggregate cross-correlation across all videos averaging to near zero. In short, kama muta experiences as such are invariably positive, with no essential negativity.

None of the vernacular English terms have denotations that exactly correspond with their nearest translations in any other language. This is illustrated in Figure 7.2, which schematically indicates the idea that one-to-one translations do not exist. (Figure 7.2 is purely schematic; I do not know just how these terms

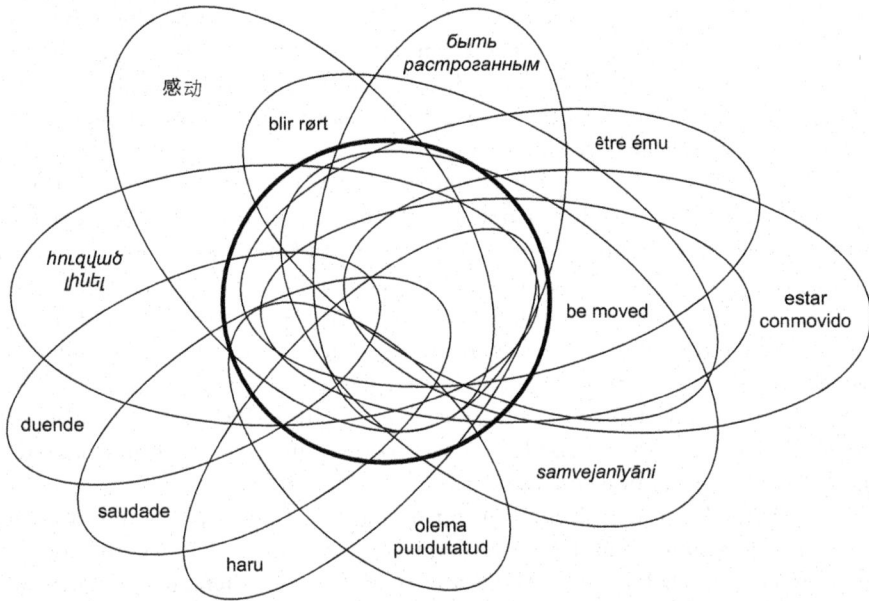

FIGURE 7.2 Schematic of the denotational fields of vernacular terms related to kama muta experiences in different languages. Dark circle indicates the kama muta experience. NB: this figure is not intended to accurately represent the correspondence among these terms, but merely to suggest the conceptual issue of lexical mapping across languages.

intersect, and in any case, presumably could not depict their intersection in just two dimensions.) Figure 7.2 includes only a few of the languages I have investigated, and only one word from each language, although, as in English, there are often several words with different foci, used in different contexts, that intersect the kama muta construct. Each term in each language maps in a somewhat indeterminate manner somewhat distinctive, culturally-constructed and culturally-delineated events and experiences. It is striking that there *are* words in many languages in several distinct language families that denote a large part of the field of kama muta experiences, although I have not found and do not expect to find any that correspond one-to-one with the kama muta construct as we define it.

Though schematic rather than accurate in detail, these Venn diagrams iconically depict a fact with crucial methodological implications. Because there is no English vernacular lexeme whose denotational field corresponds exactly with kama muta, one cannot rely on labels alone to identify instances of kama muta. And using different vernacular 'synonyms' to identify emotional experiences leads to somewhat different emotional experiences. Moreover, none of the vernacular lexemes in any language that best translate any of these English lexemes have quite the same denotational field as the lexemes in any other language: their meanings differ. So if one asked speakers of different languages about their experiences of events that they label with vernacular lexemes in their language that approximately translate, say, *be moved*, the referent affective experiences differ because the definitions of the words differ. Within any one language community or across languages, vernacular lexemes are not sufficient for accurate, valid identification of instances of kama muta.

Nonetheless, most languages have one or more vernacular lexemes that typically – though not invariably – denote kama muta experiences, though the usage of the lexemes may be limited to certain contexts. In German the most common phrases approximately denoting the kama muta experience are *bewegt sein* (literally, 'be moved,' as a thing would be physically displaced by an external force) and *gerührt sein* (literally, 'to stir,' as in stirring a pot); Dutch phrases are *ontroering, ontroerd zijn*, and *geraakt zijn*. The Norwegian is *blir rørt*; Swedish, *bliver rört*; Danish, *blir rörd*; all of these Scandinavian phrases mean 'be stirred,' as a liquid would be stirred. Norwegians also use *beveget* (literally 'moved,' somewhat old-fashioned), and speak of *ømhet*, 'tenderness.'

In French, the principal emotion terms that have the greatest intersection with the kama muta experience are cognates of the English move and touch: *émouvoir* (to be moved: *être ému*) and *toucher* (with the same literal meanings as the English lexemes). French also say *s'attendrir*, 'to feel tender emotions such as those toward an infant, or nostalgic memories'[2] (Claparède 1930).

Likewise, the Spanish lexeme that generally denotes kama muta is *estar conmovido* (literally, 'be moving with'); similarly, the Portuguese is *comovido (comover)*, and the Italian *commuovere/commozione (commuoversi)*.

In Russian (a Slavic language in the Indo-European family), the closest term and most commonly used term is быть растроганным *(byt' rastrogannym*; literally, 'be touched'). In Croatian (also a Slavic language), the most relevant lexemes are *dirnut/a* and *ganut/a*. *Dirnut* and *ganut* are also used in Serbian, and Konecni (2005) offers the Serbian words *drljivost* and *dirnutost*.

The Pāli term that definitely denotes kama muta is *samvejanīyāni* (literally, 'agitated' or 'quickly moved'; see Chapter 12).

These words in Indo-European languages all have the literal meaning of passive physical displacement, being touched, or being stirred. It is intriguing that the English word *move* derives from the Old French *mouvoir*, 'to move, get moving, set out; set in motion; introduce.' The source of *mouvoir* and the cognate terms in Spanish, Portuguese, and Italian is the same as the word *émouvoir* and *emotion*, the Latin *ex-* 'out' + *movere*, 'to move (out), set in motion; remove; disturb; agitate' (Onions 1966; Harper 2016). English *emotion, motion, motive, moment*, and *momentum* have the same Proto-Indo-European root **meue-* 'to push away'. From this root also comes the Sanskrit *muta*, 'moved,' as in the phrase *kama muta*, 'moved by love' (Onions 1966; Harper 2017).

Contemporary Hindi/Urdu (also an Indo-European language) speakers have difficulty coming up with a lexeme for kama muta. However, there was one notable exception. I showed a 23-year-old female bilingual respondent the

Thai Medicine video that we have quite effectively used to evoke kama muta in thousands of experimental participants, and when I asked her how it made her feel, she responded *"chhooliyah"* (perhaps better transliterated as *choo liyaa*, छू लिया). *Choo liyaa* literally means 'touched.' The respondent explained her response to the video "I connected very well because I felt it in my heart." She further explained "I felt touched. I felt love and gratitude. The strongest feeling would be feeling touched." Asked for examples of instances when one would be likely to experience this, she indicated,

> When a baby is born. When someone expresses & confesses their love to you for the first time. When you listen to a song or watch a movie that you can really connect to on another level. When you see a loved one get married. When your kids choose you over everything!

Asked specifically about the characteristic sensations, responding on a scale of 0 to 3, the respondent indicated 2's for "goosebumps or chills," "a warm feeling in the center of the chest," and "some feeling in the center of the chest" (as well as 1 for "chills or shivers"). The respondent showed moderate but not intense "moist eyes or tears" (the respondent was not asked about this sign). Asked about the quotations from the informant (without mention of the sensations of signs), Gyanam Mahajan, a bilingual Hindi language professor, indicated that *choo liyaa* is a variant of *choo gayaa*, छू गया, '(went and) touched (me).' Confirming the respondent's statement, she wrote "yes, it is 'in the heart' or affecting the heart. Although I am unable to separate out the emotion feeling from a physical sensation felt in the heart." This clearly indicates that *choo liyaa* and *choo gayaa* denote prototypical kama muta. Which is intriguing because among a score of Hindi speakers to whom I have described the emotion or to whom I have shown our videos, including bilingual professors, this is the only respondent who came up with the lexeme. After an hour of discussion of the kama muta concept and situations that evoke it, one language professor came up with the (Bollywood based?) lexeme *dil ko chuu lenaa*, 'touched at the heart.' The experiences denoted by Hindi/Urdu *dil ko chuu lenaa* include the 'awww, how cute' response to infants and cuddly young animals.[3]

Moving beyond the Indo-European language family, I find that there are vernacular terms for kama muta experiences in the three Uralic languages. In Estonian, people say *olema puudutatud* (literally 'being touched') and *olema liigutatud* ('being moved'), as well as *olema hingepõhjani liigutatud* ('to be moved to the bottom of one's soul') and *olema pisarateni liigutatud* ('to be moved to tears'). Similarly, in Finnish, 'moving' is *liikuttava* and 'moved' is *liikuttunut*; a term for this emotion when it is more intense *koskettaa*, 'to touch' and *koskettava*, 'touching'; again, these words have the literal physical meanings of their English glosses. In Hungarian, there is *megérintett* (literally, to 'move'), and *megérint* (literally, 'to touch'); *megható* means 'very touching' and *meghatódott* means that someone is 'moved by an experience.' The Uralic languages also have terms for the emotion evoked by perception or thought of a cute human or animal infant. Vivian Bohl told us

> In Estonian, we have a verb *heldima* to describe what happens to people in such situations. A person can be *heldinud* — it means that one has an emotional response to something cute or sweet — it can also be a memory [compare English *nostalgia*]. The noun for the emotion would be *heldimus*. To me, it has a little bit of a flavour of being oversensitive to kindness, cuteness or sweetness — almost as if you would feel a bit embarrassed if others see that you are *heldinud*. I guess the word comes from the root *hell*, which means tender in Estonian. So when you are *heldinud*, you are being made tender, perhaps even soft or fragile, by what you experience.
>
> *Heldima* is to make oneself *heldinud* by means of experiencing or witnessing something. A typical scene that comes to mind would be a grandmother looking at grandchildren doing something cute.

Similarly, asked about the emotion evoked by kittens, a Finnish linguist told us that in Finnish one would say *heltyä*, which means 'to become gentler, to soften.' One dictionary defines *heltyä* as *liikuttua*, which means 'to become emotionally moved.' She also said that a synonym of *söpö*, which means cute, is *hellyyttävä*, 'making you feel feelings of sweet tenderness.' (Naively, it sounds that it might be that Estonian *heldima*, *heldinud*, and *heldimus* share a common *hel* 'tender, soft, or fragile' root with Finnish *heltyä* and *hellyyttävä*.) Also asked about the emotion evoked by kittens, Anna Pásztor told us that in Hungarian one would use the noun *elérzékenyült*, which means 'becoming very soft and tender in a sentimental way.' It comes from *érzékeny*, 'sensitive.'

In Telegu (a Dravidian language), Tanvi Sakhamuru told us, people say that seeing an adorable kitten, infant, or toddler makes the perceiver feel *muddu vastundi* (ముద్దూ వస్తుంది), 'a kiss is coming.' Less literally, it means 'the feeling of endearment/tenderness (towards someone or something) is approaching the speaker.' It is associated with a warm feeling in the chest and being choked-up. In other contexts, Tanvi Sakhamuru told us, Telugu *kadilinĉcindi* (కదిలించింది) denotes kama muta, for example, in response to a speech or story, and equally denotes spatially 'moved' – passive physical displacement occurring at a given moment in time. So a tree branch may be *kadilinĉcindi* by the wind, or one's elbow *kadilinĉcindi* by someone or something. A less common lexeme is *chalinchindi poyanyu*, 'I (the viewer/perceiver) am moved.' It also refers to passive physical motion, but typically sudden displacement with a bounce back, as when someone or something moves an earring, or the wind blows the branches of a tree. Though less used than *kadilinĉcindi*, *chalincindi* implies a stronger emotion. One Telugu–speaking informant from Hyderabad told us, after watching a video that shows a couple's first kiss and then their kisses across the decades of their life,[4] that her emotion could be labeled *guṇḍe niṇḍipōyindi*, గుండె నిండిపోయింది, literally 'heart is filled up.' This lexeme is also used to mean that someone or something has filled a physical container or any sort with a liquid, a substance, or objects. Telegu speakers who feel kama muta may also say *hrudayam pulak-inchindi*, 'my heart was (happily) startled'; it is used only about positive experiences. *Gunde* denotes the anatomical heart, while *hrudayam* is a more 'spiritual' word for 'heart' or 'soul' without a definite anatomical locus. Watching three videos we selected to evoke kama muta, the mean rating of 21 fluent Tamil speakers on *kadilincindi poyanyu* was 4.1; on *chalinchindi poyanyu* 3.6; on *gunde nindipōyindi* 4.1; on *hrudayam pulakinchindi* 4.0.[5]

In Hebrew (a Semitic language in the Afro-Asiatic family), the closest equivalent to kama muta is נוגע ללב (pronounced approximately *noge'a lalev*) literally, 'touches the heart,' where נוגע is the verb of physical contact between objects.

In Turkish (a Turkic language) the closest term is *duygulanmak*, although this term may be less frequently used and less retrievable for Turks than corresponding terms in some other languages. After Fiske gave a talk to social and clinical psychologists at Istanbul Bilgi University, the audience discussed with each other at length whether there is a Turkish lexeme for kama muta, and if so, what the 'right' term is.

In Mandarin (a Sino-Tibetan language), the phrase that most nearly corresponds to kama muta, is *gǎn dòng* 感动 (in traditional script, 感動; literally, 'to feel movement'). One informant said that he thinks of 感动 as 'in the heart.'

In Korean (a Koreanic language), written with the same characters, it is *gam dong*.

In Japanese (a Japonic language), written with the same characters, it's pronounced *kando* (noun, 'the state of being moved'), *kandō-suru* (感動する, 'to move [one's] senses or emotion'), or, more emphatically, *kokoro o ugokasareru* ('something moved my heart') (see also Tokaji 2003).

In Tahitian and Tikopian (Polynesian languages in the Austronesian family), the corresponding word is *arōfa*, although the term may also be used for attitudes of compassion that are not as brief as an emotion.

In Malay (a Malayo-Sumbawan language in the Austronesian family) *tersentuh* nicely captures the sense of kama muta (Shaver, Murdaya, & Fraley 2001). One might say *Dia tersentuh dengan ke-hangat-an yang ditunjukkan penduduk kepada=nya*, 'He was touched by the warmth that the inhabitants felt [directed] toward him.' Dan Fessler (personal communication 9 April 2017) explained, "'sentuh' literally means 'touch'. The 'ter' prefix indicates that the individual was the passive object of an action that lacked an actor – so, in both literal and figurative meaning, *tersentuh* is exactly the same as touched." Another term that translates *moved* is *terharu* (see Chapter 2, and the blog post in Chapter 5 about Indonesia's badminton victory); the emotion so denoted is a cousin of compassion and pity (Shaver, Murdaya, & Fraley 2001). When people tell someone about a *terharu* experience, they often put a hand to their heart. Kama muta is one of the few emotions that Indonesians readily reveal that they feel. After I showed her The Kiss, one informant told us that Malay speakers also could label the emotion *menyentuh hati*, literally, 'touched my heart.' Shaver et al. also note a similar expression: "*Getar hati* means feeling moved (in the heart) and is often associated with love, although a person can be moved in other ways as well" (2001:213). (In the dialect spoken in Bengkulu Province, southwestern Sumatra, Dan Fessler explained that there is also a term, *gelinggaman*, for the feeling evoked by anything that causes shivers up the spine: whether being overcome by the cuteness of a baby, or fear, or disgust.)

In Thai (of the Kra-Dai language family), the lexeme that would commonly be used for kama muta is สะเทือนใจ, *sathuean jai*; *sathuean* literally means 'to shake, quake, tremble, or vibrate,' and *jai* is 'heart, spirit, spiritual center or core, soul, inner being, mind.' One can also say สะเทือนอารมณ์, *sathuean arom*, where *arom* is 'mood, temper, emotion, spirits, disposition, affect.'

Basque is a language isolate, unrelated to any other known language. The synonyms *ikutu* and *ukitu* are used for kama muta; both mean 'touched.' Both words would be felicitous to denote either kama muta or physical contact, such as being touched by the branch of a tree. One can also say, *bihotzean ikutu/ukitu* or *bihotz-ukitu*, 'touched the heart'; *bihoz dardaratu*; 'shake the heart'; or *bihozberatu*, 'heat the heart.'

These respective terms in these various languages do not denote precisely the same range of affective experiences; they are by no means exact translations of each other. It appears that people sometimes use each term to denote other emotions, and the key terms I have listed above are not the only terms people use for this emotion. Figure 7.2 illustrates this schematically. A crucial point for the study of emotions is that no one vernacular term in any language precisely delineates the phenomenon or the phenomenology of the emotion construct we are concerned with, an issue that I will take up below. But while the center and scope of these terms vary somewhat, it is noteworthy that in so many cultures, speakers in distinct language families recognize a CS-intensification emotion and have words or phrases that refer to it, along with its characteristic bodily symptoms. Deeper exploration in most languages would doubtless reveal in each congeries of terms that intersect more or less like the English ones diagrammed in Figure 7.1.

There is a remarkable pattern in lexemes for kama muta across quite a number of languages from various subfamilies of Indo-European, from all three Uralic languages, in Basque, from languages in the Dravidian, Afro-Asiatic, Kra-Dai, and Austronesian language families, and also in the Sino-Tibetan, Japonic, and Koreanic families (all three of which use the same 感动 characters for it and have homologous pronunciations). The lexemes that prototypically denote kama muta literally mean to <u>physically 'move,' 'touch,' or 'stir'</u>— and sometimes, 'touch the heart.' This is likely to be the result of convergent construction of the respective terms, rather than either a common deep etymology or borrowing, since these language families have been distinct for several thousand years and the terms in the respective language families are phonetically dissimilar.

In other words, across cultures and languages, speakers have independently invented, adopted, and maintained for many centuries words for kama muta based on the same two closely related physics metaphors: passive displacement of a solid or liquid, and passive contact. These lexemes are so deeply based that contemporary speakers of these languages often do not recognize that they are metaphors. Indeed, these are not secondary representations metaphorically removed from the primary lexical representations of kama muta by an explicit analogy; they are the direct and primary signs for denoting it.

I cannot say if our small convenience sample is at all representative of the 7,100 living languages in about 152 families (Simons & Fennig 2017) and the innumerable others that have died without a trace. But it seems that these passive displacement and passive contact metaphors must have independently and frequently been invented, adopted, diffused, and perpetuated. This implies that these metaphors resonate with widespread – probably universal – aspects of the cognitive representation of kama muta.

However, there are also many languages that do not use these metaphors to denote kama muta.

Related to the lexical representation of kama muta as the sense of passive contact are haptic 'softness' and delicacy terms such as English *tender* feelings, French *s'attendrir*, Estonian *heldinud*, Finish *heltyä*, Hungarian *elérzékenyült*. Consider the etymology of the English word.

tender (adj.)

'soft, easily injured,' early 13c., from Old French *tendre* 'soft, delicate; young' (11c.), from Latin *tenerem* (nominative *tener*) 'soft, delicate; of tender age, youthful,' from a derivative of PIE root ***ten-** 'to stretch,' on the notion of 'stretched,' hence 'thin,' hence 'weak' or 'young.' Compare Sanskrit *tarunah* 'young, tender,' Greek *teren* 'tender, delicate,' Armenian *t'arm* 'young, fresh, green.'

Meaning 'kind, affectionate, loving' first recorded early 14c. Meaning 'having the delicacy of youth, immature' is attested in English from early 14c. Related: Tenderly; tenderness. Tender-hearted first recorded 1530s.

(Harper 2016)

From the same root come the care-taking words *tend* and *attend to* (Partridge 1958).

So the lexical representation of kama muta as the sensory experience of passive contact extends in some languages, at least, to the feeling that one is soft, and somehow – perhaps because of not being hard, and hence being weak or vulnerable – young. It is interesting that both Indo-European and Uralic languages have apparently independently converged on this soft/young/vulnerable/affectionate manner of speaking of kama muta, especially when it is evoked by cute infant humans or animals. I have not yet searched for this 'tenderness' etymological metaphor across other language families.

What sort of sensation of being displaced does 'moved' represent: the vestibular, proprioceptive, or visual? Does the root of the metaphor reference the whole body being displaced, or some organ or appendage? If the 'moving' is something internal, what could it be? People feeling kama muta who say they are 'moved' do not seem to be referencing anything like intestinal peristalsis, and aside from such gut feelings, what other internal motion sensations can people feel? The diaphragm and chest muscles move as people breathe, and people experiencing kama muta often take and hold a deep breath. But breathing sensations are much more pronounced in other emotions such as fear. People have little sense of the *motion* of their blood, and nothing else of any appreciable mass within the body actually moves except muscles. More broadly, why is the generic English word, *emotion*, derived, via Latin, from a Proto-Indo-European root meaning 'move'? The same questions arise about being 'stirred': the only thing that people can actually feel churning in their bodies are their stomachs and intestines, which again do not seem to be the references of 'stirred.'

Likewise, what sort of 'touch' is the root of that metaphor? There are several senses of touch on the skin, based on neurons tuned respectively to warmth, cold, pain, deep pressure, light touch to body hairs or the skin surface, and gentle caressing. Does being emotionally 'touched' feel like one of these in particular, or all of them? There is also the feeling of goosebumps (piloerection, horripilation), which can be evoked by light or caressing touch, or sensual arousal, but goosebumps are also evoked by cold, fear, and the uncanny, and, subjectively, goosebumps do not seem to be the sensation that 'touched' references.

Then there is the mysterious sensation in the center of the chest that occurs in kama muta experiences, often referenced as *heartwarming* or *touching one's heart*. But just what is this sensation: what is happening in the center of the chest, and what sensory system is detecting it (or spoofing it)? In any case, English, Japanese, Hebrew, and (though less accessible) Hindi–Urdu have kama muta terms whose literal meaning is passive contact with the heart. Other languages may, as well.

Just as there are many sensations of being displaced, disturbing a liquid, or being contacted that could be metaphorical roots for *moved*, *touched*, and *stirred*, these particular words for kama muta are a small subset of the many words denoting the general concepts of being displaced, disturbing a liquid, or being contacted. Why are these particular terms used, rather than their near synonyms? What does it mean that in English, for example, we may say that a person feeling kama muta is *moved*, but not *shoved*, *displaced*, *relocated*, *repositioned*, *shifted*, *pulled*, *hauled*, or *dragged*? Why does *be moved* mean something so different from *be manipulated*? To be *moved* is not to have *moved on* or *moved up*, nor, of course, to have *moved in*, *moved out*, or *moved away*. We say a person feeling kama muta is *stirred*, but not *swirled*, *splashed*, *blended*, *beaten*, *whisked*, or *whipped.* Why does it mean something entirely different to say that a person is *stirred* than to say they are *mixed up, disturbed,* or *shaken?* It's wonderful to *stir* people, but not so nice to *stir up* trouble. Why do we say a person feeling kama muta is *touched,* but not that the person is *bumped, shoved, poked, tapped, prodded, banged, bashed, beaten, slapped, spanked, punched, stabbed, speared,* nor *stroked, massaged, caressed, hugged, kissed, fondled, cradled,* or *patted?* Why does saying that you were *touched* mean something so different from saying you were *contacted, tickled, rocked, struck,* or *had a close brush?* Why is it nice to *feel touched,* but unpleasant to deal with a *touchy* person? We could say that a person feeling kama muta is *gripped,* but not *squeezed.* Music can *grab* a person or *have a hold on* them, but those lexemes are broader than *touched.*

There are many other nuances. While in most contexts in French *être touché* means 'to be touched' in the emotional sense, in the context of sophisticated French and English repartee, *touché!* means 'you got me, you scored with that comeback' (based on conventions for winning and ending a sword duel by drawing first blood, and later, scoring points in fencing). Furthermore, being gently touched by a person can be very appealing, but unwanted or illegitimate gentle touching can also be extremely transgressive, upsetting, polluting, even disgusting. Why does the kama muta term *touching* build on the appealing aspect of touch and ignore the gross, violent, and transgressive? In general, higher-ranking persons may touch subordinates, but not vice versa, so why does the *touching* metaphor not evoke this hierarchical meaning of social contact?

As I write this, I'm watching a mother gently bouncing her infant, as parents so often do. For the infant, being bounced means that you are safe in your caretaker's arms or wrapped against her body (in addition to rocking, she may be walking, digging, grinding, pounding, etc.). For the infant, being touched (as a discrete action on a discrete patch of skin, rather than continuous whole body contact) means, that you are being caressed, groomed, or cleaned. Is that what makes the *moved* and *touched* metaphors so widespread? This might be the basis for the metaphor either through individual learning from experience, or by triggering some phylogenetically deeper mammalian innate releasing mechanism. However, this can't occur through explicit autobiographical memories from infancy, since those memories are invariably lost.

Any theory of the metaphors used to denote kama muta needs to answer such questions. I don't have definite answers. It is mystifying that these metaphors can be so widespread, and so specific, yet so opaque to introspection. Especially so because the terms for kama muta aren't simply metaphors – *moved, stirred,* and *touched* are the most basic and direct ways of characterizing the emotion. Speakers rarely notice that they are using a metaphor, and often can't easily think of any other way to label their kama muta. It would provide deep insight into the phenomenology, cognitive representation, and dynamics of kama muta (and by extension other emotions) if we could answer these questions about emotion language.

Most languages have broad terms for feelings, affect, emotion, or responses to social interaction; these terms encompass kama muta along with many or all other feelings. But not all languages have words that are even approximately focused on kama muta; many lack any lexeme specifically delineating kama muta and distinguishing it from most other emotions. However, speakers of Hebrew, Bikol, and Hindu/Urdu who have no accessible words of kama muta nevertheless report that they <u>feel</u> this emotion; some feel it frequently and sometimes intensely.

The question this raises is whether, and if so how, subjective kama muta experiences differ depending on whether or not a person's culture and language explicitly identify kama muta and represent it as a distinct emotion with one or more specific lexemes used to denote kama muta. As we have begun to see in the previous chapters and will see more clearly in the chapters to come, there is considerable cultural shaping of the sorts of experiences that evoke the emotion, the meaning of experiencing it, and the implications of various kinds of persons experiencing it. It is hard to imagine that this doesn't affect how kama muta <u>feels</u>. Certainly having a relatively specific vernacular lexeme for kama muta must make it easier for people to reflectively notice the experience, encode and retrieve it from memory, and communicate about it.

Finally, I should reiterate that the referent of any given lexeme depends on the dialect and historical moment, the speaker's idiolect, the speech situation, and the speaker's intent. Meaning is always indexically dependent on the manner in which an utterance is linked to the context of speech: the meaning of a word depends on who is speaking, who are the addresses(s) and listener(s), the speaker's relationship with them, what the speaker and others have said and plan to say, to whom it might be reported, and so forth. So what Figure 7.1 and Figure 7.2 show as sharp static lines are really fuzzy ever-shifting borders. In contrast, the purpose of the scientific term *kama muta* is to consistently and precisely denote one well-defined construct regardless of who uses it when. Only a scientific term can do this.

The epistemological implication of all this as that if the same psychological process operates in all cultures, we cannot identify its occurrences by relying <u>exclusively</u> on lexical labels (on the general point, see Scherer 2005; Paulhus & Vazire 2007; Coppin & Sander 2016). So how can we know whether and where kama muta occurs across cultures? By using a set of convergent indices, including, but not limited to, lexical labels. We conducted a study to identify kama muta among 3542 speakers of 15 languages in 19 countries (Zickfeld et al. 2019). While the labels for kama muta differ, in every place there are strong correlations among the facets of kama muta: the appraisal that a CS relationship has suddenly intensified, the characteristic sensations and signs, the positive valence of the emotion, the desire to give it to others and experience it together with others, the motivation to devote and commit to CS, and labels that translate *being moved*, *touched*, *heart-warming*, or *heart-touching*. In conjunction with each other, these facets form a gestalt, a whole, an entity: the kama muta emotion. This entity is clearly evident in every population we have studied.

The lexical fallacy: Using vernacular words as psychological constructs

The diversity of the manifestations of kama muta makes studying it challenging, exciting, and potentially contentious. One aspect of this is that the kama muta construct may not correspond with intuition, introspection, or the folk psychology of any particular person or culture at any particular point in history. Vernacular languages and folk psychology may pick up on adventitious features of kama muta experience, defining lexical and conceptual categories that, to the person reflecting on them, intuitively feel distinct. Moreover, folk names for kinds of kama muta experiences tend to be context-based, so that, for example, kama muta evoked by memory of CS is called *nostalgia*, kama muta evoked by a nationalistic ritual might be called *patriotism*, kama muta evoked by the excited identification with one's team – among teammates or by fans with the team and each other – may be called *team spirit* or eponymously named after the team, kama muta evoked by a romantic novel is *sentimentalism*, kama muta evoked by feeling suddenly one with Jesus is *being touched by the Spirit*, but kama muta evoked by cute kittens has no name at all in English. The nomenclatural taxonomy of the speaker's language makes the lexically distinguished manifestations of kama muta feel intuitively distinct, real, natural, and absolute, despite the relativistic fact that different languages sort kama muta experiences into different categories (cf. Wierzbicka 1999). And, indeed, there <u>are</u> subjectively real differences in the kama muta experiences evoked by different sorts of intensifications of different sorts of CS relationship. Nonetheless, whatever the lexically afforded, intuitively felt, or explicitly articulated folk distinctions among kinds of kama muta experiences, it is essential to keep in mind what I set out in Chapter 4: that all result from the sudden intensification of CS relationships, all motivate devotion and moral commitment to CS relationships, all are positive experiences that people want to give to and experience with others, and when sufficiently strong, all tend to evoke elements of the same constellation of physical sensations.

Like any other scientifically defined mental state or experience, the kama muta construct as a category may not respect the culturally informed intuitions of everyone (or anyone) who experiences kama muta. If one informant feels that the phenomenological qualia of his experience at a particular moment at a wedding (or at weddings in general) differ from the phenomenological qualia of his experience at a particular moment when holding his baby (or when holding babies in general), does his report of this introspection imply that the experiences must be classified as different emotions? Or that they are different emotions <u>for him</u>, regardless of whether (some or all) other informants report that their own wedding experience(s) feel pretty much the same as their baby-holding experience(s)? One could make the reports of introspections the topic of study in their own right, ignoring – or just putting aside – any other properties and processes of the experiences. That is, the phenomenology of an individual's or set of people's emotional experiences is a legitimate object of research. One could reflect on and strive to describe one's own experiences, without regard to how generalizable these are. But while we aim to take reports of experience seriously as <u>one</u> important source of information about emotions, we do not make it our primary, let alone exclusive, source for characterizing kama muta. Crucially, moreover, we do not define our construct with respect to folk taxonomies, or reflective recognition or labelling of sensations and situations. While many emotion researchers focus on vernacular naming of sensations, or sensations-in-situations, we neither define our construct that way nor restrict our research to lexicalization. Though I respect lexicography as an important pursuit, I am not a lexicographer; my aim is not to produce definitions of the usage of vernacular lexemes (words or phrases). My aim is to understand psychological, social, and cultural processes. For more on the pitfalls of using vernacular lexemes as scientific constructs, see Online Note 7.1 and Fiske 2019.

We have already come upon something else that makes it problematic to simply assume that words are in one-to-one correspondence with psychological phenomena. Languages such as ancient Greek, Hindi/Urdu, and Bikol do not have any word that denotes anything like kama muta, but speakers of these languages seem to <u>feel</u> kama muta readily enough. More generally, if we rely on the lexicon of any one language to provide an exhaustive list or classification of emotional phenomena, we will certainly fail to identify some. Tahitians have neither words nor concepts for sadness about separation or grief at the loss of a loved one (Levy 1973). English-speakers don't have a name for their emotional responses to cuteness, though, as I noted, Uralic languages do have words for it. English has no good word for the emotional experience of the uncanny, though Tahitian does (Levy 1973). It is extremely unlikely that there is any language that has specific and precise names for all human emotional experiences.

Zickfeld et al. (2017) reviewed the literature that is based on the variously defined – and often undefined – psychological concepts of *being moved*. We found that most researchers simply assume that whatever English speakers verbally label *being moved* <u>is</u> the emotion, entirely ignoring contextual, age, gender, dialectical, and historical differences in usage of the lexeme. Conversely, researchers ignore the differences among the myriad overlapping English lexemes that they might have used as alternatives to *being moved*. *Touched* is not quite the same as *moved*, nor is *heart-warmed*, let alone *stirred, enraptured, tender feelings*, et cetera; given that they are not perfectly synonymous, what is the basis for choosing one of these lexemes while ignoring all of the others? No theorist justifies or even considers the notional use of this one particular vernacular English lexeme as their concept. Consequently, most researchers take it for granted that for valid measurement of the concept, it is sufficient to have participants rate lexical labels alone; relatively few researchers systematically measure their constructs with reference to other facets of the emotion.

Researchers further ignore the great variety of ways that different languages taxonomize the affective realm. If we take any vernacular emotion word in any given language and find its best translation in another language, the meanings of the respective words are tied into their respective cultures in unique ways. English *anger* would have to be translated in Ilongot (an Austronesian language of the Philippines) as *liget* (Rosaldo 1980). However, *liget* prototypically motivates courageous disdain for the danger of climbing high in trees to lop off the branches with stone axes. Moreover, the paradigm of *liget* is the motivation that arises in young men when a loved one has died, driving them to gather to find an elder to lead them, go stealthily out into the forest, find a random stranger, cut off his or her head, and triumphantly toss it. Pruning trees and headhunting are not within the scope of actions that English speakers would anticipate being motivated by *anger*. Few English speakers value anger, but Ilongots prize *liget* as an essential, virtuous, awesome emotion. The Ilongot who doesn't get fiercely angry on appropriate occasions is disdained and disparaged. Should scientists select *anger*, *liget*, both, or neither as naming a universal emotion? The Moose of Burkina Faso (again note the pronunciation, **MOH**-say) use the verb *zoe* and the noun *dabeem* for what they feel in the presence of a charging elephant and what they feel in the presence of a great and benign chief. English distinguishes between *fear* and *awe*. Should we adopt the English nomenclature or the Moore? In either case, should a dictionary be the source of our psychological concepts?

The **lexical fallacy** consists of reification of vernacular lexemes as scientific constructs. We should not heedlessly assume that everyday word usage reveals natural kinds of psychological entities. In particular, there are no valid grounds for the ubiquitous practice of obliviously adopting the affect types and taxonomy implicit in the contemporary English lexicon (see Online Note 7.1; Fiske 2019).

Any and all of these properties of vernacular lexemes makes them unsuitable for scientific analysis or communication. That's why every major theoretical advance requires the coinage of new scientific terms for its new constructs. This is the case in every science. There are innumerable valid scientific phenomena that no vernacular lexeme precisely delineates. By the same token, we needed a technical term to denote our construct, so we borrowed the Sanskrit for 'moved by love' and called it *kama muta*. This term is a scientific term denoting our construct, just as 'anterograde amnesia' or 'prion' denote other scientific constructs. By denoting the construct with a term from a dead language unfamiliar to most readers, we avoid the ambiguity, errors, confusion, distortions, and distractions that would result from using a vernacular term from a living language. It should go without saying that we use *kama muta* <u>as</u> a scientific construct; we are not making any claim about Sanskrit speakers' varying uses of this phrase thousands of years ago. Its original South Asian meaning seems to have been in the same ballpark as our construct, but that doesn't really matter. In the context of our theory, kama muta means whatever we want it to mean.

By coining a universal scientific term to denote this emotion construct, we emphatically do not mean to imply that the situations that elicit kama muta, its subjective phenomenology, its meaning, its performance, or consequent actions are <u>identical</u> in every respect in every instance in every culture. There <u>are</u> remarkable consistencies, resulting from psychological and developmental processes shared by all humans. And there are remarkable differences. <u>Our theory aims at explaining these consistencies, while also explaining what varies from context to context and from culture to culture.</u> Something of the nature of the consistencies and the variation has already emerged in the preceding chapters, and we will see much more about what is the same and what varies in every chapter to come. In Chapters 10 and 17 I will systematically conceptualize the nature of the universality and the nature of the cultural particularity, and how they emerge together out of the psychocultural and social relational mechanism of kama muta.

The inadequacy of natural language to delineate emotions is a widespread theme in literature. In a famous dialog in *Faust* (von Goethe 1808), Margaret asks Faust whether he believes in God. And instead of telling the truth, which is that he does not, Faust talks about love and kama muta, implying that this is the real thing and more important. He basically says: I love you, and I move you, and when you are moved and touched by my love, that is enough you need to know about me, there is no need for me to believe in God. And while making this point, he also implies that what other people call God is just love and kama muta.[6]

> Faust: Are not my eyes reflected in yours?
> And don't all things press
> On your head and heart,
> And weave, in eternal mystery,
> Visibly: invisibly, around you?
> Fill your heart from it: it is so vast,
> And when you are blessed by the deepest feeling,
> Call it then what you wish,
> Joy! Heart! Love! God!
> I have no name
> For it! Feeling is all:
> Names are sound and smoke,
> Veiling Heaven's bright glow [*Glut*, characterized by heat, not luminance]
>
> Margaret: That's all well and good, I know,
> The priest says much the same,
> Only, in slightly different words.
>
> Faust: It's what all hearts, say, everywhere
> Under the heavenly day,
> Each in its own speech:
> And why not I in mine?
>
> *(Goethe 1808, Scene 19, lines 3446–3465)*

Vernacular names and folk models of and for emotions should not be adopted as scientific models, but they are an important topic of scientific research in their own right (see, for example, Lutz 1988; White & Kirkpatrick 1987). We need dictionaries, as well as thicker sociolinguistic descriptions. Moreover, folk models of emotions inform how people respond to events, including the meanings, sensations, motives that their experiences evoke. People do not fully understand the causes of their emotions, but their implicit and explicit ideas, their practices and institutions, definitely <u>affect</u> what emotions they experience, when, and how. There are also perceptual aspects of folk models, facilitating (or constraining) the identification and interpretation of emotions. For example, as I discussed in Chapter 2, the common contemporary Western folk model of tears (and, derived from the folk model, the prevalent scientific assumption as well) is that tears are an index of 'sadness.' That is, people tend to 'see' sadness when they perceive tears in others, or themselves. This can be described as an appraisal or attribution, but it is generally so 'direct' that it makes sense to describe it as apperceptive. As we have seen, this folk model is misleading – people often cry in joyful kama muta. But if we ask people to recall how they felt on a previous occasion, does the belief that tears index sadness make people recall or report tearful kama muta experiences as more sad and less joyful than they actually were? Do people's ideas about tears affect how they interpret others' kama muta? Or affect their understanding of what they themselves are feeling? Again, if people judge that tears are un-manly indications of being soft and lacking self-control, men may be less likely to report or even remember their kama muta tears.

It is not only the lexical labels for kama muta that vary across contexts, persons, cultures, and history. Kama muta is always culturally informed and oriented in many other respects as well, which I will address in Chapters 10 and 17.

Methodological challenges

So kama muta is not always whatever people call *being moved*, or *gǎn dòng* (感动), or denote with any particular vernacular term in any language. And what people label *being moved*, or *gǎn dòng*, isn't always kama muta. Furthermore, in some languages there is no specific word for kama muta that distinguishes it from many other emotions. Well, then, how can we study it? How can we know when the feeling that a person is experiencing or remembering is kama muta? How can we recognize kama muta when we see it, when people talk about their experiences, or when we read others' reports of what they observed?

To identify instances of kama muta and discriminate kama muta from other emotions we need to obtain convergent evidence. We need to triangulate, looking for events in which people

1. Participate in or observe sudden intensification of CS relationships, <u>and</u>
2. Experience a set of collectively distinctive bodily sensations, <u>and</u>
3. Indicate that they feel *positive*, want to give the emotion to others, want to experience it with others, <u>and</u>

4. Suddenly become motivated to devote and (re)commit themselves to CS relationships, <u>and</u>
5. <u>If</u> there are accessible lexemes in the person's language, they denote the experience with a word or phrase that belongs to the set of partial synonyms *moved, touched, stirred, heart-warming, heart-touching, tenderness, mystical ecstasy,* or their translations in other languages—especially when the terms are based on passive motion or contact.

Although each of these five kinds of evidence is a strong indicator none is sufficient on its own. In practice, each of them is reliable, but not flawless, because we need to rely on self-report to know whether people are experiencing some of the sensations, and whether they perceive sudden intensification of CS. Moreover, some people rarely experience any sensations, while some languages contexts: consider the lack of a clear label for the emotions evoked by cute kittens or kids.

When we have clear evidence that an event has all five of these features, or clearly has most of them, we can be confident that we have an instance of kama muta. And indeed our scores of studies, now with over 10,000 participants, consistently find that these five indicators are correlated with each other when people watch a range of videos, or report their everyday experiences (Seibt et al. 2016; Schubert et al. 2016; Seibt et al. 2017). The latter study showed this cohesion across five nations and languages. In the Zickfeld et al. (2019) study, we found that these indicators were highly intercorrelated in 19 samples of 15 languages, with 3,542 participants. That is, when a person has any one of the indicators of kama muta, they are very likely to have each of the others at the same time. The appraisal that CS has suddenly intensified, certain lexical labels, a characteristic set of sensations, positive valence and the desire to share the emotion, and motives to devote and commit to CS occur together, as an integrated and cohesive constellation.

However, in naturally occurring experiences, some or all these indicators may not be reported or discernable. Typically we can't directly identify all of these features when observing everyday behavior; likewise, ancient texts and even ethnographies typically don't provide direct, complete, or compelling evidence about all five of these facets of experiences. Furthermore, the bodily sensations and signs evidently occur only when kama muta is fairly intense; in the milder instances that probably make up the vast majority of kama muta experiences, many (most?) people do not seem to often experience <u>any</u> of these sensations or signs. Moreover, a person experiencing an emotion, or an observer, may not be aware of a sensation, may be dimly aware of a sensation but not attend to it sufficiently to encode it as a meaningful aspect of experience in long-term memory, may interpret a sensation as something else, may not be able to retrieve the sensation as an aspect or instance of that lexically encoded emotion episode, or may wish or need to report it as something else. That is, sensations of an emotion may go unnoticed, be forgotten, go unreported, or be reported as something else.

Moreover, native speakers of a language don't agree very well about what counts as an instance of any descriptor (S. T. Fiske 1986; D. W. Fiske 1995). What counts as *to weep?* What counts as *pleurer?* Are *chills, thrills, goosebumps* all the same, or are they three different sensations? Or two? English speakers are neither clear nor in complete agreement in their use of these words. Participants responding to items may not agree about the meanings of these terms, or even use them consistently. Individuals use language differently on different occasions, and no two people use a language in quite the same way. Dialects vary, along with local practices of language use. As Donald Fiske showed, people don't consistently register, encode, or reliably recall events or experiences corresponding even to common folk terms for psychological states (Fiske 1981). So we should not expect informants' memories to be sufficiently well organized to permit systematic or valid encoding, retrieval, or enumeration of all instances of being *moved* or being *angry.* Does anyone keep a tally of each type of emotion they experience? To the extent that emotions, their features, their eliciting conditions, their moral implications, or their motivational affordances do not become encoded in declarative semantic or narrative memory, or are encoded in a distorted or inconsistent manner, explicit language will be an inadequate or even deceptive guide to emotions.

Yet most research on kama muta must extensively rely on self-report, whether we are doing ethnographic research, reading ethnographies, interviewing, conducting surveys, reading blogs, or asking experimental participants to rate what they perceive or feel. The questions we ask informants, respondents, and participants have to be simply formulated in everyday language. Whether we ask informants to tell us about their experiences in an unstructured format, to name their emotions, to tell us whether they perceive sudden CS intensification, to describe their sensations or others' symptoms, to tell us about or rate their motives, our inquiries have to be expressed in everyday, nontechnical language, and any verbal responses they provide will likewise be expressed in the vernacular. To talk with English-speaking respondents, we and they have to use terms such as *moved, touched, cuteness, nostalgia, goosebumps, choked-up.* Experimental participants aren't familiar with the communal sharing construct, so we can't simply ask them whether a communal sharing relationship has suddenly intensified – even if they understood the subtleties of our conceptualization of 'intensification,' which they don't. This means that the respondents' language and folk models mediate their interpretation, encoding, and recall of their own emotional experiences and the experiences they observe. So we come up against all of the factors that make the use of vernacular language for scientific description so problematic. This makes it all the more essential to use all five of the criteria together to convergently identify instances of kama muta.

There is another issue with self-report measures. Kama muta generally (perhaps always) lasts only for seconds, or at most a minute or two. If respondents or participants are rating an entire event or stimulus of longer duration, their ratings of the kama muta moment will be diluted or confounded with their ratings of whatever emotions or affects they experienced before or after the kama muta moment. Indeed, the narratives that evoke kama muta most consistently and strongly typically do so by evoking anxiety, sadness, or other forms of distress about whether communal sharing will ever arise or be restored (Fiske, Schubert, & Seibt 2017a). We use videos of this sort because they so effectively and reliably evoke kama muta – for a moment at the end. The same issue arises in ratings of some kinds of personal experiences: think of the hours of pain, fear, and frustration of childbirth, culminating, perhaps, in a moment of joyous kama muta. It is often difficult for participants to rate just this kama muta moment, isolated from the entire narrative or episode as a whole.

There are two other methodological strategies we can use to transcend the problematics of methods that rely on ordinary language. Neither of these other strategies can replace the language-based methods, because neither is infallible. But the errors and biases that each entails are different and largely independent of the language-based methods. So whenever possible, we can use one or ideally both to complement the verbal methods. We can seek convergence not only among the verbal methods, but among the verbal methods and the other two. The first complementary strategy is to search for direct physiological indicators of kama muta. Many decades of research seeking distinctive physiological profiles for specific emotions has failed to identity any, perhaps in part because the vernacular terms used as scientific constructs may not be valid natural kinds. Regardless, self-report and attention to our own sensations strongly suggest that kama muta <u>may possibly</u> have a unique physiological profile, consisting of tears, throat construction, goosebumps or chills, a sensation in the upper center of the chest, a deep breath and pause in breathing, activation of the biceps and wrist and shoulder rotator muscles that move the palm to the upper chest, followed by a sensation of buoyancy and exhilaration. We don't know what causes the chest sensation, buoyancy, and exhilaration, or what sensory systems detect them. But it does seem that, in principle, one could objectively measure most of these physiological signs. If so, then their co-occurrence would constitute the distinctive physiological signature of kama muta.

The other essentially non-verbal method is at the opposite end of the epistemological spectrum: it is entirely subjective. We believe that we, our research assistants, and others who study kama muta, know it when they feel it. We believe that our reflective awareness of the emotion is a valid method for detecting it. Our awareness is not based on introspection about the psychosocial or psychophysiological <u>mechanisms</u>, but we don't rely on such process introspection, which may indeed be impossible. After the fact, we can analyze much of the social psychology, but the sensation of kama muta is something that we simply <u>feel</u> in the moment, and can reliably recall. We have come to be discerning connoisseurs of this emotion, to the point where our reflective awareness appears to be reliable and valid. Every colleague, research assistant, and student we have worked with fairly quickly becomes capable of recognizing her own kama muta experiences and reliably distinguishing them from other emotions. It doesn't seem to be difficult for intelligent, self-aware people to do. If indeed our reflective awareness of kama muta is both reliable and valid, that allows us to use participant observation as a method.

To do participant observation, the ethnographer not only watches for the situations and signs of kama muta in others, but attends to *her own* emotions and sensations. Then she attempts to identify what evoked her kama muta. After this, she can explore what these emotions and sensations reveal about what her informants may be experiencing. Are informants also perceiving a CS relationship to have suddenly intensified? Was there an evocative act of consubstantial assimilation, such as commensalism or blood mixing? Are informants weeping or putting their hands to their chests? Are they labelling their experiences with words that literally denote passive displacement, agitation of a liquid, or touch? If the participant observer is truly participating in the social relationships that her informants participate in and she notices that she feels kama muta, she can hypothesize that her informants may feel kama muta as well. Then she can observe to see whether she can confirm this. She can also use mostly non-verbal analytic methods to deduce whether her feeling of kama muta can be extrapolated to her informants. Is there other evidence that they perceived a CS relationship to intensify suddenly? Do the informants perform more compassionate, kind, generous actions that indicate increased devotion and commitment to the relevant CS relationships? She can sit in and listen to her informants' conversations, gossip, and commentary on the event. And finally, she can interview them. Here we are back to words, but no longer relying on informants' words alone.

Objective physiological assessment of kama muta in the laboratory may be possible before long. If so, sooner or later it may be possible to develop compact, mobile, and relatively unobtrusive systems that could continuously assess physiological signs of kama muta in everyday life. But participant observation is available now, and it works fine in everyday life. Throughout the book you will see phenomena that have been illuminated already by focused participant observation at one site on one practice, consisting of 100 hours over ten weeks. No one has yet done a long-term, comprehensive, or in-depth participant observation ethnography of kama muta in any culture, but I hope anthropologists will do so.

Neither participant observation nor physiological measurement can be done in cultures, institutions, or practices that no longer exist. These methods won't tell us whether the formation of host-guest *xenia* relationships evoked kama muta in ancient Greece, or whether contemporaries of the Buddha felt kama muta when they observed his compassion. For that we have to rely on written reports and art, together with careful comparisons to congruent contemporary experiences. But it is very much worth the effort to explore past cultures to see whether, where, and how people experienced kama muta; we need to know whether and in what respects the culturally-shaped experiences of kama muta may change over time. Historical texts and accounts also reveal significant practices, institutions, roles, narratives, and artifacts that evoke kama muta, illuminating both cultural evolutionary processes and, conversely, how malleable the psychosocial mechanism of kama muta is.

As we compare what emerges from each of the methods – noting convergence or incongruities – we refine our ontology. That is, we add, subtract, or revise the features that we theorize define kama muta experiences. Then we take these new criteria for identifying kama muta experiences back to the field, the lab, or the interview. That is, our methods depend on our conception of what kama muta is. Thus we develop our epistemology, figuring out better ways detect and to recognize kama muta motes. These new results enable us to better characterize kama muta. Thus ontology and epistemology progress in a dialectic interchange, enabling us to bootstrap our way toward an understanding of kama muta. However, the epistemology becomes especially complex when we adopt the ontological position that emotions are likely to be polythetic categories, which are fundamentally characterized by a total 'score' based on the total degree of presence of features from a weighted list. (The diagnoses of psychological disorders in the 5th edition of the *Diagnostic and Statistical Manual* of the American Psychiatric Association are formulated somewhat like this.) For example, we might say that a person experiences kama muta if their total score is ≥10, where the score is the sum of the intensity of features from a list of eight, with each feature weighted differently. Perhaps warm fuzzy feelings in the chest might be weighted more than crying, and crying more than being choked-up. The weight of a feature might be multiplied by its intensity, such that, for example, if a person is crying intensely, it would count more than if a person merely had moist eyes. A valid ontology may require an even more complex criterion: for example, we may want to say that a person is experiencing kama muta only if their total score is ≥10 *and* at least two of a set of five key features are present. Then no matter how intense features 6–8 are, this isn't an instance of kama muta unless two of the following are present: a warm feeling in the center of the chest, crying, goosebumps, feeling choked-up, and feeling buoyant. Or the score could be computed as an interaction such that a warm feeling in the chest, crying, and buoyancy occurring together might be given a score greater than the sum of the scores of the three components when they occur alone. Such an ontology – which I think is valid for emotions and many other psychological entities – is an epistemological challenge because when we start to investigate some phenomena that might constitute 'an emotion,' we don't know a priori how to identify the features, let alone how to weight or combine them, and whether some number of some set of the features is crucial. Of course, this would not be an issue if the emotional experience were characterized by necessary and sufficient features such as a unique 'facial expression,' but I don't believe this is true of kama muta (or perhaps any emotion). Reviewing the related concept of 'elevation,' Pohling and Diessner (2016) and Thomson and Siegel (2016) likewise conclude that it has no distinct facial expression.

All of this is to say that we should expect kama muta to vary across time, across cultures, across different communal sharing relationships, and across contexts – but the variants should still be clearly and definitely recognizable as kama muta because they all share most of the common features of the natural kind. Kama muta certainly varies in intensity, probably along dimensions such as attentional awareness, joyfulness, each physical sensation, and motivational impact. It may vary in unknown respects as a function of the kind of CS relationship that intensifies, how the CS intensifies, or the amplitude of the intensification. Nevertheless, the person's apperception of intensification of a CS relationship is always the cause of kama muta. So if we construe kama muta broadly and dynamically so as to include its cause, CS intensification can be regarded as its one necessary feature. In this respect, kama muta is similar to social scientific constructs such as 'language' and 'marriage.' They are natural kinds that have evolved so that they must be realized in culture-specific forms – they cannot be implemented without the proper cultural precedents, prototypes, and precepts that complete them (see Fiske 2000 and Online Note 7.2).

In Chapters 10 and 17, I'll present a more comprehensive theory of the psychological, social, cultural, and evolutionary aspects of kama muta processes. But we already have all the theory we need for now to provisionally support our explorations of kama muta across a great variety of practices, institutions, roles, narratives, and artifacts in diverse cultures throughout history. Let's begin by looking at kama muta in Western arts.

Online notes

7.1 Why not to base scientific constructs on everyday language.
7.2 Natural kinds of human mental systems that have evolved to be necessarily realized in culture-specific forms.

Notes

1 We suppose that what we have to say about *kama muta* pretty much applies to the nomenclature of other emotions, and indeed all psychological processes, but we will satisfy ourselves here by focusing on kama muta alone. In Chapter 19 (see Table 19.1) we broaden our purview to briefly consider how we can apply our ideas about kama muta to other social-relational emotions. For more on this, see Fiske 2019.
2 www.larousse.fr/dictionnaires/francais.
3 After watching the "Thai Medicine" video, one male Hindi and English bilingual informant from Uttar Pradesh reported no sensations but labeled his feeling as भावपूर्ण, *bhavapoorn*, 'poignant.'
4 https://www.youtube.com/watch?v=MH-Bm7V6_Vg.
5 My thanks to Tanvi Sakhamuru for identifying these lexemes, and then collecting ratings of the videos, in the framework of an independent study she did with me. The videos, used in many of our studies, were Thai good deeds; Thai medicine; and the clip from *Wall-E* in which Wall-E, having failed to recognize Eve, suddenly recognizes her when they kiss.
6 Beate Seibt and Thomas Schubert provided the interpretation of the German, which I here quote in A. J. Kline's translation. Note the references to sensations in the heart.

8

THE ARTS OF KAMA MUTA

Over the past few years, as my Kama Muta Lab colleagues and I learned to recognize kama muta, we were astonished to discover it in so many contexts in so many cultures. Whenever we thought of a practice or institution in which CS often suddenly intensified, we investigated it – trying to be cautious and skeptical. Yet, over and over again, wherever we found CS suddenly intensifying, we found good evidence for kama muta. One of our most exciting discoveries was how central kama muta is to the arts: we now think that the experience of kama muta may be a large part of what draws people to create and to enjoy literature, painting, and dance.[1] We saw in Chapter 3 that kama muta is pivotal in the *Odyssey*. In this chapter, let's sample sentimental literature, melodrama, poetry readings, Internet glurge, painting and sculpture, tattoos, and dance. That's a ridiculous scope for one chapter, but our aim is simply to suggest the significance of kama muta in the arts. In Chapter 6, we saw that people design oratory, political spectacle, and marketing to evoke kama muta that moves people to act in ways the designer intends. In this chapter, we explore artistic evocation of kama muta for its own esthetic sake. But I begin with an intermediate case: a novel with political aims whose remarkable impact occurred through the kama muta it evoked.

Uncle Tom's Cabin and *Tortilla Flat*

Seeking the experience of being moved for its own sake is thus the principal problem its critics perceive to be at the heart of what we have called 'active' sentimentality. The sin consists in overlooking the values revealed by the experience of being moved and focusing rather on the emotional experience itself. However, the existence of such 'misuses' of the experience of being moved does of course not tell against our claim that 'being moved' is a precious experience that can help us discover or rediscover what gives our lives significance. This is precisely why sentimental people seek it: to feel as if their lives have depth and significance. However, they are, the critics of sentimentality will say, looking in the wrong place, for it is the value the experience gives access to that lends it importance, not the experience itself.

(Cova and Deonna 2014:465)

Florian Cova and Julien Deonna's critique of sentimentality is one that many critics share, but perhaps it is too harsh, for two reasons. First, what is wrong with having eudemonic feelings, even if an experience does not change one's life? Second, there is no inherent "sin" in an emotion that generates devotion and commitment to CS; on the contrary, kama muta is a virtue! Ethical judgments aside, in fact today in the US, 74.7% of a nationally representative US sample of 3006 people report having been previously "moved, touched, or inspired" by reading a book (Raney et al. 2018; perhaps the other 25.3% haven't read a book lately).

Valuing and cultivating kama muta in the arts and life is at the heart of 'romantic' cultural movements: to a considerable degree, romanticism consists of highly valuing kama muta and the arts and practices that evoke it. Consider Britain and America from the 1740s to the 1780s, when a new genre became popular: sentimental literature that made the reader cry in compassion for the characters' suffering – and was intended to do just that (Dixon 2015:96–107).

This kind of weeping was new, and became a recognized characteristic of eighteenth-century culture. It was just one part of a world of moral weeping which extended from condemned criminals to their judges, chaplains, and executioners, and from philosophers, preachers, and philanthropists to prostitutes, forgers, highwaymen, and thieves.

(Dixon 2015:96)

Also poets: Robert Burns was moved to tears by the Bible, Shakespeare, and sentimental novels (Dixon 2015:97). The male protagonist of Henry Mackenzie's very popular 1771 novel, *The Man of Feeling*, became the prototype of tears "interpreted as signs of virtue, tenderness, and humanity" (Dixon 2015:98); "the manly tear was a gesture arising from a universal love of humanity" (2015:100).

From what I can tell, what critics call 'sentimental' literature typically evokes kama muta in the reader, and it appears that evoking kama muta is generally the sentimental author's intent (see Fiske, Schubert, & Seibt 2017a). Mendelman (2014:698) characterizes this mode:

sentimentalism refers to the literary mode whose conventions emphasize feeling—physical sensation and emotional intuition—as a source of knowledge, meaning, and interpersonal connection. Nineteenth-century sentimentalism typically links this sensibility to femininity, domesticity, intimate attachment, religious morality, and related values like sympathy, chastity, and self-sacrifice. Nineteenth-century sentimental plots commonly reward the latter values (often with marriage as the happy ending) and punish their opposite with death. Nineteenth-century sentimentalism also reinforces these values through tropes of embodiment, ranging from the excessive (fainting, weeping, fleeing) to the more subtle (a touch, a gaze, a beating heart).

Harriet Beecher Stowe did not invent sentimental literature, but she mastered it and deployed it with far-reaching effect. In her 1852 novel *Uncle Tom's Cabin*, Beecher Stowe evoked kama muta in her readers to move them to abolish slavery. That is, she used the narrative devices I discussed in Chapter 3 strategically, for her political purposes. In mid-nineteenth century America, many white Americans had only the most limited sentiments of CS solidarity with negro Americans, especially slaves. Harriet Beecher Stowe appreciated that white American support for the abolition of slavery could be nurtured by evoking third-person kama muta through scenes of intensifying CS relationships between whites and negroes, including scenes in which the reader would understand that the protagonists felt first- or second-person kama muta. She maximized the affordance of kama muta by making Eliza, the white main character, cute, and at the same time leading the reader to strongly identify with her. The scenes of love and devotion between Eliza and the negro characters evoked readers' third-person kama muta and at the same time their first-person kama muta toward the negro characters.

   Uncle Tom's Cabin was extraordinarily popular when it came out, and is arguably the most politically influential novel ever written. Its popularity and its stirring mobilization of abolitionist sentiments seems to have resulted precisely because of the strong kama muta that it evoked. The outline of the plot is that the slave Uncle Tom rescues a little white girl, Eva, from drowning; Eva persuades her wealthy, plantation-owning father to buy Tom, so Tom becomes the coachman to Eva's family. Then Eva falls ill and is going to die. Yet rather than feel frightened or sorry for herself, Eva transcends her illness, compassionately caring for those around her. In one scene, Topsy, a non-Christian orphan slave girl, believes that she is unlovable and refuses to be 'good.' Eva suggests that Miss Ophelia would love her if only she were good, and Topsy replies,

> "No; she can't bar [bear] me, 'cause I'm a nigger!—she'd's soon have a toad touch her! There can't nobody love niggers. ... "
>
> "Oh, Topsy, poor child, I love you!" said Eva, with a sudden burst of feeling, and laying her thin, white hand on Topsy's shoulder: "I love you, because you haven't had any father, or mother, or friends;—because you've been a poor, abused child! I love you, and I want you to be good. I am very unwell, Topsy, and I think I shan't live a great while; and it really grieves

me, to have you be so naughty. I wish you would try to be good for my sake;—it's only a little while I shall be with you."

The round, keen eyes of the black child were overcast with tears;—large, bright drops rolled heavily down, one by one, and fell on the little white hand. Yes, in that moment, a ray of real belief, a way of heavenly love, had penetrated the darkness of her heathen soul! She laid her head down between her knees, and wept and sobbed,—while the beautiful child, bending over her, looked like the picture of some bright angel stooping to reclaim a sinner.

(Beecher Stowe 1852:314–315)

Before dying, Eva performs an evocative act of consubstantial assimilation, giving a lock of her hair to each of the family slaves, appealing to them to become Christian so they can meet her in heaven. And in the end we see that Eva's loving kindness as she lay dying has changed the white woman Miss Ophelia, who never could stand Topsy.

"Topsy, you poor child," she said, as she led her into her room, "don't give up! *I* can love you, though I am not like that dear little child; I do, and I'll try to help you to grow up a good Christian girl."

(Beecher Stowe 1852:334)

(For more on how Stowe depicts and evokes what is clearly kama muta, see Tompkins 1985.)

While few books have had the social and political influence of *Uncle Tom's Cabin*, sentimental literature has been popular for centuries around the world. I look forward to the prospect of literature scholars examining the role of kama muta in this aspect of oral and written narrative (on this, see Fiske, Schubert, & Seibt 2017a). One of the many things that future research might illuminate concerns the kinds of CS relationships that readers imagine being both desirable and problematic, hence affording kama muta experiences. For example, what made white American readers in the 1850s disposed to accept, and indeed cherish, Eva's relationships with her slaves? How do readers in each culture imagine such CS relationships might be intensified? It seems likely that giving and keeping locks of hair may evoke kama muta in other cultural contexts, though perhaps not in South Asian cultures where another person's hair is commonly felt to be polluting.

* * * * * *

Story tellers universally evoke kama muta in their characters and their listeners or readers by reuniting lovers, family members, or comrades, as Hogan (2003) and Booker (2004) show, and with scenes of amazing devotion and love, as in *Uncle Tom's Cabin*. In another very popular political novel, *The Grapes of Wrath* (1939), John Steinbeck's migrants, displaced from their land by the Depression, drought, and industrial agriculture, are brought together by their common suffering and fear. In desperate need, they support and care for each other, share their meager resources, and offer each other solace and comfort. Steinbeck's purpose is to celebrate this communal sharing among the destitute, and to advance it as a political agenda – political, yet personal, in the daily face-to-face relationships of those whose common cause is survival. In the final scene, a young woman has been abandoned by her new husband, and her newborn has died. She and her parents, barely getting by as peach pickers, have been flooded out of the boxcar they inhabit. Reaching a barn on high ground, they find a man and his daughter inside. The man is dying of starvation because he has been giving what little food he had to his daughter. Indeed, no one has any money or food. The young woman' parents bring her to the starving man, and she suckles him.

Compassionate friendship, in all its complications and conflicts with other motives, is the core theme of Steinbeck's novels. In *Of Mice and Men* (1937), George's devotion to Lennie commits him, finally, to kill Lennie to save him from being lynched – thereby sacrificing his only friend.

With humorous sympathy, Steinbeck's *Tortilla Flat* (1935) explores kindness. The book is about the ambiguity about what is manipulative pretense, what is genuine caring, and how the two co-exist in the same friendship. Intriguingly, the characters in the novel experience kama muta in response to both true kindness and to instrumental deceptive kindness. Indeed, they understand and tolerate each other's selfish motives, knowing that they can trust each other to be there when needed. More than in his later books, in *Tortilla Flat* Steinbeck explicitly portrays his characters' emotions. Danny has unexpectedly inherited two houses. He takes one and lets his friends Pilon, Pablo, and Jesus Maria rent the other, though in fact they are unable to pay any rent at all. Their friendship with Danny is perpetually undermined by their tenant to landlord relationship and, especially, their subordination to him because of their debt. Then, in a careless accident, they have burned the house down. Pilon, Pablo, and Jesus Maria feel remorseful about having burned down the house Danny gave them to stay in, yet very relieved that they no longer are Danny's tenants – they will no longer owe him rent. So now they can just be his friends again. This is the kama muta moment – the fire has ended their market pricing and authority ranking debtor relationship with Danny, instantly restoring the communal sharing of their close friendship. Later Danny's friends have an apparent moment of reflexive kama muta evoked by their sudden love for themselves; see Online Note 8.1 for this touching passage.

What Steinbeck depicts in a number of passages is the experience of first-person kama muta evoked by characters' intensifying CS relationships though their own kindness. In the concluding chapter of *Tortilla Flat*, Danny is depressed, feeling oppressed with all the friendship that he feels to be smothering. He seeks freedom, moves out of his house, and starts raiding his friends, stealing their meager possessions. People perceive his brooding sadness and decide to throw a giant party for him at his house. Everyone in town puts themselves out to contribute. While the townspeople decorate Danny's house and bring food for a great feast, Danny's friends make a rare sacrifice for his party: they take it upon themselves to go to work, actually earning money, cutting squid so they can buy wine for the party. After they finish the day's work they buy wine and, splattered with squid, they head home to the party, with a proud solidarity that Steinbeck compares to Napoleon's victorious soldiers.

> At five-thirty the friends marched up the hill, tired and bloody but trium-phant. So must the Old Guard have looked when they returned to Paris after Austerlitz. They saw the house, bursting with color. They laughed, and their weariness fell from them. They were so happy that tears came into their eyes.
>
> *(Steinbeck 1935:190)*

While first-person kama muta is common, for example, when seeing or holding an infant or kitten, I have identified very few other instances of <u>reflexive</u> kama muta evoked by a person's own generosity. (One case is an ancient Jain text from northeast India that prescribes feeling kama muta at the opportunity and then at the experience of giving to mendicant monks; other cases may occur in self-com-passion meditation and training. See Chapter 12.) But it may be that this kind of reflexive kama muta is actually more common than it appears. Perhaps one would find more such cases by eliciting kama muta experiences that people call *pride* – of the self-loving sort Danny's friends feel as they proudly arrive with their wine for the splendid party that they have initiated and sacrificed for, and realize that the whole town has joined them in creating this wonderful gift for Danny.

Steinbeck's omniscient narrator represents Danny, Pilon, Jesus Maria, Pablo, and the Pirate as almost childlike in their simple psychology of desire, deceit, trust, and affection; today it would be controversial to write what would be judged as a racist depiction of Mexican-Indian-Americans – and the entire com-munity of "Tortilla Flat." Indeed, some critics initially saw and some still see the book as White stereotyping of the Californian underclass. But from very early in the book it becomes clear to the reader that these characters are allegories for humankind. They are represented so sympathetically that even their alcoholism is touching. The narrator clearly loves Danny, Pilon, Jesus Maria, Pablo, and the Pirate, almost as God would, and like God, the reader comes to love them for the innocent, vulnerable, and weak humans they are. They aren't Mexican, Indian, Californian, and not merely uneducated and unemployed bums, or just cute – they are simply human. They are the reader, and they are everyman. By the kama muta that Steinbeck evokes, the reader comes to feel compassion for them, and through them, for humankind.

'Romanticism' is another genre in which kama muta is not just salient, but highly sought after. Kama muta is the core emotion of the mid-eighteenth cen-tury German *Sturm und Drang* movement, including Goethe's novels, and the subsequent plays of Schiller (see online note 2.5).

The melodrama of superheroes and fighting machines

While media create many emotions that attract audiences, it seems that kama muta is a mainstay of most, especially in what are called 'romantic' periods and genres. The invention of photography, sound-recording, cinema, radio, television, and their digitalization opened up new visual and auditory channels for evoking kama muta, simultaneously satisfying and whetting the public appetite for experiencing the emotion. These technologies created opportunities to attract huge audiences seeking kama muta, and hence for producers, directors, writers, and actors to make prodigious fortunes and achieve unprecedented fame.

Yet the popular appeal of simple narratives that so readily and reliably evoke kama muta seems to be a major reason why critics devalue literature that focuses on evoking kama muta, at least when it is evoked in trite ways, dismissively calling it *sentimental*. Similarly, critics denigrate media whose principal theme is evoking kama muta though the standard plots; critics disdainfully label such movies and television *melodrama*. Probably critics' disdain reflects how easy it is to evoke kama muta with standard plots, without requiring creative subtlety – critics judge that there's nothing to admire when yet another rendition of the same storyline produces the same emotion again, as usual. It is ironic that this emotional theme is not valued by elite sophisticates precisely because it <u>is</u> unabashedly emotional, despite the fact that melodrama may explore major social divides, and even show how they can be transcended.

> In the past when melodramas have succeeded in moving viewers ... the sexual, racial, and gender problems of American history have found their most powerful expression.
>
> *(Williams 1998:82)*

And in contemporary global culture in general, kama muta in response to fiction is regarded as a feminine emotion, not a noble one. At any rate, the doyens of modern Western high culture disparage sentimental literature and melodrama (especially *romance novels* and *tear-jerking movies*) to the point where people are often embarrassed to acknowledge consuming and enjoying them. But this has not always or everywhere been the case. (See Online Note 2.5 for some of the vicissitudes of Western European standards concerning the evocation and performance of kama muta.) However, our aim is to understand what evokes this emotion, along with the cultural meanings of evoking, feeling, and performing it – not to judge the cultural artifacts and practices that evoke kama muta, much less to evaluate the creative subtlety of particular works.

Sculpture, painting, photography, sound-recording, cinema, radio, television, and video go beyond what a narrative can do to evoke kama muta: they can show moving faces and postures; precisely convey voice qualities; visually depict touching suffering, injuries, and illnesses; vividly represent dangers, obstacles, and determined efforts to overcome them. Furthermore, film, television, and video often add evocative music to augment or complement the plot. In this chapter, let's sample some of the kinds of melodrama that evoke kama muta, continuing the focus on plot and dialog that I began in the preceding analysis of literature.

Melodrama typically consists of a narrative in which the viewer identifies with a victim or victims beset by dangers or obstacles, especially derision, exclusion, ostracism, or loss of crucial relationships. The viewer is shown the pathos of the protagonist's loss of CS and is encouraged to identify with her struggle to regain the lost CS, or to forge new CS relationships. The tense climactic scene is typically a cliffhanger in which the protagonists are struggling against danger or uncertainty, fighting against the world in order to restore the CS they need. For example, a woman is ostracized when she loses her virtue, but may ultimately find new love and a new home (Williams 1998). Restoring the victim to love and familial inclusion in the primary community Williams (1998) calls "retrieval of innocence."

> The most classic forms of the mode are often suffused with nostalgia for rural and maternal origins that are forever lost yet—hope against hope—refound, reestablished, or, if permanently lost, sorrowfully lamented.
>
> *(Williams 1998:65)*

And when re-found, re-established, or mnemonically re-experienced in nostalgic lament, this sudden revival of CS evokes kama muta in the viewer.

Heroes and other admirable characters show their virtue by great kindness or generosity, by abnegation, by courageously taking risks or accepting suffering, or by sacrificing themselves for others – the precise indices of extraordinary CS that evoke kama muta. An American informant mentioned these scenes:

- The moment in *Spider-Man: Homecoming* (2017), taken straight out of Amazing Spider-Man No. 33—an iconic, character defining moment in the comic—when young Peter Parker is buried under a mountain of rubble, crying in pain and terror. The audience is suddenly uncomfortably aware of the fact that the superhero is just a vulnerable 15-year-old kid. However, he somehow finds the strength to lift the rubble through sheer determination—because he knows that people will get hurt if he doesn't stop the bad guy.
- The death of tragic villain Erik Killmonger in *Black Panther* (2018). King T'Challa fulfils his dying cousin/foe's final wish—to watch a Wakandan Sunset. Poignantly, Killmonger says 'Bury me in the ocean with my ancestors that jumped from ships, because they knew death was better than bondage.'
- Captain America's reunion with his (now elderly) love interest Peggy Carter.
- Captain America's reunion with his (now brainwashed) best friend (whom he believed to be long-dead)—and when Bucky finally begins to recognize him and remember his own identity.

(Rowan Hong)

Contemporary movies and other media frequently attract viewers by evoking kama muta. When asked to recall a *meaningful* movie and describe how they felt, American participants described feelings of *warmth, tenderness, compassion, poignancy, empathy, tenderness, sympathy, inspiration,* or *feelings of being moved or touched* (Oliver and Hartmann 2010). Conversely, Oliver, Hartmann, and Woolley (2102) found that movies that participants said made them feel *touched, moved, emotional, compassion, inspired, and tender* were ones that they also rated as *meaningful*. Meaningful films evoked reports of *tears* or *crying, lump in the throat, chills,* and *rising or open chest*. Participants who watched the meaningful films subsequently rated themselves higher on motivation to *be a better person, do good things for other people, seek what really matters,* and *live my life a better way.* Bartsch, Kalch, and Oliver (2014) also report media experiences that people describe as *moving, tender,* and *poignant.* These responses evoked by meaningful films are, respectively, the labels, sensations, and motives of kama muta. Janicke and Oliver (2017) showed that viewing meaningful films evoked feelings labelled *touched, moved, emotional, meaningful, compassion, inspired,* and *tender;* those feelings in turn made people feel more *connected* with others in general, with family, and with a higher power; feel more *compassionate* toward close others; and report more motivation to *love humanity.* In Chapter 11 I will return briefly to the sense of meaningfulness, knowing, or gnosis in kama muta experiences, including the most extreme ones.

Chick flicks and *tear-jerking* movies are created to evoke kama muta to attract female viewers, especially. Many Pixar and Disney movies are designed to evoke kama muta; animated movies do this in part by the cuteness of key the protagonists, using neotenous faces based on the *Kindchenschema* that Lorenz (1943, 1988:164–165) identified. But many violent movies are also constructed to evoke kama muta in viewers, although the men they are aimed at try not to cry, and might deny being inclined to. In action and violence movies, typically what evokes kama muta in the viewer is the hero's risking or sacrificing himself for his buddies or his community; compassion for the hero's suffering for his buddies or his community; the hero's vulnerability and even neediness (concealed by his toughness, determination, and courage); or a combination of these three triggers. For example, in *Rambo: First Blood Part II*, Rambo recognizes that he has been selected for the mission to rescue prisoners of war because he is expendable, explaining "expendable": "It's like … someone … invites you to a party, and you don't show up; doesn't really matter." After Rambo goes through hell, willingly risking his life and accepting pain and suffering to save American prisoners of war, the movie ends with this exchange:

Trautman:	The war, everything that happened here may have been wrong, but dammit, don't hate your country for it!
Rambo:	Hate? I'd die for it!
Trautman:	Then what is it you want?

Rambo: I want ... what they want, and every other guy who came over here, and spilt his guts and gave everything he had ... wants ... for our country to love us ... as much as we love it. That's what I want.

This is a kama muta moment when stolid men may shed tears. Even the toughest men, though capable of great violence and fully prepared to die for what they believe in, need love and belonging. That's touching, as we say in vernacular English.

Moreover, even when abandoned and alone, or facing certain death, in melodrama and often in fact, brave men will do their duty and sacrifice themselves to save the communities they love. Courageous women in melodrama are often depicted as deeply and truly dedicated to morality, but ultimately putting love ahead of social norms; think of Shakespeare's *Romeo and Juliet*. When they commit themselves to love above all else, the audience may feel kama muta. In the classic 1952 Western movie, *High Noon*, Marshal Will Kane has married a Quaker Pacifist, Amy Fowler Kane; he is retiring and they are about to leave town. But Frank Miller, a vicious killer whom Kane sent to jail, has been released and is coming with his gang to get revenge. Amy pleads with Will to leave town, as planned, and when he refuses, announces that she will leave at noon, with or without him. Will says he will not run away, and goes all over town seeking men to back him up. In cowardice, everyone refuses, failing to support the man who saved them from Miller in the first place. So Will faces the Miller gang alone – expecting to sacrifice himself for honor and to protect the town that will not help protect themselves. In the shootout, Will kills two of the gang, but is wounded and about to be killed. But Amy, having heard the gunfire, has leapt off the departing train and run to be with Will. Putting her love before her religious convictions, she picks up the gun of one of the men Will has shot, and she shoots and kills the man who is about to kill Will. Then, grabbed as a shield by Frank Miller, she claws Miller's face, making him push her away, enabling Will to shoot and kill Frank. Finally, their love having overcome all, Will and Amy catch the next train, so they can, as Williams (1998) would put it, 'retrieve their innocence.'

In these and innumerable other media portrayals, the audience feels kama muta by seeing, reading about, or hearing of a protagonist struggle valiantly against obstacles, bravely take risks, face hardship with determination, bear pain with courage, and ultimately, perhaps, sacrifice him- or herself for what is right – especially to protect the community and the ones they love. This is a common variant of Hogan's (2003) *heroic* narrative prototype and Booker's (2004) *overcoming the monster* plot that I discussed in Chapter 3. But much more than in traditional oral literature, in modern melodrama kama muta is evoked through the audience's compassion for the meritorious suffering of the heroes and heroines. Feeling for the neediness and vulnerability of the innocent or noble hero, empathically sensing her or his fear and pain, the audience may feel a kind of protective, nurturant CS, and hence, if that comes on suddenly, first-person kama muta. The CS relationship, and hence the kama muta affordance, is especially strong when the audience identifies with the protagonist's hardships, suffering, fear, and their isolation, loneliness, or feeling of rejection. When the audience has experienced something very similar to the protagonist's experience, that connects them in CS, as we saw in Chapter 5 where we looked at support and recovery groups. In a nationally representative US sample of 3,006 people, 87% report having been previously "moved, touched, or inspired" while watching a movie, and 80% while watching television (Raney et al. 2017). Courageous self-sacrifice evokes the viewers' kama muta whether the brave and bloodied heroes are humans or machines, even when the heroes are violent. Online Note 8.2 presents Michelle Piazza's sensitive analyses of her own kama muta responses to vulnerable, suffering action heroes and robots.

Indeed, kama muta is evoked by the counter-intuitive emergence of love between assemblages of robotic hardware, as in the touching scenes in *Wall-E*. Eve is simply a head with one enormous eye – a supernormal *Kindchenschema*. But after rebooting, Wall-E doesn't remember Eve – until they kiss. And whoever expected to see robots holding hands! It's so cute! Awww.

Reading poetry

Suffering often isolates the sufferer – she feels separated from others who aren't feeling her pain. Others can't understand, they don't know what it feels like. Moreover, other people often are uncomfortable dealing with those who are suffering, may feel disgusted by aspects of a person's disability or illness, may avoid them, and may blame or taunt them for their suffering; the suffering is a stigma, and may lead to effective exile (Ricoeur 1967). The sufferer's loneliness can be transcended by telling others about the suffering and separation – if listeners or readers are moved by the account because they themselves have suffered similarly. Even if the audience has not had a truly similar experience, evocative songs, stories, or performances may enable the audience to empathically feel the pain of the performer, identifying and connecting with her. When this happens, sorrow and suffering create bonds among those who identify with each other through the experience they share in life or imagination. Among the most lonely sorrows are the death of someone you love, separation from them, betrayal of an intimate relationship or its termination. They are difficult to tell, but the telling potentially transcends the teller's sorrow if the tale moves the audience to feel one with the teller. This may often motivate people to create art, and attract audiences to participate in moving art of all kinds. Let's consider, for example, poetry.

Poetry may be written to evoke kama muta, in some instances by explicitly or symbolically representing kama muta experiences, in other instances by recounting the experiences of love, loss, or suffering that the reader or listener may identify with. Taylor Henry's (2015) participant observation revealed that poets reading their poems in a Los Angeles poetry lounge frequently recounted sad or stressful social experiences that the audience found moving. Another female UCLA student who often attended such poetry readings provided the following self-report:

> Having just experienced the breakup of a short, but very much hoped for relationship, my intention in visiting the lounge was to have a tear-free night out with friends. In many ways, however, my awakening to poetry and spoken word was the opposite of emotionally distracting. A particularly moving poem was delivered by a girl I had never met and wouldn't have expected to relate to. But when she spoke, it was like she was reciting something I had written. Listening to her talk about the heartbreak of a relationship destined to fail, the embarrassment of being the one left longing, and "wrinkles around blue green eyes," brought tears to my eyes and made my throat tight. Acknowledging my own disappointment, empathizing with her sadness, and most importantly, realizing that there was someone else who felt the way I did – someone suffering the same lonely, heavy, melancholy brokenness – was incredibly moving. Though our connection was a result of mutual unhappiness, it was a relief to find that I was not alone. While my experience inspired me to return to the lounge regularly, after a few visits I became accustomed to the various poetic styles and their standard of emotionally dense subject matter, and gradually found myself less moved.

A regular at one Los Angles poetry lounge, asked one night after the open mic what had moved him, immediately mentioned a poem read by a 15-year-old girl on her frustration with high school: how she feels stifled by busywork, misunderstood by her teachers, and miles ahead of her peers (Henry 2015). Though the poet and listener come from very different backgrounds (female versus male, teenaged versus middle-aged, white versus mixed ethnic minority, upper-middle class versus working class upbringing), the listener said he could relate to her because he had also felt advanced and out of place in high school. When the poet was describing her feelings, the listener said he got goosebumps and was moved by the sudden emotional connection he felt with her, despite their many differences. This feeling seems to be part of what makes people write and read or listen to poetry.

> "The abortion I had at 18 was the best decision I've ever made. Yet." These words grabbed me as I stood in the audience of a poetry reading on campus. This statement was an anonymous secret that had been selected to be made into a poem that the poet was about to recite to us. Onlookers wrapped their

arms around one another, and some who were standing took a seat. We all seemed to be settling in for this emotional sharing. The poem, inspired by the secret, began with "We went on passing like two ships in the night ... now, sweetheart, listen ... " It was a poem for an unborn child and all of the things that his father would do in the future because he couldn't have that child. In the future when he was ready for children he would "love them twice as hard just for you." My eyes tingled with the nearness of tears and I had goosebumps on my arms and legs although it was a warm evening. Looking around, I believe it touched others as much as it did for me. As the night went on, more writers shared a plethora of others' anonymous secrets and the poems they inspired. Yet that first one stuck with me because of the poet's emotions and those it evoked in the crowd. When the event came to a close, a young man approached the speaker and said "I felt ... I felt ..." with glossy eyes and his hand to his chest. "I don't feel that [stuff], man."

(Autumn McGrath)

Art, narrative, news, and ordinary conversation can kama muta us when we suddenly discover that we share with others a deeply defining aspect of ourselves. The more profound the connection, the more kama muta we are. A person is especially kama muta when she realizes that an identity-essential experience or feeling that she believed was hers alone, separating her from everyone, actually connects her with others who have had similar experiences and felt the same. In this poetry lounge, poets and audience discover that the misfortunes that define me also define you: we are not alone. When the listener, perhaps hiding similar secret humiliating and demeaning traumas that isolate her, identifies with the distress expressed by an appealing other, this evokes the listener's first-person kama muta. Even when the listener does not share the specific experiences recounted, an appealing other who is in distress, especially expressing loneliness and need for care, evokes second-person kama muta.

Some kinds of poetry only indirectly allude to suffering, longing, or loss, evoking kama muta with more subtlety. And poetry need not be one-way communication from poet to audience; the interlocutors may reciprocally link their poetry, as in Japanese *haikai*, which may have been a kama muta evoking practice; see Online Note 8.3. Haiku emerged from the isolation of the first verse of *haikai*. The prototype for haiku is the juxtaposition of two images. There is an instant when the reader perceives the implicit hidden link between two images in a haiku, and through that link, connects with the poet's experience (see especially the *haiku of* Bashō 1994). This is called the 'haiku moment'; often it may be a kama muta moment. Moreover, classical haiku (*hokku*) typically consists of simultaneously metaphoric and metonymic identification of the poet with a natural organism, a natural event, a season (often signifying transience, departure, and separation), and 'nature,' or the cosmos as a whole. The sensitive reader identifies with all of these. In addition, haiku often expresses loneliness, which itself may evoke kama muta in the listener.

Great classical haiku

> realizes the oneness of human and nature, or the undifferentiated nature of human feelings and the feelings of natural events, objects, and creatures. This in itself is an embodiment of Bashō's poetics. ...
>
> Such nondifferentiation can probably be better captured by understanding the poem as a global metaphor derived from a global blend, which inherits partial structure from all of the inputs—the passing spring season, crying birds and weeping fish, but which also has emergent structure of its own—the revelation of the unity of feelings in nature and humans.
>
> *(Hiraga 1999:468)*

Hiraga footnotes this passage with a comment on Bashō's poetics: "what a poet must do is to be one with what Basho calls *zoka*, that is, the poet must fuse with nature. Then we come to real enlightenment. For Basho, haiku is a realization of such unity" (Hiraga 1999:468). With a cultured sensibility, similar sentiments may emerge when looking at great Japanese paintings (with or without poetic text), participating in a tea ceremony, or entering a garden.

And then, in nearly every language, there is love poetry. Imagine that Shakespeare had written this poem for you:

> If I should think of love
> I'd think of you, your arms uplifted,
> Tying your hair in plaits above,
> The lyre shape of your arms and shoulders,
> The soft curve of your winding head.
> No melody is sweeter, nor could Orpheus
> So have bewitched. I think of this,
> And all my universe becomes perfection.
> But were you in my arms, dear love,
> The happiness would take my breath away,
> No thought could match that ecstasy,
> No song encompass it, no other worlds.
> If I should think of love,
> I'd think of you.

Romanticism in literature and in facets of high culture waxes and wanes; Online Note 2.5 discusses modern vicissitudes of this in Europe, including the *Sturm und Drang* movement in Germany.

"Guaranteed to make you cry:" Sharing glurge on the Internet

I was sitting next to my mother in the living room when she turned to me and said, "You have to watch this video! You're totally going to cry!" I agreed but thought to myself that I definitely wouldn't cry because I had seen so many of these videos in the past. I sat and watched as a young girl held her father's hand as he walked her to school. She stopped him to give him a letter she had written: her dad was smartest, he was funniest, and he was the kindest ... but at the end of the list, she had written "but my dad is a liar." Confusion and sadness swept across his face as he looked at his little girl. The scene flashed to her father running from job to job, trying to look his best to find a better job, not eating so that she could eat, and using what little he had to buy her a special treat. The little girl's voice softly narrated each scene. She said her dad was a liar because he said he wasn't tired, he wasn't hungry, and he wasn't sad. After reading this letter, with tears in his eyes, he looks at his daughter while she has her back turned to him a few feet away, nervous about what he will think. She turns to him and the moment their eyes meet, my heart jumped in my chest, my throat felt choked up, and tears that had already been slowly forming flooded my eyes and rolled down my cheeks. They strongly embraced, her father crying as he held her. My mom was right, I was totally going to cry! I thought that after viewing the video, I had to share it with someone. I called my step-dad over and told him he had to watch it and warned him that he would cry. He said that these types of videos always got him. We sat and watched it again and we both cried. I thought I would be okay to watch it again! We talked afterwards and as he wiped away his tears, my step-dad said it was right when the father and daughter look at one another that he couldn't hold it in any longer.

(Autumn McGrath)[2]

Much of what is *shared* on social media, as well as feature stories on news shows often seem to be popular because they evoke kama muta. In a nationally representative US sample of 3,006 people, 63% report having been previously "moved, touched, or inspired" by online videos, 78% by reading a news story, and 53% by something on a social media site (Raney et al. 2017). There is a new word, *glurge*, for "sickly-sweet" "inspirational" stories in e-mail or social media posts, often featuring "puppies, kitties, children with disabilities, puppies and kitties with disabilities, and Jesus" (Mikkelson 2015).[3] It's a synonym of *sappy*. Glurge may be fictional, but one typical true story tells of premature twins, one of whom, Kyrie, was thriving while the other, Brielle, was in critical condition. Having tried everything else to aid the distressed twin, a nurse broke hospital rules and put Brielle in Kyrie's incubator, right next to her. Kyrie placed her arm around Brielle, who quickly settled in and began to recover.

Is there any reader who has not viewed or shared innumerable social media posts what evoke kama muta – viewed and posted them simply *because* they evoke kama muta? If not, just Google "guaranteed to make you cry"; there are many sites that collect the best of these. They're guaranteed to make your eyes wet, and make you want to look at them again alongside your friends and family.

If I were writing for readers in another world, I'd write a long chapter on the practices of Internet *sharing*, showing how kama muta motivates social media posting and viewing. But social media touches nearly every contemporary reader, so perhaps I can simply suggest that readers reflect on their everyday Internet sharing.

Emotibytes: Off-the-shelf emotions-on-demand

Observing others suddenly intensifying CS evokes third-party kama muta. Presumably, humans have always told stories that evoke third-party kama muta in listeners. But communication technologies lead far beyond direct observation and listening. Writing, printing, art, theater, photography, audio-recording, radio, television, cinema and video, digital representation and the Internet, and now virtual reality technology enable people to intentionally evoke kama muta in people who are not present in the same place or at the same time. Moreover, these technical media make pre-packaged kama muta and other emotions available off the shelf, on demand. Let's call these packaged, labeled, and clickable (or orderable from Amazon) emotion-inducing media *emotibytes*. Emotibytes include podcasts, television shows, movies, poems, books, social media posts, and so on. Humans can now order up the emotion they want to experience at any moment by getting a suitable emotibyte. This changes emotional experience profoundly.[4]

First, it vastly extends the role of story-teller, making many professional roles for artists, actors, writers, directors, producers, make-up and costume designers, sound and lighting and editing professionals, distributors, critics, and so forth. Generating kama muta has become a highly developed craft and a highly valued art. In the last two decades, social media has made everyone on the Internet a potentially story-teller to everyone else. The 'authenticity' and 'realism' of amateur posts on social media give them a potential to evoke kama muta through a different sort of identification than professional media productions afford.[5]

These technological developments make emotions – through the off-the-shelf packages that evoke them – more frequently accessible; more readily storable and hence technically 'memorable'; more readily given to others; more transmissible over long periods of time, long distances, and across cultures. Simultaneously, these technologies also make emotions rather easily anticipated, and much more likely to provoke semantic reflection – consciousness – and esthetic, social, and moral evaluation. Want to have a good kama muta cry? Go to a tear-jerking chick-flick. Want to feel nostalgic kama muta? Go look at old photographs of your children. Want to feel loving kama muta? Put your headphones on and listen to your favorite love song on your playlist. Want to feel the warmth and uplifting optimism of kama muta? Type "kittens" into Google. Feel angry at your parents? Listen to some heavy metal, or play a first-person shooter videogame. Through this voluntary selection, people become proficient at thinking about what emotions they would like to feel. And it makes people expect that they should be able to find content that will afford certain emotions – especially kama muta. People become accustomed to choosing their emotions.

Emotibytes afford 'regulation' of one's own emotions. And they facilitates regulation of others' emotions, as in strategic evocation of emotions as a form of social influence in politics and marketing. Want to evoke kama muta to move customers to buy your products or voters to go to the polls and cast their votes for you? Make a moving commercial. Emotions, no longer something that just happens to one, become something that one intends, gives, and promotes.

These technologies saturate experience with selected and perfected emotibyte stimuli. Like pornography or candy, the experiences are supernormal stimuli (Tinbergen 1953), more evocative than most ordinary experiences. These extraordinary prototypes of kama muta become standards for experiencing 'natural,' 'everyday' kama muta – which may pale by comparison. On the other hand, these extraordinary prototypes may make evident the emotional potentials of everyday life. Seeing perfect kama muta occasions in media, people can appreciate analogous experiences in their own lives. Does exposure to highly selected or staged third-person kama muta make 'ordinary' everyday experiences more banal? That is, does it provide an 'unrealistically' high standard for 'real' experience? Or, on the contrary, does it make people more appreciative of 'natural' kama muta experiences, because they come to see kama muta as something to appreciate, something everyone cares about, something to preserve?

Exposure to kama muta in emotibytes pushes people to reflect on everyday natural experiences, considering how they appear to others, seeing them as potential emotibytes to share. That is, even beyond the ubiquitous sharing of mundane experiences, *special moments* become events to self-consciously perform in order to photograph them or post them on social media. Performances are shaped to match ideal prototypes from cinema, television, and social media. Performing the event so as to record it enables a great many people to 'participate' in it, while it enables the performers to tailor their online personas, presenting the self they want others to see. So now people stage a homecoming or puppy-gift for YouTube posting. Weddings increasing resemble a Hollywood movie shoot – complete with retakes. Along with this staging of events to maximize their evocative potential, photographic and digital representations of kama muta events supplant the episodic neurocognitive memory system, and transform joint discursively constructed memories by framing them with reference to shared media representations.

Professionally produced media emotibytes and social media emotibytes provoke commentary in which people discursively create prescriptive standards for evoking and experiencing kama muta. Perhaps one judges and comments that, 'This instance is trite – it's an unimaginative replication of the old prototype.'

'This instance gives the prototypes and precedents a remarkable new twist.' 'This instance is manipulative.' 'This person or actor isn't convincing – her performance of kama muta isn't persuasive.' 'This cute child's sweet kindness is *sooo adorable!*' All social media have comment functions, and the numbers of *likes* and *shares* matter a great deal. This technological platform for commenting, and attending to each other's comments makes kama muta the object of extensive public (as well as private) consideration that it would not otherwise receive. There is a great deal more discussion of kama muta than there could have been before the invention of writing, printing, art, theater, photography, audio-recording, radio, television, cinema and video, digital representation, and the Internet.

Information and communication technologies also expose people to emotibytes of kama muta-evoking events in the lives of strangers and people from other nations and cultures. Where formerly kama muta was limited to the sudden intensification of CS among family and friends, we now experience it when we see people all over the world be extraordinarily kind, when we see cute children in places we've never been. This may foster CS with strangers, widening the moral circle (Singer 2011).

In association with this, digital 'sharing' of emotibytes becomes a way to sustain or enhance social relationships, and even initiate new ones. Each person's recorded or reported kama muta experience has the potential to be the medium for relating to far-flung social media 'friends,' while complementing the other practices that comprise face-to-face relating.

In recent years digital off-the-shelf kama muta emotibytes have become readily available on-demand. Does this sate people, giving them a surfeit of kama muta that dulls its impact? Or is the appetite for kama muta stimulated by its 'consumption,' so that frequent experience of 'perfected' kama muta makes people more hungry for it? Does the great increase in exposure to kama muta increase people's connoisseurship, making them more selective, or more appreciative, or more able to appreciate its nuances? Either way, emotional life is transformed by saturation with emotibytes. No longer primarily something that just happens to a person, emotions have become an intentional choice. And recently, with the advent of *trigger warnings*, people sometimes can choose not to experience aversive emotions.

Touching painting and sculpture

In Chapter 1 I showed that people often feel kama muta when they suddenly feel one with infants, cute animals, nature, or the cosmos. I suggested that when things or events that evoke kama muta are represented in photographs, paintings, woodcuts, lithographs, reliefs, and sculptures, viewers may respond with kama muta. Of course, in some respects art is less vivid and real than reality, but in other respects art may be *more* evocative. The sensitive and skilled artist may be able to optimize the features of a scene that are likely to evoke kama muta, especially when artist and viewers belong to a cultural tradition that has cultivated emotional responses to particular themes. For example, the image of a mother holding an infant may evoke mild kama muta in some, especially when the artist optimizes the *Kindchenschema* (Lorenz 1943, 1988:164–165) so that the super-cute infant releases extra-strong caring responses. But if the artist communicates to a Christian audience that the mother is the Virgin Mary and the infant is Jesus, the audience is reminded of stories of their great suffering and sacrifices for humankind. If at some point liquid tears appear on a statue or painting of Mary, as has repeatedly occurred, the flowing tears may evoke even stronger feelings of compassionate kama muta for her (sometimes along with sadness about her suffering). Likewise, an artist depicting to a Buddhist audience the story of a past life of the Buddha evokes an appreciation of the Buddha's limitless compassion for all beings. When a viewer is steeped in transcendentalism, her response to a painting of a mysterious landscape is informed by her cultural sensitivities: the painting resonates with prototypes and precedents of transcendental kama muta. A contemporary environmentalist may feel kama muta when standing in Yosemite Valley, or when gazing at Ansel Adams's photographs of it. John Muir shapes the emotional views they share.

Art in the European Middle Ages was mostly religious art, intended to evoke religious sentiments, especially kama muta. Art was intended to display Christ's crucifixion as the ultimate gift of love, and the analogous suffering of the saints; viewers were supposed to feel kama muta for the sacrifices that had been made for them. Other images depicted the Madonna or Mary Magdalene weeping, calling for the viewers' compassionate kama muta. Art was supposed to make viewers cry, and perhaps it often did. Then with the rationalizing move of the middle Italian Renaissance, art and religious accounts moved from these themes to others less moving – art became 'art,' no longer aiming to move and no longer moving viewers to tears (Elkins 2001:161). During the Renaissance, elite Europeans generally 'controlled' their emotions and cried less. However, a few recent and contemporary painters such as Rothko still aim to make people weep. Some viewers report that they weep at Rothko's huge paintings that may suddenly envelope the viewer in a disquieting "ecstasy" (Rothko's term), "hemmed in, threatened by fusion, by an absorptive, smothering unity" (Breslin 1993:280, quoted in Elkins 2001:18). Some viewers may somehow feel "at home" as a part of a Rothko painting or other works (Elkins 2001:180). As one modern art lover wrote,

> I think people cry at paintings because of a sense of recognition, even if they have never seen the pictures before. There is a sudden total identification, which makes time stand still and city noises hush, and makes one dwell within the picture … It is the recognition of something similar, the experience of being part of it, and maybe even a feeling of grace, a moment of unforgettable happiness.
>
> *(Excerpt from Mary Muller letter to Elkins, 2001:251)*

Far from Rothko's abstractions, many of Norman Rockwell's illustrations appear to have been expressly intended to evoke kama muta. Indeed, representational art may be created by the artist to share with the viewer the artist's kama muta experience. For one artist's motives, see Online Note 8.4.

When Marina Abramovic performed "The Artist Is Present" at the Museum of Modern Art, New York in 2010, she simply sat on a chair, looking across the table at anyone who took a turn sitting there, while viewers observed them. Francine Prose wrote a review blog for the New York Review of Books, entitled "When Art Makes Us Cry:" "For at least some of those viewers who gave themselves over to their silent communion with the artist, the experience seemed to have been one of great intimacy" (Prose 2012). Some viewers had traveled far to commune with Abramovic, seeking "a few minutes of transcendence by staring into the eyes of an artist whose sole mission, during those months, was to register their presence, to sit there, and look back." In her review, Prose indicates that Abramovic's performance art did more than "touch" the viewers; it inspired an extreme emotion that overcame many of them. Prose equates this emotion to the feeling of being "profoundly moved" that she felt when she herself contemplated Caravaggio's "The Flagellation of Christ" in the dim silence of the Capodimonte Museum in Naples, a feeling she also attributes to "a young priest kneeling and weeping in front of a fresco depicting the Crucifixion in Rome's church of San Clemente" whom she observed. Then she mentions the impact of Rothko's painting. Prose goes on to write about how deeply moved she also was by Song Dong's exhibit of her mother's ordinary household objects, "an immensely touching statement about family, time, memory, about what can be saved and what will inevitably be lost."

As they looked at Abramovic sitting in her "The Artist is Present" performance, many viewers at the Museum of Modern Art cried. Then one day her former life partner Ulay (Frank Uwe Laysiepen), with whom she had lived and performed for 12 years, but then parted from 22 years before, appeared and sat across from her. Abramovic then stirred for the first time; she reached her hand out to him. That event is so evocative that we use the video of it as a reliable kama muta stimulus in our experiments[6] (for background, see Blinderman 2013).

People in contemporary cultures create many things that lack both the esthetic quality and the prestige of 'art' but may evoke kama muta nonetheless. A young child draws a picture of her family and shows it to her parents; people knit or otherwise devote time and care to making a personal present; a friend makes a meal and brings it to a family with a newborn, or to someone who is ill. Simply making someone's favorite meal or pastry, thoughtfully bringing or sending flowers, or writing a thank you or condolence note may make the recipient feel a bit kama muta. It is moving to be appreciated, especially in crisis. When the dying St Francis thanked his faithful donkey for carrying him on his missions, it is said that the donkey cried (Bough 2011:153–155). One may feel kama muta when friends and family throw a surprise party, or when co-workers or employers express their affection at a retirement party and give a heartfelt retirement gift, a plaque, or award. A lover who serenades his true love may sing badly, but his serenade may still seem charming to her. The greeting card industry is substantially built on kama muta: purchased – or more evocatively, homemade – statements of love and devotion at Valentines, birthday, anniversary, mother's and father's day may touch the recipient if they are especially apt and seem to be 'from the heart' of the sender.[7] On the other hand, when the recipient appraises any of these presentations as trite, generically banal, or as an empty, merely pro-forma gesture, the recipient may be disappointed and even hurt – and the presenter consequently embarrassed.

Some widespread genres of folk art and crafts appear to be intended to evoke kama muta, such as American 'Home Sweet Home' embroidery and handcrafted slogans and proverbs intended for entrances and parlors. One of the most intriguing folk art media for kama muta is tattooing. People have tattoos for many reasons, but one of the classic genres consists of tattoos that declare love, celebrate shared identity-forming experiences, display gang membership, or commemorate deceased loved ones. Such tattoos inscribe kama muta experiences on the body, where they afford recurrent experiences of it. Online Note 8.5 presents an intriguing example, the tattoo of a gibbon whom the bearer loves and her account of her motives for getting several such tattoos.

Moving dancers, actors, and other artists

> "That's my job!"
> *(Famous actress, when told about the emotion we're studying)*

In conjunction with our research, Benedicte H. Walle, who herself was a dancer, interviewed three Norwegian professional dancers. All reported that they sometimes felt *rørt* or *beveget* (moved or touched), occasionally to tears, when watching dance performances, and also sometimes when teaching dance or taking dance workshops. Moreover, they had these feelings sometimes when performing, especially if the audience was 'getting' what they were performing. Two of them spontaneously mentioned that after watching some dance performances they wanted to (and often did) hug or massage the dancers. Kama muta appeared to be an important aspect of being a dancer and being in the dance world. Here are translations of two excerpts from two of the interviews:

Do you ever have the feeling of being moved [*rørt*]?
   Quite often. I can feel extremely moved. I had one very strong experience a couple of weeks back. I was participating in a workshop at school. The instructor guided us through an improvisation session, focusing on "lust/temptation" very intensely. We were told to imagine a movement that we really wanted

to do, and pay attention to what happens in your body before we give in to this "impulse" or lust, if you want … We worked on this for a REALLY long time – trying to detect the sensations, impulses and processes that happen before we perform the desired behaviour. And then, after pulling this out in what felt like forever, he told us "let go." And I totally let go of all control – it just felt so right/great! It was such a strong moment! It was a very special experience. I started crying/was tearing up, felt warm, I was shivering, and I noticed my voice got a bit deeper when I was talking. I was so emotional. The instructor came over and asked me if I was ok (apparently the others in the room did not have the same reaction), which I was – I was feeling great! I didn't really understand what was happening, I couldn't "place" my emotions, but I think I was feeling moved [*rørt*], among other things.

On a different occasion I was very moved during my exam performance, on stage with my fellow dancemates. I think it was this strong sense of presence. "YES, I know this – I know what I'm doing." I felt safe, and wanted to share what we created with others. I can feel moved when I see that on stage – that people invite the audience/or fellow dancers in the studio to take part in what the dancer is doing/experiencing/communicating. …

If I go to see a performance by myself and I feel moved by the dancers on stage, I feel really happy and have no problem with approaching the dancers afterwards to say "thank you" – I might even steal a hug. The same goes for the general audience. After watching a moving performance, it is generally easier for me to approach and make contact with other people from the audience. I just imagine that we're more "in the same space," we shared this experience. Before the performance we were more "separated"/individual. Afterwards I feel like we're more "in sync" in our minds, attention wise and emotionally.

I don't start crying that easily – I'd rather start laughing or giggling.

> (Norwegian professional dancer, interviewed and
> translated by Benedicte H. Walle)

Another Norwegian professional dancer, discussing when she's moved (*rørt*), told Benedicte,

If everything goes well together – the music and the movements are in some sort of harmony (*hvis det klaffer*), or if the choreography has a particularly strong expression (*sterkt uttrykk*), I can get goosebumps. But the really moving moments occur more often when tenderness (*ømhet*) is expressed on stage. As if there is a certain "nerve" between, say, two of the dancers' bodies on stage. …

Last week a 75-year-old lady held a workshop at KhiO [Oslo National Academy of the Arts]. She was sort of an "alternative" dancer, all about freeing yourself from "shape," mastery and understanding. … Receive the impulses in your entire "cellular" body. I was so moved when I saw her dance. This old person moving in a non-typical way. At one point, she started singing as well. It just seemed so liberating. And I just sat there, watching her, and I couldn't help it, I was crying.

The last day of the workshop, we were all sitting in a circle (12 people). And then she told us to sing out loud, simultaneously – like really loud – and make up our own words, just whatever we felt like. I was like a kindergarten-feeling (*barnehagefølelse*). And I started crying. I got a lump in my throat, felt warm. It was a very strange experience, and I'm not sure why this affected me the way it did.

Why do you think you felt moved on these occasions? I'm not sure, but it just felt very real/genuine (*ekte*). It was something different. Nice and childish. We all became sort of vulnerable.

It was just a moment of love (*kjærlighet*) to each other, to that old lady.

(Ellipses in original transcription)

Dance audiences report kama muta, too. For example, ballet bloggers report many performances that gave them goosebumps or moved them to tears.[8]

* * * * *

Emotions don't just happen to people – people aren't merely passive responders to random events. People actively construct emotional experiences. They do so as a means to enhance or transform authority ranking relationships, for example, in political oratory that evokes kama muta to mobilize followers. They do so as a means to enhance or transform market pricing relationships, for example, in marketing that evokes kama muta to attract customers. Moreover, as we have seen in this chapter, people come together to collaboratively construct emotional experiences more or less for their own sake. So people set up and attend boxing matches to create aggressive anger experiences, or set up and attend comedy clubs to create humorous amusement experiences. Kama muta theory posits that people want to experience kama muta themselves, evoke kama muta in others, and experience kama muta together with others. As we're seeing throughout this book, people devote a lot of their time, effort, and resources to this. But by themselves people wouldn't be able to figure out very well <u>how</u> to experience, evoke, or share kama muta – and they don't discover on their own how to do it. Just as people depend on their culture to be able to obtain and cook food, they largely depend on their culture to experience, evoke, and share kama muta. Just as no individual in one lifetime could invent agriculture, no individual could devise and perfect the narratives, practices, institutions, roles, and artifacts that people in any culture use to experience, evoke, and share kama muta. Sentimental literature and poetry, components of the Internet and its social media glurge, wedding rings and lockets, touching painting and sculpture, dance, and some genres of music have culturally evolved in large part because they enable people to experience, evoke, and share kama muta. People sometimes experience kama muta in random events, but most of the most intense kama muta is the product of social activities organized according to cultural schemas that have been perfected by myriads of contributors, often over many generations. Every culture offers a great many tools for crafting kama muta. We depend on those tools and use them frequently.

Expertise in these tools seems to be vital to certain social roles, including some of the most prominent professions in contemporary society. We haven't yet done extensive research on the intentions of writers, social media posters, painters, sculptors, actors, singers, dancers, or musicians; we look forward to hearing their voices. One can write or dance to evoke many emotions or other responses, and become a specialist in evoking any. However, provisionally I suggest that evoking kama muta seems to be a central goal of many writers, social media posters, painters, sculptors, actors, singers, dancers, and musicians, and not just a personal goal. It is a vital component of many of the roles in these vocations (in the formal sociological sense of *role*). That is, a large part of many of these social roles consists of developing and perfecting cultural tools for crafting kama muta. That is an important part of what many people go into these roles to do, and what others expect and reward them for doing. An actor or musician – or at least a certain kind of actor or director, or in certain *roles* (in the performance sense) is someone who should use a particular type and set of her culture's tools for evoking kama muta. If she does it well, she hopes to work with people in complementary roles such as stage manager, producer, costume designer, ticket vendor, fan or audience member, media purchaser, reviewer, et cetera. All of them depend on her skill at evoking kama muta, as she depends on them to perform the *movie* script or *concert* score.

An actor who was taking a research seminar on kama muta told us about a kama muta experience that was important in her choice of her career:

> Some quick backstory— my life's purpose is to perform, and I discovered this at the age of eleven in my first outside-of-school community production, in this case *Peter Pan*. Although I was in the chorus, or perhaps especially because I was in the chorus, I discovered complete fulfillment and camaraderie with everyone involved and knew that I would do this, this magic, for the rest of my existence. Flash forward some six years of development and passion for the craft, and my last production before going away to college is, coincidentally, with the same production company and the same musical that started it all, only this time, my director has entrusted me with the role of the scourge of the sea, Captain Hook himself. Often we would

have schools buses in from all around the Peninsula, and afterwards on these school performance days we would come out after the show and greet our audience in costume and in character. I remember a particular day when I was "Arrrrr-ing" it up with some particularly adorable middle-schoolers, when all of a sudden a small toddler, couldn't have been more than three or four, approaches me all on his own decked out in full Captain Hook cosplay. We lock eyes, and wordlessly he slowly lifts his hook, reaching to about my mid-calf. I smile, and ever so slowly bend down, and touch my hook to his. For a moment, the earth stands still. There is an understanding. And then, contented, he goes on his merry way.

(Jill Galbraith)

People listening to music, playing music, or singing in a chorus often report that they were *moved*, or use terms in Swedish and other languages that often denote kama muta (Gabrielsson 2011; Crafts, Cavicchi, & Keil 1993; Scherer & Zentner 2001). And music often causes sensations typical of kama muta, such as goosebumps or tears (Juslin & Laukka 2004; Konečni 2005; Bicknell 2009:46– 60; Grewe, Kopiez, & Altenmüller 2009; Laeng et al. 2016; Hodges & Sebald 2010:292; Huron & Margulis 2010; Benedek & Kaernbach 2011; Nusbaum et al. 2014; Menninghaus et al. 2015; Wassiliwizky et al. 2015; Eerola & Peltola 2016; Wassiliwizky et al. 2017a; Wassiliwizky 2017b; Mori & Iwanaga, 2017). Choral singers and musicians have told us about intense experiences of kama muta – experiences that motivate their engagement in music-making. Sometimes the CS that suddenly intensifies is between musicians and audience, sometimes among the musicians or singers, sometimes among the audience, sometimes with the composer or even with the music itself. Unfortunately space does not permit exploring musical kama muta in this book, but I hope to do so in future work.

When humans developed the technologies to smelt and forge iron, and devised the artifacts that could be made with iron, iron became an important medium for many aspects of social life: hunting, butchering, cooking, farming, fighting, and so forth. Analogously, when humans developed the narratives, practices, institutions, roles, and artifacts for evoking kama muta, kama muta became an important medium for the many aspects of social life I explore in this book. The role of the blacksmith is to forge tools and weapons out of iron, which are then used by people in other roles such as hunter, warrior, farmer, cook, or trader. Likewise, the role of many kinds of writers, composers, and choreographers is to craft kama muta tools which are then used by people in other roles such as publishers and booksellers; producers and musicians, dancers, and actors; along with their critics and, of course, audiences and fans. The development of iron technologies transformed human society and everyday life. In different but still substantial ways, the development of kama muta technologies also transformed human society and everyday life – and continues to do so.

One kind of transformation is the creation or reinforcement of communities. At performances and in virtual communities, shared kama muta experiences of narrative and performing arts create CS communities that identify with each other and the community as a whole. These communities include event audiences, festival attenders, fan clubs and book clubs, literature and arts majors and professors, as well as imagined communities that never gather in one pace. When one person discovers that another has felt kama muta to the same work of art, writer, composer, performer, or even genre, one feels some CS solidarity with them. Anderson (2006) argues that the reading of common works is crucial to the creation of nationhood, and one could argue that shared kama muta film, television, radio, and musical experiences are important roots of national identity, along with cross-national arts genre identities, such as fans of Delta blues or baroque. Many people all over the world feel more or less connected with the United States, because of their kama muta experiences listening to (or performing) American music, watching American television and movies, and reading American literature. People may develop many other cross-national bonds though their kama muta experiences with the literature and arts of other nations; conversely, regional music can play a role the maintenance of ethnic and national identities among emigrants in various diaspora. Pinker (2011) argues that the decline in violence during the modern era is partly a result of the growth of empathic mutual understanding developed through reading enabled by the printing press and later technical advances. More generally, perhaps, compassionate motives toward helping rather than harming are fostered specifically by kama muta in reading and other arts. In music, one can think of George Harrison's 1971 Concert for Bangladesh, Bob Geldof and Midge Ure's Band Aid 1984–2104 recordings and concerts, the 1985 *We Are the World* recording, the 2005 Live 8 concerts, and many others.

At a more dynamic, fine-grained, short-term level of analysis, writing and the performing arts nicely exemplify the creation and diffusion of kama muta-inducing institutions and practices. Artists may be motivated to create works of art to 'share' their own experiences: suffering, sorrow, struggles, loss, or love conquering all. Evoking such sentiments in the audience affords the artist the opportunity to feel kama muta, while the audience, recognizing and identifying with the artist's experience, likewise feels kama muta. Audience members' actual and anticipated kama muta experiences may motivate them to purchase and read books, attend performances, purchase recordings, and in some cases become performers or writers themselves, further diffusing and promoting homologous kama muta-inducing practices. Feeling kama muta, the audience seeks to repeat the experience and to tell others of it so as to re-evoke kama muta in both teller and listener or message recipient. Feeling kama muta together in an audience makes the feeling stronger and better, so people invite their CS associates to attend such performances or even to read texts aloud together. Of course, an artist who successfully evokes kama muta and so attracts a large audience also gains authority ranking status and market pricing benefits.

Kama muta is one of the fruits of the arts, and thus provides a seed from which the arts grow. Simply put, without kama muta there would be less art, and less engagement in it.

Online notes

8.1 Kama muta moments in Steinbeck's *Tortilla Flat.*
8.2 Kama muta responses to vulnerable, suffering action heroes and robots.
8.3 Potential kama muta in composing poetry together.
8.4 Painting to share the artist's kama muta experience.
8.5 A tattoo inscribed to preserve and evoke kama muta.

Notes

1 In a separate work in preparation, we analyze how the psychological disposition for kama muta culturally selects for kama muta-displaying and kama muta-evoking vocal practices such as ululation, ritual weeping, lament, song, and instrumental music.
2 The video (a commercial): https://m.youtube.com/watch?v=_0iR6KFCxkQ.
3 http://www.urbandictionary.com/.
4 This section was inspired by discussions with Sami Amadha.
5 I thank Jana Gallus for these last two insights.
6 https://www.youtube.com/watch?v=sLbFugaFyAA.
7 In the 2013 Spike Jonze movie *Her*, the protagonist Theodore works for a company that writes 'personal' letters for its clients—letters that are intended to evoke kama muta in their recipients, and that evoke kama muta in Theodore's cowriters themselves. The letters initially move the movie viewer, too, until the viewer discovers that Theodore's letters are not addressed to his own loved ones, but are mere commodities he produces for a salary.
8 http://www.balletcoforum.com/index.php?/topic/4609-goosebumps/.

9

DISASTERS, MEMORIALS, AND MEMENTOS

On 15–16 December 2014, when an Islamic extremist held ten hostages in a Sydney café, many in Sydney and elsewhere in Australia expected a backlash against Muslims. To indicate they would accompany any Muslim on public transport (or drive them), within two hours 40,000 Australians tweeted #IllRideWithYou, and 110,000 more tweeted the hashtag in the next two hours (Alexander 2014). People in Sydney put "I'll ride with you" stickers on their backpacks to make their offer to any Muslim who saw them.

> The spark was this post on Facebook by Rachael Jacobs, who said she'd seen a woman she presumed was Muslim silently removing her hijab while sitting next to her on the train: 'I ran after her at the train station.' I said 'put it back on. I'll walk with u.' She started to cry and hugged me for about a minute - then walked off alone'.
>
> *(Alexander 2014)*

When terrorists killed the staff of Charlie Hebdo on 7 January 2015, a great many people around the world put up "Je suis Charlie" (I am Charlie) signs or tweeted the message. After 13 November 2015, when terrorists killed 130 people in Paris, Parisians immediately began Tweeting "#PorteOuverte," offering to take in to their homes anyone who needed safe shelter, or who simply couldn't get home while all public transportation was shut down. Again, there were innumerable vigils all over the world, along with tweets and signs saying "Pray for Paris."

Similarly, after the 14 July 2016 Bastille Day truck attack in Nice, Niçoise offered sanctuary to all by tweeting "PorteOuverte." On 13 August 2016, when a man killed an imam and his assistant in Queens, New York City, thousands of New Yorkers and people elsewhere tweeted "#IllWalkWithYou," offering to accompany Muslims going to or from their mosques. Here are three of the tweets:

> #IllWalkWithYou is trending and my heart is bursting out with so much love for humanity right now seriously I am in tears. (06:46, 14 August 2016)
>
> i clicked on the #IllWalkWithYou tag to see what it meant and now i'm almost crying because sometimes i forget people can still be decent (06:46, 14 August 2016)
>
> I'm big and tall and scary looking, and I love you and I want you to feel safe #IllWalkWithYou (06:45, 14 August 2016)

On the days after each of these attacks, in scores of cities around the world thousands of people held vigils, and they placed candles, laid flowers and other offerings, and left notes at spontaneous memorial sites. While I don't yet know, it is easy to imagine that the compassionate kama muta experience is an important motivation for many people to tweet offers of shelter, protection, and support, and to attend vigils. Furthermore, it seems that many people feel kama muta when they learn of these tweets, attend vigils, make offerings and leave notes at spontaneous memorial sites, see these sites, or see videos of the vigils. What we will now see is that many people definitely feel kama muta when these practices are materialized in memorial architecture.

Monuments and memorial sites[1]

On *Día de Muertos*, the Mexican Day of the Dead, people build personal shrines to deceased loved ones. These shrines often include the favorite foods or drinks of the departed.

> One of the largest Day of the Dead celebrations in Los Angeles – one which I attend every year – is held at the Hollywood Forever Cemetery. Some of the shrines there are large, elaborate and perhaps something closer to "art" than "memorial." My own experience, however, has been that the majority are intimate displays of love for dearly departed kin, and quite often bring spectators to tears. These deeply personal memorials typically contain family photographs, offerings of food, and, most importantly, some of the deceased's most cherished possessions. A father's writing desk. His favorite hat. A grandmother's cash register from the shop she had been so proud to own. While it is believed that the deceased will be happy to find their favorite belongings when they return from the dead, it is also possible that the work of selecting and lovingly displaying these objects rekindles feelings of closeness – and, perhaps, kama muta – for the living.
>
> (Michele Piazza)

Closely related to private shrines are the roadside memorials (Spanish *descanso*) often erected for loved ones who die in motor vehicle accidents, and the informal memorials erected in Northern Ireland at sites of sectarian killings (Santino 2004; Sloane 2005). The creation of or visits to such shrines may be moments of kama muta. Likewise, in rural New Mexico personal memorials for loved ones who have died of heroin overdose are often decorated with crosses made from empty syringes (Garcia 2010) – objects which injected substances into the loved-one's body. Addiction here is spoken of as 'inherited' through the mystical transference of some addicted essence in the blood. Many of the addicts Garcia worked with emphasized how injecting heroin together with family members fostered feelings of closeness among them, and that physical withdrawal from the drug required and elicited family care and affection. So these syringes come to represent familial bonds. These memorials are places of reunion for family and close friends, when mourners both reconnect with the deceased and reaffirm their bonds with one other by injecting heroin together. Garcia's ethnography does not include descriptions of weeping or anything else which might support the idea that mourners feel kama muta when erecting these shrines, visiting them, or injecting together, but perhaps they do. I will consider the 'religious' aspects of love for the deceased in Chapter 16.

Other objects may mediate mournful kama muta after the sudden death of a beloved public figure, such as Princess Diana; her mourners turned out by the thousands with 'gifts' of flowers, balloons, stuffed animals, and handwritten letters, among other things (Sloane 2005). Similar memorials are often created by communities immediately following natural disasters and acts of terrorism (Sloane 2005). Irizarry (2014) noted, for example, the visual similarity between private memorials in Japanese Buddhism and the spontaneous shrines which appeared across Japan following the devastating 2011 earthquake and tsunami in Japan. After the 1995 bombing of the Oklahoma City federal building, many people made votive offerings of flowers, letters, and other personal items along a stretch of fence in front of the bomb site and at other local sites (Oklahoma City National Memorial & Museum 2015).

An informal interview with a friend who moved to Oklahoma City shortly after the 1995 bombing articulates the arresting experience of being 'moved by love' following the tragic events, and how it fostered a feeling of 'oneness' with his new community:

There was this long fence, this long walkway in front of the building, and it was just covered in pictures and letters and teddy bears and flowers. And that was really moving. […] I mean … that this thing happened was horrible. But then there was this outpouring of support from people. People in the community, people from outside of the community. And it feels kind of wrong to say this, but I had just moved there, and there was such a coming together of people in this really intense and powerful way, and I felt excited to be part of that. Excited is the wrong word. But, no, excited is the right word. I felt like I was just wrapped up in the middle of this really strong outpouring of communal support and I was also a part of that. Which felt really good, even though it feels wrong to say 'good.'

(Michele Piazza)

In an interview with Wired.com, designer Tom Hennes described how a visit to the spontaneous memorial "room" created at Ground Zero for victims' families was the first, crucial step in planning and designing the official 9/11 Memorial Museum (Kuang 2014):

> The windows and walls were ... papered over with remembrances. To glimpse Ground Zero at all, you had to peer through the narrow spaces between pictures of people who had died. Many were small framed photos like the ones you'd see on a nightstand; a few were kids' drawings with pictures stapled to them. At the center of the room was a podium bearing an oversize guest book filled with notes written to the dead ... [T]he notes were written in the present tense; one woman wrote to a relative asking for his approval of her new boyfriend, whom she'd brought with her.

Designers translated this spontaneous memorial room into the official memorial gallery:

> Upon entering, you are surrounded by the faces of those who died, shown in mounted photos ... from floor to ceiling ... In the center are the four walls of another, smaller room ... In the space between the outer and inner walls there are waist-high tables ... with touchscreen versions of the portraits ... Touch one and you can see more pictures of that person, audio recordings of their family's remembrances, and an obituary. ... You can then choose to project or play those items in the inner room. ... The entire space is designed for eye contact, like a Quaker meetinghouse: On the perimeter, you meet the gazes of the other visitors. The experience is communal but also intimate.

(Kuang 2014)

The Vietnam Veterans Memorial, the memorial at 9/11 Ground Zero in New York, and the memorial for victims of the 2011 earthquake and tsunami in Japan all consist of low horizontal forms with black reflective surfaces inscribed with the names of the dead. A survey of TripAdvisor reviews reveals that many visitors to the Vietnam Veterans Memorial experience an incredible sense of intimacy when seeing their own reflections alongside the reflections of others in the reflective black stone. I can attest that seeing one's own image superimposed on the names of those who died – who in some sense died for me – is a profound experience.

Not only is the Memorial an object of frequent ceremony and frequent visitation (more than 2.5 million visitors and 1,100–1,500 reunions per year), it is also an object with which visitors enter into active and affective relationships. These relationships have thwarted all original intentions as to what the Memorial should be and represent. Conceived as something to be passively looked at and contemplated, the Vietnam Memorial has become an object of emotion. This is not the case for the Memorial site as a whole, just the wall and its names. The names on the wall are … traced by the moving finger … caressed … reproduced on paper by pencil rubbing and taken home. And something is left from home itself – a material object bearing special significance to the deceased or a written statement by the visitor or mourner. The dedications of the aggrieved are a spectacle that to many is more moving than the Memorial wall itself. […] when the Memorial's grounds are deserted, its wall appears less magnetic, less moving, less memorable.

(Wagner-Pacifici and Schwartz 1991; see also White 1999)

Visitors report desiring to touch the names on the wall, tell of the tears they often shed there, and the feeling of "inspiration" they leave with (TripAdvisor). This suggests that the emotion which characterizes many people's experience at the Memorial – whether in response to its design, spontaneous shrine, or interactions between visitors – might be kama muta. And indeed many people specifically report being "moved" (TripAdvisor) by the monuments at Ground Zero and in Japan. Leaving offerings of flowers, photos, notes, or candles attests to the visitors' kama muta, while perhaps also further evoking kama muta by augmenting the donors' bonds with the deceased.

During my many visits to the Imperial War Museum in London – which had recently been redesigned to serve as a *non*-site-specific memorial for British military – I found it was the "authenticity" and intimacy of the personal objects and handwritten letters on display which "moved me to tears." I do not believe that transcriptions or reproductions would allow for the same feeling of connectedness to individuals whose lives I can only imagine. Similarly, a fellow student recently remarked to me that, at the Holocaust Museum in Washington, D.C., it was a large display of victims' *shoes* – some of the few original artifacts on display – which had elicited, for her, the strongest feeling of kama muta.

(Michele Piazza)

Kama muta is definitely prominent in the millions whose *hearts reached out* to the victims and survivors, as I observed in the previous chapter, and this is the impetus for the spontaneous temporary memorials consisting of messages, photos, flowers, candles, and offerings. This may be the impetus giving rise to permanent memorial edifices. But behind all this, it seems that the collective disasters which architectural monuments memorialize are extremely powerful kama muta moments for the survivors who suffered in them. Shared danger, fear, loss, and suffering create extraordinarily intense CS relationships, making a community of love. The evidence is not clear whether, how, or to what extent kama muta is involved in generating these wonderful communities of love, or results from the loving communion. But I would expect a lot of kama muta in earthquakes, massive fires, aerial bombardment, and other sudden collective disasters because they immediately create exceptionally intense CS, as Online Note 9.1 describes.

Coming to stand at the site of a loved one's death, at their grave, in front of their clothing or hand-written texts, or in front of their name on a memorial – simply being there – may evoke kama muta more strongly than just recalling the CS relationship. One's palpable presence at the site of mass death and destruction, or at a war memorial, may evoke kama muta even when one doesn't have any direct 'personal relationship' with the dead. The visitor may be moved by their sacrifice or their suffering. Visiting a memorial can be a kind of pilgrimage (see Chapter 14). Being present at the place puts a person in material contact with the dead, physically linking the body of the visitor with the body of memorialized person. It is a kind of consubstantial assimilation, as conformation systems theory would conceptualize it – mutual contact with the place or artifact materially links their bodies (Fiske 2004b; see Rozin, Millman, & Nemeroff 1986; Rozin et al. 1989). Likewise, a mourner 'contacts' the dead and connects herself with them by placing a handwritten note, a photograph, a cuddly teddy bear, a candle, or a flower on the site where the person stood or died, or simply where others are placing offerings. The moment of contact may be a moment of intensification of their CS relationship.

Social relationships are radically transformed at death, but typically the living sustain relationships with the dead for years, a lifetime, even multiple generations. At a funeral, viewing, or memorial service; when visiting the deceased's grave; at the anniversary of a death; at family gatherings and holidays; when visiting the home of the deceased or places that were important to them; or at any point when simply remembering the dead, the living person's relationship with the dead may be revived. The living person *feels* the relationship. When this relationship is CS and its felt re-emergence is sudden, the living person may experience kama muta.

The memorial sites discussed above function in conjunction with periodic rites. Many nations hold public memorial days to remember and celebrate soldiers who died for their motherland; these may evoke kama muta (Claparède 1930). People often sustain their relationships with a person after the person dies, and in some cultures this is elaborated and emphasized so as to become what we recognize as 'religion.' For example, in much of African, the respect and obedience due to elders, along with the elders' responsibility to guide, protect, and discipline their juniors, does not end with the elders' death (Kopytoff 1971). After a Moose adult dies, family members and friends come to talk to him or her for three or four days before she is buried, converse with him or her when she is about to be carried to the grave, and finally say goodbye just before the tomb is closed. In many other cultures, too, people worship dead family members, sometimes including children, siblings, and spouses, as well as 'ancestors.' Such worship may include speaking (sometimes as 'prayer') to the dead, offering them food or flowers, or, in some cultures, expressing the living persons' desire to be reunited in the afterlife. The living may consult the dead through spirit mediums who speak in their voices (Bourgignon 2008, Lewis 2003; see Online Note 3.3). It appears that all of these sorts of moments of reconnection with deceased loved ones may often evoke kama muta. For example, a film on a Balinese spirit medium shows a father apparently feeling kama muta when, through the medium, he speaks with his dead child (Connor, Asch, & Asch 1986).

Immediately following the death of a loved one, a Japanese Buddhist family will hold a wake or *tsuya* (Irizarry 2014), during which the body is displayed in front of a uniquely constructed altar *(saidan)*, alongside temporary versions of two important memorial artifacts: a portrait of the deceased, called an *iei*, and a memorial tablet called an *ihai*. The family will later install permanent versions of the *iei* and *ihai* in their home, "communicating" the deceased's "presence and involvement in the life of the family." These objects allow the living to continue participating in a CS relationship with the deceased, as family members regularly share stories with the deceased and seek out their advice. Japanese Buddhists do not believe that the *iei* or the *ihai* actually contains the deceased's spirit *(hotoke*; Irizarry 2014). These memorial objects are merely conduits for interaction in the CS relationship; it is a history of caring for these objects which binds people to them emotionally. So a memorial photograph which has been lovingly placed in the home, gently touched, and regularly dusted has a singularity; its 'biography' renders it irreplaceable. The loss of such a memorial object is considered a "social and moral failure" by those charged with its care (Irizarry 2014:181). Likewise, recovery of a lost *iei* or *ihai* is experienced as something of a family reunion, as it enables "reestablishment of familiar affective relationships" (Irizarry 2014).[2] It seems to us likely that interactions with the *iei* or the *ihai* may often either result from or lead to kama muta *(kando)*, and if *iei* and *ihai* were lost or possibly destroyed in an earthquake or fire, for example, their recovery would likely evoke *kando* or even be vocalized by *kokoro o ugokasareru* ('something moved my heart').

S. Megan Heller, a psychological anthropologist who attends and studies Burning Man, described a related experience with her five-year-old daughter at BEquinox, another desert event that is organized by Los Angeles-area Burners.

> I rejoined my daughter, whose fingernails had been painted while I was chatting. She insisted on applying pink nail polish to my toenails. Afterward, we started walking together toward the effigy, Earthstar [which was to be burned at the culmination of BEquinox], pushing the baby's stroller in front of us. Immediately, however, we encountered an interactive art project. It was a

large purple-and-black board with teardrop-shaped pieces of paper pinned to it. My daughter, recognizing this as an invitation to participate, asked to write on one of the teardrops herself. A sign near the board instructed participants to share a story of grief on one of the pieces of paper. I read the sign aloud to her and explained what "grief" means, and then I helped her write her story with the pens provided. This is what she had me write: "Grandpa – Why did you die before I was born? I wanted to meet you. Love, Sophia." Then she took the pen from me and drew several smaller teardrops on the paper.

I was quite moved by her unprompted memorial to my dead father. I remembered grieving when he was ill, lamenting how he would never know my children. Actual tears welled in my eyes as I pinned my daughter's story to the board. My father's ashes dwell in a box in our living room; this conspicuous location was inspired by my time in Japan with a Japanese host family who kept an ancestral shrine in their living area.

(Heller 2016:187)

Objects of affection

Humans imbue artifacts, natural objects, places, and substances with all sorts of social relational meaning (Csikszentmihalyi & Rochberg-Halton 1981; Appadurai 1988). People can constitute the four basic forms of social relationships through, respectively, the transfer of commodities (market pricing), matching gifts (equality matching), tribute and largesse (authority ranking), or kind sharing (communal sharing; Fiske 1991, 2004a). To mediate social relationships, objects don't have to be transferred from one person to another: material substances and things can be money or investments (market pricing), ballots or straws that each one draws to determine an outcome (equality matching), icons of status or subservience (authority ranking), family meals or essences of kinship (communal sharing).

Significantly for our present concerns, material things may suddenly create a new CS relationship; decisively renew, restore, or redress a dormant or problematic CS relationship; or dramatically deepen an ongoing CS relationship. Think of the food and fuel supplied in the Berlin airlift or disaster relief, a beautiful bouquet of apology, an unexpected and especially thoughtful gift, or an engagement ring. In interviews with 315 adults and children from 82 upper-middle and lower-middle class families living in a northern metropolitan area, Csikszentmihalyi and Rochberg-Halton (1981) asked "What are the things in your home that are special to you?" In their responses, 82% named at least one thing that was meaningful because of its significance for a relationship with one or more members of their immediate family. In addition, 23% named things that were meaningful because they represented relationships with kin outside the immediate family, ancestors, or in-laws. Also, 40% indicated at least one object whose significance derived from a relationship with someone else (non-kin). Again, 74% named objects that represented memories, and 40% listed at least one gift. Respondents valued even most of their artworks not primarily for their esthetic qualities: "Instead, art was valued primarily because it recalled memories of events, family, and friendship" (Csikszentmihalyi & Rochberg-Halton 1981:178). "All this adds up to the fact that the emotional integration of the home is concretely embodied in household objects" (Csikszentmihalyi & Rochberg-Halton 1981:165). Perhaps sometimes looking at, holding, wearing, or sitting in some of these objects evokes kama muta.

All it takes to indexically evoke a communal connection is touching something that has been in contact with the person one loves. Kama muta may be evoked by cooking 'grandma's goose' recipe, eating it together, or in rituals of food sharing, such as an American bride and groom feeding each other their wedding cake, or at marked holiday meals. The indexical consubstantial assimilation occurs though one person's contact with or ingestion of a meaningful substance that another has contacted or is contacting, has ingested, or is ingesting, making the people socially equivalent though the shared substance they have taken into their bodies (Miller, Rozin, & Fiske 1998; Fiske 2004b; Fiske & Schubert 2012). When this is suddenly felt to intensify the CS between the participants, they are likely to feel kama muta.

The kama muta of things can be first-, second-, third-party, or the *we* of first-person plural. A person could be kama muta when they give a bodily organ that saves the recipient's life (Ferguson 2015), when they receive the organ, or when they learn of someone's giving it. Combinations are common. When an aunt gives a nephew a holiday present the nephew has been wishing for and the nephew is overjoyed, both the child and the aunt may experience kama muta, along with the child's parents who observe this. When a messenger delivers unexpected candy or flowers, the recipient may experience kama muta, which sometimes may evoke kama muta in the messenger.

Ordinary objects that another person wore or used may easily become emblems of a relationship with the person; holding, putting on, or looking at such an object may suddenly evoke intense affective memories of the relationship, and thus kama muta. People often keep objects for their 'sentimental value,' especially objects that were worn, used, or touched by someone the keeper loves or admires (Newman, Diesendruck, & Bloom 2011; Belk 1988). Such objects mediate CS relationships between the original user(s) and the current user according to a principle of 'once in contact, always in contact' (Rozin, Millman, & Nemeroff 1986). Hence wearing a piece of the loved one's jewelry or clothing feels like having that person touch the wearer, where touch is an act of consubstantial assimilation constituting and representing the CS relationship (Fiske 2004b; Fiske & Schubert 2012). Or the object may be felt to be a conduit for some sort of physical 'essence' of the other (Rozin, Millman, & Nemeroff 1986; Rozin et al. 1989) where this quasi-material essence is again a form of consubstantial assimilation making the two persons one. When people perceive an object in this way, seeing it or touching it may suddenly revive the CS relationship, evoking kama muta. English speakers may label their feeling *nostalgia* (see Chapter 7).

An American flag always drapes the coffin of an American solider; when he is buried, the flag is ceremoniously folded in the required manner and presented to the next of kin. Holding this flag may evoke kama muta then and again afterwards, I imagine. Many cultures practice rituals in which a deceased person's identify-defining possessions are handed over to his or her heirs. Certainly people tend to treasure their parents' or ancestors' jewelry, lace, medals, silver, hand-made quilts, and of course, their portraits or photographs; opening a trunk in the attic and taking this out may evoke kama muta, especially when these things were forgotten and rediscovered. I know that wearing a deceased parent's sport coat can evoke a little kama muta. I feel a bit of kama muta when I sit in my father's rocking chair, or sit in the chair in which my grandfather (whom I never met) is seated in a photograph of him in his college room. Returning to one's childhood home or the home of one's ancestors may also evoke kama muta. More prosaically, a basketball, musical instrument, or old car may be treasured because it indexes wonderful communal experiences – times when the person felt truly together with teammates, band members, or travel mates. At times, picking up the basketball, playing the instrument, working on or driving the car may evoke kama muta. Rummaging in the attic, uncovering a child's toys or christening gown may bring tears of nostalgic kama muta – and perhaps one may feel that when finding the stuffed animal who was once one's constant companion.

Every year, at Christmas, my mother and I bring out my great uncle's stopwatch to time the baking of cookies. The digital egg timer which sits on the counter year-round probably keeps better time, and is certainly easier to operate, but using my great uncle's stopwatch feels as though we are including him in the tradition. The feeling of warmth in my chest and the slight chill I experience each Christmas when I first wrap my hand around this small, sturdy artifact have not diminished over the years. To hold my uncle's stopwatch always brings me immediately back to the smell of his home, the sound of his voice, the look of pure joy on his face when he would watch unsuspecting visitors choke on his infamous moonshine.

(Michele Piazza)

The body of the deceased affords the most direct consubstantial assimilation with him. In some cultures, survivors bury the dead in the floors of their homes, or in crypts in the churches where they worship; this placement affords many moments of material reconnection. There are cultures in which a widow wears her deceased husband's jawbone on a necklace and carries his skull behind her in a net bag; do widows feel kama muta sometimes when they put these on in the morning? Even the bones of a stranger can be evocative.

> I was in India not long ago. ... One day I wandered into a park, and this park had a little science museum in the back. ... there was a human skeleton. And above the human skeleton, written in English and in Hindi, was this sign; it said:
> 'Please see toward me. I was as you are. You have to be as I am. Hence, love all.'
> And it was very moving. I remembered it quite vividly.
>
> *(Siegel 2014)*

In a number of cultures in New Guinea and elsewhere, female mourners, unwilling to be separated from the deceased and appalled at the prospect of letting him or her simply rot away, eat the deceased (Gillison 1983; Lindenbaum 1979). Do they feel kama muta when they do this, or when they recall that their family member remains a part of them? Are their feelings anything like the feelings of worshippers consuming their god? Do Christians occasionally feel kama muta when they ingest the consecrated wafer and wine of the Eucharist, constituted as the blood and body of Christ? What do the devout feel when they touch the container in which a saint's relic is preserved? We'll look at kama muta in these and other religious practices in Chapters 12–16.

To create or preserve CS relationships with the living or the dead, people often actively seek to give or receive objects imbued with a desired partner's essence: wedding rings, for example. The CS relationship may be transitively reinforced by giving a ring worn by one's mother or ancestor, or the bride's wearing something that her mother wore at her wedding. Throughout Ireland there is a tradition of tying pieces of fabric to the branches of specially designated "rag trees" when a CS relationship is in jeopardy, such as when a loved one departs or is ill or in danger (Santino, 2004). The fabrics are chosen for the essence embedded within them – some part of the person's identity – such as a baby's bib, or the scrap of a loved one's favorite T-shirt. It is believed that a prayer or wish for restoration of the CS relationship will come true as the fabric decomposes (Santino 2004).

To evoke kama muta, material stuff does not have to consist of discrete objects. Returning from a long and hazardous journey, with a surge of kama muta, a traveler may kiss the soil of his homeland. One can feel kama muta when setting foot in a holy place where a savior or prophet once stood. Nor does the stuff have to be palpable: the smell of autumn leaves or the scent of fields of lavender may evoke kama muta in an emigrant who remembers home – sometimes, perhaps, without the traveler noticing what has evoked his nostalgia.

Memorials and mementos are mental reunions. In Chapter 3 I observed that when reunions restore CS relationships that were challenged or problematic, the reunited typically feel kama muta, along with their kin and friends, and the audience. Death, time, and other kinds of separation challenge CS relationships, but the CS can be revived in places that connect the persons, or by contact with material objects that bridge the gap between the dead and the living.

* * * * *

In sudden disaster, people immediately intensify communal sharing relationships with just about everyone; they rescue, shelter, give, and share. The CS relationships that arise from disaster are extraordinarily strong, and they accompany an almost euphoric and nearly unique sense of meaningfulness – incongruously, disaster is a peak experience (see Chapters 1 and 9). This may be mediated by kama muta, but we don't have evidence regarding the presence or absence of its characteristic physical sensations in survivors who were in jeopardy. The wider public response to disaster definitely comprises kama muta generated by feelings of identification with, and compassion for, the victims and survivors. Huge numbers of people are motivated to make donations or even travel to the site to provide aid. On social media people offer shelter or offer to accompany and protect potential victims. People gather to weep in heartwarming candle-lit vigils, laying flowers and messages at spontaneous memorials. The sensations are salient, while the devotion and commitment motives are plainly demonstrated. An eventual result of this (along with other contributing factors) is the construction of permanent memorial structures and exhibits that are expressly <u>designed</u> to evoke kama muta in visitors. Apt memorial architecture and exhibits draw visitors in to connect with the victims, heroes, and rescuers. Standing on the actual ground where victims died, touching their names on a memorial, being in proximity to the clothes they wrote or the letters they wrote, and looking at their photographs provides a consubstantial connection, assimilating the viewer's body to the victims' bodies. This evokes a mnemonic feeling of CS with the victims, generating kama muta. Handling or wearing mementos, visiting a grave or the site reminiscent of an important CS relationship do the same thing in much the same way.

* * * * * *

Evoking kama muta is an important implicit aim of life-cycle ceremonies such as weddings, along with their artifacts such as albums and videos. Likewise, evoking kama muta is an important implicit or explicit aim of patriotic ceremonies such as national day celebrations and commemorative rites (Claparède 1930), along with their memorials in enduring stone and bronze. Funerals and memorial rites have similar functions of restoring bonds among the living, as functionalist anthropologists have long pointed out. These rituals and artifacts grow out of the kama muta propensity of *Homo movens*. I suppose that a species without the capacity for kama muta would not have such rituals or artifacts.

Online notes

9.1 Collective response to terrorism and disaster.

Notes

1 This section draws directly and extensively from field notes and an independent study research paper written by Michele Piazza, who kindly agreed to their use.
2 This paragraph consists mostly of a lightly edited excerpt from a 2015 independent study paper by Michele Piazza, reproduced here with her permission.

10

THE KAMA MUTA EXPERIENCE IS GENERATED BY A CULTURALLY TUNED PSYCHOLOGICAL MECHANISM, THE *PSYPE*

We have now considered how kama muta arises in a range of situations in a range of cultures. I will present many more in the following chapters. But before we go further, we should stop to more precisely characterize just what kama muta <u>is</u>. Describing where kama muta occurs and what it looks like in its various contexts – its 'natural history' – is a crucial aspect of characterizing what a human emotion is. Though that natural history is missing from most accounts of emotion constructs, I believe that one doesn't know what an emotion is until it has been studied in its natural settings across history and cultures. That's why so much of this book is devoted to such ethnographic, historical, and contemporary descriptions. Kama muta isn't simply its manifestation among people watching YouTube videos, although that's <u>one</u> manifestation of it. We don't know kama muta until we recognize it wherever it appears, appreciate how its manifestations vary, and understand what is the same across those cultural and contextual manifestations. If we don't know kama muta in Los Angeles cry dates and Japanese cry parties, in responses to narratives and poetry, in winner weeping, in Greek recognition reunions, in oratory and marketing, in patriotic ceremonies and memorials, in Buddhist Jātaka stories, in South Asian laments, in Amazonian greeting with tears, we simply don't know kama muta. Or perhaps I should say, we have a simplistic parochial understanding of it. We don't know what a planet is if we only know Earth. It's the same with kama muta – we don't know what kama muta is if we only know contemporary Americans responding to YouTube videos. That's not an unreasonable place to start, but we can't <u>stop</u> there.

In Chapter 4 I sketched the core of kama muta theory: it occurs when a communal sharing relationship suddenly intensifies, increasing the prospects for communal sharing. We've begun to see some of the kinds of CS relationships that can be involved, and some of the processes that can bring about sudden intensification. In succeeding chapters, we'll see a lot more of both. In Chapter 4

I posited that the function of kama muta is to focus a person's attention on the CS intensification and motivate them to devote and commit themselves to CS. We've seen a number of the CS relationships that people devote and commit to, and ways that they do – although that's what we know least about, because motives are often hard to track and are not included in reports of events that launch the motives. So I've sketched the basic theory, which is consistent with what we've seen in the cultural practices, institutions, roles, narratives, and artifacts we've explored so far, as well as those we'll encounter in later chapters. But we can go much deeper, now we have an overview of the natural history of kama muta. So let's dig down to the next level.

What sort of entity is this emotion? Up to this point I've been taking for granted some intriguing ontological matters that we ought to deal with. It's time to more fully articulate our constructs. I will argue that it is a universal, evolved, adaptive psychological system – so it is a natural kind, but a natural kind that, like language, can only be realized in specific cultural systems that generate unique, culturally informed, social relational experiences. This means that we can aptly describe kama muta as a function, in the mathematical sense, mapping propitious moments in CS relationships onto fruitful motives to enhance CS relationships. I will consider what that implies about the ethnological and historical knowledge we need to characterize the kama muta function. Then we will consider how kama muta is situated among emotions whose function – in the adaptive sense – is to motivationally regulate social relationships. The conceptual tools I develop in this chapter will enable us to more precisely describe kama muta events and their eliciting conditions, to better understand what this emotion is, and to see more clearly what it is doing.

The psychological mechanism for kama muta is a function mapping communal sharing intensifications onto motivations

To understand any emotion, we need some sort of general theory of emotions that orients us; conversely, developing knowledge about any one emotion informs our general theory of emotions. In particular, we want to know what sort of thing a social emotion is, and where kama muta belongs in that general category. There are some basic questions we need to ask. Are social emotions simply the denotations of vernacular words, so that study of emotions is based on semantics – on dictionary definitions? That's what many emotion theorists have assumed, while in Chapter 7 I argued that one needs scientific constructs of emotions that are distinct from the meanings of everyday words. Social emotions are social relational processes, involved in the orientation and transformation of relationships. But how? In shaping social emotions, how does the biological process of natural selection interact with the social psychological process of cultural selection? Why are there so many powerful cultural practices, institutions, narratives, and artifacts that so effectively evoke certain emotions? How is the cultural diversity of such practices grounded in the innate psychology of emotions? I begin to address these issues here.

I posit that for any social or moral emotion there is a psychological process consisting of a function (in the mathematical sense) mapping a domain of social relational circumstances onto a range of sensations, performances, and motives. The function responds selectively to relevant inputs (the domain of the function), generating adaptive output (the range or image of the function) that operates to orient or transform the relevant social relationship.

For example, consider a simplified version of the function of a non-social emotion, 'fear.' The function may be such that when minimally frightened or in the presence of people one wants to impress, one approaches the threatening stimulus to explore or confront it. Yet when alone, the same level of minimal fear might lead to avoidance. When caring for one's child, the presence of even an extremely fear-inducing threat might lead to the parent attacking the threat, willing to sacrifice herself to protect her child. The output – physical signs, motives, speech, and actions – differs according to the input, such that the output is generally adaptive with respect to the input. "Adaptive" means not simply some sort of invariant response, but output that is tuned to 'work well' for the person in a particular culture, community, network of relationships, and social situation.

The emotion-generating mapping function naturally changes as the brain and body develop in conjunction with experience in a particular environment. How the function changes will be contingent on an interaction between the neurocognitive biology of the developing brain and the sociocultural and physical environment in which the mechanism develops. In genetics an environmental response function built into the biology of the ontogeny of the organism is called a *reaction norm*.[1] It is an evolved adaptation, functioning to increase fitness in the most prevalent past environments. The reaction norm of an emotion-generating mechanism is an ontogenetic meta-function that shapes the adult function so as to map the domain of experience onto the resultant range of emotional sensations, performances, and motives. So, for example, depending on one's childhood experience, a person might learn various responses to someone threatening them: flight, laughing at them, asking their pardon, appealing to one's buddies, calling the police, threatening harm to the person, or immediate and disproportionate violence.

It's important to distinguish specific instances of an emotion from this mapping function – called the *graph* of the emotion: for example, if we call both the graph and a particular token 'fear,' it may not be clear what we're referring to. In our case we need to distinguish instances of kama muta from the mapping function that develops, elaborating and transforming over the lifespan according to its cultural reaction norm. So let's call the mapping function the **psy**chological **p**roclivity to the **e**motion; for short, the *psype* (pronounced 'sipe'). In the language of complementarity theory (Fiske 2000), the psype is a *mod*, although I now incorporate into the mod concept its reaction norm – the ontogeny of the psype function in response to experience. A mod is a mechanism that has evolved to presuppose and require cultural complements that specify how, when, and with whom it operates. That is, the mod requires local precedents, prototypes, paradigms, precepts, principles, and prescriptions (called *preos*) that complete it by specifying the exact form of the adult function.[2] The psype is a disposition, a proclivity, a potential, an affordance which exists before, during, and after any particular experience of the emotion. Like any other component of psychology, of course, this disposition is part of a system that includes neural substrates and networks, physiological and hormonal mechanisms. The psype is not a simple binary on/off switch, not even a transducer like a volume control. Rather, it is a function, with a domain and a range that are informed by cultural experiences. The psype must actively and discerningly search for, discriminatingly attend to, sensitively interpret, accurately encode in memory, reliably recall, and subtly analyze and map selected aspects of the CS relationships it encounters (directly or through verbal reports). Having done so, it must map these aspects of CS encounters onto potential realizations of kama muta, and generate those kama muta experiences when socioculturally appropriate. The psype generates each particular kama muta experience with respect not just to the immediate events, but with reference to a lifetime of culturally shaped social encounters.

A **psype** is a psychological function that maps changes in the prospects for a social relationship onto emotions that motivate fruitful tactics to transform that social relationship beneficially. The domain (input) of psype is the social relational situations that it looks for, attends, and responds to. The range (output, image) of a psype is the emotions, motives, and performances (displays) that it generates. That is, the range of a psype are the motes it generates (see below). Psypes are necessarily tuned to a person's culture, social relational history, needs and intentions; otherwise, they would not enhance either fitness or well-being.

At any point in the life-cycle, when exposed to a circumstance within its domain, the psype generates a token of the emotion. So if this is the fear psype, when a contemporary passenger on an airliner hears over the loudspeaker, "This is the captain speaking. Sorry folks – we've run out of fuel," the psype generates a set of sensations and thoughts, evokes a certain sort of performance, and motivates a set of actions.[3] To clearly denote the thoughts, feelings, sensations, motives, and actions of a particular person on a particular occasion, I'll call that a **mo**mentary experience and performance of th**e e**motion; for short, a *mote*. The term *mote* is intended to resonate with *emote*, *motive*, and the Sanskrit *muta* (as well as the dictionary definition of the vernacular word *mote*, 'a tiny bit, a speck'). It's obvious that an occurrence of a psychological event, the mote, is distinct from the functional mechanism that generates it, the psype. This terminology is necessary to distinguish between the enduring, evolved, but culturally attuned psype and the myriad momentary and particular experiences that the psype engenders because the English vernacular word *emotion* conflates the two.

Any person's mote may be affected by others' motes, and may correspond closely to others' motes, but I define 'a mote' as the thoughts, feelings, sensations, performances, motives, and actions of one person at one moment. In other words, a mote is the product of the psype function shaped by a person's ontogeny in one or more particular cultures, operating on any given occasion in a manner that is typically highly attuned to the relevant cultural preos. (Responses by young infants and people with severe mental disorders are among the partial exceptions to this cultural sensitivity.)

Motes are the output of psypes: a mote is the emotional event generated by a specific psype on a particular occasion. A mote comprises the phenomenological experience, sensations, performances (displays), motives, evaluations, labels, and meanings of the experienced event. It is inherently culturally informed. The core of a mote is the motivation to beneficially transform a social relationship in accord with the manner in which the prospects for the relationship have changed.

Figure 10.1 is a schematic representation of the kama muta psype function. On the left is the domain of the psype: its input consist of perceived intensifications

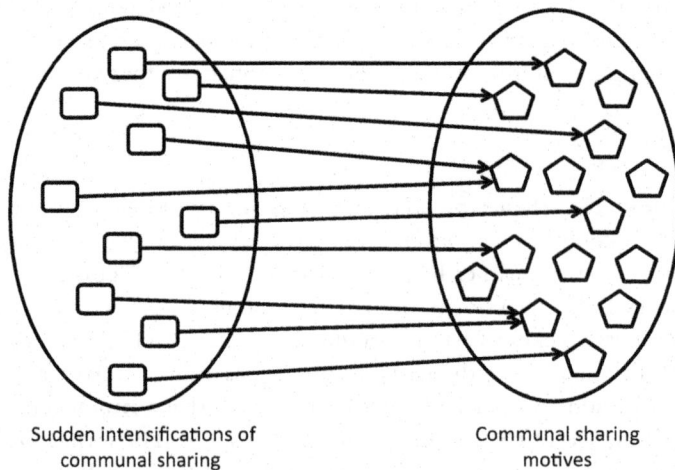

Sudden intensifications of
communal sharing

Communal sharing
motives

FIGURE 10.1 The kama muta psype as it maps all sudden intensifications of communal sharing to which it responds.

of CS. The arrows represent the function mappings. On the right are the CS motives that are generated. For graphical simplicity, the figure represents sudden intensifications of CS as discrete elements. However, it is likely that the psype comprises both discrete and continuous dimensional graphing; that is, both the sudden intensifications of CS and the resulting motives may differ not only typologically, but also at the same time vary along one or more dimensions. Note that the figure represents the possibility that two or more different kinds of sudden intensification may map onto the same motivation. Also, in depicting a motive to which there are no arrows, Figure 10.1 also represents the fact that kama muta is not the sole source of CS motives. In interpreting this figure, keep in mind that the pentagon that represents each sort of CS motive will consist of an integrated configuration of several devotions and commitments. For example, when a bride and groom feel kama muta at the moment they are wed, they are likely to feel committed to live together; to take care of each other in sickness and in health; to be sexually faithful; to conceive, love, and raise children together; to be cordial to and supportive of each other's kin, and so forth. In the figures, all of the motives that compose this configuration are represented as a single pentagon, even though they involve a number of CS relationships. Moreover, while the range (image, output) of the psype is labelled "motives," each of the pentagons also comprises sensations, performances (displays), and evaluations of the experiences.

Each <u>instance</u> of a CS intensification mapping onto CS motives, et cetera, is a mote; for graphical simplicity, Figure 10.1 shows categories or types of motes, as if they were distinct kinds. But it is a graphical simplification, not meant to imply that motes can in fact be categorized into discrete kinds. There may or may not be a valid taxonomy of motes, of one or more hierarchical (nested) levels; there may or may not be continuous parametric variations among motes, generating a valid dimensional space. I don't know yet.

One can imagine that Figure 10.1 represents what this book ideally would be, if we knew all there is to know about kama muta; each rectangle, arrow, and pentagon represents one of the topics in this ideal book, or, let us say, the complete characterization of kama muta. One rectangle, arrow, and pentagon represents the mapping of the romantic narrative prototype, another is cry dates, another is kama muta-inducing oratory, another kama muta-based marketing, et cetera.

In any case, this figure enables us to see something important: to understand kama muta experiences, we need to characterize the psype function that generates it. <u>A valid characterization of the psype function requires an extensive inductive synthesis of the entire domain of circumstances in which people experience the whole gamut of human kama muta experiences</u>. Observing any one specific circumstance and the particular kama muta experience it generates tells us very little about the function, which is a mapping from a domain of many processes, circumstances, or events onto a range of kama muta motes.

Compare Figure 10.1 with Figure 10.2, which represents the activity of the kama muta psype in one particular culture. Any particular culture implements

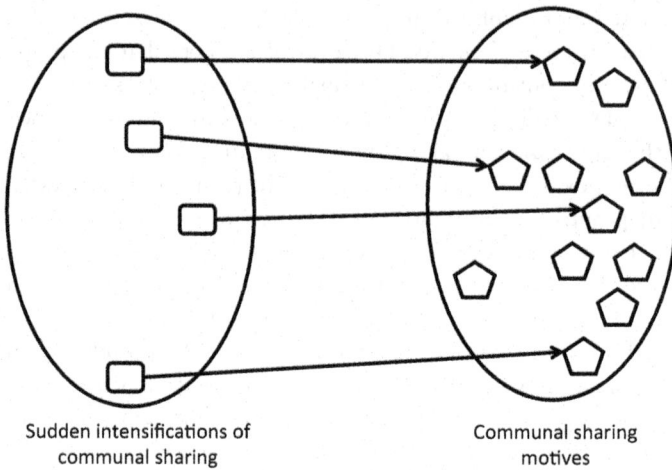

Sudden intensifications of
communal sharing

Communal sharing
motives

FIGURE 10.2 The kama muta psype as it maps the sudden intensifications of communal sharing that actually occur in a particular culture.

CS relationships in only some of the innumerable ways they can be implemented; for example, the culture may have blood–brotherhood but not *compadrazgo*, host-guest *xenia* bonds, lineages, or age-sets. It may not have marketing or winner weeping. Epistemologically, what this means is that researchers cannot characterize the psype function based on data only from, say, university students in a few cultures. There is no way to determine the mapping (the *graph*) of CS intensifications onto motives without knowing the full diversity of CS intensifications that occur in a multitude of greatly varying cultures and historical periods. If we have only the observations shown in Figure 10.2, we don't know the kama muta function – we can't specify its graph. We don't know the reaction norm. This is true whether our data are from ethnological and historical comparison, participant observation, survey, interviews, or experiments – but it's especially a problem when we are limited to experimental data. Why? For two reasons. First, experimenters are likely to fiddle around until they finally find one effective way of inducing an emotion with just a few stimuli of a very few kinds. For example, watching videos. It's hard to make a paradigm work reliably, so once a lab gets the effects it hopes for, it is rare for the lab, or even the entire field, to explore many more experimental designs that may evoke the emotion – but often, for unknown reasons, fail to do so. So they study minor variations on one rectangle, one arrow, and one pentagon; often they are not aware of any of the others, so their model doesn't encompass them. Second, ethnologists, historians, participant observers, and interviewers stumble onto all kinds of things that they had never imagined. It's a big, complex world, far beyond the imagination of researchers who don't explore it thoroughly. Assuming that the psype is an adaptation selected to work well over its entire domain, the more of its domain we know, the better we can understand the adaptive function of the psype. And mathematically, the more varied observations we have on its domain, its range, and the mapping between them, the more constrained are the possible functions that describe the process that produces the observations.

Human psychology, especially social relational psychology, is evolutionarily adapted to function in, and with respect to, a cultural framework. What is adaptive in one culture is maladaptive in another. Moreover, much of what makes many human psychological processes adaptive is their facilitation of beneficial social relationships. The fundamental relational models are universal, but the specific implementations of them that enable beneficial coordination vary greatly from situation to situation and culture to culture (Fiske 1991; Fiske & Schubert 2012). Indeed, much of human psychology presupposes and depends on socially transmitted preos – i.e., culture (Fiske 2000). The best understood example is language; whatever the mechanisms and motives for developing linguistic capabilities, those mechanisms and motives function precisely to enable and reliably realize the development of proficiency in the specific language(s) of the community in which a particular child finds herself. If there is such a thing as universal grammar, no-one speaks it, or could possibly speak it; it's utterly indeterminate until completed by the cultural complements it requires (in generative linguistics, called *principles and parameter setting*). It is not possible to determine the nature of the language learning mechanisms and motives without studying a wide variety of languages within and across historically related families. Moreover, one cannot say what human language is if one studies only one or a few related languages, or even a small sample of language families. Similarly, only meticulous induction based on precise, reliable, and valid descriptions of kama muta across widely varying circumstances in diverse cultures will enable us to characterize the function that maps history and circumstances onto kama muta emotional experiences and their meanings. This is the only way to understand how the psype works and thus what kama muta *is*.

We have seen, and will see in subsequent chapters, that there are innumerable preos with reference to which the kama muta psype is implemented – and must be implemented. That is, in order to realize kama muta in any specific instance, certain parameters must be set, prototypes imitated, precedents followed, paradigms conformed to, precepts respected. Without these preo specifications, the kama muta psype graph cannot be determined. The kama muta psype ontologically depends on preos that we can heuristically taxonomize into five categories:

1. Emphasis, elaboration, and orientation:
   A. **What intensifications of CS relationships are culturally salient?**
   B. What are the **cultural cues** that intensify CS, or signal its intensification?
   C. **What secondary CS relationships are people motivated to create**, seek, or enhance as a result of experiencing kama muta in a primary relationship?
   D. **Which sensations and signs** of kama muta are culturally salient?

2. Meanings, significance:
   E. **When and why is who expected to seek to experience kama muta?**
   F. What are the **implications** of experiencing kama muta?
   G. In particular, when and how does experiencing kama muta **shape the self or transform identities**?
   H. When and why do people **communicate about** their experiences or others' experiences of kama muta, and how do they represent it? (see part 4)
3. Institutions, practices, roles:
   I. What are the **ordinary contexts and activities** in which people most often experience kama muta?
   J. What **social systems and processes** are designed or function to evoke kama muta?
   K. How do certain people **become proficient** evokers or experiencers of kama muta?
   L. Are there **specialized roles** in which people are responsible for experiencing or evoking kama muta?
4. Art, artifacts, technologies, architecture:
   M. What material **arts, objects, and mechanisms** do people use to evoke kama muta?
   N. What **buildings and landscapes** do people use to evoke kama muta?
   O. What forms of oral or written **literature** do people use to evoke kama muta?
   P. What sorts of **performances** do people use to evoke kama muta?
   Q. What sorts of **images**, film, and video do people use to evoke kama muta?
5. Recognition and ritualization:
   R. To what degree are what aspects of what sorts of kama muta motes **explicitly identified** as articulable cultural constructs ('hypercognized')?
   S. What sorts or aspects of kama muta motes are *not* **explicitly recognized** or named ('hypocognized')?
   T. What articulated **ethnopsychological conceptions or erudite models** do people use to understand kama muta?
   U. What sorts of kama muta experiences, sensations, or signs are **identified and categorized** as other emotions (such as 'sadness,' 'joy,' or 'awe'?
   V. How is kama muta **linked, combined, conflated, and configured** in relation to other emotions and mental states or processes?
   W. What sorts of kama muta motes are **fluid, informal, and ad hoc**?
   X. How is the kama muta psype **ritualized** into predictable, controlled, expected, required, explicitly significant ceremonies?
   Y. How does the culture **attenuate, enhance, or inform the phenomenological experience** of kama muta motes and the signs people exhibit?

These questions are about the domain (input) of the psype, and its range (output). Until we answer these questions, we do not know what the psype accepts as input, that is, what activates it, what it responds to. And we don't know what actions it maps onto. Without knowing that, we just do not know what the psype graph is. That is why we need broad and deep ethnological and historical research to understand the psychology of this emotion, or any other.

There are many species of plants and animals that reproduce asexually, generating clones of themselves – in optimal environments. But the same species reproduces sexually in harsh or uncertain environments. Similarly, there are fish that are female as long as a male is with the school, but become male if there are no other males around. If we studied such species in just one environment, under one set of stable conditions, we would completely fail to understand their reproductive biology – or their psychology. Humans have evolved the extraordinary adaptation of learning from each other by observing and imitating. That is, culture. Moreover, humans are uniquely dependent on their culture; we can only speak the particular language(s) we have been exposed to – and without this exposure we cannot develop language at all. Similarly, humans are often utterly committed to their kin group or community, sometimes even ready to die for it. But what constitutes the kin group – for example, descent along the paternal versus maternal line – totally depends on cultural learning. The propensity for self-sacrificial loyalty is an innate evolved psychological system, but that system is always oriented with respect to specific cultural precedents, prototypes, precepts, and paradigms. Loyalty exists only as loyalty to a particular culturally constituted social entity. Just as there is no generic, universal language, there is no realization of communal sharing outside of particular equivalence relations in particular communities in particular cultures. Communal sharing is always devotion to some culturally constituted essence of some particular culturally delineated set of persons.

But regardless of this, CS relationships are essential to the existence of any community: for the most part, a community is a set of people who coordinate in CS. Most of its constituent groups consist of CS relationships. Groups (including dyads) can consist of coordination based on each of the four relational models: followers of a leader, peers who have equal rights (e.g., voters), or participants in a market. However, on the whole, CS-based groups are the most prevalent, most motivating, and most significant. Because of the devotion and commitment that emerge from kama muta motes, the kama muta psype is a major mediator of many – perhaps most – CS dyads and groups. Cultural practices that evoke kama muta are major enablers of many CS groups, and indeed many groups would probably not survive without the devotion and commitment these practices evoke. Different societies are composed of different CS groups, and the salient groups in any society change over time. Culturally evolved practices, institutions, roles, arts, and artifacts evoke kama muta-devotion and commitment to particular CS relationships; thus the cultural practices that evoke kama muta determine the dynamically crystallizing and dissolving equivalence sets that are the most basic aspects of social structure. Thus kama muta-evoking practices substantially shape societies, helping to give each its own particular form.

In some contemporary societies, people are linked by national identity afforded by flags, memorial sites, patriotic ceremonies, oratory, and other things that evoke kama muta. In most historical societies, there were no such practices evoking kama muta motives toward the imagined community that is the nation, and hence without this nationalism there were no nations. In some societies, people are linked in congregations and religions by narratives, rituals, hymns, art, and religious leaders who evoke kama muta; in other societies that lack these cultural systems, there are no strong religious CS groups. Today, sets of people are connected by the kama muta that a band or singer evokes in them, and the performances or recordings these fans share with each other. In cultures without these performance practices and digital artifacts, there is nothing driving any such kama muta, and there are no such groups. *Uncle Tom's Cabin* is a narrative that is designed to evoke kama muta, dependent on literacy and the printing press: it evoked kama muta that afforded whites' feelings of loving-kindness toward slaves, fostered the abolitionist social movement, and moved the nation toward a civil war. Without this narrative and the artifacts that disseminated it, history might have followed another path. When charities create kama muta-evoking posters or commercials of hungry children, refugees, or endangered animals that enhance viewers' CS sentiments toward these needy targets, they create care and solidarity that would not have existed otherwise, and that indeed historically did not previously exist. When a greeting card evokes kama muta or a kama muta social media post initiates a new friendship or group, CS bonds are created or renewed that would not have been without such artifacts. Presenting an engagement ring, proposing marriage and accepting, participating in a wedding, and celebrating anniversaries may evoke kama muta that considerably strengthens the CS bonds uniting the couple with each other and with their friends and kin. Without these practices and artifacts, perhaps marriages would be less intimate and less stable. Without the kama muta-evoking practices so pivotal to addiction and support groups, it seems that such groups would have fewer and less committed members.

I discussed in Chapter 7 the fact that vernacular words make poor scientific constructs. Nevertheless, vernacular lexemes, folk concepts, folk theories and discourse about emotions (let's call them folk models) influence psypes and are crucial to people's folk understandings of motes. Indeed, folk models provide the cultural framework with reference to which people interpret their own and others' motes. Since the interpretation of a mote – its meaning – is integral to the experience, folk models inform every mote. Folk models may tell a person in a certain role in a certain situation that they ought to experience a mote, or must *be* experiencing it, and may actually be more or less sufficient to evoke the emotion. Conversely, folk models may lead a person to conclude that they are not experiencing any emotion – 'How could I, a *man*, be moved by this nonsense!'

In short, every psype operates within, through, and with reference to a specific culture (or combination of cultures). Many psychological proclivities are not manifest at birth but emerge and mature along with the development of the brain and experience in the cultural world, so that they *never* appear in any raw acultural form. <u>This means that the nature of a psype graph cannot be determined independently of its culturally varied manifestations</u>. If the scientist observes the expression of a psype only in one culture (or set of closely related cultures) it is impossible to identify the psype function – the graph that maps its domain onto its range. This poses a huge epistemological challenge – especially since most psychological proclivities which have been studied across cultures have been shown to manifest themselves in atypical, extreme, and peculiar ways in contemporary educated Western persons (Henrich, Norenzayan, & Heine 2010).

But, as I began to discuss in Chapter 7 with regard to lexical labels, this also creates an epistemological challenge problem because one cannot know a priori just how a psype will manifest itself in the motes of particular cultures, making it problematic to compare manifestations of 'the same' psype across cultures. Indeed, even within one culture how do we know that any two motes are motes of the same psype? To make matters more difficult, every thought, feeling, act, or practice is likely to be jointly shaped by the interaction of multiple converging or conflicting psychological proclivities: we cannot expect to find a lot of 'pure' ideal types in the real world. Kama muta may occur simultaneously with other emotions such as *awe* or *fear* or *joy*, and different combinations are likely to be differentially afforded by particular practices in specific cultures.

So emotion researchers must do a lot of boot-strapping, dialectical, trial-and-error, feeling-our-way as we go (see Fiske, Schubert, & Seibt 2017a). Sometimes we'll go astray. While there is no straightforward way around this problem, we can navigate – as navigators always attempt to do – using multiple convergent systems of reckoning, as I discussed in Chapter 7. When attempting to identify kama muta motes, we can get our bearings by integrating indications of CS-intensification, the characteristic kama muta sensations, positivity of the experience and the desire to share it, motivation to enhance CS, and labelling with terms that are likely to mean *be moved*, *be touched*, *be stirred*, or *heart-warming*. Until we use these criteria to get our bearings and search out kama muta motes in diverse cultures and contexts, we simply don't know just what the kama muta psype is.

To understand the world, we need to know it. We cannot explain anything without knowing what it is: its features and dynamics across its full natural range. This is what ethnology gives us, in conjunction with history: a more or less comprehensive description of the range of behaviors, practices, and institutions of interest. But then, and only then, we need more. We need representative surveys, systematic behavioral sampling from everyday life, and controlled experiments. Ethnology provides minimal evidence about incidence or contingent rates; for this we need surveys and behavior sampling. And the natural world is usually too complex to enable one to establish causal mechanisms with any certainty; for this we need experiments in which researchers compare behavior when only the putative cause varies, while everything else is held as constant as possible. Our experiments do that. We hope to do more surveys and behavior sampling, but in the meanwhile the complementarity of the inferences we can make from ethnology and experimentation enables us to draw fairly strong conclusions. The scientific community can draw still stronger conclusions if anthropologists now do participant observation focused on kama muta in diverse cultures, and other laboratories independently replicate and extend our findings.

To fully understand the social functions, the psychology, and the cultural implementation of the kama muta psype, we will also need to work out its biology: the genetics, hormones, neuroanatomy (central and peripheral), along with its phylogeny – its homologues and analogs in primates and other socially-bonding species. If the kama muta construct is valid, then the neurocognitive mechanisms, the functional neuroanatomy, the neurochemistry and psychophysiology should be very similar in Andaman weeping reconciliations, charismatic Christians being touched by the Spirit, Americas watching Pixar movies, and nationalists visiting war shrines. Indeed, finding such similarities would be strong confirmation of the validity of the construct. In any case, to deeply understand kama muta, we need to delineate its neurobiological and psychophysiological substrates. Is it associated with increased levels of peripheral and CNS oxytocin or vasopressin, prolactin, serotonin, dopamine, mu-opioids, or other endogenous opioids? Is kama muta associated with activation of the agranular insulae? How does kama muta affect heart rate, blood pressure, breathing, skin conductance, and skin temperature? What is going on near the sternum that makes kama muta *heartwarming*? These questions can only be fully addressed with reference to their cultural, social, psychological, phylogenetic, and ontogenetic contexts. Ultimately our successors will work out the genetics and epigenetics of kama muta. But kama muta is not reducible to its biology; the biology subserves the social psychological and cultural functions of kama muta. The biology of kama muta has evolved to respond to very specific sociopsychocultural situations, and to generate behavior that is flexibly adaptive to those situations.

The kama muta psype is a natural kind, culturally informed by precedents, prototypes, precepts, and other *preos*

Cultural, historical, and situational variety in human action is often interpreted as evidence for pure constructionism, based on the assumption that variation implies some sort of cultural arbitrariness free of any biopsychological constraint or foundation. The ubiquity of genetic reaction norms, along with many kinds of adaptive flexibility in animals with little or no culture, show that variation does not imply the absence of biopsychological foundations. Nonetheless, many social scientists who emphasize the importance of culture, history, and individual agency – and who value choice and insist upon moral responsibility – typically oppose theories of evolved biopsychological foundations for action. Theories of evolved biopsychology are condemned as reductionist, meaning that such theories either ignore or deny cultural and historical variability and particularity, agency, and moral responsibility. In contrast, kama muta theory posits that it is precisely the evolved biopsychology of the kama muta psype that generates the diversity and particularity of kama muta motes. The kama muta function is adaptive at the level of evolutionary natural selection and at the level of social-relational functioning precisely because, and only if, the psype is subtly attuned to culture, community, context, and agentic intentionality. The function is culturally and socially informed. It could not work otherwise.

Evolutionary psychologist generally posit that there are evolved, innate, discrete neurocognitive modules to 'solve' every specific 'adaptive problem' faced by each species, including humans (Barkow, Cosmides, & Tooby 1995). If this were generally true, it might be taken to imply that, since humans have the 'problem' (or rather, opportunity) of discriminatively bonding with daughters, sons, mothers, fathers, husbands, wives, older and younger brothers, older and younger sisters, older and younger co-wives or co-husbands, stepmothers and stepfathers, stepdaughters and stepsons, several sorts of cousins, two sets of grandparents, mothers in law, fathers in law, brothers in law, sisters in law, age-mates, blood brothers, *compadres*, *xenia*, friends, allies, community, war bands, work parties, et cetera, *Homo movens* would have a specific adaptive module for bonding with each of these. There are different factors affecting the costs and benefits of CS bonds with each sort of partner or group, and in each case different indicators of these costs and benefits, so it might seem adaptive to have a distinct specialized module for each. However, such modules would be highly specialized and hence, ipso facto, inflexible. They would not enable the formation of new kinds of CS bonds when new opportunities arise, much less the ready invention of propitious new kinds of CS relationships. Moreover, the strict interpretation of evolutionary modularity theory seems to imply that there must be a distinct module specialized to form every kind of CS bond that exists, or has existed, in every culture. Obviously this is absurd. What evidently exists is one kama muta psype that has evolved to be generative, sensitively responding to consubstantial assimilation and other signs indexing opportunities for any kind of propitious CS. The niche that *Homo movens* has created for itself consists of flexible, generative, recursively complex sociality (Fiske 2000). The psype is innately attuned to cultural precedents, prototypes, precepts, paradigms, and parameters for the locally important kinds of CS, and the locally significant indices of their meaningful intensification. This means that, on the whole, it tends to be adaptive in every culture, tending to enhance fitness no matter what sorts of CS relationship are locally beneficial, and no matter what particular acts of consubstantial assimilation, or other signs, index CS intensification.

In stark contrast to evolutionary modularity theories, some psychological theories of emotion posit that there is a two-dimensional space in which emotions vary continuously, with particular vernacular languages more or less arbitrarily marking out regions of that space with emotion labels. In contrast, I posit that discrete psypes exist, each of which consists of a function mapping new information onto adaptive tactics. In the social-relational domain, psypes are attentive to changes in the prospects for relationships, mapping new information onto new tactics. I am not particularly concerned with the semantics of vernacular languages – I'm not aiming to write a dictionary of emotion words in natural languages – but I agree with the dimensional theorists that the emotion labels are somewhat arbitrary, vary across languages, and do not necessarily or validly denote discrete kinds. However, in contrast to sociocultural constructionists, interpretivists, and dimensionalists, I posit the existence and universality of discrete kinds of psypes and distinct types of motes.

To be precise, I posit that the kama muta psype is a natural kind: a distinct type of universal emotion mechanism. A natural kind is not simply defined by the coordinates of the space it occupies in a system of continuous dimensions. Geometrically speaking, a natural kind is not a polytope such as a polygon in two dimensions, or a polyhedron in three dimensions. In particular, kama muta does not consist of some amount of other emotions such as sadness, happiness, and surprise (even if sadness, happiness, and surprise themselves actually <u>are</u> valid psypes, which I doubt). Nor is kama muta simply a temporal transition from one natural kind to another – say, from sadness to happiness, from challenge to affirmation of a core value, or from observing a transition from a neutral state to fulfillment of a supererogatory moral virtue. Kama muta is, indeed, a dynamic process, but it is a systemically integrated dynamic process, distinct from other social psychological processes. Either a CS relationship suddenly intensifies, or it does not; either devotion and commitment to the CS relationship increase, or they do not. There are qualitative differences – differences in kind – between intensifying CS and intensifying any other type of relationship, and between motives to devote and commitment to CS versus devoting or committing to other types of relationship. Kama muta motes vary greatly in intensity, but they are categorially distinct from other emotions. Of course, people may experience kama muta at the same time that they experience other emotions, and these mixtures may have interesting properties of their own. But the co-existence of multiple emotions in one person at the same point in time does not imply that there is a continuum from one emotion to the other. Perhaps one could define a metric of the relative intensities at any point in time in any one person of, say, kama muta and jealousy. Such a measure would be a continuous variable. Likewise, one can define a metric of the relative concentration of sodium and potassium in a substance, but that doesn't imply that there is a continuum of any sort from sodium to potassium; they are distinct elements.

A number of researchers have argued that emotions are <u>not</u> natural kinds, but are merely arbitrary linguistic labels based on culturally constituted, culturally specific taxonomies of affect (Russell et al. 1995; Russell 2003, 2009; Wierzbicka 1999; Barrett, Wilson-Mendenhall, & Barsalou 2015; Wilson-Mendenhall & Barsalou 2016; Feldman-Barrett 2017). In these perspectives, emotions are individual or collective folk-<u>conceptualizations</u> of states of the body in a given context. I agree that languages vary greatly in their labeling of emotions, and throughout this book point out that in English and other languages, kama muta is labelled differently in different contexts (with substantial variation over time and dialect). But note that the scholars who have argued that emotions are arbitrary cultural-linguistic constructions conceptually <u>define</u> 'emotion' as linguistic-conceptual labeling of sensations in context. I have no quarrel with scholars using any definition of emotion they choose; there's no problem defining 'emotions' as 'the everyday folk labelling of affective states in situations.' In contrast, we define kama muta as a <u>configuration</u> of appraisal, sensations, positivity, motives, and labels (if any).

> In our theory, a kama muta mote is a kama muta mote regardless of how or whether any person labels it in any particular dialect of any language in any particular context in any particular culture. In some cases, a kama muta mote may occur without any conscious attention to it. You may feel kama muta without being aware of it, let alone conceptualizing or naming it. Or you may feel kama muta without being able to articulate what you are feeling – you may not be able to put a name to it. You probably give kama muta motes different names on different occasions. Within and across cultures, people have innumerable names for kama muta motes (none of the labels used exclusively for kama muta). Whatever people call it or don't call it, kama muta is kama muta.

Labels are methodologically useful clues, and as I explored in Chapter 7, there are patterns in the labels for kama muta that across language families and cultures: it is often denoted using metaphors of passive motion, passive contact (sometimes *touching the heart*), passive stirring, or warmth in the 'heart'. But while words are culturally constituted, in our conceptualization, 'emotions' are not merely words, nor are they processes of naming. There is far more to kama muta than its verbal labels, and kama muta occurs whether a person names it or not. In many contexts in many cultures, it has no accessible name. Conversely, lexemes such as *being moved* do not always denote kama muta; people sometimes say they are *moved* by something that makes them *sad*, by something that *awes* them, or by something that makes them *outraged*. Kama muta is a natural kind, but that natural kind is not reducible to the usage of lexemes that may or may not name it. Nor is kama muta a culturally constituted category in anyone's folk psychology.

In one sense, this entire book is an argument that the category of kama muta motes is a natural kind. But it is helpful to state the arguments succinctly, all in one place. In brief, there are at least nine, and likely ten, major reasons to believe that the kama muta psype and the category of kama muta motes are natural kinds:

1. In many languages from different language families the vernacular terms that approximately denote kama muta are based on similar physical metaphors of passive motion, contact, or stirring, and sometimes warmth and/or sensations in the center of the chest attributed to the heart. This convergence of metaphors across many languages implies a universal phenomenology that has been very widely and consistently experienced (see Chapter 7 and also Fiske, Schubert, & Seibt 2017a, 2017b).

2. When the emotion is strongly felt, informants within and across cultures report similar sensations: tearing or crying; goosebumps or chills; warmth or other feelings in the center of the chest; hand(s) to the center of the chest; a deep and prolonged breath; mild choking constriction of the esophagus, associated with difficulty speaking or speaking with a creaky voice; and certain distinctive high-pitched utterances such as *awww*; often followed by buoyancy, lightness, or exhilaration. These sensations are very highly correlated with each other in the context of #3 (Seibt et al. 2016; Schubert et al. 2016; Seibt et al. 2017).

3. Informants report these sensations specifically when their own CS relationships or CS relationships they observe or hear about suddenly intensify. The intensification of CS consists of the sudden creation, strengthening, renewal, or repair of CS relationships, or vivid memories or imagination of CS relationships, especially against a background of possible breakdown of CS, barriers to CS, separation, or loss (Seibt et al. 2016; Schubert et al. 2016; Seibt et al. 2017).

4. Informants within and across cultures develop similar motives when they have kama muta motes. These motives are:
   A. The desire to hug, hold, snuggle, caress (or pet), stay with, feed, or eat with the one(s) who evoke kama muta. These are the components of consubstantial assimilation, posited to be the primary mode of constituting CS.
   B. The desire to renew or reinforce CS relationships with others in other ways, such as being with, expressing affection for, and taking care of them.
   C. These are accompanied by subjective affective devotion and moral commitment to the CS.

5. Kama muta motes are 'positive,' appealing,' 'rewarding' experiences:
   A. People seek to experience kama muta motes.
   B. People want to repeat motes they have experienced.
   C. People are eager to tell others about their mote, and to tell or transmit the events that evoked it to people they like.
   D. People desire to experience the mote jointly, together with others – by joining in the performance of it, or by listening to or watching the performance along with others, especially with people with whom they already have some sort of CS.

    E. Experiencing a kama muta mote together tends to reinforce CS relationships among participants.

6. In all cultures there are important practices, institutions, roles, arts, narratives, and artifacts that operate to evoke, express, and transmit kama muta (Fiske, Schubert, & Seibt 2017a, 2017b). While these cultural forms are embedded in their own particular cultural matrices, they often evoke kama muta in audiences or participants from other cultures. These practices, institutions, roles, arts, narratives, and artifacts have rather congruent forms across cultures. Quite commonly, people admire and respect the persons, activities, and things that are especially capable of evoking kama muta motes.

7. In all cultures there are apparently prototypes, precedents, and precepts indicating who should experience kama muta motes in what circumstances, who should avoid it, and guiding evaluation of the significance of evoking, experiencing, and displaying motes. For example, preos may indicate that women should seek and display kama muta motes more than young men; preos may indicate that motes should be displayed only in the privacy of the family; that motes should be experienced in relation to a divinity, or in relation to one's nation.

8. In all of the cultures I have investigated, kama muta operates recursively: people feel kama muta motes when they see or hear about others' motes, or even when they hear about hearing about others' motes. That is, kama muta is contagiously transitive.

9. Natural kinds have substantial, regular, distinctively patterned links with other natural kinds. In this case, one of those distinctively patterned links is with a relational model: kama muta is the experience of the sudden intensification of communal sharing, and motivates commitment to communal sharing relationships (see Fiske, Schubert, & Seibt 2017a, 2017b). And we see in many chapters of this book that kama muta is distinctively linked to a great many significant cultural attitudes, cultural models, roles, institutions, practices, narratives, and artifacts. Kama muta motes are common and often intense at major life-cycle transitions, including birth, various forms of christening and confirmation, school graduation, birthdays, marriage proposals, weddings, anniversaries, and funerals. Kama muta also appears to be common and sometimes intense at reunions and leave-takings, when someone is remarkably hospitable to strangers, or when someone is extraordinarily generous or kind. Kama muta motes are common at collective events such as national days, memorial commemorations, and moments of social mobilization. People often experience remarkable kama muta in certain kinds of religious practices oriented toward a loving god, and at the culmination of pilgrimage. Human and animal infants and other cute agents also evoke kama muta motes in many perceivers. Also, some kinds of music and dance definitely evoke kama muta. It seems that kama muta sometimes motivates people to compose, sing, play, or listen to music, to dance, or to

attend dance performances. The fact that kama muta frequently occurs at these and many other objectively identifiable social events further establishes it as a natural kind.

10. Although it is not yet definitely established, a tenth kind of evidence potentially validates the supposition that the kama muta psype is a natural kind. An extension to relational models theory, conformations systems theory, posits that people understand, create, communicate, and modulate CS relationships through consubstantial assimilation (Fiske 2004b; Fiske & Schubert 2012). Consubstantial assimilation consists of making or apperceiving participants' bodies to be essentially the same by touch, synchronous movement, intimate sex, giving birth, nursing, feeding, commensalism, and modifying or marking bodies alike, especially genital modification. To the extent that future research shows that consubstantial assimilation especially consistently and strongly activates the kama muta psype, this will further solidify its status as a natural kind.

Taken together, these nine or ten kinds of evidence imply that the kama muta psype and kama muta mote are natural kinds. Methodologically, they also function as convergent indicators of the kama muta mote, and therefore of the operation of the kama muta psype (see especially Seibt et al. 2017; Zickfeld et al. 2019). That is, in scores of experiments with several thousand participants in 15 languages in 19 countries, we consistently find strong associations connecting the appraisal of perceived intensification of CS, the characteristic sensations, the labels, positivity, and the motivation to devote and commit to CS. Quantitatively, these five features occur together. Beyond this experimental evidence, all of our other kinds of data show that these five features form a coherent whole with the other features listed above which we have not yet measured experimentally.

Any indicator – any method for identifying whether something is present and how much there is of it – has inherent sources of error and bias. One component of the indicator, one hopes, is the construct being measured, but there are innumerable other components of the indicators, many of which are unknown and none of which enter into the indicator in fully knowable ways. This means that the researcher using only one indicator can never know whether the construct even exists or is merely an illusion of the measurement process. And if the construct exists and is present in the instances examined, the user of only one indicator cannot know its magnitude, because with only one indicator, there is no way of isolating the contribution to that indicator of the construct, as distinct from the contribution of all the unknown sources of error and bias (Campbell & D. W. Fiske 1959; D. W. Fiske 1986). Only when the 'edges' of several indicators align, marking the same boundary of the entity, can one make a valid inference that the entity is a discrete category, rather than a continuum in one or more dimensions (Ruscio, Haslam, & Ruscio 2006; Haslam, Holland, & Kuppens 2012). Separately, our nine or ten indicators of kama muta are each fallible evidence for the existence (and strength) of a kama muta mote. When many or all of them are present, that provides convergent evidence for the existence of a mote. To the extent that these indicators co-vary with each other more strongly than with indicators of other emotions, that pattern validates both the kama muta construct and these indicators of it.

There is also an basic ontological aspect of observing an entity in many contexts. When the same entity is consistently reported in a great variety of contexts across history and cultures, one becomes more confident that the observations are valid. This confidence is greatly increased when the entity consistently occurs just when the theory predicts that it will, and only when the theory predicts that it will (see J. S. Mills' 1882 method of difference and method of similarity). We should be suspicious about the reality of something that occurs only in unique or unpredictable circumstances, or a supposed entity that lacks constant and comparable features across its putative apparitions. So we need to look everywhere and ask, Do kama muta motes occur whenever CS relationships suddenly intensify – regardless of the specifics of the CS relationships and regardless of the features of the participating individuals? Do kama muta motes occur only when CS relationships intensify suddenly, but not in any other circumstance? Do this generality and this specificity hold up across history, across very diverse cultures, across diverse CS relationships, and across diverse intensification processes? If so, it makes sense to say that kama muta motes are a natural kind, generated by a natural kind of biologically evolved psype, often triggered by practices, institutions, roles, narratives, arts, and artifacts that are culturally adapted to that psype.

I predict that eventually it will be possible to discover genetic, epigenetic, and ontogenetic processes giving rise to the kama muta psype. There are, of course, crucial neuroanatomical and neurochemical systems involved, which must be somewhat distinctive to the kama muta psype. But at this point we know virtually nothing about the biology. However, we do not need to identify such biological markers to know that kama muta is a natural kind. Moreover, the kama muta psype and its motes cannot be reduced to biology, and the biology itself cannot logically be isolated from their social psychology, relationships, and culture. That is because the function of that biology is to respond to and regulate psychological states and social actions – and to do so in a culturally informed manner.

Of course, kama muta motes do share some features with other states; people may shed tears or get goosebumps when they are afraid. People may shed tears of pain, and even frustration. People like to share jokes and tales about near-disasters, not just kama muta. In the material world, lithium shares some properties with sodium; both trees and houses provide shade; men and women have some important features in common. But despite sharing tears and goosebumps, fear and kama muta are distinct and discrete emotions; there is no dimensional continuum from kama muta to fear. It is precisely the <u>conjunction</u> of its polythetically defining features that indicates the existence of a kama muta mote.

However, it is interesting to consider whether kama muta has flavors within its boundaries; does the father's feeling on being reunited with his family when he returns from war have the same flavor as the father's nostalgia about his wartime comradeship, his response to the snuggly kitten, his feelings at the conclusion of a Pixar movie, or his rapturous feeling of being touched by the Holy Spirit? These experiences all result from sudden intensification of CS relationships, their physical sensations are pretty much the same, and they all increase devotion and commitment to the CS relationships in which they occur. Of course these experiences differ greatly in intensity, target, and cultural meaning, but how different are their essential phenomenologies? They may have different flavors. It is also possible that there are intensity thresholds across which quantitative differences in the strength of the emotion produce qualitative differences in its phenomenology, its performance, and its motivational impact.

Since it's important but not obvious, I should elaborate a bit on the ninth feature that indicates that the kama muta mote is a natural kind – is that it has substantial, regular, distinctively patterned links with other natural kinds. Natural kinds are players in the natural world: they cause and are caused by other natural kinds, and occur in positional relations with other natural kinds (Fiske, Schubert, & Seibt 2017a, 2017b). There is much yet to be discovered about how kama muta motes interact with other natural kinds, but I can make some general points. Activation of the kama muta psype is afforded by the prior or concurrent activation of other psypes: the kama muta psype is affected by its position in syntactical structures. Emotional syntax may include co-occurrence, temporal sequences, or patterns of hierarchical nesting. Kama muta psype may fit in distinct syntagms (positional relations in a sequence or other structure) or paradigms (systematic contrasts between possible alternatives in a sequence or other structure). For example, the sudden intensification of CS is afforded by prior feelings of separation sadness, anxiety about whether the partners will be (re)united, or fear of obstacles to the relationship. Kama muta is often followed by excited, 'happy,' or comfortable moods. Perceiving others' kama muta may evoke kama muta in the observer, and people often seek to experience or re-experience kama muta with CS partners or in CS groups – which leads to further intensification of *those* CS relationships, and hence further kama muta. In paradigmatic narratives, when protagonists battle obstacles to reunion with a loved one, there are just two prototypical endings: joyous kama muta union, or a tragic ending. Synchronically, there may be simple affordances such that kama muta facilitates or is facilitated by the experience of other concurrent emotions. Conversely, perhaps kama muta may inhibit or be inhibited by other emotions such as anger or disgust, if those emotions are in some way incompatible with kama muta. In short, like other natural kinds, kama muta occurs in characteristic combinations and sequences with other natural kinds. And kama muta exists as a natural kind for the same reasons that other natural kinds exist. Online Note 10.1 analyzes why natural kinds exist, including natural kinds of psychological mechanisms.

Any sort of understanding, whether nomothetic or idiographic, depends on valid identification of the entities in the world whose tokens (instances) have maximally consistent properties, while the entities have maximally consistent causal, functional, and pattern-positional relations with other valid entities. Without identifying such entities, explanation or any other sort of understanding is impossible. Interpretive approaches are not exempt; however particular and subjective, interpretations are only meaningful if they show connections among real entities. Our aim is to establish the explanatory usefulness of the kama muta psype and mote constructs.

Narrower constructs: Bits of kama muta

A number of researchers have presented categories of emotional experiences that we identify as typically consisting of instances kama muta. But in each case, the proposed category consists of a subset of the natural kind that we posit to be kama muta motes. For example, as I mentioned in Chapter 1, Marshall (2005) wrote a perceptive account of "mystical encounters with the natural world." His description of the phenomenology is illuminating, but he did not recognize that these mystical encounters with nature consist of the same physical sensations, of the same feeling of sudden union, of the same type of joy, and evoke the same sort of motives to devote and commit to the CS relationship with nature that occur with humans and deities. Nor did he recognize that *nature* is an historically-situated cultural construct. So Marshall does not appreciate the larger system that these 'nature' experiences belong to, and does not recognize their source in the natural kind that is the kama muta psype. The same is true of most of the other phenomena I have explored in this book: peak experiences, sentimentality in literature and recognition reunions, and the many studies of tears: scholars have theorized these phenomena far too narrowly because they were not aware of the common features they each share with all of the others. Similarly, Menninghaus and others have shed quite a lot of light on 'chills' that occur when listening to music (Panksepp 1995; Laeng et al. 2016; Konečni 2005; Juslin & Laukka 2004; Hodges & Sebald 2010:292; Huron & Margulis 2010; Benedek & Kaernbach 2011; Nusbaum et al. 2014; Menninghaus et al. 2015; Wassiliwizky et al. 2015; Wassiliwizky et al. 2017a; Wassiliwizky et al. 2017b; Eerola & Peltola 2016; Mori & Iwanaga, 2017). What seems problematic to us is the apparent assumption that 'chills' are markers for a distinct emotion. It seems to us that some of the chills that some of these researchers report are likely evoked by *awe* at the grandeur and magnificence of some of musical pieces they explore. It is also well known that fear can evoke chills, as can the feeling of the uncanny (Levy 1973), or the sound of chalk squealing on a blackboard. But even granting the likelihood that most of the chills and goosebumps studied in this music literature result from kama muta, in order to understand why people get chills and goosebumps listening to music, we need to understand what else, beyond music, evokes kama muta chills.

These studies nicely spotlight the chills experience, raising interesting possibilities about the qualities of music that may evoke chills. But they do not explain why chills are associated with the other sensations that accompany chills, they largely ignore the feeling of CS oneness that activates the kama muta psype, and often they do not consider the motives that ensue – or mention but do not fully explain them. By focusing on chills in response to music, Menninghaus and the other chills researchers miss what we perceive to be the big picture. As researchers in the early stages of research on any topic, we all are like the blind people in the fable describing an elephant: one identifies something like a rope (the tail), one something like a leaf (the ear), another something like a tree trunk (a leg), another something like a hose (the trunk), et cetera. Each of these perceptions is <u>part</u> of the elephant truth, necessary but not sufficient to understanding what an elephant is.

Marshall (2005) restricts his purview to experiences that occur in response to nature, and Menninghaus and the others cited above largely restrict their purview to chills responses to music. We shall see in Chapters 12–15 that a great many writers have restricted their scope to experiences either evoked by religious practices or interpreted as encounters with divinity. Nearly all writers focused on such religious experiences, often labelled *mystical*, have further limited their field of view to motes that are both rare and exceptionally intense. I find the same unnecessarily narrow perspective among the scholars whose work on "peak experiences" we looked at in Chapter 1 (Maslow 1962, 1970; Keutzer 1978, Wuthnow 1978; Davis 1998; Woodward, Findlay, & Moore 2009; Hoffman, Iversen, & Ortiz 2010; Hoffman, Garg, & González-Mujica 2013; Ho et al. 2013). Likewise, as I show in Online Note 4, by a priori restricting herself to "transcendent ecstasy," Laski (1961, 1980) prevents herself from extending her insights into commonplace emotional experiences that are similar in kind. Presupposing that rare and intense emotional experiences are categorically distinct from more common and milder emotions, all of these researchers fail to appreciate that the sensations, pleasurable quality, and motives of these extraordinary experiences are qualitatively continuous with ordinary emotions. Such narrow restrictions of the researchers' field of view are blinders that artificially prevent them from seeing the whole of the phenomenon. Similarly, as we mentioned in Chapter 4, some scholars have isolated the extremes of relationship intensification, naming them "elevation" or "being moved," assuming without explanation that exceptional moral acts evoke an emotion that differs from the emotions of everyday relationship intensification (Haidt 2000, 2003a, 2003b; Haidt & Keltner 2004; Cova & Deonna 2014; Cova, Deonna, & Sanders 2017; see also Menninghaus et al. 2015). Conversely, Haidt posits that <u>any</u> kind of moral excellence evokes "elevation," while Cova and Deonna posit that realization of <u>any</u> core value evokes "being moved." So their theories imply that in seventeenth century England, the crowds gathered to observe the moral beauty of the realization of their core value of just punishment for treason must have felt elevation and been moved while watching a traitor being hanged and then, while still alive, slowly drawn, and then quartered.

In contrast, we believe that only intensification of CS elicits kama muta – even when the intensification is ordinary connection with one's dogs when coming home from work, or simply seeing kittens online. But, unlike Cova, Deonna, and

Haidt, we believe, and our studies confirm, that the intensification must be sudden. Gradual intensification is lovely, but doesn't evoke the emotion. Moreover, as we indicated, the goodness doesn't have to be passively observed in others: a person may also experience kama muta when they kindly give something, or are grateful to receive something – or just feel one with their chorus.

We laud research that is precisely focused on a specific context, temporal period, or culture; often the only feasible way to dig deep is to sink a narrow borehole. There is much to be learned from DeMares's (2000) collection of peak experience triggered by encounters with cetaceans, Russo's (2012) accounts of responses to solar eclipses, and Yaden and colleagues' (2016) collation of astronauts' experiences viewing the earth from space. But when we put these studies together, connecting them to each other to understand how they are similar and how they differ, our insight is much greater than the sum of the insights from the separate studies considered independently. Furthermore, even if our primary interest is specific to human interactions with cetaceans, or what it's like to see the earth from space, our understanding of these particular moments will be much fuller by comparing and contrasting them to each other, thereby putting them in their proper context. And our understanding of each and all will be further deepened by recognizing how they fit together as special cases of kama muta motes, all generated by the kama muta psype. This is one of the major aims of this book: connecting these particulars to show how they fit together into one natural kind, kama muta. We hope that this integration of what were previously studied as disparate phenomena is a large part of what makes it rewarding to read this large book.

We do not conclude that feeling CS with a dolphin is identical to feeling CS with the earth, or that either is identical to feeling CS with one's newborn, or to every other peak or mystical experience. Dolphins are not planets; infants are not divine love. But to cogently contrast them we need to compare them. We can only understand their differences with reference to what they have in common. And they have a lot in common.

Social emotions are immediate proxies for the long-term benefits of social relationships

Let's place kama muta psypes and motes in a wider context. Why do people have psypes for social emotions? The answer is simple: dispassionate human cognition involves many biases that are likely to lead to defection from beneficial social relationships, free-riding, laziness, or succumbing to immediate temptation, resulting in the attenuation or loss of those relationships – or punishment for violating them. There are many temptations to defect in order to gain immediate short-term and subjectively certain rewards, or avoid immediate short-term costs. When they don't lead to outright defection, common biases in human cognition tend to result in neglect of social responsibilities, poor social performance, or abandonment of important partners. In short, dispassionate cognition results in termination of important relationships or relationships degrading to the point that they lose any value. This occurs because people respond too strongly to immediate and subjectively certain non-social rewards and benefits, excessively discounting the long-term and uncertain rewards and benefits, and failing to invest consistently in social relationships.

> Dispassionate people make poor social partners, and they suffer the consequences of isolation, exile, or worse. Social emotions remedy this adaptive problem by functioning as present motivational proxies for the long-term expected value of social relationships (Keltner & Haidt 1999; Fiske 2002, 2010).

Compared to nearly any other vertebrate and certainly to any other primate, social relationships are uniquely crucial for human fitness (and psychological well-being), but the benefits of relationships depend on commitment (Schelling 2007; Hirshleifer 1987; Frank 1988; Nesse 2001). Social relational emotions motivate the devotion and commitment that is essential to enable people to reap the eventual harvest of loyal devotion. In particular, the kama muta psype is like a switch turning on an electromagnet: it pulls a person toward a partner whom they had been more weakly attracted to until the psype was activated.

> Kama muta is a 'wake-up call,' impelling people to attend to potentially vital CS relationships that are newly promising. It jolts people out of their complacency, so they reinvigorate CS relationships that they had been taking for granted or were not aware of. It may jump-start auspicious new CS relationships, pulling people to engage in relational opportunities they would otherwise have passed up. The kama muta psype may also reconnect people who have been separated, who offended each other, who quarreled, or whose relationship simply languished, renewing commitment when there is good cause for rededication. It may further tighten already close bonds when it is propitious to do so. CS relationships require a lot of attention, effort, patience, perseverance, consistency, self-control – and sometimes painful, exhausting, or otherwise costly altruism. The kama muta psype motivates the necessary investment. (For a similar theorization of other 'self-transcendent' emotions such as compassion, gratitude, and awe, see Stellar et al. 2017).

The pervasiveness of kama muta demonstrates that CS relationships frequently intensify in large, abrupt steps – steps that consist of mutual recalibration of commitment, indicating that CS commitment is frequently refreshed by demonstrations of old, new, or potential partners' commitment to CS relationships. The existence and the benefits of appropriate mutual commitment to CS (and other) relationships is well understood (Schelling 1980; Hirshleifer 1987; Frank 1988; Nesse 2001). The puzzle has been to understand how people make such mutual commitments without exposing themselves to defection or free-riding. Typically, game theory models of commitment have implicitly assumed that it is binary: people commit or defect. The dynamics of kama muta evidently provide a major part of the answer to this puzzle: people frequently renew commitments mutually and incrementally when either party engages in a significant CS-renewing or CS-creating act. Unlike a brass lock of love on a bridge, CS commitment isn't eternal – it requires constant refreshing.

Drivers: Institutions, practices, narratives, roles, art, and artifacts whose function is to evoke the psype

The domain of a psype is the set of circumstances that activate the psype. The domain of the kama muta psype includes many everyday events in which the sudden intensification of a CS relationship is fortuitous. We may walk by a cute sleeping infant, or happen to hear a toddler tell her mother, "Mommy, I love you so much!" In a night-time storm on a lonely road you crash your bicycle and injure yourself; someone hears your cries and comes out, helps you up, brings you in out of the storm, gives you dry clothes, cleans and binds up your wounds, and feeds you soup. These events, like all events, are culturally organized, but they are not organized as they are <u>because</u> they are likely to evoke kama muta. However, many of the occasions that activate the kama muta psype <u>are</u> structured to evoke kama muta. There are innumerable cultural artifacts, architectures, arts, narratives, practices, roles, and institutions whose <u>function</u> is to evoke the kama muta psype, producing kama muta motes. We will call these **drivers**. They are cultural entities that have been specifically selected by cultural evolution to evoke a particular sort or set of motes. Often there is no little or no intentional, reflective design behind cultural selection; but there is a cultural-evolutionary feedback loop such that consequences of past practices become causes of future practices. Through intentional, reflective, planned design, together with haphazard variation with selective retention of effective variants, such artifacts, architectures, arts, narratives, practices, roles, and institutions culturally evolve. Instances of this special class in the domain of a psype we will call its drivers.

A **driver** is an historically situated, culturally constructed device in the domain of a psype that exists precisely because (or partly because) the corresponding psype responds to it strongly so as to yield motes that in some manner have contributed to culturally reproducing the driver.

The cultural function of a kama muta driver is to evoke kama muta; kama muta drivers have culturally evolved under selection by the kama muta psype. In other words, kama muta drivers are cultural adaptations to the kama muta psype: they are invented, reproduced, and diffused because they are supernormal activators of the psype. That is, they activate the psype more strongly than many events that have not culturally evolved to activate it.[4]

Evoking kama muta is one of the major functions of drivers such as the prototypical narratives and basic plots such as the homecoming scenes in the *Odyssey* and sentimental literature such as *Uncle Tom's Cabin*; social media posts of cute animals, or kids' receiving puppies; lyric poetry; patriotic ceremonies and anthems; Pixar and 'chick-flick' tear-jerking movies; melodramas of superheroes who takes risks and bear pain to help others; oratory such as Martin Luther King, Jr.'s preaching; life-cycle rituals such as christenings, confirmations, weddings, birthdays, anniversaries, and funerals; memorials to wars and disasters. Indeed, most of the kama muta described in this book is generated by drivers. By the end of the book we shall see that a great many practices, institutions, roles, narratives, arts, and artifacts of most cultures consist of kama muta drivers. Drivers whose culturally evolved function is to evoke kama muta are ubiquitous, extensively elaborated, often estheticized, and often highly valued. In many cultures, many of the most basic CS relationships are created, sustained, enhanced, or redressed by kama muta drivers.

While by definition a driver is shaped by cultural selection with respect to the corresponding psype, innumerable other selective factors also give it some path-dependent, historically and culturally distinctive features. Further, a driver may be over-determined, having culturally evolved by virtue of belonging to the domain of more than one psype. That is, the same driver may function to evoke more than one emotion. For example, many types of narratives are appealing, remembered, and reproduced because they resonate with more than one emotion psype (cf. Hogan 2003 and Booker 2004). Doubtless many of the drivers we describe in this book are over-determined: the kama muta psype was the major selective force to which these drivers are adapted, but they have ancillary adaptive functions with respect to other psypes as well.

In Chapter 17 we fully explicate the dynamics of the cultural selection of drivers in conjunction with the natural selection of psypes. This co-evolution is intriguing. Though intuitive, it's somewhat complex and we don't need to trace these dynamics yet. For the time being, we just need to keep in mind the idea that the practices, institutions, roles, narratives, arts, and artifacts we are considering are drivers: their function is to activate the kama muta psype. They exist just because they do activate it: by processes of cultural selection, they arise, are reproduced, and diffuse as adaptations to the kama muta psype.

Chapter 1 mostly presented kama muta experiences that are evoked by situations that are not primarily tailored to evoke kama muta, but simply do so. But humans culturally construct innumerable practices, institutions, arts, and artifacts whose function is to evoke kama muta. For example, dogs and cats may have been domesticated in the first place in part because puppies and kittens are cute, and many breeds have been bred to enhance the kama muta-evoking cuteness *Kindchenschema* (Lorenz 1943, 1988:164–165). Pets' evocation of kama muta is a major motivation for obtaining and caring for them. Every chapter since has presented drivers whose primary function (or at least one of whose primary functions) is to evoke kama muta.

Doing, feeling, and performing

Enactments of drivers evoke kama muta, and at the same time constitute prototypes and establish precedents <u>for</u> performing kama muta motes in the future. That is, participants and observers come to expect that a person engaging in a driver is likely to display kama muta motes. Moreover, feeling kama muta is understood to index affective devotion and moral commitment to the CS relationships that are supposed to intensify when enacting the driver. For example, at an American wedding, the close female kin and friends of the bride ought to cry, because doing so shows that they love the bride and support the love between bride and groom. Crying in kama muta when reunited with an endangered loved one displays virtuous concern and love.

But just because someone <u>ought to</u> <u>*be moved*</u>, and/or the person <u>acts</u> *moved*, doesn't mean that they subjectively <u>feel</u> *moved*. That is, the precedents, prototypes, paradigms, and prescriptions may indicate that kama muta is expectable, and these drivers may afford kama muta in the specified circumstances, but the drivers as preos do not fully <u>cause</u> a person to experience it. The person performing kama muta may actually just feel empty and flat, but know that they have to go through the proper (e)motions. Furthermore, people often have multiple, more or less conflicting feelings – so they may have a kama muta mote, yet at the same time be self-consciously embarrassed at their performance, or resentful at having to do it. Culture doesn't automatically make people sincerely be what they are supposed to be, nor does it <u>make</u> people believe in the love of a deity, for example. So sometimes people make-believe. And of course people can humorously, ironically, or theatrically play at weeping; children do so, and adults may do so in bracketed contexts in which the audience knows that it is 'just a staged performance.' Likewise, kissing and hugging mean a lot, but they are not necessarily sincere; sometimes people can detect insincerity, sometimes they are fooled. Moreover, sometimes the weeper, kisser, or hugger doesn't quite know how she feels, or doesn't pay much attention to her feelings: not everyone is fully reflective all the time, or, when reflective, necessarily fully understands her own feelings. People may regard their feelings as unimportant or forgettable.

Sometimes people consciously or unreflectively react against their feelings, transforming them into their opposite, or muting their feelings to the point that they become imperceptible. So culturally mandated performances of kama muta do not always reflect phenomenological experiences of kama muta motes.

However, performing kama muta may afford experiencing it. In general, the conformation systems of the relational models affect the actor as well as on the recipient, evoking or amplifying the sentiments of both (Fiske & Schubert 2012). Imitating, playing, practicing, and performing an emotion on any one occasion, and especially practicing it repeatedly on certain types of occasion, may make the performer actually tend to feel the emotion they are performing, or feel it more fully. Emotions can be learned by classical Pavlovian conditioning to all sorts of cultural stimuli that are regularly associated with the emotion. For example, if people weep when they feel kama muta, they may learn to feel kama muta when they weep. Shame, pride, anger, and humility can be learned, and so can kama muta. So, for example, in cultures in which women practice performing kama muta, they may come to be more disposed to experience it, at least when they perform it. In cultures and contexts where men practice suppressing the experience and blocking any display of kama muta, men may become less prone to experience it. In any case, drivers typically are collective practices, so each participant is surrounded by fellow participants who seem to be experiencing kama muta. Perceiving kama muta often evokes third-person kama muta in the perceiver. And doing the same thing together – in this case, performing kama muta – affords the sense of sudden unity that evokes kama muta. So even if most or all participants start out faking kama muta, they may reciprocally evoke it in each other.

Hence, in addition to evoking kama muta directly, drivers can evoke kama muta indirectly through culturally mandated performance of it.

Perhaps the most intriguing and important of all kama muta drivers are those that evoke sudden feelings of union with deities, which I will explore in Chapters 12 to 16.

Let us summarize how we recognize instances of kama muta:

1. It occurs when people are engaged in or observe the sudden intensification of CS.
2. When kama muta is strongly felt, people feel or display some or all of the sensations and signs previously listed. We can be most confident in recognizing kama muta when a combination of these sensations or signs occur simultaneously – the stronger the signs or sensations, the more confident we can be, and the greater the number of distinct sensations and signs, the greater the intensity of kama muta.
3. In the absence of any clear physiological sensations or signs, people are likely to be experiencing kama muta if they report their experience using lexemes that they also use when reporting more intense experiences in which they do experience or display a combination of these sensations and signs.

4. People refer to their experience using lexemes whose primary meaning is 'passively being moved, touched, or stirred,' 'warming in the upper front of the chest,' or 'touching the chest/heart.'

5. When initiated by the first or second person, people feel a stronger, more enduring commitment to the intensified CS relationship.

6. The person is diffusely more open to and more motivated to engage in CS with others, e.g., by being more caring and compassionate.

7. The feeling is primarily 'positive': people tend to seek to experience or re-experience it.

8. People experiencing kama muta want to 'share' it with others: they want to have others experience it, preferably together with them; people share it especially with those with whom they relate communally.

9. People who witness kama muta are typically disposed to suddenly intensify their CS relationships with the persons exhibiting kama muta, or sometimes with others, and hence themselves tend to experience kama muta.

As a general research strategy, when we observe any of these, we start looking for the others, because we think they are features of the same emotional entity, kama muta. The more consistently we find these facets occurring together, the better our theory is validated. At the same time, we are attentively eager to discover and illuminate cultural variations in the particulars of each of these features, as well as cultural practices that are designed to evoke kama muta and exploit its motivational and behavioral outcomes.

Online Notes

10.1 Why are there natural kinds in the world?

Notes

1 A simple example that we recall from an old textbook is that different varieties of maize respond differently to variations in rainfall; each yields its maximum amount of grain in response to different amounts of rain (at different points in the season, depending on the soil, temperature, solar radiation). What's the ideal rainfall for maximum yield? It depends on the reaction norm of each variety.

2 "Adult" is a convenient way to specify the function at a given point in the life history of the individual; it does not imply that the function becomes fixed after childhood. "Ontogeny" continues throughout life. However, the lability and responsiveness of the meta-function tends to be greatest in childhood and adolescence.

3 "Certain" means 'in some sense probabilistically specifiable,' or more simply, 'characterizable.' It does not imply that a person's actions are culturally determined in any absolute sense; it does not deny personality differences or individual agency. All that it means is that in a given circumstance, psychology and culture inform and orient human action.

4 The conceptualization of culturally evolved supernormal drivers is an extension of the concept of naturally selected supernormal releasing stimuli, formulated by Tinbergen 1953; Lorenz and Leyhausen 1973.

PART IV
Religion

11

MYSTICAL RELIGIOUS EXPERIENCES

In Chapter 1 we considered the "peak experiences" that Maslow (1962, 1970) characterized. We have mentioned the "transcendent ecstasy" experiences that Laski investigated (1961, 1980; see Online Note 1.4). We can now see that both of these constructs are, for the most part, names for very intense, infrequent, life-transforming kama muta events. "Peak" and "ecstatic" experiences generally have the same features as weaker, more ordinary, and frequent kama muta motes, so we can understand them better by comprehending them in the kama muta construct. A further limitation of both constructs is that they are essentially and rather arbitrarily secular in their conceptualizations. As such, neither construct fully encompasses the panoply of intense experiences that people experience as 'religious.' In this and the following chapters we will show that a great many intense religious experiences are kama muta motes very much like secular peak and ecstatic experiences.

Let us begin with the foundational modern psychological conceptualization of religion. William James (1902:318) posited that the core of religion consists of union or communion between the individual and a deity or some more encompassing wholeness. He wrote that this communion brings "a new zest which adds itself like a gift to life, and takes the form either of lyrical enchantment or of appeal to earnestness and heroism. It brings an assurance of safety and … a preponderance of loving affections." Is he describing what we call the "exhilaration" and feeling "energized" of kama muta? He then wrote that out of this communion grows an "appeal to earnestness and heroism" and "in relation to others, a preponderance of loving affections." Is this a description of the kama muta motivation to devote and commit to CS relationships?

'Mysticism' is the concept that James and other scholars of religion use to denote the most intense experiences of CS with divinities, when the worshippers feels herself merge into the divinity, becoming one. Dissolving the boundaries of the self, one is part of the whole, in perfect union.

> This overcoming of all the usual barriers between the individual and the Absolute is the great mystic achievement. In mystic states we both become one with the Absolute and we become aware of our oneness. This is the everlasting and triumphant mystical tradition, hardly altered by differences of clime or creed. In Hinduism, in Neoplatonism, in Sufism, in Christian mysticism, in Whitmanism,[1] we find the same recurring note, so that there is about mystical utterances an eternal unanimity which ought to make a critic stop and think, and which brings it about that the mystical classics have, as has been said, neither birthday nor native land. Perpetually telling of the unity of man with God, their speech antedates languages, and they do not grow old.
>
> *(James 1902:276)*

What is the nature of this "eternal unanimity" in reports of experiences of "the unity of man with God"? Here is one man's account of such an experience attending a service of an unfamiliar religion, in a language he doesn't understand:

> The Russian Orthodox liturgy is new to me. For hours, I stand in the cathedral, amidst these Russian people, taking my cues from them as I participate in the liturgy—moving, bending, crossing myself when they do these things. My legs are tired from the standing; my heart, light and joyful. Choral singing and incense fill this large space, surrounded by candles and icons. I feel a sense of community and unity with the people and things around me. ...
>
> The liturgy ends. As the celebrants disappear into the sanctuary and close the gates and doors, I feel a sadness—a sense of loss. But now, a tall, solitary, burning candle is placed outside the holy of holies. Tears fill my eyes, and along with the tears come gooseflesh and feelings of chills and thrills—a tingling feeling in my spine, arms, shoulders, neck, and back. My breathing becomes slightly irregular. The tears intensify. I gaze at the single, tiny flame through watery eyes, as the chills continue. What has just happened has profound meaning for me. The celebrants have disappeared into the secret, holy place; they, and what they represent, are no longer accessible. Yet the single burning taper remains. ... Eventually, the tears stop; the chills cease caressing my spine. I feel a profound gratitude.
>
> *(Braud 2001:99–100)*

Mystical experiences of union with divinity, like other kama muta experiences, are nearly always joyful – indeed, people often describe their mystical experiences as *rapturous* or *ecstatic*. In addition, a fair number of accounts report being literally uplifted, levitating, or floating upward (e.g., Pike 1992:12–19, 28), corresponding to the buoyancy some contemporary informants feel in strong kama muta. For example, reports of levitation were fairly typical of thirteenth and early fourteenth century Western Christian mystics (McGinn 1998; presumably this is a self-described sensation, not something that others could observe). As we shall see in the next four chapters, across religions, tears and goosebumps are often reported as well. Furthermore, people who experience union with a divinity want to tell others about it, and often recruit or train others to enable them to experience it, too.

There is debate about whether experiences such as seeing visions, hearing voices, possession, trance, and out of body experiences are important aspects of "mysticism," per se, as a scientific construct or phenomenal category (James 1902; Otto 1932; Stace 1961; Jantzen 1989, 1990). Of course the entity with which people experience union varies greatly; it may be a deity with many qualities specific to a particular religion, or in transcendentalism and some kinds of Buddhism, it may be a monistic whole experienced in one way or another. Another discussion concerns whether, and in which respects, mystical union is ineffable, or on the contrary, descriptions of unitive experiences are accurate, however paradoxical they appear. Regardless of these issues, like James (1902), Stace (1961:110) argues that

> there is a clear unanimity of experience from Christian, Islamic, Jewish, Mahayana Buddhist, and Hindu sources, also supported by the pagan mystic Plotinus, and the modern Englishman J. A. Symonds, that there is a definite type of mystical experience, the same in all these cultures, religions, periods, and social conditions.

Stace concludes that this experience is characterized by the feeling of union, a lack of spatial or temporal locus, a sense of objectivity, "feelings of blessedness, joy, peace, happiness," and an apprehension of the experience as sacred. From the congruity of self-reports of such experiences from different sources, Stace (1961:136) concludes,

> All that the mere unanimity of mystics can by itself prove—apart from showing that they are not misdescribing what they experience—is the existence of some common and universal element in the makeup of human beings which causes them to have similar experiences.

In our terms, this "common and universal element" is the kama muta psype.

There is a near consensus in religious studies that the ephemeral emotional experience of loving oneness with divinity is a core of religion, or even <u>the</u> foundation of religion (James 1902; Stace 1961; Merkur 1999; Hood 2016). Yet as Hill (1995:355–356) notes, there is little theory about how or why mystical experiences occur, and in particular no distinct theory of religious <u>emotions</u> as such. What we aim to provide is precisely such an integrative theory of the principal religious emotion. In addition, in the following four chapters we will show that mystical experiences of unity with divinity, while exceptionally intense, are not different in kind from a great many other kama muta motes evoked by religious drivers. While most scholars of mysticism treat it as a distinct phenomenon, mystical experiences are actually just the extreme end of a continuum of sudden intensifications of CS relationships with divinities.

From an atheistic scientific perspective, what is remarkable about such motes is that people are feeling the love of a being that does not exist, and never did. Or rather, a being that is a culturally constituted driver. In many respects, motes of the sudden intensification of CS with a deity are homologous with motes based on sudden intensification of CS with absent or dead persons, with fictional characters, with living persons known only indirectly though writing or digital media, and with motes based on technical mediated interaction (e.g., writing, phone, text messages, social media) with people whom one knows or has known face to face. Beings do not need to be biologically present in order to be vividly represented social partners in rich relationships. What is also extraordinary about religious kama muta motes is that in important respects the CS that intensifies with a deity may be more perfect than CS with any mere mortal. With the flawless imagined partner, the imagined love may be flawless – and consequently the intensification of it is not limited by the imperfections of union with an imperfect human.[2] Thus for some people some of the time, these religious motes are stronger than the kama muta motes they usually feel at the sudden intensification of communal sharing relationships with other humans. Of course, the imagining human partner has flaws that could limit the perfection of the union, but the flawless love of the perfect deity may transcend the human partner's limits. Hence union-with-deity kama muta motes are sometimes extremely strong.

And they are moderately frequent in populations that have been surveyed. Keutzer (1978) asked 146 upper division college students (presumably at the University of Oregon), "With what frequency have you felt as though you were very close to a powerful, spiritual force that seemed to lift you out of yourself?" In her sample, 34% reported "once or twice," 19% "several times," and 12% "often"; only 34% indicated "never in my life" (2% "I can't answer this question." Given a non-exclusive checklist of "triggers," those who reported such experiences indicated the kinds of "events that set them off." The most common were: beauties of nature such as sunsets – 45%; moments of quiet reflection – 42%; listening to music – 32%; drugs – 22%; physical exercise – 21%; watching little children – 19%; reading a poem or a novel – 18%; your own creative work – 18%; prayer – 16%; sexual lovemaking – 14%; looking at a painting – 10%. Many respondents filled in "Other" responses, especially meditation or yoga. Reviewing 20 surveys from 1962 to 1992 using different forms of the question, Yamane and Polzer (1994) found that 20–53% of American respondents indicated that they had had some sort of personal religious experience of the ultimate. Using data from the University of Chicago National Opinion Research Center General Social Survey from 1983, 1984, 1988, and 1989, Yamane and Polzer found that "blacks, individuals living in the South and West, and those individuals with occupations scoring low on the prestige scale have a higher probability of having had an ecstatic experience" (Yamane and Polzer 1994:52). Other Protestants and Baptists were more likely to report such experiences, and to a lesser extent, so were Presbyterians, Episcopalians, and Methodists.

However, digging a bit deeper, one may find that answers to such an item overstate the incidence of profound mystical-ecstatic experiences. In a convenience sample of 302 young adults in Connecticut (44 male), Thomas and Cooper (1978) reported that 34% answered affirmatively the question, "Have you ever had the feeling of being close to a powerful spiritual force that seemed to lift you out of yourself?" But coding respondents' descriptions of the events, they found that only 5% of these (2% of the total) were "mystical" in the strict sense: "Response included expression of awesome emotions, a sense of the ineffable, feeling of oneness with God, nature, or the universe." These contrast with the 29% of reports of "being close to a powerful spiritual force" that seemed to be more routine religious feelings, or paranormal experiences that did not seem to involve union with divinity, or any intense *ecstasy*.

Knowing

Many of the less common experiences that Thomas and Cooper (1978) assessed as 'mystical' in the strict sense included description of "changed perceptions of time and surroundings and feelings of 'knowing,' coupled with a reordering of life priorities." Recall Laski's (1980) report that in transcendent experiences of *ecstasy* many of her respondents reported that one important facet was a sense of knowing or discovery. In reports of 'mystical' experiences, Otto (1932) and Stace (1961) also found that people often report a profound sense of *gnosis*, 'knowing,' though neither the mystics nor the scholars can clearly explain just what it is that mystics knew or know. However, sometimes people report that in mystical experiences they discover that 'all is one' or 'everything is connected.'

'Mystical' and 'ecstatic' experiences are, by a priori definition, extreme and relatively infrequent, but they may be one pole of a continuum with more common, less intense kama muta experiences. Research on experience watching videos and movies reveals that everyday experiences of kama muta often share with ecstatic mystical experiences the feature that they are meaningful or inspiring. Mary Beth Oliver and Tilo Hartmann (2010) asked one set of participants to name and recall a "meaningful" film, and another set to recall a "pleasurable" film they had seen in the past, providing open-ended accounts of their feelings when they had watched it. Those who described memories of meaningful films were more likely to describe feelings of *warmth, tenderness, compassion, poignancy, empathy, tenderness, sympathy, inspiration,* or *feelings of being moved or touched*. Conversely, Oliver and Anne Bartsch (2011) showed that moves that people found *moving* were also more meaningful, and seemed to afford wisdom. Replicating this, Oliver, Hartmann, and Woolley (2012) showed that movies that participants said made them feel *touched, moved, emotional, compassion, inspired, and tender* were ones that they also rated as *meaningful*. They also found that compared to pleasurable films, meaningful films evoked more reports of *tears* or *crying, lump in the throat, chills, and rising or open chest* (although the difference in *warmth in chest* was not significant). Participants who were asked to describe meaningful films subsequently rated themselves higher on motivation to *be a better person, do good things for other people, seek what really matters,* and *live my life a better way.* These responses evoked by meaningful films are, respectively, the labels, sensations, and motives of kama muta. Similarly, Bartsch, Kalch, and Oliver (2014) found that media experiences that people describe as *moving, tender,* and *poignant* make people more 'reflective.' Janicke and Oliver (2015) showed that portrayals of connectedness, love, and kindness (i.e., CS) are more prominent in meaningful films than in pleasurable films. Further, they found that viewing meaningful films evoked higher ratings of *touched, moved, emotional, meaningful, compassion, inspired,* and *tender*; those feelings in turn made people feel more *connected* with others, with family, and with a higher power; feel more *compassionate* toward close others; and report more motivation to *love humanity.* In short, contemporary media that evoke kama muta are felt to be *meaningful* and media that are *meaningful* evoke kama muta. Or at least participants' culturally-informed <u>representation</u> of experiences denoted *meaningful* are characterized by kama muta features. Either way, these media experiences seem to be mild instances of the extreme emotion that mystics describe themselves feeling in the ecstasy of union with divinity or the ultimate.

Perhaps it's a bit counter-intuitive, even blasphemous, to propose that the same kama muta emotion that Pixar movies, popular music, and YouTube and Instagram content often evoke is also the hallmark of the most profound religious experiences – despite the differences in intensity and cultural significance. But that is the implication of the convergence between the conclusions of theorists of mystical and ecstatic experiences and results of quantitative research on media. This fits with what we saw in Chapters 1 and 8, where we found that meaningful peak experiences, along with responses to universally appealing themes in literature (including sentimental literature), are forms of kama muta. In Chapters 12–16 we will see that kama muta motes are at the core of the world religions, and that it seems that these religions endured and diffused across the globe in large part <u>because</u> they evoke kama muta.

It appears that some drugs, especially MDMA (Ecstasy, Molly) and psilocybin, whose effects are sometimes described as analogous to religious raptures, may afford strong kama muta experiences. Several informants have reported that when intoxicated with MDMA they and others have had stronger or more intense kama muta experiences than they otherwise would have had, usually in conjunction with electronic dance music or evoked by co-participation in a rave or concert. This may be a principal appeal of MDMA. Online Note 11.1 analyzes the similarities between kama muta motes and MDMA experiences; the following account of a first MDMA experience captures the kama muta mote.

I began to direct my attention to my surroundings and experienced an immense shift. It felt like I had suddenly crashed into a wall of emotion and sensation – It was as if some invisible barrier had been knocked down and I found myself plugged into some unifying, magnetic force that operated between me and my surroundings. I felt so close and connected to everything – my boyfriend, his cat, the couch. I felt calm yet tingly, hot and cold, all at the same time. When looking down at my arm, I saw goosebumps. I recall rubbing my boyfriend's arm, placing my hand on his knee and us both commented on the intense charge that it sparked. Because of the romantic nature of our relationship, such touching eventually led to us having sex. However, this feeling of love and connectedness was hardly of a sexual nature – such acts felt to be more of a result of wanting to intensify this closeness opposed to reaching any level of sexual gratification. In fact, it almost seemed to take me out of it. … Everything felt new and exciting, much like the euphoric lens one sees the world through when falling in love, with its difference being that its source was everything around me.

(Madeline McMurray)

To posit that mystical experiences of union with divinity, ecstasy, and peak experiences, along with inspirational, eudemonic, self-transcendent experiences with media, are motes of kama muta is not to minimize or ignore, let alone deny, the diversity of cultural prototypes, paradigms, precepts, and precedents that shape the experience. Some students of mysticism, rather than focusing on the consistencies across cultures, have used the evidence to argue that personal experiences of union are immanently cultural (Katz 1983; Proudfoot 1985). I agree, but I do not think that the culturally informed aspects of kama muta mystical motes imply that the psype is not universal. I am of the school of thought formulated by William James in the earlier quotation: the phenomenology of such experiences is based on universal psychology (or true encounters with divinity), and only subsequently <u>interpreted</u> by the person (and others) according to their cultural conceptions of worship and divinity. Again, I don't see these views as mutually exclusive: belief in the possibility of union, and the particular feeling of union, are based on cultural preos of union with a particular, culturally constituted deity. But it is an innate kama muta psype that <u>affords</u> each and every kama muta mote that occurs in union with each particular culturally constituted being, or in merging with a culturally-constituted, inchoate, transcendent wholeness or cosmos. This is consistent with the possibility that some scholars have advanced that there are degrees or sequences of mystical experience, as well as meaningful dimensions or types of mystical experiences; see Online Note 11.2.

In the following five chapters we will look at kama muta motes across the world's religions, and we will see that they are central to major traditions of Christianity, Islam, Vaishnavism (a strain of Hinduism), Buddhism, Jainism, and, across religions, arrival at the destinations of pilgrimage. Obviously, however, kama muta is not the only significant emotion that religious adherents experience in any religion. Some religious experiences involve mild or intense experiences of other emotions, without any kama muta. People feel religious *guilt, shame, disgust, anger, envy*, and so forth. Where kama muta experiences occur, they may be organized in a dynamic process in which other emotions proceed or follow it. For example, a set of religious practices may evoke compassionate sorrow, which, at least ideally, quickly transform into love, evoking kama muta. In the Abrahamic religions we often see a thoroughly explicated cultural prototype and precept in which fear of the wrath of God should transform into trusting devotion to his will, which should then turn into sorrowful contrition for one's sins of disobedience, and finally become grateful envelopment in God's boundless, forgiving love. It is at this last point that people experience kama muta. In Christianity a major variant of this well-articulated model is grieving *compassionate* sorrow for Christ's self-sacrificing suffering, which turns into loving devotional union with Him – and at that moment, kama muta. Conversely, the kama muta experience of suddenly feeling divine love may persuade a worshipper of the truth of the Bible and motivate her to adopt a region's doctrines and formally affiliate with that religious institution (see Chapter 15). A similar sequence structures Shia *muharram*, except that participants feel compassionate sorrow and devotional union with Hussain ibn Ali, his family, and followers (see Chapter 13).

As I mentioned above, in addition to, or instead of, communal sharing relations with deities, people also have authority ranking relationships with many deities, and these authority ranking relationships generate a distinct emotion. In the authority ranking aspects of worshippers' relationships with such deities, the deities must be shown respect and must be strictly obeyed; religiosity consists of following the deity's will. A person or community who disobeys such a deity fears his wrath. The classic account of this is Rudolf Otto's (1950 [1917]) characterization of two types of relationship with God: the attraction of *mysterium fascinans* (enchanting, fascinating mystery), which he contrasts with the *mysterium tremendum* (awe-inspiring, dreadful mystery; the Latin *tremendum* literally refers to 'trembling'). The *mysterium tremendum* aspect of a deity is totally other, completely distinct from the self. What it inspires is not the ordinary fear of natural dangers, but numinous dread of the wrath of God. (In Otto's original German, this dread is *Scheu*, and in characterizing God's wrath, Otto references the Greek οργή.) This kind of mystical experience, Otto (1950) writes, is the experience of *tremenda majestas* (awful majesty), terror-inspiring, consisting of a feeling of humility and abasement. The worshipper feels that he is nothing, facing the superiority of a supreme being. It is the experience of being daunted, overwhelmed, overpowered, by a great and unapproachable force, an omnipotent energy. In our theoretical framework, mystical fascination is a CS relationship, while mystical *tremendum* or magisterial mysticism is an authority ranking relationship. Consistent with relational models theory (Fiske 1991, 1992), Otto's account here shows many facets of the iconic physics of magnitudes and dimensions, which is the conformation system of authority ranking (Fiske 2004b). That is, the worshipper cognizes, communicates, and constitutes his relationship to the deity as contrasts along physical dimensions: ABOVE–BELOW, LARGER–SMALLER, GREATER FORCE–LESSER FORCE, MANY–ONE, TEMPORALLY PRECEDENT–TEMPORALLY SUBSEQUENT, LUMINOUS–DIM, LOUD–QUIET.

Congruent with Otto's account of *mysterium tremendum* or *tremenda majestas*, but using English vernacular terms, I posit that when a person's subordination in an authority ranking relationship with a deity suddenly intensifies, the person experiences an emotion that can be approximately glossed as *awe*.[3] "Awe" is a sister emotion to kama muta, evoked by the sudden intensification of the worshipper's authority ranking relationship with the deity above him. Worshippers often feel awe at the greatness, power, and infinite wisdom of supreme deities. Awe also occurs when suddenly impressed by impersonal entities such as nature or the cosmos (cf. Laski 1980:151–154). And motes of awe also occur, or course, when encountering a great and revered human person, far above oneself. Awe and kama muta both can be very intense when people participate in certain religious drivers, but certainly neither is restricted to religious contexts (see Chapter 19).

* * * * * *

In Chapter 12, we look at Hinduism and Buddhism; in Chapter 13, Islam; in Chapter 14, pilgrimage and religious self-injury. In Chapter 15 we will look at kama muta in Christianity, with a particular focus on the meaning of tears, which were often interpreted as indexing devotion to Jesus, or as a gift from God, demonstrating His compassion. Then, having considered all this material, we will be prepared in Chapter 16 to further analyze the loci of kama muta drivers in the constituents of religion. And in Chapter 16 I will link our theory and evidence with Emile Durkheim's (1912) theory of religion, focusing on the correspondence between his concept of "collective effervescence" and our concept of kama muta. The history of the meanings of religious tears will lead us to the meanings of other tears, their ritualization, and their esthetics.

Online notes

11.1 Mystic chemistry: The effects of MDMA and psilocybin.
11.2 Mystical variations, combinations, and related religious emotions.

Notes

1 The transcendental oneness with nature expressed and exemplified by the poet and essayist Walt Whitman (1819–1892).
2 Rowan Hong suggests that "This is why so many fanboys and fangirls of fictional characters feel such a close connection to their Anime 'waifus' and 'husbandos'."

3 The vernacular term *awe* is not always used to denote the emotion of sudden intensification of subordination (Fiske 2019). *Awe* is sometimes used to denote the kama muta experience of oneness with nature or the cosmos. And terms other than *awe* may be used for sudden intensification of subordination, including *fear*, for example. So research on the emotions of authority ranking intensification will require precise technical terms for these emotion constructs, and cannot rely on vernacular terms from any language.

12

HINDUISM AND BUDDHISM

Like the other world religions, Hinduism and Buddhism are complex and variegated; even if I were writing an encyclopedia, and not just a short chapter, I could not hope to plumb their depths or encompass many of their variants, let alone their historical vicissitudes. Rather, here and in our exploration of the other world religions, our aim is to discover salient drivers that trigger the kama muta psype to generate culturally and historically distinctive motes with particular meanings. What are some of the common drivers that evoke kama muta toward Hindu deities or tales of the Buddha's loving-kindness? What are some of the major precedents, prototypes, paragons, and other preos that complement the kama muta psype, completing it so as to constitute specific, culturally, and socially situated motes? In short, just how do Hindus and Buddhists suddenly intensify their CS relationships with immaterial beings? We will only reconnoiter, but we can get the lay of the land. Our hope is that this scouting report will provoke expert scholars to extend, correct, and fill in the precise details of this preliminary sketch map.

Bhakti: Sacred erotic love for Krishna

For many centuries in South Asia a major form of religious devotion has been *bhakti* (Tamil *pattar*), which consists of an ultimately intimate CS relationship with a divinity. *Bhakti* is integral to Hindu and Sikh traditions, but by no means limited to these (Lorenzen 2004; Schweig 2005). The earliest preserved textual precedent for *bhakti* is the Upanishads (various unknown dates, beginning a few centuries BCE, from what is now northern India). *Bhakti* is "not only devotion, but sharing – a love relationship in with the devotee both gives and receives" (McDaniel 1989:3). Prototypical *bhakti* is often represented as mystical union. "In devotional ecstasy there is a permeability and openness uniting the person and the divinity, a sharing of love between them" (McDaniel 1989:3). In one of the core precedents for Hindu kama muta, the *Bhagavad Gītā* (9.29), Krishna, the paragon of *bhakti*, says to Arjuna

> Those who worship me with devotion [*bhakti*],They are in me, and I in them.

In her review of the literature on *bhakti*, Frazier (2013:102) writes that *bhakti* literally means "a sharing, a division, or the relation of a part or an attribute to something larger" and evokes "tantric notions of sharing one's self with another." In further consonance with the constitutive semiotics of consubstantial assimilation (Fiske 2004b; Fiske & Schubert 2012), *bhakti* concerns "'commensality,' the sharing of comestibles by a community as a way of marking their kinship" (Novetzke 2007:262). Frazier (2013) characterizes, or cites researchers who characterize, *bhakti* as denoting "participation," "attachment, trust, and devotion," "salvation by grace," "affection, love, adoration," "sharing of (divine) being" (2013:102); as "a kind of *experience* – one in which the quality of emotional intensity predominates" (2013:104); "loving engagement," "communal, sense-rich, passionate practice" (2013:105); "intimate sharing," the deity or guru to whom a worshipper is devoted "entering him through yogic possession, yoking him to himself, and liquefying the inner organ (*atahkarana)* of selfhood and drawing it into his own self" (2013:106); adoration with aspects corresponding to every form of human love, "comfort in maternal protection," "irresistibly charmed" (2013:107), "participatory or shared divinity" (2013:109); identifications "that lead to a form of divine union," "remaking the self into part of a shared whole" (2013:110). In short, the concept of *bhakti* encompasses both the CS relationship and its sudden intensification, kama muta.

And indeed, the classical texts highlight both tears and goosebumps as identifying features of moments of intense *bhakti*, which is a feeling of the heart. The text that focuses most closely on *bhakti* toward Vishnu is the *Bhāgavata Purāṇa*, probably dating from the ninth century or earlier, with possible Tamil roots; see Hardy (1983). Sometimes the text refers to Vishnu as such, and sometimes names him as his Krishna avatar. The *Bhāgavata Purāṇa* says "A heart that is not moved by hearing Viṣṇu's names is a heart of stone. When one's heart is moved, tears come to one's eyes and the hairs on one's body stand erect" (2.3.24; Lorenzen 2004:194). Sanskrit includes several terms that specifically denote hair standing up due to bliss, rapture, delight, or love, including *hṛṣta-romā* and *pulaka-aṅgī*. Indeed *hṛṣta-romā* means literally 'having hairs that are thrilled' or 'joyful' (Schweig 2005:144–145, 274; Jamieson, personal communication). Goosebumps or body hair standing up are central to the representation of the experience of union with Vishnu/Krishna, and in fact the *Purāṇa* stories are narrated by Sūta, who is "called Romaharṣaṇa because he made his listeners' hair (*roman/ loman*) stand on end with his engaging narrative skill" (Rao 2004:103). Indeed Romaharṣaṇa's own hair is said to have stood erect when he originally heard the tales from their source, Vyāsa. In other words, piloerection was an oral and then textual prototype and precedent for the bodily sensation of loving union with Vishnu/Krishna, the paragon of love.

The most often read, the longest, and the most pivotal part of the *Bhāgavata Purāna* is Book 10, which recounts the erotic love of some cow-herd girls (*gopi*) for Krishna. When the *gopi* or other devotees of Krishna encounter him,

> their eyes overflow with tears, and their body hairs stand on end ... Bliss spreads throughout the three worlds ... and, in some of the most beautiful verses of the text, even the natural world is thrown into a stunned rapture simply by hearing the sound of Kṛṣṇa's flute.
>
> *(Bryant 2003:xxxii–xxxiii)*

Calves cry, trees shed tears of honey and "'bristle with ecstasy'," while rivers horripilate lotus blossoms. (In translations of South Asian texts the English term used for goosebumps or piloerection is 'horripilation.') The earth itself erects its hair – trees – from the touch of Krishna's feet (2003:131; X.30.10; see also 1.40, 21.8 & 30.12, 35.9). Throughout Book X, horripilation or tears, commonly both, are the signs of blissful union with Krishna (see Book X, 21.9, 13, & 19; 32.8, 38.26; 38.26 & 35; 39:56–57; 40.28; 71.25–26). Conversely, at one point (X.5.21) in the *Bhāgavata Purāna*, the love of his cow-herd girls for him moves Krishna himself to tears (Schweig 2005:276). In another episode in the following book of the *Bhāgavata Purāna*, Krishna preaches

> Without the bristling of the hair of the body, without the mind dissolving, without being inarticulate [choked up?] because of tears of joy, without *bhakti*, how can the heart be purified?
>
> He whose voice is stammering [from emotion, because of being choked up?], whose thought dissolves, who repeatedly weeps and sometimes laughs, who, shameless, sings and dances,—such a person, attached by *bhakti* to me, purifies the world.
>
> *(*Bhāgavata Purāna XI.14.23–24, translated by Hopkins 1966:9; rectangular brackets by the present author)*

In passages such as this, the prototype for bhakti includes piloerection and tears of joy, and also something about the heart, laughter, singing, and dancing. This prototype is depicted not only in texts, but in art: Krishna and the cow-herd girls, often represented as dancing together, are a common subject of traditional and modern South Asian images, including temple sculpture and relief depictions (Ghosh 2010). There is also a tradition of Indian dance depicting the love between Krishna and the *gopis*; their erotic love is a prototype of union between the worshipper and Krishna. Online Note 12.1 examines this *bhakti rasa* in Krishna worship, showing why many instances so labeled are probably kama muta motes.

The representations of kama muta in Book X of the *Bhāgavata Purāṇa* correspond closely to other paradigmatic North Indian Sanskrit texts, as well as South Indian Dravidian texts which seem to have been among the sources of some of the Sanskrit texts. The *Mahabharata* (the great Sanskrit epic with roots in the eighth century BCE, written down by the fourth century BCE) tells of a guru, Upamanyu, undeviatingly devoted to Shiva for many years, to whom Shiva finally appears with an entourage of other deities. Shiva praises Upamanyu's steadfast devotion, and in consequence Upamanyu is overcome with kama muta. "Eventually, with a voice chocked [sic] with tears and the hairs on his body standing erect, Upamanyu is able to offer prayers to Śiva and receive benedictions and blessings from him" (Sutton 2005:158). In another passage, Upamanyu, who loves Shiva beyond any concern with the lowest rebirth, is quoted describing his experience of another appearance of Shiva with his consort Umā, in which he is also choked-up:

> O lord, when I was addressed by Mahādeva (Śiva) in this way, tears of ecstasy welled up inside me and the hairs of my body stood erect. With my knees bent, bowing down again and again, I then spoke to the Lord with my words faltering due to ecstasy.
>
> *(Sutton 2005:161)*

Similarly, in another passage in the *Mahabharata*, in response to Krishna's devotion, Shiva appears to him, whereupon Krishna's body hair stands up and he is unable to pray to Shiva because his voice is choked with emotion (Sutton 2005:158).

Sutton compares these set of three signs of devotion in the North Indian Sanskrit Mahabharata with the more widely acknowledged Tamil sources:

> This we find both from Kṛṣṇa and more especially from Upamanyu who experiences the standing erect of his bodily hairs, weeping with ecstasy and an inability to speak coherently due to excessive emotions. All three of these symptoms are found in writings of the Ālvārs and in the Bhāgavata Purāṇa as signs of emotional agitation due to the overwhelming mood of devotion that carries away the mind of the bhakta [worshipper in the *bhakti* mode].
>
> *(Sutton 2005:163)*

Likewise, Keller (1984) describes the works of the three major sainted poets of the early (seventh to ninth centuries) *bhakti* (in Tamil, *pattar*) tradition of Tamil Shiva worship. These poets wrote about the personal, interior experience of being possessed by Shiva in an exalted, often tumultuous possession (see also Hardy 1983). The poets describe the relationship with Shiva as also an authority ranking relationship in which they clung to his feet, were his servants or slaves. But this authority ranking aspect seems to have been distinct from the 'love' (*aṇpu*) aspect of the relationship which predominated in their *pattar* devotion. The poets wrote that Shiva made the worshipers his, acquired them, made them resemble him, and they aimed to obliterate any perception or thought of anything other than Shiva and their love for him. Tamil worshippers incorporated Shiva into themselves and dissolved into Shiva, absorbed by him. Shiva loved his worshippers as they loved him, and he gave them food, health, joy, security, refuge, certainty – and he abolished the burden of karma (Keller 1984:11). They characterized Shiva as their honey and ambrosia. These Tamil Shiva devotees reported the experience of an 'interior liquefied' as they chanted and ecstatically danced together for Shiva. *Pattar* worshippers 'melted' in tears of communion with Shiva. (Perhaps the Tamil lexemes translated as 'interior liquefied" and being 'melted' are references to feelings of warmth in the center of the chest?) Traditionally, true *pattar* devotees were recognizable by ten signs: passionate feelings of being carried away by love, agitated and trembling body, staggering walk followed by fainting and collapsing to the ground, hot and sweaty limbs, quavering or failing voice [choked up?], stammering voice [again, choked up?], quivering lips, goosebumps, and face flooded with tears of unbearable, overwhelming emotion (Keller 1984:9–10). The Tamil poets often mention worshippers' collective tears alternating with loud laughter and exultation in sweetness. For more details on the signs and sensations of kama muta in South Asia, see Online Note 12.2.

Tears and piloerection are the signs of a strong kama muta motes in a famous eleventh century Sanskrit story that tells of King Sahasrānīka's Queen Mrigavati and their son being taken away due to a curse. The King is "tortured with the fire of separation." But when he learns that the Queen and their children are in a hermitage, he immediately makes his way there and is finally reunited with them.

> And the hermit handed over to him that Queen Mrigavati with her son, regained by the king after long separation, like tranquility with joy. And that sight which the husband and wife obtained of one another, now that the curse had ceased, rained, as it were, nectar into their eyes, which were filled with tears of joy. And the king embracing that son Udayana, whom he now beheld for the first time, could with difficulty let him go, as he was, so to speak, riveted to his body with his own hairs that stood erect from joy.
>
> *(Tawney 1924:120)*

The later Vaiṣṇava texts set out devotional practices in which the person becomes deeply involved though their body, evoking a true emotion of love (*bhāva bhakti*) for Krishna (McDaniel 1989:42). Passing through the stages of firm faith, genuine liking, and attachment, the devotee finally reaches the stage of *prema*, intense love, characterized by a feeling of possession toward Krishna and total bodily and mental burning desire for him. At this point the partially ecstatic devotee's symptoms are mild pallor, tears, and horripilation (McDaniel 1989:42). For example, in 1894 a Bengali Vaiṣṇava saint, Gaur Kiśora Dās Bābājī, who went partially or fully naked, using discarded pots and the clothing of corpses, was known for going into *bhāva* states in which he ate raw and dirty foods, which he also offered up to his personal deity. When he made this offering, "his voice became choked, and his body turned bright red and began to swell, while tears flowed from his eyes in streams, soaking his face and chest. Seeing these signs of love, Lalitā-dīdī was amazed" (McDaniel 1989:54, translating and quoting Dāsa, n.d.:40). In the late nineteenth century, a Bengali Vaiṣṇava saint, Vijayakṛṣṇa, was also known to sob and become drenched in tears when he worshipped, sometimes "covered with gooseflesh" or with his hand shaking extremely rapidly (McDaniel 1989:66). A third Bengali Vaiṣṇava saint, Jagadbandhu, organized groups to sing the name of Lord Hari (Krishna) in order to save the world from Kālī Yuga. When he sang in this collective worship, he was observed to sweat, shed tears, horripilate, and shiver (McDaniel 1989:71).

The sacred text of one school of Śākta, the *Kulārṇava Tantra*, prescribes a ritual, Kulācāra, consisting of drinking alcohol to intoxication and engaging in sexual relations in order to realize the god and goddess, Śiva and Śākti.

> The ritual links wine, women, and forbidden foods with the divine, and all things become allowable. The mere mention of the Kulācāra caused thrills in those who have experienced its joys: 'When the *kula* is praised, [those] whose hair stands on end, whose voices shake with emotion, and who shed tears of joy, they are the best of devotees.'
>
> *(McDaniel 1989:111, quoting from the Sanskrit*
> Kulārṇava Tantra *IX.86)*

These texts show that for perhaps more than two millennia, texts and contemporary reports of Hindu worship represented kama muta as the ideal experience of sudden intensification of CS with their highest deities. In Hinduism and in certain traditions of South Asian goddess worship, extreme kama muta experiences are manifested in tears, choking, and goosebumps, and, when especially ecstatic, sometimes in trembling, pallor, fainting, perspiration, vigorous movements, loud non-linguistic utterances, immobility, collapse, and fainting. Other South Asian signs of kama muta include dishevelment, specifically loosening of the *sari* knot and flowers dropping from loosening hair (Hardy 1983:529). Some texts locate kama muta in the 'heart,' but most do not localize it. In some texts, the prototype for kama muta emphasizes warmth and further stages of fiery heat, but without specifying whether this sensation is localized in any particular part of the body.

The prototype of Krishna worship is a specific form of CS: erotic heterosexual *bhakti* love. The prototype of the Krishna-worship kama muta mote is the first- and second-person intensification of love for, from, and with Krishna. Does sudden intensification of other forms of religious CS also evoke kama muta? In what respects are Hindu kama muta motes distinctive, and what features do they have in common with kama muta motes of other religions?

Buddhism

Compassion can evoke kama muta. In many studies, now involving thousands of participants, we have found that the personality trait of empathic concern is correlated – with a coefficient of $r = .32$ to .35 – with ratings of *being moved or touched* by several videos, and also consistently correlated with reports of warm chest, tears, and goosebumps to these videos (results from the first 16 studies are reported in Zickfeld et al. 2017; results from 19 more studies are in Zickfeld et al. 2019). The items in the empathic concern scale ask about typical responses to others' suffering and distress, while our video stimuli often depict little or no suffering or distress – and none at the moment when people report being most *moved or touched*, and when their sensations are strongest (Schubert et al. 2016). The foundation of Buddhism is loving-kindness, especially toward those who are suffering or in distress. So I would expect to find kama muta salient in Buddhist accounts of loving-kindness when a compassionate person's heart goes out to a needy person or other being.

In Buddhism, the prototype of CS is the Buddha's *karuṇā* – compassionate loving-kindness for all beings. *Karuṇā* is CS, but based on entirely different preos from the erotic *bhakti* 'love' CS of Krishna worship. While *bhakti* is being erotically drawn out of the self toward a marvelously loving being, *karuṇā* is a deep empathy for the need of others, evoked by their suffering.

In contrast to the first- and second-person *bhakti* kama muta of Shiva/Krishna worship, the principal prototype and precedent of the Buddhist kama muta mote is <u>third-person</u> kama muta when observing, hearing, or reading about the paragon Buddha's paradigmatic loving-kindness. A secondary but essential precedent is first-person kama muta that occurs when the Buddhist attains deep compassionate loving-kindness (*karuṇā*), as the Buddha did. The precept is that first-person kama muta should also occur at the culmination of pilgrimage to sacred places associated with the Buddha.

> The Pali account of Buddha's death in 'The Discourse on the Great Decease' (Mahāparinibbāna Sutta) mentions four places that a person should 'see and be moved by' (*dassanīyāni saṃvejanīyāni*): the place where Buddha was born, the place where he attained enlightenment, the place where he delivered his first sermon, and the place where he passed away.[1]
>
> *(Eckel 2005:116)*

In Vedic literature, *dassanīyāni*, 'seeing,' is not merely visual, but approaches touching or "participating in his or her nature ... [and is a] powerful experience of communion" (Eckel 1992:138). Pāli is the language of the principal Buddhist texts. The Pāli term *saṃvejanīyāni*, 'moved' (based on a root *vij*, meaning 'quickly moved'), prevalent in early Buddhist texts, denotes the kama muta mote in this context. Being *saṃvejanīyāni* is "often connected to the experience of profound meditative absorption (Sanskrit *dhyāna*, Pali *jhāna*), seeing/

meeting the Buddha, hearing the Dharma (his teachings), or witnessing some act of wisdom, kindness, or compassion" (Robert Buswell, personal communication, 2015). Weeping and piloerection are both commonly mentioned as manifestations of *samvejanīyāni*. As in the Sanskrit and Hindi texts, in the Pali texts, horripilation is "conceived to be occasioned by, and to express, exquisite delight" when "enraptured" (Thompson 1846:416; see also Tawney 1924:120 footnote).

A *bodhisattva* (Pali *bodhissata*) is a person with great compassion for all others' suffering, on the threshold of the end of the Buddhist path, nirvana. The sign (*liṅga*) that a *bodhisattva* is irreversibly on the path to full enlightenment "are the tears and horripilation that occur spontaneously in a true bodhisattva who hears a particular Mahāyāna sutra [aphorism of the Buddha] for the first time, or when listening to an explanation of *bodhiccta* and *śūnyatā*" (Buswell & Lopez 2013:474–475). These terms apparently denote forms of CS: *bodhiccta* consists of the wish to become enlightened by true compassion for all beings, together with detachment from illusion of a bounded, inherently separate self. *Śūnyatā* means emptiness, non-selfness, such that one loses the sense of being a distinct being apart from others. This is a third Buddhist precedent and precept of kama muta, in which the intensification of CS is the dissolution of the boundaries that separate the self from the totality of being, so that all is one. This resembles the "oceanic feeling" described by Roman Rolland (cf. Koestler 1954:351–352; Griffiths et al. Jesse 2006; Bolender 2010:104–111; Tylša, Páleníceka, & Horáceka 2014).

And it is not just *bodhisattva* who experience this. Weeping and goosebumps of kama muta are often described in tales of ordinary people's encounters with the Buddha or his teachings. Jātaka stories recount the past lives of the Buddha. The most famous, composed before the third century BCE, tells of the penultimate incarnation of the Buddha as King Vessantara. With absolute compassionate generosity he gives away anything that anyone asks of him, even giving to his enemies his own rain-making magic white elephant. As a result, his subjects send him and his family into exile, entailing a long, arduous journey. When his two hungry children see trees on a mountainside laden with fruit, they cry with hunger. Seeing the children weeping, the trees are distressed (*ubbigga* in Pāli, *udvigna* in Sanskrit) and bend over so that the children can reach their fruit. Observing this horripilating (*loma-hamsana* in Pāli, *loma-harsana* in Sanskrit) act of kindness to her children, Queen Maddī is moved to praise them: "This is an horripilating miracle!" (Dhammarama & Bareau 1963:341–342; from Jātaka 547, *Jātaka*: Volume VI, 479–593). Another tale of the Buddha's past lives tells about the perfect equanimity of Bodhisattva Mahā-Lomahaṃsa; his name means 'Great Goose-bump' or 'Great Hair-raised' (Dhammarama & Bareau 1963:387; from Jātaka 94, *Jātaka*: Volume I, 389–391). (Recall earlier, the narrator of the *Purāṇa* stories, Sūta, who was called Romaharṣaṇa, because of his own hair standing up when he heard from Vyāsa the stories of union with Vishnu/Krishna, and the piloerection he evoked in his listeners when he retold the stories.)

In one Jātaka tale (in this case probably dating before the fifth century CE), in his incarnation as Prince Sutasoma, the Buddha gives his word to the cannibal

Kalmāṣapāda that he will return after meeting another obligation. Although dubious, Kalmāṣapāda releases him. When Prince Sutasoma does in fact return and tells the cannibal of his history of integrity and good works, Kalmāṣapāda is overcome by Sutasoma's calm, fearless goodness. "Tears of gladness filled Kalmāṣapāda eyes when he heard this. His hair bristled, and he came out in goose pimples. The darkness of his evil nature vanished as he looked at the Buddha" (Khoroche 1989:58–59).

In these texts, the essence of the Buddha is that he evokes kama muta by his perfectly selfless kindness, generosity, and trustworthiness. In this tradition, the paradigm is that learning of the Buddha's great CS *karuṇā* compassion evokes third-person kama muta, the paragon emotion of Buddhism.

Ciji in Contemporary Taiwan

These texts are preos; although they take the form of narrative descriptions, we cannot confidently make direct inferences about the emotions or actions of Buddhists two millennia ago. However, kama muta is still at the core of major strands of contemporary Buddhism. Let's look at just one sect, devotees of Ciji, a movement founded by the Venerable Zhengyan, a Taiwanese Buddhist nun. Followers are dedicated to helping the poor, to providing medical care through their two large hospitals in which they tend to the ill, and to disaster relief. They are known for often crying when they encounter the needy people they serve. Women devotees describe themselves as people who love to cry or sob (Minnan *aikhau;* Mandarin *aikuae;* Huang 2003). Ciji women also sometimes cry (and may nearly faint) when chanting Buddha's or Bodhisattvas' names or in the presence of Buddha or Bodhisattva statues. Much of this crying is "contagious": when one woman starts weeping, her peers are moved to weep with her. Male devotees rarely do.

Three Ciji women tell what they felt when they sobbed:

1. Every time I chanted a Buddha's name, I felt I was embraced by someone, someone I could rely on, someone in front of whom I could act like a spoiled child. I could cry like a baby.
2. I felt close to Buddha, as if I was taken care of and protected by Buddha. I felt cozy and safe.
3. [When entering the 'compassion gate' into the Ciji Abode] I felt as if I was seeing home, as if I had finally returned home. I couldn't stop crying then … I also cried at home when I chanted sutras.

(Huang 2003:84; ellipses in Huang)

Likewise, when first encountering the Venerable Zhengyan, many people weep, later reporting that they felt ecstatic; some even weep when first hearing her on a tape or simply viewing her photograph. Women giving testimonials at Ciji gatherings are often overcome by tears, while the listening congregation sobs.

Selections of tearful declarations of transformation are broadcast on the Ciji television station, distributed on cassettes, and depicted in printed publications. Huang (2003) describes the closing ritual of the Ciji annual gathering: each member in turn lights the candle of another, until everyone holds a burning candle; many weep.

Huang (2003:84) characterizes Ciji crying as redemptive, as ecstatically embodying "the selfless experience that stands at the core of the charismatic experience." Moreover, Huang (2003:84) posits that these experiences generate the CS devotion and commitment that characterizes kama muta: "such ecstasy has a transcendental transformative effect on the followers and leads thousands of them to spend their lives bound together to carry out the leader's mission" of care for the ill, the destitute, and the victims of disaster.

> Many followers, especially the early followers, who cried whenever they saw the Venerable Zhengyan, asked Zhengyan for an explanation. Zhengyan said it is the *yuan* (bonds, or relationship) between them, deeply fixed in a past life or several past lives. 'It's like a lost wanderer who finally found his or her family after a long journey. You cry when you finally see your family after a long absence.'
>
> *(Huang 2003:84)*[2]

Goosebumps do not seem to be mentioned in the Ciji literature. This is intriguing, given their prominence in the Pail and Sanskrit literature, but may simply reflect that Ciji arose in Taiwan; the Venerable Zhengyan and her followers are not likely to be familiar with the Pali or Sanskrit literature of India. Of course, the salience of crying in Ciji prototypes, precedents, prescriptions, and personal accounts does not mean that Ciji do not experience goosebumps, warm chests, deep and paused breath, buoyancy, exhilaration, and other kama muta sensations. But because the crying preos define Ciji as a CS group and as a compassionate experience, Ciji are sure to direct their attention to their own crying, to episodically encode their experiences <u>as</u> crying events, and then to make crying especially salient when they constructively remember and recount these experiences. Because goosebumps, warm heart, deep and paused breath, exhilaration, and buoyancy are absent from the defining narratives that are the paradigmatic precedents for their kama muta experiences, these sensations have little or no meaning, and hence are likely to be pretty much ignored.

Furthermore, it is plausible to imagine that practice perfects feeling in conjunction with particular performances of it (see Chapter 10). That is, it may be that people enrich their experience of kama muta and refine their cultural display of it by observing admired paragons, imitating them, and practicing the performance of the indexical signs of kama muta that correspond to local cultural preos. In this case, Ciji devotees may become more prone to cry, and cry more effectively, the more they engage in the practice and feel kama muta as a result. Additionally, it is certainly conceivable that there are genetic, physiological, dietary, or ecological affordances that make some sensations more prominent in some populations than in others (for relevant phenomena, see Chiao et al. 2012; Chiao 2015).

The kama muta of Ciji devotees grows out of *karuṇā*, compassion for suffering, which is a key prototype of Buddhist kama muta. In that respect, it somewhat resembles something I will discuss in the next chapter and Chapter 15: kama muta of Shia in *majlis* remembrance of the martyrdom of Hussain ibn Ali and his family and followers, and the kama muta of Christian remembrance of Jesus on the cross. All involve compassionate loving and even identification. However, compassion for the present suffering of ordinary mortals is the focal source of Ciji kama muta, while much of Shia and Christian kama muta grows out of gratitude for and identification with the suffering of specific sacred beings who sacrificed themselves for the worshipper many centuries ago. Likewise, reading or hearing Pali texts evokes kama muta at the compassionate sacrifices of the Buddha for the benefit of others, but in contrast to Shia and Christian kama muta focused on the death of the sacred figures, in the Jātaka tales the Buddha is not the victim of violence.

Ciji kama muta is primarily first-person, emerging from the devotees' compassion for suffering and need. The kama muta of Shia majlis sorrow for the suffering of Hussain ibn Ali, and the kama muta of Christian sorrow for the suffering of Jesus on the cross, are primarily second-person gratitude responses to the voluntary martyrdom of the sacred beings for the worshipper: Jesus, saints, and Hussain died for the worshipper. For readers of Buddhist and Krishna classical texts, kama muta is primarily third-person kama muta, responding to tales of the first-person and second-person kama muta experienced by persons whose CS relationships intensified. It is likely that a Buddhist also experiences kama muta when he merges his individual self into the transcendent whole, and it seems that Krishna worshippers also experience kama muta when they feel themselves to be in loving union with Krishna.

Meditation is essential to Buddhism, and important kinds of meditation, such as *Maitrī* and *Gtong Len*, consist in fostering compassion. I imagine that kama muta may arise out of such meditation, since its aim is cultivating love towards others whom the mediator did not previously love. Online Note 12.3 explores more deeply the issue of when meditation or mindful self-compassion evoke kama muta.

Meditative practices derived from Buddhism and the premises of mindfulness are being incorporated into Western psychotherapy (Hayes, Follette, & Linehan 2004; Hoffman, Grossman, & Hinton 2011; MacBeth & Gumley 2012). Mindfulness is especially prominent in Dialectical Behavioral Therapy (DBT; Linehan 1993; see Chapman 2006 for a review), Acceptance and Commitment Therapy (Hayes, Strosahl, & Wilson 1999), and Gestalt Therapy (see Brownell 2010 for an overview). Mindfulness and the establishment of mindfulness practices is contemporary psychological practice and research has long been promoted by Jon Kabat-Zinn through his program of Mindfulness-based Stress

Reduction (Kabat-Zinn 1990). Using elements of this, Mindfulness-based Cognitive Therapy (Segal, Williams, & Teasdale 2002) was specifically developed for patients with depression (see also Hayes, Follette, & Linehan 2004).[3]

As I observed in Chapter 5, kama muta may occur in any kind of psychotherapy when the patient's CS relationship with the therapist suddenly intensifies. But there is another kind of CS that can occur in therapies derived from mindfulness practices. Mindful self-compassion and other therapies aimed at cultivating self-compassion seem particularly likely to afford opportunities for sudden intensification of CS <u>with the self</u> (Gilbert 2005; Neff, Kirkpatrick, & Rude 2007; Neff 2011; Germer & Neff 2013). Mindful self-compassion fosters the feeling of shared humanity, recognizing that all people are imperfect, unable to attain everything they want – and all people suffer. Imperfection, disappointment, and suffering are essential aspects of life that we share with all. Mindful self-compassion also fosters self-kindness. "Self-kindness entails being warm and understanding toward ourselves when we suffer, fail, or feel inadequate, rather than flagellating ourselves with self-criticism. ... With self-kindness, however, we soothe and nurture ourselves when confronting our pain" (Germer & Neff 2013:656–657). Reflexive kama muta motes probably occur when a patient suddenly loves herself. Victoria Schönefeld, a clinical psychologist who studies kama muta, reports her own experience of mindful self-compassion.

Some time ago, I started with daily meditation. I found a lovely meditation program online, which offers a variety of audio files with guided meditations on different topics. All these meditations are based on the concept of mindfulness and compassionate living, where self-compassion, self-love, and self-acceptance play a key role. So I did several guided meditations on the importance and benefits of self-love, and heard about several imagination techniques to enhance these qualities. At this point, I understood the concept of self-love on an abstract level, but little did I know that the feeling was still missing. Then there was one day, when I sat on my meditation cushion on the balcony, enjoying the first warm days of spring during my daily sitting meditation. The guided meditation on that special day also addressed the topic of self-love and self-acceptance once again. And then I suddenly felt it. At this very moment, I experienced a wave of self-love and self-acceptance. I started crying, and tears were running down my cheeks. I was deeply moved by the experience, that I was able to love myself, which I never thought was possible. It was a deeply comforting feeling to experience this quality and intensity of unconditional love – and it emerged from within myself! This moment was crucial for me, because I never felt this way for myself before. It showed me that self-acceptance and self-love are possible. From my experience, developing true self-love is a long journey, maybe a lifelong one. But from this

> moment on, self-compassion, tender feelings for myself, self-forgiveness, and self-acceptance were much easier to access, and were able to grow.

In my opinion, discovering and fostering self-love, self-compassion, and self-acceptance is also a crucial element in psychotherapy. Especially clients who suffer from low self-esteem, or strong self-devaluations, can benefit extraordinarily. There are cases where self-compassion can enable or facilitate access to other therapeutic processes of significant importance. For example, the exploration of emotions in certain situations can be blocked, if the client considers them as "wrong," "forbidden," "weak" and so on, like sadness or anger. Developing self-acceptance, self-compassion, self-forgiveness – and eventually, even self-love – can help to make these important reflections easier. During my psychotherapist education, I was very grateful for the chance of self-experience – where therapists in training attend psychotherapy sessions themselves. Within these sessions, I experienced several moments of kama muta myself, elicited by the experience of self-love and self-acceptance. In my own work with clients, I was also able to witness moments of kama muta, when I could assist a person to discover a self-loving, self-compassionate side. These were very moving, precious moments for me as well, and I consider these moments crucial for the therapeutic process.

(Victoria Schönefeld)

Moments of self-love may also occur in Dialectical Behavioral Therapy (DBT), whose inventor, Marsha Linehan, herself suffers from borderline personality disorder (Linehan 1993; Bedics et al. 2012). Helping patients to love themselves is a central aim of DBT. Linehan traces DBT to a personal experience she had while praying:

'One night I was kneeling in there, looking up at the cross, and the whole place became gold — and suddenly I felt something coming toward me,' she said. 'It was this shimmering experience, and I just ran back to my room and said, "I love myself." It was the first time I remember talking to myself in the first person. I felt transformed.'

(Quoted in Carey 2011)

Jainism

Generosity is crucial for Jains, and they take great joy in both giving and observing others giving. In Jain stories, when people see someone give an especially meritorious gift, observers participate in the giver's joy, acclaiming "'Wonderful! A gift! A gift!'" (Heim 2004:153, note 27, citing Balbir 1982:149). But Jain prototypes go beyond this sort of third-person response. For example, a ninth century Jain commentator, Siddhasena Gaṇin, emphasized the supreme importance of giving joyfully, not resentfully, to mendicant monks. From the moment one sees mendicant monks approaching one should be pleased, thinking only of one's good fortune in having the opportunity to give one's possessions to the monks. He wrote:

> This is what it means to want to give. One wants to give upon seeing a monk or when he asks, and one should have supreme joy and horripilation. Indeed one should horripilate in this way also when giving and having given — at all three times

(that is, in anticipation, when making the gift, and when recalling one's generosity; Heim 2004:43; from Balbir 1982:148f.).

As Heim (2004:43) puts it, "The donor should be moved by his or her own generosity." In another passage, Siddhasena Gaṇin goes further: taking into account the time, place, and worthiness of the recipient, with a feeling of esteem for the recipient, with a mind full of love and joy, the donor of a gift should be "covered in a cloak of horripilation" as the donor experiences (in Heim's words) "an emotional and physical thrill" (Heim 2004: 95–96). Recall that in Chapter 8, I reviewed how, in *Tortilla Flat*, Steinbeck (1935) similarly depicts Pilon, Pablo, and Jesus Maria's kama muta motes evoked by their own generosity or kindness. Reflexive kama muta probably also occurs occasionally when one nostalgically imagines oneself as an innocent child, or sees cute photos or videos of oneself as a young child.

* * * * * *

The erection of body hair is emphasized much more and is much more prevalent in these Hindu and Buddhist texts than in Islamic or Christian texts. It is intriguing that Sanskrit-speakers and later contemporary South Asians regarded piloerection as the most important sign of the virtuous experience of kama muta, difficult as it is to perceive in people who do not typically have very thick dark hair on very pale skin. For comparison, research participants from the US, Norway, Portugal, Israel, and China who watch videos or record events in their lives do not report goosebumps or chills more frequently or more strongly than tears, and report both tears and goosebumps slightly less than warm or other feelings in the chest. In social media and in our interviews with Americans and Norwegians, tears and warm feelings in the chest are at least as salient as goosebumps. So the salience of piloerection in Hindu texts is intriguing. Weeping is also prominent in the Hindu and Buddhist texts. But these texts are not surveys or samples of behavior; we cannot infer that piloerection was the modal or sensorially dominant response of Sanskrit or Tamil-speaking or recent worshippers. Indeed, from these texts we cannot make any inferences about frequencies or strength of kama muta sensations. These texts present models <u>for</u> action, not models <u>of</u> action: these texts are precedents, prototypes, and paradigms for kama muta motes, telling the reader what they should experience and what their sensations mean. As such, the texts tell us what signs of kama muta are significant to the writers and hence to the readers who model their actions and understandings after the texts.

Regardless of how people actually behaved, these texts demonstrate that for over two thousand years prominent South Asian religious writers and their readers explicitly but selectively <u>represented</u> some of the characteristic sensations and signs of kama muta, claimed that these sensations and signs occurred when devotees experienced union with divinity, regarded this as the ideal response, and declared that it was proof of loving union with divinity. These signs and sensations were important preos that presumably afforded emotional experiences and shaped the meanings people gave to what they and others experienced.

Furthermore, despite uncertainty about the personal emotional experience of kama muta in Hinduism, Buddhism, and Jainism, the texts clearly delineate the principal drivers of kama muta in these religions, or at least ideal precedents and precepts for the drivers. The most immediate driver is the third-person observation, hearing of, or reading narratives of love (*bhakti*) or compassionate loving kindness (*karuṇā* and *maitrī*). At the next level, based on these respective prototypes, key drivers are oneself <u>being</u> in love with Krishna, and for Buddhists and Jains, <u>performing</u> acts of compassionate kindness. Albeit rarely experienced, the paragon driver is the transcendent, quiet rapture of dissolving the boundaries that separate the individual self, so that one becomes one with the all. The texts present numerous narratives of such events.

Online notes

12.1 *Bhakti rasa* in Krishna worship.
12.2 The signs and sensations of kama muta in South Asia.
12.3 Can meditation or mindful self-compassion evoke kama muta?

Notes

1 For kama muta in Christian and Muslim pilgrimage, see Chapter 14.
2 The Yellow Bridge dictionary gives the apparently relevant meaning of *yuán* as 'circle, round'; it defines 团圆, *tuányuán*, as 'to have a reunion.'
3 Thank you to Victoria Schönefeld for suggesting several of these references.

13

ISLAM

Five times a day Muslims are called to pray. When beautifully sung, sometimes the call to prayer (*adhān* or *azān*) "penetrates the heat," stirs the soul and evokes kama muta as a soothing feeling of spiritual peace and relaxation (Akbari 2015a). Some even weep while listening, feeling a connection with God, remembering the inevitability of death but at the same time feeling peaceful reassurance and gratitude for God's merciful forgiveness. One American informant said that listening to *adhān* gives her a warm feeling in her heart traveling down her body. Another said it makes her feel calm; she feels the love and warmth of Allah in the *adhān*. Entering a beautiful mosque apparently sometimes evokes mild kama muta, too, and it seems that collective prayer may do so. After praying together, worshippers may stay in the mosque to read the Qur'an; for some, this reading sometimes also evokes kama muta. This is visible in their tears, along with their reports of shivers, and their explanations that they are crying at the beauty of the passages, crying from the feeling of closeness to Allah and other religious figures, from Allah's sweetness, and from the happiness they feel as they read. These drivers afford kama muta to all Muslims, and in addition, some strands of Islam incorporate even stronger drivers.

In addition to Ramadan fasting, some Muslims fast for one or more days of Muharram, when Shias in particular commemorate the death of Muhammad's grandson Hussain ibn Ali, his family and supporters at Karbala in 680 CE (Pinault 1992; Chelkowski 2010). Shia identify themselves with Hussain ibn Ali as the legitimate heir of the Prophet, while Sunnis identify themselves with the lineage of Yazid, the powerful heir who sent a large army to kill Hussain and his small group of followers. Muharram is a rite of mourning for the martyrdom of Hussain, his family, and followers at Karbala, but at the same time, for Shia, a celebration of his moral victory in defending and preserving what Shia define as true Islam (Hyder 2006:51). Consequently some communities at some points in history – today especially in rural areas – have made Muharram something of a festival or even carnival – a "mixture of grief and elation" (Wolf 2000:101). Shia women, especially, but also men, weep profusely during Muharram gatherings, and often sigh. But this is not pure grief – it is also an indexical conformation of identification with and thankfulness for the sacrifice of Hussain and his family (on the concept of *conformation system*, see Fiske 2004b; Fiske & Schubert 2012). At the same time, Muharram is the performance of solidarity with all Shia across all time, a feeling of collective pride in being Shia (Pinault 1992; Hyder 2006:50; Aghaie 2009). One influential authority explains the CS-constitutive signifi- cance of weeping for Shia:

> The life, progress, and glory of any community depends upon a passion for unity among its members and their wise organization. The stronger the passion for unity and the wiser the organization the more progressive and glorious will be the community. What sows the seed of passion for unity and organization in the community and helps it to germinate and develop is this very practice of weeping and wailing which has earned for us [Shia] the nickname 'the Community of Weepers.' ... All of the symptoms of unity and cooperation in the community ... are either the direct product or the indirect result of this same practice of weeping and wailing. It is so, because the only asset in the treasure house of the community which keeps alive and alert our congregational feelings and excites them whenever nec- essary is this practice of weeping and wailing and the various rituals con- nected with it and it is this practice which is the vital force behind all the symptoms of unity in the community.
>
> *(Ameed 1974:75–76)*

> Weeping and wailing is certainly a purpose of our condolatory rituals [*maj- lis*] in so far as rituals move us to weeping and wailing but this is not the final or ultimate purpose of the rituals. The ultimate purposes of weeping and wailing are unity in the community and its organization, preservation of record of the great deeds of the Ahle Bait, (A.S.), smooth propagation of our religion and producing of eloquent speakers and eminent poets in the community [who in turn can move the community to solidarity through weeping]. [The Ahle Bait, تيبلا لها, are the family of Muhammad; here, especially referencing the martyrs of Karbala.]
>
> *(Ameed 1974:80)*

At *majlis*, the mourning gatherings of Muharram, preachers recite elegies that "can be extremely heartfelt and moving" and "typically move the audience to tears" (Blomfield 2010:313). Howarth (2005:168) quotes a Hyderabad preacher who succinctly states the meaning of *majlis* weeping: "The meaning of life is an open book of love. The perfection of the return to God is love, and the perfec- tion of love is the shedding of tears for the sufferings of Husayn." Hence sermons at *majlis* are expressly structured so as to evoke weeping; it is the preacher's responsibility to represent the suffering at Karbala so vividly that the congregation sobs (Pinault 1992:116–117; Howarth 2005). This weeping is meritorious, conferring *savab*, merit that counts toward admission to heaven (Pinault 1992:116). Religious leaders or lay speakers evoke weeping by reciting poetry about the sacrifice that Hussain made of himself, his family, and his band of followers. "Highlighting poignant kinship bonds, *majlis* poetry articulates and elicits tearful expressions of love for Ḥusain, encouraging listeners to participate in the bereavement and separation experiences by the *imam* [Ḥusain] and his family" (Bard 2005:149). *Majlis* preaching and poetry poignantly recount the thirst of Hussain and his family in the Karbala desert, and some Shia perceive their tears as providing water that Hussain and his family drink to assuage that thirst (Bard 2005:149, 157). For these believers, weeping forges a direct bond of consubstantial assimilation when they feel their essential body substances nurture the martyred Hussain and his family. These bonds may be even stronger when young male participants in *matam* cut their foreheads with swords and repeatedly strike their backs with chains laced with sharp blades. It seems likely that many rituals of collective religious self-injury and even solitary self-mortification may evoke kama muta, although the evidence does not definitely establish this. Online Note 13.1 describes apparent kama muta in *majlis* during *muharram*, and in self-injury in rituals of other religions.

Sufi chanting and moving together

Majlis affords sudden intensification of CS with Hussain and his family, *ahl al-bayat*, and at the same time, but secondarily, with co-participants and Shia performing *majlis* everywhere. In contrast, the singular aim of Sufism is union with Allah, when the separate individual self disappears in His encompassing being. "The goal is the fusion and merging with the Absolute and the Divine" (Frembegen 2009:1). "Mystics are touched and moved by Him, pervaded by the awareness of God" (2009:4). The Sufi mystic seeks God's care and love: "The mystical path (*tariqa*) to the experience of unity leads to one's own heart where one finds God" (2009:5). There are elements of overwhelming *awe* in the encounter with God, but the core is the longing for Him that leads the mystic to submerge his will and his ego until he "is finally touched by God who now resides in his heart" (2009:6), so that he reaches "union with the Divine Beloved (*fana*)" (Frembegen 2009:6). Sufis may also seek annihilation of the self in union with the Prophet, or with the living saint who guides them.

"In one way or another love, the capacity of one spirit (*ruh*) to join selflessly with another, forms the basis for nearly all Sufi discourse and practice" (Frishkopf 2001:243). Love is the

> desire for unification with the beloved, even to the point of self-sacrifice. In the most extreme degrees of love ('*ishq* or *wajd*), the lover loses his or

her individual attributes and becomes assimilated within the beloved, a condition technically known as *fana'* (annihilation). A Sufi may seek *fana'* in his shaykh, or in the Prophet, but the highest form of *fana'* is in Allah. On a lower plane, Sufi love is manifested as selfless generosity, tolerance, compassion, and empathy for others, regardless of their religious affiliations. Nearly all Sufi poetry speaks about love, longing, or praise for the beloved, and the Sufi is often called a *muhibb* (pl. *muhibbin*), or *'ashiq* (pl. *'ashiqin*); both words mean 'lover.'

(Frishkopf 2001:244)

Fanā', annihilation with/in becoming one with another, is the pinnacle of *ḥāl* – union with Allah, with the Prophet, or even with a saint.

The literature of Sufism ... is above all the literature of *ḥāl*. It is a literature which reflects of the deepest longings and yearnings of the human soul for God and communicates the ecstasy of union with the Beloved and nostalgia of separation from the Reality which is the source of all that is beautiful and all that can be loved.

(Nasr 1999:3)

Ḥāl is transitory state of the soul, experienced as momentary mystical emotion (Ansu 1980 60ff.). The fourteenth century Sufi Jurjānī wrote that *ḥāl* "is echoed in the heart without affectation. It is not earned or acquired, whether it be happiness or sadness, contraction or expansion or composure" (quoted in translation by Nasr 1980:61). Its essential character is that it is a gift from God in his generosity, received by the human heart, which enables a person to connect to God. *Ḥāl* is

an occasional spark of the divine light which for the moment illuminates his soul and puts him in a state beyond himself. A *ḥāl* is a divine gift which can come both to the beginner upon the Path and to the most advanced Sufi possessing a high station. In fact occasionally it can also come to the uninitiated if he be spiritually disposed to the reception of the grace of Heaven. The divine grace (*barakah*) flows too strongly in the arteries of the Universe not to touch occasionally even men who are not following the Way. The expansion of the soul and the sense of joy it experiences in seeing beautiful face or hearing a lovely melody ... foreshadow the *ḥāl* of those travelling upon the path.

(Nasr 1980:62)

Noting that *ḥāl* quickly passes, Nasr (1980:63) quotes in translation the Sufi poet Sa'di's characterization of *ḥāl* as "leaping lightening." It is momentary. This moment in Sufi worship is also denoted by *jadhbah* and *mjdhub*, 'rapture or overpowering attraction to God' (the words also denote a person in such a state).

While essentially linking the individual worshiper to Allah, or the Prophet, or a saint, the moment of ecstatic union is often realized collectively, by listening to, and sometimes collectively singing, sacred songs, often while participants perform rhythmic movements in synchrony with the song and with each other. In some cases participants do not know the language (usually Arabic) in which they are singing in unison, and they may also chant the thousand names of Allah, or even otherwise meaningless utterances. Because the experience of union with Allah is the personal concern of the individual herself, while they are singing, Sufi worshippers tend to avoid direct gaze that would indicate they are observing anyone. But when a participant feels the kama muta of union with divinity, one or another quality of their voice is likely to reveal the experience to all. This stimulates all who hear it.

Tears are definite signs of the rapturous union of *ḥāl*. For example, a tenth century Sufi writer, drawing on and then directly quoting a ninth century Sufi writer analyzing types of weeping, states that

> weeping from God is fear of God's chastisement and grief at being kept apart from him. Weeping toward God is the yearning of lovers to meet their Beloved. Weeping over God results from separation after arrival or from 'weeping in joy at the arrival at Him, when he embraces [the seeker] in kindness like a suckling child nursing at the breast of its mother.'
>
> *(Chittick 2005:135; the quoted segment is from Abū Nasr al-Sarrāj 1914:229)*

Similarly, an influential twelfth century Sufi writer "typically associates weeping with the fire of love and the burning of the heart," and writes about how Allah, "the Exaltation of Unity," loves those who grievingly weep (Chittick 2005:141, 142).

On the way to merging with Allah, Sufis may seek to merge with the Prophet Mohammed, a union conceived in several ways: "The terms used for this contact vary – vision (*ru'yā*), annihilation (*fanā'*), witness (*mushāhada*), meeting or joining (*jam'* or *ijtimā'*), and union (*ittiḥād*)" (Hoffman 1999:364). Sufis also may seek to merge with saints or religious guides, who mediate further union with god. Thus it seems likely that they may also experience some kind of kama muta when this occurs. For example, Ibn Qunfudh, a pilgrim, recounts an encounter in 1367–1368 in the south of Morocco with the saint Abū 'l-Ḥasan Yūsuf al-Ṣnhāī, who constantly wept when he heard a verse of the Koran, a teaching of the Prophet, or the words of a Sufi master. The saint's weeping evoked tears in those who observed his tears. When the saint embraced the pilgrim and caressed him with his blessed hand, the saint cried and the intensity of the saint's spiritual state made the pilgrim shiver (Calasso 2000a:47, 2000b:452). The same encounter and others of its ilk involved the saint offering the pilgrim food from his own hands. Other pilgrims also recounted how the exquisite hands of such a saint physically touched a follower (Calasso 2000b:447).

The tears of saints were perceived as purifying tears of joy, pity, remorse for sins, religious scruples, and fear of god and god's punishment – and the texts report that various saints' tears made observers cry in turn (Ferhat 2000:463). Quite generally in medieval Sufi texts, the ideal expression of religiosity was the tears of the saint, the tears of his disciples when they saw him cry, the tears of pilgrims in Mecca jamming into the Ka`ba, tears of the crowds shoving up to embrace the tomb of a saint, tears of preaching imams moved by their own virtuous speech, the unrestrained sobbing of imams' listeners, and the tears of the convert who chooses to abandon the world to give himself to god (Calasso 2000b:452–453). One famous mystic poet, enraptured by *sama`* music and his own singing, is said to have become so ecstatic "that his long hair stood on end" (Frembegen 2009:173). When the mystic becomes one in CS with God, "a characteristic of this rapture was the inner ecstatic heat which is described in Persian as 'glowing red' (*surkh*)" (Frembegen 2009:177).[1] These signs appear to index kama muta motes.

These textual events are paradigms for Sufi followers; presumably they afford and shape the emotional experiences of those followers. But even without knowledge of the texts, or any semantic belief in Islam, simple direct participation in the synchronous movement and chanting in a Sufi mosque can evoke kama muta motes. Singing or chanting in unison and synchronous rhythmic movement apparently make participants feel that their bodies are one and the same, through the medium of consubstantial assimilation, the conformation system that mediates CS. While the semantics of the words or even the motions may augment this consubstantial assimilation for those with declarative knowledge of the language, it is the synchrony itself that indexically makes participants' bodies merge into one. What is especially intriguing about Sufi kama muta drivers is that experiencing the kama muta that this musical, vocal, and kinetic consubstantial assimilation <u>with other worshippers</u> affords the perception of becoming one <u>with Allah</u>, not just with their fellow participants. Vocal and motor synchrony with fellow humans generates the feeling of *ḥāl, fanā', wajd, jadhbah, mjdhub*, or *ittiḥād* with the divine – somewhat like singing in a Christian church choir. Sufi worshippers on three continents report kama muta experiences – even when they don't speak the language in which they are worshipping. Online Note 13.2 illustrates kama muta in Sufi worship in California, Paris, and Morocco – among participants who don't speak Arabic, the language in which the worship is conducted.

* * * * *

Sufi synchronous movement, chanting, lyrics, and music, as well as the more secular musical genres intimately linked with these practices, consistently evoke transitory states that are evidently kama muta motes. And not incidentally, but functionally: these practices are precisely shaped to evoke kama muta motes. Culturally salient exemplars, explicit semantic prescriptions, cultivated perceptual skills, emotional conditioning, and other mnemonic systems are integrated into this cultural elaborated evocative system. These preos provide a multi-faceted model for evoking kama muta: together they compose a potent driver. Moreover, participants expressly engage in these events in order to experience kama muta.

Let us now turn to two other practices that evoke kama muta in several world religions. After that, in Chapter 16, I pause, take a step back, and consider what religion is, and what role kama muta plays in it.

Online notes

13.1 Apparent kama muta in *majlis* during *muharram*, and in self-injury in rituals of other religions.
13.2 Kama muta in Sufi worshipers in California, Paris, and Morocco – who don't know the language.

Note

1 Compare with Mormons' experience of 'burning in the bosom,' a sign of deep religious connection with God, and John Wesley's pivotal moment when he felt his "heart strangely warmed." See Chapter 16.

14

KAMA MUTA IN PILGRIMAGE

What evokes kama muta is the sudden intensification of a communal sharing relationship. Kama muta in turn motivates devotion and commitment to communal sharing relationships. So if we are searching for religious kama muta drivers, we should look where people go to get close to divinities, affirm their piety, suddenly consecrate their fidelity to a divine being – and establish their solidarity with fellow worshippers. This is just what pilgrimage is, in all world religions. So our theory predicts that kama muta should appear at the culmination of pilgrimage, and I looked to see whether it did. In some cases it clearly does. In other cases the evidence I have found so far does not show whether kama muta is present or not, but field researchers who speak the relevant languages may discover it.

Among Christians who have faith in the boundless love of the Virgin Mary, many want to make pilgrimages to see and touch relics or places where she appeared. Pilgrims are "moved by Mary," whom they perceive as a loving mother (Hermkens, Jansen, & Notermans 2009:6). But pilgrims' CS may also intensify with others. For example, pilgrims visiting Lourdes today cry during the rituals they participate in there in part because of the CS they feel with fellow participants (present and past), or when they think about family members who have died (Notermans 2007, 2008). Again, at many of the churches of Jerusalem,

> pilgrims are deeply moved by their ritual encounters with Christ's trials and tribulations, with the life of the Virgin, and with the fate of the apostles: they weep, meditate serenely, empathize in agony, speak in tongues, chant and sing. In the exquisite Norman Church of Saint Anne, for example, situated in a peaceful garden off the busy Via Dolorosa and renowned for its acoustic qualities, parties of pilgrims take turns singing hymns in its unadorned limestone nave, and for that moment their voices make the

ancient church their own. The song of the singers is richly amplified by the curved stone surfaces of the apse walls and vaulted roof. The sheer splendor of the sound resonates within the pilgrims, arousing 'spiritual' euphoria and, often, tears.

(Marchand 2016:80)

Pilgrims, generally, are hopeful of an encounter with the divine—a sublime connection between themselves and their God, or the attainment of deep and moving pathos for the suffering of their Lord, Jesus Christ.

(Marchand 2016:81–82)

Yet while many of them do have such experiences at other Jerusalem churches, for various reasons, Marchand notes, they generally do <u>not</u> have them at the focal place where they expect to: the Holy of Holies, the Church of the Holy Sepulcher. Expectation, hope, placement, and sensation of place are important to experiencing kama muta, but not sufficient.

Muslims making the *hajj* frequently weep when they first see the Ka'ba (Wolfe 1997). For example, writing of his own visit in 1853, Richard Burton reports, "A wonderful desire and love impel men from distant regions to visit the holy spot, and the first sign of the Ka'abah causes awe and fear, horripilation and tears" (Burton 1906:325). But is it just 'fear' and awe the hajjis feel, or kama muta together with awe? In a 2 September 2011 blog, Atif Ibrahim wrote,

The first time I visited the Kaaba, it was not crowded. I was fascinated by the pure white lightings surrounding everywhere. When I saw the Kaaba, to me, it looked like it was touching the skies, covering everything around it. I could see nothing but It. I could not hear anything around me and goosebumps were covering my whole body. I had to hold on to something in order not to fall on my knees. I could not speak. My strength was gone and my body was shaken. All of a sudden, I started saying prayers of gratefulness and praise. If I could wash myself with the tears I wept, they could've covered all of my body.

I lifted my head up feeling like I became a new person. I felt as if my sight was glowing with the image of the pure Kaaba. My ears started sensing the sounds of everyone else around me saying their prayers loudly. My heart was flickering as if it will fly out of my ribcage from joy and happiness.

I approached the Kaaba very slowly out of fear and awe of Allah's majesty. When I reached the Black Stone, I kissed it right away. My prayers preceded my tears as I walked around it with my bowed head. I felt shy around Allah. I roamed around and my emotions of fear and hope, love and affection, respect and honor, and desire and awe wandered around with me.[1]

This reads like a combination of kama muta and *awe*. In the same blog, on 2 February 2011 a "Student of Jurisprudence" posted:

> The first time I visited was when I was 13 years old. There were fancy lightings that were nicely organized all around to reflect on the Kaaba in unity. With all this glory, I felt goosebumps around my body. I was shaking to the greatness and majesty of the place. My tears were frozen.

On the same date, "Harvest of Paradise" wrote,

> The first time I saw the Kaaba, I had the most magnificent feelings. My heart was beating fast and all my emotions got mixed up with thankfulness, happiness, fear, timidness, and longing. My tears were flowing out of my eyes and I felt strangely relieved after. I forgot everything about life and let it all go behind me.

Waleed Samih Abd-Alal, wrote in an 11 November 2010 blog,

> Can you believe you're watching the Kaaba ... ?
>
> Chilling goose-bumps, awed hearts, eyes overflown with tears, and those with delicate hearts cry intensely once they see the Kaaba ... you go speechless, and you find yourself unconsciously floating around this ancient glorious structure.
>
> You fill your eyes up with the sight of the Kaaba like a person who has longed for his loved one for a long time, and once you saw him, you were reassured that his beauty remained the same, untouched by the dust of the days and years that have passed by. ...
>
> You want to stare at it well. . to close your eyes and try to imagine these invaluable moments of faith. . the moment Prophet Abraham was building it. . these sincere universal moments to which the land, mountains, trees and rocks shake and the hearts tremble. . these emotions felt by Prophet Abraham when he was lifting the first building blocks to establish this sacred architecture, when his heart was filled with love, honor, loyalty and gratitude towards Allah. . the moment he was weeping while his son was helping him.
>
> When I saw the Kaaba, my body was shivering, my heart was shaking, my eyes were flooding with tears, I was weeping, and words were stuck in my throat, unable to come out. [double ellipses in original].[2]

These self-reports are doubtless influenced by social desirability, but nonetheless they suggest that when pilgrims arrive at the Ka'ba, while many feel *awe* from the sudden intensification of their relationship with the immense grandeur of Allah iconically materialized in the massive Ka'ba, many also feel kama muta from their suddenly intensified feeling of union with Allah, and perhaps sometimes with fellow hajji.

What do the tens of millions of Hindu Kumbha Mela pilgrims feel when they bathe together in one of the sacred rivers? I predict they often experience kama muta motes, not least because immersion in the holy waters is an act of consubstantiation: the body is in total contact with the divinity. But I have not yet located accounts of Hindu pilgrims' experiences, nor have I yet found reports from Buddhist pilgrims. As I noted in Chapter 12,

> The Pali account of Buddha's death in 'The Discourse on the Great Decease' (Mahāparinibbāna Sutta) mentions four places that a person should 'see and be moved by' (*dassanīyāni samvejanīyāni*): the place where Buddha was born, the place where he attained enlightenment, the place where he delivered his first sermon, and the place where he passed away.
>
> *(Eckel 2005:116)*

So, they theoretically should be, but <u>are</u> Buddhists typically *samvejanīyāni* when they arrive at these holy sites?

Pilgrimage cries out for participant observation ethnographic study. A key question is whether, where kama muta is salient at the culmination of pilgrimage, it is an important <u>goal</u> of pilgrimage. Do reports of kama muta experiences motivate new pilgrims? Do imaginative hopes of kama muta with a loving deity lead people to attempt pilgrimage? In short, is the quest for kama muta a motivational cause of pilgrimage?

Notes

1 http://www.mediumd.com/forum/archive/index.php/t-2654.html. This quotation and the following ones are translations from the Arabic by Mariam Bakheet, who located the blogs; she was blind to our kama muta theory. Ellipses in the Abd-Alal post are in the original. Note that in this and other experiences, pilgrims may have motes of kama muta along with motes of the sudden intensification of authority ranking relationships; see Chapter 19.

2 http://www.alukah.net/spotlight/0/27272/#ixzz3nknh3PHN.

15

MILLENNIA OF MEANINGS OF CHRISTIAN TEARS

Up until now, exploring the cultural drivers and other circumstances of kama muta, I have been focusing on what it is that activates the kama muta psype, asking 'What makes people feel kama muta motes?' In the rest of the book I will continue to explore the domain (input) of the kama muta psype function, surveying the myriad cultural drivers of kama muta. But henceforth I will also be examining the range (image, output) of the function, asking 'What is the significance of feeling or performing kama muta motes – what do the motes mean in various cultures and contexts?' As far as the sources permit, I will consider the motives that emerge from kama muta. And beyond motives, I will consider the consequences of kama muta motes, their impact. A great place to start is by tracing 1700 years of meanings ascribed to Christian kama muta weeping in the eastern and northern Mediterranean, Western Europe, Britain, and North America. Tears usually are the most visible sign of kama muta – they are more apparent to observers than warm feelings in the chest, goosebumps, changes in breathing, buoyancy, or exhilaration. The visibility of tears, and perhaps their effect on the weeper's vision, makes the weeper especially self-conscious about them.[1] Together, these reciprocal facets of the salience of tears make them specially likely to be endowed with cultural significance as signs of devotion and commitment. This social sign potential is reinforced by the fact that tears are bodily excretions, yet they do not evoke disgust. As substances from the body, tears are effective media of consubstantial assimilation: they can form bodily connections that link people socially. Finally, tears are not just readily understood as signs of kama muta – tears also tend to <u>evoke</u> compassionate kama muta in the perceiver who sees tears as an index of vulnerability and need. In Chapter 2 I posited that tears are a plea for love – for compassion and caretaking. Tears mean 'I need you, take care of me, comfort me.' Indeed, we can reasonably posit that <u>crying is an attempt to evoke kama muta</u> in receptive perceivers. This is consistent with what we have now seen in Islam and Vaishnavism, when tears are, in part, appeals for divine love. If tears are not only symptoms of kama muta motes, but also tend to elicit kama muta in sympathetic perceivers, that makes them doubly interesting.

Many infant birds and mammals utter distress calls that function to elicit care, feeding, or protection from mothers, and in a few species, from fathers too, and in still fewer species, from siblings or other kin as well. Human infants likewise cry for kin care. Secretions from mammalian tear ducts lubricate and clean the eyes, but so far as is known, only humans also shed tears to appeal for care; apparently all human infants do so. In humans, crying and tears are closely associated. Working with these biological proclivities, cultures have evolved practices, narratives, and arts of tears and weeping. These crying constructions are often strongly evaluated: prescribed or proscribed, and judged according to age, gender, race, sanity, health, social class, and context. Moreover, cultures provide paradigms and precepts for attributing meaning to tears and weeping; there are ready heuristics for making inferences about the crying person and the dynamics of her social relationships. Because the roots of tears and crying are in universal human psychobiology, they offer a clear-cut framework for studying how culture builds on the psychobiology of the kama muta psype, and how this changes though history.[2] In short, tears and crying show how, and to what extent, the sensations and signs of kama muta are endowed with cultural meaning and serve as the material for crafting cultural constructions of all sorts.

To begin with, I will treat moist eyes, tears, crying, sobbing, and weeping as simply different degrees of the same sensation and sign, encompassing all of them under the rubric "tears." In this chapter, our focus is on how cultures endow tears with cultural meanings and how these meanings transform over time. People understand tears to be indices or performances of 'emotion' and of vital social relationships, so tears can be endowed with deep moral significance. We will see in this chapter that tears may be regarded as indices of weakness, lack or loss of self-control, irrationality, and femininity; or, conversely, as indices of sophisticated, cultured, masculine sensibility. Tears may attest to patriotic political allegiance, or to warm, sincere friendship. Tears may be understood as attestations of true religious devotion and commitment, and/or as gifts from God, and hence as manifestations God's favor. In some contexts, weeping has been construed not only as a communicative <u>sign of</u> devotion to certain communal sharing relationships, but to some degree weeping <u>constitutes</u> those communal sharing relationships in which it is expected: those who weep are thereby united with God, as well as with the congregation and with the community of tradition – those who have wept and those who will weep. On the other hand, in many contexts in some eras in some cultures, for children or adults of one or both genders, tears have been regarded as indices of pitiable immaturity, contemptible ill-breeding, deplorable weakness, lamentable and shameful lack of self-control, irrational sentimentality, or soft feminine fragility. I will explore all of these variants of meaning in the Christian context in this chapter. For many more details of the history of the meanings of kama muta tears in European art, politics, and personal relationships, see Online Note 2.5.

Communal sharing is the core of New Testament Christianity. The Christian ideal is a loving union with Jesus and communion among all Christians; in this chapter we will see that when this happens suddenly, Christians may experience kama muta. Roman Catholics also may experience kama muta when they attend to the suffering, loss, commitment, and encompassing love of the Virgin Mary, or of saints. Much of the available evidence consists of theological texts representing paragons, prototypes, precedents, precepts, paradigms – the preos that specified how, why, why, and with whom Christians should experience kama muta motes. In the background of these theological preo texts, we can sometimes discern ideal models of the drivers that are supposed to evoke Christian kama muta. Also, we can assume that there is some sort of dialectical interplay between preos and the actual motes. Hence while third-person, and even first-person, accounts of kama muta motes operate as preos for the successors who hear or read about them, I assume that they are also often memories of actual experiences. Of course, memories are constructed using sociocultural schema consisting of preos, but one root of such memories is the sensations of the actual experience. So while we look at drivers and preos over the millennia, we can also make some qualified inferences about actual Christian kama muta motes, not just the cultural prototypes for them.

The Christian fathers of the first centuries after Jesus articulated the idea of tears as an index of the desire for CS with God, manifested in *penthos* (repentance, mourning for sin).

> The Greek terms πένθος [*penthos*], κατάνυξις (*compunction*), πόθος (*yearning*), and λύπη (*grief*) are all relevant here, and it soon becomes evident that their meanings overlap. Grief for sin may be variously described as mourning, weeping, compunction, or remorse. What unites these expressions is that each is speaking of a heartfelt sorrow, expressed by actual tears, or a desire to weep, which is generated by and expressive of the mystery of divine participation. Such grief is never despair, self-pity, or mourning for human losses. … It is the purified passion experienced by the penitent who, through the pricking of conscience, accepts his or her need to repent, in order to be restored to God. … Living out [*penthos*] enables him or her to participate in the sufferings of Christ; it restores the penitent to kinship with the Father.
>
> *(Hunt 2004:3)*

That is, to be restored to oneness with God, the worshipper had to sincerely regret his or her sins, and that regret was itself an important step toward union with God. One corollary of this was that beginning in the fourth century, "crying became an officially recognized form of worship" (Elkins 2001:152).

The 'compunctive' tears of moral remorse that devout Christians shed in worship were more true than their verbal prayers.

> Your tears are not your own: they always belonged to God, and the only way to show Him that you love Him is to let Him release His tears so that they can go back to Him. … Compunctive tears are a bittersweet flood, mingling joy and grief, desire, repentance, penance, devotion, love, and hope.
>
> *(Elkins 2001:152)*

Shedding tears as consubstantial assimilation to enhance the CS relationship with God is notable, since tears were the sole manifestation of the body positively regarded by the church (Nagy 2000:416).

Sixth century writers continued to consider tears to be an index of God's grace and indeed to be a crucial mediator of the worshipper's relationship with God (McEntire 1990). Around 591 CE, Pope Gregory I (Saint Gregory the Great) wrote that one must go beyond fear of damnation.

> Once we envision the choirs of angels, and fix our gaze on the endless vision of God, the thought of having no part in these joys makes us weep more bitterly than the fear of hell and the prospect of eternal misery did before. Thus the compunction of fear, when perfect, leads the soul to the compunction of love.
>
> *(Gregory, Book III of the* Dialogi, *translated and*
> *quoted by McEntire 1990:50–51)*

The unspeakable joy of love between worshipper and God cannot be concealed; it expresses itself in tears, Gregory wrote in the *Moralia* (XXIV, vi, 10; translated and quoted by McEntire 1990:51). Tears of spiritual joy, Gregory wrote, come from the longing for God, in contrast to the tears of spiritual sadness at regret for past sins (Nagy 2004:125). Interestingly, church doctrine explicitly recognized and approved of the desire to share kama muta with others and the converse tendency toward third-party kama muta experiences when observing others' kama muta: medieval theologians recognized that the "weeping spiritual seeker could give the gift of tears to another" (Nagy 2004:127).

Saint John Climacus (Klimakos) of Mt Sinai, writing around 600 CE, wrote that tears of godly sorrow produce not only joy, even spiritual laughter (Hunt 2004:86–88), but "By open repentance the soul is broken and refined; it is brought to a certain unity, I will even say a commingling with God, by means of the water of genuine sorrow." (Step 25, 6, 989D, translation by Moore 1959: 84). He wrote that penitent mourning erodes the self, enabling the weeper who grieves for his sins and thereby loses his sense of self to "become incorporated into the earthly community of the monastery, and the pneumatic community of Christ and his saints" in the intimacy of divine love (Hunt 2004:236).

In Syria in the seventh century or earlier, Isaac of Nineveh wrote of torrents of tears as an especially genuine form of prayer, replacing verbal prayer when the worshipper reached a stage of ecstatic incorporation (Hunt 2004:140). Joyful, sweet, warm tears may be evoked "'from a fervent love of God which inflames the soul,' and then the worshipper 'cannot endure (any longer) without weeping continually as a result of its sweetness and delight'" (*Second Part*, XVIII, 5; translation from Brock 1995:67, quoted by Hunter 2004:143). Isaac also wrote that these joyful higher order tears are accompanied by a sensation of gentle warmth (in the center of the chest, perhaps?) (*Book of Grace* 4, 21, cited by Hunter 2004:156).

Hagiographies from the sixth through the eighth centuries emphasizing the spirituality of tears were mostly limited to tales about monastic Carolingians, while the tears of other saints were mentioned simply as habitual characteristics of no great significance (Nagy 2000). But by the late ninth century, tears came to be regarded as crucial evidence of the grace and sanctity of any saint. And then, as a consequence, worshipful weeping increasingly came to be <u>prescribed</u> for all. Shedding tears of consubstantial assimilation to God became a prototype and precedent for how to constitute the Christian's relationship with Him. Symeon the New Theologian, a Byzantine writing in the late tenth to early eleventh centuries, declared that tears index the presence of God within the worshipper, constituting a second baptism, so Symeon enjoined that one should never receive communion without weeping (Hunter 2004:202, 215, 240).[3] Symeon wrote that the essential truth of Christianity "depended on direct, personal experiences of incorporation with God," evinced by tears (Hunter 2004:219). "From the beginning of the Middle Ages, religious weeping during the celebration of the Mass contributed to a priest's honor and was seen as a sign of his devotion," though it was never obligatory (Nagy 2004:127). In the European High Middle Ages, consequently, it was common for bishops to weep when they said mass, and priests cried during their private prayers as well (Dixon 2015:22). Similarly, the eighteenth century Revolutionary French people construed tears as the true sign of personal friendship and of patriotic commitment to the new, collectively constituted nation; see Online Note 2.5. One of the most remarkable instances occurred in 1792. Each member of the Legislative Assembly placed his hands on the new Constitution of France and swore allegiance to it. "According to Robespierre, many of them wept tears over it and covered it with kisses" (Vincent-Buffault 1986:85). Conversely, when Rousseau and Diderot had a falling-out in 1757, they each complained that the other no longer shed tears over their friendship – their letters arrived completely dry (Vincent-Buffault 1986:25–27).

Climacus, Isaac, Symeon, and other early theologians posited that weeping for sin transforms the human being "through incorporation into the Body and Church of Christ." Weeping transforms the embodied person by "uniting it beyond its anthropological divisions, and mirroring in its unity the divine unity of the Godhead and creation itself" such that the weeper achieves *theosis* – coming into union with God (Hunt 2004:241). Similarly, writing in Normandy in the early eleventh century, Italian-born John of Fécamp felt his tears to be the medium of his CS relationship with God and proof of it.

> Sweet Christ, good Jesus, as I desire, as I seek with my whole mind, give me your holy and sacred love, that it may replenish me, keep me, and possess me. And give me a visible sign of your love, a wet fountain of continually flowing tears, that these very tears also may clearly proclaim your love to me and that they may say how much my soul loves you since because of too much sweetness of your love, my soul cannot keep itself from tears. … Give me, I beg, internal tears from the whole of my interior affections, which might loosen the chains of my sins, and might always replenish my soul with heavenly delight. … I ask you, good Jesus, for these your most precious tears, and through your compassion … give me the pleasantness of tears, which my soul desires and hungers so much for, because if you do not give it, I am unable to have it, except through your Holy Spirit who softens hearts which are hard from sins, and punctures to tears. Give me the gift of tears, just as you have given it to our fathers whose footsteps I ought to follow in, that I may lament all my life just as they lamented both night and day. … Therefore, give me the gift of tears, blessed and beloved God, because of the sweetness of your love, and the remembrance of your mercies, prepare this table for your servant in your sight.
>
> *(Fécamp,* Patrologia Latina *158:892–894, translated and quoted by McEntire 1990:54)*

This passage shows that some theologians, at least, treated tears as sustenance, an essential substance that is given and shared like a commensal meal. Likewise, in the late twelfth century, Guigo II (of Chartreuse, in southeastern France) wrote about how joyfully sweet it is to experience God, describing tears as honey and milk from the breast of God given to the worshipper's soul to drink, and as the bread which sustains the worshipper day and night (McEntire 1990:72). Feeding and commensalism are characteristic media of consubstantial assimilation (Fiske 2004b).

Weeping was not limited to church services. Many late Medieval paintings depicted compunctive weeping, and by the later Middle Ages art also came to focus on the depiction of the crucified Jesus, Mary (often weeping), or saints being martyred. Looking at these images often made people weep, on occasion moving viewers to the point of collapse (Elkins 2001). From time to time up to the present day, images or sculptures of Mary have shed liquid (usually bloody) tears seen as miraculous demonstrations of Mary's love and loss, and her profound connection with Jesus; such tears presumably evoke especially strong kama muta in perceivers, probably often together with *sorrow, awe,* and even *pride* that it is 'our' Mary who is blessed with these miraculous tears.

Sermons in the English Lambeth Homilies (written around 1200 CE, partly from earlier sources) focus more on penitent tears; one sermon distinguished penitent tears from tears wept for the sins of fellow Christians or tears from loathing of the world, commending the most sacred tears as those expressing longing for heaven, connecting the weeper with the Holy Ghost (McEntire 1990:122). Tears of longing for heaven lead to salvation – the soul's eternal union with God. And, says a thirteenth century text, tears touch God, moving him to grant our prayers (McEntire 1990:126). In thirteenth century hagiography, tales of women "almost incapacitated through floods of tears" from meditating on the Passion of Christ were a legitimating index of their being recipients of God's grace. "The tears that spilled out from the eyes signified the spiritual fulfillment of contact with the ineffable. This union with God was an ultimate and prized connection, giving a foretaste of heaven on earth" (Knight 2012:136–137). God's Gift of Tears was visible "proof that union had been achieved" (Knight 2012:139).

Around the thirteenth century, the English church, in particular, gradually assumed authority over these compunctive tears, so that the priest became the judge of whether tears truly expressed penitential contrition (McEntire 1990:164ff.). By the thirteenth century in continental Europe as well, tears became routinized, and hence generally ceased to be crucial evidence of grace (Nagy 2000). Fourteenth century English texts shift to describing and prescribing tears as expressions of loving compassion for Jesus's suffering on the cross. However, shedding such tears can be transformed from mere expression of compassion to an act of identifying with Christ's tears upon the cross and gratitude for his merciful sacrifice for the sins of men – and, moreover, such tears simultaneously become a sign of God's grace (McEntire 1990:126–147). Tears also cleanse, purifying the weeping worshipper (McEntire 1990:144). In some southern European traditions, participants' tears were necessary to safeguard the community (see Online Note 15.1).

It is notable that along with endless floods of tears at the mystical experience of union with God, some English, Italian, and other saints are reported to have felt an intense but agreeable burning sensation in the chest (Cohen 1996). Likewise, the early fourteenth century English mystic Richard Rolle of Hampole, describing his own experience as *Incendium Amoris* (The Fire of Love), wrote:

> I was more astonished than I can put into words when, for the first time, I felt my heart glow hot and burn. I experienced the burning not in my imagination but in reality, as if it were being done by a physical fire. I was really amazed by the way the burning heat boiled up in my soul and (because I had never before experienced this abundance), by the unprecedented comfort it brought. In fact, I frequently felt my chest to see if this burning might have some external cause.
>
> *(Cohen 1996:447, quoting Deanesly's [1981:93]*
> *quotation of Rolle)*

Contemporary European Roman Catholicism is less weepy than it has been at times in the past, but people still sometimes weep or get goosebumps at mass, especially when taking the Eucharist (for a sample of self-reports, see Fulwiler's 2007 blog). Consuming the body and blood of Christ is quintessential consubstantial assimilation, making the bodies of Christ and worshipper one, and hence making their persons one in CS. For the person who feels that drinking Christ's blood and ingesting his body make them corporeally one with Christ, the Eucharist is a sudden intensification of CS.

We cannot identify with certainty the emotion that is described and prescribed in such texts, but evidently tears were regarded as a reliable index of the sudden intensification of CS with God, and conversely, such tears moved God to love the weepers. These tears were said to move others. Tears are a bodily substance that God gave to worshippers, who shed them for God, thus linking them through consubstantial assimilation. So it looks as though worshippers often experienced kama muta, and were admonished to feel it. This does not exclude their feeling other emotions toward God, such as *sadness* or *horror* at the suffering of Jesus on the cross, or sadness at the separation between living humans on earth and God in heaven. Probably many Christians sometimes felt fearful *awe*, *guilt*, and *shame*. But the texts emphasize tears that index sudden love of God, tears that were at the same time an appeal for God's love and a gift from God.

In sum, the argument is this: strong kama muta usually produces tears. Syrian and European Christians recognized tears as the primary symptom of kama muta evoked by love for God, distinguished these kama muta tears from others, and interpreted such compunctive tears as the sign of repentance for the separation from God that followed sin. Partly through this inference, it seems, weeping in a person's relationship with God came to be seen as evidence demonstrating the avidity and validity of the weeper's love for God. Increasingly, however, early Christian writers also began to interpret kama muta tears as a gift from God to the weeper: they were a sign of God's grace. From that meaning developed the prescription that one *should* shed kama muta tears in prayer or when taking communion – beyond words or other actions, tears themselves came to be the most genuine, heartfelt medium of loving union with God. Tears indicated love in both directions. As a bodily substance, tears that were at once of and from God, shed though the body of the worshipper, make God and worshipper one being in CS. But eventually this emphasis on and valuation of tears receded, especially in Northern Europe and in conjunction with the initial shift to the Protestant doctrinal emphasis on belief as the essence of religion.

In Scotland and then in North America in the eighteenth and early nineteenth centuries, evangelical Presbyterians and Methodists held revival camp meetings that evidently evoked intense kama muta motes in participants. Online Note 15.2 describes the sometimes ecstatic kama muta in that emerged in this evangelical collective worship. At these revivals, weeping eyes and melting hearts were everywhere; whole assemblies wept together (Schmidt 2001:119, 138, 158, 212). One of the most famous British Methodist preachers, George Whitefield, was especially known for sermons that made his audiences weep – and made him weep, too, so that he had to pause until he got his voice back (implying that he was choked up; Dixon 2015:73). Attending the communions in 1742 near Cambuslang, Scotland, Catherine Cameron, an educated daughter of a gentleman, wept and trembled at the thought of Christ's sacrificial suffering:

> The whole communion occasion represented so much to her that she was moved to the gate of heaven, to the edge of final transcendence. Having met with Christ in this love feast, she longed for the dissolution of her body and for final union with her beloved [Christ].
>
> *(Schmidt 2001:120–121)*

Sermons captured another sensation of kama muta: they "spoke of Christ's love warming the heart as the wine warmed the stomach" (Schmidt 2001:197). Indeed, in 1738 it was a warm feeling in the center of the chest that affirmed to John Wesley that he was saved. He was listening to a reading of Luther's preface to the Epistle to the Romans about how faith leads to salvation.

> About a quarter before nine, while he was describing the change which God works in the heart through faith in Christ, I felt my heart strangely warmed. I felt I did trust in Christ, Christ alone, for salvation; and an assurance was given me that he had taken away my sins, even mine, and saved me from the law of sin and death. I began to pray with all my might for those who had in a more especial manner despitefully used me and persecuted me. I then testified openly to all there what I now first felt in my heart.
>
> *(Wesley Center Online)*

"Wesley interpreted faith as a sensible experience" and reverently preached this to his many followers (Dryer 1983:20). This heartwarming direct experience of divine love was so important that Methodists have celebrated it for 280 years as Aldersgate Day. Note that the Mormons later also adopted this sensation, which they call *burning in the bosom*, as the unmistakable sensation of divine love.

In America, the precedential prototype of revival was the Cane Ridge sacrament of 1801. This collective communion is now recognized as the start of the Second Great Awakening. Thomas Cleland reported his experience at Cane Ridge, enthralled by a text from the Song of Songs:

> My heart was melted! my bosom heaved! my eyes, for the first time, were a fountain of tears. I wept till my handkerchief was saturated with my tears.
>
> *(Schmidt 2001:169)*

Especially given the salience in Methodism of Wesley's report of his experience, it is plausible to interpret these reports of 'melting hearts' as references to warm feelings in the center of the chest. In any case, what struck contemporary observers in both Scotland and America was not just the tears, but the participants' "shaking, leaping, dancing, jerking the head backward or forward and from side to side, twitching, swooning, and rhapsodic bodies" (Schmidt 2001:xviii). Participants rolled on the ground, moved about on all fours barking and growling, ran, laughed, and sang (xx, xxiv). Then many fainted or collapsed and lay still on the ground for minutes or hours. Some went into trance-like states, heard voices, or saw visions (2001:145). In some participants some of these behaviors sometimes continued for some time after the four-day meetings. Many participants reported a feeling of awakening, release, relief, renewal, and revival afterwards (2001:154), which corresponds to the buoyant exhilaration characteristic of strong kama muta. "For many the refreshening lasted a great while, perhaps carrying the pilgrim through until the next sacramental occasion," invigorating the participant for weeks or months, though generally "the infusion of grace that the sacramental season offered was far from inexhaustible. ... The effect of the sacramental season on these evangelicals, even when intense and satisfying, often wore off quickly" (Schmidt 2001:155). Revivals evolved into evangelical preaching at mass venues and giant churches, where worshippers continued to have kama muta motes, which probably motivated attendance and strengthened religious commitment. Kama muta at revivals often involved extreme ecstatic movement, often followed by torpor. It is intriguing to consider how the psype combines with specific cultural precedents and prototypes to generate ecstatic movements and torpor. Online Note 15.3 offers some accounts of this remarkable sequence at revivals.

For centuries the most prominent sensation-sign of kama muta was tears, but then in early modern Northern Europe, the tears dried up for a few centuries. Then in the Great Awakenings of Europe and North America (c. 1731–1755, c. 1790–1840, c. 1850–1900, and c. 1960–1980), worshippers joined in collective emotional revival gatherings, which consisted in part of tears and warm hearts, along with new ecstatic enactments and exhilarated invigoration, according to new preos. The drivers were dramatic preaching and mass commensal communion at camp meetings. Thus in Western Christianity over the centuries there has been a cycle consisting of movement towards individual or collective exhilarating kama muta experiences and then back toward less emotional, routinized, more textual, oral, and belief-oriented, more private and sedate worship. Alongside these cycles were some steadily spreading ecstatic worship movements. Beginning in the nineteenth century, the Holiness movement, and then the twentieth century Pentecostal movement, continuously steadily spread this passionate, exhilarating form of worship, especially among poor rural US Southerners – its essence and its "'greatest joy' being that of spiritual communion with God" (Griffith 1998:220).

In addition to and in between worship gatherings, otherwise isolated women in these religious milieux increasingly connected in print, likely evoking each other's kama muta with their letters (see Online Note 15.4).

Contemporary Christianity

Intense experiences of divine love are common in the United States today. Lee, Poloma, and Post (2013) commissioned a 2009 random telephone sample of 1208 US respondents. When asked "How often do you feel God's love for you directly?," 14% selected "most days," 36% "every day," and 9% "more than once a day." Other US surveys have yielded similar results (Lee, Poloma, & Post 2013:252). Responding to three items about experiences where they felt "everything seemingly disappears except the consciousness of God," "the unmistakable presence of God during prayer," and any experience of "the unmistakable presence of God," 89% reported that they had had such an experience at least once (Lee, Poloma, & Post 2013:118). Moreover, 25% reported "the unmistakable presence of God" most days, every day, or several times each day. Interpreting these results we should keep in mind that Lee, Poloma, and Post's survey had a response rate of 36%. It seems likely that religiosity affected willingness to respond to the survey, in which case these figures are overestimates. Also, respondents may have felt a demand to answer affirmatively to these questions to please the researchers, or wished to respond affirmatively in order to present themselves in a socially desirable light. But even with these caveats, it appears that Americans often have experiences of divine love that seem likely to involve kama muta motes.

In Pentecostal, charismatic, and other new paradigm churches today, the sudden experience of union with divinity, and conversion experiences in particular, are called *coming to Jesus*, being *touched by the Spirit*, being *possessed by the Holy Spirit*, or being *baptized in the Spirit*. Being *born again* denotes many of these experiences. Churches aiming to foster intense, joyful, intimate personal relationships with God are growing rapidly. Tanya Luhrmann describes their worship.

> The congregant prays. He closes his eyes, and he yearns for God. His songs of worship, whether in home fellowship accompanied by a guitar or led by a rock band in a weekend service, are simple lyrics of love and longing. In either, he sings for perhaps half an hour, swaying back and forth, eyes shut, hands held up, palms outward, his face content or sometimes wet with tears. These are meant to be moments of prayerful ecstasy.
>
> *(Luhrmann 2004:147)*

Although Luhrmann's description here is accurate for each churchgoer, it ignores the communal nature of the worship, with worshippers singing, swaying, gesturing, and weeping *together*. She captures the interaction among congregants somewhat more clearly in her account of one Chicago church:

> Each Sunday-morning service began with 30 minutes of prayerful singing described by the church as 'worship,' and every service ended in a call for people 'who need prayer' to come up front to get prayer. Indeed, there was

a 'prayer team' chosen by and trained within the church, and as the service drew to a close one saw 20–30 people up at the front of the room, their hands on each other's shoulders, with those who were praying speaking aloud and those who were being prayed for standing with tears running down their face.

(Luhrmann, Nussbaum, & Thisted 2010:69)

What Luhrmann is describing seem to be culturally informed, institutionally scripted, and highly valued kama muta motes that are evidently the goal and the peak experience of worshipers. Worshippers suddenly feeling divine love would be likely to have some of the signs of kama muta motes even without any cultural prototype, paradigm, or precept, but the culture of these churches perhaps facilitates these signs, certainly draws attention to them, and endows them with definite meaning.

The Vineyard network of churches is one of the largest systems in this movement. "In a church like the Vineyard, Christians are supposed to experience themselves as unconditionally loved"; the experience of this God-given feeling is the "heart" (Luhrmann 2012:101, 107). Congregants learn to experience this feeling through a number of unnamed practices, including "crying in the presence of God" (Luhrmann 2012:111). In the church Luhrmann studied,

They cried a lot. People cried when other people prayed out loud over them. When people went up for prayer at the end of church, someone from the prayer team would stand by them, take a look at their face, and as often as not go over in a businesslike way to tug a tissue out of the box on the amplifier and then walk the congregant over to the side as the band picked up again. People cried at the sermons. They cried in house group. The pastors would sometimes cry as they stood before the congregation. At one conference I attended, four men spoke, one after the other, and every last one of them wept by the time he was done. Crying when people prayed over you was so common that not to cry turned you into a social category. 'You know,' someone would say, 'the kind of person who never cries when you pray for them.' If people didn't cry when others prayed for them, it became something they had to explain. ...

And as people cried as others prayed over them, those who were praying aloud were asking God to make them feel safe, loved, and protected—wrapped in his arms, soothed by his embrace, washed by his forgiveness. I came to think of these events as prayer 'huddles': one person in the center usually crying and in distress; the rest of the group crowded around with their hands on the person or (if they could not reach) their hands on the people who were touching the person in the center, as if the physical connection carried a supernatural connection. (Many of them believed it did.)

(Luhrmann 2012:112)

Luhrmann notes that people also cry when they feel saved, even though they don't know why they are crying. This prototypical Holy Spirt experience also involves a feeling sometimes described as a feeling of electricity on your body (Luhrmann 2012:146), which is probably the thrills/chills/goosebumps feeling of kama muta. And then they feel the post-kama muta buoyancy:

> They also talk about feeling light and free ... [A male informant describes it:] 'It just felt like every single thing I had piled on top of me was gone. What I'd said—"Yes, I accept Christ my Lord and Savior"—it didn't mean a ton to me. But I felt that a million pounds on me were gone, just after I said it.'
>
> *(Luhrmann 2012:144)*

This informant reported that on a later occasion, at the end of the experience when he first truly felt God's presence, he "felt absolutely weightless" (Luhrmann 2012:145).

Choral hymns may evoke kama muta most among the singers or with the listeners. Consider the signs of kama muta in this account of a Ghanaian church and its televised worship.

> Charismatic churches ... share an emphasis on experience and, in particular, on the sense of being touched by the Holy Spirit, as crucial to the conversion process. The touch of God through the Spirit makes a fundamental change in a born-again Christian's life. This experience is commonly expressed in terms of tactile sensation, of feeling. ... On a video tape showing a miracle healing service, the popular miracle preacher Dag Heward-Mills, for instance, preaches: 'I see the healing of the Lord moving into your body right now. Some of you may feel it like a warm passing through. Or something you feel, but you don't know what it is.' Testimonies captured on this video include people describing their experiences to the audience as feeling heaviness, heat or coldness in particular parts of the body or as 'just feeling something.' Other frequent descriptions include the feeling of electricity running through the body or having goose pimples. ... Much of religious performance is literally tactile. Laying on of hands, applying anointing oil to various parts of the body, falling to the floor, clapping, stamping, going down on one's knees, holding hands among the congregation.
>
> *(De Witte 2011:495–496)*

Charismatic and Pentecostal worship is often characterized by worshippers' participatory action, performing mutually resonant recursive kama muta motes. Online Note 15.5 describes an occasion where this evidently occurs in a church in Accra, Ghana.

Attending a service at a charismatic Christian church, I was unsure of what to expect. I was brought by a friend who offered to help me with my research. Although I am not religious myself, I still feel very open to spirituality and think that it is a wonderful thing for many. However, I wasn't ever able to feel that myself. At the end of the sermon the pastor asked us to bow our heads and pray with him for anyone who felt it was time to recommit and come home to Jesus. All of our eyes were closed while soft music played. I found myself wanting someone to come home to Jesus and feel the deep love that the sermon had emphasized—though I wasn't certain *why* I felt this way. No one came forward, but as we lifted our heads the pastor announced that there was one family who had scheduled a baptism. A young mother climbed into the small white pool and prayed aloud, telling God that she was ready to commit to Him and that she wanted the rest, repentance, and quiet that only He could give to her. Holding their infant daughter her husband stood beside her, trying to hold back his tears. When she said that she was ready to accept Jesus into her heart, her husband softly jumped up and down with teary eyes. The pastor, praying, submerged her, and as she arose he loudly said 'raised to walk in the newness of LIFE!' I was lost in those moments, totally focused and absorbed. I had chills from her prayer because she seemed like she was *so* genuinely ready for that love. I found myself smiling and when I turned to my friend, I saw that she was beaming, with tears streaming down her face. I looked around and many people seemed moved by this woman's plunge into the newness of life. I couldn't help the tears that were ready to spring from my own eyes and a light happiness in my heart.

(Autumn McGrath)

Outside of churches *per se*, religious social movements and autobiographical books foster similar kama muta motes in union with divinity. Likewise, religious movements such as Aglow International promote worship practices characterized by joyful tears, hugs, and kisses (described in Online Note 15.6).

Interviewing 27 participants in a white, middle-class Pentecostal church in Western New York State about their worship experiences, Inbody (2015) found that 21 (and he himself, as well) reported religious experiences in which they felt goosebumps, tingles, or similar sensations. All 27 had experienced what Ingold calls "emotional energy" on some occasions when participating in the energetic congregational singing that is accompanied by a loud band with heavy percussion. Ingold doesn't specify how he identified reports of emotional energy, except that it is "felt" and "bodily"; perhaps in some instances it corresponds to our participants' reports of exhilaration. Inbody specifically asked whether people had experienced tingling, and posed his question about goosebumps with reference to the pastor's reporting that "some people say that when God speaks to them, they get goosebumps." On at least some occasions in church worship, nine informants reported feeling emotional energy as tingling (6), goosebumps (4), shivers (1), or heat (3). In private religious experiences, 12 reported somatic experiences: goosebumps (10), tingling (3), chills (2), or heat (1). In response to other questions, participants mentioned feeling "peace that persisted through stressful circumstances" (14), joy (12), comfort (10), love of the Father (9), feeling a connection (5), or sensing "power" (4). A number of participants interpreted these sensations as "sensing God's presence," as God "speaking" to them, or as feeling "anointed by the Holy Spirit". They sometimes made the interpretation that this church explicitly taught – that these sensations indexed God's coming to support them when "summoned by the participants responding to trying circumstances through engaging in a purposeful activity (e.g., fervently reading the Bible)" (Inbody 2015:346). But many, including two pastors, also expressed skepticism about whether these sensations resulted from God's presence rather than something in the mundane context.

Kama muta is also manifest among Jehovah's Witnesses, often when reading alone.

> Jehovah's Witnesses treasure God's Word, the Bible, and highly value an accurate, clear translation. … The branch office in Russia has been receiving many letters of appreciation for the complete Russian edition of the New World Translation. 'Although I have read the Bible many times,' wrote one woman, 'reading this translation is like reading the Bible for the first time! Sometimes my eyes fill with tears and a shiver of excitement runs down my spine as the Bible's message touches my heart.'
>
> (2009 Yearbook of Jehovah's Witnesses:12)[4]

Kama muta apparently is also central to the Church of Jesus Christ of Latter-day Saints, but their primary focus is not tears, but the heat they feel in the chest. Mormons report that they experience religious revelation – a communication from the Spirit – as a "burning in the bosom." Burning in the bosom is "a feeling of comfort and serenity. That is the witness many receive. That is the way revelation works" (Oaks 1997). Indeed, Mormons cite the experience of "a burning in the bosom" as the basis of their faith, scripturally based on *Doctrine and Covenants* sections 8–9, where Joseph Smith says

> But, behold, I say unto you, that you must study it out in your mind; then you must ask me if it be right, and if it is right I will cause that your bosom shall burn within you; therefore, you shall feel that it is right. But if it be not right you shall have no such feelings.

Many Mormons connect this with Luke 24:32, in which, after the crucifixion, two women speak to a man, walk and eat with him, and then suddenly recognize him as the resurrected Jesus. After he disappears, "They asked each other, 'Were not our hearts burning [*kaio*] within us while he talked with us on the road and opened the Scriptures to us?'"

Mormons also recognize crying and choking up as manifestations of "being touched by" the Holy Spirit. And they report goosebumps or chills when they are touched by the Spirit – when they feel the Holy Ghost. The blog "Holy Ghost/Burning in the Bosom"[5] reports "the goosebumps and tearfulness I experience when someone speaks in a testimony meeting," and tells of

> a young Chinese investigator who asked the missionaries teaching her, 'Why do I feel cold every time I read the Book of Mormon? Every time I even touch this book, I feel cold, and I don't understand that.' I promise you that no missionary had taught this girl to expect a cold feeling in association with the Book of Mormon. This is not part of our language of the Spirit at all. It was only with patient listening that they could discern that this cold feeling she was struggling to describe in English was not negative in any way for her, but rather the feeling we might describe as goosebumps, a concept they had never discussed and for which they had no mutual vocabulary.

Another Mormon blogger, a young Hmong woman, writes

> I always had good feelings when I read the book and the feelings came as goosebumps that made me have the chicken skin. I remember one particular moment when the missionaries taught me about the prophet Joseph Smith (who I've never heard of) and I felt a sudden rush of goosebumps throughout my whole body as they shared with me the story of Joseph Smith. I didn't just feel the goosebumps once but twice! We all feel the Holy Ghost differently. This is the Spirit to me.[6]

In short, while Mormon doctrine acknowledges tears and goosebumps or chills as legitimate signs of the presence of the Holy Ghost in a person, following Joseph Smith's revelatory precept, "burning in the bosom" is the prototype for the experience, based on the precedent of Luke's gospel and on Joseph Smith's precept. Unlike weeping among early and medieval Christians, the warm feeling is simply valid evidence, not a channel that mediates the CS connection with God. And unlike tears, a burning bosom is not visible to others, so while the sensation legitimates for the individual the inference that the Spirit is present, others must rely on that individual's testimony that s/he was touched by the Spirit. However, burning in the bosom is more than a sign of the Spirit; it is proof of the truth of Smith's revelations as recorded in the *Doctrine and Covenants*. Moreover, the sensation does not merely communicate this fact, proving the truth of his revelations and his status as prophet, and signaling the fact of the experiencer's own union with God, it is <u>constitutive</u> of those relationships. Burning in the bosom <u>is</u> God's love, corporally known. A Mormon friend tells us that kama muta is also common in the congregation when people witness.

Some churches recognize chills as the focal validating sign of divine union – in conjunction with practices related to breathing. In Brazil, participating in Padre Marcelo Rossi's Catholic Charismatic Renewal services in person, on television, or on the radio, thousands of worshippers engage in rhythmic synchronous breathing, mediated by fingering their ten-bead Byzantine rosaries and coordinated with the singing of Padre Marcelo (de Abreu 2008). As they breathe in and out in time to the sound of Padre Marcelo's voice, they mentally repeat alternating prayers. Recorded on hit CDs and played on his popular radio station, many of his songs have the strong dancing beat of techno music. In his live services in São Paulo, Padre Marcelo directs what he calls the "aerobics of Jesus":

> he shouts, 'now,' 'sing it,' 'up! up!' 'beautiful,' 'don't stop,' 'ah!' 'shake it up,' he directs the entire choreography of breath. To the extent that Catholic Charismatics describe the Holy Spirit according to the notion of *pneuma*, the Greek word for 'lungs,' 'air,' or 'breath,' Padre Marcelo operates as a kind of angel who both embodies and organizes among his followers the cosmic exhalations of the Spirit. He does not really sing. He either reads or simply initiates the sentences so as to help recall the lyrics. Like a coach, he often blows a whistle in order to mark the rhythms of both sound and movement. There are moments when the gentle swaying and waving, up-and-down movements of the multitude visually resonates with the very breathing dynamics that are being vocally emitted. When this occurs, their movements resemble the wind blowing through the thick canopy of a forest. …
>
> As adherents improve their ability to use their voice and control their breath in prayer, they experience feelings of intense love and joy.
>
> *(de Abreu 2008:68)*

Then the worshippers feel the goosebumps that index for them the presence of the Spirit, they weep, and they tremble. And then they are doused.

> When, because of the tears and sweat, temperature rises in the sanctuary, Padre Marcelo opens the sanctuary's sprinklers. As the thin stream of water pours down, a cooling mist arises, mimicking the ecology of the rainforest itself. When temperatures get even hotter, Padre Marcelo takes five buckets of water and splashes them over his followers, while in praise they go on branching their arms. Quakes and tremors ensue. By quaking and shivering, the divine's overwhelming presence disperses across the skin.
>
> *(de Abreu 2008:72)*

In these practices, Padre Marcelo directly induces what may correspond to the kama muta sensation of deep and paused breathing, together with the experience of pneumatic motor synchrony. And then he directly induces chills by using sprinklers and dousing with buckets of water. Do these manipulations of kama muta sensations evoke kama muta through the mechanism of classical Pavlovian conditioning?

* * * * * *

The various forms of passionate or ecstatic collective Christian and Muslim religious kama muta share some basic features. In general, observing others' kama muta often evokes kama muta in the participant observer. Furthermore, the kama muta that is evoked by intensification of their CS relationship with God is greatly enhanced by *collectively* experiencing that relationship with the deity, and the kama muta evoked by it: each participant's sense of their own union with the deity is amplified by resonance with the others' manifestations of this sense of union. Seeing others weeping or exhibiting other vocal and bodily signs of kama muta, each participant's mirrored feelings are modeled, reassured, bolstered, validated, legitimated. Moreover, when each participant senses that her personal kama muta experience with the deity is shared with all of the others – that they are experiencing this same profound connection with the deity – this commonality in turn quickly bonds the participants in a new, renewed, or intensified group CS relationship, evoking an often enthralling second-order kama muta in and among them.

In Chapter 5 I noted American and British judges' reports that when a defendant is convicted of homicide and then forgiven by the family of his victim, the defendant often cries in apparent kama muta. For Christians, a defining feature of God is that He is ready to forgive all sinners if they acknowledge their sinfulness, repent, accept His love, and commit to obeying him. Being forgiven by a limitlessly loving God is likely to evoke kama muta. One institution where this may frequently occur is in the confessional, when the priest officially expresses God's unconditional love for the sinner. People often go to confession because they perceive themselves to have committed a sin that separates them from God, so that their contrition, confession, and absolution removes this barrier, restoring their relationship to God (Kettunen 2002:18, 23). Guilty secrets isolate a person: "The possession of secrets acts like a psychic poison that alienates their possessor from the community" (Jung 1954:55, quoted in Todd 1985:43). Until a person confesses his guilt, "an impenetrable wall shuts him off from the vital feeling that he is a man among other men" (Jung 1954:58, quoted in Todd 1985:43). Jung wrote, "The tremendous feeling of relief which usually follows a confession can be ascribed to the readmission of the lost sheep into the human community. His moral isolation and seclusion, which were so difficult to bear, cease" (Jung 1961:192, quoted in Todd 1985:42).[7] The moment a person confesses, feels absolved, and experiences this renewed and reaffirmed CS relationship with a loving God, they may feel kama muta. In the 1880s, Norwegian Protestant theologian Knud Krog-Tonning, ministering to a prison workhouse, adopted the practice of hearing confession and pronouncing absolution. He later reported what he observed when he gave absolution: "I remember eyes that radiantly met mine through tears of joy, and hands stretched out in fervent thanks for such an act" (Krog-Tonning 1906, cited in translation by Berggren 1975:13).

One priest portrays the ideal confession:

> Those who visualize confession in colors, and with sympathy, see a sinner, broken and despondent, entering a Catholic Sanctuary with faltering steps to unburthen his soul to a wise and kindly priest, who is vowed to secrecy and eager to bestow the balm of encouragement. They find much beauty and pathos and holiness in the scene. The priest, his face averted, listens with solicitude. The sinner, with bowed head, reveals the troubles of his anguished heart and finds hope and comfort in so doing. Presently the priest raises his hand to bestow absolution, and tears of joy fill the penitent's eyes. He feels an inexpressible lightness of heart, and goes forth to face life with new courage. His step is firm as he leaves the church, and he murmurs to himself, 'That man was a saint, God bless him.'
>
> *(Barrett 1928:188–189)*

On the basis of his extensive experience on both sides of the confessional, Barrett goes on to show in how many ways this cultural folk epitome is far from everyday reality. But even if Barrett was, and is, correct – and even though in many parts of the world, contemporary Catholics don't often go to confession – it is still interesting to observe that kama muta is a keystone of the *ideal* of confession, even to those who don't go, or who do go, but typically experience it differently.

Overall, what we see when we look at the big picture is that in many eras Christians have noted that when they suddenly feel one with God they weep, feel warmth in the chest, and, in recent accounts, get goosebumps or chills. Moreover, Christians often have adopted these indexical signs and sensations as performatively constitutive of love for God and God's love for the worshippers: true communion. To weep, get goosebumps, or feel warmth in the chest is to be one with God: if a person has these sensations in the context of religiously oriented or framed practices, then God loves them and they love God. These indexically constitutive signs are the sensations of love, and the proof of it. They validate the truth, the reality, the personal immediacy of union with divinity. These sensations are aspects of consubstantial assimilation, the conformation system of CS between humans and God: they are a primary medium of cognizing, communicating, constituting, and conducting CS. At the same time these sensations are an essential conduit for cultural reproduction and diffusion of CS religion, because they are the preos through which people discern the cultural implementations of CS in the domain of relationships with God. That is, at any given time in history in any given community, any of these signs of kama muta may be the medium through which, by observation and imitation, people learn to be religious. Observing and imitatively participating in weeping, chills, and warm hearts, people in practice become Christian.

Over the centuries of Christianity, the salience and value of emotionally mediated CS relationships with God have waxed and waned repeatedly. When they waned, they were largely supplanted by less evocative ritual performances, or, later, by doctrinally mediated belief; subsequently these in turn have been displaced again by kama muta-mediated relationships with God. I have no explanation to propose for these historical dynamics (they aren't regular enough to call them cycles), though an explanation of some sort would likely draw on updated psychosocial versions of Max Weber's concepts of tradition, charisma, and routinization (Weber 1978 [1922]). When CS relationships have been the crux of Christianity, I also cannot say why certain kama muta sensations emerge to be more salient, more elaborated, and more valued in certain eras and traditions, but less so in other periods or places. Tears are the sign of kama muta that is most visible to others, and perhaps in some sense more tangible to the person herself, so they afford cultural elaboration, and have been the index of Christian devotion and grace for much of its two millennia. But on the other hand, tears alone do not distinguish between kama muta, sorrow, loss, regret, pain, and fear; so it is not entirely obvious why they would be adopted and elaborated to the extent they often have been. In Chapter 12 I noted the salience of goosebumps in South Asian texts representing sudden intensification of CS relationships with divinities. I cannot account for these apparent differences in the religious representations of kama muta. In any case, when reading texts or self-reports, the absence or rarity of mention of a sensation does not imply the absence or rarity of that sensation in the experience being reported. So I don't know yet whether experiences of kama muta are more uniform than the texts that represent them.

However, I would expect that the cultural significance of a sensation should substantially affect a person's sensitivity to any sensation, their attention to it, their memory of it, and their disposition to report it – not to mention the more or less conscious intention to construct the experience or confabulate it. Sensitivity to a valued kama muta sensation in oneself, abetted by observation and others' reports and praise, may enable a person to practice and learn to feel a particular sensation. If your peers and those whom you admire put their hands to their heart and utter a high-pitched 'Awww' when they see kittens, you are likely to imitate them, which may affect your experience of kittens, and even of yourself as a person who adores kittens. If the paragons, prototypes, precedents, and precepts in your community represent tears as the index of truly loving God and of God's gift of grace to the tearful worshipper, that is likely to facilitate your shedding tears, and/or inform your interpretation of your own tears. In short, cultural preos may affect the person's construction of their emotional experience.

There is a particularly striking facet of the question of how the innate social biopsychology of the kama muta psype enables and more or less constrains the cultural evolution of the performance of its sensations and signs: how do people generate extreme kama muta behaviors? At moments when CS with divinity suddenly intensifies, along with the 'standard' signs and sensations of kama muta,

Sufi texts and contemporary reports of responses to *qawwal* musical engagement in Pakistan and India report trembling, ecstatic movement, shouting, and making non-linguistic sounds (Qureshi 1995:60, Frembegen 2009:172–173). These signs, sometimes followed by fainting or torpor, were reported in Methodist revivals, and occur in contemporary Pentecostal and charismatic worship (see Online note 15.3). But we have not observed any of these signs in response to our experimental stimuli, or in diary self-reports from Norwegian students. Is this because responses to our experimental stimuli and events represented in our small experience-samples do not include extremely strong kama muta? I can only speculate on how and with what degree of cultural flexibility extreme kama muta is linked to hyperactive gesticulation and locomotion, loud non-linguistic vocalization, and subsequent quiescence or unconsciousness. I imagine that these actions are especially potentiated by exceptionally intense kama muta. But I imagine that the performance of these extreme actions, like its other sensations and signs, is substantially informed by cultural precedents, prototypes, precepts, or paradigms.

Further exploration will likely reveal kama muta-evoking practices in Cabalistic and Hasidic Judaism, Sikhism, strains of Vedanta and Tantric Hinduism, Taoism, and/or in Confucian ancestor worship. Online Note 15.7 considers some reasons to expect kama muta in Hasidic or Cabalistic Judaism and other religions.

* * * * *

Among the many thousands of variant religions that humans have constructed, only a few have persisted for many hundreds of years or spread across the world: the most enduring and widespread are Hinduism, Buddhism, Christianity, and Islam. The great majority of contemporary humans are engaged to a greater or lesser degree in one or more strands of these religions. (If we add environmentalism, we encompass even more of the human population.) Why? What is it that makes people so much more likely to participate in, recruit others to join, and reproduce these religions so much more than the innumerable others that have sprung up over the millennia? There must be multiple factors involved, which only the most extensive and fine-grained ethnographies and experiments could establish. But in the preceding chapters I have explored one thing that is characteristic and perhaps rather distinctive of these world religions – something that makes people pay attention to them, attracts people to participate, motivates recruitment of others to participate, draws people to participate together with their close associates, and moves people to re-enact their experiences in these religions. Kama muta. The occasional experience of kama muta seems to motivate much of the enduring devotion and commitment to at least these and probably some other religions. So perhaps the affordance of kama muta is largely responsible for the cultural selection that has made these particular religions have such an enormous sociocultural advantage over all the myriad other religions of the earth which only rarely or weakly evoke kama muta. I will generalize this observation in Chapter 17.

Online notes

15.1 Religious weeping to protect the community.
15.2 Kama muta in evangelical collective worship.
15.3 Fervent worship and torpor.
15.4 Kama muta letters to denominational publications.
15.5 Worshipful participatory action in Ghana.
15.6 Worshipful tears, hugs, and kisses.
15.7 Kama muta in Hasidic or Cabalistic Judaism and other religions.

Notes

1 They also make tears attractive, amenable topics for academic study, so there is far more research and writing on tears than on any of the other sensations and signs of kama muta. This made tears a natural path for us to pursue in our own ethnological and historical search for cases of kama muta. The history of the meanings of tears in Europe is particularly well attested, but we have numerous ethnographic accounts to draw on as well.

2 These dispositions are universal, but not uniform. Virtually all human infants shed tears and cry. But from birth, and progressively more thereafter, individuals greatly vary in their disposition to do so, and in what situations evoke tears or cries. Doubtless there are variations among populations, as well.

3 Evidently communion can indeed evoke kama muta in some contemporary Christians. Describing Maltese Catholics, Mitchell (1997:90) reports that "Many informants said that they felt a tingling sensation, or feeling of warmth, as they ingested the Host and internalized Christ." At confirmation, too, Maltese reported experiencing "a kind of shock, or tingling, that emanated from the Archbishop's hand and filtered down into their whole body. They would never forget it" (Mitchell 1997:86).

4 From Watchtower Online Library: http://wol.jw.org/en/wol/d/r1/lp-e/302009016#p59. *The Doctrine and Covenants of The Church of Jesus Christ of Latter-day Saints Containing Revelations Given to Joseph Smith, the Prophet, with Some Additions by his Successors in the Presidency of the Church*, 1981. Salt Lake City, UT: Intellectual Reserve.

5 http://en.fairmormon.org/Holy_Ghost/Burning_in_the_bosom.

6 http://www.mormon.org/me/80kt.

7 Jung said this also occurs in psychotherapy, where the patient's disclosures create a "moral bond" that is a crucial aspect of the transference relationship. We read examples of this in Chapter 5. As we indicated, sometimes – perhaps typically – something like this also occurs in addiction recovery groups such as Alcoholics Anonymous.

16

THE LOCUS OF KAMA MUTA IN RELIGION

While I do not need, wish, or know how to formulate a general theory of religion, it will situate what I am proposing about religion if I map where in religion kama muta does and does not tend to occur. As a useful heuristic for present purposes, we can analytically distinguish among five strands of religion (ignoring for our purposes its arts, artefacts, and architecture). First, some strands of religions comprise belief in doctrine, such that religion comprises declarative allegiance to a set of propositions. This strand consists of explicit semantic conceptions. While supported by texts and other physical artifacts, along with social practices, the mnemonic form of this corresponds to the declarative (explicit) semantic memory system (on memory systems from a cognitive science perspective, see Schacter & Tulving 1994; Squire & Knowlton 1995). The essence of this strand is the study of texts, especially those conveying the will of the deities, and/or the declaration, 'I believe ... .' Kama muta motes may occur here, but not often.

A second strand of religion consists of cosmological narratives that account for the origins and nature of the world. These stories explain how people, animals and plants, geological features, social relationships, and society come into being, and what will eventually happen to them. The origins and fates of humans are almost always explained in terms of social relational dynamics – as moral processes. This strand corresponds to the second declarative mnemonic system, episodic memory (Schacter & Tulving 1994; Squire & Knowlton 1995). Cosmology rarely evokes kama muta motes.

A third core of religious thought and practice nearly everywhere consists of concepts and practices concerning the moral meaning of misfortune, suffering, and death: ways of answering the question when things go wrong, 'Who did what wrong?' This question motivates engagement in practices such as divination, consultation with oracles, or invoking spirits to possess someone so as to explain who is at fault, what they have done wrong, and what needs to be done to rectify the wrong. Misfortune, suffering, and death may be construed as indices of human transgression of social relationships with immaterial beings such as elves or fairies, ancestors, ghosts, spirits, sentient places such as springs or mountains, or powerful deities. Bad things also may be interpreted as morally imminent sanctions for violation of taboos. Or the bad things that happen to people may be blamed on the wrongdoing of witches or sorcerers who are attacking the more or less innocent victim. Having attributed blame, the diviner, oracle, or spirit (speaking through a medium) then prescribes a ritual or offering to redress the disrupted relationship. Motes of *outrage* and *fear* are common responses to misfortune, but kama muta is not. However, the experience of suffering <u>together</u>, with mutual compassion, support, and identification, can evoke strong kama muta.

A fourth strand of religion is the precise and timely performance of ritual practices, together with rigid avoidance of commission of any tabooed actions. Adherence to the rituals, and avoidance of transgressing any taboos, are regarded as essential for fostering well-being, subsistence, and for avoiding misfortune. Collective rituals may be primarily or entirely construed as perpetuating a traditional practice as such, replicating what has been done before and hence reproducing the participants' communal identity. But many ritual practices are also intended to constitute social relationships with immaterial beings. The mental aspect of this corresponds to the implicit (non–declarative) mnemonic system called procedural memory (Mauss' "techniques du corps" and "habitus," Merleau-Ponty's "praktognosia," Ryles' "knowing how."). And there is a facet of anxiety here, as well. Kama muta often occurs when people perform rituals together, or when a person feels that she is enacting a ritual as her ancestors or identity group always have.

The fifth strand is engagement in social relationships with immaterial or other special beings: forming, committing to, sustaining, enhancing, renewing, and redressing felt relationships. People relate to high gods, ancestors, and less exalted deities, saints, spirits, totems, elves, and such. People also engage in relationships with supernaturally acting human beings such as living gurus and charismatics, witches, or sorcerers, and to immaterial social aspects of the earth, mountains, rivers, springs, oceans, trees, and other landscape features. Although relationships with deities, ancestors, and other immaterial beings are often the most salient aspects of religion, researchers have generally paid little attention to the social relationships as such. Researchers have generally aimed at explaining 'belief in' supernatural beings and the features that people attribute to such beings (see especially Guthrie 1995; Boyer 2001). But people's concepts of the characteristics of supernatural beings are often vague, inconsistent, and rather peripheral to their primary concerns about <u>relating</u> to the beings. Social emotion motes frequently occur in relationships with immaterial beings and the deceased.

Pilgrimage is a vital practice in relationships with religious beings in many religions. As we saw in the preceding chapter, at the culmination of pilgrimage, kama muta motes are common when CS relationships suddenly intensify with those beings and among the pilgrims.

These are the five principle cognitive and behavioral strands that collectively characterize religion as religion. In any given religious community at any point in history – and in any individual at any moment – these five strands vary greatly in their relative elaboration and valuation, in how loosely or closely intertwined they are, and in the manner in which they are intertwined. Although religions differ and shift over time in their emphasis (cf. Whitehouse 2004), in general semantically formulated doctrine and prayer, performative ritual, and avoidant taboos, misfortune interpretation, cosmology, and relations with supernatural being are more or less integrated.

Within the fifth strand, relationships with immaterial beings, four fundamental types of relationships occur: communal sharing, authority ranking, equality matching, and market pricing (Fiske 1991, 1992, 2004a). CS and authority ranking relationships are the most prevalent and important in religion. In authority ranking, humans respect and may obey beings who guide and protect them. In CS, humans seek a loving communal sharing mode of mutual love or even merging with a divinity. As we've observed, such CS relationships are particularly characteristic of certain prominent traditions in the world religions, including Marian, Charismatic, and Pentecostal Christianity; Muslim Sufism, and Shia Muharram commemoration; Hindu Vaishnavism; Buddhism; Jainism; and, it seems, Hassidic and Kabalistic Judaism. People may also have equality matching and market pricing relationships, for example, with fairies, elves, and the like. There may be distinctive emotions that occur respectively when each of four fundamental types of relationships suddenly intensify with an immaterial or material being. But for sure, when the CS relationship with an immaterial being suddenly intensifies, people feel kama muta. That is a key place that kama muta occupies in religion.

Kama muta also occurs within the fourth strand, ritual and taboo. Performing religious rituals enacts the participants' corporate identity; by participating in the ritual, participants collectively constitute themselves as 'we who perform these rituals' – and identify with deities. Rituals intensify CS through its conformation system, consubstantial assimilation: making people feel that their bodies and therefore, indexically, their social selves are one. People create this corporeally mediated sense of social unity by moving in rhythmic synchrony together, singing or chanting in unison, wearing the same identity-marking clothes or accoutrements, eating or drinking commensal communion, and gentle touch.[1] Also, when ritual participation revives participants' emotional memories of past family or congregational CS, they may have nostalgic kama muta motes: when a child is baptized or confirmed, when people are married in church, or singing holiday hymns, for example. To a greater or lesser degree, simply gathering and worshipping together, in any manner, whether highly predictable and strictly structured or not, may evoke some kama muta in some participants sometimes.

And of course it is not only <u>religious</u> rituals that evoke kama muta. Participation in mass events of all sorts can evoke solidarity and collective identity: being among fans at a sports event, participating in a demonstration, parading on a national day (Neville & Reicher 2011; Páez & Rimé 2014). It appears that this CS is generated by the kama muta – Páez and Rimé call it "emotional communion" – that these events evoke: "in collective emotional experiences, an attunement with the group develops from which shared emotions and identity fusion emerge" (Páez & Rimé 2014:206). Based on field studies of natural events and one naturalistic experiment, Páez and Rimé (2014:215) conclude that,

> Globally, evidence supports Durkheim's ideas that emotional communion is at the heart of social rituals. Collective gatherings reinforce affects, social integration, and social beliefs, and these effects are stronger in participants experiencing higher emotional communion and fusion of identity with the group.

(For experimental studies on related emotional sources of spirituality and belief in the benevolence of others, see Van Cappellen et al. 2013.)

Taking a large view of the concept of 'ritual' appropriate for present purposes, intensification of CS may also occur through singing of chanting in unison, as in a chorus, Sufi *dikr*, or Shi'a *muharram*, or from other aspects of collective worship practices.

As I mentioned, kama muta motes sometimes occur in the framework of the third strand, moral attributions about misfortune, suffering, and death. When bad things happen, people tend to think that someone (not necessarily the unfortunate persons) must have done something bad. To find a legitimate attribution about who did what wrong, people in most cultures consult a diviner or oracle; use a spirit medium to consult their deceased family members, ancestors, local spirits, or various deities; assert that the suffering is due to karma from a past life; anticipate that the innocent sufferer will enjoy a perfect existence in heaven and the evil perpetrator will suffer eternal agony in hell; or try to come to terms with the idea that God has acted morally, but the moral meaning of the suffering is ineffable. These attributions do not intensify any CS relationship, so they do not evoke kama muta. However, the feeling of suffering <u>together</u> sometimes evokes kama muta (see Chapters 5 and 9 and Online Note 13.1). Moreover, Christians often feel kama muta when they attend to their belief that Jesus died for their sins and that those who follow Him will be welcomed into heaven, rather than being eternally damned, as they otherwise deserve for their sins. Many Christians believe that people are punished in this life for their sins, but such punishments are averted or ended when they avow their love and faith in Jesus; sudden appreciation of divine forgiveness certainly affords kama muta.

Perhaps in a somewhat similar manner, some Buddhists may welcome suffering when they appreciate that suffering helps them appreciate that life is suffering, which can only be transcended when one dissolves the self in the ultimate unity of all. I don't know whether Buddhists experience kama muta at this realization. In Yap, though not construed as specifically religious, suffering connects people as an index of the work the sufferers have done to care for others (Throop 2010). Likewise, as presented in Chapter 9, the encounter with war memorials or participation in ceremonies dedicated to those who have suffered and died for the survivors often evokes kama muta. So sometimes, in various ways, addressing the moral meanings of suffering does lead to the sudden intensification of some CS relationships with immaterial beings.

Many traditional local religions involve spirit possession, spirit mediumship, or shamanism (Connor, Asch, & Asch 1986; Bourgignon 2008; Lewis 2003). In these religious practices an ancestor, deceased family member, local spirit, deity, or other immaterial being (hereafter, 'spirit') takes over the central person, who then speaks or acts as that spirit. Often, there is a sort of dissociation in which the possessed person afterwards does not recall what she said or did. In many cases possession, mediumship, or shamanism are oriented to healing the person who is taken over. In these and other cases, through the medium or shaman the spirit may reveal the moral responsibility for a misfortune, suffering, or death, or reveal whether it is propitious to build a house in a particular location, marry a particular person, depart on a journey, carry out a ritual, or engage in a particular project. The spirit may indicate that in order to redress transgressions or moral failures, the spirit himself or other supernatural beings need to be propitiated with specific offerings or sacrifices at certain places on certain days. Or the possessed person may need to dedicate herself to the possessing spirit. In all of these practices, the agency and sometimes voice of the shaman, medium, or possessed person is subjectively replaced by the agency or voice of the possessing spirit. Despite the superposition of the spirit, ghost, or deity on the possessed person, our impression from ethnographies and videos is that generally the medium does not experience her relationship with the being that possesses her as a CS relationship. Most often, it seems that the spirit is the master, taking over and controlling the possessed person, medium, or shaman; it is an authority ranking relationship. Occasionally the spirit is not a superior being but something more like a peer to humans, and the relationship between spirit and possessed person, medium, or shaman seems to be akin to an equality matching or even market pricing relationship in which humans and possessing beings give and get, quid pro quo. But the ethnographies and theories of these religious practices have tended to focus on the morphology of the behaviors and on cognitive aspects, including subjective perspectives and verity of belief; other approaches have compared these practices to schizophrenia and dissociative identity disorder.

At present, all I can say is that I do not know of any evidence for kama muta motes occurring in these forms of spirit-possession religion – with one exception. When a spirit medium is possessed by the spirit of a deceased loved one, the sudden felt presence of the loved one may evoke kama muta in the family consulting the medium (Connor, Asch, & Asch 1986). In some cultures, probably, kama muta is especially likely when the deceased communicates vulnerability and dependence on her living family, telling them she needs them to perform certain rituals to take care of her, or make offerings to feed her. Or when she simply communicates love and longing.

Figure 16.1 represents this analysis of how kama muta is situated in religion. Of course, the figure is intended to capture the predominant patterns of kama muta's loci in religion, so it schematically simplifies, leaving out various nuances and complexities. Online Note 16.1 goes into some of the details and subtleties of the religious contexts of kama muta.

Collective effervescence in communal sharing with immaterial beings and fellow worshippers

Like most psychological processes, the workings of the kama muta psype are not directly accessible to consciousness; people don't necessarily know how the psype works, and sometimes don't even know what has triggered it. Phenomenologically, this means that a person (or set of persons) may experience kama muta motes without consciously knowing why. And concordantly, they may misunderstand why they experience a mote, for example, using an incorrect folk-psychological theory. Often it is easy to reflectively recognize and to linguistically articulate what happened to evoke the emotion, but that inferential process occurs 'outside' of the psype function itself. So it is possible to make provenance errors, attributing the emotional experience to a CS partner, relationship, or act of intensification other than those which actually evoked it. In any case, it is interesting to speculate on the functions of kama muta-mediated devotion and commitment to immaterial beings. Online Note 16.2 explores some of the facets of CS relationships with culturally constituted immaterial beings.

Thus it happens that people don't know why they are crying, why they are choked-up, why they have goosebumps, or why they have warm feelings in the chest; they may not be able to make sense of wanting to hug someone or call their grandmother. On the other hand, there may be familiar cultural prototypes, precedents, paradigms, and precepts for the sensations and lexical labels that do indicate when one should experience it, why one experiences it, and more generally what the experience means. These preos guide the attributions that people make in interpreting the experience, including the inferences they make about what CS relationship has intensified, and what intensified it. Likewise, the preos orient the resultant devotion and commitment to the culturally appropriate CS relationships.

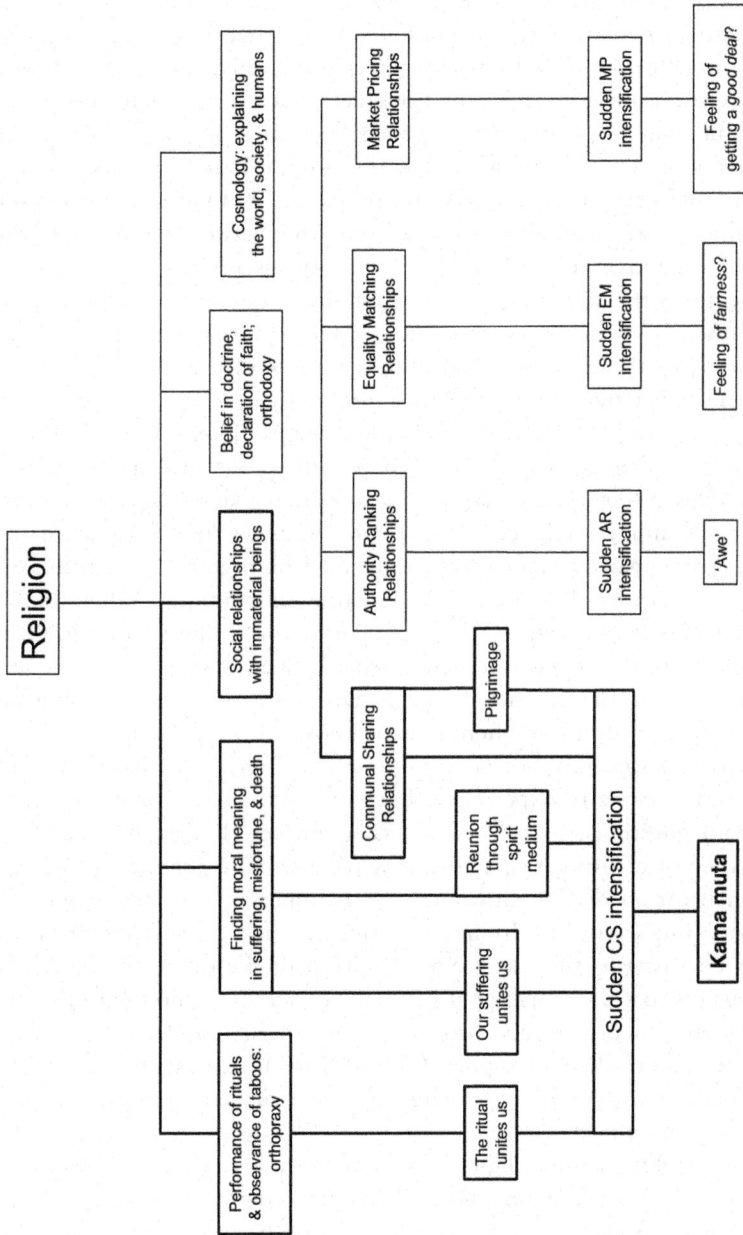

FIGURE 16.1 The principal contexts of kama muta in religion.

In important respects, this conceptualization of culturally enabled and informed kama muta motes is an updating, based on contemporary cognitive science, of Emile Durkheim's (1912) theory of religion. Although nominally eschewing psychological explanation, Durkheim posited that participation in religious rituals evokes "collective effervescence" that bonds participants into a social unit. Durkheim did not characterize the sensations of this emotion, and indeed did not report any direct observations as grounds for his theories. But the unexplained term "effervescence" sounds a bit like goosebumps or chills, or bubbly feelings in the chest.[2] Durkheim based his theory on (and repeatedly illustrates it with details from) Spencer and Gillen's ethnographies of Australian aboriginal cultures. Drawing on these ethnographies, Durkheim posits that collective effervescence results from assembling in one place and participating in the same actions and thoughts together – in annual gatherings, at funerals, or in responses to threatened or actual community danger. Participating in these driver rites, people transcend their separate selves so that they feel that they merge together into a larger whole that encompasses them in something beyond their individual selves. This super-excites them, makes their sensations exceptionally vivid, and re-energizes people for their everyday lives. Effervescence affords extraordinary action such as culturally approved self-injury, violence, or sexual license; at exceptional moments, it stimulates participants to take revolutionary action together. Collective effervescence is a feeling of being enveloped in an ineffable transcendent immortal whole that people perceive as a deity, but is actually the society itself. (See Online Note 16.3 for reasons to believe that collective effervescence refers to kama muta motes.) In intriguing respects, Durkheim is positing the emotional equivalent of the cognitive phenomenon known as source-memory error in which a person sincerely but falsely 'remembers' an event that they did not directly and personally experience, but construct in imagination based on inputs from questions, narratives, or other sources (Loftus 1980, 2015). An emotional error of this sort may occur when a worshipper experiencing sudden intensification of CS with fellow worshippers misattributes her consequent kama muta mote to divine love. But this may be infrequent. What is certainly pervasive is that the (re)presentation of the deity, the deity's love, and the means that the worshipper may take to achieve union with the divinity all depend on precedents, prototypes, paradigms, and precepts that the culture provides to the worshipper. Online Note 16.4 presents the case that it is the kama muta psype that generates the solidarity emerging from engagement in certain rituals.

It is not straightforward to align a century-old sociological concept based on secondary analysis with a contemporary psychological construct based on an integration of focused ethnographies, interviews, diary studies, experiments, and extensive ethnological and historical comparison. But Durkheim posited that when people come together to perform religious rituals they feel a collective effervescence that generates social solidarity. That sounds like kama muta. It is the sudden experience of being part of the group, of belonging, of the shared mental state that he calls col-lective conscience in and of mechanical solidarity – the bond among people who feel they are equivalent. The kama muta psype is the mechanism that enables rituals to function to create, renew, and enhance social solidarity. Online Note 16.5 makes the case that it is precisely the kama muta psype that is the mechanism behind the social solidarity function of rituals.

Cultural selection of religious kama muta drivers

As I depicted in Figure 16.1, there is more to religion than kama muta drivers and motes, and unlike Durkheim, I do not propose that rites of collective effer-vescence – kama muta drivers – comprise the fundamental or original form of religion. I do not offer a general theory of religion. But I do propose a theory of how kama muta drivers are selected and shaped by cultural evolution. Many religious practices evoke kama muta, particularly practices whose aim is union with divinity but which simultaneously strengthen the CS bonds among the worshippers. The deep, intrinsically meaningful rapture of kama muta, as well as its milder forms, attracts people: people want to experience kama muta again and again. So people are drawn to whatever ritual practices, music, costumes, movements, arts, and architectures evoke kama muta; people vividly remember and eagerly create and re-enact them. Furthermore, people want to talk or sing or write about kama muta – it's a feeling that people like to tell others about, partly because telling about it re-evokes it, and partly because people want to give this beautiful feeling to others. All this attracts others, resulting in the diffusion of religious practices evoking kama muta. Moreover, feeling kama muta together, the kama muta resonates and reverberates. This further moti-vates people to recruit new participants – to proselytize. Feeling kama muta together often suddenly intensifies CS among those sharing the experience, creating kama muta anew. This recursion makes a congregation. Thus sudden CS solidarity evokes kama muta that generates enduring devotion and moral commitment to the CS relationship.

In this manner the naturally selected kama muta psype culturally selects for kama muta drivers: the psychological proclivity for kama muta catalyzes the cul-tural reproduction of religious systems that evoke kama muta. At the same time, but much more slowly, when these kama muta-evoked CS bonds, practices, and institutions enhance the reproductive success of the participants, natural selec-tion increases the prevalence and fervor of kama muta, along with the craving for it. Thus the fitness benefits of kama mute drivers becomes the cultural niche to which the psype (gradually) adapts by natural selection. Cultural selection for drivers is orders of magnitude faster than the genetic selection for which cultural selection is the adaptive environment. But in a co-evolutionary process that links the two levels, kama muta is both root and fruit of major strands of the world religions: it is probably the crucial emotional factor in the perdurance and wide diffusion of the few world religions (see Online Note 16.5).

The innate, biologically evolved psype is the niche to which many other drivers culturally adapt – religious kama muta drivers are not the only ones that occupy this niche. Chapter 17 presents the detailed dynamics of this cultural selection.

Online notes

16.1 Details and subtleties in religious contexts of kama muta.

16.2 CS relationships with culturally constituted immaterial beings.

16.3 The kama muta psype generates collective effervescence motes.

16.4 The kama muta psype is the mechanism behind the social solidarity function of rituals.

16.5 Why a few religions spread around the world.

Notes

1 This effect of synchronous action is not limited to religious contexts; see Brown 2013; Launay, Tarr, & Dunbar 2016; Rennung & Göritz 2016. Four year-olds who sing together act more prosocially: Kirschner & Tomasello 2010. See Fiske 2004b for an overview.

2 Durkheim's programmatic goal was to develop sociology as a paradigm in which properties and variation in the structures of society are explained in terms of other properties and variations of the social structures. He showed that phenomena such as national rates of suicide could be explained in this way. It is ironic that his theory of religion as the worship of the immortal society itself rests on the deduction that social solidarity ultimately depends on a social psychological process: the ritual evocation of collective effervescence – a motivating emotion. For recent thoughts and references on effervescence, see Nikolas 2001.

PART V
The big picture

17

PSYCHOLOGICAL, SOCIAL, CULTURAL, AND EVOLUTIONARY DYNAMICS OF KAMA MUTA

In this chapter I present a more detailed exposition of kama muta theory, generalizing what we observed about kama muta psypes, motes, and drivers. I will explicate more precisely the processes that I explored in Chapter 10 through which the natural selection of the psype, the cultural selection for diffusion of drivers, and the social relations of CS are all part of a more or less integrated system. In constant interaction, they shape each other, but on different time scales: CS relationships intensify in a moment; drivers reproduce and diffuse over hours and years; the cognitive neurobiology of the psype evolves over many generations. Together, the biology, psychology, and social processes integrally shape kama muta motes.

The drivers of kama muta culturally evolve as adaptations to the psychology of the psype, and indeed depend on the niche that the psype provides: the drivers only exist because the psype enables them to be noticed, remembered, and replicated. Conversely, the psychology of the kama muta psype has biologically evolved to respond to culturally propitious intensifications of culturally important CS relationships. And natural selection has formed the psype so that it functions to generate culturally apt motives to devote and commit in culturally efficacious manners to culturally implemented intensifications of CS. This cultural attunement is precisely what makes the psype so beneficial to fitness: in a great many respects the kama muta psype is functionally dependent on cultural preos. These precedents, prototypes, precepts, parameters, and paradigms indicate whether a CS relationship exists, when it suddenly intensifies, what sort of devotion and commitment are appropriate, and how to perform the mote. In the most basic situations such as holding one's newborn or reuniting with a loved one, the psype functions with only moderate reference to cultural drivers. But in many other contexts, the psype is deaf, blind, and mute without cultural preos to activate and orient it. In these respects, the psype is analogous to the human language capacity that enables each person to develop the capacity to speak a particular, culturally transmitted language. Like the language capacity, the kama muta psype has biologically evolved to function in conjunction with cultural preos – and functions primarily in response to them. Let's consider the details of these psychological, social relational, cultural evolutionary, and biological evolutionary processes.

The co-adaptation of the psype and its drivers

Kama muta responses to sudden increases in CS intensity evoke motivational commitment to CS relationships. These CS motives enhance biological fitness when participation in the CS relationships is beneficial. This is how the psychological processes that evoke kama muta – the psype – evolves by natural selection. However, the type of partners, types of circumstances, and types of CS relationships that contribute to survival and reproductive success vary greatly as a function of how a person's community and network implement CS, in conjunction with their behavioral ecology. It is not adaptive to commit to just any CS relationship with just anyone under any circumstance. Furthermore, acts that suddenly intensify CS in one culture may not do so in another. Likewise, motivation to devote and commit to CS relationships must be tailored to generate the kinds of acts that are effective, recognized, and appreciated in precisely this type of relationship in this community. It is maladaptive to over-commit to CS relationships that are particularly vulnerable to free-riding or defection. But conversely, it is also maladaptive to fail to make the most of opportunities to fully engage in CS relationships that are likely to be beneficial. Furthermore, one's own defection or free-riding on beneficial CS relationships is likely to lead to potentially deleterious punishment or exclusion from such relationships. This means that CS devotion and commitment must be modulated to be congruent with the expected consequences of over- or under-committing. (In statistical test terms, fitness is maximized when the costs of Type 1 errors match the cost of Type 2 errors, while reducing both as far as feasible. That is, natural selection should minimize and balance the costs of mistakenly perceiving a propitious CS opportunity when there is actually no good opportunity, on the one hand, and, on the other hand, failing to recognize a propitious CS opportunity that actually presents itself.) Natural selection favors variants of the psype that effectively discriminate between the intensifications of the specific CS relationships to which commitment in this culture has expected benefits and the intensification of the specific CS relationships to which commitment has expected costs. So natural selection will shape the psype to be discriminating, responding to culturally propitious inputs and mapping them onto culturally effective inputs, motivated to a culturally and contextually fitting degree.

Once such an innate psype begins to function, it provides psychosocial niches that select for the emergence and selection of cultural institutions, roles, practices, arts, and artifacts that utilize the psype to reproduce – kama muta drivers of the myriad sorts I have surveyed in this book. Some of these drivers may contribute to the biological fitness of the persons who respond to them, some may be fitness-neutral, and some may be deleterious to the biological fitness of their carriers. In ecological terms, as forms of symbiosis, these are, respectively, mutualistic, commensal, and parasitic kama muta drivers. Kama muta drivers evolve through cultural evolution that is orders of magnitude more rapid than genetic evolution, so parasitic drivers do emerge. However, in the long run, if the total net effect of all the kama muta drivers in a population is deleterious, variants of the psype that respond to such drivers will be deselected and disappear. Only if all the diverse drivers circulating in a population taken together have a net positive effect on biological survival and reproduction will a culturally sensitive kama muta psype be selected for and persist. Since presumably all of the existing drivers – mutualistic, commensal, and parasitic – compete with each other to occupy the niche(s) that the psype provides, it is not clear what competitive processes among drivers, if any, would result in a stable equilibrium of net positive impact on biological fitness.

However, there must be an arms race in which rapid cultural evolution of drivers easily keeps up with the slow biological natural selection of the psype, such that there are always drivers that are tuned and tailored to whatever psype is evolving. While some of these drivers will likely be mutualistic or commensal, some more recently emerged drivers will be parasites that decrease the biological fitness of their human hosts. However, parasites and hosts typically co-evolve to reduce virulence, because a living, active, relatively healthy host will generally spread far more parasites for far longer than a dead host. So there is some overlap in the adaptive 'interests' of parasites and hosts, both benefiting from the viability of the host, such that whatever equilibrium is reached, if any, should be at a point where the net biological fitness effect of all kama muta drivers is at least somewhat positive. A process of biological natural selection, albeit slow, should tend to make the psype 'immune' to drivers that are deleterious to biological fitness, and, conversely, make the psype especially responsive to drivers that are especially beneficial. That is, parasitism may evolve into commensalism and even mutualism. Likewise, drivers that enhance the biological fitness of the people 'infected' with them are thereby more likely to have more opportunities to diffuse and be transmitted to succeeding biological generations. But there is no reason to expect all kama muta drivers to have fitness benefits, in part because newly evolved kama muta drivers, like new pathogens, may not yet have co–evolved with the psype to reduce their virulence. And because there may be ways for drivers to reproduce culturally despite killing or sterilizing their human hosts.

Regardless of any temporary equilibrium that may emerge, the kama muta psype and driver always function as adaptive environments for each other, co-evolving to presuppose, depend on, and mesh each other in many respects. For a more precise and detailed graphical visualization of the systemic dynamics, see Online Note 17.1, which depicts the processes in a comprehensive series of diagrams.

The psype itself

Having mapped the entire system of psychology, social relations, cultural selection, and biological evolution, let us look at core of the system, the psype itself. The figures in the supplementary materials represent where the psype fits in the larger system, molded by evolutionary processes so as to respond to culturally propitious CS relationships. The figures show that the psype generates brief motes, which motivate more enduring CS devotion and commitment. But what actually goes on 'inside' the psype on any given occasion? We've noted many instances and described in general terms how the psype operates. Now let's put it under a microscope and observe what goes on in the fraction of a second after it recognizes the potential to intensify a CS relationship. After all the cases we've examined and our reflections on them, we can model the functioning of the psype quite precisely.

Figure 17.1 represents the psychological processes that comprise the psype, indicating the essential ones with solid lines, while other very common but not essential processes are drawn as dotted lines. Kama muta occurs when there is the potential to create, renew, or intensify a CS relationship with some being or entity. That is, there is a prospect for the person to develop a new or newly propitious CS relationship. This is indicated in Figure 17.1 by the box, **Representation of CS opportunity.**

1. What creates the representation of a new or suddenly better prospect for CS can be:
    a. The person encounters (perceives, reads, hears of) a 'passive' or even unknowing target being who is an appealing or 'attractive' CS partner. For example, an observed being is potentially 'loveable' because it is cute, vulnerable, or innocently needy; when the observer is responsive we may say that her *heart goes out* to the adorable, helpless target. Another case is that the person remembers intense CS with some being, feeling *nostalgia*, hopefully imagines intense CS. A third is that the person simply has the opportunity to initiate loving-kindness toward other beings who are not necessarily needy, but whom the person can benefit. In these instance, the person has the opportunity to intensify CS with a being who itself has not explicitly or directly acted to initiate the intensification, and who, indeed, may not be aware of the person. If kama muta occurs in these circumstances, it is what I have called 'first-person kama muta,' evoked without the target making any overt overture toward the person.
    b. The person observes or learns of some other being's CS relationship with a third being (e.g., someone is kind to someone, returns home, or makes a great sacrifice for the community). There is the potential for the person to imaginatively identify with one or more of the observed persons, and hence vicariously experience their kama muta. Observing

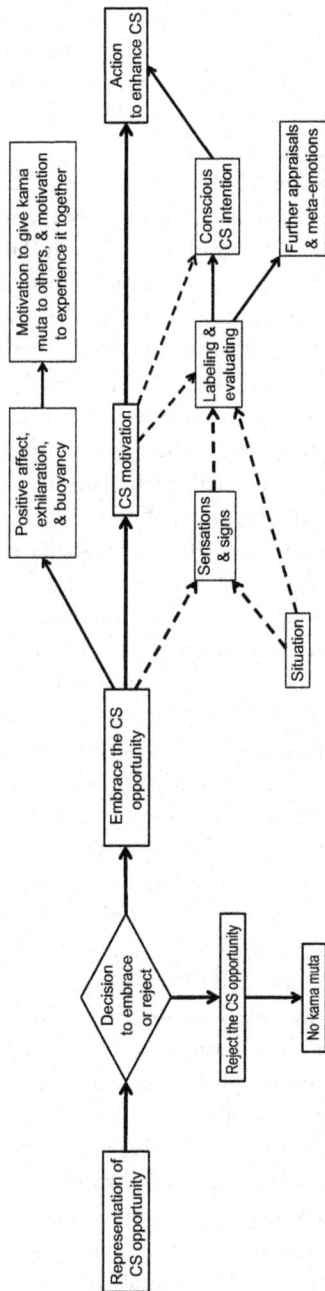

FIGURE 17.1 The processes within the kama muta psype. Time and psychological process go from left to right, the whole process often occurring in less than a second. (The vertical dimension of the figure has no significance.) Only the psychological processes of the psype are represented; ontogenetic, social relational, cultural, and biochemical processes are ignored. The mote consists of everything after "Embrace the CS opportunity."

the intensification of a CS relationship between/among others may stimulate the observer to remember, imagine, or hope for a promising CS relationship of her own. Or the observed kama muta affords the observer's suddenly intensified affection for the observed person(s). When it occurs though this process, this is what I call 'third-person kama muta' – it is evoked by observing, hearing about, or reading of other's kama muta. Third-person kama muta can be considered a special case of first-person kama muta because in neither case does the target (or targets) initiate any CS toward the observing person.

c. Some other being(s) initiate(s) a CS relationship with the person by an act or offer of compassion, kindness, welcome, or inclusion; by self-sacrifice for the person or their CS group; by incorporating the person in a ritual of belonging; by consubstantial assimilation, et cetera. If the person takes this opportunity to intensify the potential CS, this is what I have called 'second-person kama muta' – the other initiates the sudden intensification of CS with the person who feels it.

d. The person acts together with others, for example, dancing or making music together, rowing or marching in synchrony, making love, suffering, or facing danger together, fighting or winning a match together, sharing ritual food. The mutual participation, the doing and being together – typically in the medium of consubstantial assimilation – has the potential to suddenly intensify CS. If kama muta occurs through this process, it is 'first person plural kama muta' – the sense of being *we* is evoked by the joint action, mutually mirrored.

Most cases of sudden intensification of CS occur through at least one of these processes, but they are not mutually exclusive. However, the taxonomy is not exhaustive, and it may not be possible to develop an exhaustive list of the occasions that afford sudden intensification of CS.

All four of these processes are culturally imbued, although the figure does not represent this: the psype enhances biological fitness when it facilitates attention to sudden intensification of the specific CS relationships that have expected survival and reproductive benefits in each particular culture and context, and when it motivates culturally and contextually apt and efficacious devotion and commitment. That is, the psype is attuned to cultural preos, and must be culturally attuned to be biologically adaptive. The culture affords the beings and entities with whom a person can form a CS relationship, along with the specific nature of the equivalence that comprises the CS relationship. The culture also affords the occasions for – and indices of – suddenly propitious opportunities for CS intensification. There are myriad culturally evolved institutions, roles, practices, narratives, arts, and artifacts whose primary function is to evoke kama muta – these drivers are culturally adapted to the niche provided by the psychological system for kama muta – the psype. Conversely, the innate psype has biologically evolved to be sensitive to cultural drivers and cultural indices (constitutive signs) of sudden intensification of culturally significant CS. This means that psype and drivers are symbiotic; they are mutually co-adapted. This symbiosis is often mutualistic; the biological reproduction of the psype is enhanced by the drivers, while the cultural reproduction of the drivers is enhanced by the psype. However, because the cultural evolution of the drivers is orders of magnitude faster than the biological evolution of the psype, some drivers may be parasitic on the driver; they may reduce its inclusive fitness. (It is not known whether any drivers incorporate any ways of resisting such cultural parasitism.)

2. The person may or may not 'accept,' any of these potential intensifications of CS. This selectivity is indicated by the diamond, **Decision to accept or reject.** This 'decision' need not be conscious, and typically is not; the selectivity may even be inconsistent with reflective, articulable judgments. So a person can apperceive or ignore a potential intensification of CS. If they perceive the potential, they may not be aware of perceiving it. Then they 'accept' or 'reject' the opportunity, but again, they may not be consciously aware of 'making a decision' – it does not require reflection. Even when the person is conscious that there was a 'choice' of whether to intensify CS, they may still not know how or why they made the choice.

I don't know what moderators affect the 'acceptance' or 'rejection' of potential intensifications of CS. There may be larger contextual factors that people implicitly or explicitly use to determine whether a potential intensification is propitious in various respects. Probably the output of this 'decision' process is not dichotomous, but rather is some sort of degree of 'acceptance.'

This 'decision' process is very rapid, perhaps occurring in much less than one second. The rapidity of the 'decision' likely reflects two aspects of the psype. First, while CS varies in intensity, it is cognitively, affectively, motivationally, morally, and behaviorally binary. In an essential sense, a person either is equivalent to some set of beings, or the person is not equivalent. One cannot be somewhat equivalent. Formally, there are only two states: equivalent or not, without any stable middle ground. (This is a formal mathematical property of equivalence relations, and loosely analogous with certain quantum states in physics, where a particle may be in either of two quantum states, or in either of two places, but cannot be in-between them.) Psychosocially and subjectively, one does not move gradually between separate and united: the transition is instantaneous.

The rapidity of the kama muta response is also functional, in two respects. The phylogenetic origin of kama muta is likely to be maternal bonding, which then in a few mammals eventually evolved into pair-bonding, paternal bonding, and bonding of sibling helpers. This bonding must be immediate: mammalian newborns need dedicated care from the moment of birth. Any delay in caring for the newborn may be fatal. *Homo sapiens* later evolved indefinitely flexible kama muta bonding, expanding the formerly narrowly targeted infant- and partner-limited mechanism so as to be able to connect a person with any CS partner. But while kama muta biologically evolved to become more flexibly targeted, incorporating cultural preos, the instantaneous core mechanism remained the same.

This instantaneity is not just a conservative holdover from maternal, partner, paternal, and sibling-helper bonding. When the opportunity occurs to create a propitious new CS relationship or intensify an existing one, any hesitation in doing so may be interpreted by the partner(s) as equivocation, implying less than wholehearted commitment. Delay implies hesitancy, and hesitation implies indecision, which in turn implies a calculative weighing of the benefits and costs of the relationship – and a difficult decision, at that. Conditional calculativeness is inconsistent with the all-or-none, we-are-one, all-in nature of CS, so a person who delays the performance of kama muta appears uncommitted and untrustworthy – they certainly have reservations about committing to the CS relationship. Delay evokes doubt: is the slow responder sincere and whole-hearted? If you return from a tour of combat and your partner doesn't immediately cry and hug and kiss you, you wonder whether she really loves you still, or even wants you back at all. If you are exceptionally kind to someone and they don't immediately emote their appreciation, you wonder whether they truly do appreciate it. It's best to cry right away when your parents give you a puppy. After a few seconds, it's too late to make a convincing display of kama muta; a deferred response does not appear *spontaneous* and *heart-felt*. So evolutionary processes, supported by cultural selection and learning, keep the kama muta response rapid.

This instantaneity tells us that, whatever the cognitive and affective neurobiology of the kama muta mechanism turns out to be, it operates as a discrete function, not a continuous one; the output domain has only two elements: devoted commitment exists, or not. This dichotomous instantaneity is consistent with some mechanisms and not others; we can narrow the search to mechanisms that operate as on/off switches, ignoring rheostat-like continuous transducers. However, some other mechanism nonetheless yields a continuously varying intensity of the resultant affect and motivation. One can model this with a digital switch that turns an electrical current on, in series with a rheostat, for example, an analog dimmer that continuously modulates the brightness or heat output. In many cars, dashboard lights work like this, as do both the heater and the air conditioner. One sets the heater to off or on; if it's on, one sets the heat anywhere in a continuous range. Kama muta is the switching on of the digital on/off switch. This digital switch must be distinct from, but functionally in series with, an analog device that determines how strong the resultant motivation is, along a continuous dimension of intensity across different CS relationships and, in each relationship, continuously varying in degree over time, as well as in duration.

This fact that the kama muta psype operates quite rapidly and quite consistently also implies that the kama muta psype is a well-organized and somewhat autonomous system that does not require a very extensive or open-ended processing network. That is, it has a certain degree of modularity at the operational level. Over the longer term, the psype is culturally informed and oriented, but on each occasion, it quickly and efficiently uses the cultural information that it has previously absorbed. In this respect, it is like the language system. The psype function picks up a culturally relevant input from its domain and almost immediately generates a culturally appropriate output from its range. It does so having already incorporated and tightly integrated into itself the cultural precedents, prototypes, and paradigms that it needs to recognize culturally relevant CS intensifications and generate culturally apt and efficacious motives and actions. The rapidity with which the psype operates is clear evidence that these preos are already integrated into the psype: the psype doesn't have to take the time to search for them, and it doesn't produce the uncertain and variable output that would result from an ad hoc search on each occasion for the precedents, prototypes, and paradigms whose guidance it requires. The psype is well-prepared, evolutionarily, ontogenetically, and culturally; hence it is fast yet consistently accurate.

3. The person may **Reject the CS opportunity**, in which case no kama muta mote occurs. For example, someone may be remarkably kind to you but there are factors that influence you to spurn the opportunity to intensify a CS relationship, so you don't actually experience second-person kama muta. However, a person may reflectively reject the CS opportunity – for example, when he judges a narrative to be trite or a commercial to be manipulative – but the psype may be triggered nonetheless, evoking a mote that the person finds embarrassing or perplexing.[1]

4. The person may **Embrace the CS opportunity**. If so, the following steps very rapidly ensue:

Embracing the prospective CS relationship (CSR) generates CS motivation: affective devotion and moral commitment to the CSR, indicated in the Figure as **CS motivation**. That is, the person starts or intensifies her/his engagement in the CSR. This devotion and commitment motivation may be fairly short-lived, or may endure indefinitely, but even when it does not long endure it persists beyond the emotion moment. This motivation, even if not conscious, leads to action to realize the newly auspicious prospects for CS.

We don't yet understand what determines how strong this motivation is and how long it endures. Are strength or duration directly predicted by subjective intensity of the emotion, or the number and intensity of the sensations and signs?

The devotion and commitment may be focused almost exclusively on the specific CSR that initially intensified, or these motives may be more diffusely oriented to encompass other actual and potential CSRs. In some degree, the motivation may possibly extend to all possible CSRs, but is unlikely to extend equally to all. We don't yet understand the typical degree of specificity of focus, or what sociocultural and psychological factors determine how narrowly the CS motives are oriented. Nor do we know, when the CS motives are broad, what affects their selective orientation toward certain CSR possibilities.

5. Embracing the prospective CSR tends to generate sensations: a warm or other positive feeling in the center of the chest, moist eyes or tears, being choked-up or having a lump in the throat, goosebumps or chills, a deep and then paused breath, placing the palm(s) over the center of the chest, sometimes uttering an exclamation such as *Awww!*, and in some cultures lamentation or ululation. In Figure 17.1, this is indicated as **Sensations & signs**. The arrow from **Suddenly embracing CS** to **Sensations and signs** is dashed to indicate that the person does not get all the characteristic sensations or signs, and may not have any of them.

6. If the sensations, gesture, or utterance occur, they afford the person's **Labeling & evaluating** their emotion, but, as indicated by the dashed line, a person could have sensations or show signs without **Labeling** and without **evaluating** their emotion. **Evaluation** need not be conscious (and could well be modeled as a distinct box of its own), but is facilitated by conscious **labeling**.

   As I have observed in many practices, the culturally informed **Situation** alone may be sufficient to generate the signs of kama muta, such as ululation, lamentation, or weeping (for example, in greeting or in worship). In any case, any **Labeling & evaluating** a person does, they always do with respect to the **Situation**, not just the **Sensations & signs** alone. Linking the feeling of **CS motivation** with the **Situation** may enable the person to perform the **Labeling & evaluation** of their emotion, even in the absence of any **Sensations & signs** (or, even if sensations or signs occur, in the absence of any awareness of or attention to them).

7. **Labeling & evaluation** facilitate the person's **Consciousness CS intention** to work out tactics for investing in the new or newly intensified CSR, which may include verbal communication of affective devotion and moral commitment ('I love you so much!'). In any case, **Consciousness CS intention** leads to **Action to enhance CS** in accord with the relevant cultural preos. The motives that kama muta generates are culturally informed because the nature of the devotion and commitment that are appropriate to a given CSR depends on the culture: there are culturally diverse ways to sustain CSRs.

   That is, the sensations mobilize conscious intentions and deliberate tactical thinking. In effect, the sensations make people notice and reflect, 'Oh, wow! This is important! I really do care about this person/group/entity! What shall I do to devote myself to her/it?' Furthermore, the salience of the sensations makes the event memorable.

   Conscious awareness also affords verbal labeling, folk-psychological conceptualization of the state, along with statements of affective devotion and moral commitment. (This naming and linking to folk concepts – and only this – are just what many emotion researchers mean by the term *emotion*. In contrast, I don't construe explicit naming and categorizing as essential to the psychosocial-cultural processes we conceptualize as kama muta. Labeling and identification of the mote can certainly occur, but it doesn't always occur; a kama muta mote exists whether the person experiencing it names and categorizes it or not.) Reflective awareness is also *one* medium for invoking preos indicating how best to devote and commit. But the emotion can occur without any subjective bodily sensations or any apparent gestures or facial expressions.

The person may label the emotion with a gender-, context- and partner-appropriate lexeme. The person may note their emotionality without naming it. The person may notice it but later forget it. The person may not consciously attend to the 'emotionality' of the experience at all.

8. **Labeling & evaluation** also result in **Further appraisals** of the emotional state and any display of its **Sensations & signs** in the **Situation**. These appraisals generally generate **meta-emotions** such as 'embarrassment' or 'pride' about feeling or displaying the **Sensations & signs** in the **Situation**.

   If others perceive perceptible signs of kama muta in the person, the perceivers are likely to make culturally informed attributions and evaluations about the person's state, traits, and relationship(s). Tears are especially likely to be interpreted as indexing the person's CS devotion and commitment. Moreover, perceiving a person's tears or other signs is likely to evoke kama muta in observers (and those who hear reports of the tears, goosebumps, or other signs). These processes are not shown in Figure 17.1, which depicts only the psychological processes 'within' the person. If others perceive perceptible signs of kama muta in the person, the perceivers are likely to make culturally informed attributions and evaluations about the person's state, traits, and relationship(s).

9. Generally, the prospects for the new or newly enhanced CSR make the person feel **Positive affect, exhilaration, & buoyancy**, shown by the box at the top of the figure. The buoyancy or exhilaration may begin immediately, or begin slightly later; they may endure for minutes or hours after the emotional experience proper. This in turn generates **Motivation to give kama muta to others, & motivation to experience it together**. This is what is colloquially known as *sharing*, for example, in social media. Although these arrows and boxes in the figure represent these steps as a separate process, distinct from the other sensations and motives, it is also possible that they are more integrated into the processes shown along the bottom of the figure. We need further evidence to explore whether **Positive affect, exhilaration, & buoyancy** are indeed the principal sources of the **Motivation to give kama muta and the motivation to experience it together**.

This entire dynamic process is the psype. It is culturally attuned – and that cultural attunement is what makes the psype fitness-enhancing. The attunement is necessary for it to function adaptively in each and every culture.[2] This attunement is inherent in every step of the psychological process, so in the figure the cultural aspects are not separately represented as such.

The psychology of the psype, depicted here, works through neural and chemical systems, with roots in genes and development. It is not reducible to just functional anatomy and neurochemistry, but the psype operates in a medium that is not merely social and cultural, but simultaneously biological. At some point we hope that the biology of the kama muta psype will be illuminated, revealing how its biology, social psychology, and cultural aspects are integrated. That means that the biology of the psype is sensitively attuned to social relations and culture – we will not understand its biology until we understand that attunement.

Arriving here, we can more deeply appreciate a point made in the Preface and elaborated in Chapter 10: we cannot properly characterize the kama muta psype without identifying the domain of the function. That is, the psype is a mechanism that responds to all the sorts of intensification of all the implementations of CS analyzed in this book. If we only knew kama muta motes in recognition reunions, we would fundamentally misunderstand what they are. If we construed kama muta as a religious emotion per se (let alone an emotion peculiar to, say, charismatic religion), we would fail to understand what the kama muta psype is – and fail to appreciate just what its motes are, too. If we limited our view to *nostalgia*, we would imagine what kama muta motes are by their nature mnemonically generated, which is not the case. As I pointed out in the Preface, if we theorized an emotion that consists of responses to art that people label *moving* (e.g., Konečni 2005), posited that there is a distinct emotion people label *being moved* that occurs specifically when core values are challenged but realized (Cova & Deonna 2014), or theorized an emotion that is uniquely evoked by perception of morally beautiful events (Haidt & Keltner 2004), we would be doing what the blind men feeling different parts of an elephant did. To understand the nature of the kama muta psype, we must know that it responds to all sorts of intensifications of myriad CS relationships. And to appreciate the phenomenology of the experience of kama muta motes in any of the contexts where they occur, we must know those motes to be qualitatively similar to kama muta motes in all of the others. Similar, but at the same time having features specific to the person, context, relationship, and culture. That's what makes ethnology necessary: we cannot know what kama muta is if we know it only within the limits of a few contexts in a few cultures.

Online notes

17.1 A graphical depiction of the co-adaptational processes.

Notes

1 In 2009, Thomas Schubert and Beate Seibt noticed what we now call kama muta in themselves when watching a video clip of Susan Boyle singing "I Dreamed a Dream" in *Britain's Got Talent*. In 2012 Thomas brought up a perplexing and intriguing experience of crying at trite moves in conversations with Beate Seibt and Alan Fiske. Those discussions were the seed from which our research and conceptualization of kama mute grew.

2 Of course, the psype evolved to be adaptive functionality on the whole – to have **expected** contributions to fitness in the totality of situations that evoked it in the past in the entire human population. Parasitic drivers may be deleterious in particular cases, or even on the whole in given society at given point in history.

18

THE JOYS OF KNOWING KAMA MUTA

Conclusions we can draw

I hope that the research presented in this book, along with our ongoing studies, establishes the plausibility, promise, and appeal of kama muta theory. I hope that it also provides a model for a fruitful approach to other emotions that mediate other transitions in CS, and transitions in other social relationships (see Chapter 19). The conclusions I believe can be drawn from this research are as follows:

1. Kama muta is a distinct emotion.
2. It occurs frequently in a wide variety of cultures throughout history.
3. It occurs in a great many domains of social life, in all sorts of communal sharing relationships – whenever they suddenly intensify.
4. It is not a location in a continuous multi-dimensional emotional space. Rather, it is distinct entity that consists of the experience of a distinct dynamic function mapping the intensification of communal sharing relationships onto motives to devote and commit oneself to promising communal sharing relationships.[1]
5. It roughly corresponds with common vernacular lexemes in many, though not all, languages – often several lexemes in the same language, each denoting the emotion in a different context – but probably does not correspond one-to-one with everyday language usage of any term in any natural language.
6. It is not experienced when other kinds of social relationships suddenly intensify and is not evoked by other social events.
7. The psype is highly attuned to the cultural significance of specific transitions in particular CS relationships in each social domain. Likewise, the

psype is tuned to generate motives to devote and commitment to CS <u>in culturally apt and efficacious manners</u>.

8. The psype is an evolved adaptation, selected because it motivates people to devote and commit to CS relationships that are 'expected' to be fitness-beneficial <u>in the particular cultural, historical, domain, and practice milieu</u>.

9. Kama muta is often so mild that it goes unnoticed, or is not remarked on, or is quickly forgotten. But when it is intense it may be a peak experience, shaping the life course and transforming perceptions and values.

10. When it is intense, it often, but not invariably, involves some combination of a warm or other feeling in the center of the chest, tears or weeping, goosebumps or chills, a constricted or creaky voice, taking a deep breath and a short pause in breathing, or holding the palm(s) against the chest. Immediately after an intense kama muta experience, people may feel buoyant (light, floating), and also refreshed, energized, exhilarated.

11. Kama muta is a positive experience that people enjoy, like to create, seek out, strive to repeat, want to transmit to others (especially those with whom they have CS relationships), and want to experience together with others.

12. Nevertheless, because it sometimes occurs when strong CS occurs in the foreground against a background of problematic or lost CS or separation, kama muta may occur alongside the poignant sadness of longing for the missing CS, or even desperate fear for the welfare of the lost loved one. Thus while kama muta itself is always positive, it may occur during events that are, overall, distressing.

13. The social significance of experiencing or displaying kama muta differs across cultures, history, domains of life, practices, and gender. It has a great many culturally imbued meanings, each linked to a resonating web of implications.

14. An enormous number of social institutions, practices, roles, arts, and artifacts have culturally evolved to evoke and orient kama muta. A great many of these drivers are widespread and enduring frameworks for social life, shaping human lives and social structures. Some are local or transitory. The niche to which these drivers are culturally adapted is the innate, biologically evolved psype.

15. Kama muta is significant in many disparate social domains: oral narrative, literature, popular video, television, movies, music, politics and oratory, religion, social movements, war, sports, marketing, family life, friendship, life-cycle rituals, religion, and perhaps collective disaster.

16. Kama muta motes can be reliably identified in self-reports. In particular, the KAMMUS is a valid measure of kama muta; with care and insight, it can be translated into many languages other than English and appropriately used in other cultures to measure the same motes (see especially Seibt et al. 2017; and Zickfeld et al. 2019). The KAMMUS identifies kama muta from self-report of the five principal aspects of the mote: perceived sudden intensification of CS, bodily sensations and signs, CS devotion and

commitment motivation, positivity (independent of negativity), and vernacular labels.

17. Metatheoretically, the insights of kama muta theory suggest the fruitfulness of analyzing the functional dynamics of transitions in social relationships. That is, kama muta theory suggests that many sociomoral emotions – some heretofore hardly envisioned – may consist of the experience of motives that activate and orient adaptive social relational tactics.

18. Again metatheoretically, kama muta theory indicates how fitness-adaptive psychological mechanisms may select for the cultural evolution of drivers that, taken all together over many generations, enhance biological fitness. However, drivers may sometimes diffuse and endure through culture-evolutionary mechanisms that reduce the inclusive fitness of their practitioners. Thus, the symbiosis between psype and drivers may be mutualistic, or the rapid cultural evolution of drivers may allow them to be parasitic on the psype that slowly evolves though biological natural selection. In any case, many culturally-informed social practices – drivers – evidently arise and persist because they resonate with the psychology of the disposition to kama muta.

19. Epistemologically (and rhetorically), I hope that this book illustrates how illuminating and fruitful it is to combine the methods of hypothesis-testing experimentation analyzed with sophisticated statistical analyses, ethnological comparison across cultures and history, focused *participant* observation ethnography, interviewing, survey and diary methods, and reflective attention to individual subjective experience.[2] Each approach has merits that complement the limitation of the others, so they combine synergistically. In isolation, none is sufficient unto itself.

20. I hope to have intimated something of the esthetic virtues of kama muta motes. Becoming more aware of, and sensitive to, kama muta adds something to the quality of life, and the meaning in it.

21. If kama muta is a uniquely evoked by sudden intensification of CS, then kama muta motes are valid indices of CS.

Consider this last point carefully. This book documents evidence of kama muta motes occurring across a very wide range of domains in quite diverse cultures across thousands of years. In nearly all instances described, there is strong evidence that the kama muta motes result from the sudden intensification of CS; and there are <u>no</u> instances where kama muta occurs but CS intensification definitely does not. This very consistent association between kama muta motes and CS means that a kama muta mote is a reliable and valid indicator of CS, and more particularly, of sudden intensification of CS. That is, it seems that in future research of all sorts, kama muta motes can be used as indicators of CS: where kama muta occurs, we can confidently infer that people are relating according to CS. Furthermore, if we observe kama muta, we can infer that people have become (more) devoted and morally committed to their CS relationships. Since CS relationships are coordinated mental states and hence not always clearly apparent to observers – and never constantly visible at every moment – it is useful to know this. In fact, our own search for kama muta motes led us to discover (and then independently confirm) sudden intensifications of CS in many places where, when we started, we had had no idea that CS existed at all. For example, performing or listening to music, listening to great oratory, visiting memorial monuments, and sports victories.

Why does understanding kama muta matter?

What difference does it make whether we understand kama muta, or not? It is an intellectual joy to study and illuminate it, that's for sure. Curiosity is a worthy motive, the intrigue of exploration is exciting, and the esthetics of elegant explanation is exalting. But in a world with millions of suffering people and portents of ecological or political catastrophe, is studying kama muta merely a selfish indulgence of the ivory tower? Does it make any practical difference? Can knowledge of kama muta enhance human, animal, or global welfare?

Most of the suffering and stress in the world today are direct or indirect products of insufficient compassion, or products of the hatred and denigration that are opposites to compassion. There are sufficient resources and means to feed and house everyone in the world, provide good medical care, education, and employment – if we cared to do so. The better we understand the major sources of loving-kindness, the better our chances of fostering it. If we were better able to evoke more kama muta with the vulnerable and needy, and with our enemies, we could better evoke the motivation to care for them.

Knowledge of kama muta safeguards us from being manipulated by it in marketing, politics, and mobilization for violence. We can resist it when we recognize it.

The feeling that someone cares for you – that someone is *there for you* – is crucial for psychological well-being. Furthermore, as I will consider in the next chapter, the perception of social support has a huge effect on health and survival. Kama muta experiences may mediate the feeling that someone is there for you, and if it does, we need to know all about how to foster the kama muta experiences that do that. In Chapter 5 and Online Note 5.1, I considered anecdotal evidence that mutual kama muta experiences in psychotherapy may be pivotal moments that generate trusting therapeutic bonds that facilitate progress. Likewise, kama muta experiences may motivate participation in, and perhaps even complement, addiction recovery groups. Kama muta may be important in other support groups and everyday friendship, marriage, and family bonds. Indeed, parents' and other caretakers' kama muta experiences with infants and children may motivate dedicated, devoted care for them. I don't know if they do, but if so, then we need to understand how those bonding experiences come about and how they function to heal and to protect.

And not just that. It is an end in itself. So we need to know how to craft and cherish it. Kama muta is a common joy, enhancing the quality of mundane life;

the more we develop our sensitivity to and appreciation of it, the more vibrant the joy. When it is exceptionally strong, as a secular peak experience or as mystical religious ecstasy, it can be one of the most wonderful experiences of a lifetime, and sometimes transformative. At every level, it contributes to making life meaningful. The more we understand about kama muta, the more we will be able to cultivate this aspect of the good life. And we need to know how to combine it with the other ingredients for the complete good life in the wholly good society. Or the best we can do.

The ostensive characterization of kama muta

From the discovery of kama muta in all of the different human activities that this book covers, we reveal something they all have in common – and that we humans all have in common. Who knew that seeing cute kittens, singing, listening to Martin Luther King, Jr., and visiting the Vietnam Veterans Memorial all had something fundamental in common? Who knew that reading *Uncle Tom's Cabin* and reaching a holy site of pilgrimage could evoke the same emotion? Who knew that there might be a common motivation for going to a Pixar movie, attending AA meetings, and mutual aid in collective disasters? Who knew that people would experience Krishna worship, holding their newborn baby, and winning an Olympics event in significantly similar ways? Kama muta is something humans everywhere and across history evidently experience, whether they express, share, and further evoke it by ululating, with tenderly murmuring *Awww!*, or fangirls' *squee!* screaming, or ritual weeping, or *being slain in the Spirit* and collapsing into torpor. For that matter, for many of us it's an eye-opener to realize that tears are often an indexical sign of suddenly intensified love – as are goosebumps and chills. Kama muta is all over the place, once we learn to recognize it.

So, just what <u>is</u> kama muta? I have defined it processually as something caused by sudden intensification of CS relationships, and in turn causing renewed affective devotion and moral commitment to CS relationships. I have defined it phenomenologically as a joyful, short-lived feeling that, when intense, is accompanied by some sort of often warm feeling in the chest, tears, goosebumps or chills, and being choked-up, followed by feelings of buoyancy and exhilaration. I have depicted its dynamic processes graphically. And in the course of this book I have also defined it ostensively, by induction, delineating it though the various practices in which it commonly occurs. That is, I can define kama muta as that which occurs in the kinds of events we have observed in this book, along with many others as yet unverified.

Not everyone experiences kama muta motes when they encounter all such circumstances. But it is clear that kama muta is prevalent across cultures and throughout history, and there is every prospect that further research will discover additional major kama muta-inducing practices in contemporary cultures and at other times in other places. What has already emerged, in any case, is the approximate topography of vast regions of the landscape of the domain (input) and range (image or output) of the kama muta psype function: especially the sorts of practices, institutions, roles, narratives, arts, and artifacts that have culturally evolved as culturally selected adaptations to the niche afforded by the kama muta psype.

The first and most crucial step in understanding an emotion (or any psychological process) is identifying it in the world and characterizing its ecology. <u>We simply don't know what an emotion is until we know where it occurs and what it looks like in its various occurrences across the epochs and cultures of *Homo movens*</u>. Conversely, when we learn to recognize the emotion in a great many manifestations across truly diverse settings, we come to discern what it is. So to inductively enumerate the occasions when kama muta motes emerge is to ostensively define it – kama muta is that which occurs in these situations. It is what they have in common. To get the big picture, we need to see everything together: the image on the puzzle that makes sense of all the bits of color does not appear until all the pieces have been found and fitted together.

Beyond the inductive-enumerative ostensive characterization that this provides, the assimilation of all of these phenomena into one construct, kama muta, is immediately meaningful in several respects. It provides a more parsimonious, simpler, and clearer understanding of human affect and social relations: what we previously perceived as many distinct, unrelated phenomena we can now recognize as variant instances of the same emotion. This reveals a pattern, an order, an entity that makes sense of what was otherwise inchoately incoherent. What previously appeared to be scores of distinct phenomena are discovered to be all manifestations of the same one. Or rather, they have a common foundation, a common core. As I proposed in the Preface, one might even say that kama muta 'explains' occurrences of these practices, somewhat as Newton's law of gravity nomothetically explains the motions of the planets, ballistic trajectories, tides, flotation, and the oscillation of pendulums – by describing them all as particular instances of $F = G\, m_1 m_2 / r^2$. With elegant parsimony the Newtonian 'law' of gravity accurately <u>describes</u> a huge range of phenomena. Similarly, consider the discovery that genes are composed of DNA that provides a four-base code (adenine, thymine, guanine, and cytosine) for transcribing proteins. This is an elegant, simple, but encompassing description of a fundamental biological process. By revealing parsimonious coherence underlying what hitherto appeared to be innumerable inchoate processes organizing different aspects of living organisms, DNA provides a parsimonious characterization of them all. I hope that, in a small way, kama muta provides an analogous account of a common mechanism of seemingly diverse sorts of human bonding.

Assimilating these phenomena motivates closer comparison among them: we now appreciate that we should look closely for further <u>similarities</u> among them that we have not yet recognized. For a start, we should search in each case for features that we have recognized in other cases, to see how consistent the manifestations of kama muta are. Conversely, we now see that we must fully characterize and explain the <u>differences</u> among these instances: if they are all instances of kama muta, then how and why do they differ in evoking conditions, phenomenology, cultural construal and elaboration, the orientation and form of the CS motives they evoke, and the particular CS relationships they foster? Bringing together these seemingly disparate phenomena into a single coherent kama muta concept makes it possible to begin to precisely yet parsimoniously <u>describe the function</u> that maps the domain of evocative events onto the range of CS motives and performances of kama muta. To characterize the function, we need to know all of its mappings, hence its entire domain and range. Only when one has identified the entire domain and range of cultural phenotypes on which natural selection of the kama muta psype operates can one analyze the ways the culturally-informed and oriented psype is adaptive in terms of biological fitness. That is, the kama muta psype is beneficial to the frequency-weighted integral of the CS relations it supports, so we must know what these CS relationships actually are in order to correctly describe how the psype evolved (and the selective pressures it currently faces). Similarly, recognizing that all these seemingly disparate phenomena are cultural implementations of the same psype enables researchers to explore the phylogeny and ontogeny of the kama muta psype. The more we know about the current end–points of the phylogeny and ontogeny of the psype, the better we can understand the processes that led to them.

Likewise, this integration makes it possible to properly describe and analyze how the cultural drivers that generate these diverse manifestations of kama muta arise, reproduce, diffuse, and transform through cultural evolution. How does the kama muta psype engender the cultural evolution of these sorts of narratives, practices, institutions, roles, and artifacts? When are the drivers and psype mutualistic, when are the drivers psychoculturally parasitic on the evolving driver, and how does the psype resist parasitism? Furthermore, this integration enables us to investigate how kama muta drivers integrate with other social, political, religious, and economic institutions and practices. It also makes it possible to explore how kama muta motes link with other emotion motes – what combinations of kama muta and other emotions tend to arise and become symbiotic? Metaphorically, if kama muta is an elemental emotion, what is its combinatorial 'chemistry'?

Finally, consider the most purely idiographic account of a particular event in unique circumstances in the life of a singular individual or specific community at one historical moment in a distinctive culture. Just to be intelligible, the identification of the event must use descriptors that situate it by comparing and contrasting it with other phenomena. Hence, understanding the event is only possible with reference to some general account of human being and becoming. That is, any understanding must be based on general principles of how the constituents of human beings affect each other, and how one thing leads to another. Even the most radical social-constructionist account must identify the materials from which people construct an event. Even an account of the most arbitrary, purely conventional symbolic processes must identify how people can generate and interpret such symbols, and what responses to such symbols they are capable of – and prone to. The terms kama muta psype, driver, and mote provide a language for describing the affective and motivational aspects of certain kinds of social events, together with their sources and consequences. For example, to describe and understand a Krishna worshipper's experience on a particular occasion, we need a conceptual language for that experience and its sociocultural ecology; kama muta theory provides that conceptual language. Kama muta theory provides concepts for representing and comprehending what happened on 28 August 1963 on the steps of the Lincoln Memorial in Washington, DC, when Martin Luther King, Jr., said "I have a dream" to 250,000 people. The event was unique, but we need kama muta concepts to compose a precise and valid description of what that event was, including just how it was unique. Kama muta theory enables us to compare and contrast that event with Abraham Lincoln's Gettysburg Address, with an occurrence of Krishna worship, with a viewing of cute kittens on YouTube, or with a reading of the *Odyssey*.

In short, sketching the big picture provides perspective that enriches comprehension of the specific phenomena, whose elucidation in turn illuminates the big picture. The more we learn about and compare particular times and places, the deeper our understanding of humanity. The more we understand humanity, the better we understand particular acts of particular humans. Understanding psychology helps us to understand cultures, because neither functions apart from the other. Our hope is that the better we understand the big picture of kama muta as a human social emotion, the greater the insights we can have into particular cultures, institutions, practices, roles – and into specific events and persons. Our nomothetic approach inductively builds on meticulous descriptions of specific persons in specific events at unique moments in history in unique cultures. Conversely, I believe that the general theory that I inductively construct from these particulars provides context for them. That is, the nomothesis provides an essential framework for the comparison and contrast essential to the idiographic. We can only understand a particular moment by recognizing how it resembles and how it differs from other potentially comparable moments. For this, we need a framework, and the more explicit the framework, the more support it provides.

In order to understand the phylogeny, natural selection, neuroanatomy, neurochemistry, ontogeny, social psychology, sociology, and cultural construction of any of the manifestations of kama muta motes, we must recognize the entire scope of phenomena that are kama muta motes. For example, a theory intended to explain why people are 'moved' by certain videos cannot be valid unless the theory also accounts for why people commonly have similar (albeit more intense, and differently significant) kama muta motes when feeling loving union with Krishna, when reunited with a loved one, when visiting a memorial, when listening to dancers sing in a Kaluli longhouse or hearing the birds singing outside it.

Provocations

I hope that our research indicates the synergy among ethnology, history, linguistic investigation, ethnography, interviewing, surveys, diary studies, ad hoc collation of media materials, and online and laboratory experiments. Our experience is that they are complementary, fitting together to enable the construction of a much more valid, nuanced, and complete understanding than any one approach could provide on its own, unsupported by the others. There are many kinds of understanding, theoretical explanation, and interpretation. Though emphasizing nomothetic concerns, this book attempts to balance the complementary merits and challenges of nomothetic, descriptive, idiographic, and interpretive frameworks. And these approaches <u>are</u> complementary. They fit together, despite considerable rhetoric that treats them as incompatible or even mutually invalidating. Today the scientific metaparadigm is often seen as antithetical to interpretive and critical approaches. But in my view, the deepest understanding emerges from their synthesis. Scientific explanations are only valid to the extent they are based on, and consistent with, observations of myriad particular instances, so in the social sciences scientific explanations depend on research that coherently builds on detailed accounts of the particulars of social life in the widest possible range of human communities. A theory must integrate and be consistent with the details of the myriad phenomena it purports to encompass and integrate. Conversely, any attempt to describe, interpret, or critique particular events, persons, relationships, practices, institutions, or communities must use descriptive, interpretive, or critical constructs that have wide applicability and meanings that are consistent across the innumerable contexts in which the constructs may be used. To say what is happening, why people are doing something, or what is wrong with what is going on, we need concepts that enable us to characterize, contrast, compare – and, if that is the aim, go on to judge. If the essential concepts have no clear and consistent meanings, and do not clearly denote objectively observable facts, the description, interpretation, or critique have no definite meaning.

I hope that this book makes a plausible, preliminary case that kama muta motes can be compared across persons, contexts, cultures, and historical periods. All kama muta motes are not identical, but in important respects they are equivalent – they tend to share many characteristic features, and these features cohere (they are highly correlated across instances, and functionally related as phases of a single process). Kama muta psypes are shaped and oriented by the cultures in which they develop, but the starting point for the cultural formation of the innate psype is likely much the same in all infants, within a range of initial individual differences. Then there are general principles that determine the ways in which culture ontogenetically informs and orients kama muta motes. The drivers of kama muta are wonderfully diverse, with intriguing cultural peculiarities, but all drivers afford sudden intensification of CS. Accepting these conclusions makes it possible to describe, interpret, and critique any instance of kama muta, and do so fruitfully, while rejecting these conclusions makes description, interpretation, and critique not only futile, but incoherent – unintelligible. Each kama muta driver has distinctive facets, but it functions in a manner that corresponds to other drivers, tapping human psypes that maintain and reproduce every driver. Each post-infancy kama muta psype is distinctly shaped by experience with the cultural drivers and preos the person has encountered, but it belongs to a definite set of systems with consistent dynamics, such as responsiveness to acts of consubstantial assimilation. To understand any driver, psype, or mote, we need to recognize it as an instance of its kind and see how it operates in relation to the CS–driver–psype–mote system.

A theory is a provocation. Our theory should incite readers to reconsider what they know. Each reader knows much that I do not know, so each reader can bring new evidence to bear on kama muta theory. And every reader can look at the world they know through the lens of kama muta theory – perhaps to see in a new light what's been there all along. I hope the theory will provoke every observer, every thinker, every researcher who reads this to search for new evidence and arguments for and against the theory. How well does it fit what we as an intellectual community know? What fruitful new questions does it ask about familiar phenomena? What intriguing new facts and features does it excite us to search for? What does the theory fit well – what does it explain parsimoniously and elegantly? What are the boundaries of the theory – what are its limits? What sorts of phenomena does the theory only incorporate awkwardly, incompletely, approximately, or contingently? In this book I propose that kama muta is salient, pervasive, and frequent in many experiences, events, and practices. This is a provocation: I hope each reader will bring into the discussion new evidence, new perspectives, and new reasoning about these and other cases. The nature of every instance presented in this book can be better characterized by experts who know the languages of the texts or do fieldwork in the communities explored here. The book surely leaves out many apposite and illuminating manifestations of kama muta. The theory is imperfect and can surely be transcended. In all these respects, I hope this book inspires – or provokes – readers to go beyond it.

A theory raises a question, opening our eyes to possibilities that otherwise wouldn't have been considered. Here the new question is, 'In this event, is anyone having a kama muta mote?' If so, what CS relationship has suddenly intensified? Why and how has it suddenly intensified? What motives and actions does the kama muta mote engender? What meanings do people make of their mote? Without kama muta theory, we wouldn't think to ask such questions, so we probably wouldn't notice the phenomenon. We would certainly miss crucial features. And we might notice some of the features of a kama muta mote, but misinterpret them; for example, we might see tears and attribute them to sadness. The theory prompts us to keep a lookout for kama muta, and then recognize it when it appears.

Notes

1 For the distinctions between taxons (discrete categories) and dimensions, see Ruscio, Ruscio, & Haslam 2006; Haslam, Holland, & Kupens 2012.
2 We also believe that experience-sampling methods will yield their own invaluable complementary insights, but have not yet worked out how to do experience-sampling of occasional brief emotions.

19

THE ADVENTURES OF THE UNKNOWN

What we don't know about kama muta far exceeds what we do know. We don't know whether other mammals (or even birds) have homologous emotions, though they definitely do have maternal bonding, and in some cases pair-bonding to mates and/or paternal bonding or sibling bonding to infants. My dogs seem to be very pleased when I come home; is canid tail-wagging a sign of a kama muta-like emotion? Canids and a few other highly social pack-pod-troop mammals apparently have a reunion emotion that may be substantially homologous with kama muta. But we don't know precisely how *Homo movens* – which is perhaps as apt a name for our species as *Homo sapiens* – evolved our uniquely generative, flexible, culturally sensitive kama muta psype. We don't know anything for sure about the ontogeny of kama muta. We don't know anything about its neuroanatomical substrates, although I might imagine that the insula is important, at least in mediating the consubstantial assimilation that is the conformation system of CS (Fiske 2004b; Fiske & Schubert 2012). We don't know anything about the neurochemical mediation of kama muta, though I can imagine that it may involve some interaction among oxytocin, arginine vasopressin, estrogen, μ-opioids, dopamine, and other hormones, perhaps including an inhibitory role for androgens. Presumably the CS devotion and commitment motives that result from kama muta, when they are strong, involve changes in hormone levels. We don't know how menarche, male sexual maturation, or diurnal, menstrual, menopausal, and other life history processes alter proclivities to experience kama muta, how stress may do so, or how administration of contraceptive hormones, Pitocin, or steroids may do so. Kama muta motes presumably involve the parasympathetic system including activation of some specific subset of the vast bundle of neurons called the vagal nerve. But we don't know how kama muta motes generate the set of sensations they do, including goosebumps and chills, which are products of the sympathetic nervous system.

As I mentioned in Chapter 2, one of the sensations of kama muta motes is enigmatic: what is the *warm fuzzy* feeling perceived as in the heart or the center of the chest? Humans have no known warmth receptors anywhere in the thorax, and in any case it is not evident what would warm up in a kama muta mote, how it would warm up, or, functionally, why anything should warm up.

There is one particular set of mysteries whose solution would likely illuminate many questions about kama muta: why do <u>sudden</u> intensifications of CS evoke kama muta, while slower, incremental increases in CS do not? Concomitantly, why is kama muta so brief? What are the functions and the processes that makes the proclivity to kama muta selectively responsive to rapid change, make it fast-acting, and make it fleeting? *Anger, grief, sexual desire*, and *amusement* can have sudden onsets in response to sudden stimuli, but they can also grow slowly, and they can be sustained for hours and more. Why is kama muta different? Part of the adaptive functional answer may be that the origin and a continued core function of the kama muta psype is bonding the mother, father, siblings, grandparents, and other close kin to the newborn infant. Newborns need immediate, intensive, and arduous care, so the mechanism that motivates that care must immediately generate strong motives. Indeed, many mammals, including many social mammals, are aversive to most close contact, treating nearby conspecifics as threats or treating small mammals as prey; this disposition must be instantly counteracted and replaced by nurturance.

Why does kama muta seemingly only occur in response to <u>sudden</u> intensification of CS? Granted that it mediates new or increased devotion and commitment, why is there a mechanism that responds specifically to instantaneous affordances, and that responds <u>immediately</u>? What's the rush about responding to a reunion, an extraordinarily kindness, heroic sacrifice, a pledge of love, being forgiven, or the discovery that someone shares your experience of trauma? In these situations, any delay in responding with devotion and commitment to the CS relationship is likely to be seen by partners and observers as wavering, as equivocation, as vacillation – thinking too long implies weighing the decision, implying less than full devotion and less than certain commitment. Slow to commit means half-hearted or conditional commitment. Which means people can't count on you; if you're not dedicating yourself immediately and completely, you can't be trusted. Imagine that you propose marriage, and your potential partner mulls it over for several minutes or longer. There may also be adaptively and sociopsychologically important circumstances in which great beneficence or courageous help lead to rapid formation of coalitions. People remember who <u>first</u> pledged support, who initially joined them when it was still risky. So responding rapidly may get one securely on the inside of the right side.

Do comparatively slow intensifications of CS – occurring gradually over many minutes, hours, or longer – evoke the same levels and kinds of CS motivation as the rapid intensifications that evoke kama muta? Or are there differences in the nature of the affective devotion and moral commitment emerging with kama muta motes, compared to the features of the motives that develop more gradually? Conversely, what is the role of kama muta in creating and sustaining CS? Do (some sorts of) CS relationships 'need' repeated reinvigoration by kama muta? Is the CS created or reinvigorated by kama muta in any way different from CS that develops without kama muta?

Even when we figure out why the kama muta psype is so responsive to sudden CS intensification, many questions about the mapping function will remain. Are kama muta sensation intensity and number (of different sensations) linearly related to the <u>rate</u> of CS intensification (acceleration), to the amount of intensification, or neither? What about the motives that emerge? Does the psype response depend on the absolute level of CS at the beginning or end of the change? How do these functions vary by context and culture?

Another question is why kama muta involves bodily sensations that only the person herself detects; what is the function of goosebumps and warm feelings in the chest? In particular, how are the emergent motives related to sensations? I myself, and some (perhaps 5–10%) of our experimental participants, have no perceptible sensations in most moderate kama muta experiences. That is, we often feel subjectively *moved*, et cetera, and motivated to devote and commit to CS, without any perceptible bodily sensations. Are those people who typically experience kama muta sensations still equally motivated to devote and commit to CS on the occasions when CS suddenly intensifies but they nonetheless perceive no sensations? If so, what is the function of the sensations, and of the signs such as *awww* vocalizations or ululation, tears, and movement of the palm to the chest? Would blocking interoception of kama muta sensations reduce or eliminate either the subjective awareness of kama muta motes and/or the ensuing CS motives? This raises another question: Are the kama muta motes that are <u>marked by sensations</u> only the tip of the iceberg? Do relatively small or slow intensifications of CS often evoke CS devotion and commitment without any subjective sensations?

The security of feeling that one is 'in' or 'has' CS relationships, that one belongs to something enduring that transcends the individual self, seems to have an effect on mood. This may be why kama muta motes are exhilarating – even beyond the moment of the emotion proper. Beyond this, do kama muta motes, as such, have other specific effect on moods? How are kama muta motes related to the several types of depression, bipolar disorder, and anxiety?

It is quite possible that kama muta experiences have profound effects on health and longevity. The perception of social support – the feeling that people (at least one person) is there for you, that someone cares, that you are not alone – affects morbidity and mortality from nearly every disease and disorder (for meta-analyses and reviews, see Chida et al. 2008; Greenwood et al. 1996; Barth, Schneider, & von Kanel 2010; Garssen & Goodkin 1999; Holt-Lunstad, Smith, & Bradley 2010; Pinquart & Duberstein 2010). The magnitude of the effect of social support on morbidity and mortality are greater than the effects of regular exercise, greater than the effects of optimal weight versus obesity, greater than the effects of excessive alcohol use versus abstinence, and greater than the effects of abstaining from ever smoking, or ceasing moderate levels of smoking (Doll et al. 1980; Jacobs et al. 1999; Calle et al. 1999; Kuriyama 2006; Kodama et al. 2009; Holt-Lunstad, Smith, & Bradley 2010). The effects of social support are not due to the practical services that family and friends provide – it is the psychological feeling that people are there for that reduces rates of illness and death by 25–40%. Because the kama muta mote is precisely the wonderful feeling that people are there for you, that you are connected, that you belong, it is plausible to imagine that the frequency and intensity of such motes might mediate the effects of social support on health. Furthermore, kama muta motes evoked by fiction, videos, television, radio, cinema, deities, nature, music, dancing, sports, pets, patriotism, participation in social movements, and online forums that link otherwise isolated people might well have an additional health effect on top of the effect of kama muta motes with friends and kin. It would be important to sort out the relative health benefits of these various kinds of CS relationships, and whether, when, and how kama muta mediates such benefits.

Whatever its effects on mortality and morbidity, kama muta motes seems to enhance overall life satisfaction and well-being, and to contribute especially to making life meaningful.

Awe at the sudden intensification of authority ranking

Communal sharing is one of the four fundamental relational models with which people coordinate social interaction in all sorts of domains in all cultures. CS is an equivalence relation, in which people organize some aspect(s) of interaction by treating members of a group as socially equivalent in some respect. Another of the four relational models is authority ranking: social coordination based on a linear ordering of persons, offices, social groups, or social categories, where the asymmetries are regarded as legitimate, natural, or inevitable (Fiske 1991, 1992, 2004a). In authority ranking relationships, the subordinate(s) owe respect or even reverence, deference, and obeisance. They are committed to support, follow, and, often, to obey. The complementary responsibilities of a superior are to guide wisely, to protect and look out for, to stand up and speak out for her followers. The superior decides and decrees what is right and what is wrong; subordinates must follow these edicts. But the superior's edicts must be wise and lead to the good.

Sudden intensification of CS activates the kama muta psype, triggering kama muta motes. What happens when authority ranking relationships suddenly intensify? When a person is shown great respect and deference; wins a significant election, award, promotion, or contest; graduates or receives a degree; is appointed to an important position; succeeds to a title or high office; triumphs in battle, or in some other culturally meaningful way rises in a hierarchy, they feel an emotion that is approximately denoted in English as 'pride' (for academic work that takes this English lexeme as a psychological construct, see Tangney 1999; Lewis 2000; Tracy & Robins 2007). This is the sudden intensification of authority ranking looking down – a relational transition in which the person assumes or augments legitimate superiority over subordinates. Laski (1980:151–153) calls this experience of one's magnificence and superiority when 'sitting on top of the world' the "Napoleonic experience." It occurs when one triumphs, she says; for example, when one gives a lecture or performance that holds an audience spellbound. She contrasts this feeling of dominance with both transcendent "ecstasy" and the opposite of ecstasy, "desolation."

Looking 'up,' a person feels what English speakers often call *awe* when he meets or learns about someone who greatly outranks him or whom he greatly admires and looks up to, when he is enormously impressed by someone's incredible performance, when he sees someone wield great social power, or when he imagines a mighty deity. Weber (1978 [1922]) called awe–evoking qualities and transcendent triumphs "charisma," analyzing how charisma attracts followers, facilitates overthrow of existing leaders, confers legitimacy, and makes people obey the particularistic arbitrary will of the charismatic leader. Weber infers from historical sources that charisma only endures so long as the leader continues his exceptional successes and overawes any resistance.

Innumerable religious speakers and writers have expatiated on the emotion of recognizing or even encountering a supreme god. In some languages and cultural contexts, this feeling of smallness, abject inferiority, and utter dependence on the arbitrary whim of a high god is characterized as *fear*. Indeed, in some languages the same lexeme is used for attitudes toward ordinary human superiors and toward immediate physical dangers. For example, in the Moore language of the Moose of Burkina Faso, to respect an authority is *zoe*, 'fear,' sometimes used with the object *dabeem* ('fright') as in *m zoeta dabeem*, 'I am awed, I respect' – literally, 'I fear fright' (where the person who is the object of the emotion is contextually understood). (Compare this with Kant's [1790/1987:119–120] discussion of fear of God.)

A person, alliance, or organization who can evoke a lot of *awe* intensifies their superior authority ranking position, consolidating or increasing their prestige. Consequently, a great many practices, institutions, artifacts, and edifices have culturally evolved to evoke awe. These are constructed on the basis of the conformation system of AR, the iconic physics of dimensions and magnitudes (Fiske 2004b). A person evokes awe by appearing to be (or intrinsically associated with things that are) bigger, higher, more numerous, louder, brighter, or have more force/strength/power. Subordinates feel awe when they encounters human works that make them feel small: when they stand before a gigantic statue of a god, come up to a massive mound, pyramid, or ziggurat; look up at an astounding tower or skyscraper; see and enter a great cathedral or mosque whose ceiling is high above them; or walk under a monumental portal or arch. This is something like what Kant meant by the judgment or feeling of the sublime – perception of something "large absolutely [*schlechthin, absolut*], in every respect (beyond all comparison)" (Kant 1790/1987:105). Awe is evoked by going up a slope, climbing ramps or stairs, and looking up a person on a dais wearing a crown or headdress that adds to their stature. A person appears great when seated on a huge horse, tall camel, great elephant – or in a big automobile or stretch limousine, or part of an imposing procession. Saluting guns, drums, great gongs or bells, trumpet blasts, and brass bands inspire awe. Pageantry with massed marchers or huge moving objects is awesome. Historically, paramount leaders, high priests, and elites have dressed in regalia that shines brilliantly in sunlight, and indeed the Incas sheathed their temples and palaces inside and out with gold alloy plates that dazzled the populace. All of these practices, artifacts, and architectures function to evoke awe, which is why they were invented, diffused, replicated, and elaborated.

Likewise, much of the language of *awe* is the language of physical magnitudes and dimensions (Fiske 2004b). In English, an awesome person and their performances are 'huge'; 'great'; 'head and shoulders above the rest'; 'at the top' and 'above' competitors; 'brilliant'; 'stellar'; 'powerful'; 'a force to be reckoned with'; an 'enormous,' 'gigantic,' 'tremendous,' 'magnificent,'[1] 'thunderous,' or 'resounding' success.

It appears that there is a distinct emotion evoked by all of these ways of suddenly intensifying authority ranking. Subjectively and conjecturally, the physical sensations of *awe* seem to include two of the sensations of kama muta; goosebumps or shivers, and a gasp (sudden deep intake of breath) perhaps by a drawn-out vocalization such as 'wow.' However, awe does not seem to evoke tears, feelings in the center of the chest, or subsequent buoyancy. Awe probably activates the sympathetic nervous system more than the parasympathetic system that is likely the core of kama muta physiology (except for the goosebumps and chills). (For other conceptualizations of 'awe,' see Keltner and Haidt 2003; Konečni 2005, 2011.)

I imagine that awe motivates effort to reinforce, sustain, and deepen authority ranking relationships, and moral commitment to do so. I suspect that, like kama muta, there are first-, second-, and third-person experiences of awe. In the first-person, one can put oneself in the way of an awesome encounter, for example, by attending a speech, concert, or religious service; and in these and other situations one can facilitate the potential for awe by assuming a humble attitude, putting oneself at another' s feet or, in some domains in some cultures, prostrating oneself in reverence or worship. Religious institutions focused on authoritarian high gods foster first-person awe. In the second-person, a charismatic person can initiate an interaction with the person or display their greatness. Observers of sports and other contests experience third-person awe when they see impressive performances and striking victories, and a listener or viewer may be awed by magnificent status-enhancing acts of characters in narratives, videos, television, or movies. Third-person awe will be especially frequent where people have technologies and practices that make performances vivid to their audiences, where cultural practices hype 'record-breaking' performances, and where there are institutions that attract, train, select, employ, and present extraordinary performers – such as the contemporary professional sports industry. Myths about heroic, herculean exploits and movies about superheroes will also evoke awe, though perhaps mostly in children (though superheroes seem to often evoke kama muta in adult viewers). But all of this remains to be studied systematically.

Our point is simply that there are definite conceptual grounds for positing the existence and importance of an emotion of sudden intensification of authority ranking, and there are ample ethnological indications that there are widespread practices and institutions that function to evoke awe. Research on such an emotion construct should not rely on a vernacular lexeme from English or any other natural language, of course – here I use the term *awe* only provisionally. We in the Kama Muta Lab are provisionally using the ancient Greek word sebomai to name the emotion of sudden intensification of authority ranking in a subordinate.

Are there distinct emotions mediating each kind of transition of each relational model?

Social and moral emotions are the experience of motivations that are the proxies in the immediate present for the long-term expected fitness value of relational tactics, informed and oriented according to what is adaptive in a particular socio-cultural milieu (Fiske 2002, 2010; Keltner & Haidt 1999). So I would expect to find a distinct emotion mediating each basic kind of transition in each fundamental type of social relationship.

Recall from Online Note 1.4 Laski's (1961, 1980) exposition of transcendent ecstasy. She also briefly sketches a larger scheme of emotions. She posited that one can have the opposite of ecstasy, the momentary feeling of "desolation," consisting of terrifying, dark loneliness (1961:160–170, 1980:79ff). Laski asserts that the triggers for desolation are people and places that one finds repulsive, including the maimed, ill, dying, or ugly, along with dilapidated, horrifying locations, prisons, and the like. Whatever disgusts one is a trigger for desolation; for Laski this includes the poor, needy, children, and aged relatives! In our framework, "desolation" is the feeling of not having needed CS connections; the sense of separation or otherness. Finally, Laski notes a third emotion, the sudden feeling of superiority that she calls the "Napoleonic experience" (1980:151–153). We might also call it *pride*, occurring when one 'rises' in an authority ranking relationship.

Let's systematically construct a matrix of relational dynamics. First, consider the basic transitions that a person must be motivated to respond to appropriately. Nurturance and commitment to a CS relationship are adaptive under certain sociocultural conditions, while under other conditions, it is adaptive to reduce efforts to participate in a CS relationship, or, in other conditions, to terminate it. In other sociocultural conditions, it is adaptive to punish a CS partner – or a third party. Then there are conditions in which one has transgressed an important CS relationship, so it is imperative to redress it: one should 'make it up to' the partner and persuasively commit to refraining from further transgressions. When one loses a good and vital CS relationship one must reorient, lower one's expectations for the future, retrench, plead for support from existing CS partners, and eventually seek new CS relationships with good prospective partners. This suggests that people should experience the respective adaptive motives needed to capitalize on these changes – challenges and opportunities – as distinct emotions of attenuating, terminating, punishing, redressing, or mourning CS. The same kind of analysis and synthesis that we are doing for kama muta, the emotional experience of the motivation to engage more deeply in a CS relationship, could be done for each of these other emotions

I considered above the emotion of *sebomai* at sudden intensification of subordination in an authority ranking relationship, and briefly mentioned the emotion of sudden elevation to a (more) superior position. In addition, just as in CS relationships, we should expect that there should be distinct emotions evoked by, respectively, others' transgression of authority ranking, one's own prospective or actual transgression of the relationship, the necessity to terminate a deleterious relationship, and the unwanted attenuation or loss of the relationship. The emotions for each of these transitions when the person is in the superior position should be distinct from the emotions when the person is in the subordinate position in the authority ranking relationship.

Equality matching, the third fundamental relational model, consists of coordination with respect to socially meaningful additive intervals, with even balance as the reference point. Examples are turn-taking, even distribution and evenly matched contribution, in-kind one-for-one balanced reciprocity, tit-for-tat vengeance, voting, and fair lotteries. Equality matching also has its sudden intensifications, transgressions by self and by partners, intentional termination, and attenuation or loss. Each of these is likely mediated by its own emotion, generating the functional motives to support effective action.

The fourth fundamental type of coordination is market pricing (which is by no means limited to material transactions, let alone literal 'markets' or monetary 'prices'). Market pricing is coordination with reference to socially meaningful proportions, rates, or ratios. Thus it manifests as many sorts of cost-benefit analyses, consideration of whether what one contributes is *worth it* in proportion to what one receives in return, punishment or reward to proportion to just desert, or utilitarian moral reasoning. And obviously in tithes, taxes, prices, wages, rents, interest rates, discount rates, and so forth. Market pricing, too, also has its sudden intensifications, transgressions by self and by partners, intentional termination, and attenuation or loss.

Good relationships of each of the four fundamental types are adaptively beneficial at the level of natural selection, health, psychological well-being, and happiness. So we would expect the regulation of each relational model to depend on functional emotions. Table 19.1 illustrates this theoretical taxonomy of social-relational emotions. As initial, albeit tentative, starting points for generating intuitions about the subjective feeling of these emotions, some English lexemes are provisionally indicated, although I expect that none corresponds closely (certainly not one-to-one) with the scientific construct that we need to formulate. All of the illustrative terms have vague and diverse meanings, so most cells

TABLE 19.1 Theoretical emotions mediating relationship transitions

	Suddenly create or intensify	Other transgresses: Desire to punish	Self transgresses: Rectify, make amends	Self terminates or attenuates	Mourn separation or loss
Communal Sharing	**Kama muta**	Disgust, bitterness	Shame	Coldness	Grief
Authority Ranking down ↓	Pride, pity	Rage	Humiliation	Contempt	Dejection
Authority Ranking up ↑	Awe	Righteous rebellion	Guilt	Disdain, belittlement	Abandonment
Equality Matching	Comradeship	Retaliatory payback	Embarrassment	Disappointment	Missing
Market Pricing	Avarice	Cheated anger	Indebtedness	Devaluation	Destitution

Note: Authority Ranking down refers to the emotions of the superior, while Authority Ranking up refers to the emotions of the subordinate. The vernacular names given for all cells are merely suggestive placeholders, and not always apt; there are no precise or consistent English vernacular lexemes for the actual emotions (see Chapter 7).

do not have particularly apt names in English. Ultimately we need a technical vocabulary that will enable conceptual precision and prevent the misconstrual that inevitably results from using vernacular terms, but we do need an initial terminology to begin the discussion. In the meanwhile, we should use these terms in scare quotes ('humiliation') to indicate their technical usage.

Consider the first row: kama muta we have considered; look at the next cell. When a partner 'cheats,' a cowardly soldier runs from battle, or a traitor defects, his CS partner(s) feel *betrayed*, *hurt*, and *disgusted*. This emotion differs from non-social disappointment and anxiety, and contrasts with the emotions that a person feels when he himself violates the CS. Likewise, the emotional response to a partner's CS betrayal differs from the emotion one feels in an authority ranking relationship when disobeyed or disrespected, and from the emotion a follower feels when his leader fails to guide wisely, protect, and stand up for her followers. The emotion of being betrayed in CS is also distinct from the feeling of being let down when an EM partner fails to reciprocate, fails to do his share, or fails to take his turn at an onerous task. Despite being labelled in English with the same term, when one discovers one has been *cheated* in a market pricing deal, the emotion one experiences is entirely different from the emotion of discovering a CS partner *cheating*, or the CS emotion one feels seeing a member of one's platoon cowering in a hole when he should have your back. All of these emotions motivate punishment of the transgressing partner, as well as evoking distrust and leading to attenuation of the violated relationship. But they are not the same, because the relationships are fundamentally different.

When one violates a CS relationship oneself, one feels *shame* – one doesn't want to be seen and doesn't feel that one can be with one's partner(s). This emotion of wanting to hide and keep away from partners differs from the feeling of humiliation when one has failed one's followers and no longer deserves their respect. It is also dissimilar from the emotion of *guilt* when one has disobeyed one's superior. And it is unlike the *embarrassment* a person feels when they fail to help a friend who helped them, or when they fail to make a contribution that matches what others have contributed. All of those emotions of personal transgression in the other three relationships contrast with the market pricing violation emotion of being caught making fraudulent claims about a product or swindling clients in a Ponzi scheme. And so forth. Each of these 25 emotions must motivate different relational tactics. It seems that the more psychopathic a person, the weaker these emotions would be, and the weaker the consequent motives. Indeed, perhaps deficits in these emotions constitute the core of psychopathy, antisocial personality disorder, and the early symptoms of fronto-temporal disorder (see Fiske 2002, 2010). These emotions may also be diminished in autism-spectrum disorders.

It is certainly conceivable that this taxonomy is too coarse. Perhaps the emotional responses to one's partners' lazy, inept, or half-hearted performance of their relational responsibilities differ from one's emotional responses to outright relationship-destroying transgressions. Presumably the emotion one feels when one's partner fails to do the dishes is quite distinct from the emotion one feels when one finds him in bed with someone. Perhaps there is more than a difference in degree; the hurt may be qualitatively distinct. Likewise one's shame at failing to do the dishes may differ in kind from the shame at being found in bed with someone. Again, the emotional experience of the motivation to back away from a CS relationship – just 'needing some space' – may differ from the acute emotion of wanting to 'break up' forever and never see the partner again. The grief of temporary separation may have qualities that differ from the grief of permanent loss, and the emotions of permanent loss may differ depending on whether the partner is obliged to leave unwillingly, dies, 'breaks up' with one to take up with another partner, or simply ends the CS relationship by neglect. There is the further question of whether the grief from 'breaking up' with a partner at one's own initiative differs from the grief when one's partner initiates the 'break-up' against one's wishes, or, again, when the break-up is mutually desired.

So perhaps this table needs more columns. It could even need more rows, if, for example, some of the emotions of romantic and sexual CS dynamics differ from the emotions of the transitions in other CS relationships. It appears that kama muta is qualitatively the same in both types of CS, but the other dynamic emotions could differ. This table represents the most parsimonious analysis, which I propose until both rigorous theoretical analyses of the functions of these emotions and solid empirical evidence show that there are more than these 25 relational dynamic emotions. In any case, I hope that this table offers a foundational matrix for discovery. This is not yet a periodic table of emotions, but perhaps we can get there eventually.

Of course, while I posit that these 25 emotions are analytically and qualitatively distinct, that does not imply that they typically occur in isolation. Emotions in the same row are especially likely to co-occur. Similarly, oxygen is a distinct element, but oxygen atoms are usually found in compounds with hydrogen, carbon, metals, et cetera.

These 25 posited sociomoral emotions may vary considerably within and across cultures in their incidence and modal intensity, largely as a function of the respective functional significance of the dynamic transitions in relational motives. For example, in a given culture, the opportunity to create a new market pricing relationship or intensify an existing one may be relatively important, or it may be unimportant. Again, for example, the functional social significance of one's own transgression of an authority ranking relationship with a superior may be great in a culture and domain in which authority ranking is crucial, but comparatively minor in another domain, another culture, or another point in history. The intensity of the emotions should correspond, reflecting how much such transgressions matter. In a hunting and gathering society in which people minimize and avoid authority ranking, it may be rare to experience the emotion of transgressing an authority ranking relationship with a superior.

More significant, all of these emotions must be modulated by cultural precedents, prototypes, paradigms, precepts, and parameters. That is, preos must sensitize the respective psypes to culturally and contextually significant signs of transitions in locally important relationships. Other preos must orient the psype to generate motives to act aptly; the tactics that are effective in one context of one culture at one point in history may backfire in others.

It remains to be seen whether every emotion has a distinctive or even perceptible set of sensation and signs. Sensations and signs are not essential to the functioning of 'emotions' as I use this term.

Beyond the emotions that dynamically motivate tactical reallocation of effort at moments of relational transition, during periods of relational stability people may experience subtler but more enduring moods, or dispositions toward particular partners, that dispose them to sustain important relational equilibrium strategies. That is, while relational changes require prompt action, people also need to adapt as well as possible to relational equilibria. Moods and interpersonal dispositions may motivate effective relationship-sustaining strategies.

A final touch

We of the Kama Muta Lab hope that our research, presentations, publications, and this book in particular help people to appreciate kama muta. Recognizing it makes life richer. The deeper our understanding of kama muta, the deeper our potential enjoyment of it and the more meaningful it can be. Let us cultivate opportunities to experience, give, and share kama muta. Let us savor its delights together. May it connect us all, and may it ever remind us how loving and kind humans often are, and always can be.

Note

1 From "Latin *magnus* 'great, large, big' (of size), 'abundant' (of quantity), 'great, considerable' (of value), 'strong, powerful' (of force); of persons, 'elder, aged,' also, figuratively, 'great, mighty, grand, important'" (Online etymological dictionary).

GLOSSARY OF THEORETICAL
CONSTRUCTS

authority ranking an asymmetrical relation in which the subordinate owes
deference, respect, and allegiance to a superior who takes responsibility
for providing wise guidance, leadership, and protection (Fiske 1991, 1992,
2004a). It differs from 'power' because is not based on pure force or coer-
cion, and because participants perceive it to be morally legitimate. One of
the four fundamental and universal relational models.

awe An English vernacular word that typically denotes the sudden intensi-
fication of a subordinate's authority ranking relationship with a superior.
Some other languages denote this emotion with a lexeme meaning 'fear.'
See pp. 336–339.

communal sharing (CS) a social relation in which participants treat each other
as equivalent in respect to some aspect of their coordination (Fiske 1991,
1992, 2004a). Loosely speaking, *love*, in a broad sense. Participants attend
to and are motivated by what they have in common, which they typically
feel to be some common bodily essence. Involves feelings of belonging,
closeness, connection, shared identity, compassion, and kindness. One of the
four fundamental and universal relational models. Sudden intensification of
communal sharing usually evokes kama muta. See pp. 61–63.

consubstantial assimilation perceiving or making bodies equivalent, so that
individuals become socially equivalent. The indexical conformation system
(see below) of communal sharing. See pp. 73–75.

conformation system The primary, natural, maximally evocative semiotic-
constitutive medium in which people mentally and communicatively represent, actively create, and modulate a specific relational model (Fiske 2004b).
Also is the semiotic medium in which children expect to find and do discover the preos necessary to implement that specific relational model, and
hence the medium in which the local implementations of that relational
model are culturally replicated and diffused. The conformation system
for authority ranking is iconic physical dimensions and magnitudes. The
conformation system for equality matching is concrete operations that are

ostensive operational definitions of even balance. The conformation system of market pricing is abstract symbols, in the narrow sense of signs whose meaning is based on arbitrary conventions.

CS abbreviation for communal sharing (see above).

driver A cultural practice, institution, role, artifact or art whose function is to evoke an emotion such as kama muta. Through cultural evolution, drivers adapt to the niche provided by the psype (see below). That is, the more a driver evokes the psype, the more people are likely to invent, attend to, remember, re-enact, seek to participate in, communicate about, and recruit other participants to join in the driver. Drivers and psype are symbiotic, often mutualistic. But, culturally evolving faster than the biological evolution of their psype, drivers may also be parasitic, diminishing participants' survival or reproduction. See pp. 232–234.

equality matching social coordination based on a standard of even balance, with additive-subtractive differences from even balance (Fiske 1991, 1992, 2004a). Social coordination based on one-to-one correspondence. Examples are turn-taking, balanced in-kind reciprocity, tit-for-tat exchange, one-person one-vote elections, fair lotteries, evenly matched contributions, and even distributions. 'Equality' in this relational model means 'distinct but evenly matched,' in contrast to the equivalence of communal sharing in which participants become one, losing their individuality when they merge into a transcendent social dyad or group that envelopes them. One of the four fundamental and universal relational models.

indexicality The semiotic constitutive aspect of consubstantial assimilation (see above), in which participants' bodies and bodily substances (including what they ingest) constitutively represent their social selves (Fiske 2004b). The concept was first set out as an aspect of the representationality of communicative and cognitive signs by C. S. Pierce (1931–1958, 1985). People primarily represent and create communal sharing relationships indexically. Indexical constitutive acts and perceptions are maximally evocative of kama muta.

kama muta The positive emotion evoked by the sudden intensification of communal sharing, marked by characteristic sensations and signs, motivating affective devotion and moral commitment to communal sharing. In English, often (though not invariably) denoted by *moved*, *touched*, feeling *tenderness*, or labeling experiences as *heart–warming* or *stirring*. In specific contexts, may be identified as *nostalgia, rapture, patriotic pride, team spirit*. Generally encompasses the psype and motes, and sometimes the drivers. See especially pp. 90–92.

market pricing cooperatively coordinating with reference to ratios, proportions, or rates (Fiske 1991, 1992, 2004a). Does not intrinsically involve selfishness, maximization, competitiveness, or individualistic orientation. Examples include fair proportionality in penalties and rewards, cost/benefit calculations of what one gives and gets out of relationships, utilitarian moral reasoning, and all other calculations of the relative worth of unlike entities. Need not involve money, transactions, or material goods, but encompasses monetary prices, wages, rents, taxes, tithes, and interest rates. One of the four fundamental and universal relational models.

mote A particular occurrence of an emotion such as kama muta; an event or episode that is an instance of the emotion. Characteristically momentary, although the motivations that emerge from a mote may be enduring. See pp. 209–212.

mod   An innate psychological system or propensity that can be implemented only with respect to a certain class of cultural preos that complement it (Fiske 2000). That is, the mod has evolved in the context of cultural preos, and its realization depends on those preos to function. Hence, to be used to generate action, understand, motivate, and evaluate social action – to enable cooperative coordination – a mod needs the complementary preos. Examples include the human language learning system, the respective cores of each of the four fundamental relational models, and the kama muta psype in its raw state as it reaches maturity early in ontogeny. Strictly speaking, a mod is the psychological system before it encounters the preos it seeks and depends on. The mod together with a cultural- and context-specific set of necessary complementary preos is called a 'cultural coordination device.' See pp. 208–209.

mutualism   A form of symbiosis in which participation is mutually beneficial. In the context of the co-evolution of psype and drivers, mutualism occurs when the psype favors the cultural evolution (diffusion, reproduction) of a driver, while the driver favors the inclusive biological fitness (survival, reproduction) of the genes that produce the psype. See pp. 310–311.

parasitism   A form of symbiosis in which participation benefits one party at the expense of the other. In the context of the co-evolution of psype and drivers, parasitism occurs when a driver reproduces culturally to the detriment of the genes that produce the psype. That is, engaging in the driver (participating, re-enacting, recruiting others) decreases the biological fitness of the participants. Drivers can be parasitic on a psype because the cultural evolution of drivers is orders of magnitude more rapid than the biological evolution of a psype. However, natural selection favors psypes that evolve 'immunological' mechanisms to defend against parasitic drivers. See pp. 310–311.

preo   A culturally-transmitted complement to a mod, required by the mod to function (Fiske 2000). Preos take many semiotic forms including precedents, prototypes, paradigms, parameters, precepts, prescriptions, and proscriptions. A mod is indeterminate until coupled with preos that complete it by specifying with whom, when, where, and how the mod operates. The kama muta psype mod can only function with reference to preos that indicate what communal sharing relationships are propitious. The kama muta psype mod also needs preos that indicate what sorts of consubstantial assimilation or other signs index intensification of communal sharing relationships. And the mod can only operate in conjunction with preos that specify how to effectively devote and commit to the relevant communal sharing relationships. See p. 310.

psype   The psychological system that, in response to a transition in a social relationship, generates a mote. Thus a psype can be formally analyzed as a function that maps its domain (input) of relational transitions onto a range (image, output) of affective devotion and moral commitment to some set of relationships. The domain of the kama muta psype is comprised of sudden intensifications of communal sharing relationships; its range consists of effective forms of devotion and commitment to appropriate communal sharing relationships. To be precise, one should distinguish between two states of the kama muta psype. The first, the mod, is the psype's innate, ontogenetically undifferentiated, pre-cultural, indeterminate form. The second is the psype coupled to the cultural preos it depends on to function as a specific cultural coordination device. See pp. 309–310.

relational model A fundamental, universal model of, and for, cooperative social coordination (Fiske 1991, 1992, 2004a). People use relational models to generate, understand, and evaluate social interaction. Although they have evolved as adaptations that generally enhance biological fitness, subjectively, relational models are intrinsically-motivated ends in themselves. There are four relational models: communal sharing, authority ranking, equality matching, and market pricing. Though the mods of the relational models are innate, to function to coordinate any actual social interaction on any occasion, each mod must be operationalized through cultural preos that specify how, when, where, and with whom to implement the mod. When they do not use any relational model to coordinate, people may simply treat others as mere material objects or as agents with no moral standing (like ants); I call this a "null" interaction. A person (such as one with a high degree of psychopathy) may understand the relational models, recognizing others' relational model motivation and moral engagement, but himself feel no intrinsic relational motivation or moral engagement; then the person interacts instrumentally in an "asocial" model.

REFERENCES

Abou Zahab, Mariam 2008. 'Yeh Matam kayse ruk jae?' ('How Could this *Matam* Ever Cease?'): Muharram Processions in Pakistani Punjab. In Knut A. Jacobson, Ed., *South Asian Religious Display: Religious Processions in South Asia and the Diaspora* (pp. 104–114). Oxford: Routledge.

Abū Nasr al–Sarrāj (10th century) 1914. *Kitāb al–luma'*. Edited by R. A. Nicholson., Leiden: Brill.

Abu–Lughod, Lila 1986. *Veiled Sentiments: Honor and Poetry in a Bedouin Society*. Berkeley, CA: University of California Press.

Abu–Lughod, Lila 1993. Islam and the Gendered Discourses of Death. *International Journal of Middle East Studies* 25(2):187–205.

Agbetsoamedo, Yvonne, & Francesca Di Garbo 2015. Unravelling Temperature Terms in Sɛlɛɛ. In Maria Koptjevskaja-Tamm, Ed., *The Linguistics of Temperature* (pp. 107–127). Amsterdam: John Benjamins.

Aghaie, Kamran Scot 2009. The Women of Karbala: Ritual Performance and Symbolic Discourses in Modern Shi'*a Islam*. Austin: University of Texas Press.

Akbari, Mersalla 2015a. Undergraduate Research Paper on Muslim Call to Prayer and Prayer, Based on Participant Observation and Interviewing, Working Under the Supervision of Alan Fiske, UCLA Department of Anthropology.

Akbari, Mersalla 2015b. Undergraduate Research Paper on Ghazals Among Afghanis in Southern California, Based on Participant Observation and Interviewing, Working Under the Supervision of Alan Fiske, UCLA Department of Anthropology.

Alcoholics Anonymous 2001. *The Big Book*. Fourth Edition. New York, NY: A.A World Services.

Alexander, James 1846. Introduction. In Philip Doddridge, Ed., Thoughts on Sentimental Occasions. Philadelphia, PA: William S. Martien. [Quoted in Schmidt 2001].

Alexander, Ruth 2014. Sydney Cafe: Australians say to Muslims "I'll Ride With You". BBC News 15 December 2015. http://www.bbc.com/news/blogs–trending–30479306 Accessed 3 September 2019.

Algoe, Sara B., & Jonathan Haidt 2009. Witnessing Excellence in Action: The "Other-praising" Emotions of Elevation, Gratitude, and Admiration. *The Journal of Positive Psychology* 4(2):105–127.

Ameed, Syed Mohammad 1974. The Importance of Weeping and Wailing in our Condolatory *Observance*. Karachi: Peermahomed Ebrahim Trust.

Ameka, Felix K. 2015. "Hard Sun, Hot Weather, Skin Pain: The Cultural Semantics of Temperature Expressions in Ewe and Likpe (West Africa). In Maria Koptjevskaja-Tamm, Ed., *The Linguistics of Temperature* (pp. 43–72). Amsterdam: John Benjamins.

American Psychiatric Association 2013. *Diagnostic and Statistical Manual of Mental Disorders, 5th Edition: DSM–5*. Washington, DC: American Psychiatric Association.

American Rhetoric 2019. Jesse Jackson 1988 Democratic National Convention Address. https://www.americanrhetoric.com/speeches/jessejackson1988dnc.htm

Anderson, Benedict 2006. *Imagined Communities: Reflections on the Spread of Nationalism.* Revised Edition. London: Verso.

Anderson, Gary A. 1991. *A Time to Mourn, A Time to Dance: The Expression of Grief and Joy in Israelite Religion.* University Park, PA: The Pennsylvania State University Press.

Andrabi, Zoya 2014. Is Understanding Everything? Undergraduate Independent–Research Paper Based on Participant Observation and Interviewing in Southern California. Available from Alan Page Fiske.

Anonymous 1981. From W. S. Merwin and J. Moussaieff Masson, editors and translators, *The Peacock's Egg: Love Poems from Ancient India.* San Francisco, CA: North Point Press. Poem on pp. 170–171.

Appadurai, Arjun 1988. *The Social Life of Things: Commodities in Cultural Perspective.* Cambridge: Cambridge University Press.

Arficio, Haile Bubbamo 1973. Some Notes on the Traditional Hadiya Women. *Journal of Ethiopian Studies* 11(2):131–155. http://www.jstor.org/stable/41988261

Asch, Solomon E., & Harriet Nerlove 1960. The Developmenbt of Double Function Words: An Exploratory Investigation. In Bernard Kaplan & Seymour Wapner, Eds., *Perspectives in Psychology: Essays in Honor of Heinz Werner* (pp. 47–60). New York: International Universities Press.

Atintono, Samuel Awinkene 2015. The Semantics and Metaphorical Extensions of Temperature Terms in Gurenɛ. In Maria Koptjevskaja-Tamm, Ed., *The Linguistics of Temperature* (pp. 73–106). Amsterdam: John Benjamins.

Atkinson, Jane 1984. "Wrapped Words": Poetry and Politics among the Wana of Central Sulawesi, Indonesia. In Donald Lawrence Brenneis & Fred R. Myers, Eds., *Dangerous Words: Language and Politics in the Pacific* (pp. 33–68). New York: New York University Press.

Atkinson, Max 1984. *Our Masters' Voices: The Language and Body Language of Politics.* London: Methuen.

Austin, John L. 1975. *How To Do Things with Words.* 2nd Edition. Edited by J. O. Urmson and Marina Sbisà. Cambridge, MA: Harvard University Press.

Ayoub, Mahmoud M. 1978. *Redemptive Suffering in Islam: A Study of the Devotional Aspects of Ashura in Twelver Shi'ism.* The Hague: Mouton.

Bain, Alexander 1859. *The Emotions and the Will.* London: John W. Parker & Sons. https ://books.googleusercontent.com/books/content?req=AKW5Qad7awj6Qp-Kd4Nl4 4aTuCGYiUhoplTzwOesCLSsNwhHzSIYoI8VNzcFvLlDNacRZW5briVX41dtg YKQ44At4_S8wjTogmhOBszdKSa3OVPnwgNvHHGdwwKMzQ0m5Rn2o9Mt 2NQyX0_PEuRrxKmRw5kPH4iQlpbJLoBHz-tCn8ykzpOj8aF8ZkAwF1NDzWvc 27ZuM5qLw85u94X344UdsfHUXTWaKhSG_6jL5c45nDMAAEaHbZCvDcJ 6ZeeuAdtlOaNmvQgGl72QpcaQu6rfz8KjIiZ68g

Balbir, Nalini, Editor and Translator, 1982. *Dānâṣṭakakathā: Recueil Jaina de Huit Histoires sur le Don.* Série in-8o; fasc. 48. Paris: Collège de France, Institut de Civilisation Indienne.

Balsters, Martijn J., Emiel J. Krahmer, Marc G. Swerts, & A. J. Vingerhoets 2012. Emotional Tears Facilitate the Recognition of Sadness and the Perceived Need for Social Support. *Evolutionary Psychology: An International Journal of Evolutionary Approaches to Psychology and Behavior* 11:148–158.

Banks, Caroline Giles 1996. "There Is No Fat in Heaven": Religious Asceticism and the Meaning of Anorexia Nervosa. *Ethos* 24:107–135.

Bard, Amy C. 2005. "No Power of Speech Remains": Tears and Transformation in South Asian *Majlis* Poetry. In Kimberley Christine Patton & John Stratton Hawley, Eds., *Holy Tears: Weeping in the Religious Imagination* (pp. 145–164). Princeton, NJ: Princeton University Press.

Bard, Amy C. 2010. Turning Karbala Inside Out: Humor and Ritual Critique in South Asian Muharram Rites. In Selva J. Raj & Corinne G. Dempsey, Eds., *Sacred Play: Ritual Levity and Humor in South Asian Religions* (pp. 161–184). Albany, NY: State University of New York Press.

Barkow, Jerome H, Leda Cosmides, & John Tooby 1995. *The Adapted Mind: Evolutionary Psychology and the Generation of Culture*. Oxford: Oxford University Press.

Barnhill, David Landis, translator. 2004. *Bashō's Haiku: Selected Poems by Matsuo Bashō*. Albany, NY: State University of New York Press.

Baron, Zach 2014. Where the Wild Things of Viral. GQ 4 March 2014 2:00 am. http://www.gq.com/story/buzzfeed–beastmaster–profile–march–2014 Accessed 3 September 2019.

Barrett, E. Boyd 1928. The Drama of Catholic Confession. *The Journal of Religion* 8:188–203.

Barrett, Lisa Feldman 2017. *How Emotions Are Made: The Secret Life of the Brain*. New York: Houghton Mifflin Harcourt.

Barrett, Lisa Feldman, Christine D. Wilson-Mendenhall, & Lawrence W. Barsalou 2015. The Conceptual Act Theory: A Road Map. In Lisa Feldman Barrett & James A. Russell, Eds., *The Psychological Construction of Emotion* (pp. 83–110). New York: Guilford Press.

Barth, J, Schneider, S, & von Kanel, R. 2010. Lack of Social Support in the Etiology and the Prognosis of Coronary Heart Disease: A Systematic Review and Meta–analysis. *Psychosomatic Medicine* 72:229–238.

Bartsch, Anne, Anja Kalch, & Mary Beth Oliver 2014. Moved to Think: The Role of Emotional Media Experiences in Stimulating Reflective Thoughts. *Journal of Media Psychology* 26(3):125–140.

Bashō, Matsuo 1994. *The Essential Haiku: Versions of Bashō, Buson, and Issa*. Edited and translated by Robert Hass. New York: Ecco (Harper Collins).

Basile, Christopher, & Janet Hoskins 1998. Nusa Tenggara Timur. In Terry Miller, Ed., *Garland Encyclopedia of World Music Volume 4: Southeast Asia*. New York: Routledge. http://glnd.alexanderstreet.com/view/329157

Batson, C. Daniel 1991. *The Altruism Question: Toward a Social–Psychological Answer*. Hillsdale, NJ: Erlbaum.

Batson, C. Daniel 2010. Empathy-Induced Altruistic Motivation. In Mario E. Mikulincer & Phillp R. Shaver, Eds., *Prosocial Motives, Emotions, and Behavior: The Better Angels of Our Nature* (pp. 15–34). Washington, DC: American Psychological Association.

Batson, C. Daniel, Jacob Håkansson Eklund, Valerie L. Chermok, Jennifer L. Hoyt, & Biaggio G. Ortiz 2007. An Additional Antecedent of Empathic Concern: Valuing the Welfare of the Person in Need. *Journal of Personality and Social Psychology* 93:65–74. doi:10.1037/0022-3514.93.1.65

Batson, C. Daniel, Janine L. Dyck, J. Randall Brandt, Judy G. Batson, Anne L. Powell, M. Rosalie McMaster, & Cari Griffitt 1988. Five Studies Testing Two New Egoistic Alternatives to the Empathy-Altruism Hypothesis. *Journal of Personality and Social Psychology* 55(1):52–77. doi:10.1037/0022-3514.55.1.52

Batson, C. Daniel, Jim Fultz, & Patricia A. Schoenrade 1987. Distress and Empathy: Two Qualitatively Distinct Vicarious Emotions with Different Motivational Consequences. *Journal of Personality* 55:19–39. doi:10.1111/j.1467-6494.1987.tb00426.x

Beck, Jerome, and Rosenbaum, Marsha 1986. *The Pursuit of Ecstasy: The MDMA Experience*. Albany, NY: State University of New York.

Bedics, Jamie D., David C. Atkins, K. A. Comtois, & Marsha M. Linehan 2012. Treatment Differences in the Therapeutic Relationship and Introject During a 2-Year Randomized Controlled Trial of Dialectical Behavior Therapy Versus Nonbehavioral Psychotherapy Experts for Borderline Personality Disorder. *Journal of Consulting and Clinical Psychology* 80:66–77. doi:10.1037/a0026113

Beecher Stowe, Harriet 1852. *Uncle Tom's Cabin*. Boston: Houghton Mifflin.

Belk, Russell W. 1988. Possessions and the Extended Self. *Journal of Consumer Research* 15(2):139–168.

Benedek, Mathias, & Christian Kaernbach 2011. Physiological Correlates and Emotional Specificity of Human Piloerection. *Biological Psychology* 86:320–329.

Benedict, Ruth 1922. The Vision in Plains Culture. *American Anthropologist* (New Series) 24:1–23.

Berggren, Erik Gustav Alexius 1975. *The Psychology of Confession*. Leiden: Brill.

Berry, Diane S., & Leslie Zebrowitz McArthur 1985. Some Components and Consequences of a Babyface. *Personality and Social Psychology* 48:312–323. doi:10.1037/0022-3514.48.2.312

Bershad, Anya K., Jessica J. Weafera, Matthew G. Kirkpatrick, Margaret C. Wardled, Melissa A. Millera, & Harriet de Wit 2016. Oxytocin Receptor Gene Variation Predicts Subjective Responses to MDMA. *Social Neuroscience* 11(6):592–599. doi:10.1080/17470919.2016.1143026.

Bhāgavata Purāṇa, n.d. Book X and parts of Book XI translated by Edwin F. Bryant as *Krishna: The Beautiful Legend of God: Srimad Bhagavata Purana*. London: Penguin.

Bicknell, Jeanette 2009. *Why Music Moves Us*. Houndmills, Hampshire, England: Palgrave Macmillan.

Biten, Ali Furkan 2016. Personal oral Communication, 16 November 2015.

Bligh, Michelle C., & Jeffrey C. Kohles 2009. The Enduring Allure of Charisma: How Barack Obama Won the Historic 2008 Presidential Election. *Leadership Quarterly* 20:483–492.

Bligh, Michelle C., Jeffrey C. Kohles, & James R. Meindl 2004. Charisma Under Crisis: Presidential Leadership, Rhetoric and Media Responses Before and After September 11 Terrorist Attacks. *Leadership Quarterly* 15:211–39.

Blinderman, Ilia 2013. In Touching Video, Artist Marina Abramović & Former Lover Ulay Reunite After 22 Years Apart. From *Art, Life*, 2 December 2013. Read on *Open Culture*. http://www.openculture.com/2013/12/artist–marina–abramovic–former–lover–ulay–reunite.html; Accessed 3 September 2019.

Blomfield, Bridget 2010. From Ritual to Redemption: Worldview of Shi'a Muslim Women in Southern California. In Zayn Kassam, Ed., *Women and Islam* (pp. 303–324). Santa Barbara, CA: Greenwood.

Bolender, John 2010. *The Self–Organizing Social Mind*. Cambridge, MA: MIT Press.

Booker, Christopher 2004. *The Seven Basic Plots: Why We Tell Stories*. London: Continuum.

Bosworth D. A. 2015. Weeping in Recognition Scenes in Genesis and the Odyssey. *The Catholic Biblical Quarterly* 77:629–639.

Bough, Jill 2011. *Donkey*. London: Reaktion.

Bourgignon, Erika 2008. Spirit Possession. In Conerly Casey & Robert B. Edgerton, Eds., *A Companion to Psychological Anthropology: Modernity and Psychocultural Change* (pp. 374–388). Malden, MA: Wiley–Blackwell.

Bowern, Claire, & Laura Kling 2015. Bardi Temperature Terms. In Maria Koptjevskaja-Tamm, Ed., *The Linguistics of Temperature* (pp. 815–831). Amsterdam: John Benjamins.

Bowers, Faubion 1996. *The Classic Tradition of Haiku: An Anthology*. Mineola, NY: Dover.

Boyer, Pascal 2001. *Religion Explained*. New York: Basic Books.

Bradley, M. M., & P. J. Lang 2007. The International Affective Picture System (IAPS) in the Study of Emotion and Attention. In J. A. Coan & J. J. B. Allen, Eds., *Handbook of Emotion Elicitation and Assessment* (pp. 29–46). Oxford: Oxford University Press.

Braud, William 2001. Experiencing Tears of Wonder–Joy: Seeing With The Heart's Eye. *Journal of Transpersonal Psychology* 33:99–111.

Bravo, Gary L. 2001. What Does MDMA Feel Like? In Julie Holland, Ed., *Ecstasy: The Complete Guide* (pp. 21–38). Rochester, VT: Park Street Press.

Bremmer, Jan N. 2007. Greek Normative Sacrifice. In Daniel Ogden, Ed., *A Companion to Greek Religion*. Malden, MA: Blackwell.

Breslin, James 1993. *Mark Rothko: A Biography*. Chicago, IL: University of Chicago Press.

Briggs, Charles L. 1993. Personal Sentiments and Polyphonic Voices in Warao Women's Ritual Wailing: Music and Poetics in a Critical and Collective Discourse. *American Anthropologist* 95:929–957.

Brock, Sebastien, translator. 1995. *Isaac of Nineveh (Isaac the Syrian): The Second Part*, Chapters 4–41, Corpus Scriptorium Christianorum Orientalium 554–5, Scriptores Syri 224–5. [Quoted by Hunter 2004]

Brosig, Benjamin 2015. Temperature Terms in Khalkha Mongolian. In Maria Koptjevskaja-Tamm, Ed., *The Linguistics of Temperature* (pp. 570–593). Amsterdam: John Benjamins.

Brown, Daniel James 2013. *The Boys in the Boat: Nine Americans and Their Epic Quest for Gold at the 1936 Berlin Olympics*. New York: Penguin.

Brown, Peter 1988. *The Body and Society: Men, Women, and Sexual Renunciation in Early Christianity*. New York: Columbia University Press.

Brownell, Philip 2010. *Gestalt Therapy: A Guide to Contemporary Practice*. Springer.

Bryant, Edwin F. 2003. *Krishna: The Beautiful Legend of God: Śrīmad Bhāgavata Purāṇa, Book X*. London: Penguin Books.

Brykina, Maria, & Valentin Gusev 2015. Temperature Terms in Nganasan. In Maria Koptjevskaja-Tamm, Ed., *The Linguistics of Temperature* (pp. 537–569). Amsterdam: John Benjamins.

Buckley, Ralf C. 2016. Aww: The emotion of perceiving cuteness. *Frontiers in Psychology* 7(1740). doi:10.3389/fpsyg.2016.01740

Buddhaghosa, Bhadantácariya 2010 [original text 5th century CE]. *The Path of Purification (Visuddhimagga)*. Translated by Bhikkhu Ñáóamoli. Kandy. Sri Lanka: Buddhist Publication Society. In print. http://www.accesstoinsight.org/lib/authors/nanamoli/PathofPurification2011.pdf

Burton, Richard Francis 1906. *Personal Narrative of a Pilgrimage to Al–Madinah and Meccah*, Volume 2. London: George Bell and Sons.

Buswell, Robert E., Jr., & Donald S. Lopez Jr. 2013. *The Princeton Dictionary of Buddhism* Princeton, NJ: Princeton University Press.

Cairns, Douglas 2013. A Short History of the Shudders. In Angelos Chaniotis & Pierre Ducrey, Eds., *Unveiling Emotions II, Emotions in Greece and Rome: Texts, Images, Material Culture* (pp. 85–107). Stuttgart: Franz Steiner Verlag.

Calasso, Giovanna 2000a. La dimension religieuse individuelle dans les textes musulmans médiévaux, entre hagiographie et littérature de voyages: les larmes, les émotions, l'expérience. *Studia Islamica* 91:39–58. http://www.jstor.org/stable/1596268

Calasso, Giovanna 2000b. Les Sourires et les Larmes: Observations en Marge de Quelques Textes Hagiographiques Musulman. *Al–Qanṭara: Revista de Estudios Arabes* 21:445–456.

Calle, E. E., Thun, M. J., Petrelli, J. M, Rodriguez, C., & Heath, C. W. 1999. Body–Mass Index and Mortality in a Prospective Cohort of US Adults. *New England Journal of Medicine* 341:1097–1105.

Campbell, Donald T., & Donald W. Fiske 1959. Convergent and Discriminant Validation by the Multitrait–Multimethod Matrix. *Psychological Bulletin* 56:81–105.

Kanʿān, Tawfīq. 1931. Unwritten Laws Affecting the Arab Woman of Palestine. *Journal of the Palestine Oriental Society* 11:172–203.

Caplan, A. P. 1976. Boys' Circumcision and Girls' Puberty Rites among the Swahili of Mafia Island, Tanzania. *Africa: Journal of the International African Institute* 46: 21–33.

Carey, Benedict 2011. Expert on Mental Illness Reveals Her Own Fight. *New York Times* 23 June, Page A1. https://www.nytimes.com/2011/06/23/health/23lives.html

Carroll, Lewis (Charles Lutwidge Dodgson) 1897 (1871). *Through the Looking Glass, and What Alice Found There*. Philadelphia, PA: Henry Altemus.

Carruthers, Peter 2011. *The Opacity of Mind: An Integrative Theory of Self-Knowledge*. Oxford: Oxford Unversity Press.

Cerletti, A. 1958. Étude Pharmacologique de la Psilocybine. In R. Heim & R. G. Wasson, Eds., *Les champignons hallucinogènes du Mexique* (pp. 268–271). Paris: Museum de Historie Naturelle. Cited in Passie et al 2002.

Chapman, Alexander L. 2006. Dialectical Behavior Therapy: Current Indications and Unique Elements. *Psychiatry* 3(9):62–68.

Chapman, Mark D. 2005. Why Do We Still Recite the Nicene Creed at the Eucharist? *Anglican Theological Review* 87(2):207–223. http://www.anglicantheologicalrevie w.org/read/article/387/

Chelkowski, Peter J. (Ed.) 2010. *Eternal Performance: Taʿziyeh and Other Shiite Rituals*. London: Seagull.

Chiao, Joan Y. 2015. Current Emotion Research in Cultural Neuroscience. *Emotion Review* 7:280–293.

Chiao, Joan Y., Katherine D. Blizinsky, Vani A. Mathur, & Bobby K. Cheon 2012. Culture–gene Coevolution of Empathy and Altruism. In Barbara Oakley, Ed., *Pathological Altruism* (pp. 291–299). Oxford: Oxford University Press.

Chida, Yoichi, Mark Hamer, Jane Wardle, & Andrew Steptoe, J. 2008. Do Stress–Related Psychosocial Factors Contribute to Cancer Incidence and Survival? *Nature Clinical Practice Oncology* 5:466–475.

Chinyowa, Kennedy 2001. The Context, Performance and Meaning of Shona Ritual Drama. In Lokangaka Losambe & Devi Sarinjeive, Eds., *Pre–colonial and Post–colonial Drama and Theatre in Africa* (pp. 3–13). Claremont: New Africa Books.

Chittick, William C. 2005. *Weeping in Classical Sufism*. In Kimberley Christine Patton & John Stratton Hawley, Eds., *Holy Tears: Weeping in the Religious Imagination* (pp. 132–144). Princeton, NJ: Princeton University Press.

Christian, William A., Jr. 1982. Provoked Religious Weeping in Early Modern Spain. In J. Davis, Ed., *Religious Organization and Religious Experience* (pp. 97–114). London: Academic Press.

Germer,K. Christopher , & Kristin D. Neff. 2013. Self-Compassion in Clinical Practice. *Journal of Clinical Psychology: In Session* 69(8), 856–867.

Churchhill, Winston 1940. We Shall Fight on the Beaches. Speech to the House of Commons on 4 June 1940. International Churchill Society. https://winstonchurchill. org/resources/speeches/1940-the-finest-hour/we-shall-fight-on-the-beaches/

Cialdini, Robert B., Richard J. Borden, Avril Thorne, Marcus Randall Walker, Stephen Freeman, & Lloyd Reynolds Sloan 1976. Basking in Reflected Glory: Three (Football) Field Studies. *Journal of Personality and Social Psychology* 34(3):366–375.

Claidière, Nicolas, & Dan Sperber 2007. The Role of Attraction in Cultural Evolution. *Journal of Cognition and Culture* 7:89–111.

Claparède, Édouard 1930. L'émotion "Pure". *Extrait des Archives de Psychologie* 22:333–347.

Clark, Donald Lemen 1922. *Rhetoric and Poetry in the Renaissance: A Study of Rhetorical Terms in English Renaissance Literary Criticism*. New York: Columbia University Press. http://www.gutenberg.org/files/10140/10140-h/10140-h.htm#foot352

Clark-Decès, Isabelle 2005. *No One Cries for the Dead: Tamil Dirges, Rowdy Songs, and Graveyard Petitions*. Berkeley, CA: Cambridge University Press.

Cohen, Emma, Roger Mundry, & Sebastian Kirschner 2013. Religion, Synchrony, and Cooperation. *Religion, Brain & Behavior*. doi:10.1080/2153599X.2012.741075

Cohen, Esther 1996. Fire and Tears: The Physical Manifestations of Conversion. *Dimensione e Problemi della Ricerca Storica* 2:235–241. http://dprs.uniroma1.it/sites/default/files/241.html

Cohen, Esther 2010. *The Modulated Scream: Pain in Late Medieval Culture*. Chicago, IL: University of Chicago Press.

Combs-Schilling, M. E. 1989. *Sacred Performances: Islam, Sexuality, and Sacrifice*. New York: Columbia University Press.

Coogler, Ryan, Director 2018. *Black Panther*. Produced by Marvel Studios and distributed by Walt Disney Studios Motion Pictures.

Connor, Linda, Patsy Asch, & Timothy Asch 1986. *Jero Tapakan: Balinese Healer: An Ethnographic Film Monograph*. Cambridge: Cambridge University Press.

Conrad, Bettina 2006. "A Culture of War and a Culture of Exile": Young Eritreans in Germany and their Relations to Eritrea. *Revue Européenne des Migrations Internationales* 22(1):59–85.

Conti, Natale 2006. *Natale Conti's* Mythologiae. Books I–IV. Translated and Annotated by John Mulrayan and Steven Brown. Tempe, AZ: Arizona Center for Medieval and Renaissance Studies. On Cupid, see especially Chapter 14, pp. 330ff.

Coppin, G., & Sander, D. 2016. Theoretical Approaches to Emotion and its Measurement. In H. Meiselman, Ed., *Emotion Measurement* (pp. 3–30). Cambridge, MA: Woodhead Publishing.

Cova, Florian, & Julien A. Deonna 2014. Being Moved. *Philosophical Studies* 169:447–466. doi:10.1007/s11098-013-0192-9

Cova, Florian, Julien A. Deonna, & David Sander 2017. "That's Deep!": The Role of Being Moved and Feelings of Profundity in the Appreciation of Serious Narratives. In Donald R. Wehrs & Thomas Blake, Eds., *The Palgrave Handbook of Affect Studies and Textual Criticism* (pp. 347–369). doi:10.1007/978-3-319-63303-9_13

Cox, K. S. 2010. Elevation Predicts Domain-Specific Volunteerism 3 Months Later. *The Journal of Positive Psychology* 5(5):333–341. doi:10.1080/17439760.2010.507468

Creider, Chet A. 1977. Towards a Description of East–African Gestures. *Sign Language Studies* 14:1–20. https://muse.jhu.edu/article/507190/pdf

Csikszentmihalyi, Mihaly, & Eugene Rochberg-Halton 1981. *The Meaning of Things: Domestic Symbols and the Self*. Cambridge: Cambridge University Press.

Cuddy, Amy J., Susan T. Fiske, & Peter Glick 2007. The BIAS Map: Behaviors from Intergroup Affect and Stereotypes. *Journal of Personality and Social Psychology* 92:316–348. doi:10.1037/0022-3514.92.4.631

Culture Gabfest on Slate Plus, March 9, 2016, with Julia Turner, Dana Steven, Stephan Metcalf, and Carl Wilson. http://www.slate.com/articles/podcasts/culturegabfest/2016/03/the_culture_gabfest_answers_a_listener_question_about_art_that_makes_them.html

Dale, Katherine R., Arthur A. Raney, Sophie H. Janicke, Meghan S. Sanders, M. S., & Mary Beth Oliver 2017. YouTube for Good: A Content Analysis and Examination of Elicitors of Self-Transcendent Media. *Journal of Communication* 67:897–919. doi:10.1111/jcom.12333

Daniel, Michael, & Victoria Khurshudian 2015. Temperature Terms in Modern Eastern Armenian. In Maria Koptjevskaja-Tamm, Ed., *The Linguistics of Temperature* (pp. 392–439). Amsterdam: John Benjamins.

Darkwa, Asante 1985. Traditional Music and Dance in Luo Community Life. Anthropos 80:646–653.

Darwin, Charles 1872. *The Expression of the Emotions in Man and Animals.* London: John Murray. http://darwin-online.org.uk/content/frameset?pageseq=1&itemID=F1142&viewtype=text

Dāsa, Haridāsa n.d. *Śrī Śrī Gauḍīya Vaiṣṇava Jīvanī.* Volume 2. Navadvīpa: Hribol Kuṭhir, 465 Gaurābda. [quoted in McDaniel 1989].

Davis, John 1998. The Transpersonal Dimensions of Ecopsychology: Nature, Nonduality, and Spiritual Practice. *The Humanistic Psychologist* 26(1–3):69–100. doi:10.1080/08873267.1998.9976967

de Abreu, Maria José A. 2008. Goose Bumps All Over: Breath, Media, and Tremor. *Social Text* 25(96):59–78.

de Sousa, Hilário, François Langella, & N. J. Enfield 2015. Temperature Terms in Lao, Southern Zhuang, Southern Pinghua and Cantonese. In Maria Koptjevskaja-Tamm, Ed., *The Linguistics of Temperature* (pp. 594–638). Amsterdam: John Benjamins.

de Waal, Frans 1996. *Good Natured: The Origins of Right and Wrong in Humans and Other Animals.* Cambridge, MA: Harvard University Press.

de Witte, Marleen 2011. Touched by the Spirit: Converting the Senses in a Ghanaian Charismatic Church. *Ethnos: Journal of Anthropology* 76:489–509. doi:10.1080/00141844.2011.620711

Deanesly, M. (Ed.) 1981. The Incendium Amoris of Richard Rolle, Manchester, 1915, prologue; English version, *The Fire of Love and the Mending of Life.* Edited and translated by M.S. del Mastro. Garden City, NY: Image Books.

Delmonico, Neal 2007. Chaitanya Vaishnavism and the Holy Names. In Edwin Francis Bryant, Ed., *Krishna: A Sourcebook* (pp. 549–575). Oxford: Oxford University Press.

DeMares, Ryan 2000. Human Peak Experience Triggered by Encounters with Cetaceans. *Anthrozoös* 13(2):89–103.

Desjarlais, Robert R. 1991. Poetic Transformations of Yolmo 'Sadness'. *Culture, Medicine and Psychiatry* 15:387–420.

Dhammarama, P. S., & André Bareau 1963. Les récits canoniques du Cariyāpitaka et les Jātaka pāli. Traduction du Cariyāpitaka. *Bulletin de l'Ecole Française d'Extrême-Orient* 51(2):321–390. doi:10.3406/befeo.1963.2085

Diduk, Susan 2004. The Civility of Incivility: Grassroots Political Activism, Female Farmers, and the Cameroon State. *African Studies Review* 47(2):27–54. doi:10.1017/S0002020600030845

Dijker, Anton J. M. 2014. A Theory of Vulnerability-based Morality. *Emotion Review* 6:175–183. doi:10.1177/1754073913514120

Dissanayake, Ellen 2000. Antecedents of the Temporal Arts in Early Mother–Infant Interaction. In Nils L. Wallin, Björn Merker & Steven Brown, Eds., *The Origins of Music* (pp. 389–410). Cambridge, MA: MIT Press.

Dixon, Thomas 2015. *Weeping Britannia: Portrait of a Nation in Tears.* Oxford: Oxford University Press.

Doll, Richard, Gray, Richard, Hafner, Barbara, & Richard Peto 1980. Mortality in Relation to Smoking – 22 Years Observations on Female British Doctors. *British Medical Journal* 280:967–971.

Dreyer, Frederick 1983. Faith and Experience in the Thought of John Wesley. *The American Historical Review* 88(1):12–30. http://www.jstor.org/stable/1869343

Dulaney, Siri, & Alan Page Fiske 1994. Cultural Rituals and Obsessive-Compulsive Disorder: Is There a Common Psychological Mechanism? *Ethos* 22:243–283.

Dundes, Alan 1980. *Interpreting Folklore.* Bloomington, IN: Indiana University Press.

Durkheim, Émile 1912. *Les Formes Élémentaires de la Vie Religieuse: Le Système Totémique en Australie.* Paris: Le Livre de Poche. Translated by Joseph Ward Swain as *The Elementary Forms of the Religious Life.* 1915. London: George Allen.

Eckel, Malcolm David 1992. *To See the Buddha: A Philosopher's Quest for the Meaning of Emptiness.* New York: HarperCollins.

Eckel, Malcolm David 2005. Hsüan–tsang's Encounter with the Buddha: A Cloud of Philosophy in a Drop of Tears. In Kimberley Christine Patton, John Stratton Hawley, Eds., *Holy Tears: Weeping in the Religious Imagination* (pp. 112–131). Princeton, New Jersey: Princeton University Press. The cited passage is footnoted to indicate that the source is Dīgha Nikāya XYI.5.8.

Eerola, Tuomas, & Henna-Riikka Peltola 2016. Memorable Experiences with Sad Music—Reasons, Reactions and Mechanisms of Three Types of Experiences. *PLoS One* 11(6):e0157444. doi:10.1371/journal.pone.0157444

Efran, Jay S., & Timothy J. Spangler 1979. Why Grown–Ups Cry: A Two–Factor Theory and Evidence from *The Miracle Worker. Motivation and Emotion* 3:63–72.

Ehrenreich, Barbara, Elizabeth Hess, & Gloria Jacobs 1992. Beatlemania: Girls Just Want to Have Fun. In Lisa A. Lewis, Ed., *The Adoring Audience: Fan Culture and Popular Media* (pp. 84–106). London: Routledge.

Ekman, Paul 1992. An Argument for Basic Emotions. *Cognition and Emotion* 6:169–200.

Elkins, James 2001. *Pictures and Tears: A History of People Who Have Cried in Front of Paintings.* New York: Routledge.

Eller, Jack David 2010. *Cruel Creeds, Virtuous Violence: Religious Violence across Culture and History.* Amherst NY: Prometheus.

Epps, Patience 2015. Temperature Terms in Hup, a Nadahup Language of Amazonia. In Maria Koptjevskaja-Tamm, Ed., *The Linguistics of Temperature* (pp. 792–811). Amsterdam: John Benjamins.

Evans-Pritchard, Edward E. 1956. *Nuer Religion.* Oxford: Clarendon Press.

Farès, Bichr 1932. *L'Honneur chez les Arabes avant L'Islam.* Paris: Librarie D'Amerique et D'Orient Adrien–Maisionneuve.

Feldman Barrett, Lisa 2017. *How Emotions Are Made: The Secret Life of the Brain.* Houghton Mifflin Harcourt.

Ferguson, Eamonn 2015. Mechanism of Altruism Approach to Blood Donor Recruitment and Retention: A Review and Future Directions. *Transfusion Medicine* 25:211–226.

Ferhat, Halima 2000. Le Saint et Son Corps: Une Lutte Constante. *Al–Qanṭara: Revista de Estudios Arabes* 21:457–469.

Finseth, Ian Frederick 1995. "Liquid Fire Within Me": Language, Self and Society in Transcendentalism and early Evangelicalism, 1820–1860. M.A. Thesis in English, University of Virginia. http://xroads.virginia.edu/~ma95/finseth/thesis.html

Fishman, Sterling 1964. The Rise of Hitler as a Beer Hall Orator. *The Review of Politics* 26:244–256.

Fiske, Alan P. 1991. *Structures of Social Life: The Four Elementary Forms of Human Relations.* New York: Free Press (Macmillan).

Fiske, Alan Page 1992. The Four Elementary Forms of Sociality: Framework for a Unified Theory of Social Relations. *Psychological Review* 99:689–723.

Fiske, Alan P. 2000. Complementarity Theory: Why Human Social Capacities Evolved to Require Cultural Complements. *Personality and Social Psychology Review* 4:76–94.

Fiske, Alan P. 2002. Moral Emotions Provide the Self–Control Needed to Sustain Social Relationships. *Self and Identity* 1:169–175.

Fiske, Alan P. 2004a. Relational Models Theory 2.0. In Nick Haslam, Ed., *Relational Models Theory: A Contemporary Overview* (pp. 3–25). Mahwah, NJ: Erlbaum.

Fiske, Alan P. 2004b. Four Modes of Constituting Relationships: Consubstantial Assimilation; Space, Magnitude, Time and Force; Concrete Procedures; Abstract Symbolism. In N. Haslam, Ed., *Relational Models Theory: A Contemporary Overview* (pp. 61–146). Mahwah, NJ: Erlbaum.

Fiske, Alan P. 2010. Dispassionate Heuristic Rationality Fails to Sustain Social Relationships. In Andrea W. Mates, Lisa Mikesell & Michael Sean Smith, Eds., *Language, Interaction and Frontotemporal Dementia: Reverse Engineering the Social Brain* (pp. 199–241). Oakville, KY: Equinox.

Fiske, Alan P. 2011. Metarelational Models: Configurations of Social Relationships. *European Journal of Social Psychology* 42:2–18. doi:10.1002/ejsp.847.

Fiske, Alan Page 2019. The Lexical Fallacy in Emotion Research: Mistaking Vernacular Words for Psychological Entities. In press, *Psychological Review.*

Fiske Alan P., & Lisa Schubert 2012. How to Relate to People: The Extra–Terrestrial's Guide to *Homo sapiens.* In Omri Gillath, Glenn Adams, & Adrianne D. Kunkel, Eds., *Relationship Science: Integrating Evolutionary, Neuroscience, and Sociocultural Approaches* (pp. 169–195). Washington, DC: American Psychological Association.

Fiske, Alan P., & Nick Haslam 2005. The Four Basic Social Bonds: Structures for Coordinating Interaction. In Mark Baldwin, Ed., *Interpersonal Cognition* (pp. 267–298). New York: Guilford.

Fiske, Alan Page, Thomas W. Schubert, & Beate Seibt 2017a. The Best-Loved Story of All Time: Overcoming All Obstacles to Be Reunited, Evoking Kama Muta. *Evolutionary Studies in Imaginative Culture* I:67–70.

Fiske, Alan Page, Thomas W. Schubert, & Beate Seibt 2017b. The Sudden Devotion Emotion: Kama Muta and the Cultural Practices Whose Function Is to Evoke It. *Emotion Review.* doi:10.1177/1754073917723167

Fiske, Alan Page, Thomas W. Schubert, & Beate Seibt 2017c. "Kama Muta" or "Being Moved by Love": A Bootstrapping Approach to the Ontology and Epistemology of an Emotion. In Julia Cassaniti & Usha Menon, Eds., *Universalism without Uniformity: Explorations in Mind and Culture* (pp. 79–100). Chicago, IL: University of Chicago Press.

Fiske, Donald W. 1986. Specificity of Method and Knowledge in Social Science. In Donald W. Fiske and Richard A. Shweder, Eds., *Meta–theory in Social Science: Pluralisms and Subjectivities* (pp. 61–82). Chicago, IL: University of Chicago Press.

Fiske, Donald W. (Ed.) 1981. *Problems with Language Imprecision*. San Francisco: Jossey–Bass.

Fiske, Susan T. 1995. Words! Words! Words! Confronting the Problem of Observer and Self Reports. In Patrick E. Shrout & Susan T. Fiske, Eds., *Personality Research, Methods, and Theory: A Festschrift Honoring Donald W. Fiske* (pp. 221–240). Hillsdale, NJ: Erlbaum.

Fiske, Susan T. 2010. Envy up, Scorn Down: How Comparison Divides Us. *American Psychologist* 65(8):698–706. doi:10.1037/0003-066X.65.8.698

Fiske, Susan T. 2012. Warmth and Competence: Stereotype Content Issues for Clinicians and Researchers. *Canadian Psychology/Psychologie Canadienne* 53:14–20. doi:10.1037/a0026054

Föllinger, Sabine 2009. Tears and Crying in Archaic Greek Poetry (especially Homer). In Thomas Fögen, Ed., *Tears in the Greco–Roman World* (pp. 17–36). Berlin: Walter de Gruyter.

Fortes, Meyer 1987. *Religion, Morality, and the Person: Essays on Tallensi Religion*. Edited by Jack Goody. Cambridge: Cambridge University Press.

François, Alexandre 2015. Temperature Terms in Northern Vanuatu. In Maria Koptjevskaja-Tamm, Ed., *The Linguistics of Temperature* (pp. 832–857). Amsterdam: John Benjamins.

Frank, Robert H. 1988. *Passions Within Reason*. New York: Norton.

Frazer, James George 1918. *Folk–lore in the Old Testament: Studies in Comparative Religion Legend and Law*. London: Macmillan.

Frazier, Jessica 2013. Bhakti in Hindu Cultures. *The Journal of Hindu Studies* 6:101–113. doi:10.1093/jhs/hit028

Fredrickson, Barbara L. 2013. Positive Emotions Broaden and Build. *Advances in Experimental Social Psychology* 47:1–53.

Frembegen, Jurgen Wasim 2009. *Journey to God: Sufis and Dervishes in Islam*. Oxford: Oxford University Press.

Frijda, Nico H. 1988. The Laws of Emotion. *The American Psychologist* 43:349–358.

Frijda, Nico H. 2001. Foreword. In Ad J. J. M. Vingerhoets & Randolph R. Cornelius, Eds., *Adult Crying: A Biopsychosocial Approach* (Vol. 3, pp. XII–XVIII). Hove, UK: Brunner–Routledge.

Frijda, Nico H. 2006. *The Laws of Emotion*. Mahwah, NJ: Erlbaum.

Frishkopf, Michael 2001. Tarab in the Mystic Sufi chant of Egypt. In Sherifa Zuhur, Ed., *Colors of Enchantment: Visual and Performing Arts of the Middle East* (pp. 233–269). Cairo, Egypt: American University in Cairo Press.

Fruyt, Michèle 2013. Temperature and Cognition in Latin. http://www.paris-sorbonne .fr/IMG/pdf/Temperature-m_fruyt.pdf

Fulwiler, Jennifer 2007. Crying at Mass. Fulwiler, Conversion Diary blog. http://www .conversiondiary.com/2007/07/crying–at–mass.html Accessed 3 September 2019.

Gabrielsson, Alf 2001. Emotions in Strong Experiences with Music. In Patrik N. Juslin & John A. Sloboda, Eds., *Music and Emotion: Theory and Research* (pp. 431–449). New York, NY, US: Oxford University Press.

Gabrielsson, Alf 2011. *Strong Experiences with Music: Music Is Much More than Just Music*. Roy Bradbury, translator. Oxford, England: Oxford University Press.

Gainsford, Peter 2003. Formal Analysis of Recognition Scenes in the "Odyssey". *The Journal of Hellenic Studies* 123:41–59.

Garcia, Angela 2010. *The Pastoral Clinic: Addiction and Dispossession along the Rio Grande*. Berkeley, CA: University of California Press.

Garssen, Bert, & Karl Goodkin 1999. On the Role of Immunological Factors as Mediators Between Psychosocial Factors and Cancer Progression. *Psychiatry Research* 85:51–61.

Gathigia, Moses Gatambūki, 2010. Metaphors of Love in Gikūyū: Conceptual Mappings, Vital Relations and Image Schemas. Linguistics PhD Thesis, School of Humanities and Social Sciences, Kenyatta University. http://ir-library.ku.ac.ke/bitstream/handle/123456 789/12099/Metaphors%20of%20love%20in%20gik%20y%20.....pdf?sequence=1

Germer, Christopher G., & Kristin D. Neff 2013. Self-Compassion in Clinical Practice. *Journal of Clinical Psychology: In* Session 69(8):856–867.

Gernet, Louis 1932. You–You: en marge d'Hérodote. In *Cinquantenaire de la Faculti des Lettres D'Alger (1881–1931).* Articles publiés par les professeurs de la faculté. Algiers. Université d'Alger. Faculté des lettres et sciences humaines, Société historique algérienne, France: Premier ministre. Direction de l'information légale et administrative. [cited in Jacobs 2008; not accessed by present authors].

Ghosh, Pika 2010. Swayed by Love: Dance in the Vaishnava Temple Imagery of Bengal. In Pallabi Chakravorty & Nilanjana Gupta, Eds., *Dancing Matters: Performing India* (pp. 150–168). London: Routledge.

Gilbert, Paul (Ed.) 2005. *Compassion: Conceptualisations, Research and Use in Psychotherapy.* London: Routledge.

Gillison, Gillian 1983. Cannibalism among Women in the Eastern Highlands of Papua New Guinea. In Paula Brown and Donald Tuzin, Eds., *The Ethnography of Cannibalism* (pp. 33–50). Washington, DC: Society for Psychological Anthropology.

Glocker, Melanie L., Daniel D. Langleben, Kosha Ruparel, James W. Loughead, Rubin C. Gur, & Norbert Sachser 2009. Baby Schema in Infant Faces Induces Cuteness Perception and Motivation for Caretaking in Adults. *Ethology* 115:257–263.

Glucklich, Ariel 2001. *Sacred Pain: Hurting the Body for the Sake of the Soul.* New York: Oxford University Press.

Goddard, Cliff 2014. Interjections and Emotion (with Special Reference to "Surprise" and "Disgust"). *Emotion Review* 6:53–63. doi:10.1177/1754073913491843

von Goethe, Johann Wolfgang 1774/1999. *Die Leiden des jungen Werther.* Stuttgart, Germany: Philipp Reclam jun. Translated by R.D. Boylan as *The Sorrows of Young Werther,* http://www.gutenberg.org/ebooks/2527.

von Goethe, Johann Wolfgang 1808. *Faust.* Translated by A. S. Kline, *Faust, Parts I and II.* Poetry in Translation. http://www.poetryintranslation.com/PITBR/German/Fa usthome.php

Goff, Barbara 2004. *Citizen Bacchae: Women's Ritual Practice in Ancient Greece.* Berkeley, CA: University of California Press.

Goldberg, Harvey E. 1973. Cultural Change in an Israeli Immigrant village: The Twist in Even Yosef. *Middle Eastern Studies* 9:73–80.

Gombrich, E. H. 1966. Ritualized Gesture and Expression in Art. *Philosophical Transactions of the Royal Society of London. Series B, Biological Sciences* 251(772):393–401.

Gottschall, Jonathan, et al. 2003. Patterns of Characterization in Folktales Across Geographic Regions and Levels of Cultural Complexity. *Human Nature* 14:365–382.

Gowack, Paul, & Valerie A. Valle 1998. The Experience of Feeling Grace in Voluntary Service to the Terminally Ill. In Ron Valle, Ed., *Phenomenological Inquiry in Psychology: Existential and Transpersonal Dimensions* (pp. 373–386). New York: Springer Science & Business Media.

Granqvist, Hilma 1965. *Muslim Death and Burial: Arab Customs and Traditions Studied in a Village in Jordan.* Helsinki: Helinsingfors.

Greenwood, D. C., Muir, K. R., Packham C. J., & Madeley, R. 1996. Coronary Heart Disease: A Review of the Role of Psychosocial Stress and Social Support. *Journal of Public Health Medicine* 18:221–231.

Greer, George, & Tolbert, Requia 1986. Subjective Reports of the Effects of MDMA in a Clinical Setting. *Journal of Psychoactive Drugs* 18:319–327.

Grewe, Oliver, Reinhard Kopiez, & Eckart Altenmüller 2009. The Chill Parameter: Goose Bumps and Shivers as Promising Measures in Emotion Research. *Music Perception: An Interdisciplinary Journal* 27:61–74.

Griaule, Marcel 1965. *Conversations with Ogotemmêli: An Introduction to Dogon Religious Ideas*. (Published for the International African Institute). Oxford: Oxford University Press.

Griffith, R. Marie 1997. *God's Daughters: Evangelical Women and the Power of Submission*. Berkeley, CA: University of California Press.

Griffith, R. Marie 1998. "Joy Unspeakable and Full of Glory": The Vocabulary of Pious Emotion in the Narratives of Pentecostal Women, 1910–1945. In Peter N. Stearns and Jan Lewis, Eds., *An Emotional History of the United States* (pp. 281–240). New York: New York University Press.

Griffiths, R. R., W. A. Richards, U. McCann, & R. Jesse 2006. Psilocybin Can Occasion Mystical–Type Experiences Having Substantial and Sustained Personal Meaning and Spiritual Significance. *Psychopharmacology* 187(3):268–283. doi:10.1007/s00213–006–0457–5

Grima, Benedicte 1992. *The Performance of Emotion among Paxtun Women: "The Misfortunes which Have Befallen Me"*. Austin, TX: University of Texas Press.

Guthrie, Stewart 1995. *Faces in the Clouds: A New Theory of Religion*. Oxford: Oxford University Press.

Haberman, David L. 2003. *The Bhaktirasāmṛtasindu of Rūpa Gosvāmin*. New Delhi: Indira Gandhi National Center for the Arts, and Motilal Banarsidass Publishers.

Hagemeyer, Birk, Michael Dufner, & Jaap J. A. Denissen 2016. Double Dissociation Between Implicit and Explicit Affiliative Motives: A Closer Look at Socializing Behavior in Dyadic Interactions. *Journal of Research in Personality* 65:89–93. doi:10.1016/j.jrp.2016.08.003

Haidt, Jonathan 2000. The Positive Emotion of Elevation. *Prevention & Treatment*, 3(1). doi:10.1037/1522–3736.3.1.33c

Haidt, Jonathan 2003a. Elevation and the Positive Psychology of Morality. In C. L. M. Keyes & J. Haidt, Eds., *Flourishing: Positive Psychology and the Life Well–lived* (pp. 278–289). Washington DC: American Psychological Association. Retrieved from http://drdavidlawrence.com/wp–content/uploads/2015/12/Flourishing–Positive–psychology–and–the–life–well–lived

Haidt, Jonathan 2003b. The Moral Emotions. In R. J. Davidson, K. R. Scherer & H. H. Goldsmith, Eds., *Handbook of Affective Sciences* (pp. 852–870). Oxford: Oxford University Press.

Haidt, Jonathan, & Dacher Keltner 2004. Appreciation of Beauty and Excellence [Awe, Wonder, Elevation]. In Christopher Peterson & Martin E. P. Seligman, Eds., *Character Strengths and Virtues* (pp. 537–551). Washington, DC: American Psychological Association Press.

Haldane, J. A. 1965. Musical Themes and Imagery in Aeschylus. *The Journal of Hellenic Studies* 85:33–41. http://www.jstor.org/stable/628806

Hamde, Kiflemariam. 2009. Constructing Cultural Identity for the 'Good' Life: The Case of Blin Culture Community in Stockholm. In Maddy Janssens, Dino Pinelli, Dafne C. Reymen & Sandra Wallman, Eds., *Sustainable Cities: Diversity, Economic Growth and Social Cohesion* (pp. 77–92). Northampton, MA: Edward Elgar.

Hanich, Julian, Valentin Wagner, Mira Shah, Thomas Jacobsen, & Winfried Menninghaus 2014. Why We Like to Watch Sad Films: The Pleasure of Being Moved in Aesthetic Experiences. *Psychology of Aesthetics, Creativity, and the Arts* 8(2):130–143. doi:10.1037/a0035690

Hanlon, Charlotte, Rob Whitley, Dawit Wondimagegn, Atalay Alem, & Martin Prince 2009. Postnatal Mental Distress in Relation to the Sociocultural Practices of Childbirth: An Exploratory Qualitative Study from Ethiopia. *Social Science & Medicine* 69:1211–1219.

Hardy, Friedhelm 1983. *Viraha–Bhakti: The Early History of Kṛṣṇa Devotion in South India.* Oxford: Oxford University Press.

Harper, Douglas 2016. Online Etymological Dictionary. http://www.etymonline.com/

Haslam, Nick, E. Holland, & P. Kuppens 2012. Categories Versus Dimensions in Personality And Psychopathology: A Quantitative Review of Taxometric Research. *Psychological Medicine* 42:903–920. doi:10.1017/S0033291711001966

Hayes, S. C., V. M. Follette, & M. Linehan Eds. 2004. *Mindfulness and Acceptance: Expanding the Cognitive-Behavioral Tradition.* Guilford.

Hayes, S. C., K. D. Strosahl, & K. G. Wilson 1999. *Acceptance and Commitment Therapy: An Experiential Approach to Behavior Change.* Guilford.

Heber, Levi Y. n.d. Additional Sephardic Circumcision Customs: The customs of Sephardim and Oriental Jews at a Brit Milah. Chabad.org http://www.chabad.org/library/article_cdo/aid/144126/jewish/Additional–Sephardic–Circumcision–Customs.htm

Heim, Maria 2004. *Theories of the Gift in South Asia: Hindu, Buddhist, and Jain Reflections on Dāna.* New York: Routledge.

Heller, S. Megan 2016. Memories of Burning Man. In Clare L. Boulanger, Ed., *Reflecting on America.* 2nd Edition (pp. 181–192). Milton Park, Abingdon: Taylor & Francis.

Hemacandra n.d. From W. S. Merwin and J. Moussaieff Masson, editors and translators, *The Peacock's Egg: Love Poems from Ancient India.* San Francisco: North Point Press. Poem on pp. 106–107.

Henderson, Clara, & Lisa Gilman 2004. Women as Religious and Political Praise Singers within African Institutions: The Case of the CCAP Blantyre Synod and Political Parties in Malawi. *Women and Music: A Journal of Gender and Culture* 8:22–40. doi:10.1353/wam.2004.0007

Hendriks, Michelle C. P., Marcel A. Croon, & A. J Vingerhoets 2008. Social Reactions to Adult Crying: The Help–Soliciting Function of Tears. *The Journal of Social Psychology* 148:22–42. doi:10.3200/SOCP.148.1.22-42

Henrich, J., Steven J. Heine, & Ara Norenzayan 2010. The Weirdest People in the World? *Behavioral and Brain Sciences* 33:61–135.

Henry, Taylor 2015. Kama Muta in a Poetry Lounge. Paper written for undergraduate independent study course under the supervision of Alan Page Fiske, Department of Anthropology, UCLA.

Heritage, John, & David Greatbatch 1986. Generating Applause: A Study of Rhetoric and Response at Party Political Conferences. *American Journal of Sociology* 92:110–157.

Hermkens, Anna–Karina, Willy Jansen, & Catrien Notermans 2009. Introduction: The Power of Marian Pilgrimage. In Karina Hermkens, Willy Jansen, & Catrien Notermans, Eds. *Moved by Mary: The Power of Pilgrimage in the Modern World* (pp. 1–13). Burlington, VT: Ashgate.

Hess, Eckhard H. 1973. *Imprinting: Early Experience and the Developmental Psychobiology of Attachment.* New York: Van Nostrand Reinhold.

Hill, Peter C. 1995. Affective Theory and Religious Experience. In Ralph W. Hood, Jr., Ed., *Handbook of Religious Experience* (pp. 353–3770. Birmingham, AL: Religious Education Press.

Hinn, Benny 1990. *Good Morning, Holy Spirit.* Nashville, TN: Thomas Nelson (Harper Collins).

Hiraga, Masako K. 1999. "Blending" and an Interpretation of Haiku: A Cognitive Approach. *Poetics Today* 20:461–481.

Hirshleifer, Jack 1987. On the Emotions as Guarantors of Threats and Promises. In John Dupré, Ed., *The Latest and the Best: Essays in Evolution and Optimality.* Cambridge, MA: MIT Press.

Hitler, Adolf 1939. *Mein Kampf.* Translated under the auspices of Dr. Alvin Johnson. (New York: Reynal & Hitchcock). Quoted in Fishman 1964.

Ho, Man Yee, Sylvia Xiaohua Chen, Edward Hoffman, Yanjun Guan, & Valentina Iversen 2013. Cross–Cultural Comparisons of Adults' Childhood Recollections: How are Peak–Experiences Described in China and Portugal? *Journal of Happiness Studies* 14:185–197. doi:10.1007/s10902–012–9323–9

Hodges, Donald A., & David Sebald 2010. *Music in the Human Experience: An Introduction to Music Psychology.* New York, NY: Routledge.

Hoffman, Morris B. 2014. *The Punisher's Brain: The Evolution of Judge and Jury.* Cambridge: Cambridge University Press.

Hoffman, Stegan G., Paul Grossman, & Devon E. Hinton 2011. Loving-Kindness and Compassion Meditation: Potential for Psychological Interventions. *Clinical Psychology Review* 31:1126–1132.

Hoffman, Valerie J. 1999. Annihilation in the Messenger of God: The Development of a Sufi Practice. *International Journal of Middle Eastern Studies* 31:351–369.

Hoffman, Edward, Neeta Relwani Garg, & Jenniffer González–Mujica 2013. Tears of Joy in India. *Indian Journal of Positive Psychology* 4(2):212–217.

Hoffman, Edward, Valentina Iversen, & Fernando A. Ortiz 2010. Peak–experiences among Norwegian Youth. *Nordic Psychology,* 62(4):67–76.

Hogan, Patrick Colm 2003. *The Mind and Its Stories: Narrative Universals and Human Emotion.* Cambridge: Cambridge University Press.

Holland, Julie 2001a. The Godparents of MDMA: An Interview with Ann and Sasha Shulgin. In Julie Holland, Ed., *Ecstasy: The Complete Guide* (pp. 58–65). Rochester, VT: Park Street Press.

Holland, Julie 2001b. MDMA and Society: Introduction. In Julie Holland, Ed., *Ecstasy: The Complete Guide* (pp. 346–349). Rochester, VT: Park Street Press.

Holt–Lunstad, Julianne, Smith, Timothy B., & Layton J. Bradley 2010. Social Relationships and Mortality Risk: A Meta–Analytic Review. *PLoS Med* 27(7):e1000316.

Homer 2007. *The Iliad.* Rodney Merrill, translator. Ann Arbor: University of Michigan Press.

Homer, n.d. [2018] *The Odyssey.* Translated by Emily Wilson. New York: Norton.

Hood, Ralph W. Jr. 2016. The Common Core Thesis in the Study of Mysticism. *Religion.* Oxford Research Encyclopedias. doi:10.1093/acrefore/9780199340378.013.241 http://religion.oxfordre.com/view/10.1093/acrefore/9780199340378.001.0001/acrefore–9780199340378–e–241#ref_acrefore–9780199340378–e–241–note–93 Accessed 3 September 2019.

Hopkins, Thomas J. 1966. The Social Teaching of the Bhāgavata Purāṇa (pp. 3–22). In Milton Singer, Ed., *Krishna: Myths, Rites, and Attitudes.* Westport, CT: Greenwood Press.

Howarth, Toby M. 2005. *The Twelver Shī'a as a Muslim Minority in India: Pulpit of Tears.* London: Routledge.

Huang, C. Julia 2003. Weeping in a Taiwanese Buddhist Charismatic Movement. *Ethnology* 42:73–86.

Hubert, Henri, & Marcel Mauss 1899. Essai sur la Nature et la Function du Sacrifice. *Année Sociologique* 2:29–138. Translated by W. D. Halls as Henri Hubert and Marcel Mauss 1964. *Sacrifice. Its Nature and Function.* Chicago, IL: The University of Chicago Press.

Hudson, W. H. 1918. *Far Away and Long Ago: A History of My Early Life.* New York: Dutton.

Hume, David 1777. *An Enquiry Concerning the Principles of Morals.* London: A. Millar. http://www.davidhume.org/texts/epm.html

Humphrys, Keith 2000. Community Narratives and Personal Stories in Alcoholics Anonymous. *Journal Of Community Psychology* 28:495–506.

Hunt, A. N. 2015. Traces of Transcendence: C. S. Lewis and the Ciphers of Being. *Sehnsucht: The C. S. Lewis Journal* 9:47–74.

Hunt, Hannah 2004. *Joy–bearing Grief: Tears of Contrition in the Writings of the Early Syrian and Byzantine Fathers.* Leiden: Brill.

Huron, David, & Elizabeth Hellmuth Margulis Musical Expectancy and Thrills. 2010. In Patrik N. Juslin & John L. Sloboda, Eds., *Handbook of Music and Emotion: Theory, Research, Applications* (pp. 575–604). Oxford, England: Oxford University Press.

Huyser–Honig, Joan 2006. The Case for Reciting Creeds in Worship. Interview with Albert Aymer. Posted by the Calvin Institute of Christian Worship, 31 March 2006. http://worship.calvin.edu/resources/resource–library/the–case–for–reciting–creeds–in–worship/

Hyder, Syed Akbar 2006. *Reliving Karbala: Martyrdom in South Asian Memory.* Oxford: Oxford University Press.

IJzerman, Hans, & Gün R. Semin 2009. The Thermometer of Social Relations: Mapping Social Proximity on Temperature. *Psychological Science* 20:1214–1220. doi:10.1111/j.1467–9280.2009.02434.x

Inbody, Joel 2015. Sensing God: Bodily Manifestations and Their Interpretation in Pentecostal Rituals and Everyday Life. *Sociology of Religion* 76(3):337–355. doi:10.1093/socrel/srv032

Irizarry, Joshua A. 2014. Signs of Life: Grounding the Transcendent in Japanese Memorial Objects. *Signs and Society* 2(S1):S160–S187.

Jacobs, David R., Jr., Hisashi Adachi, Ina Mulder, Daan Kromhout, Alessandro Menotti, Aulikki Nissinen, & Henry Blackburn for the Seven Countries Study Group. 1999. Cigarette Smoking and Mortality Risk: Twenty–five–Year Follow–up of the Seven Countries Study. *Archives of Internal Medicine* 159:733–740.

Jacobs, Jennifer E. 2007. 'Unintelligibles' in Vocal Performance at Middle Eastern Marriage Celebrations. *Text & Talk* 27:483–507.

Jacobs, Jennifer E. 2008. *Ululation In Levantine Society: The Cultural Reproduction of an Affective Vocalization.* Ph.D. dissertation, Department of Anthropology, University of Pennsylvania.

James, William 1890. *Principles of Psychology.* New York: Henry Holt.

James, William 1902. *The Varieties of Religious Experience: A Study in Human Nature.* Edited and Annotated for the World Wide Web by LeRoy L. Miller. https://www.worldu.e du/library/william_james_var.pdf Accessed 3 September 2019.

James, William 1906. On Some Mental Effects of the Earthquake. *Youth's Companion,* 7 June. Reprinted in *William James: Writings 1902–1910,* Library of America, 1987.

Janicke, Sophie H., & Mary Beth Oliver 2017. The Relationship Between Elevation, Connectedness, and Compassionate Love in Meaningful Films. *Psychology of Popular Media Culture* 6:274–289. doi:10.1037/ppm0000105

Janicke, Sophie Helga, Diana Rieger, & Winston Connor III 2018. Finding Meaning at Work: The Role of Inspiring and Funny YouTube Videos on Work-Related Well-Being. *Journal of Happiness Studies* 20(2):619–640.

Janicke-Bowles, Sophie H., Thomas W. Schubert, & Johanna K. Blomster 2020. Kama Muta as an Eudaimonic Entertainment Experience. In P. Vorderer & C. Klimt, Eds., *Oxford Handbook of Entertainment Theory*. Oxford: Oxford University Press.

Jantzen, Grace M. 1989. Mysticism and Experience. *Religious Studies* 25:295–315.

Jantzen, Grace M. 1990. Could There Be a Mystical Core of Religion? *Religious Studies* 26:59–71.

Jones, L. Fran 2001. Women and Music around the Mediterranean. In Karin Pendle, Ed., *Women and Music: A History*. 2nd Edition (pp. 422–437). Bloomington: Indiana University Press.

Jorgensen Joseph G. 1972. *The Sun Dance Religion: Power for the Powerless*. Chicago, IL: University of Chicago Press

Joyce, Rosemary, Richard Edging, Karl Lorenz, & Susan Gillespie 1991. Olmec Bloodletting: An Iconographic Study. In V. Fields, Ed., *Sixth Palenque Roundtable, 1986*. Norman, OK: University of Oklahoma Press. http://www.mesoweb.com/pari/publications/RT08/Bloodletting.pdf

Jung, Carl G. 1954. *Problems of Modern Psychotherapy*, Collected Works, Volume16. New York: Pantheon Books.

Jung, Carl G. 1961. *The Theory of Psychoanalysis*, Collected Works, Volume 4. New York: Pantheon Books.

Juslin, Patrik N. 2013. From Everyday Emotions to Aesthetic Emotions: Towards a Unified Theory of Musical Emotions. *Physics of Life Reviews* 10(3):235–266.

Juslin, Patrik N., & Petri Laukka 2004. Expression, Perception, and Induction of Musical Emotions: A Review and a Questionnaire Study of Everyday Listening. *Journal of New Music Research* 33(3):217–238. doi:10.1080/0929821042000317813

Juvonen, Päivi, & Ahti Nikunlassi 2015. Temperature Adjectives in Finnish. In Maria Koptjevskaja-Tamm, Ed., *The Linguistics of Temperature* (pp. 491–536). Amsterdam: John Benjamins.

Kabat-Zinn, Jon 1990. *Full Catastrophe Living: Using the Wisdom of Your Body and Mind to Face Stress, Pain, and Illness*. Delacorte.

Kaeppler, Adrienne L., Peter Russell Crowe, Vida Chenoweth, & Lamont Lindstrom 1998. Vanuatu. In Adrienne L. Kaeppler, Ed., *Garland Encyclopedia of World Music, Volume 9: Australia and the Pacific Islands*. http://glnd.alexanderstreet.com/view/332658

Kakridis, Hélène J. 1963. *La Notion de L'Amitié et le L'Hospitalité chez Homère*. H Bibliothke tou Philologou, ar 9. Thessaloniki: Βιβλιοθήκη το Φιλολόγον.

Kant, Immanuel 1790/1987. *Critique of Judgment*. Translated by Werner S. Pluhar. Indianapolis, IN: Hackett.

Kapchan, Deborah 2009. Singing Community/Remembering in Common: Sufi Liturgy and North African Identity in Southern France. *International Journal of Community Music* 2:9–23.

Karthaus, Ulrich 2000. *Sturm und Drang: Epoche–Werke–Wirkung*. München: C.H. Beck.

Katz, Steven T. (Ed.) 1983. *Mysticism and Religious Traditions*. Oxford: Oxford University Press.

Kaulfers, Walter Vincent 1931. Curiosities of Colloquial Gesture. *Hispania* 14(4):249–264.

Keating, Caroline F., David W. Randall, Timothy Kendrick, & Katherine A. Gutshall 2003. Do Babyfaced Adults Receive More Help? The (Cross-Cultural) Case of the Lost Resume. *Journal of Nonverbal Behavior* 27:89–109. doi:10.1023/a:1023962425692

Keenan, Elinor 1975. A Sliding Sense of Obligatoriness: The Polystructure of Malagasy Oratory. In Maurice Bloch, Ed., *Political Language and Oratory in Traditional Society* (pp. 93–112). London: Academic Press.

Keller, Carl–A. 1984. Aspiration Collective et Experience Individuelle dans la Bhakti Shivaite de l'Inde du Sud. *Numen* 31(1):1–21.

Keltner, Dacher, & Jonathan Haidt 1999. Social Functions of Emotions at Four Levels of Analysis. *Cognition and Emotion* 13:505–521. doi:10.1080/026999399379168

Keltner, Dacher, & Jonathan Haidt 2003. Approaching Awe, A Moral, Spiritual, and Aesthetic Emotion. *Cognition and Emotion* 17:297–314.

Kendon, Adam 1984. *Gesture: Visible Action as Utterance*. Cambridge, England: Cambridge University Press.

Kendon, Adam 2004. *Gesture: Visible Action as Utterance*. Cambridge: Cambridge University Press.

Kettunen, Paavo 2002. The Function of Confession: A Study Based on Experiences. *Pastoral Psychology* 51:13–25.

Keutzer, Carolin S. 1978. Whatever Turns You On: Triggers to Transcendent Experiences. *Journal of Humanistic Psychology* 18 (3):77–80.

Khamis, Vivian 2012. Impact of War, Religiosity and Ideology on PTSD and Psychiatric Disorders in Adolescents from Gaza Strip and South Lebanon. *Social Science and Medicine* 74:2005–2011.

Khoroche, Peter 1989. *Once the Buddha Was a Monkey: Ārya Śūrya's Jātakamālā*. Chicago, IL: University of Chicago Press:

King, Martin Luther 2007. *The Papers of Martin Luther King, Jr., Volume IV: Symbol of the Movement, January 1957–December 1958*. Edited by Clayborne Carson, Susan Carson, Adrienne Clay, Virginia Shadron, and Kieran Taylor. Berkeley: University of California Press.

Kirkpatrick, John 1985. Some Marquesan Understandings of Action and Identity. In Geoffrey White & John Kirkpatrick, Eds., *Person, Self, and Experience: Exploring Pacific Island Ethnopsychologies* (pp. 80–120). Berkeley, CA: University of California Press.

Kirschner, Sebastian, & Michael Tomasello 2010. Joint Music Making Promotes Prosocial Behavior in 4-Year-Old Children. *Evolution and Human Behavior* 31:354–364.

Klam, Mathew 2001. Experiencing Ecstasy. *New York Times Magazine* 21 January, 38–43, 64, 68, 72, 78–79.

Klostermaier, Klaus 1974. The Bhaktirasāmṛtasindhubindu of Viśvanātha Cakravartin. *Journal of the American Oriental Society* 94(1):96–107. http://www.jstor.org/stable/599733

Knight, Kimberley–Joy 2012. Si purose calcina a'propi occhi: The Importance of the Gift of Tears for Thirteenth–Century Religious Women and their Hagiographers. In Elina Gertsman, Ed., *Crying in the Middle Ages: Tears of History* (pp. 136–155). New York: Routledge.

Kodama, Satoru, Saito, Kazumi, Tanaka, Shiro, Yachi, Yoko, Asumi, Mihoko, Sugawara, Ayumi, Totsuka, Kumiko, Shimano, Hitoshi, Ohashi, Yasuo, Yamada, Nobuhiro, & Sone, Hirohito 2009. Cardiorespiratory Fitness as a Quantitative Predictor of All–Cause Mortality and Cardiovascular Events in Healthy Men and Women: A Meta–analysis. *JAMA–Journal of the American Medical Association* 301:2024–2035.

Koestler, Arthur 1954. *The Invisible Writing: Being the second volume of Arrow in the Blue, an autobiography*. London: Collins & Hamish Hamilton.

Koestler, Arthur 1964. *The Act of Creation*. New York: Macmillan.

Kofksy, Frank 1973. *Black Nationalism and the Revolution in Music*. New York: Pathfinder. [quoted in Berliner 1994].

Köllner, Martin G., & Oliver C. Schultheiss 2014. Meta-analytic Evidence of Low Convergence Between Implicit and Explicit Measures of the Needs for Achievement, Affiliation, and Power. *Frontiers in Psychology* 5, article 826. doi:10.3389/fpsyg.2014.00826

Konečni, Vladimir J. 2005. The Aesthetic Trinity: Awe, Being Moved, Thrills. *Bulletin of Psychology and the Arts* 5(2):27–44.

Konečni, Vladimir J. 2011. Aesthetic Trinity Theory and the Sublime. *Philosophy Today* 55(1):64–73.

Konstan, David 2009. Meleager's Sweet Tears: Observations on Weeping and Pleasure. In Thomas Fögen, Ed., *Tears in the Greco–Roman World* (pp. 311–533). Berlin: Walter de Gruyter.

Koptjevskaja-Tamm, Maria 2015. Introducing "The Linguistics of Temperature." In Maria Koptjevskaja-Tamm, Ed., *The Linguistics of Temperature* (pp. 1–40). Amsterdam: John Benjamins.

Kopytoff, Igor 1971. Ancestors as Elders in Africa. *Africa* 41(2):129–142.

Kosslyn, Stephen M., Giorgio Ganis, & William L. Thompson 2001. Neural Foundations of imagery. *Nature Reviews Neuroscience* 2:635–642.

Kosslyn, Stephen M., William L. Thompson, & Giorgio Ganis 2006. *The Case for Mental Imagery*. Oxford: Oxford University Press.

Kottler, Jeffrey A. 1996. *The Language of Tears*. San Francisco, CA: Jossey-Bass.

Krajeck, Amy J. 2009. The Things They [All] Carried: Discovering Themes through Imagined Stories of Votive Offerings. *The English Journal* 99(2):42–47.

Krieglmeyer, Regina, Jan De Houwer, & Roland Deutsch 2013. On the Nature of Automatically Triggered Approach–Avoidance Behavior. *Emotion Review* 5(3):280–284. doi:10.1177/1754073913477501

Kringelbach, Morton L., Eloise A. Stark, Catherine Alexander, Marc H Bornstein, & Alan Stein, A. 2016. On Cuteness: Unlocking the Parental Brain and Beyond. *Trends in Cognitive Sciences* 20:545–558. doi:10.1016/j.tics.2016.05.003

Krog-Tonning, Knud 1906. *En Konvertits Erindringer* [A Convert's Recollections]. Copenhagen: Høst & Son.

Kryvenko, Anna 2015. In the Warmth of the Ukrainian Temperature Domain. In Maria Koptjevskaja-Tamm, Ed., *The Linguistics of Temperature* (pp. 300–332). Amsterdam: John Benjamins.

Kuang, Cliff 2014. The Near Impossible Challenge of Designing the 9/11 Museum. Wired.com, May.

Kuipers, Joel C. 1999. Ululations from the Weyewa Highlands (Sumba): Simultaneity, Audience Response, and Models of Cooperation. *Ethnomusicology* 43:490–507.

Kuriyama, Shinichi 2006. Impact of Overweight and Obesity on Medical Care Costs, All–Cause Mortality, and the Risk of Cancer in Japan. *Journal of Epidemiology* 16:139–144.

Laeng, Bruno, Lisa Mette Eidet, Unni Sulutvedt, & Jaak Panksepp 2016. Music Chills: The Eye Pupil as Mirror To Music's Soul. *Consciousness and Cognition* 44(Supplement C):161–178.

Laham, Simon M., Yoshihisa Kashima, Jennifer Dix, & Melissa Wheeler 2015. A Meta-Analysis of the Facilitation of Arm Flexion and Extension Movements as a Function of Stimulus Valence. *Cognition and Emotion* 29:1069–1090. doi:10.1080/02699931.2014.968096

Lakoff, George, & Mark Johnson 2003. *Metaphors We Live By*. Chicago, IL: University of Chicago Press.

Langlois, Judith H., Jean M. Ritter, Rita J. Casey, & Douglas B. Sawin 1995. Infant Attractiveness Predicts Maternal Behaviors and Attitudes. *Developmental Psychology* 31:464–472.

Larsen, Thomas J. 1979. Hambukushu Girls' Puberty Rites. *Botswana Notes and Records* 11:33–36.

Laski, Marghanita 1961. *Ecstasy in Secular and Religious Experiences*. Los Angeles, CA: Jeremy P. Archer.

Laski, Marghanita 1980. *Everyday Ecstasy*. London: Thames & Hudson.

Launay, Jacques, Bronwyn Tarr, & Robin I. M. Dunbar 2016. Synchrony as an Adaptive Mechanism for Large-Scale Human Social Bonding. *Ethology* 122: 779–789.

Le Buzz 2016. Dimitri Payet Scores Wondergoal Winner for France, Then Breaks Down in Tears. Eurosport 10th June 2016 – 10:14 pm http://lebuzz.eurosport.co.uk/viral/wow–what–a–moment–dimitri–payet–scores–wondergoal–winner–for–france–then–breaks–down–in–tears–15078/

Le Guen, Olivier 2015. Temperature Terms and Their Meaning in Yucatec Maya (Mexico). In Maria Koptjevskaja-Tamm, Ed., *The Linguistics of Temperature* (pp. 742–775). Amsterdam: John Benjamins.

Lee, Dorothy D. 1959. *Freedom and Culture*. Englewood Cliffs, NJ: Prentice Hall.

Lee, Matthew T., Margaret M. Poloma, & Stephen G. Post 2013. *The Heart of Religion: Spiritual Empowerment, Benevolence, and the Experience of God's Love*. Oxford: Oxford University Press.

Lester, Rebecca J. 1995. Embodied Voices: Women's Food Asceticism and the Negotiation of Identity. *Ethos* 23:187–222.

LeVine, Robert A. 1984. Properties of Culture: An Ethnographic View. In Robert A. LeVine & Richard A. Shweder, Eds., *Culture Theory: Essays on Mind, Self, and Emotion* (pp. 67–87). Cambridge: Cambridge University Press.

Levinson, Jerrold 2006. Emotion in Response to Art. In Jerrold Levinson, Ed., *Contemplating Art: Essays in Aesthetics* (pp. 39–55). Oxford: Oxford University Press. (Essay originally published in 1997.)

Levy, Robert I. 1973. *Tahitians: Mind and Experience in the Society Islands*. Chicago, IL: University of Chicago Press.

Lewis Michael 2016. Self-conscious Emotions: Embarrassment, Pride, Shame, and Guilt. In Lisa Feldman Barrett, Michael Lewis, & Jeannette M. Haviland-Jones, Eds., *Handbook of Emotions*. 4th Edition (pp. 792–814). New York: Guilford Press.

Lewis, I. M. 2003. *Ecstatic Religion: A Study of Shamanism and Spirit Possession*. 3rd Edition. New York: Routledge.

Lienhardt, Godfrey 1961. *Divinity and experience: The Religion of the Dinka*. Oxford: Oxford University Press.

Liljegren, Henrik, & Naseem Haider 2015. Facts, Feelings and Temperature Expressions in the Hindu Kush. In Maria Koptjevskaja-Tamm, Ed., *The Linguistics of Temperature* (pp. 440–470). Amsterdam: John Benjamins.

Lindenbaum, Shirley 1979. *Kuru Sorcery: Disease and Danger in the New Guinea Highlands*. Palo Alto, CA: Mayfield.

Linehan, Marsha M. 1993. *Cognitive-Behavioral Treatment of Borderline Personality Disorder*. New York: Guilford Press.

Lockwood, Hunter, & Susanne Vejdemo 2015. 'There Is No Thermostat in the Forest" – the Ojibwe Temperature Term System. In Maria Koptjevskaja-Tamm, Ed., *The Linguistics of Temperature* (pp. 721–741). Amsterdam: John Benjamins.

Loftus, Elizabeth F. 1980. *Memory*. Reading, MA: Addison-Wesley.

Loftus, Elizabeth F. 2015. Planting Misinformation in the Human Mind: A 30-Year Investigation of the Malleability of Memory. *Learning and Memory* 12:361–366.

Lorenz, Konrad 1943. Die angeborenen Formen möglicher Erfahrung. *Zeitschrift für Tierpsychologie* 5:235–409. doi:10.1111/j.1439–0310.1943.tb00655.x

Lorenz, Konrad, & Paul Leyhausen 1973. *Motivation of Human and Animal Behavior: An Ethological View*. New York: Van Nostrand Reinhold.

Lorenz, Konrad 1988. *The Foundations of Ethology*. Translated by Konrad Lorenz and R. W. Kickert. New York: Springer.

Lorenzen, David N. 2004. Bhakti. In Sushil Mittal and Gene Thursby, Eds., *The Hindu World* (pp. 185–209). New York: Routledge.

Ludolphus de Saxonia 1502–1503. *Vita Cristi Romãçado por Fray Ambrosio* I–IV. Alcalá. [Cited in Christian 1982].

Luhrmann, Tanya M. 2012. *When God Talks Back: Understanding the American Evangelical Relationship with God*. New York: Knopf.

Luhrmann, Tanya M., Howard Nusbaum, & Ronald Thisted 2010. The Absorption Hypothesis: Learning to Hear God in Evangelical Christianity. American Anthropologist 112:66–78.

Luraghi, Silvia 2015. Asymmetries in Italian Temperature Terminology. In Maria Koptjevskaja-Tamm, Ed., *The Linguistics of Temperature* (pp. 333–353). Amsterdam: John Benjamins.

Lutz, Catherine A. 1988. *Unnatural Emotions: Everyday Sentiments on a Micronesian Atoll and their Challenge to Western Theory*. Chicago, IL: University of Chicago Press.

Lutz, Catherine A. 1995. Need, Nurturance, and the Emotions on a Pacific Atoll. In Joel Marks & Roger T. Ames, Eds., *Emotions in Asian Thought: A Dialog in Comparative Philosophy* (pp. 235–252). Albany: State University of New York Press.

Lutz, Catherine, & Lila Abu–Lughod (Eds.) 1990. *Language and the Politics of Emotion*. New York: Cambridge University Press.

MacBeth, Angus, & Andrew Gumley 2012. Exploring Compassion: A Meta-Analysis of the Association Between Self-Compassion and Psychopathology. *Clinical Psychology Review* 32:545–552.

Mahmood, Saba 2001. Rehearsed Spontaneity and the Conventionality of Ritual: Disciplines of "Ṣalāt". *American Ethnologist* 28:827–853.

Marchand, Trevor H. J. 2016. Place Making in the "Holy of Holies": The Church of the Holy Sepulcher, Jerusalem. In Jon P. Mitchell & Michael Bull, Eds., *Ritual, Performance and the Senses* (pp. 63–84). London: Bloomsbury.

Marcus, Cressida 2002. In Praise of Women: The Veneration of the Virgin Mary in the Ethiopian Orthodox Church. *Journal of Ethiopian Studies* (Special Issue on Gender and Christianity) 35(1): 9–26.

Marmor–Lavie, Galit, & Gabriel Weimann 2008. Intimacy Appeals in Israeli Televised Political Advertising. *Political Communication* 25(3):249–268. doi:10.1080/10584600802197327

Marshall, Paul 2005. *Mystical Encounters with the Natural World: Experiences and Explanations*. Oxford: Oxford University Press.

Maslow, Abraham 1962. *Toward a Psychology of Being*. Princeton, NJ: Van Nostrand.

Maslow, Abraham 1970. *Religions, Values, and Peak–Experiences*. New York: Viking.

Mawere, Munyaradzi, Cosmas M. Mukombe, & Christopher M. Mabeza *Memoirs of an Unsung Legend, Nemeso*. Bamenda: Langaa.

McDaniel, June 1989. *The Madness of the Saints: Ecstatic Religion in Bengal*. Chicago, IL: University of Chicago Press.

McDougall, William 1919. *An Introduction to Social Psychology*. 14th Edition. London: Methuen. Reprinted 2001 by Batoche Books Kitchener, Ontario. http://socserv2.socs ci.mcmaster.ca/econ/ugcm/3ll3/mcdougall/socialpsych.pdf

McDougall, William 1923. *Outline of Psychology*. New York: Charles Scribner's Sons.

McEntire, Sandra J. 1990. *The Doctrine of Compunction in Medieval England: Holy Tears*. Studies in Medieval Literature 8. Lewiston, NY: Edwin Mellen Press.

McGinn, Bernard 1991. *The Foundations of Mysticism: Origins to the Fifth Century*. Volume 1 of *The Presence of God: A History of Western Christian Mysticism*. New York: Crossroad.

McGinn, Bernard 1998. *The Flowering of Mysticism: Men and Women in the New Mysticism—1200–1350*. Volume 3 of *The Presence of God: A History of Western Christian Mysticism*. New York: Crossroad.

McNeill, William H. 1995. *Keeping Together in Time: Dance and Drill in Human History*. Cambridge, MA: Harvard University Press.

Mendelman, Lisa 2014. Feeling Hard–Boiled: Modern Sentimentalism and Frances Newman's *The Hard–Boiled Virgin*. *American Literary History* 26:693–715.

Mendoza–Denton, Norma 2011. The Semiotic Hitchhiker's Guide to Creaky Voice: Circulation and Gendered Hardcore in a Chicana/o Gang Persona. *Journal of Linguistic Anthropology* 21:261–280. doi:10.1111/j.1548–1395.2011.01110.x

Menninghaus, Winfried, Valentin Wagner, Julian Hanich, Eugen Wassiliwizky, Milena Kuehnast, & Thomas Jacobsen 2015. Towards A Psychological Construct of Being Moved. *PloS One* e0128451. doi:10.1371/journal

Menninghaus, Winfried, Valentin Wagner, Eugen Wassiliwizky, Thomas Jacobsen, & Christine Angela Knoop 2017. The Emotional and Aesthetic Powers of Parallelistic Diction. *Poetics* 63:47–59. doi:10.1016/j.poetic.2016.12.001

Merkur, Dan 1999. *Mystical Moments and Unitive Thinking*. Albany: SUNY Press.

Metraux, Alfred 1947. Mourning Rites and Burial Forms of the South American Indians. *América Indígena* 7:744.

Middleton, John 1960. *Lugbara Religion: Ritual and Authority among an East African People*. (Published for the International African Institute.) New York: Oxford University Press.

Mikkelson, David 2015 Rescuing Hug. http://www.snopes.com/glurge/healinghug.asp Accessed 3 September 2019.

Milano, Dominic 1984. Jazz Pianist and Psychiatrist Denny Zeitlin on the Psychology of Improvisation. *Keyboard* 10(no. 10, October):30–35. [quoted in Berliner 1994].

Mill, John Stuart 1882. *A System of Logic, Ratiocinative and Inductive*. Eighth Edition. New York: Harper.

Mill, John Stuart 2002 [1843]. *A System of Logic*. Honolulu, HI: University Press of the Pacific.

Miller, Lisa, Paul Rozin, & Alan Page Fiske 1998. Food Sharing and Feeding Another Person Suggest Intimacy: A Study of American College Students. *European Journal for Social Psychology* 28:423–436.

Mitchell, Jon P. 1997. A Moment with Christ: The Importance of Feelings in the Analysis of Belief. *The Journal of the Royal Anthropological Institute* 3:79–94. http://www.jstor.org/stable/3034366

Momondo.com 2016. The DNA Journey. Video at https://www.momondo.com/letsopenourworld/dna. Accessed 3 September 2019.

Monglond, André 1966. *Le Maître des Âmes Sensibles*. Volume II of Le Préromantisme Français. Paris: Librarie José Corti.

Montiglio, Silvia 2013. *Love and Providence: Recognition in the Ancient Novel*. Oxford: Oxford University Press.

Moore, Archimandrite Lazarus 1959. *The Ladder of Divine Ascent. St. John Climacus*. London: Harper.

Moors, Agnes 2010. Theories of Emotion Causation: A Review. In Jan De Houwer & Dirk Hermans, Eds., *Cognition and Emotion: Reviews of Current Research and Theories* (pp. 1–37). New York: Psychology Press.

Morgan, Louis Henry 1871. *Systems of Consanguinity and Affinity of the Human Family*. Washington, DC: Smithsonian Institution Contributions to Knowledge XVII.

Mori, Kazuma, & Makoto Iwanaga 2017. Two Types of Peak Emotional Responses to Music: The Psychophysiology of Chills and Tears. *Scientific Reports* 7. https://doi.org/10.1038/srep46063

Morris, Ryan 2015. Meals on Wheels. Undergraduate Student Independent Study Ethnography, Department of Anthropology, UCLA.

Muir, John 2004 (originally published 1911). *My First Summer in The Sierra*. Mineola, NY: Dover.

Murray, Colin 1980. Sotho Fertility Symbolism. *African Studies* 39:65–76.

Mwansa, Dickson M. 2014. *The Family Question and Other Plays*. Bloomington, IN: Xlibris.

Myrick, Jessica Gall 2015. Emotion Regulation, Procrastination, and Watching Cat Videos Online: Who Watches Internet Cats, Why, and to What Effect? *Computers in Human Behavior* 52:168–176.

Nabokov, Vladimir 1948. Butterflies. *New Yorker* June 12 issue. https://www.newyorke r.com/magazine/1948/06/12/butterflies-vladimir-nabokov

Nadel, S. F. 1954. *Nupe Religion: Traditional Beliefs and the Influence of Islam in a West African Chiefdom*. London: Routledge & Kegan Paul.

Nagy, Piroska 2000. *Le Don des Larmes au Moyen Âge: Un Instrument Spirituel en Quête d'Institution (Ve – XIIIe Siècle)*. Paris: Albin Michel.

Nagy, Piroska 2004. Religious Weeping as Ritual in the Medieval West. *Social Analysis: The International Journal of Social and Cultural Practice* 48:119–137.

Naiden, F. S. 2013. *Smoke Signals for the Gods: Ancient Greek Sacrifice from the Archaic through Roman Periods*. Oxford: Oxford University Press.

Naish, Stephen Lee 2015. Crying at Robots: Emotional Responses to Artificial Intelligence. 3:AM Magazine. 22 June 2015. http://www.3ammagazine.com/3am/ crying–at–robots–emotional–responses–to–artificial–intelligence/

Napoli, Philip M. 2011. *Audience Evolution: New Technologies and the Transformation of Media Audiences*. New York: Columbia University Press.

Nārāyaṇa, Bhaktivedānta (Editor & translator) 1996. *Drop of the Nectarine Ocean of Bhakti–rasa*. Translation of Viśvanātha Cakravartī Thākura's *Sri Bhakti–rasamrta–sindhu–bindu*. Mathurā: Gauḍīya Vedānta Publications.

Nasr, Seyyed Hossein 1980. *Living Sufism*. London: George Allen & Unwin. [Originally published in 1972 as *Sufi Essays*.]

Nasr, Seyyed Hossein 1999. Persian Sufi Literature: Its Spiritual and Cultural Significance. In Leonard Lewisohn, Ed., *The Heritage of Sufism: Volume II The Legacy of Medieval Persian Sufism (1150–1500)* (pp. 1–10). Oxford: Oneworld.

Neale, Steve 1986. Melodrama and Tears. *Screen* 27(6):6–23.

Neff, Kristen D. 2011. Self-Compassion, Self-Esteem, and Well-Being. *Social and Personality Psychology Compass* 5(1):1–12. doi:10.1111/j.1751-9004.2010.00330.x

Neff, Kristen D., Kristin L. Kirkpatrick, & Stephanie S. Rude 2007. Self-Compassion and Adaptive Psychological Functioning. *Journal of Research in Personality* 41:139–154.

Nelson, Judith Kay 2005. *Seeing Through Tears: Crying and Attachment*. New York: Routledge.

Nelson, Timothy J. 1996. Sacrifice of Praise: Emotion and Collective Participation in an African–American Worship Service. *Sociology of Religion* 57:379–396.

Nesse, Randolph 2001. *Evolution and the Capacity for Commitment*. New York: Russell Sage.

Neubauer, Eckhard, & Veronica Doubleday n.d. Islamic Religious Music, II. Sufism and Popular Islam, 4. 'Mawlid'. In *Oxford Music Online*. Oxford: Oxford University Press.

Neville, Fergus, & Stephen Reicher 2011. The Experience of Collective Participation: Shared Identity, Relatedness and Emotionality. *Contemporary Social Science* 6:377–396. doi:10.1080/21582041.2012.627277

New York Times 1988 (July 20). A Jackson Sermon Turns Former Foes into Cheering Fans. Quoted in Shamir, Arthur, & House 1994.

Newman, George E, Gil Diesendruck, & Paul Bloom. 2011. Celebrity Contagion and the Value of Objects. *Journal of Consumer Research*, Inc. 38:215.

Ngũgĩ, wa Thiong'o 1997. *Petals of Blood*. London: Heinemann.

Nicolas, Mariot 2001. Les formes élémentaires de l'effervescence collective, ou l'état d'esprit prêté aux foules. *Revue Française de Science Politique* 51:707–738. doi:10.3917/rfsp.515.0707

Niles, Lyndrey A. 1984. Rhetorical Characteristics of Traditional Black Preaching. *Journal of Black Studies* 15:41–52.

Nittono, Hiroshi, Michiko Fukushima, Akihiro Yano, & Hiroki Moriya 2012. The Power of "Kawaii": Viewing Cute Images Promotes a Careful Behavior and Narrows Attentional Focus. *PLoS One*, 7:e46362. doi:10.1371/journal.pone.0046362

Norenzayan, Ara 2013. *Big Gods: How Religion Transformed Cooperation and Conflict*. Princeton, NJ: Princeton University Press.

Notermans, Catrien 2007. Loss and Healing: A Marian Pilgrimage in Secular Dutch Society. *Ethnology* 46:217–233.

Notermans, Catrien 2008. Local and Global Icons of Mary: An Ethnographic Study of a Powerful Symbol. *Anthropos* 103:471–481.

Novak, Michael 1993. *Joy of Sports: Endzones, Bases, Baskets, Balls, and the Consecration of the American Spirit*. Revised Edition. Lanham, MD: Rowman & Littlefield.

Novetzke, Christian Lee 2007. Bhakti and Its Public. *International Journal of Hindu Studies* 11:255–272. http://www.jstor.org/stable/25691067

Ntshinga, Thabazi 2009. Song Texts and the Ambiguities of Oral Performance. *Muziki: Journal of Music Research in Africa* 6(1):36–48.

Nusbaum, Emily C., Paul J. Silvia, Roger E. Beaty, Chris J. Burgin, Donald A. Hodges, & Thomas R. Kwapil 2014. Listening Between the Notes: Aesthetic Chills in Everyday Music Listening. *Psychology of Aesthetics, Creativity, and the Arts* 8:104–109.

Oaks, Dallin H. 1997. Teaching and Learning by the Spirit. *Ensign* March. https://www.lds.org/ensign/1997/03/teaching–and–learning–by–the–spirit?lang=eng

Ohnuki–Tierney, Emiko 2002. *Kamikaze, Cherry Blossoms, and Nationalisms: The Militarization of Esthetics in Japanese History*. Chicago, IL: University of Chicago Press.

Olaveson, Tim 2003. 'Connectedness' and the Rave Experience: Rave as New Religious Movement? In Graham St John, Ed., *Rave Culture and Religion* (pp. 83–104). London: Routledge.

Oliver, Mary 1986. *Dream Works*. Boston: Atlantic Monthly Press.

Oliver, Mary Beth B., Keunyeong Kim, Jennifer Hoewe, Mun-Young Chung, Erin Ash, Julia K. Woolley, & Drew D. Shade 2015. Media-Induced Elevation as a Means of Enhancing Feelings of Intergroup Connectedness: Media-Induced Elevation. *Journal of Social Issues* 71(1):106–122. doi:10.1111/josi.12099.

Oliver, Mary Beth, & Anne Bartsch 2011. Appreciation of Entertainment: The Importance of Meaningfulness via Virtue and Wisdom. *Journal of Media Psychology* 23(1):29–33. doi:10.1027/1864-1105/a000029

Oliver, Mary Beth, & Arthur A. Raney 2011. Entertainment as Pleasurable and Meaningful: Identifying Hedonic and Eudaimonic Motivations for Entertainment Consumption. *Journal of Communication* 61:984–1004. doi:10.1111/j.1460-2466.2011.01585.x

Oliver, Mary Beth, & Tilo Hartmann 2010. Exploring the Role of Meaningful Experiences in Users' Appreciation of "Good Movies". *Projections* 4(2):128–150. doi:10.3167/proj.2010.040208

Oliver, Mary Beth, Tilo Hartmann, & Julia K. Woolley 2012. Elevation in Response to Entertainment Portrayals of Moral Virtue. *Human Communication Research* 38:360–378.

Olivier J.–P. 1986. Cretan Writing in the Second Millennium B.C. *World Archaeology* 17:377–389.

Olsen, Miriam Rovsing 2001. Music in Performance: A Wedding in the Atlas Mountains. In Virginia Danielson, Scott Marcus, & Dwight Reynolds, Eds., *Garland Encyclopedia of World Music Volume 6: The Middle East.* New York: Routledge. http://glnd.alexande rstreet.com/view/330327

Onion, The 2016. Universe Feels Zero Connection to Guy Tripping On Mushrooms. http://www.theonion.com/article/universe–feels–zero–connection– guy–tripping–mushro–52749.

Onions, C. T. 1966. *Oxford Dictionary of English Etymology.* Oxford: Clarendon Press.

Otto, Rudolph 1932 [German original first published in 1926]. *Mysticism East and West: A Comparative Analysis of the Nature of Mysticism.* Translated by Bertha L. Bracey & Richenda C. Payne. New York: Macmillan.

Otto, Rudolph 1950 [German original first published in 1917]. *The Idea of the Holy: An Inquiry into the Non–rational Factor in the Idea of the Divine and Its Relation to the Rational.* 2nd Edition. Translated by John W. Harvey. Oxford: Oxford University Press.

Páez, Dario, & Bernard Rimé 2014. Collective Emotional Gatherings. Their Impact Upon Identity Fusion, Shared Beliefs and Social Integration. In C. von Scheve & M. Salmela, Eds., *Collective Emotions: Perspectives from Psychology, Philosophy, and Sociology* (pp. 204–216). Oxford, UK: Oxford University Press.

Panksepp, Jaak 1995. The Emotional Sources of "Chills" Induced by Music. *Music Perception* 13:171–207.

Panzarella, Robert. 1980. The Phenomenology of Aesthetic Peak Experiences. *Journal of Humanistic Psychology* 20:69–85.

Pardeshi, Prashant, & Peter Hook 2015. Blowing Hot, Hotter, and Hotter Yet: Temperature Vocabulary in Marathi. In Maria Koptjevskaja-Tamm, Ed., *The Linguistics of Temperature* (pp. 471–490). Amsterdam: John Benjamins.

Parrinder, Geoffrey 1976. *Mysticism in the World's Religions.* London: Sheldon.

Partridge, Eric 1958. *Origins: A Short Etymological Dictionary of Modern English.* New York: Macmillan.

Parzuchowski, Michal, Aleksandra Szymkow, Wieslaw Baryla, & Bogdan Wojciszke 2014. From the Heart: Hand Over Heart as an Embodiment of Honesty. *Cognitive Processing* 15:237–244.

Parzuchowski, Michal & Bogdan Wojciszke 2014. Hand Over Heart Primes Moral Judgments and Behavior. *Journal of Nonverbal Behavior* 38:145–165. doi:10.1007/ s10919–013–0170–0

Pascal, Roy 1952. The "Sturm und Drang" Movement. *The Modern Language Review* 47(2):129–151.

Pascal, Roy 1953. *The German Sturm und Drang.* Manchester: Manchester University Press.

Passie, Torsten, Juergen Seifert, Udo Schneider, & Hinderk M. Emrich 2002. The Pharmacology of Psilocybin. *Addiction Biology* 7:357–364.

Paulhus, Delroy L., & Simine Vazire 2007. The Self-Report Method. In Richard W. Robins & R. Chris Fraley, & Robert F. Krueger, Eds., *Handbook of Research Methods in Personality Psychology* (pp. 224–239). New York, NY: Guilford Press.

Peirce, Charles Saunders 19311958. *The Collected Papers of C. S. Peirce.* C. Edited by Hartshorne, P. Weiss, & A. W. Burks. Cambridge, MA: Harvard University Press.

Peirce, Charles Saunders 1985. Logic As Semiotic: The Theory of Signs. In R. Innis, Ed., *Semiotics: An Introductory Anthology* (pp. 1–23). Bloomington: Indiana University Press.

Pepys, Samuel 2003. *The Diary of Samuel Pepys.* Edited by Richard Le Gallienne. Introduction by Robert Louis Stevenson. New York: Modern Library (Random House).

Pérez, Regina Gutiérrez 2008. A Cross-Cultural Analysis of Heart Metaphors. *Revista Alicantina de Estudios Ingleses* 21:25–56.

Perkova, Natalia 2015. Adjectives of Temperature in Latvian. In Maria Koptjevskaja-Tamm, Ed., *The Linguistics of Temperature* (pp. 216–253). Amsterdam: John Benjamins.

Perrin, B. 1909. Recognition Scenes in Greek Literature. *The American Journal of Philology* 30(4):371–404.

Perrin, Loïc-Michel 2015. Climate, Temperature and Polysemous Patterns in French and Wolof. In Maria Koptjevskaja-Tamm, Ed., *The Linguistics of Temperature* (pp. 151–186). Amsterdam: John Benjamins.

Petje, Rebecca Mmasea 1998. A Survey of Bapedi Women's Songs. MA mini-dissertation, African Languages, Rand Afrikaanse University. https://ujdigispace.uj.ac.za/bitstream/handle/10210/7597/R.M.%20PETJE_1998_MA.pdf?sequence=1&isAllowed=y

Phaf, R. Hans, Sören E. Mohr, Mark Rotteveel, & Jelte M. Wicherts 2014. Approach, Avoidance, and Affect: A Meta-Analysis of Approach-Avoidance Tendencies in Manual Reaction Time Tasks. *Frontiers in Psychology* 5:378. doi:10.3389/fpsyg.2014.00378

Pike, Nelson 1992. *Mystic Union: An Essay in the Phenomenology of Mysticism.* Ithaca, NY: Cornell University Press.

Pinault, David 1992. *The Shiites: Ritual and Popular Piety in a Muslim Community.* New York: St. Martin's.

Pohling, Rico, & Rhett Diessner 2016. Moral Elevation and Moral Beauty: A Review of the Empirical Literature. *Review of General Psychology* 20(4):412–425. doi:10.1037/gpr0000089

Prabhupada, Bhaktivedanta 2008. *Krsna, the Supreme Personality of Godhead: A Summary Study of Srila Vyasadeva's Bhagavat Purana, 10th Canto.* Alachua, FL: Bhaktivedanta Book Trust. Accessed 3 September 2019. https://krsnabook.com/ch32.html

Preece, Rob 2012. And the Gold Medal for Sobbing on the Podium Goes to... Emotional Hurdler Felix Sanchez Lets It All Go After Winning Olympic Title in Memory of his Grandmother. *Daily Mail* 6 August, updated 7 August 2012. http://www.dailymail.co.uk/news/article-2184634/London-2012-Olympics-Emotional-hurdler-Felix-Sanchez-sobs-winning-title-second-time.html

Propp, Vladimir 1968 [originally published 1928]. *Morphology of the Folk Tale.* 2nd Edition. Translated by Laurence Scott, revised and edited by Louis A. Wagner. Austin, TX: University of Texas Press.

Prose, Francine 2012. When Art Makes Us Cry. *New York Review of Books.* 6 September 2012. http://www.nybooks.com/blogs/nyrblog/2012/sep/06/marina-abramovic-when-art-makes-us-cry/

Proudfoot, Wayne 1985. *Religious Experience.* Berkeley, CA: University of California Press.

Qureshi, Regula Burckhardt 1995. *Sufi Music of India and Pakistan: Sound, Context and Meaning in Qawwali.* Chicago: University of Chicago Press.

Racy, Ali J. 2003. *Making Music in the Arab World: The Culture and Artistry of Tarab.* Cambridge: Cambridge University Press.

Radcliffe–Brown, A. R. 1922. *The Andaman Islanders: A Study in Social Anthropology.* Cambridge: Cambridge University Press.

Rai, Tage S., & Alan P. Fiske 2011. Moral Psychology Is Relationship Regulation: Moral Motives for Unity, Hierarchy, Equality, and Proportionality. *Psychological Review* 118:57–75. doi:10.1037/a0021867

Raney, Arthur A., Sophie H. Janicke, Mary Beth Oliver, Katherine R. Dale, Robert P. Jones & Daniel Cox 2017. Profiling the Audience for Self–Transcendent Media: A National Survey. *Mass Communication and Society* 21:296–319. DOI: 10.1080/15205436.2017.1413195.

Rao, Velcheru Narayana 2004. Purāṇa. In Sushil Mittal and Gene Thursby, Eds., *The Hindu World* (pp. 97–115). New York: Routledge.

Rappaport, Julian 1993. Narrative Studies, Personal Stories, and Identity Transformation in the Mutual Help Context. *Journal of Applied Behavioral Science* 29:239–256.

Rasulić, Katarina 2015. What's Hot and What's Not in English and Serbian: A Contrastive View on the Polysemy of Temperature Adjectives. In Maria Koptjevskaja-Tamm, Ed., *The Linguistics of Temperature* (pp. 254–299). Amsterdam: John Benjamins.

Reece, Steve 1993. *The Stranger's Welcome: Oral Theory and the Aesthetics of the Homeric Hospitality Scene.* Ann Arbor, MI: University of Michigan Press.

Rennung, Miriam, & Anja S. Göritz 2016. Prosocial Consequences of Interpersonal Synchrony. *Zeitschrift für Psychologie* 224:168–189. doi:10.1027/2151-2604/a000252

Rett, Jessica 2019. The Semantics of Emotive Markers and Other Illocutionary Content. *Semantics and Pragmatics.* UCLA Department of Linguistics paper in progress.

Reynolds, Simon 1998. *Energy Flash: A Journey through Rave Music and Dance.* London: Picador (Macmillan).

Ricoeur, Paul 1967. *The Symbolism of Evil.* Translated by E. Buchanan. Boston, MA: Beacon Press.

Rinpoche, Choden 2010. *Tong Len Meditation (Meditation on Giving and Taking).* Teaching at Chokyi Gyaltsen Center, Penang, *Malaysia on 25th December 2009.* Translated by Geshe Gyalten. Transcribed and lightly edited by Ven. Osel. http://www.fpmt-cgc. org/resources/teaching/mar2010.html

Roberts, Brent W., Peter D. Harms, Jennifer L. Smith, Dustin Wood, & Michelle Webb 2006. Using Multiple Methods in Personality Psychology. In Michael Eid & Ed Diener, Eds., *Handbook of Multimethod Measurement in Psychology* (pp. 321–335). Washington, DC: American Psychological Association.

Robertson Smith, W. 1957 [1889]. *Lectures on The Religion of the Semites: The Fundamental Institutions.* New York: Meridian Library.

Rockefeller, Marilyn Moss, & Joan Johnson–Freese 2013. Dancing for Democracy: Understanding Malawi's First Female President. *Orbis* 57:268–281.

Rodrigues, Hillary Peter 2003. *Ritual Worship of the Great Goddess: The Liturgy of the Durgā Pūjā with Interpretations.* Albany, NY: State University of New York Press.

Rosaldo, Michelle Z. 1980. *Knowledge and Passion: Ilongot Notions of Self and Social Life.* Cambridge: Cambridge University Press.

Rosaldo, Michelle Z. 1984. Words That Are Moving: The Social Meanings of Ilongot Verbal Art. In Donald Lawrence Brenneis & Fred R. Myers, Eds., *Dangerous Words: Language and Politics in the Pacific* (pp. 131–160). New York: New York University Press.

Rotella, Sebastian 2004. Taking Iraqi Customs to Heart. *Los Angeles Times*, 27 March 2004. https://www.latimes.com/archives/la–xpm–2004–mar–27–fg–heart27–story. html

Rothman, Joshua 2014. Live from the Moon. *New Yorker.* https://www.newyorker.com/ books/joshua–rothman/live–moon

Roulon-Doko, Paulette 2015. Lexicalisation of Temperature Concepts in Gbaya (an Ubanguian language of C.A.R.). In Maria Koptjevskaja-Tamm, Ed., *The Linguistics of Temperature* (pp. 128–150). Amsterdam: John Benjamins.

Rozin, Paul, Carol Nemeroff, Marcia Wane, & Amy Sherrod 1989. Operation of the Sympathetic Magical Law of Contagion in Interpersonal Attitudes among Americans. *Bulletin of the Psychonomic Society* 27:367–370.

Rozin, Paul, Linda Millman, & Carol Nemeroff 1986. Operation of the Laws of Sympathetic Magic in Disgust and Other Domains. *Journal of Personality and Social Psychology* 50:703–712.

Ruscio, John, Nick Haslam, & Ayelet Meron Ruscio 2006. *Introduction to the Taxometric Method: A Practical Guide.* New York: Routledge.

Rushkoff, Douglas 2001. Ecstasy: Prescription for Cultural Renaissance. In Julie Holland, Ed., *Ecstasy: The Complete Guide* (pp. 350–357). Rochester, VT: Park Street Press.

Russell, R. V. 1916. *The Tribes and Castes of the Central Provinces of India.* London: Macmillan.

Russell, James A. 2003. Core Affect and the Psychological Construction of Emotion. *Psychological Review* 110(1):145–172.

Russell, James A. 2009. Emotion, Core Affect, and Psychological Construction. *Cognition and Emotion* 23:1259–1283.

Russell, James A. José-Miguel Fernández-Dols, Anthony S.R. Manstead, & Jane C. Wellenkamp 1995. *Everyday Conceptions of Emotion: An Introduction to the Psychology, Anthropology and Linguistics of Emotion.* NATAO ASI Series. Dordrecht: Kluwer Academic.

Russo, Kate 2012. *Total Addiction: The Life of an Eclipse Chaser.* Heidelberg: Springer.

Ryan, Pauline M. 1981. An Introduction to Hausa Personal Nomenclature. *Names* 29(2):139–164.

Saitz, Robert L., & Edward J. Cervenka 1972. *Handbook of Gestures: Columbia and the United States.* 2nd Edition. The Hague: Mouton.

Salmon, Christopher 1953 The Trumpets Have Sounded – A Spectator's Impressions of June 2. BBC Radio Third Program, Saturday, June 6, 21:45.

Salamon, Justyn 2015. Temperature Domain in West Greenlandic. In Maria Koptjevskaja-Tamm, Ed., *The Linguistics of Temperature* (pp. 703–720). Amsterdam: John Benjamins.

Salmond, Anne. 1974 Rituals of Encounter among the Maori: Sociolinguistic Study of a Scene. In Richard Bauman & Joel Sherzer, Eds., *Explorations in the Ethnography of Speaking* (pp. 192–212). Cambridge: Cambridge University Press.

Salzberg, Sharon 1995. *Lovingkindness: The Revolutionary Art of Happiness.* Boston, MA: Shambhala Publications.

Santino, Jack 2004. Commemoratives, the Personal, and the Public: Spontaneous Shrines, Emergent Ritual, and the Field of Folklore. *The Journal of American Folklore* 117:363–372.

Sauder, Gerhard 1974. *Empfindsamkeit: Voraussetzungen und Elemente.* Stuttgart: Metzler.

Schacter, Daniel L. and Endel Tulving 1994. *Memory Systems 1994.* Cambridge, MA: MIT Press.

Schapper, Antoinette 2015. Temperature Terms in Kamang and Abui, two Papuan languages of Alor. In Maria Koptjevskaja-Tamm, Ed., *The Linguistics of Temperature* (pp. 858–885). Amsterdam: John Benjamins.

Schelling, Thomas C. *Strategies of Commitment and Other Essays.* Cambridge, MA: Harvard University Press.

Scherer, Klaus R. 2005. What are Emotions? And How Can They Be Measured? *Social Science Information* 44(4):695–729. doi:10.1177/0539018405058216

Scherer, Klaus R., & Marcel R. Zentner 2001. Emotional Effects of Music: Production Rules. In Patrik N. Juslin & John A. Sloboda, Eds., *Music and Emotion: Theory and Research* (pp. 361–392). Oxford, England: Oxford University Press.

Schiller, Friedrich 1782/2014. *Die Räuber*. Stuttgart, Germany: Philipp Reclam jun. Translated by D. Widger as *The Robbers*. http://www.gutenberg.org/ebooks/6782

Schiller, Friedrich 1784/2014. *Kabale und Liebe*. Stuttgart, Germany: Philipp Reclam jun. Translated by T. Riikonen and D. Widger as *Love and Intrigue*. http://www.gutenberg.org/ebooks/6784

Schmidt, Leigh Eric 2001. *Holy Fairs: Scotland and the Making of American Revivalism*. 2nd Edition. Grand Rapids, MI: Eerdmans Publishing.

Schnall, Simone, Jean Roper, & Daniel M. Fessler 2010. Elevation Leads to Altruistic Behavior. *Psychological Science*, 21:315–320.

Schroedel, Jean, Michelle Bligh, Jennifer Merolla, & Randall Gonzalez 2013. Charismatic Rhetoric in the 2008 Presidential Campaign: Commonalities and Differences. *Presidential Studies Quarterly* 43:101–128.

Schubel, Vernon James 1993. Religious Performance in Contemporary Islam: Shi'a *Devotional Rituals in South Asia*. Columbia, SC: University of South Carolina Press.

Schubert, Thomas W., Janis H. Zickfeld, Beate Seibt, & Alan Page Fiske 2016. Moment-to-Moment Changes in Feeling Moved Match Changes in Closeness, Tears, Goosebumps, and Warmth: Time Series Analyses. *Cognition and Emotion*. doi:10.1080/02699931.2016.1268998

Schweig, Graham M. 2005. *Dance of Divine Love: The Rāsa Līlā of Krishna from the Bhāgavata Purāṇa, India's Classical Sacred Love Story*. Princeton, NJ: Princeton University Press.

Scorgie, Fiona 2013. Virginity Testing and the Politics of Sexual Responsibility: Implications for AIDS Intervention. *African Studies* 61(1):55–75. doi:10.1080/00020180220140073

Sedikides, Constantine, & Tim Wildschut 2017. Finding Meaning in Nostalgia. *Review of General Psychology*. doi:10.1037/gpr0000109

Segal, Z. V., J. M. Williams, & J. D. Teasdale 2002. *Mindfulness-based Cognitive Therapy for Depression: A New Approach to Preventing Relapse*. Guilford.

Seibt, Beate, Roland Neumann, Ravit Nussinson, & Fritz Strack 2008. Movement Direction or Change in Distance? Self- and Object-Related Approach–Avoidance Motions. *Journal of Experimental Social Psychology* 44:713–720. doi:10.1016/j.jesp.2007.04.013

Seibt, Beate, Thomas W. Schubert, Janis H. Zickfeld, & Alan Page Fiske 2016. Interpersonal Closeness and Morality Predict Feelings of Being Moved. *Emotion* 17:389–394. doi:10.1037/emo0000271

Seibt, Beate, Thomas W. Schubert, Janis H. Zickfeld, & Alan Page Fiske 2018. Touching the Base: Heart-Warming Ads from the 2016 U.S. Election Moved Viewers to Partisan Tears. *Cognition and Emotion*. doi:10.1080/02699931.2018.1441128

Seibt, Beate, Thomas W. Schubert, Janis H. Zickfeld, Lei Zhu, Patricia Arriaga, Cláudia Simão, Ravit Nussinson, & Alan Page Fiske 2018. Kama Muta: Similar Emotional Responses To Touching Videos across the US, Norway, China, Israel, and Portugal. *Journal of Cross–Cultural Psychology* 49:418–435.

Shamir, Boas, Michael B. Arthur, & Robert House 1994. The Rhetoric of Charismatic Leadership: Theoretical Extension, a Case Study, and Implications for Research. *Leadership Quarterly* 5:25–42.

Shaver, Philip, R. Upekkha Murdaya, & R. Chris Fraley 2001. Structure of the Indonesian Emotion Lexicon. *Asian Journal of Social Psychology* 4:201–224.

Shaw, Samuel 1847. *The Life and Journals of Major Samuel Shaw*. Edited by Josiah Quincy. Boston, MA: Crosby and Nichols.

Sherman, Gary D., Jonathan Haidt, Ravi Iyer, & James A. Coan 2012. Individual Differences in the Physical Embodiment of Care: Prosocially Oriented Women Respond to Cuteness by Becoming More Physically Careful. *Emotion* 13:151–158.

Shimbun, Chunichi 2013. Participants Ease Stress Levels at Crying Events. *Japan Times* 22 June. Evening Edition. http://www.japantimes.co.jp/news/2013/06/22/national/participants–ease–stress–levels–at–crying–events/#article_history

Shindo, Mika 2015. Subdomains of Temperature Concepts in Japanese. In Maria Koptjevskaja-Tamm, Ed., *The Linguistics of Temperature* (pp. 639–665). Amsterdam: John Benjamins.

Shirane, Haruo 2000a. Beyond the Haiku Moment: Basho, Buson & Modern Haiku Myths. New Zealand Poetry Society. https://poetrysociety.org.nz/affiliates/haiku-nz/haiku-poems-articles/archived-articles/beyond-the-haiku-moment-basho-bu son-modern-haiku-myths/ Originally published in *Modern Haiku* XXXI:1.

Shisler, Famee Lorene 1942. The Technique of the Portrayal of Joy in Greek Tragedy. *Transactions and Proceedings of the American Philological Association* 73:277–292.

Shweder, R. A. 2014. The Tower of Appraisals: Trying to Make Sense of the One Big Thing. *Emotion Review* 6:322–324.

Shweder, R. A., J. Haidt, R. Horton, & C. Joseph 2008. The Cultural Psychology of the Emotions. Ancient and Renewed. In M. Lewis, J. M. Haviland–Jones & L. F. Eldman Barrett, Eds., *Handbook of Emotions*. 3rd Edition (pp. 409–427). New York: The Guilford Press.

Siahaan, Poppy 2015. Why Is It Not Cool? Temperature Terms in Indonesian. In Maria Koptjevskaja-Tamm, Ed., *The Linguistics of Temperature* (pp. 666–699). Amsterdam: John Benjamins.

Siegel, Ronald D. 2014. *The Science of Mindfulness: A Research–Based Path to Well–Being*. Lecture 20: Growing Up Is Not Easy: Facing Impermanence. Course No. 9303. Chantilly, VA: The Great Courses (The Teaching Company).

Sikhosana, Eugenia Lindiwe Zamandelu 2002. A Critical Study of the Contemporary Practice of Ululation (Ukukikiza) and its Current Social and Cultural Values Among the Zulus. Ph.D. dissertation, Department of IsiZulu Namagugu at the University of Zululand.

Simão, Cláudia, & Beate Seibt 2014. Gratitude Depends on the Relational Model of Communal Sharing. *PLoS One* 9(1):e86158. doi:10.1371/journal.pone.0086158

Simão, Cláudia, & Beate Seibt 2015. Friendly Touch Increases Gratitude by Inducing Communal Feelings. *Frontiers in Psychology* 6, article 815. doi:10.3389/fpsyg.2015.00815

Simons, Gary F., & Charles D. Fennig (Eds.) 2017. *Ethnologue: Languages of the World*. 20th Edition. Dallas, TX: SIL International. http://www.ethnologue.com

Singer, Peter 2011. *The Expanding Circle: Ethics, Evolution, and Moral Progress*. Princeton, NJ: Princeton University Press.

Sizer, Sandra 1978. *Gospel Hymns and Social Religion: The Rhetoric of Nineteenth–Century Revivalism*. Philadelphia, PA: Temple University Press.

Slater, Matt 2012. Sir Chris Hoy Leads GB to Cycling Gold in Men's Team Sprint. BBC Sport 2 August. http://beta.bbc.com/sport/0/olympics/18912106

Sloane, David Charles 2005. Roadside Shrines and Granite Sketches: Diversifying the Vernacular Landscape of Memory. *Perspectives in Vernacular Architecture* (Vernacular Architecture Forum) 12:4–81.

Sloboda, John 2000. Music and Worship: A Psychologist's Perspective. In Jeff Astley, Timothy Hone & Mark Savage, Eds., *Creative Chords: Studies in Music, Theology and Christian Formation* (pp. 110–125). Herefordshire: Gracewing.

Smith, Aaron C. T. 2006. 'Just Think It': The Neural and Spiritual Correlates of Football Consumption. In M. Nicholson, R. Hess, & B. Stewart, Eds., *Football Fever: Moving the Goalposts* (pp. 31–45). Melbourne: Maribyrnong Press.

Solnit, Rebecca 2009. *A Paradise Built in Hell: The Extraordinary Communities that Arise in Disaster*. New York: Penguin.

Sorin–Barreteau, Liliane 1996. *Le Langage Gestuel des Mofu–Gudur au Cameroun*. PhD Thesis, Université Paris V – René Descartes. London: Mandaras Publishing Electronic Publication.

Sperber, Dan 1996. *Explaining Culture: A Naturalistic Approach*. Hoboken, NJ: Wiley.

Squire, Larry R., and Barbara J. Knowlton 1995. Memory, Hippocampus, and Brain Systems. In Michael S. Gazzaniga, Ed., *The Cognitive Neurosciences* (pp. 825–838). Cambridge, MA: MIT Press.

St. Michel, Patrick 2015. Crying It Out in Japan: Tokyo gets into Communal Bawling. *Atlantic* May 2015 issue. http://www.theatlantic.com/magazine/archive/2015/05/crying–it–out–in–japan/389528/

Stace, Walter T. 1961. *Mysticism and Philosophy*. London: Macmillan.

Stanley, Alessandra 2016. Hillary's New Go–To Gesture: Hand to the Heart. *New York Times* Style section, 5 August. http://www.nytimes.com/2016/08/07/style/hillary–clinton–hand–on–heart–michelle–obama.html?_r=0 A version of this article appears in print on 7 August 2016, on page ST8 of the New York edition with the headline: Hillary Clinton and the Political Gesture du.Jour.

Stathi, Katerina 2015. Temperature Terms in Modern Greek. In Maria Koptjevskaja-Tamm, Ed., *The Linguistics of Temperature* (pp. 354–391). Amsterdam: John Benjamins.

Steinbeck John 1935. *Tortilla Flat*. New York: Penguin.

Steinbeck, John 1937. *Of Mice and Men*. New York: Covici–Friede.

Steinnes, Kamilla Knutsen 2017. *Too Cute for Words: Cuteness Evokes the Kama Muta Emotion and Motivates Communal Sharing*. Master Thesis in Social Psychology, Department of Psychology, University of Oslo. https://www.duo.uio.no/handle/10852/57260

Steinnes, Kamilla K., Johanna H. Blomster, Beate Seibt, Janis H. Zickfeld, & Alan Page Fiske 2019. Too Cute for words: Cuteness Evokes the Heartwarming Emotion of Kama Muta. *Frontiers in Psychology*. https://doi.org/10.3389/fpsyg.2019.00387

Stellar, Jennifer E., Amie M. Gordon, Paul K. Piff, Daniel Cordaro, Craig L. Anderson, Yang Bai, Laura A. Maruskin, & Dacher Keltner 2017. Self-Transcendent Emotions and Their Social Functions: Compassion, Gratitude, and Awe Bind Us to Others Through Prosociality. *Emotion Review* 9:200–207. doi:10.1177/1754073916684557

Stevenson, Robert Louis 1881 (1923). *Samuel Pepys*. In Robert Louis Stevenson, Ed., *Familiar Studies of Men and Books* (pp. 252–282). New York: Charles Scribner's Sons.

Strathern, Andrew 1975. Veiled Speech in Mount Hagen. In Maurice Bloch, Ed., *Political Language and Oratory in Traditional Society* (pp. 185–204). London: Academic Press.

Strick, M., & J. Van Soolingen 2017. Against The Odds: Human Values Arising in Unfavourable Circumstances Elicit the Feeling of Being Moved. *Cognition and Emotion*. doi:10.1080/02699931.2017.1395729

Strick, M., H. L. de Bruin, L. C. de Ruiter, & W. Jonkers 2015. Striking the Right Chord: Moving Music Increases Psychological Transportation and Behavioral Intentions. *Journal of Experimental Psychology: Applied* 21(1):57–72. doi:10.1037/xap0000034

Sullivan, Shirley D. 1988. *Psychological Activity in Homer: A Study of Phren*. Ottawa: Carleton University Press.

Sullivan, Shirley D. 2000. *Euripides' Use of Psychological Terminology*. Montreal: McGill–Queens University Press.

Sutton, Nicholas 2005. A Note on the Development of Emotional Bhakti: Epic Śaivism in the Mahābhārata. *Annals of the Bhandarkar Oriental Research Institute* 86:153–166. http://www.jstor.org/stable/41692394

Swora, Maria Gabrielle 1984. Narrating Community: The Creation of Social Structure in Alcoholics Anonymous Through the Performance of Autobiography. *Narrative Inquiry* 11:363–384.

Swora, Maria Gabrielle 2004. The Rhetoric of Transformation in the Healing of Alcoholism: The Twelve Steps of Alcoholics Anonymous. *Mental Health, Religion and Culture* 7:187–209.

Tan, Ed S. H, & Nico H. Frijda 1999. Sentiment in Film Viewing. In Carl Plantinga & Greg M. Smith, Eds., *Passionate Views. Film, Cognition and Emotion* (pp. 48–64). Baltimore, MD: John Hopkins University Press.

Tan, Ed S. H. 2009. Being Moved. In David Sander & Klaus R. Scherer, Eds., *Companion to Emotion and the Affective Sciences* (p. 74). Oxford, UK: Oxford University Press.

Tangney, June Price 1999. The Self-Conscious Emotions: Shame, Guilt, Embarrassment and Pride. In Tim Dalgleish & Mick Power, Eds., *Handbook of Emotion and Cognition* (pp. 541–568). Malden, MA: Wiley.

Tawney, Charles H. (Translator) 1924. *The Ocean of Story*, Volume 1. Translation of Somadeva's *Kathā Sarit Sāgara*. Edited by N. M. Penzer. London: Charles J. Sawyer.

Tegnaeus, Harry 1952. *Blood Brothers: An Ethno-Sociological Study of the Institutions of Blood-Brotherhood with Special Reference to Africa*. New York: Philosophical Library.

The Doctrine and Covenants of The Church of Jesus Christ of Latter–day Saints Containing Revelations Given to Joseph Smith, the Prophet, with Some Additions by his Successors in the Presidency of the Church 1981. Salt Lake City, UT: Intellectual Reserve.

Thomas, L. Eugene, & Pamela E. Cooper 1978. Measurement and Incidence of Mystical Experiences: An Exploratory Study. *Journal for the Scientific Study of Religion* 17:433–437. http://www.jstor.org/stable/1385407

Thompson, John Thomas 1846. *A Dictionary in Hindee and English*. Calcutta: Baptist Mission Press.

Thompson, Stith 1957. *Motif–Index of Folk–Literature*. Revised and enlarged edition. Bloomington, IN: Indiana University Press.

Thomson, A. L., & J. T. Siegel 2016. Elevation: A Review of Scholarship on a Moral and Other-Praising Emotion. *The Journal of Positive Psychology* 12(6):628–638. doi:10.1080/17439760.2016.1269184

Thomson, A. S. 1859. *The Story of New Zealand*. London: John Murray.

Thomson, Andrew L., & Jason T. Siegel 2013. A Moral Act, Elevation, and Prosocial Behavior: Moderators of Morality. *The Journal of Positive Psychology* 8(1):50–64. doi:10.1080/17439760.2012.754926

Thornton, Thomas F., & Ishmael Hope 2014. "Our Tears Never Left This Ground", An Appreciation of Tlingit Ritual Oratory. *AlterNative* 10(2):99–109.

Throop, Jason 2010. *Suffering and Sentiment: Exploring the Vicissitudes of Experience and Pain in Yap*. Berkeley, CA: University of California Press.

Tinbergen, Niko 1953. *The Herring Gull's World*. London: Collins.

Tiwary, K. M. 1978. Tuneful Weeping: A Mode of Communication. *Frontiers: A Journal of Women Studies* 3(3):24–27.

Todd, Elizabeth 1985. The Value of Confession and Forgiveness According to Jung. *Journal of Religion and Health* 24:39–48.

Tokaji, Akihiko 2003. Research for Determinant Factors and Features of Emotional Responses of "Kandoh" (the state of being emotionally moved). *Japanese Psychological Research* 45:235–249.

Tolbert, Elizabeth 1990. Women Cry with Words: Symbolization of Affect in the Karelian Lament. *Yearbook for Traditional Music* 22:80–105.

Tolbert, Elizabeth 2007. Voice, Metaphysics, and Community: Pain and Transformation in the Finnish-Karelian Ritual Lament. In Sarah Coakley, Kay Kaufman Shelemay, Eds., *Pain and Its Transformations: The Interface of Biology and Culture* (pp. 147–165). Cambridge, MA: Harvard.

Tompkins, Jane 1985. *Sensational Designs: The Cultural Work of American Fiction* 1790–1860. New York: Oxford University Press.

Tracy, Jessica L., & Richard W. Robins 2007. Emerging Insights Into the Nature and Function of Pride. *Current Directions in Psychological Science* 16(3):147–150. doi:10.1111/j.1467-8721.2007.00493.x

Trepp, Anne–Charlott 1994. The Emotional Side of Men in Late Eighteenth–Century Germany (Theory and Example). *Central European History* 27(2):127–152.

Trigger, Bruce G. 2003. *Understanding Early Civilizations: A Comparative Study.* Cambridge: Cambridge University Press.

Turner, Victor 1970. *The Forest of Symbols: Aspects of Ndembu Ritual.* Ithaca, NY: Cornell University Press.

Tylša, Filip, Tomáš Páleníčeka, & Jiří Horáčeka 2014. Psilocybin – Summary of Knowledge and New Perspectives. *European Neuropsychopharmacology* 24(3):342–356.

Urban, Greg 1988. Ritual Wailing in Amerindian Brazil. *American Anthropologist* 90:385–400. http://www.jstor.org/stable/677959

van Beek, Walter E. A. 2012. From Ritual to Performance — The Dynamics of Dogon Bajani. In Daniela Merolla, Jan Jansen, & Kamal Naït–Zerrad, Eds., *Multimedia Research and Documentation of Oral Genres in Africa: The Step Forward* (pp. 21–38). Zurich: LIT Verlag.

Van Cappellen, Patty, Vassilis Saroglou, Caroline Iweins, Maria Piovesana, & Barbara L. Fredrickson 2013. Self-Transcendent Positive Emotions Increase Spirituality Through Basic World Assumptions. *Cognition & Emotion* 27:1378–1394.

van Dijkhuizen, Jan Frans 2009. Partakers of Pain: Religious Meanings of Pain in Early Modern England. In Jan Frans van Dijkhuizen & Karl A. E. Enenkel, Eds., *The Sense of Suffering: Construction of Physical Punishment in Early Modern Culture* (pp. 189–220). Leiden: Brill.

Vejdemo, Susanne, & Sigi Vandewinkel 2016. Extended Uses of Body-Related Temperature Expressions. In Päivi Juvonen & Maria Koptjevskaja-Tamm, Eds., *The Lexical Typology of Semantic Shifts* (pp. 249–284). Berlin: Walter de Gruyter.

Vincent–Buffault, Anne 1986. *The History of Tears: Sensibility and Sentimentality in France.* London: Macmillan.

Vingerhoets, Ad J. J. M., & Lauren M. Bylsma 2015. The Riddle of Human Emotional Crying: A Challenge for Emotion Researchers. *Emotion Review* 8(3):207–217.

Volk, Anthony, & Vernon L. Quinsey 2002. The Influence of Infant Facial Cues on Adoption Preferences. *Human Nature* 13:437–455. doi:10.3389/fpsyg.2017.00439

Vuoskoski, Jonna K., & Tuomas Eerola 2017. The Pleasure Evoked by Sad Music Is Mediated by Feelings of Being Moved. *Frontiers in Psychology* 8. www.frontiersin.org/articles/10.3389/fpsyg.2017.00439/full

Wagner–Pacifici, Robin, & Barry Schwartz 1991. The Vietnam Veterans Memorial: Commemorating a Difficult Past. *American Journal of Sociology* 97:376–420.

Walker, Alan 1987. *Franz Liszt, The Virtuoso Years (1811–1847).* 1Revised Edition. Ithaca, NY: Cornell University Press.

Wassiliwizky, Eugen, Valentin Wagner, Thomas Jacobsen, & Winfried Menninghaus 2015. Art-elicited Chills Indicate States Of Being Moved. *Psychology of Aesthetics, Creativity, and the Arts* 9:405–416.

Wassiliwizky, Eugen, Thomas Jacobsen, Jan Heinrich, Manuel Schneiderbauer, & Winfried Menninghaus 2017. Tears Falling on Goosebumps: Co–occurrence of Emotional Lacrimation and Emotional Piloerection Indicates a Psychophysiological Climax in Emotional Arousal. *Frontiers in Psychology* 8. https://doi.org/10.3389/fpsyg.2017.00041

Wassiliwizky, Eugwn, Stefan Koelsch, Valentin Wagner, Thomas Jacobsen, & Winfried Menninghaus 2017. The Emotional Power of Poetry: Neural Circuitry,

Psychophysiology, Compositional Principles. *Social Cognitive and Affective Neuroscience* 12:1229–1240.

Weber, Max 1978 [originally published 1922]. *Economy and Society.* Translated by Guenther Roth and Claus Wittich. Berkeley, CA: University of California Press.

Webster, Wendy 2005. *Englishness and Empire, 1939–1965.* Oxford: Oxford University Press.

Weidman, Aaron C., Conor M. Steckler, and Jessica L. Tracy 2017. The Jingle and Jangle of Emotion Assessment: Imprecise Measurement, Casual Scale Usage, and Conceptual Fuzziness in Emotion Research. *Emotion* 17:267–295. doi:10.1037/emo0000226

Wesley Center Online. John Wesley the Methodist. http://wesley.nnu.edu/john-wesley/john-wesley-the-methodist/chapter-vii-the-new-birth/

White, Geoffrey M. 1999. Emotional Remembering: The Pragmatics of National Memory. *Ethos* 27:505–529.

White, Geoffrey M., & John Kirkpatrick 1987. *Person, Self and Experience: Exploring Pacific Ethnopsychologies.* Berkeley: University of California Press.

Whitehouse, Harvey 2004. *Modes of Religiosity: A Cognitive Theory of Religious Transmission.* Walnut Creek, CA: AltaMira.

Wierzbicka, Anna 1991. *Cross–Cultural Pragmatics: The Semantics of Human Interaction.* Berlin: Mouton de Gruyter.

Wierzbicka, Anna 1999. *Emotions Across Languages and Cultures: Diversity and Universals.* Cambridge: Cambridge University Press.

Wiesenfeld, A. R., & R. Klorman 1978. The Mother's Psychophysiological Reactions to Contrasting Affective Expressions by Her Own and an Unfamiliar Infant. *Developmental Psychology* 14:294–304.

Wilce, James M. 2009. *Crying Shame: Metaculture, Modernity, and the Exaggerated Death of Lament.* Malden, MA: Wiley.

Wildschut, T., C. Sedikides, J. Arndt, & C. Routledge 2006. Nostalgia: Content, triggers, functions. *Journal of Personality and Social Psychology* 91:975–993. doi:10.1037/0022–3514.91.5.975

Wildschut, T., C. Sedikides, C. Routledge, J. Arndt, & P. Cordaro 2010. Nostalgia as a Repository of Social Connectedness: The Role of Attachment–Related Avoidance. *Journal of Personality and Social Psychology* 98:573–586. doi:10.1037/a0017597

Wilkins, David P. 1992. Interjections as Deictics. *Journal of Pragmatics* 18:119–158.

Williams, Helen Maria 2001. *Letters Written in France.* Edited by Neil Freistat & Susan S. Lanser. Peterborough, Ontario: Broadview Press.

Williams, Linda 1998. Melodrama Revised. In Nick Browne, Ed., *Refiguring American Film Genres* (pp. 42–88). Berkeley, CA: University of California Press.

Williams–Jones, Pearl 1975. Afro–American Gospel Music: A Crystallization of the Black Aesthetic. *Ethnomusicology* 19(3):373–385. http://www.jstor.org/stable/850791

Willison, John 1720. *A Sacramental Catechism: Or, A Familiar Instructor for Young Communicants.* Edinburgh: Samuel Willison and Co. [Quoted in Schmidt 2001].

Wilson, Jonathan 2016. Dimitri Payet's Tears of Joy Put a Huge Smile Back on Face of France, a Nation Tormented by Tragedy. Eurosport 11/06/2016 at 16:20.

Wilson, Scott 2015. Only in Japan: Rent a Hot Guy to Make You Cry then Wipe Your Tears Away. *Rocket News 24,* 17 September. http://en.rocketnews24.com/2015/09/17/only-in-japan-rent-a-hot-guy-to-make-you-cry-then-wipe-your-tears-away/

Wilson-Mendenhall, Christine D., & Lawrence W. Barsalou 2016. A Fundamental Role for Conceptual Processing in Emotion. In L.F. Barrett, M. Lewis, & J.M. Haviland-Jones, Eds., *Handbook of Emotions.* 4th Edition (pp 547–563). New York: Guilford Press.

Wolf, Richard K. 2000. Embodiment and Ambivalence: Emotion in South Asian Muharram Drumming. *Yearbook for Traditional Music* 32:81–116. http://www.jstor.org/stable/3185244

Wolf, Richard K., & Zoe C. Sherinian 1999. Tamil Nadu. In Alison Arnold, Ed., *Garland Encyclopedia of World Music, Volume 5: Southeast Asia*. New York: Routledge. http://glnd.alexanderstreet.com/view/329850

Wolfe, Michael (Ed.) 1997. *One Thousand Roads to Mecca: Ten Centuries of Travelers Writing about the Muslim Pilgrimage*. New York: Grove Press.

Woodward, Anne J., Bruce M. Findlay, & Susan M. Moore 2009. Peak and Mystical Experiences in Intimate Relationships. *Journal of Social and Personal Relationships* 26:429–442. doi:10.1177/0265407509339994

Wright, Matthew 2005. The Joy of Sophocles' Electra. Greece & Rome 52(2):172–194.

Wuthnow, Robert 1978. Peak Experiences: Some Empirical Tests. *Journal of Humanistic Psychology* 18(3):59–75.

Yaden, David B., Jonathan Iwry, Kelley J. Slack, Johannes C. Eichstaedt, Yukun Zhao, George E. Vaillant, Andrew B. Newberg 2016. The Overview Effect: Awe and Self–Transcendent Experience in Space Flight. *Psychology of Consciousness: Theory, Research, and Practice* 3:1–11.

Yamagata, Naoko 1994. *Homeric Morality*. Leiden and New York: E. J. Brill.

Yamane, David, & Megan Polzer 1994. Ways of Seeing Ecstasy in Modern Society: Experiential-Expressive and Cultural-Linguistic Views. *Sociology of Religion* 55:1–25. http://www.jstor.org/stable/3712173

Yan, Yunxiang 2009. The Good Samaritan's New Trouble: A Study of the Changing Moral Landscape in Contemporary China. *Social Anthropology* 17:9–24. doi:10.1111/j.1469-8676.2008.00055.x

Young, Michael W. 1999. Feasting Friends, Eating Enemies: Amity and Enmity in Kalauna. In John R. Campbell & Alan Rew, Eds., *Identity and Affect: Experiences of Identity in a Globalising World* (pp. 105–125). London: Pluto Press.

Zaehner, Robert C. 1957. *Mysticism, Sacred and Profane: An Inquiry into Some Varieties of Praeternatural Experience*. Oxford: Clarendon.

Zaehner, Robert C. 1960. *Hindu and Muslim Mysticism*. London: Athlone.

Zeid, Abou A. M. 1966. Honour and Shame among the Bedouins of Egypt. In Julian G. Peristiany, Ed., *Honour and Shame: The Values of Mediterranean Society* (pp. 243–259). Chicago, IL: University of Chicago Press.

Zhang, Lucy 2012. A Cultural Comparison of Spatial Metaphors in Chinese and English. Linguistics Honours Thesis, University of Michigan. https://deepblue.lib.umich.edu/bitstream/handle/2027.42/91856/lcyzhao.pdf;sequence=1

Zhou, X., C. Sedikides, T. Wildschut, & D.–G. Gao 2008. Counteracting Loneliness: On the Restorative Function of Nostalgia. *Psychological Science* 19:1023–1029. doi:10.1111/j.1467–9280.2008.02194.x

Zickfeld, Janis H. 2015. Heartwarming Closeness: Being Moved Induces Communal Sharing and Increases Feelings of Warmth. Master thesis at Department of Psychology, University of Oslo. http://urn.nb.no/URN:NBN:no–52508

Zickfeld, Janis H., Thomas W. Schubert, Beate Seibt, & Alan Page Fiske 2017. Empathic Concern Is Part of a More General Communal Emotion. *Frontiers in Psychology*. doi:10.3389/fpsyg.2017.00723

Zickfeld, Janis H., & Thomas W. Schubert 2018. Warm and Touching Tears: Tearful Individuals Are Perceived as Warmer Because We Assume They Feel Moved and Touched. *Cognition and Emotion* 32:1691–1699.

Zickfeld, Janis H., Thomas W. Schubert, Beate Seibt, & Alan Fiske 2018. *Moving Through the Literature: What Is the Emotion Often Denoted Being Moved? Emotion Review* 11(2):123–139.

Zickfeld, Janis H., Thomas W. Schubert, Beate Seibt, Blomster et al. 2019. Kama Muta: Conceptualizing and Measuring the Experience of *Being Moved* Across 19 Nations and 15 Languages. *Emotion.* 19:402–424.

Zúñiga, Fernando 2015. Temperature Terms in Mapudungun. In Maria Koptjevskaja-Tamm, Ed., *The Linguistics of Temperature* (pp. 776–791). Amsterdam: John Benjamins.

INDEX